David Farwell   Laurie Gerber
Eduard Hovy (Eds.)

Machine Translation and the Information Soup

Third Conference of the Association
for Machine Translation in the Americas
AMTA'98
Langhorne, PA, USA, October 28-31, 1998
Proceedings

Springer

Series Editors

Jaime G. Carbonell, Carnegie Mellon University, Pittsburgh, PA, USA
Jörg Siekmann, University of Saarland, Saarbrücken, Germany

Volume Editors

David Farwell
New Mexico State University, Computing Research Lab
Box 30001 / 3CRL, Las Cruces, NM 88003, USA
E-mail: david@crl.nmsu.edu

Laurie Gerber
SYSTRAN Inc.
7855 Fay Avenue, Suite 300
P.O. Box 907, La Jolla, CA 92037, USA
E-mail: lgerber@systransoft.com

Eduard Hovy
University of Southern California, Information Sciences Institute
4676 Admiralty Way, Marina del Rey, CA 90292-6695, USA
E-mail: hovy@isi.edu

Cataloging-in-Publication Data applied for

Die Deutsche Bibliothek - CIP-Einheitsaufnahme

Machine translation and the information soup : proceedings ; Langhorne, PA,
USA, October 28 - 31, 1998 / David Farwell ... (ed.). - Berlin ; Heidelberg ;
New York ; Barcelona ; Hong Kong ; London ; Milan ; Paris ; Singapore ; Tokyo :
Springer, 1998
  (... Conference of Association for Machine Translation in the Americas, AMTA ... ; 3)
  (Lecture notes in computer science ; Vol. 1529 : Lecture notes in artificial
  intelligence)
  ISBN 3-540-65259-0

CR Subject Classification (1998): I.2.7, H.3, F.4.3, H.5, J.5

ISBN 3-540-65259-0 Springer-Verlag Berlin Heidelberg New York

© Springer-Verlag Berlin Heidelberg 1998
Printed in Germany

Typesetting: Camera ready by author
SPIN 10692906   06/3142 – 5 4 3 2 1 0   Printed on acid-free paper

Machine Translation and the Information Soup!

Over the past fifty years, machine translation has grown from a tantalizing dream to a respectable and stable scientific-linguistic enterprise, with users, commercial systems, university research, and government participation. But until very recently, MT has been performed as a relatively distinct operation, somewhat isolated from other text processing.

Today, this situation is changing rapidly. The explosive growth of the Web has brought multilingual text into the reach of nearly everyone with a computer. We live in a soup of information, an increasingly multilingual bouillabaisse. And to partake of this soup, we can use MT systems together with more and more tools and language processing technologies—information retrieval engines, automated text summarizers, and multimodal and multilingual displays. Though some of them may still be rather experimental, and though they may not quite fit together well yet, it is clear that the future will offer text manipulation systems that contain all these functions, seamlessly interconnected in various ways.

What is the position today? What opportunities and challenges of multilinguality exist on the Web? How can we adapt existing technology to address all languages? This conference offers invited speakers, papers, panels, and plenty of time for professionals in machine translation to learn about the issues, think about them, and discuss them with colleagues and friends. All of this in a pleasant setting. We hope you enjoy it!

This year, as you see, the AMTA conference proceedings have a new format. We are very happy in having secured an agreement with Springer-Verlag, based in Heidelberg, to publish our conference proceedings in the book format from now on. This means that AMTA papers will be distributed on a far wider scale than before. We hope that the format pleases you.

AMTA is fortunate in having a diverse membership of lively, involved, and friendly people. Without them, conferences such as these would be impossible to organize and awful to attend. Great thanks are due to David Farwell of the Computing Research Laboratory (CRL) of New Mexico State University and Laurie Gerber of SYSTRAN Software Inc., who together assembled an extremely interesting and diverse program, containing more papers and more tutorials than any previous AMTA conference. Of special note are the sessions devoted to user studies, an area underrepresented in past years. Linda Fresques and Helen Fleishenhaar of CRL assisted in various ways. We thank the CRL and SYSTRAN in allowing their staff to devote some time to organizing the conference.

The program committee are to be thanked for their reviewing and the comments that helped authors improve all the papers accepted: William Albershardt (US Dept of Defense), Scott Bennett (Logos Corp.), David Clements (Globalink Inc.), Bonnie Dorr (University of Maryland), David Farwell (NMSU Computing Research Laboratory—co-chair), Pascale Fung (Hong Kong University of Science and Technology), Laurie Gerber (SYSTRAN Software Inc.—co-chair), Kurt

Godden (General Motors Corp.), Bonnie Glover Stalls (USC Information Sciences Institute), Viggo Hansen (Hofman-Bang A/S), Stephen Helmreich (NMSU Computing Research Laboratory), Eduard Hovy (USC Information Sciences Institute), Lori Levin (CMU Language Technologies Institute), Susann Luperfoy (then of MITRE Corporation), Elliott Macklovitch (Université de Montréal), Ingrid Meyer (University of Ottawa), Mary Ellen Okurowski (US Dept of Defense), Patricia O'Neill-Brown (US Dept of Commerce), Boyan Onyshkevych (US Dept of Defense), Fred Popowich (Simon Fraser University), Randall Sharp (Universidad Autónoma Nacional de México), Beth Sundheim (NCCOSC RDTE), Virginia Teller (Hunter College, CUNY), Jin Yang (SYSTRAN Software Inc.).

One of the hallmarks of a good conference is the memorability of its invited speeches. With the speakers and topics selected by the program chairs, this conference can't go wrong! Many thanks to the invited speakers, and also to the tutorial presenters and the panelists, who put a lot of work into preparing their presentations!

The local arrangements are in many ways the most harrowing and difficult aspects of organizing a conference. Martha Palmer, Jennifer MacDougall, and Elaine Benedetto, the Local Arrangements Committee, have done a tremendous job, and deserve special thanks. Their attention to the banquet and special events must be particularly recognized, for this is often what helps make a gathering memorable. AMTA gratefully recognizes your work!

The exhibits were managed by Kimberly Kellogg Belvin, who eagerly located exhibitors and arranged exhibition space, computers, and all the seemingly little things that together sum to a smooth and professional presence. Advertising, mailings, and early registration were ably handled by the AMTA Registrar, Debbie Becker, whose continued service to AMTA is appreciated very much.

Several corporations were kind enough to sponsor portions of the conference. Many thanks to SYSTRAN Inc., Logos Corp., Globalink Inc., and the University of Pennsylvania's Institute for Research in Cognitive Science for their generous donations.

May this conference help you enjoy the variety and spice of the Information Soup!

Eduard Hovy
Conference Chair
Marina del Rey, August 1998

Tutorial Descriptions

MT Evaluation

John S. White
Litton PRC, Fairfax, VA, USA

Evaluation has always been a fundamental part of the MT discourse. Yet many participants in the field will claim that there is no generally agreed upon method for evaluation. In part, this sense springs from the realization that there are different purposes for MT, different interests of the participants in the process, radically different theoretical approaches, and, of course, different languages. Also, MT evaluation has some unique difficulties over evaluations of other language systems; in particular, there is never a single 'right' translation, and therefore never a solid ground truth against which MT output may be compared. This tutorial faces all of these issues, discussing the different evaluation needs of different MT stakeholders, the problems of using subjective judgments for evaluation, and a variety of classic and new approaches to evaluation.

Survey of Methodological Approaches to MT

Harold Somers
UMIST, Manchester, England

This tutorial presents various approaches to the problem of Machine Translation taking us from early methodological approaches, through the 'classical' architectures of 1970s and 1980s MT systems to the latest ideas, ending with a consideration of some outstanding topics for MT researchers. On the way we also consider how various external factors (use and users) affect MT system design. The tutorial is divided into six topics, as follows:

1. Historical perspective
2. Second generation: Transfer versus interlingua, rule-based systems
3. Making life easier I: sublanguage and controlled language systems
4. Making life easier II: Tools for translators
5. New paradigms: EBMT and statistical MT
6. Hard problems don't go away

Survey of (Second) Language Learning Technologies

Patricia O'Neill-Brown
U.S. Department of Commerce, Washington, DC, USA

Computer Assisted Language Learning (CALL) Programs come in all shapes and sizes these days. They are on the Web and they are on your software store shelf. In this tutorial, we work through a variety of CALL programs and see what they have got to offer to you as the MT developer, whether you are in the beginning or advanced phases of system development. The tutorial will be divided into 4 topics:

1. Identifying and locating CALL programs: Where do you find them?
2. What is out there: Developing a taxonomy of CALL programs
3. Reviewing the reviews on CALL: Evaluating the evaluations and making the most out of them
4. The value of CALL to MT development: What can the MT developer get out of CALL that cannot be obtained elsewhere?

Ontological Semantics for Knowledge-Based MT

Sergei Nirenburg
Computing Research Lab, New Mexico State University, Las Cruces, NM, USA

The idea of representing a source text in a language-neutral format and then generating the target text off the latter is simple and well known. The devil, as always, is in the details. Ontological semantics is a computational-linguistic theory devoted to the issues of deriving, representing and manipulating meanings of concrete natural language texts. While the theory can serve as the basis for many information technology applications, in the area of machine translation it is buttressed by a detailed and tested development methodology developed in the framework of the Mikrokosmos R&D project. This tutorial will address the following topics:

1. Introduction to the concerns, assumptions, content and justification of ontological semantics. Comparison of ontological semantics with other semantic theories
2. The body of the theory
3. Methodological issues
4. Status of theory and methodology development
5. Applications of ontological semantics outside machine translation

Cross Language Information Retrieval

Gregory Grefenstette
Xerox Research Centre Europe (XRCE), Grenoble, France

Contrary to fears and beliefs of five years ago, the WWW will not be an English-only resource. Information is readily accessible in growing numbers of languages. Cross Language Information Retrieval (CLIR) supports the view that foreign language documents are sources of information and not just noise to be eliminated.

This tutorial will present CLIR techniques and recent experiments attacking the problems raised trying to access documents written in one language by a query expressed in another.

The tutorial will be divided into four parts, as follows:

1. The science of information retrieval
2. Why CLIR is not information retrieval and is not machine translation
3. Linguistic techniques for CLIR
4. Experiments and results

Speech to Speech Machine Translation

Monika Woszczyna
Carnegie Mellon University, Pittsburgh, PA, USA

With the introduction of commercial text dictation systems (such as Dragon Naturally Speaking) and text translation systems (e.g., IBM Personal Translator), two important technologies in natural language processing have become available to the general public. However, speech translation cannot be reduced to just speech recognition and text translation. Utterances that occur in unrehearsed, spoken dialogs are very different from written text. For such spontaneous input, speech recognition systems have a higher error rate and conventional text translation systems often fail due to ungrammaticalities, missing punctuation, and recognition errors. To make full use of all information present in the speech signal, a more integrated approach to speech translation is required.

The main section of the tutorial covers common approaches and problems in speech recognition and speech translation. Some algorithms used in speech translation systems are explained in more detail to provide a better understanding of the problems and possibilities. A description of past, present, and future speech translation systems with video and/or live demonstrations rounds off the tutorial.

Multilingual Text Summarization

Eduard Hovy and Daniel Marcu
USC/Information Sciences Institute, Marina del Rey, CA, USA

After lying dormant for over two decades, automated text summarization has experienced a tremendous resurgence of interest in the past few years. This tutorial reviews the state of the art in automatic summarization, with particular emphasis on multilinguality, to the extent this has been addressed to date. The tutorial begins by outlining the major types of summary, then describes the typical decomposition of summarization into three stages, and explains in detail the major approaches to each stage. Next, discussion turns to the difficult issue of evaluation—measuring how good a summary is. Finally, we outline the major open problems and research challenges that remain to be solved.

Panel Description

A Seal of Approval for MT Systems

Eduard Hovy (moderator)

MT may not yet be a household term, but it is rapidly moving in that direction. Thanks to the World Wide Web, the need for occasional translation in the home or the monolingual workplace is increasing. The presence of translation systems on the Web—especially when partnered with Web access engines—makes it increasingly easy for the general public to access them.

Unfortunately, the occasional user is hardly likely to understand what MT is all about, and is in no position to distinguish the good MT from the bad. And it is quite likely that bad MT—not just low-quality output, but dishonorable business practice such as misleading advertising and worse—may proliferate.

The traditional hurdles that weeded out armchair MT and ensured that only serious MT practitioners eventually made it in the business are falling away. This will happen even more if current research in natural language processing succeeds in making it relatively easy to build a quick-and-dirty MT system with little effort, using Web-based resources, in only a few months or even weeks.

What can we, as a community, do?

One response is to create a Seal of Approval, a tangible marker that indicates to the public at large that any software so marked has been recognized by AMTA or the IAMT. Though such a seal may not have any legal force, it could be registered with consumer watchdog agencies such as Consumer Reports and Better Business Bureaux, and could set an example for other software products in general.

The experts invited to this panel will discuss the feasibility of a Seal of Approval. Many perplexing questions must be solved, including:

- What are the criteria for approval? Do they apply only to the software, or also to the company creating and/or selling it?
- Who administers the tests? How frequently?
- Should there be only one seal, or various levels or ratings within the seal? How would a multi-level rating scheme differ from a normal evaluation?
- How do we prevent unscrupulous companies from simply using the seal?

Panelists (at time of printing):
Eduard Hovy (USC/ISI), president, AMTA (chair)
John Hutchins (University of East Anglia), president, EAMT
Bente Maegaard (CfS, Copenhagen), MT evaluation expert
L. Chris Miller (MCS, Washington), PC MT expert
Reba Rosenbluth (SYSTRAN Inc.), MT seller
Hozumi Tanaka (TITech), representing president IAMT and AAMT
Muriel Vasconcellos, past president, IAMT and AMTA
John White (Litton PRC), MT evaluation expert

Panel Description

The Forgotten Majority: Neglected Languages

Laurie Gerber (moderator)

The number of the world's languages spoken today is estimated to be between 3000 and 8000. Machine translation efforts have focused on a small set of these, many of them closely related Indo-European languages. Commercial MT systems exist for only 30–40 languages as a source or target, with the vast majority focusing on fewer than 10 languages. Why so few?

This panel seeks to address:

1. Economics of MT development: What conditions are necessary to justify the investment in MT for minority languages?
2. Resource constraints: Can methods be devised to handle new languages cheaply and quickly, despite the lack of electronic (or even printed) resources?
3. Theoretical considerations: Will work on new language families expose gaps in MT theory?
4. The role of public policy in language engineering: If "HLT is the key that can open the door to a true multilingual society," what are the risks of marginalization and isolation for language groups that are not included?
5. Linguistic minorities within societies: Can MT help meet the legal and administrative needs of states with large immigrant communities?
6. The role of MT preservation of endangered languages: Can loss of languages be slowed with MT?

Panelists (at time of printing):
Laurie Gerber (SYSTRAN Software Inc.), chair
Scott Bennett (LOGOS Inc.)
Denis Gachot (SYSTRAN Software Inc.)
Sergei Nirenberg (Computing Research Laboratory, NMSU)
John O'Hara (Globalink Inc.)
Harold Somers (UMIST)
Peter Wilkniss (CATANAL Project)

Panel Description

Breaking the Quality Ceiling

David Farwell (moderator)

Recent advances in MT have perhaps enabled us to acheive large-scale, low-quality MT faster, but they have failed to improve the quality of translation, say, for the purpose of dissemination.

In the session, panelists representing different approaches to MT will discuss the sorts of barriers their approaches must overcome to achieve high (or at least much improved) quality, and identify potential breakthroughs and how far they will take us. Specifically, each panelist will outline the basic characteristics of a core approach to MT, describe the associated quality pitfalls, and suggest ways to overcome those pitfalls. In passing, participants may directly address the question of what quality is and, possibly, discuss various various 'hybridizations' of approaches in relation to overcoming pitfalls.

Panelists (at time of printing):
David Farwell (Computing Research Laboratory, NMSU), chair
Christian Boitet (University of Grenoble), structural-transfer-based MT
Sergei Nirenburg (Computing Research Laboratory), knowledge-based MT
Harold Somers (UMIST), example-based MT
Dekai Wu (Hong Kong University of Science and Technology), statistical MT

Table of Contents

System Descriptions

A Statistical View
on Bilingual Lexicon Extraction:
From Parallel Corpora to Non-parallel Corpora

Pascale Fung

Human Language Technology Center
Department of Electrical and Electronic Engineering
University of Science and Technology (HKUST)
Clear Water Bay, Hong Kong
pascale@ee.ust.hk

Abstract. We present two problems for statistically extracting bilingual lexicon: (1) How can noisy parallel corpora be used? (2) How can non-parallel yet comparable corpora be used? We describe our own work and contribution in relaxing the constraint of using only clean parallel corpora. **DKvec** is a method for extracting bilingual lexicons, from noisy parallel corpora based on arrival distances of words in noisy parallel corpora. Using **DKvec** on noisy parallel corpora in English/Japanese and English/Chinese, our evaluations show a 55.35% precision from a small corpus and 89.93% precision from a larger corpus. Our major contribution is in the extraction of bilingual lexicon from non-parallel corpora. We present a first such result in this area, from a new method–**Convec**. **Convec** is based on context information of a word to be translated. We show a 30% to 76% precision when top-one to top-20 translation candidates are considered. Most of the top-20 candidates are either collocations or words related to the correct translation. Since non-parallel corpora contain a lot more polysemous words, many-to-many translations, and different lexical items in the two languages, we conclude that the output from **Convec** is reasonable and useful.

1 Introduction

Bilingual lexicon extraction using large corpora is a relatively new area of research where the curve of progress has been positively steep since the beginning. The initial breakthrough in the area came from using statistical information of word features from clean, parallel corpora for automatic term translation. A parallel corpus is a pair of translated texts. A clean corpus is one which contains minimal translation noise such as when a sentence in one text is not translated in the other, or when the sentence boundary is not clear. Most parallel corpora are cleaned up by manual preprocessing to eliminate such noise. The most common word feature used is the co-occurrence of words in parallel sentences. Given a bilingual corpus where pairs of translated sentences are aligned, co-occurring words across the two languages in the text are extracted and matched by using correlation measures.

Efforts in using clean, parallel corpora for translation have been met with some objections in the research community. One main objection came from the fact that restricting the resources to clean, parallel corpora is too constraining. Therefore, we want to extract statistical word information from different types of real world data, including parallel but noisy corpora, as well as non-parallel texts of monolingual data from the same domain.

Another constraint of previous algorithms is their implicit reliance on common character sets between parallel corpora. So, another goal for us is to develop robust algorithms which can process languages that do not share etymological roots, such as Chinese and English, or Japanese and English.

In this paper, we present our view and our solutions to these problems. We show how word occurrence frequency, position, distance, context of the words, and dictionary seed words are used in different algorithms targeted at extracting bilingual lexicon from clean parallel corpora, noisy parallel corpora, and from non-parallel yet comparable corpora.

2 Bilingual lexicon extraction from parallel corpora

Algorithms for bilingual lexicon extraction from parallel corpora exploit the following characteristics of translated, bilingual texts:

1. Words have **one sense** per corpus
2. Words have **single translation** per corpus
3. **No missing translations** in the target document
4. **Frequencies** of bilingual word occurrences are **comparable**
5. **Positions** of bilingual word occurrences are **comparable**

Most translated texts are domain-specific, thus their content words are usually used in one sense and are translated consistently into the same target words. Pairs of sentences from both sides of the translated documents contain the same content words, and each word occurs in approximately the same sentences on both sides. Once the corpus is aligned sentence by sentence, it is possible to learn the mapping between the bilingual words in these sentences.

Sometimes lexicon extraction is a by-product of alignment algorithms aimed at constructing a statistical translation model [2–4, 12, 23, 32]. Others such as [6, 7] use an EM-based model to align words in sentence pairs in order to obtain a technical lexicon. Some other algorithms use sentence-aligned parallel texts to further compile a bilingual lexicon of technical words or terms using similarity measures on bilingual lexical pairs [21, 25, 29]. Yet others focus on translating phrases or terms which consist of multiple words [6, 25, 29].

The main inspiration for our work [10, 14], to be described in the following section, comes from [21] who propose using word occurrences patterns and average mutual information and t-scores to find word correspondences as an alternative to the IBM word alignment model. Given any pair of bilingual words, their occurrence patterns in all sentences are transformed into binary occurrence vectors, where the presence of a word in sentence i assigns a 1 to the i-th dimension of the binary vector w.

The correlation between a word pair is then:

$$W(w_s, w_t) = \log_2 \frac{\Pr(w_s = 1, w_t = 1)}{\Pr(w_s = 1)\Pr(w_t = 1)}$$
$$= \log_2 \frac{a \cdot (a + b + c + d)}{(a + b) \cdot (a + c)}$$

A word pair is considered only if their $t > 1.65$ where

$$t \approx \frac{\Pr(w_s = 1, w_t = 1) - \Pr(w_s = 1)\Pr(w_t = 1)}{\sqrt{\frac{1}{a+b+c+d}}\Pr(w_s = 1, w_t = 1)}$$

This work laid the basis for other translation algorithms using correlation scores.

2.1 DKvec: From clean parallel corpora to noisy parallel corpora

Our work in bilingual lexicon extraction is motivated by the need to handle parallel corpora which do not have clear sentence boundaries, which contain many insertion or deletion *noise*, which consist of language pairs across families. These corpora are difficult to align. **DKvec** [10, 13, 14] is an algorithm which, instead of looking at the position vector of a word, looks at the arrival distance vector of the word and compares it with that of target words. An arrival distance vector is a vector whose values are the positional differences between two successive occurrences of the word in the text. It is based on the notion that while similar words do not occur at the exact same position in each half of the corpus, distances between instances of the same word are similar across languages. Dynamic time warping (DTW) is used to find a mapping between arrival distance vectors. Matched word pairs are then used to align the noisy parallel corpus by segments, taking into account insertion and deletions. From the aligned corpus, words are represented in the word position binary vector form and are matched using Mutual Information score, much like the approach in [12, 21]. Fig. 1 shows recency vectors of some words and Fig. 2 shows the DTW path between the words *Governor* in English and Chinese.

We tested the algorithm on a noisy parallel corpus of English and Chinese texts, and another one of English and Japanese texts. Our algorithm yields a 55.35% precision in technical word translation for the small English/Japanese corpus. In the English/Chinese version we collected translations of 626 English words and suggested candidate translations for 95 English term translations. Word translations were evaluated as 89.9% accurate. Our algorithm produces a suggested word list for each technical term in the English/Chinese corpus and improved human translator performance by an average of 47%.

Fig. 1. Recency vector signals showing similarity between *Governor* in English and Chinese, contrasting with *Bill* and *President* in English

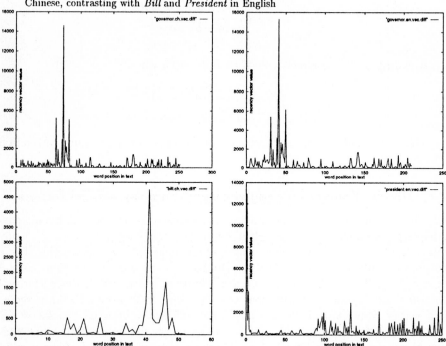

Fig. 2. Dynamic Time Warping path for *Governor* in English and Chinese. The axes represent the lengths of the two texts.

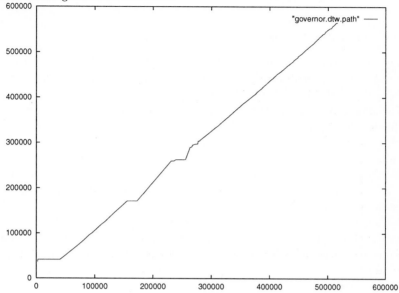

3 Bilingual lexicon extraction from non-parallel corpora

The very trend of using bilingual parallel corpora for machine translation was started by Jelinek's group formerly at IBM. Their work, and others which followed, are based on the conjecture that there must always exist a parallel corpus between any pair of languages for which *"mutual translation is important enough"*. In fact, organizations such as the Linguistic Data Consortium have been dedicating resources to *collect* such parallel corpora in different language pairs. However, acquiring and processing of parallel corpora is labour-intensive and time-consuming. It is still unlikely that one can find parallel corpora in any given domain in electronic form. Whereas even labour-intensive effort is certainly necessary and worthwhile for building baseline bilingual lexicons, we believe that there is an even larger corpora resource which is under-exploited—monolingual texts forming non-parallel yet comparable corpora.

With the advent of Internet technology and the World Wide Web, it has become obvious that such type of non-parallel, comparable corpora are more abundant, more up-to-date, more accessible than parallel corpora. Such corpora can be collected easily from downloading electronic copies of newspapers, journals, articles, and even books from the World Wide Web. At any given time, there are a lot more comparable corpora available than parallel corpora. At any given time, there are always a larger number of new words in comparable corpora than in parallel corpora because there is a delay in "time-to-market" for parallel corpora due to the human translation process. There is a great potential for one to obtain a mapping between bilingual word pairs from these non-parallel but comparable texts in the source language and the target language.

3.1 Comparable corpora

Unlike parallel corpora, which are clearly defined as translated texts, there is a wide variation of *nonparallelness* in monolingual data. Nonparallelness is manifested in terms of differences in *author, domain, topics, time period, language.*

The most common text corpora have nonparallelness in all these dimensions. The higher the degree of nonparallelness, the more challenging is the extraction of bilingual information. Parallel corpora represent the extreme example where all dimensions of nonparallelness except the language are reduced to zero. At the other extreme, newspapers from different time periods have different authors, sometimes cover different domains, and even have very different perspectives on the same events leading to topical differences. Such a corpus is nevertheless a desirable source of bilingual information, especially for new words.

As the nonparallelness of the texts increases, it is more difficult to find statistical usage patterns in the terms. Nonparallelness leads to the following characteristics:

1. Words have **multiple senses** per corpus
2. Words have **multiple translations** per corpus
3. Translations might **not exist** in the target document
4. **Frequencies** of occurrence **not comparable**
5. **Positions** of occurrence **not comparable**

Because of the above, bilingual lexicon extraction from non-parallel corpora is a far more difficult task than that from parallel corpora. Hence, we need a departure from the general paradigm of statistical methods applied to parallel corpora. We have been studying this problem since 1995 [9, 11, 15, 16] and have discovered the following characteristics of comparable corpora:

1. For the same topic, words have **comparable contexts** across languages
2. Words in the same domain and the same time period have **comparable usage** patterns (e.g. Zipf's law)

In the following sections, we describe a new method, **Convec**, which finds translation *candidates* for new words from online newspaper materials. When the source word is unambiguous, the top candidate is usually the correct translation. When the source word is polysemous, or has multiple translations, then the top candidates include other words which are collocations of the correct translation.

3.2 Convec: Moving on to non-parallel corpora

Content information of a monolingual text and context information of its words have been used in algorithms for author characterization from documents [26], document categorization from queries [1, 5, 24, 27, 30] and sense disambiguation between multiple usages of the same word [8, 20, 19, 17, 18, 22, 28, 33]. We propose to use context information of a word to find its counter part in the other language in a comparable corpus.

Our goal is to find translation or translation candidates for new words which are not found in an online dictionary, and then use the result to augment the dictionary, in order to improve the quality of a broad-coverage English-Chinese MT system at the Human Language Technology Center [31].

As an example, while using this MT system, we discovered that it is unable to translate the word *flu* which nevertheless occurs very frequently in the texts. Other words it cannot translate include names of politicians and public figures which only recently start to appear frequently in the news, medical and technical terms which are used in the context of recent events. In the following sections, we use *flu* and the discovery of its translation as a tutorial example to describe our algorithm.

3.3   The algorithm

Our algorithm finds bilingual pairs of words from non-parallel, comparable texts by using an Information Retrieval (IR) approach. It extracts the context of an unknown word in the source language and treats that as a *query*. It then looks at the *documents*—contexts of all candidate translations in the target language, and finds the translation in the *document* which best matches the *query*. Using the example of *flu* → 流感/*liougan*, our algorithm discovers this translation by matching the context of *flu* to that of 流感/*liougan* found in different English and Chinese newspaper articles in Hong Kong. Table 1. shows some occurrences of *flu* in the English newspaper.

Table 1. Contexts of *flu* from English newspaper articles

effect businesses avian flu
responsible called bird flu resulted
vaccine combat bird flu ready
The government handled bird flu crisis health
bird flu crisis
The deadly bird flu spread
VACCINE combat bird flu ready summer
THE government handled bird flu crisis health
bird flu crisis
THE deadly bird flu spread
possibility bird flu transmitted humans
This bird flu able
He cited bird flu evidence need change No
After avian flu subsides scientists expect
If bird flu struck Hong Kong
bird flu monetary turbulence soon Moreover
THE bird flu caused concern people Hong Kong

Algorithm

1. Precompile context vector models of all unknown words W_e in the source language
2. Precompile context vector models of all candidate translation words W_c in the target language
3. For all W_e, W_c, compute $similarity(W_e, W_c)$.
4. Rank the output according to this similarity score.
5. (I)Choose the N highest ranking W_c as translation candidate for W_e.
6. (II) Choose the M highest ranking (W_e, W_c) as new lexicon entries for the bilingual dictionary

3.4   Finding the TF of words

If we collect all the words in the context of *flu* and count their occurrence frequency **in the context of** *flu*, then we will get the list partially shown in Table 2. This frequency is the word **term frequency (TF)**. The right side of the table shows the most frequent words in the context of 流感/*liougan*. Note the similarity in the two lists.

Table 2. Words in the context of *flu*/流感 are similar.

English	TF	Chinese		TF
bird	284	事件	(event)	218
virus	49	病毒	(virus)	217
people	45	政府	(establishment)	207
Sydney	38	感染	(contraction)	153
scare	32	表示	(denote)	153
spread	19	沒有	(doesn't_exist)	134
deadly	19	病人	(invalid)	106
government	16	專家	(consultancy)	100
China	14	部門	(branch)	96
new	13	染上	(catch)	93
crisis	13	醫院	(hospital)	92
outbreak	12	情況	(circumstance)	90
hospital	12	處理	(deal_with)	89
chickens	9	醫生	(doctor)	49
spreading	8	染上	(infected)	47
prevent	8	醫院	(hospital)	44
crisis	8	沒有	(no)	42
health	8	政府	(government)	41

3.5   Mapping context words using bilingual dictionary

To establish the fact the contexts of *flu/liougan* are similar, we need to find a mapping between the *context words* in the left and right columns of Table 3. This is achieved via an online dictionary—the same one used by the MT system. It goes without saying that only known words are considered in the context vector. So for example, *virus* is found in the dictionary and it is considered a common word between the vectors of *flu/liougan*, whereas even though the name of the Chief Executive appears in both contexts, they are not used as seed words since they are unknown to the dictionary. In total, there are 233 common seed words shared by *flu/liougan*.

Table 3. Some of the 233 common seed words shared by 流感 and *flu*.

Common Index	Chinese word	English word
10614	以往	formerly
10677	出售	for_sale
10773	自由	free
1107	合併	amalgamate
11156	恢復	get_over
11682	香港	H.K.
11934	主管	head
1197	分析	analysis
12229	假日	holiday
12345	醫院	hospital
12635	抵抗力	immunity
12723	好轉	improve
1276	發言人	announcer
12968	之外	infra
13039	調查	inquire_into
12345	醫院	hospital
13845	實驗室	lab
23306	病毒	virus

Table 5. shows that the contexts of *flu* and another unrelated word, *shop* are not similar. Consequently, we found only 41 common seed words shared between *shop/liougan*.

3.6 Finding the IDF of words

We could proceed to compute the similarity of context vectors based on the frequency of the common words they share. However, there is a problem with using TF only. Note that in the example of *flu/liougan*, their common words, such as *virus, infection, spread* are mostly content words highly related to the usage of *flu/liougan* themselves, whereas words such as *discuss, fall, forward, frequently* which are shared by the context vectors of *shop/liougan* have much more general usage. We want to emphasize the significance of common words such as *virus, infection, spread* and deemphasize that of *discuss, fall, forward* by using another frequency, the Inverse Document Frequency (IDF). IDF accounts for the overall occurrence frequency of a context words in the *entire corpus*:

Table 4. Words in the context of *shop/*流感 are not similar.

English	TF	Chinese		TF
pet	5	事件	(event)	218
nine	4	病毒	(virus)	217
here	4	政府	(establishment)	207
ago	4	感染	(contraction)	153
stopping	3	表示	(denote)	153
six	3	沒有	(doesn't_exist)	134
reduce	3	病人	(invalid)	106
owner	3	專家	(consultancy)	100
business	3	部門	(branch)	96
walk	2	染上	(catch)	93
terminate	2	醫院	(hospital)	92
talk	2	內地	(inland)	91
square	2	情況	(circumstance)	90
space	2	處理	(deal_with)	89

Table 5. Some of the 41 common seed words shared by 流感 and *shop*.

Common Index	Chinese word	English word
10363	討論	discuss
13048	下降	fall
14472	引言	forward
14756	不時	frequently
15357	才	gift
15582	過去的	gone
17960	有關連的	incident
17995	包	include
18475	內	inside
20818	本地	local
21699	出售	market
22737	月	month
25320	物主	owner
26245	寵物	pet
26987	小灘	pool
27032	一般的	popular
27413	提出控告	prefer
27633	五月	price

$$IDF = \log \frac{n_{max}}{n_i} + 1$$

where n_{max} = the maximum frequency of
any word in the corpus
n_i = the total number of occurrences
of word i in the corpus

3.7 Similarity measures

Now we can visualize the context vector for *flu* to have the dimension of the bilingual dictionary we use, in this case, 20,000. The i-th dimension of this vector is $w_i = TF_i \times IDF_i$. It is zero if the i-th word does not appear in the context of *flu*. Similarly we obtain the context vectors of all unknown words in the source language and context vectors of all candidate words in the target language.

To locate translation candidates for *flu*, we have to compare the context vector of *flu* with context vectors of all Chinese words. The most common similarity measure used in the IR community is the Cosine Measure. We use one of the variants of the Cosine Measure:

$$S(W_c, W_e) = \frac{\Sigma_{i=1}^{t}(w_{ic} \times w_{ie})}{\sqrt{\Sigma_{i=1}^{t} w_{ic}^2 \times \Sigma_{i=1}^{t} w_{ie}^2}}$$

where $w_{ic} = TF_{ic} \times IDF_i$
$w_{ie} = TF_{ie} \times IDF_i$

3.8 Confidence

In using bilingual seed words such as 病毒/*virus* as "bridges" for word translation, the quality of the bilingual seed lexicon naturally affects the system output. First, segmentation of the Chinese text into words already introduces some ambiguity of the seed word identities. Secondly, English-Chinese translations are complicated by the fact that the two languages share very little stemming properties, or part-of-speech set, or word order. This property causes every English word to have many Chinese translations and vice versa. In a source-target language translation scenario, the translated text can be "rearranged" and cleaned up by a monolingual language model in the target language. However, the lexicon is not very reliable in establishing "bridges" between non-parallel English-Chinese texts. To compensate for this ambiguity in the seed lexicon, we introduce a **confidence weighting** to each bilingual word pair used as seed words. If a word i_e is the $k - th$ candidate for word i_c, then $w_{i_{t_e}} = w_{i_{t_e}}/k_i$.

The similarity score then becomes:

$$S'(W_c, W_e) = \frac{\Sigma_{i=1}^{t}(w_{ic} \times w_{ie})/k_i}{\sqrt{\Sigma_{i=1}^{t}w_{ic}{}^2 \times \Sigma_{i=1}^{t}w_{ie}{}^2}}$$

$$\text{where } w_{ic} = TF_{ic} \times IDF_i$$

$$w_{ie} = TF_{ie} \times IDF_i$$

3.9 Experimental Results

Evaluation I: unknown words In order to apply the above algorithm to find the translation for 流感/*liougan* from the newspaper corpus, we first use a script to select the 118 English content words which are not in the lexicon as possible candidates. The highest ranking candidates of 流感 are *flu, Lei, Beijing, poultry* respectively. We also apply the algorithm to the frequent Chinese unknown words and the 118 English unknown words from the English newspaper. The output is ranked by the similarity scores. The highest ranking translated pairs are shown in Table 6.

Evaluation II: known words A second evaluation is carried out on randomly selected 40 known English words from the English newspaper against 900 known Chinese words from the Chinese newspaper. This evaluation is more automatic because a dictionary can be used to find correct translations. We have added *flu*/流感 in the dictionary.

The five highest ranking candidates for *flu, shop, virus* are shown in Table 7.

For the test set of 40 English words against 900 Chinese candidates, translation accuracy ranges from 30% when only the top candidate is counted, to 76% when top 20 candidates are considered, and up to 88% when top 40 are counted. We suggest that it is not unreasonable for the system to to give 20+ translation candidates for each word when the system is used as translator-aid.

4 Discussion of results

Predictably, the characteristics of non-parallel corpora cause lexicon extraction accuracy to be lower than that obtained from parallel corpora of similar sizes. Some other errors are caused by inherent differences between English and Chinese:

1. **Polysemous words**: Online newspapers cover multiple sub-domains. There is a much higher chance for words to be used in multiple senses. In our evaluation set II, such words include *drive, behind, fine, track,* etc. We expect this type of error to reduce when we only translate domain words or terms.
2. **Many-to-many translations**: *spread* has seven Chinese equivalents and *virus* has three in our corpus. Each of the Chinese equivalent in turn has

Table 6. Convec output for unknown English and Chinese words

score	English	Chinese	
0.008421	Teng-hui	登輝	(Teng-hui)
0.007895	SAR	特區	(SAR)
0.007669	flu	流感	(flu)
0.007588	Lei	鴨	(Lei)
0.007283	poultry	家禽	(Poultry)
0.006812	SAR	建華	(Chee-hwa)
0.006430	hijack	登輝	(Teng-hui)
0.006218	poultry	特區	(SAR)
0.005921	Tung	建華	(Chee-hwa)
0.005527	Diaoyu	登輝	(Teng-hui)
0.005335	PrimeMinister	登輝	(Teng-hui)
0.005335	President	登輝	(Teng-hui)
0.005221	China	林	(Lam)
0.004731	Lien	登輝	(Teng-hui)
0.004470	poultry	建華	(Chee-hwa)
0.004275	China	登輝	(Teng-hui)
0.003878	flu	鴨	(Lei)
0.003859	PrimeMinister	建華	(Chee-hwa)
0.003859	President	建華	(Chee-hwa)
0.003784	poultry	梁	(Leung)
0.003686	Kalkanov	珠海	(Zhuhai)
0.003550	poultry	鴨	(Lei)
0.003519	SAR	葉利欽	(Yeltsin)
0.003481	Zhuhai	建華	(Chee-hwa)
0.003407	PrimeMinister	林	(Lam)
0.003407	President	林	(Lam)
0.003338	flu	家禽	(Poultry)
0.003324	apologise	登輝	(Teng-hui)
0.003250	DPP	登輝	(Teng-hui)
0.003206	Tang	唐	(Tang)
0.003202	Tung	梁	(Leung)
0.003040	Leung	梁	(Leung)
0.003033	China	特區	(SAR)
0.002888	Zhuhai	農曆	(Lunar)
0.002886	Tung	董	(Tung)

Table 7. Top five translation candidates for *flu, shop, drug*

flu	Chinese	Gloss	shop	Chinese	gloss	drug	Chinese	gloss
0.082867	傳播	spread	0.031571	商店	shop	0.056118	藥	drug
0.064126	傳染	contagious	0.014100	價格	cost	0.019768	昏睡	lethargy
0.056328	感染	contraction	0.012916	算出	$figure_{o}ut$	0.019208	查出	discover
0.054037	擴散	diffuse	0.011575	施與	send	0.017252	臀部	behind
0.046364	流感	flu	0.011552	飼養	breed	0.015905	病人	invalid

Fig. 3. Translation accuracy of N-best candidates

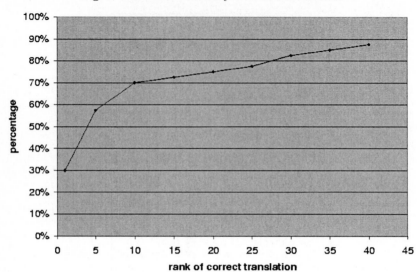

multiple English counterparts. This splits the context vectors into smaller pieces and gives lower scores to each translations. For example, all three correct translations for *virus* rank lower than another word, *contagious*. But when they are combined into a single context vector, the final score ranks first in the list.

3. **Dictionary error**: The bilingual dictionary we use is augmented by a statistical process. Its content includes many context-dependent entries in addition to human errors. This causes errors in our output as well.

4. **Missing candidate**: It is not surprising that non-parallel, comparable corpora contain a lot of un-matchable words.

5. **Chinese tokenization**: One complication in the translation process of Chinese words is that the words have no space delimiters. The tokenizer we use to insert word boundaries makes mistakes when the words are not found in its dictionary. This reduces the number of context seed words we can use for matching context vectors.

6. **Stemming**: There are mismatches between lexical types in English and Chinese. For example, the Chinese translations for *spread, spreading* are all the same, and the Chinese translations for *beauty, beautiful* and *beautifully* are often the same. To compensate for such mismatches, it might be helpful to use a stemming tool to pre-process the corpora. However, some of the morphological information might be useful for translation. So it is not clear what the optimal amount of stemming is needed for bilingual lexicon extraction.

Some of these errors can be overcome by using better tools or some learning procedures. Some others, such as the missing candidate problem, is inherent in comparable corpora. To solve this problem, the *size* of the comparable corpus has to be so large as to include all possible words.

5 Conclusion

In this paper, we present our view on the general approaches and the evolution of statistical bilingual lexicon extraction, starting from using aligned parallel corpora as resources, to noisy parallel corpora, and continuing with comparable corpora. Most importantly, we discuss the paradigm change from parallel corpora to comparable corpora and suggest a new method, **Convec**, to find bilingual lexicon in comparable corpora. **Convec** finds translations of new words by matching its context vector with that of its counterpart in the target language. We have tested this method on a comparable corpora consisting of texts from various English and Chinese newspaper articles. Two sets of evaluations are carried out. The first test set consists of all English and Chinese unknown words from the corpus. **Convec** matches most of the unknown English word to their correct translation in Chinese. The second test set consists of 40 English words matched against 900 Chinese words. Translation accuracy is 30% when top one candidate is counted, 76% when top 20 are counted and 88% when top 40 are included. Translation candidates among the top 20 are usually words related to the true translation. This means that one can refine the algorithm eventually to get better precision. We conclude that bilingual lexicons extracted from non-parallel, comparable corpora can be used to augment dictionaries containing a baseline lexicon extracted from parallel corpora, or entered by human lexicographers.

6 Acknowledgement

Students at the Human Language Technology Center, HKUST, Lo Yuen Yee and Luis Parmentier(visiting student from ENST, France), both implemented different parts of the programs for **Convec**, and Liu Yi helped with the evaluations for the output of **Convec**. The newspaper material is downloaded with a software tool developed by Xuen Yin Xia.

References

1. A. Bookstein. Explanation and generalization of vector models in information retrieval. In *Proceedings of the 6th Annual International Conference on Research and Development in Information Retrieval*, pages 118–132, 1983.
2. P.F. Brown, J. Cocke, S.A. Della Pietra, V.J. Della Pietra, F. Jelinek, J.D. Lafferty, R.L. Mercer, and P. Roosin. A statistical approach to machine translation. *Computational Linguistics*, 16:79–85, 1990.
3. P.F. Brown, S.A. Della Pietra, V.J. Della Pietra, and R.L. Mercer. The mathematics of machine translation: Parameter estimation. *Computational Linguistics*, 19(2):263–311, 1993.

4. Stanley Chen. Aligning sentences in bilingual corpora using lexical information. In *Proceedings of the 31st Annual Conference of the Association for Computational Linguistics*, pages 9–16, Columbus, Ohio, June 1993.

5. W. Bruce Croft. A comparison of the cosine correlation and the modified probabilistic model. In *Information Technology*, volume 3, pages 113–114, 1984.

6. Ido Dagan and Kenneth W. Church. Termight: Identifying and translating technical terminology. In *Proceedings of the 4th Conference on Applied Natural Language Processing*, pages 34–40, Stuttgart, Germany, October 1994.

7. Ido Dagan, Kenneth W. Church, and William A. Gale. Robust bilingual word alignment for machine aided translation. In *Proceedings of the Workshop on Very Large Corpora: Academic and Industrial Perspectives*, pages 1–8, Columbus, Ohio, June 1993.

8. Ido Dagan and Alon Itai. Word sense disambiguation using a second language monolingual corpus. In *Computational Linguistics*, pages 564–596, 1994.

9. Pascale Fung. Compiling bilingual lexicon entries from a non-parallel English-Chinese corpus. In *Proceedings of the Third Annual Workshop on Very Large Corpora*, pages 173–183, Boston, Massachusettes, June 1995.

10. Pascale Fung. A pattern matching method for finding noun and proper noun translations from noisy parallel corpora. In *Proceedings of the 33rd Annual Conference of the Association for Computational Linguistics*, pages 236–233, Boston, Massachusettes, June 1995.

11. Pascale Fung. Domain word translation by space-frequency analysis of context length histograms. In *Proceedings of ICASSP 96*, volume 1, pages 184–187, Atlanta, Georgia, May 1996.

12. Pascale Fung and Kenneth Church. Kvec: A new approach for aligning parallel texts. In *Proceedings of COLING 94*, pages 1096–1102, Kyoto, Japan, August 1994.

13. Pascale Fung and Kathleen McKeown. Aligning noisy parallel corpora across language groups: Word pair feature matching by dynamic time warping. In *Proceedings of the First Conference of the Association for Machine Translation in the Americas*, pages 81–88, Columbia, Maryland, October 1994.

14. Pascale Fung and Kathleen McKeown. A technical word and term translation aid using noisy parallel corpora across language groups. *Machine Translation*, pages 53–87, 1996.

15. Pascale Fung and Kathleen McKeown. Finding terminology translations from non-parallel corpora. In *The 5th Annual Workshop on Very Large Corpora*, pages 192–202, Hong Kong, Aug. 1997.

16. Pascale Fung and Lo Yuen Yee. An ir approach for translating new words from nonparallel, comparable texts.

17. W. Gale, K. Church, and D. Yarowsky. Estimating upper and lower bounds on the performance of word-sense disambiguation programs. In *Proceedings of the 30th Conference of the Association for Computational Linguistics*. Association for Computational Linguistics, 1992.

18. W. Gale, K. Church, and D. Yarowsky. Using bilingual materials to develop word sense disambiguation methods. In *Proceedings of TMI 92*, 1992.

19. W. Gale, K. Church, and D. Yarowsky. Work on statistical methods for word sense disambiguation. In *Proceedings of AAAI 92*, 1992.

20. W. Gale, K. Church, and D. Yarowsky. A method for disambiguating word senses in a large corpus. In *Computers and Humanities*, volume 26, pages 415–439, 1993.

21. William Gale and Kenneth Church. Identifying word correspondences in parallel text. In *Proceedings of the Fourth Darpa Workshop on Speech and Natural Language*, Asilomar, 1991.

22. M. Hearst. Noun homograph disambiguation using local context in large text corpora. In *Using Corpora*, Waterloo, Canada, 1991.

23. Martin Kay and Martin Röscheisen. Text-Translation alignment. *Computational Linguistics*, 19(1):121–142, 1993.

24. Robert Korfhage. Some thoughts on similarity measures. In *The SIGIR Forum*, volume 29, page 8, 1995.

25. Julian Kupiec. An algorithm for finding noun phrase correspondences in bilingual corpora. In *Proceedings of the 31st Annual Conference of the Association for Computational Linguistics*, pages 17–22, Columbus, Ohio, June 1993.

26. Frederick Mosteller and David L. Wallace. *Applied Bayesian and Classical Inference - The Case of The Federalist Papers*. Springer Series in Satistics, Springer-Verlag, 1968.

27. G. Salton and M.J. McGill. *Introduction to Modern Information Retrieval*. McGraw-Hill, 1983.

28. Hinrich Shütze. Dimensions of meaning. In *Proceedings of Supercomputing '92*, 1992.

29. Frank Smadja, Kathleen McKeown, and Vasileios Hatzsivassiloglou. Translating collocations for bilingual lexicons: A statistical approach. *Computational Linguistics*, 21(4):1–38, 1996.

30. Howard R. Turtle and W. Bruce Croft. A comparison of text retrieval methods. In *The Computer Journal*, volume 35, pages 279–290, 1992.

31. Dekai Wu and Hongsing Wong. Machine translation with a stochastical grammatical channel.

32. Dekai Wu and Xuanyin Xia. Learning an English-Chinese lexicon from a parallel corpus. In *Proceedings of the First Conference of the Association for Machine Translation in the Americas*, pages 206–213, Columbia, Maryland, October 1994.

33. D. Yarowsky. Unsupervised word sense disambiguation rivaling supervised methods. In *Proceedings of the 33rd Conference of the Association for Computational Linguistics*, pages 189–196. Association for Computational Linguistics, 1995.

Empirical Methods for
MT Lexicon Development

I. Dan Melamed

Computer Science Research Department
West Group
D1-66F, 610 Opperman Drive
Eagan, MN, 55123
melamed@research.westlaw.com

Abstract. This article reviews some recently invented methods for automatically extracting translation lexicons from parallel texts. The accuracy of these methods has been significantly improved by exploiting known properties of parallel texts and of particular language pairs. The state of the art has advanced to the point where non-compositional compounds can be automatically identified with high reliability, and their translations can be found. Most importantly, all of these methods can be smoothly integrated into the usual work flow of MT system developers. Semi-automatic MT lexicon construction is likely to be more efficient and more accurate than either fully automatic or fully manual methods alone.

1 Introduction

Translation lexicons are a vital component of any machine translation (MT) system. The high cost of lexicon development and maintenance is a major entry barrier for potential new vendors in the MT market, and a hindrance to growth for existing vendors. Many have tried to accelerate the MT lexicon development process by incorporating automatic methods for finding translation candidates in text corpora. Typically, these candidates are presented to a human expert for validation. Automatic methods must be accurate to be effective; otherwise, the human in the loop would spend most of her time filtering errors, instead of adding information to the MT system. Sufficiently accurate methods started to appear around 1995, and the state of the art has advanced considerably since then.

This article reviews some recently invented methods for learning translational equivalents from parallel texts (bitexts). It also suggests effective ways to integrate these methods into the MT lexicon development process. The overview is intentionally non-technical. Extensive literature reviews and technical details have been published elsewhere (Melamed, 1998, submitted).

2   How Can Existing Methods Help?

To understand how to take advantage of existing automatic methods for translation lexicon construction, it helps to think of the MT lexicon construction process as answering two questions:

1. What are the possible translations for each source word?
2. In what context are the various translations used?

Automatic methods are not yet good enough to answer Question 2 reliably. They can answer Question 1, however, given suitable bitexts. They can answer it even better when used in a semi-automatic mode with a human in the loop (see Section 6). Once the question of possible translations has been semi-automatically answered, the answer can be filtered and supplemented by hand and enhanced with context-dependent selectional preferences.

The integration of automatic methods into the MT lexicon development process has the potential to improve not only cost-efficiency, but also accuracy. This is especially true when an existing lexicon is being retargeted or specialized for a new domain. In most cases, the MT developer will not be a domain expert, and will be unable to accurately predict which entries need to be added or modified. Discrepancies between an existing translation lexicon and translation patterns in a bitext are easy to detect automatically. In the same way, automatic methods can help MT developers to keep up with rapidly evolving vocabulary.

The methods described in this paper were designed to produce probabilistic word-to-word translation lexicons. "Word-to-word" means that the lexicon does not account for how translation is influenced by context — the lexicon is just a list of word pairs, where each pair contains one word from the source language and one from the target. "Probabilistic" means that each entry in the lexicon is tagged with its relative frequency.

Translation lexicons that are probabilistic offer additional advantages. If there isn't enough time or money to enhance the lexicon by hand, then the most frequent translation in the automatically constructed lexicon is better than no translation at all. Even with a manually enhanced lexicon, frequency information can be used as a default target word selection strategy in unfamiliar linguistic contexts. The same information can also be used to produce more natural-looking language, by generating synonyms in proportion to their frequency. Perhaps most importantly, only probabilistic translation lexicons contain sufficient information to enable the automatic methods for identifying non-compositional compounds described in Section 5.

3   Translation Lexicon Construction Methods

3.1   Formalization of the Question of Possible Translations

Asking "What are the possible translations of X?" in a given bitext is equivalent to asking "What words occur as translations of some instance of X?" in the bitext. To narrow down the possibilities, we can start by asking the simpler question "What words co-occur with some instance of X?" There are different ways to define "co-occur" (Melamed, 1998). For expository purposes, let us assume that our bitext consists of pairs of aligned text segments, where each segment in a pair is the translation of the other[1]. Under this model of co-occurrence, two words co-occur if they occur in aligned segments[2]. To answer the remainder of the question of possible translations, we must pick the translations of X out of the words that co-occur with X.

Suppose we want to find the possible translations of the English word "head" and we have the bitext in Figure 1. Anyone who speaks both French and English

1. **English**: The minister nods his head.
   French: Le ministre hoche la tête.
2. **English**: The head of the company has a big head.
   French: Le chef de la société a une grosse tête.
3. **English**: My office is smaller than my boss's office.
   French: Mon bureau est plus petit que le bureau de mon chef.

Fig. 1. *An English/French bitext consisting of three aligned segments.*

should have no trouble picking out the two translations of "head" in the bitext ("tête" and "chef"). Alas, our algorithms must work without the benefit of such vast knowledge. As many others have done, we start with the following intuition: Words that are translations of each other are more likely to co-occur than other pairs of words. This intuition can lead to a very simple heuristic for linking words with their translations: Link word pairs with a probability proportional to their relative frequency of co-occurrence.

Of course, it's not that easy, if only because more frequent words are more likely to co-occur with all words, not just their translations. For example, in Figure 1, "head" co-occurs with "la" as often as it co-occurs with "tête." To account for this confounding variable, the co-occurrence counts are typically discounted in proportion to the marginal word frequencies. There are many variations on these ideas in the literature, but they all boil down to an initial similarity score $S(u, v)$ between words u and v in opposite halves of a bitext:

$$S(u, v) = f\left(\frac{c(u, v)}{c(u) \bigcirc c(v)}\right). \tag{1}$$

In Equation 1, $c(u, v)$ is the number of times u and v co-occur, $c(u)$ and $c(v)$ are the frequency counts of u and v, respectively, $\bigcirc$ is either addition or multiplication and f is some positive scaling function.

---

[1] All the methods presented here can also be based on other models of co-occurrence.

[2] Sufficiently accurate bitext mapping and alignment methods are now available for most purposes. See Melamed (1998) or Melamed (to appear) for a review.

Regardless of its exact form, the initial similarity metric in Equation 1 suffers from egregious independence assumptions. The problem with these independence assumptions is illustrated in Figure 2. The two strings represent corresponding

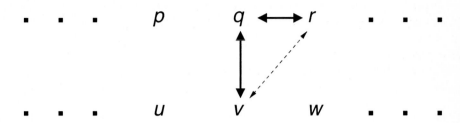

Fig. 2. *q and v often co-occur, as do q and r. The direct association between q and v, and the direct association between q and r give rise to an indirect association between v and r.*

regions of a bitext. If **q** and **v** co-occur much more often than expected by chance, then any reasonable similarity metric will deem them likely to be mutual translations. If **q** and **v** are indeed mutual translations, then their tendency to co-occur is called a **direct association**. Now, suppose that **q** and **r** often co-occur within their language. Then **v** and **r** will also co-occur more often than expected by chance. The arrow between *v* and *r* in Figure 2 represents an **indirect association**, since the association between *v* and *r* arises only by virtue of the association between each of them and *q*. Translation lexicon construction methods that do not account for indirect associations are unlikely to be very accurate.

3.2   Method A: The One-to-One Assumption

To filter out indirect associations, we can use two things we already know about bitexts. First, indirect associations are usually weaker than the direct associations on which they are based. This is a somewhat surprising consequence of the irregularities (noise) in text and in translation. If noise in the data reduces the strength of a direct association, then the same noise will reduce the strengths of any indirect associations that are based on this direct association. On the other hand, noise can reduce the strength of an indirect association without affecting any direct associations.

Another thing we know about bitexts is that most word tokens translate to only one word token. For the sake of simplicity, we shall make this one-to-one assumption about all words. Thus, we do not allow a word to translate to a multi-word phrase. The one-to-one assumption is not as restrictive as it may appear, because we are free to redefine what words are. Indeed, Section 5 describes how to construct translation lexicons whose entries may contain non-compositional compound "words" consisting of several space-delimited tokens. Initially, however, words are space-delimited character strings.

The one-to-one assumption has the following implication: If a text segment containing v is aligned with a segment containing w and w', then the entries (v, w) and (v, w') should not both appear in the translation lexicon. If both do appear, then at least one is incorrect. Think of a competition among lexicon entries where there can be only one winner. If entry (v, w) is a winner in some segment pair, then we say that v and w are linked in that segment pair. A reliable procedure for selecting the correct lexicon entry among several competitors can be a powerful lexicon cleaning agent. The tendency for direct associations to be stronger than indirect associations suggests the following heuristic: *The entry with the highest similarity score wins.*

In each pair of aligned segments, there can be as many competitions as there are words, and each candidate word pair can participate in two of them (one for each member of the pair). The outcome of the competitions will depend on the order of the competitions. So, we need a well-founded method to order the competitions within segment pairs. If we assume that stronger associations are also more reliable, then the order of the competitions can be determined by the reliability of their winners. The procedure in each segment pair (S,T) is then as follows:

1. Pick $v \in S$ and $w \in T$, such that the lexicon entry (v, w) has the highest similarity score. This entry would be the winner in any competition involving v or w. So, consider v and w linked.
2. The one-to-one assumption implies that entries containing v or w cannot win any other competition in the segment pair (S,T). Therefore, remove v from S and remove w from T.
3. If there is another $v \in S$ and another $w \in T$, such that (v, w) is in the lexicon, then go to Step 1.

The competitive linking algorithm links corresponding word tokens in the bitext. These token-level links can be counted and normalized to produce probabilities over translation lexicon entries. The overall translation lexicon construction method is illustrated in Figure 3:

1. Construct an initial translation lexicon, ordered according to some reasonable initial similarity score.
2. Armed with this lexicon, return to the bitext, and use the competitive linking algorithm to generate links among co-occuring word tokens.
3. Discard lexicon entries whose tokens are never linked.
4. Normalize the link counts $links(u, v)$ to sum to one. These normalized counts become the similarity score for the next call to the competitive linking algorithm.
5. Go to Step 2 unless the lexicon reaches a fixed point or some other stopping condition is met.

3.3   Method B: An Explicit Noise Model

Yarowsky (1993) has shown that "for several definitions of sense and collocation, an ambiguous word has only one sense in a given collocation with a probability

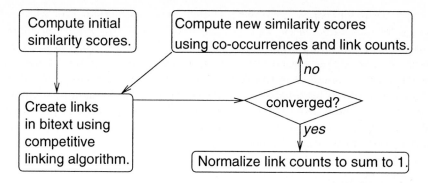

Fig. 3. *Top-level flowchart for automatic translation lexicon construction.*

of 90-99%." In other words, a single contextual clue can be a highly reliable indicator of a word's sense. One of the definitions of "sense" studied by Yarowsky was a word token's translation in the other half of a bitext. For example, the English word *sentence* may be considered to have two senses, corresponding to its French translations *peine* (judicial sentence) and *phrase* (grammatical sentence). If a token of *sentence* occurs in the vicinity of a word like *jury* or *prison*, then it is far more likely to be translated as *peine* than as *phrase*. "In the vicinity of" is one kind of collocation. Co-occurrence in aligned segments is another kind of collocation. If each word's translation is treated as a sense tag, then "translational" collocations have the unique property that the collocate and the word sense are the same object!

Method B exploits this property under the hypothesis that "one sense per collocation" holds for translational collocations. This hypothesis implies that if u and v are *possible* mutual translations, and a token u co-occurs with a token v in the bitext, then with very high probability, u and v are indeed mutual translations and should be linked. The smaller the ratio $\frac{links(u,v)}{c(u,v)}$, the more likely it is that u and v are *not* mutual translations, and that links posited between tokens of u and v are noise. Information about how often words co-occur without being linked can be used as the basis for a more accurate similarity score.

Method B improves on Method A by using a function of the ratio of links and co-occurrences as the similarity metric, instead of just normalized link counts. This similarity metric reflects an explicit noise model that can be employed the same way in translation models that are not based on the one-to-one assumption.

3.4 Method C: Pre-Existing Word Classes

The similarity metric in Method B depends only on the link frequencies generated by the competitive linking algorithm and on co-occurrence counts. All word pairs that co-occur the same number of times and are linked the same number of times are assigned the same similarity score. More accurate models can be induced by taking into account various features of the linked word tokens. For example, frequent words are translated less consistently than rare words. To account for these differences, we can condition the similarity scores on different ranges of $c(u, v)$. Similarly, the scores can be conditioned on the linked parts of speech. We can exploit word order correlations by conditioning the scores on the relative positions of linked word tokens in their respective text segments. Just as easily, we can model word pairs that coincide with entries in an on-line bilingual dictionary separately from those that do not. Almost any kind of pre-existing knowledge can be used to refine the word linking process, and thereby to produce more accurate translation lexicons.

4 Experiments

Manual evaluation of the entries in several translation lexicons is very labor-intensive. Fortunately, for automatically constructed lexicons, there is a direct relationship between the accuracy of lexicon entries and the accuracy of the links created by the algorithm in the training bitext. Using a carefully developed "gold standard" of links, I compared the accuracy of lexicon construction Methods A, B, and C with a well-known knowledge-poor baseline method. The comparison was in terms of link precision and recall, averaged into a version of the commonly used Dice coefficient. To demonstrate the power of language-specific knowledge, the experiment informed Method C with only a list of function words for both the source and target language. The results in Figure 4 demonstrate that even the smallest bit of knowledge, such as the distinction between content words and function words, can reliably boost translation lexicon accuracy. These results are statistically significant at the $\alpha = .05$ level, according to the Wilcoxon signed ranks test.

The question remains, however, whether these more accurate methods are sufficiently accurate to be useful in a semi-automatic lexicon production environment. I have carried out another experiment, designed to measure more directly the utility of these methods for the purposes of translation lexicon construction. The input to the experiment was a translation lexicon created by an earlier version of Method B[3]. I sorted the entries in the lexicon by their similarity scores. Figure 5 shows the distribution of these scores on a log scale. The log scale helps to illustrate the plateaus in the curve. The longest plateau represents the set of word pairs that were linked once out of one co-occurrence (1/1) in the bitext. All these word pairs were equally likely to be correct. The second-longest plateau resulted from word pairs that were linked twice out of two co-occurrences (2/2) and the third longest plateau is from word pairs that were linked three times out of three co-occurrences (3/3). The entries with higher similarity scores were more likely to be correct. By discarding entries with lower similarity scores, recall could be traded off for precision. This trade-off was measured at three points, representing cutoffs at the end of each of the three longest plateaus in Figure 5.

I define the recall of a translation lexicon as the fraction of the bitext vocabulary represented in the lexicon. Lexicon precision is a more thorny issue,

---

[3] *I.e.*, Method C and more recent versions of Method B should perform better.

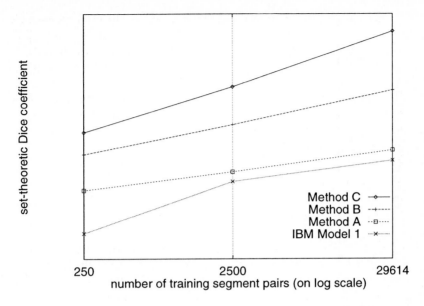

Fig. 4. *Effects of training set size and pre-existing knowledge on link accuracy.*

because people disagree about the degree to which context should play a role in judgements of translational equivalence. I manually evaluated five random samples of 100 entries from each of the lexicons resulting from the three cutoff levels. The evaluation was performed in the context of the bitext from which the lexicon was induced, using a bilingual concordancer. An entry (u, v) was considered correct if u and v ever co-occurred as direct translations of each other. Where the one-to-one assumption failed, but an entry captured part of a correct translation, it was judged "incomplete." Whether incomplete entries should be considered correct depends on the application.

For the bitext I used, the three cutoffs resulted in recall scores of 36%, 46% and 90%, which corresponded to translation lexicons containing 32274, 43075 and 88633 words, respectively. Figure 6 shows the precision of the lexicons with 95% confidence intervals. The upper curve represents precision when incomplete entries are considered correct, and the lower curve when they are considered incorrect. On the former metric, Method B can generate translation lexicons with precision and recall both exceeding 90%, as well as dictionary-sized translation lexicons that are over 99% correct.

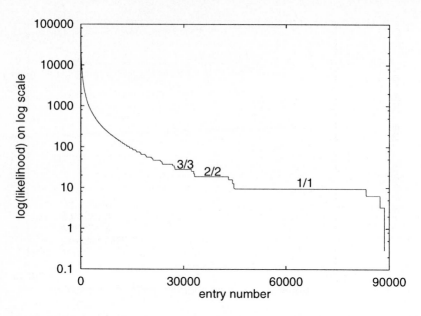

Fig. 5. *Distribution of lexicon entry similarity scores. The long plateaus correspond to the most common combinations of $\frac{links(u,v)}{c(u,v)}$: $1/1, 2/2$ and $3/3$.*

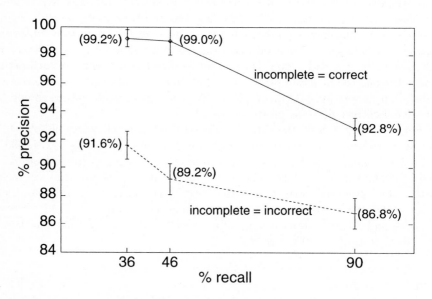

Fig. 6. *Translation lexicon precision with 95% confidence intervals at varying levels of recall.*

5   Non-Compositional Compounds

One of the most challenging aspects of translation lexicon development is finding the minimal content-bearing units of the languages in question. This task is particularly difficult in languages such as Chinese, whose written forms don't use spaces between words. Spaces in texts of languages like English offer an easy first approximation, but this approximation mis-analyzes non-compositional compound (NCC) words such as "kick the bucket" and "hot dog."

There are different kinds of non-compositionality. Word sequences such as "ivory tower" and "banana republic" are non-compositional from a monolingual perspective. Their definitions in a monolingual dictionary are unlikely to rely on their component words. However, their translations into French (*tour d'ivoire, république bananière*) can be correctly inferred word by word. These word sequences are compositional with respect to translation.

Some word sequences have the opposite characteristics. For example, the English phrase "tax system" seems perfectly compositional from a monolingual perspective, but its usual French translation is "régime fiscale." Word sequences whose translations are not typically composed of the translations of their parts are the most important from the point of view of MT system development, because failure to correctly treat such NCCs as atomic units thwarts even the simplest kind of word-to-word translation, let alone more sophisticated approaches. Non-compositionality with respect to translational equivalence is the only kind of non-compositionality that the method described below is designed to discover. Whether a given word sequence is an NCC depends on the target language.

If NCCs are not translated word-for-word, then one way to discover them is to look for word sequences in bitexts that are linked in unusual ways. For example, suppose that in addition to the aligned segments in Figure 1, our bitext contains the following aligned segment:

English: The head of the company works at the head office.
French: Le chef de la société travaille au siège.

Most instances of English "head" in the bitext are linked with either "tête" or with "chef." This last instance, however, is not. Likewise, this last instance of "office" is not linked to "bureau" as it is in the third segment pair. The collocation of these two atypical events suggests that this instance of the word sequence "head office" is translated non-compositionally. The more often this occurs with a certain word sequence, the more confident we can be that we've discovered an NCC.

These intuitions have been formalized and encoded in an iterative NCC discovery algorithm. On each iteration, the algorithm produces a large number of candidate NCCs, and then runs information-theoretic tests to predict which ones are likely to improve the accuracy of the translation lexicon. A new translation lexicon is induced on each iteration, where NCCs that have been validated on previous iterations are treated as atomic units. Thus, NCCs are not only identified, but also paired with their translations.

The algorithm can find hundreds of NCCs on each iteration. Objective evaluation on a simple word-to-word translation task has confirmed the intuition that accurate NCC recognition improves the accuracy of translation lexicon construction algorithms, and therefore also the accuracy of the resulting translation lexicons. A qualitative assessment of the NCC discovery method can be made by looking at Table 1. It contains a random sample of 20 automatically discovered English NCCs. All of the NCCs in the table are non-compositional in their bitext.

Count	NCC (underlined) in context	a translation in French text
36	*tax base*	assiette fiscale
24	*perform < GAP > duty*	assumer . . . fonction
23	*red tape*	la paperasserie
16	*heating oil*	mazout
11	*rat pack*	meute
10	nuclear *generating station*	centrale nucléaire
10	Air *India disaster*	écrasement de l'avion indien
9	*Ottawa River*	Outaouais
8	I *dare hope*	j'ose croire
7	*machine gun*	mitrailleuse
6	*cry for help*	appel au secour
5	*video tape*	vidéo
4	*shot-gun wedding*	mariage forcé
4	*Great West* Life Company	Great West Life Company
4	we *lag behind*	nous traînions de la patte
3	*en masse*	en bloc
3	*create a disturbance*	suscite de perturbation
3	*blaze the trail*	ouvre la voie
2	*weak sister*	parent pauvre
2	*swimming pool*	piscine

Table 1. *Random sample of 20 English NCCs validated by the algorithm.*

6 Integration of Manual and Automatic Methods

If we assume that the cost of computer time is negligible compared to the cost of human time, then the most efficient lexicon construction process is one that minimizes human effort. To be helpful, automation must help the lexicon developer to construct lexicon entries more quickly. In addition, the time saved by accelerated entry construction must not be wasted rejecting false candidates. Much of this paper describes how to improve automatic translation lexicon construction methods by taking advantage of pre-existing knowledge. Such knowledge is just as valuable if it is not previously encoded, but supplied on the fly by the MT developer.

These observations suggest an iterative semi-automatic lexicon development strategy:

1. Run the automatic translation lexicon construction algorithm on all available bitexts in the relevant language pair.
2. Sort the entries in the output by their similarity score, as in Figure 5.
3. Present the human developer with the sorted lexicon entries for validation, along with their bilingual contexts in a bilingual concordance.
4. The developer should continue validating entries in order down the list, until the ratio of true and false entries drops below some reasonable threshold.
5. Permanently fix the similarity scores of the rejected entries at negative infinity. This will prevent their co-occurrences in the bitext from ever being linked. Since links are very inter-dependent, this negative information should improve the average quality of entries that have not yet been presented for validation.
6. Repeat from Step 1 until valid entries become too rare to worry about.

Candidate NCCs can be validated or rejected in the same way and at the same time as candidate translations.

Conclusion

Recent years have seen significant advances in empirical methods for translation lexicon construction. The advances have come largely from insights into how to exploit what we already know about bitexts and about particular language pairs. Better informed lexicon construction methods are able to glean valuable information even from very small data sets. The knowledge need not be previously encoded; it can be infused on the fly. Therefore, the new empirical methods can be smoothly interleaved with the usual work flow of MT system developers.

Although the empirical methods have not yet been tested in a real production environment, the experiments summarized in Section 4 suggest that these methods are now sufficiently accurate to have a significant positive impact on the efficiency of MT lexicon development. In addition, these methods may be able to increase coverage and accuracy, and to provide better information about non-compositional compounds. These considerations will become more important as MT customers become more demanding and vocabulary evolution accelerates.

As evidenced by the volume of relevant papers at recent conferences, even better methods are just around the corner. Little doubt remains that empirical methods will become a favorite tool in the MT developer's toolbox. The only remaining question is who will be the first to use it to their advantage in the MT marketplace.

Bibliography

I. D. Melamed. (1998) *Empirical Methods for Exploiting Parallel Texts,* Ph.D. dissertation. University of Pennsylvania, Philadelphia, PA.

I. D. Melamed. (to appear) "Bitext Maps and Alignment via Pattern Recognition," to appear in *Computational Linguistics.*

I. D. Melamed. (submitted) "Word-to-Word Models of Translational Equivalence," submitted to *Computational Linguistics.*

D. Yarowsky. (1993) "One Sense Per Collocation," *DARPA Workshop on Human Language Technology.* Princeton, NJ.

A Modular Approach to Spoken Language Translation for Large Domains

Monika Woszczyna, Matthew Broadhead, Donna Gates, Marsal Gavaldà,
Alon Lavie, Lori Levin, and Alex Waibel

Interactive Systems Laboratories
at Carnegie Mellon University, Pittsburgh, USA
and Karlsruhe University, Karlsruhe, Germany
monika@cs.cmu.edu

Abstract. The MT engine of the JANUS speech-to-speech translation system is designed around four main principles: 1) an **interlingua approach** that allows the efficient addition of new languages, 2) the use of **semantic grammars** that yield low cost high quality translations for limited domains, 3) **modular grammars** that support easy expansion into new domains, and 4) **efficient integration of multiple grammars** using multi-domain parse lattices and domain re-scoring. Within the framework of the C-STAR-II speech-to-speech translation effort, these principles are tested against the challenge of providing translation for a number of domains and language pairs with the additional restriction of a common interchange format.

1 Introduction

Within the JANUS project [9] we have been involved in an ongoing effort to develop a machine translation system specifically suited for spoken dialogue. Spoken language is characterized by highly disfluent utterances that are often fragmented and ungrammatical. Furthermore, many communicative acts such as making a polite request involve language specific formulaic expressions. Literal translation of such utterances may not effectively convey the underlying communicative intentions of the speaker. Effective translation of spoken language must therefore be robust and capable of identifying and translating the key underlying concepts of the speaker.

In the most recent version of JANUS, our focus has been on extending the capabilities of the system to handle large and rich domains. Within the framework of the C-STAR-II speech-to-speech translation effort[1], we have been developing a translation system for the broad domain of travel planning, which contains a rich structure of sub-domains. Figure 1 shows the complete set of input and output languages that are covered by the C-STAR-II translation effort.

---

[1] C-STAR is the Consortium for Speech Translation Advanced Research. The C-STAR-II partners are: ATR, Japan; ISL, Universität Karlsruhe, Germany; ISL, Carnegie Mellon University, USA; ETRI, Korea; IRST, Italy; CLIPS-GETA, France. See http://www.is.cs.cmu.edu/cstar

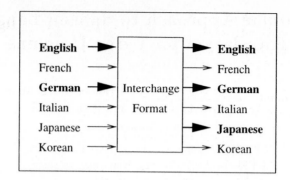

Fig. 1. C-STAR II Languages. Input and output languages analyzed by our group are marked in bold face.

The current JANUS MT system is designed around the following four main principles:

An Interlingua-based Approach: Following an interlingua-based approach allows us to easily expand our system to new languages. Since each language is usually integrated as both a source and a target language, input analyzed into an interlingua representation can then be translated back into the same language as a paraphrase of the original input utterance. This enables a user who has no knowledge of the target language to assess if the system correctly analyzed the input utterance. In our earlier work on the appointment scheduling domain (SST), the SOUP parser [5] generated an interlingua text (ILT), from which the output sentence was generated. For the translation of travel dialogues in the C-STAR project, a common interchange format (IF) for all six member sites was defined. Even though this IF differs considerably from the ILT we used for the scheduling task, our current system architecture can integrate them in a unified system as explained in more detail below.

Semantic Grammars: Semantic grammars have been shown to be effective in providing accurate translation for limited domains. They are also known to be robust against ungrammaticalities in spontaneous speech and recognition errors in speech-to-speech translation systems [6],[7],[10]. However, they are usually hard to expand to cover new domains.

Modular Semantic Grammars: In our current version of the JANUS system we have developed *modular* grammars to overcome the problems associated with expanding semantic grammars to new domains. Each sub-grammar covers the dialogue acts required for one sub-domain. An additional grammar provides cross-domain dialogue acts such as common openings and closings. All grammars share one library with common concepts, such as time expressions and proper names.

Efficient Integration of Multiple Grammars: Our current system is designed to integrate multiple domain grammars in a common analysis module. The parser analyzes the input with multiple grammars concurrently. Analyzed segments of the input are tagged with an ID that reflects the domain grammar that was used in creating the analysis. Segmentation of long utterances into a sequence of DAs is performed as part of the parsing process. The parser produces a lattice output of all possible parsable segments according to the different domain grammars. A statistical domain re-scoring procedure is then applied to the lattice, in order to reduce the level of ambiguity that arises from the combination of multiple domain grammars.

These main themes are described in greater length in the remaining sections of the paper. In Section 2 we describe the interchange format that has been developed for the C-STAR-II multi-site translation effort. In Section 3 we detail our approach for constructing modular semantic grammars which are used to extend our system coverage to new domains. We also describe in detail how these grammars are then integrated together in the runtime architecture of our translation system. In the final section we present a preview of current work on alternative backup methods for translation.

2   The C-STAR Interchange-Format

While the JANUS project has always used an interlingua for translation among multiple languages, the C-STAR project presents a special challenge by requiring an interlingua to be used at multiple research sites. It was therefore necessary to design an simple interlingua that could be used reliably by many MT developers. Simplicity is possible largely because we are working on travel planning, a task-oriented domain. In a task-oriented domain, most utterances perform a limited number of *domain actions* (DAs) such as requesting information about the availability of a hotel or giving information about the price of a hotel. These domain actions form the basis of the C-STAR interlingua, which is known as the *interchange format*, or IF. The IF does not represent the literal meaning of an utterance and is far-removed from the source language syntax. It represents only the domain action that the utterance was intended to perform. Translation via a shallow DA-based interlingua is also used in the Verbmobil project, although there it complements a transfer approach which is based on deeper semantic representations [1].

The design principles of the IF are 1) that it is based on domain actions, 2) that it is compositional, i.e. domain actions are built from an inventory of speech acts, concepts, and arguments, and 3) that it is intended to be suitable for all C-STAR languages.

A DA consists of three representational levels: the *speech act*, the *concepts*, and the *arguments*. In addition, each DA is preceded by a speaker tag (a: for agent or c: for customer) which indicates who is speaking. Plus signs ("+") separate speech acts from concepts and concepts from each other. In general the speech act and speaker information are obligatory whereas the concepts and the arguments are optional. DAs can be roughly characterized as shown in (1). However, there are constraints on the order of concepts so that not all combinations are possible.

(1)   *speaker : speech act +concept* (argument*)*

Examples (2) (3) (4) demonstrate specific DAs that are constructed according to this scheme. In example (2) the speech act is `give-information`, the concepts are `availability` and `room`, and the arguments are `time` and `room-type`. The arguments are inherited through a hierarchy of speech acts and concepts. In this case `time` is an argument of `availability` and `room-type` is an argument of room. Example (3) shows a DA which consists of a speech act with no concepts attached to it. The argument `time` is inherited from the speech act `closing`. Finally, example (4) demonstrates a case of DA which contains neither concepts nor arguments.

(2)   On the twelfth we have a single and a double available.
        `a:give-information+availability+room`
        `(room-type=(single & double),time=(md12))`
(3)   And we'll see you on February twelfth.
        `a:closing (time=(february, md12))`
(4)   Thank you very much
        `c:thank`

The DAs in the above examples do not capture all of the information present in their corresponding utterances. For instance they do not represent definiteness, grammatical relations, plurality, modality, or the presence of embedded clauses. These features are generally part of the formulaic, conventional ways of expressing the DAs in English. Their syntactic form is not relevant for translation; it only indirectly contributes to the identification of the DA.

Example (5) shows the English paraphrase, German translation, and Japanese translation for sentence (2).

(5) Input: On the twelfth we have a single and a double available.
    Paraphrase: A single and a double room will be available the twelfth.
    German: Es gibt Einzelzimmer und Doppelzimmer am zwölften.
    Japanese: １２日でしたらシングル・ダブルのどちらも空きがございます。

3   Modular Semantic Grammars

For both analysis and generation we have been developing semantic grammars. Rather than focusing on the syntactic structure of the input, semantic grammars directly describe how surface expressions reflect the underlying semantic concepts that are being conveyed by the speaker. Because they focus on identifying a set of predefined semantic concepts, they are relatively well suited to handle the types of meaningful but ungrammatical disfluencies that are typical

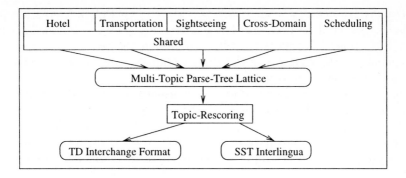

Fig. 2. Combining multiple sub-domain grammars with shared and cross domain grammars.

of spoken language, and are also less sensitive to speech recognition errors. Semantic grammars are also relatively fast to develop for limited domains, where the set of concepts being described is relatively small. However, they are usually hard to expand to cover new domains. New rules are required for each new semantic concept, since syntactic generalities cannot usually be fully utilized. For large domains, this can result in very cumbersome grammars that are difficult to expand and further develop, and which become highly ambiguous in nature.

Modularization and common libraries have long been a well-established concept in software development. Many of the advantages of modularity and shared libraries equally apply to the design of a large semantic grammar for a large domain, particularly if the domain can be dissected into multiple sub-domains. The application of these principles to the development of semantic grammars has the following advantages:

- Separating grammars for sub-domains into independent files allows several grammar developers to work independently and simultaneously without interfering with each other's grammar development.
- The sub-domain grammars draw from a shared library of rules in order to maintain consistency in the analysis of entities such as time and date phrases, auxiliary verbs, etc. The shared library and the cross-domain sub-grammar substantially reduce the effort required to expand the system to new domains.
- Separating grammar rules for different sub-domains enables the parser to tag parses of sub-utterances with the corresponding sub-domain. These tags can be used to re-score a lattice of parse trees using conditional probabilities to reduce the ambiguity introduced by expanding to new domains. Lattice re-scoring is explained in more detail in Section 3.3.

3.1 Integration of Multiple Sub-domain Grammars

Figure 2 shows the current configuration used for expanding the grammars to cover a variety of sub-grammars of the travel domain. The SOUP parser reads one sub-domain grammar at a time, and tags the concepts of each grammar with a domain tag, such as HTL (for hotel reservation), TPT (for transportation) and GTR (for general travel), in order to eliminate the possibility of conflicting concept names. All concepts in the shared grammar are left untagged so that they are accessible to all sub-domain grammars.

Since each utterance is parsed as a sequence of DAs, the parser also provides the segmentation of the utterance into DAs. Thus we do not need a separate program for segmenting spoken utterances into sentences. The DAs that comprise one utterance do not have to be taken from the same sub-grammar. The utterance in example (6) contains sub-parses from three different grammars.

(6)   Hello,
I would like to make a reservation for a flight to Frankfurt on the fifth and maybe also book a hotel room.
```
(GTR) c:greeting
(TPT) c:request-action+reservation+temporal+flight
(HTL) c:request-action+reservation+features+room
```

A considerable advantage of this approach is that grammars producing different interlingua representations can be combined into one system on the sub-utterance level, as shown in example (7), which uses IF and ILT in one utterance. This is possible because in this case the parser is working with a joint grammar that consists of non-overlapping domain-grammars. The output is a sequence of parse-trees, one for each DA in the utterance. Since each parse-tree is marked with a domain ID, it is easy to make sure that each parse-tree is handled by the appropriate mappers and generators.

(7)   I would like to make a reservation for a hotel room – do you have time on Friday?
```
(HTL) c:request-action+reservation+features+room
(SST) q_your_availability
```

3.2   Cross Domain and Shared Grammars

The goal of cross domain and shared grammars is to cover the overlap between the grammars for different sub-domains. The cross domain grammar contains grammar rules for dialogue acts that are required in a large number of different tasks. Examples for IF dialogue acts covered the cross domain grammar are:

(8)   `apologize`   (I'm sorry)
        `closing`   (bye)
        `greeting`   (hello Alex)
        `introduce-self`   (I'm Monika)
        `request-repeat`   (can you repeat that please)

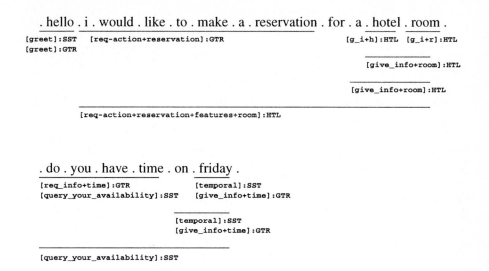

Fig. 3. DA parse lattice with multi-domain grammars.

Many of the speech acts in the cross domain grammars can be reused for new domains with only minor changes.

The shared grammars cover concepts that are used on a lower level to parse DAs in a variety of domains. Examples of concepts placed into shared grammars are date and time expressions (such as *around 5pm on Friday*) as well as lists of proper names. These grammars facilitate the expansion of the domain with new dialogue acts that are not covered by the cross-domain grammar but still contain some of the underlying concepts.

In example (6), the greeting *hello* is parsed by a cross-domain grammar, while the words *Frankfurt* and *on the fifth* are parsed by the shared grammar, in this case accessed by the sub-domain grammar for transportation.

3.3 Disambiguation with Statistical Domain Knowledge

With the expansion of our system to multiple domain grammars we have witnessed a significant increase in levels of ambiguity. It is often the case that an input utterance can consist of DAs from multiple domains. When applying the entire set of domain grammars, the utterance can be analyzed into a variety of different sequences of DAs. Disambiguating the correct sequence of DAs is crucial for correct translation.

One possible approach to disambiguation is to pre-segment the utterance in advance into sub-utterance units that are expected to belong to only one domain, and to use a domain classifier to determine the correct domain for each sub-utterance prior to or after parsing with the separate sub-domain grammars. However, this process is difficult to perform reliably, and any error in either one of the three steps would cause the translation to fail.

Since a great deal of knowledge about the DA segment boundaries and their domains is inherent in the modular parsing grammars, we have introduced a new approach to reduce the risk of miss-classifications: the SOUP parser parses complete utterances using *all* tagged sub-domain-grammars and produces a lattice of parse trees that contains all possible DA parses. Consequently, the parser also determines all possible ways of segmenting the utterance into DA-level segments. Figure 3 shows the resulting DA parse lattice for the utterance in example (7).

Using statistical domain knowledge, we then attempt to extract the best combination $\mathbf{S}$ of DA parse trees from the lattice. The goal is to find the most likely sequence of DAs $\mathbf{S} = s_1, s_2, \ldots s_N$ given the sequence of input words $\mathbf{W}$, i.e. to maximize the probability $P(\mathbf{S}|\mathbf{W})$. Unfortunately, the number of different dialogue acts is too large for robustly estimating their individual probabilities. Therefore, we collapse all DAs to just the domain $\mathbf{T}$ to which they belong, and use the domain tag probabilities instead of the DA probabilities. The domain tag for each DA is attached to the analysis, since it is derived from the sub-grammar from which the analysis was created. Thus, we search for the sequence of DAs $\mathbf{S} = s_1, s_2, \ldots s_N$, for which the corresponding $P(\mathbf{T}|\mathbf{W}) = P(t_1, t_2, \ldots t_N \mid \mathbf{W})$ is maximal. We perform this indirectly, using standard language modeling methods. First, applying Bayes rule, we have:

$$P(\mathbf{T}|\mathbf{W}) = \frac{P(\mathbf{W}|\mathbf{T}) \cdot P(\mathbf{T})}{P(\mathbf{W})} \tag{9}$$

Since $P(\mathbf{W})$ does not change once the utterance has been recognized, finding the maximal $P(\mathbf{T}|\mathbf{W})$ is the same as maximizing $P(\mathbf{W}|\mathbf{T}) \cdot P(\mathbf{T})$. Now, for any sequence of domains $\mathbf{T} = t_1, t_2, \ldots t_N$, we make an independence assumption between the word probabilities, such that the probability of a word w_i depends only on its domain t_i. Thus, for a given sequence of DAs $\mathbf{S} = s_1, s_2, \ldots s_N$, where the sequence of words W_i covered by the DA s_i is $W_i = w_{i1} w_{i2} \ldots w_{ik}$, we have:

$$P(W_i|\mathbf{T}) \approx P(W_i|t_i) \tag{10}$$
$$\approx P(w_{i1}|t_i) \cdot P(w_{i2}|t_i) \ldots P(w_{ik}|t_i)$$

Thus, for any possible segmentation of the entire input into a DA sequence $\mathbf{S}$, with corresponding domain sequence $\mathbf{T}$, we have:

$$P(\mathbf{W}|\mathbf{T}) = P(W_1, W_2, \ldots W_N \mid t_1, t_2, \ldots t_N) \tag{11}$$
$$\approx P(W_1|t_1) \cdot P(W_2|t_2) \ldots P(W_N|t_N)$$

where each $P(W_i|t_i)$ is calculated as in (10). To estimate each possible $P(w|t)$, the frequency of observing an individual word in the vocabulary for a given domain is estimated from a tagged training database.

The remaining needed probability for a sequence of domains $P(\mathbf{T})$ within one utterance is approximated by a unigram or a bigram statistic:

$$P(\mathbf{T}) = P(t_1, t_2, \ldots t_N) \tag{12}$$
$$\approx P(t_1) \cdot P(t_2) \cdot \ldots \cdot P(t_N)$$
$$\approx P(t_1) \cdot P(t_2|t_1) \cdot \ldots \cdot P(t_N|t_{N-1})$$

The search for the optimal DA sequence according to the probabilistic framework described above is performed within the SOUP parser at the end of the parsing stage. The parser then outputs a ranked list of possible DA sequences for the entire utterance.

4   Current and Future Work

The current architecture framework of the JANUS MT engine described in this paper has provided us with a solid design foundation for developing our translation system for the travel domain, which has proven to be a challenging task. Much of our current work involves incremental improvements in the coverage of our grammars and other knowledge sources and adding new languages in preparation for a thorough end-to-end evaluation. Recent preliminary end-to-end evaluations show a level of performance of about 50% acceptable translation of DAs, after about a year of system development. We aim at achieving a level of 80-90% acceptable translations within the next year.

We are also working on a number of advanced extensions to the translation system itself. These include the analysis of more advanced statistical disambiguation techniques, and the development of several alternative translation methods that we intend to combine with our grammar-based approach:

Multi-Engine Translation: Multi-engine translation was proposed by Frederking et al. [2] and has since been implemented in the Diplomat [3] and Verbmobil [11] systems. A multi-engine system applies multiple translation programs simultaneously and makes a translation by composing the best parts from the various outputs. Typically, a multi-engine system might include knowledge-based, statistical, and direct dictionary based approaches. In our case the components will be the knowledge based system described in this paper, statistical dialogue act assignment, and glossary lookups.

Combined Statistical/Grammar-based Analysis: One weakness of the grammar-based analysis system is that it is not very robust to concept phrasings that deviate significantly from those expected in the grammars, or to the occurrence of unexpected "noise" within concepts. To address this problem we are developing an alternative parsing method that combines both statistical and grammar information. Statistical information will be used in order to identify the DA, in cases where the grammar fails to do so with reasonable confidence. Using constraints from the interlingua specification, we will then predict the set of possible arguments that can our with the DA. A modified version of the grammars for parsing just argument fragments will then be used in order to extract the appropriate arguments from the utterance. Statistical identification of DAs has been investigated in the Verbmobil project [8]. Our own preliminary experiments on statistical DA extraction have shown encouraging results [4], and we are in the process of fully implementing the proposed method.

Acknowledgements

The IF formalism is the result of a close cooperation of the six C-STAR-II partners. Siemens played an important role in devising the initial format and structure. The description of the IF format is based on a specification document written by Mirella Lapata. Preliminary work on statistical DA identification was done by Toshiaki Fukada from ATR during a research term at CMU.

References

1. Thomas Bub, Wofgang Wahlster and Alex Waibel. Verbmobil: The Combination of Deep and Shallow Processing for Speech Translation. In *Proceedings of ICASSP-97*, 1997.
2. R. Frederking, S. Nirenburg, D. Farwell, S. Helmreich, E. Hovy, K. Knight, S. Beale, C. Domashnev, D. Attardo, D. Grannes, and R. Brown. Integrating Translations from Multiple Sources within the Pangloss Mark III Machine Translation', in *Proceedings of the First Conference of the Association for Machine Translation in the Americas* (AMTA-94). Columbia, Maryland, 1994.
3. R. Frederking, A. Rudnicky, and C. Hogan. Interactive Speech Translation in the DIPLOMAT Project. In *Proceedings of the Spoken Language Translation Workshop at the 35th Meeting of the Association for Computational Linguistics (ACL-97)*. Madrid, Spain. 1997.
4. Toshiaki Fukada. Statistical Extraction of Dialogue Acts for Spoken Language Translation. To appear in *Proceedings of ICSLP-98*, Sydney, Australia, 1998.
5. Marsal Gavaldà. The SOUP Home Page. June 1998.
   http://www.is.cs.cmu.edu/ISL.speech.parsing.soup.html
6. Alon Lavie, Lori Levin, Puming Zhan, Maite Taboada, Donna Gates, Mirella Lapata, Cortis Clark, Matthew Broadhead, and Alex Waibel.
   Expanding the Domain of a Multi-lingual Speech-to-Speech Translation System.
   In Proceedings of the Workshop on Spoken Language Translation, ACL/EACL-97, Madrid, Spain, July 1997.
7. Laura Mayfield, Marsal Gavaldà, Y-H.Seo, Bernhard Suhm, Wayne Ward and Alex Waibel. Parsing Real Input in JANUS: A Concept Based Approach. in *Proceedings of TMI-95*, 1995.
8. Norbert Reithinger and Martin Klesen. Dialogue Act Classification Using Language Models. in *Proceedings of EuroSpeech-97*, pages 2235–2238, Rhodes, Greece, 1997.
9. Alex Waibel. Interactive Translation of Conversational Speech, *Computer*, 29(7), pages 41–48.
10. Wayne Ward. 'The CMU Air Travel Information Service: Understanding spontaneous speech', In *Proceedings of the DARPA Speech and Language Workshop*, 1990.
11. Karsten Worm. A Model for Robust Processing of Spontaneous Speech by Integrating Viable Fragments. In *Proceedings of COLING-ACL-98*, Montreal, Canada, August 1998.

Enhancing Automatic Acquisition
of the Thematic Structure in a Large-Scale Lexicon
for Mandarin Chinese

Mari Broman Olsen, Bonnie J. Dorr, and Scott C. Thomas

University of Maryland, College Park MD 20742, USA,
molsen,dorr,scthmas@umiacs.umd.edu
WWW home page: http://umiacs.umd.edu/labs/CLIP

Abstract. This paper describes a refinement to our procedure for porting lexical conceptual structure (LCS) into new languages. Specifically we describe a two-step process for creating candidate thematic grids for Mandarin Chinese verbs, using the English verb heading the VP in the subdefinitions to separate senses, and roughly parsing the verb complement structure to match thematic structure templates. We accomplished a substantial reduction in manual effort, without substantive loss. The procedure is part of a larger process of creating a usable lexicon for interlingual machine translation from a large on-line resource with both too much and too little information.

1   Introduction

In previous work on Spanish and Arabic (Dorr et al., 1997; Dorr, 1997a), we reported the results of an acquisition process for verb databases in new languages, using automatic assignment of candidate thematic structure templates ("grids") and manual verification of the output. This paper reports on acquisition of a Mandarin Chinese verb database from an on-line resource ten times as large as those used for Spanish and Arabic (600k, rather than 60k entries). The procedure is part of a larger process of creating a usable lexicon for interlingual machine translation from a large on-line resource with both too much and too little information necessary for our interlingual machine translation system (Dorr, 1997b; Hogan and Levin, 1994).

The major contributions of this work are: (i) reducing the effect of polysemy by addressing it in the preprocessing phase, and (ii) removing a substantial subset of automatically generated thematic grids requiring manual correction, by relating thematic information incorporated in Chinese verbs to overt complements in English. Both of the above result in a reduction of 11% of material that needs to be corrected by hand: 15,565 possible candidate thematic grids. Furthermore, the separation of senses allows candidate grids to be evaluated with respect to a particular sense. Noise that is introduced from polysemy in the English glosses—by putting the grids from the 'run a machine' and 'run a race' senses into a "bag of grids"—may therefore be eliminated, as grids are tied to a particular sense. The reduction of manual effort has been accomplished without substantive loss of relevant definitions, as evaluated in a preliminary task, assigning thematic grids to verbs in 10 sentences from a corpus of 10 *Xinhua* articles.

We see this work as a step beyond that suggested by (Dorr et al., 1997), in which manual correction took place without first reducing the degree of ambiguity in the entry. Dorr et al. generated 18353 candidate thematic grids, representing 3623 verbs in the initial Spanish-English lexicon. Of that, 3025 entries were verified as correct (16.5%), and 15328 (83.5%) had to be modified in some way. There were 6082 deletions of entries, 334 reclassifications (resulting in changes of entries) and 6295 refinements of entries. The refinements included 3648 deletions of non-applicable entries; 2747 changes to prepositions, optional roles made obligatory, etc.; 2617 entries (955 verbs) deleted due to rarity of usage and/or disjointness with respect to WordNet concepts; 1213 new entries added (representing 1092 verbs not in the initial database). That is, there were a total of 9730 deletions, representing 63.5% of the required modifications, and 53% of the total number of candidate grids. Thus, an automatic process that reduces the number of deletions in a principled way would substantially reduce the manual correction process.

In the next section we describe the role of thematic grids in our system. We then describe our lexicon acquisition procedure, with respect to the verbs, detailing how we attempted to deal with polysemy and overgeneration of grids. We also report on other issues that arose in adapting the on-line resources.

2   Thematic Structure: Grids

Thematic structure serves as the interface between the syntactic component (parsing) and the lexical-semantic component, the Lexical Conceptual Structure (LCS). Verbs are assigned to classes that share syntactic and semantic behavior. That is, verbs in a class appear in the same types of sentences, with the same syntactic and semantic type of complements, represented as thematic (or "theta") roles. The syntactic and semantic behavior is abbreviated in the form of thematic grids, consisting of lists of obligatory and optional thematic roles, including agent, theme (patient), experiencer, source, goal and location.

In thematic grids, roles preceded by an underscore (_) are obligatory, and those preceded by a comma (,) are optional. A set of parentheses () indicates that the role must be expressed as a complement of a preposition or complementizer (e.g. the infinitival *to* in English). If the preposition is indicated, that preposition must be the head of the phrase. For example, the thematic grid `ag_th,src(from),goal(to)` indicates that agent and theme are obligatory, and source and goal are optional, and must be expressed by *from* and *to* prepositional phrases, respectively. Assigning this grid to the *Send* verbs, for example (class 11.1 in (Levin, 1993)), allows these verbs to appear in sentences like (1)-(4), but not (5)-(8), since the obligatory theme argument is missing.

(1) I sent the book.
(2) I sent the book to Mary
(3) I sent the book from the warehouse.
(4) I sent the book from the warehouse to Mary.
(5) * I sent.
(6) * I sent to Mary.
(7) * I sent from the warehouse.
(8) * I sent from the warehouse to Mary.

The thematic roles map directly into numbers, representing variables in the LCS. Although theta roles are theoretically unordered (Rappaport and Levin, 1988), the numbers correspond to a "canonical" linear position in a sentence and relative structural height in syntax and LCS trees. Thus 1 in the LCS corresponds to the ag(ent) thematic role and 2 to th(eme), since agents usually precede themes and occur higher in the syntactic tree. That is, in a sentence with an agent and a theme, typically the agent will be the subject and the theme the object, and both will precede other arguments.

The LCS for the above grid (simplifying irrelevant details) is given below: agent = thing 1, theme = thing 2, source preposition = thing 3, source complement of the preposition = thing 4, goal preposition = thing 5, goal complement of the preposition = thing 6. The * markers indicate where arguments are instantiated.

```
(cause (* thing 1)
   (go loc (* thing 2)
       ((* to 5) loc (thing 2) (at loc (thing 2) (thing 6)))
       ((* from 3) loc (thing 2) (at loc (thing 2) (thing 4))))
   (!!-ingly 26))
```

Thematic grids represent multiple structures; additionally, verbs in a language can take more than one thematic grid. For example, verbs like *fill, carpet, cloak* and *plug* allow the following grids, among others:[1]

(9) _ag_th,mod-poss(with) Derek filled the bucket with water.
(10) _mod-poss_th The water filled the bucket.

Other verb classes may take some of these grids but not others. Verbs like *inscribe, mark, sign, stamp* take the former, but not the latter, for example: *She signed his yearbook with her name*, but not *His name signed her yearbook*. The grids therefore group verbs by "semantic structure" (Levin and Rappaport Hovav, 1995). In contrast to "semantic content"—the idiosyncratic aspect of verb meaning—semantic structure determines syntactic patterning within and across languages (Dorr and Oard, 1998; Dorr and Katsova, 1998; Grimshaw, 1993; Pinker, 1984; Pinker, 1989).

---

[1] The mod-poss indicates a "possessed" item, paraphraseable by *have*: *The hole has water (in it)*.

Most importantly for our system, the assignment of a set of thematic grids to a verb class allows us to create the interlingual LCS structures automatically (Dorr et al., 1995). Furthermore, in selecting grids for creating LCS entries for a new language, we leverage the fact that semantic structure overlaps across languages to a large degree. The task of creating the grids is therefore reduced to automatic generation, as described in Section 4, followed by manual correction to eliminate inappropriate grids (along with other modifications, described in Section 1 above). Before we describe the automatic process, we first describe some of the pre-processing required to extract appropriate verbs.

3 Verb Selection

The assignment of thematic grids/LCS structures to verbs is one step in the creation of a lexicon from a large (600k entries) machine readable Chinese-English dictionary. The dictionary was compiled by hand, by the Chinese-English Translation Assistance (CETA) group from some 250 dictionaries, some general purpose, others domain-specific or bilingual (Russian-Chinese, English Chinese, etc.). The CETA group, started in 1965 and continuing into the present decade, was a joint government-academic project. The machine-readable version of the CETA dictionary, *Optilex*, licensed from the MRM corporation, Kensington, MD.

CETA contains some information extraneous to our purposes. Some of the 250 resources used to create the dictionary were very domain-specific, including, for example, *Collier's North China Colloquial Collection*, a publication listing many regionalisms not observed anywhere else in China, and the *Faxue Cidian*, a dictionary of legal terms from Shanghai. We eliminated many archaic and technical verbs by eliminating verbs identified by CETA as derived from these sources.[2]

Even after archaic or idiosyncratic sources were eliminated, entries varied widely in specificity, from the general verbs (and other words) to the extremely specific, as the examples below show, given with the Pinyin, definition, and simplified character representation from CETA.

---

[2] BF Chinese-English Dictionary 1978, BE same as E but Chinese-Chinese 1978, AR Atlas of the PRC 1977 (for Chinese placenames), AO Gazetteer of the PRC (also for Chinese placenames), BQ extra new entries from the first two above BE and BF CJ standardized FBIS translations of Chinese communist terms, CM specialized terms extracted from Mao's works, CU Hong Kong glossary of Chinese communist terms, EJ 1981 idiom dictionary, EK 1982 idiom dictionary, FA Foreign Exchange terms 1963, IP International political economics glossary 1980, IQ Beijing social sciences academy economics terms 1983, NA world place names 1981, PP primary political economics glossary 1956, TM McGraw-Hill general scientific and technical dictionary 1963, VF Lin Yutang's dictionary 1972, VT 1973 Beijing foreign exchange glossary, WB Liang Shih-ch'iu's traditional dictionary 1973, YG Stanford's dictionary of Chinese communist terms 1973.

(11) po4_shi3 compel 迫使
(12) po4_shi3 force 迫使
(13) ben1_pao3 run 奔跑
(14) zou3 walk 走
(15) chu1_kou3 speak[3] 出口
(16) bi1_gong1 force_the_sovereign_to_abdicate 逼宫
(17) ben1_zou3_xiang1_gao4 run_around_spreading_the_news 奔走相告
(18) ca1_la5_zhe5_zou3 walk_dragging_one's_feet 擦拉着走
(19) chui1_xu1 speak_in_favor_of_somebody_in_exaggerated_terms 吹嘘

Although CETA is large, and in some ways exhaustive, some information required by our machine-translation lexicon is not directly encoded, notably part of speech.[4] We identified the verbs by a simple process. We parsed the DEF (gloss) field in the CETA entries from the selected sources. If the English glosses began with the infinitival 'to', the whole entry was used to generate as many new verb entries as there are verbs in the DEF field. As an example, the excerpt from following entry has four subentries in its DEF field. PY gives the Pinyin representation.[5]

PY: bian1 ta4
DEF: 1. to whip, to flog 2. <fig> to chastise, to castigate

After processing, each definition has a single subsense entry, i.e. there are four subentries.

4 Pairing Verbs and Thematic Grids

4.1 English glosses

For the Arabic and Spanish lexicon, we created candidate thematic grids by pairing target language words with the thematic grids associated with their English gloss, with manual correction over a period of two weeks. We did the same initial step for Chinese, as well. However, as described above, the senses had already been separated into different subentries. We thus had candidate thematic grid sets for each sense of a given verb.

The file containing Chinese grids was created by first matching the main verb of the English glosses to one or more entries in the English grids file. Separating

---

[3] As in 'to speak ill of someone.' This meaning is the first listed, although it is less common than others, including 'exit', as in exit signs (John Kovarik, p.c.).

[4] In fact, part of speech was not included in Chinese dictionaries at all, until the mid-80s (John Kovarik, Jin Tong p.c.); how and whether to do it is still controversial (http://linguistlist.org/issues/9/9-1186.html).

[5] CETA includes other fields not listed, including HWT and HWS encoding traditional and simplified characters, STC for the Standard Telegram Code, and REF for the dictionaries the entry came from.

polysemous entries is an aid to this process, since not all grids are associated with all verb senses. For example, a wide range of grids is available for the *Run* verbs. The first numbers, again, are classes from Levin (Levin, 1993). Numbers less than 9 are classes not found in Levin that were created automatically (Dorr, 1997b).

(20) 26.3 _ag 持 chi2 run

(21) 26.3 _ag_ben_th 持 chi2 run

(22) 26.3 _ag_th,ben(for) 持 chi2 run

(23) 47.5.1 _ag,mod-loc() 持 chi2 run

(24) 47.5.1 _loc_th 持 chi2 run

(25) 47.5.1 _th_loc() 持 chi2 run

(26) 47.7 _th_goal() 持 chi2 run

(27) 47.7 _th_src(from)_goal(to) 持 chi2 run

(28) 51.3.2 _ag 持 chi2 run

(29) 51.3.2 _th,src(),goal() 持 chi2 run

In contrast, a relatively small number is available for other meanings of this character.

(30) 31.2 _exp_perc,mod-poss(in) 持 chi2 support

(31) 47.8 _th_loc 持 chi2 support

In previous work, all grids were associated with a single entry and the checker was presented with a "bag of grids", without a link to a specific meaning. Since manual separation of senses was necessary, the likelihood of human error was high: checkers would delete or retain grids depending on which sense of the verb they had in mind. In the case at hand, it turns out that 持 chi2 means 'run', as in 'run a business' or 'run a machine', whereas the theta grids were derived from the motion verb *run* in English. Should the grids prove inappropriate in the manual verification stage, they can be deleted without affecting entries with other meanings.

4.2 Automatic Modification of Candidate Grids

Each thematic grid in the initial candidate set describes the argument structure for the head verb of the gloss, in some usage of that (English) verb. To construct appropriate LCSs for the Chinese verb, these grids must be manually checked and modified where necessary. We have further parsed the DEF field to automatically make certain modifications that in earlier work had been done by hand.

For instance, the candidate set for the Chinese verb in (16) above, glossed 'to force the sovereign to abdicate,' contains the grid _ag_th,prop(to), because the English verb *force* takes an agent, theme and optional propositional complement. After parsing the gloss into subphrases, we can posit that 'the sovereign' is theme, and 'to abdicate', the propositional element. On the assumption that a gloss of this sort implies that theme and propositional element are part of the Chinese verb meaning and *not* expressed as overt complements, the grid is reduced to _ag; 'the sovereign' and 'to abdicate' are set aside, to be inserted directly into the LCS for the Chinese entry. Thus, for hand checking, we construct a grid that appears like:

(32) 002 _ag 逼宫 bi1_gong1 force_the_sovereign_to_abdicate
    (th = sovereign) (prop = to_abdicate)

Similarly, the following Chinese word receives the grid shown in (9), but with the possessional modifier `mod-poss(with)` lexicalized by the verb itself, and thus removed from the grid:

(33) 9.8 _ag_th 填土 tian2_tu3 fill_in_with_earth (mod-poss = earth)

The underlying intuition is that verbs that incorporate thematic elements in their meaning would not allow that element to appear in the complement structure: *fill_in_with_earth with gravel*, cf. English *I sodded my lawn with ivy*[6].

The matching of gloss verb-complements to thematic roles is made as follows. We first parsed the gloss with simple context-free phrase-structure rules, to retrieve a flat structure, consisting of the V and a list of complements: NPs, PPs, clauses like 'to abdicate', and predicate adverbs or adjectives, like 'weary' in 'to be weary'. PPs headed with 'of' were attached low and not considered as a VP complement, e.g. *give [an explanation of the situation]*.

Information in parentheses was ignored. Thus, had the gloss above been 'to force (i.e. the sovereign) to abdicate', we would have assumed that the Chinese verb *required* a theme argument (like 'the sovereign'), and the grid would have been _ag_th instead of just _ag. Parentheses do contain some apparently important material. For example, there is a gloss 'to kill (or catch) a tiger', which appears to condense two different senses. However, this usage of parentheses was mostly found in the sections of CETA we suppressed. A series of nouns was considered a single NP, as in 案检: an4 jian3; DEF: to investigate [a law case].

Having split the gloss into its thematic parts, we then match the PPs to thematic roles that specify the same head as the PP, and match propositional elements that have matching prepositions or particles (i.e. the 'to' in 'to abdicate'). Some grids specify roles with no particular preposition, in which case we heuristically assign roles according to this table:

from: `src` (source) or `instr`
for: `purp` (purpose)
with: `instr` or `mod-poss`
without: `mod-poss`
into, to against: `goal`
under, around, along: `mod-loc`

---

[6] We are ignoring 'cognate objects', as in *I sodded my lawn with the best sod available* (Macfarland, 1995)

Adverbs become `manner` components, in positions where they typically modify the verb ('to blindly worship foreign things'), rather than an adjective ('to be seriously ill'). The adverbial manner components become part of the LCS, if the entry passes through the hand inspection phase. A gloss that ends with a *dangling preposition* is taken as a sign that, where the English verb takes a PP, the Chinese verb fills the same role with a bare NP argument. Thus the parentheses are removed from the grid for that role (see Section 2). *Bare noun phrases* are matched to non-prepositional-phrase thematic roles. *Predicate adjectives* match `pred`, an identificational predicate—in this case, naming a property. Any material in the gloss not matching anything in the thematic grid is kept for incorporation into the LCS as a modifier.

In this manner, 11360 distinct theta role assignments were created. In some cases the original theta-roles list actually becomes empty, in which case it appears as _0, the thematic grid for verbs with no semantic arguments, such as *rain* in English *It's raining*.

After we saturate the relevant components of the thematic grids, we use the filled grids to reduce the candidate set of grids. If the set of theta roles lexicalized by a Chinese verb sense for one candidate grid (which may be the empty set) is a proper subset of that for another grid of that verb sense, then the smaller grid is discarded, resulting in an a 11% reduction in the number of entries that need to be hand-checked. Thus, if there were a thematic grid _ag_th generated for 'to force the sovereign to abdicate', it would be discarded in favor of the grid above.

Similarly, the seven candidate grids for 'to serve as a guide' reduce to one, since only one could incorporate the predicate with 'as', that from Levin class 29.6, which includes verbs like *act, behave,* and *pose* as well as *serve*:

(34) Entry HWS: 充向导
    PY: chong1 xiang4 dao3
    DEF: 'to serve as a guide'

(35) Retained:
    29.6.b _th_pred(as)

(36) Suppressed:
    13.1 _ag_goal_th (e.g. *We served them food*)
    13.1 _ag_th_goal(to) (e.g. *We served food to them*)
    13.4.1 _ag_th,mod-poss(with) (e.g. *I served him with a warrant*)
    13.4.1 _ag_th,goal(to) (e.g. *We served a warrant to them*)
    54.3 _ag_th_loc() (e.g. *We serve 114 people in this restaurant*)
    54.3 _th_poss (e.g. *This restaurant serves 114 people*)

5   Results

Using the process described above, 15565 thematic grids were eliminated, representing 11% of the total number of candidates. We began the process of manual evaluation of the theta grids, beginning with the verbs in 10 articles from *Xinhua,* comparable to the *Wall Street Journal* in content: 124 grids were suppressed for 47 verbs (29 classes), leaving 3041 grids for 263 verbs (characters, rather than definitions). A set of 51 theta grids were generated for the 13 verbs in ten sentences from these articles. Chinese speakers deleted 17 grids, or 33.3%. Although these results are a tiny subset of the full verb lexicon, this figure compares favorably to the 53% deletion required of the Spanish data. Importantly, none of the relevant grids had been discarded by our algorithm.[7]

The fact that we parsed the complement structure in the subentries alerted the language experts (John Kovarik and Mary-Ellen Okurowski, both from the Department of Defense (DOD), and Ron Dolan from the Library of Congress) to additional senses that should be eliminated from the lexicon, e.g. those not properly considered verbal. Furthermore, although we used only the most general sources, all the dictionaries included entries from both classical and colloquial Chinese. Only the latter is used in our domain. Additionally, the classical entries are often archaisms and figurative uses that would likely not have the same thematic structure, for example, the meaning 'to shelve' derived from a character meaning 'to push (down)' (PY an4). In addition, the syntactic structure assigned to the gloss demonstrated that some of the entries glossed as verbs are more appropriately treated as prepositions or prepositional phrases. Removing old and syntactically incorrect entries resulted in a further 40% reduction for verb senses in the ten articles. Since we have been generating an average of 3.3 thematic grids per sense, we have decided to do preprocessing before generating the other candidate grid sets.

6 Conclusions and Future Work

We have described a procedure for automatically reducing the amount of manual checking necessary for building the thematic grid structure for verbs in Chinese. We anticipate that this procedure will save us time over our original checking procedure. The latter, in turn, reduced the amount of time required to create thematic structure from 6 person months (for a lexicon with 60k entries and 3-4k verbs) to approximately two weeks of hand verification. The time savings for our project is even more imperative, since we expect to have almost double that size in verbs alone, even after removing inappropriate entries. The procedure described in this paper provides further streamlining for the process of acquiring large-scale lexica for NLP applications with non-optimal on-line resources.

In addressing the polysemy problem in this context, we have, as a by-product, produced a sense-to-syntax mapping, tying a verb sense/character pair to a set of grids representing syntactic as well as semantic structure. This mapping, in turn, could be used not only for machine translation, but for segmentation and word sense disambiguation algorithms for Chinese.

---

[7] The copular grid for the verb *shi4* was added to the set, using a grid assigned to other copular verbs, namely *wei2* and *zuo4*. Somewhat surprisingly, the absence of the copular grid in our candidate set resulted from an absence in CETA of the copular meaning for that verb.

Acknowledgments

This work has been supported, in part, by DOD Contract MDA904-96-C-1250. The second author is also supported by DARPA/ITO Contract N66001-97-C-8540, Army Research Laboratory contract DAAL01-97-C-0042, NSF PFF IRI-9629108 and Logos Corporation, NSF CNRS INT-9314583, and Alfred P. Sloan Research Fellowship Award BR3336. We would like to thank members of the following lab groups at Maryland: Computational Linguistics and Information Processing (CLIP), and Language And Media Processing (LAMP), particularly Galen Wilkerson for his implementation and description of verb selection, and John Kovarik, a Chinese language instructor on loan from the DOD.

References

Dorr, B. J. (1997a). Large-Scale Acquisition of LCS-Based Lexicons for Foreign Language Tutoring. In *Proceedings of the ACL Fifth Conference on Applied Natural Language Processing (ANLP)*, pages 139–146, Washington, DC.

Dorr, B. J. (1997b). Large-Scale Dictionary Construction for Foreign Language Tutoring and Interlingual Machine Translation. *Machine Translation*, 12(4):271–322.

Dorr, B. J., Garman, J., and Weinberg, A. (1995). From Syntactic Encodings to Thematic Roles: Building Lexical Entries for Interlingual MT. *Machine Translation*, 9:71–100.

Dorr, B. J. and Katsova, M. (1998). Lexical Selection for Cross-Language Applications: Combining LCS with WordNet. In *Proceedings of AMTA-98*, Lanhorne, PA.

Dorr, B. J., Marti, A., and Castellon, I. (1997). Spanish EuroWordNet and LCS-Based Interlingual MT. In *Proceedings of the MT Summit Workshop on Interlinguas in MT*, San Diego, CA.

Dorr, B. J. and Oard, D. W. (1998). Evaluating resources for query translation in cross-language information retrieval. In *Proceedings of the First International Conference on Language Resources and Evaluation*, Granada, Spain.

Grimshaw, J. (1993). Semantic Structure and Semantic Content in Lexical Representation. unpublished ms., Rutgers University, New Brunswick, NJ.

Hogan, C. and Levin, L. (1994). Data Sparseness in the Acquisition of Syntax-Semantics Mappings. In *Proceedings of the Post-COLING94 International Workshop on Directions of Lexical Research*, pages 153–159, Nicoletta Calzolari and Chengming Guo (co-chairs), Tshinghua University, Beijing.

Levin, B. (1993). *English Verb Classes and Alternations: A Preliminary Investigation*. University of Chicago Press, Chicago, IL.

Levin, B. and Rappaport Hovav, M., editors (1995). *Unaccusativity: At the Syntax-Lexical Semantics Interface*. The MIT Press, Cambridge, MA. LI Monograph 26.

Macfarland, T. (1995). *Cognate Objects and the Argument/Adjunct Distinction in English*. PhD thesis, Northwestern University, Evanston, IL.

Pinker, S. (1984). *Language Learnability and Language Development*. MIT Press, Cambridge, MA.

Pinker, S. (1989). *Learnability and Cognition: The Acquisition of Argument Structure*. The MIT Press, Cambridge, MA.

Rappaport, M. and Levin, B. (1988). What to do with θ-Roles. In Wilkins, W., editor, *Syntax and Semantics: Vol. 21, Thematic Relations*, pages 7–36. Academic Press, New York.

Ordering Translation Templates by Assigning Confidence Factors*

Zeynep Öz and Ilyas Cicekli

Dept. of Comp. Eng. and Info. Sc., Bilkent University,
06533 Bilkent, Ankara, TURKEY,
{ozzey,ilyas}@cs.bilkent.edu.tr

Abstract. TTL (*Translation Template Learner*) algorithm learns lexical level correspondences between two translation examples by using analogical reasoning. The sentences used as translation examples have similar and different parts in the source language which must correspond to the similar and different parts in the target language. Therefore these correspondences are learned as translation templates. The learned translation templates are used in the translation of other sentences. However, we need to assign confidence factors to these translation templates to order translation results with respect to previously assigned confidence factors. This paper proposes a method for assigning confidence factors to translation templates learned by the TTL algorithm. Training data is used for collecting statistical information that will be used in confidence factor assignment process. In this process, each template is assigned a confidence factor according to the statistical information obtained from training data. Furthermore, some template combinations are also assigned confidence factors in order to eliminate certain combinations resulting bad translation.

1 Introduction

Traditional approaches to machine translation (MT) require detailed knowledge about languages and the world knowledge. Therefore corpus-based machine translation is a good alternative for avoiding them. *Example-based* machine translation (EBMT) is one of the main approaches of corpus-based machine translation and originally proposed by Nagao [12]. This approach is based on the idea of performing translation by imitating translation examples of similar sentences. It involves translating the source language into the target language via remindings from the previous translation cases as stated in Brona [5]. After this proposal several machine translation methods that utilize translation examples and bilingual corpora have been studied such as [13, 15, 16, 1]. EBMT is the marriage of the MT and *Case-based reasoning* techniques (CBR). Finding the

---

* This research has been supported in part by NATO Science for Stability Program Grant TU-LANGUAGE and The Scientific and Technical Council of Turkey Grant EEEAG-244.

correspondence of units in a bilingual text, retrieving the best matches from previous translation examples, and producing the translation of the given input by using these examples are the fundamental phases in EBMT. Brown [2] and Gale [6] have proposed methods for establishing correspondence between sentences in bilingual corpora. Brown [3], Sadler [14] and Kaji [9] have tackled the problem of establishing correspondences between words and phrases in bilingual texts.

Statistical machine translation is another approach of corpus-based machine translation. Statistical MT techniques use statistical metrics to choose the best structures in the target language among all possible candidates. These techniques are useful for retrieving the best matches from the previous translation examples, which is a vital issue in EBMT. This fact motivated us to develop a machine translation system that is a combination of statistical MT and EBMT.

Using previous examples for learning from new examples is the main idea behind exemplar-based learning which is originally proposed by Medin and Schaffer [11]. This way of learning stores the examples in memory without any change in the representation. The characteristic examples stored in the memory are called exemplars.

In the translation process, providing the correspondences between the source and target languages is a very difficult task in EBMT. Although, manual encoding of the translation rules has been achieved by Kitano [10], when the corpus is very large, it becomes a complicated and error-prone task. Therefore Cicekli and Güvenir [7, 4] offered a technique in which the problem is taken as a machine learning task. Exemplars are stored in the form of templates that are generalized exemplars. A template is an example translation pair where some components (e.g., words stems and morphemes) are generalized by replacing them with variables in both sentences, and establishing bindings between variables. These templates are learned by using translation examples and finding the correspondences between the patterns in the source and target languages. The heuristic of the translation template learning (TTL) [7, 4] algorithm can be summarized as follows: Given two translation pairs, if there are some similarities in the source language, then the corresponding sentences in the target language must have similar parts, and they must be translations of the similar parts of the sentences in the source language. Similar parts are replaced with variables to get a template which is a generalized exemplar by this method. Translation examples are stored as a list of string formed by strings of root words and morphemes. In other words, the lexical level representation of the sentences are used.This representation of translation examples is suitable for learning algorithm. If we used surface level representation, the number of correspondences would be decreased and we could learn less number of generalized exemplars. For example the sentence pair **i came from school⇔ben okuldan geldim** is stored as:

i come+p from school⇔ben okul+DAn gel+DH+m

where *i, come, from, school* denote root words and *+p* denotes the past tense morpheme in English sentence, and *ben, okul, gel* denote root words and *+DAn, +DH, +m* denote ablative, past tense and first singular person morphemes in

Turkish sentence. The following translation pairs given in English and Turkish illustrates the heuristic:

I go+p to school by bus $\Leftrightarrow$ okul +yA otobüs+ylA git+DH+m

I go+p to city by bus $\Leftrightarrow$ şehir +yA otobüs+ylA git+DH+m

The similarities between the translation examples are underlined. The similarities in English are represented as **I go+p to** X^{L_1} **by bus**, and the corresponding similarities in Turkish as X^{L_2}**+yA otobüs+ylA git+DH+m** by replacing differences by variables. According to the heuristic, these similarities should correspond to each other. Here, X^{L_1} denotes a component that can be replaced by any appropriate structure in English and X^{L_2} refers to its translation in Turkish. In addition to this, it is also inferred that *school* is the translation of *okul* and *city* is the translation of *şehir*. This shows that it is possible to learn more than one template by using two translation examples.

The order of the translation templates that will be used for the translation of new sentences is an important fact for the soundness of the outputs, however, the early versions of the algorithm uses a simple criterion for the order of the translation templates inferred. We need to assign confidence factors, i.e., weights, to these translation templates to have more accurate translations. Confidence factor assignment is done by using training data and collecting some statistical information. In the learning phase of the algorithm, each template is given a template number. Since translation is bidirectional, templates (specific templates without variables and generalized ones with variables) are assigned two weights, one for left to right usage and one for right to left usage of that template by using the translation examples. In addition to these, some template combinations are also assigned confidence factors in order to eliminate bad translation results. Translation accuracy is increased by using these weights. In the translation process, the output translations which have the highest weights are selected among all possibilities. Thus, it is ensured that the correct answer will be among these selected output.

The rest of the paper is organized as follows. Section 2 explains the confidence factor assignment process to the templates. Translation algorithm is described in Section 3. In Section 4 performance results of the system are provided. Section 5 concludes the paper and gives some future directions.

2 Methods for Assigning Confidence Factors

The translation templates are ordered according to the number of terminal symbols of the templates in the previous version of TTL algorithm [7]. However, this criteria is not sufficient for large systems, and we need another method where a statistical method is a powerful candidate, in order to improve the soundness of the translation process. Therefore, in the new version of the TTL algorithm, learning translation templates is followed by a confidence factor assignment process in which each rule and some rule combinations are assigned weights. Our main resource for assigning confidence factor is the training data that is used in the learning of translation templates. This process has three fundamental parts: Confidence factor assignment to facts (i.e. specific templates without variables), rules (i.e. generalized templates in which the similarities are replaced with variables) and rule combinations. These three parts are explained in detail in the following sections.

Our translation process is bidirectional. In other words, it is possible to give an input sentence in language L_1 and obtain a translation in language L_2 and vice versa. Therefore we have templates that will be used for translation from L_1 to L_2, (left to right) and from L_2 to L_1(right to left).

2.1   Method for Assigning Confidence Factors to Facts

In this section confidence factor assignment to facts, which are the simplest case of this process, are discussed. We do not need to consider any other rule during this process and we use only the translation examples.

Consider the case that, $rule_k$ is a fact which will be used for left to right translation. Assume that, it is in the form of $X \Leftrightarrow Y$ and we have training pairs in the form of $trainpair(X_i, Y_i)$ then the confidence factor of $rule_k$ for left to right translation is evaluated as follows:

- $N1$ denotes the number of training pairs where X is a substring of X_i and Y is a substring of Y_i
- $N2$ denotes the number of training pairs where X is a substring of X_i and Y is not a substring of Y_i
- $confidence factor_{rule_k} = \frac{N1}{N1+N2}$

If $rule_k$ is a fact which will be used for right to left translation, everything will be the same except definition of $N2$

- $N2$ denotes the number of training pairs where X is not a substring of X_i and Y is a substring of Y_i

Now, we illustrate how to find the confidence factor of a fact by giving an example. Let us assume that our all training pairs are as follows:

    he come+s⇔gel+Hr
    he go+s⇔git+Hr
    book+s⇔kitap+lAr
    pen+s⇔kalem+lAr

where +Hr and +lAr denote present tense and plural morphemes in Turkish. If we want to find the confidence factor of the rule +s → **Hr** (this rule is a fact and it will be used in left to right translation) which has been learned from these training pairs, we can find its confidence factor as follows:

$N1 = 2$ from pairs 1 and 2
$N2 = 2$ from pairs 3 and 4
$confidence factor_{rule} = \frac{N1}{N1+N2} = \frac{2}{2+2} = 0.5$

If *rule* is **+s**← **+Hr**, (i.e. it is a fact and it will be used in right to left translation), we can find its confidence factor as follows:

$N1 = 2$ from pairs 1 and 2
$N2 = 0$ no such pair
$confidence factor_{rule} = \frac{N1}{N1+N2} = \frac{2}{2+0} = 1.0$

It is possible to have the same confidence factor for left to right and right to left usage of the same rule, but it is more probable to have different values. For example, in the following example we have same confidence factors in both direction.

1) if *rule* is **come**→ **gel** (i.e. it is a fact and it will be used in left to right translation), and our translation examples are the same with the previous example. Then we will find confidence factor of *rule* as:

$N1 = 1$ from pair 1
$N2 = 0$ no such pair
$confidence factor_{rule} = \frac{N1}{N1+N2} = \frac{1}{1+0} = 1.0$

2) if *rule* is **come**← **gel** (i.e. it is a fact and it will be used in right to left translation), we will find confidence factor of *rule* as:

$N1 = 1$ from pair 1
$N2 = 0$ no such pair
$confidence factor_{rule} = \frac{N1}{N1+N2} = \frac{1}{1+0} = 1.0$

2.2 Method for Assigning Confidence Factors to Rules

Assigning confidence factor to a rule, (a template that has variables in it) is a more complicated task if we try to find the confidence factor of that rule completely. Therefore, if $rule_k$ has variables which will be unified with other rules in the translation phase then we will assign a partial confidence factor to this rule by considering the parts which do not include variables according to the confidence factor formula used in the previous section. In the translation process, the variables are bound using some other rules or facts, and we find the whole confidence factor of this rule by multiplying the confidence factors of all rules which are used to bind the variables. The following is an example for this:

If $rule_k$ is

$$X^{L_1}+\mathbf{s}\Leftrightarrow X^{L_2}+\mathbf{Hr} \text{ if } X^{L_1} \Leftrightarrow X^{L_2}$$

and our training pairs are the same with the previous example. Since $X^{L_1}+\mathbf{s}$ can be a substring of left sides of all pairs and $\mathbf{X}^{L_2}+\mathbf{Hr}$ can be a substring of right sides of pairs 1 and 2 by assuming that the variables can match one or more tokens of the string (i.e. variables can not match empty string), we will get the following confidence factor for left to right usage:

$N1 = 2$ from pairs 1 and 2
$N2 = 2$ from pairs 3 and 4
$$partial confidence factor_{rule_k} = \frac{N1}{N1+N2} = \frac{2}{2+2} = 0.5$$

Since $X^{L_2}+\mathbf{Hr}$ can be a substring of right sides of pairs 1 and 2 and $\mathbf{X^{L_1}+s}$ can be a substring of left sides of pairs all pairs by assuming that the variables can match one or more tokens of a string, we will find the following confidence factor for right to left usage:

$N1 = 2$ from pairs 1 and 2
$N2 = 0$ no such pair
$$partial confidence factor_{rule_k} = \frac{N1}{N1+N2} = \frac{2}{2+0} = 1.0$$

In the translation phase, these partial confidence factors are multiplied by the confidence factors of the rules replacing variables to calculate the real confidence factor of that translation output.

2.3 Method for Assigning Confidence Factors to Rule Combinations

The most complicated task of the procedure is the assignment confidence factors to rule combinations. The reason for considering these rule combinations is the following: Although some rules or facts are assigned high confidence factors when they are considered as single rules or facts, they may have a very low confidence factor when they are used with other rules or facts. The algorithm of this assignment process is given in Table 1. The algorithm in Table 1 is used only for left to right translation. This algorithm is repeated for right to left translation by replacing X^{L_1} with X^{L_2}.

Table 1. Algorithm for assigning confidence factor to rule combinations

---

For each training pair $X^{L_1} \Leftrightarrow X^{L_2}$
- Find all corresponding $\mathbf{Xs}^{L_2}$ for X^{L_1} from training pairs
- Find all translations ($\mathbf{Ts}$) with their proofs ($\mathbf{Ps}$) of X^{L_1} from translation templates where proofs show the rules used in the translation
- For each $T_i \in \mathbf{Ts}$ do the following steps
  If $T_i \in \mathbf{Ts}$ is the same as $X_j \in \mathbf{Xs}^{L_2}$
    - Assign confidence factor of the rule combination $P_i \in \mathbf{Ps}$ as 1
  else
    - Find distances between T_i and each $X_j \in \mathbf{Xs}^{L_2}$
    - Choose the minimum distance $\mathbf{d}$ among these distances
    - Assign confidence factor of this rule combination $P_i \in \mathbf{Ps}$ as
      $$confidence factor_{P_i} = \frac{1}{1+d}$$

At this point, calculation of the minimum distance between a translation result, T_i, and a part of training pair, $X_j \in \mathbf{Xs}^{L_2}$, needs more explanation. First of all, X_j and T_i are assumed to be points whose coordinates are (Length of X_j, 0) and (Length of Similarities between X_j and T_i, Length of Differences between X_j and T_i) in a two-dimensional space, respectively. Then the distance is calculated by using the Euclidean formula for calculating the distance between two points:

$$distance = \sqrt{(Length of X_j - Length of Similarities)^2 + (Length of Differences)^2}$$

Assume that we have $\mathbf{X}^{L_1}$=you come+p and we obtained $\mathbf{Xs}^{L_2}$= {gel+DH+n, siz gel+DH+nHz} and $\mathbf{Ts}$={gel+Hr+DH+n, gel+DH+nHz} then confidence factors for rule combinations used to find translations in $\mathbf{Ts}$ are computed as follows:

1) For T_1=gel+Hr+DH+n where T_1 is found by using n rules $i_1, \cdots, i_n$, the confidence factor of the rule combinations $i_1, \cdots, i_n$ is calculated as:

- Find the distance between T_1 and X_1:
  - Since similarities between T_1 and X_1 are [gel,+DH,+n], the length of similarities is 3.
  - Differences between T_1 and X_1 are [[],[+Hr]], and the length of differences is 1, since length of [+Hr] is 1.
  - **d1**=$\sqrt{(3-3)^2 + (1)^2} = 1$
- Find the distance between T_1 and X_2:
  - Since similarities between T_1 and X_2 are [gel,+DH], the length of similarities is 2.
  - Differences between T_1 and X_2 are [([siz],[]),([],[+Hr]),([+nHz],[+n])] and the length of differences is 3, since length of [siz] is 1, length of [+Hr] is 1 and length of [+nHz] or [+n] is 1, giving a total of 3.
  - **d2**=$\sqrt{(4-2)^2 + (3)^2} = \sqrt{13}$
- **min(d1,d2)=d1**=1 and confidence factor$_{[i_1,\cdots,i_n]}= \frac{1}{1+1}$=0.5

2) For T_2=gel+DH+nHz where T_2 is found by using m rules $j_1, \cdots, j_m$, the confidence factor of the rule combinations $j_1, \cdots, j_m$ is calculated as:

- Find the distance between T_2 and X_1:
  - Since similarities between T_2 and X_1 are [gel,+DH] and the length of similarities is 2.
  - Differences between T_2 and X_1 are [([+n],[+nHz])] and the length of differences is 1, since length of [+n] or [+nHz] is 1.
  - **d1**=$\sqrt{(3-2)^2 + (1)^2} = \sqrt{2}$
- Find the distance between T_2 and X_2:
  - Since similarities between T_2 and X_2 are [gel,+DH,+nHz]] and length of similarities is 3.
  - Differences between T_2 and X_2 are [([siz],[])] and the length of differences is 1, since length of [siz] is 1.
  - **d2**=$\sqrt{(4-3)^2 + (1)^2} = \sqrt{2}$

- $\mathbf{min(d1,d2)=d1}$ or $\mathbf{d2}$ and confidence factor$_{[j_1,\cdots,j_m]} = \frac{1}{1+\sqrt{2}}$

Note that, the length of differences is calculated by choosing the maximum of lengths in difference pairs.

These rule combinations are represented as tree structures. For example if $rule_i$ has two variables that are bound to $rule_j$ and $rule_k$, then the root of the tree is assumed to be $rule_i$ and its children are $rule_j$ and $rule_k$. If $rule_j$ or $rule_k$ has variables then they become the root of that subtree and their children become the numbers of the rules that are used in the binding of their variables. This tree structure is formed recursively. The tree structure will be helpful during the translation process and its usage will be explained in the next section.

3   Translation Process by Using Confidence Factors

Translation process can be summarized by the four steps given in Table 2. We find all possible translations by using the templates obtained in our learning phase. Then these results are evaluated according to their weights. These weights come either directly from the weights of rules or rule combinations. After the evaluation of the results, the ones that have the highest weights are given as the output, and the ones with lowest weights are eliminated. Therefore the correct output is ensured to be among these selected outputs, and hopefully will be on the top of the selected outputs.

The second step of the algorithm is the most important part of the translation process. Finding the confidence factors of these results is not as simple as it seems. We need both the confidence factors of the rules and rule combinations which are calculated in the learning process. The details of these calculations are given in Table 3. The rules that are pertaining to the result are found and a tree structure is obtained from these rules as explained in Section 2.3. Then this tree structure is used for comparison. If the result does not match a rule combination that is assigned a weight in the learning phase, then the comparison continues among the subtrees.

Table 2. Translation Algorithm

- Find all possible translations and their proofs
- Find confidence factors of these results by using the confidence factors assigned in the confidence factor assignment process.
- If one result is found more than once with different weights use the average of all possibilities for confidence factor.
- Sort results according to the calculated confidence factors in descending order by using a sort algorithm

---

Table 3. Algorithm for calculating confidence factors of the translations

---

Find the translation output's confidence factor by using the previously calculated confidence factors of rule combinations

- Find the set of rule combinations (**R**) which are assigned confidence factors
- If $rp = R_i \in \mathbf{R}$ then $cf_{result} = \mathrm{cf}_{R_i}$ where rp is the resulting proof
  else $cf_{result} = \mathrm{cf}_{rp_{root}} * \mathrm{cf}_{rp_{child_1}} * \mathrm{cf}_{rp_{child_2}} * \cdots * \mathrm{cf}_{rp_{child_n}}$
  where if $child_k$ is a fact ($fact_m$), then $\mathrm{cf}_{child_m} = \mathrm{cf}_{fact_m}$
  else calculate recursively cf_{child_k} as a tree

---

4 Performance Results

In this section, the results of the simulation on small corpora are summarized. A training set of examples has contained 488 sentences. Total number of the translation templates that are learned in the learning phase is 4723. In the confidence factor assignment process 4723 templates for left to right usage (from English to Turkish), and 4723 templates for right to left usage (from Turkish to English) are assigned confidence factors. 55845 rule combinations for left to right usage and 53676 rule combinations for right to left usage are assigned confidence factors. Therefore, we obtained a total of 118967 confidence factor assignments.

Table 4. Performance Results

Type of data	Percentage of correct results in translations	Percentage of incorrect results in translations	Percentage of correct results in top 5 without weights	Percentage of correct results in top 5 with weights
Sentences selected from training data	42.0	58.0	44.0	80.0
New sentences not appearing in training data	33.0	67.0	40.0	60.0

In the translation process, we used two groups of sentences to evaluate the performance of the results. The first group of sentences are randomly selected from training data and the second group of sentences are the new sentences which do not occur in the training data. The results are obtained by using the previously assigned weights and they are sorted in ascending order according to these weights. We also produced the outputs without using the weights of the templates for comparison purposes. Then they are sent to the generator to obtain surface forms from the lexical forms. In Table 4 the results with weights and without weights are summarized. The columns denote the percentage of the correct translations among all the results, percentage of the incorrect translations, and percentage of the correct translations seen in the top five results, respectively.

5 Conclusion and Future Work

In this paper, we have presented a statistical model for assigning confidence factors to the translation templates learned by the translation model offered in Cicekli [7, 4]. This translation model learns general translation patterns from the given translation examples by using analogy principle.

The early versions of the algorithm, translation templates are sorted according to their specificities (i.e., the number of terminals in templates). Although this way of sorting gives correct results, the accuracy was not high enough.The major contribution of this paper is assigning confidence factors to templates in order to improve the accuracy. Assigning confidence factor to these rules depends on the statistical data collected from translation examples which are assumed to be grammatically correct. As mentioned before, in the translation process, the output translations which have the highest weights are selected among all possibilities. Thus, it is ensured that the correct answer will be among these selected output and at the top of the list.

The algorithm is tested on Turkish and English for illustration purposes, but it is applicable to any pair of languages. On a small set of data, learning and translation times are reasonable enough. The accuracy of the results are promising. We need to test it on very large corpora. Thus, we are trying to form a large corpus for this purpose. The learning process on a large corpus will take a considerable amount of time, but it can be tolerated since it will be done only once and increase the translation accuracy.

In the future, the system accuracy can be increased by using a human assistance for the verification of the templates, morphological analysis etc. However, in order to fully automate the system, it will be better to use some additional reliable tools for parallel text alignment, disambiguation, etc.

References

1. R. D. Brown. Example-Based Machine Translation in the Pangloss System. In *Proceedings of COLING-96*, 1996.
2. P. F. Brown. Aligning Sentences in Parallel Corpora. In *Proceedings of the 29th Annual Meeting of th ACL*, pp:169-176, 1991.
3. P. F. Brown. The Mathematics of Statistical Machine Translation: Parameter Estimation. *Computational Linguistics*, pp:233-311, 1993.
4. I. Cicekli, and H. A. Güvenir. Learning Translation Rules From A Bilingual Corpus. *Proceedings of the 2nd International Conference on New Methods in Language Processing (NeMLaP-2)*, Ankara, Turkey, September 1996, pp:90-97.

5. B. Collins, and P. Cunningham. A Methodology for Example-Based Machine Translation. *Trinity College*, Dublin, 1995

6. W. A. Gale, and K.W. Church. A Program for Aligning Sentences in Bilingual Corpora. In *Proceedings of the 29th Annual Meeting of th ACL*, pp:177-184, 1991.

7. H. A. Güvenir, and I. Cicekli. Learning Translation Templates from Examples. *Information Systems* (accepted to be published).

8. H. A. Güvenir, and A. Tunc. Corpus-Based Learning of Generalized Parse Tree Rules for Translation. In Gord McCalla (Ed) *New Directions in Artificial Intelligence: Proceedings of the 11th Biennial Conference of the Canadian Society for Computational Studies of Intelligence*, Springer-Verlag, LNCS 1081, Toronto, Ontario, Canada, May 1996, pp:121-131.

9. H. Kaji, Y. Kida, and Y. Morimoto. Learning Translation Templates from Bilingual Text. In *Proceedings of COLING-92*, pp:672-678, 1992.

10. H. Kitano. A Comprehensive and Practical Model of Memory-Based Machine Translation. In Ruzena Bajcsy (Ed.) *Proceedings of the Thirteenth International Joint Conference on Artificial Intelligence*, Morgan Kaufmann Volume 2, 1993, pp: 1276-1282.

11. D. L. Medin, and M. M. Schaffer. Context Theory of Classification Learning. *Psychological Review*, 85, 1978, pp:207-238.

12. M. A. Nagao. Framework of a Mechanical Translation between Japanese and English by Analogy Principle. *Artificial and Human Intelligence*, A. Elithorn and R. Banerji (eds.), NATO Publications, 1984.

13. V. Sadler. Working with Analogical Semantics: Disambiguation Techniques in DLT. *Foris Publications*, Dodrecht, Netherlands, 1989.

14. V. Sadler, and R. Vendelmans. Pilot Implementation of a Bilingual Knowledge Bank. In *Proceedings of COLING-90*, pp:449-451, 1990.

15. E. Sumita, H. Iida, and H. Kohyama. Translating with Examples: A New Approach to Machine Translation. In *Proceedings Third International Conference on Theoretical and Methodological issues in Machine Translation of Natural Language*, 1990.

16. E. Sumita, and Y. Tsutsumi. A Translation Aid System using flexible Text Retrieval Based on Syntax Matching. *TRL Res. Report TR-87-1019*, Tokyo Research Laboratory, IBM, Tokyo, Japan, 1988.

Quality and Robustness in MT – A Balancing Act[*]

Bianka Buschbeck-Wolf and Michael Dorna

Institut für Maschinelle Sprachverarbeitung, Universität Stuttgart
Azenbergstr. 12, D–70174 Stuttgart
{bianka;michel}@ims.uni-stuttgart.de

Abstract. The speech-to-speech translation system Verb*mobil* integrates deep and shallow analysis modules that produce linguistic representations in parallel. Thus, the input representations for the transfer module differ with respect to their depth and quality. This gives rise to two problems: (*i*) the transfer database has to be adjusted according to input quality, and (*ii*) translations produced have to be ranked with respect to their quality in order to select the most appropriate result. This paper presents an operationalized solution to both problems.

1   Introduction

Verb*mobil* is a real-time speech-to-speech translation system [7]. Its application domain is appointment scheduling and travel planning. Currently, the system includes German, English and Japanese.

The Verb*mobil* system combines different MT approaches in a multi-engine MT technology [13]. The combination of translation engines ensures that, in most cases, a translated speech output can be produced. Additionally, this architecture is used for comparing the quality and performance of the various MT approaches. The three main engines of the Verb*mobil* system are semantic-based transfer [12], statistical translation [19] and example-based translation [15] (see Fig. 1). The common base for the three translation engines is a word lattice produced by a speech recognizer which is enriched with prosodic information.

Consider the transfer module in Fig. 1. Its input is provided by various modules. First, there is a deep semantic representation provided by an HPSG grammar which integrates semantic processing [10]. Since spoken language is highly elliptical and often ungrammatical, its processing requires less exact methods. Hence, Verb*mobil* integrates two shallow processing modules: a cascaded chunk parser [1, 16], and a statistical parser [4]. They produce (partial) syntactic analyses from which a robust semantic module [18] constructs semantic structures.

As all analysis results are encoded in a common interface format (see Sect. 2), their quality can be compared. Deep analysis usually provides more reliable results than shallow analysis. However, all representations produced differ in many

---

[*] We thank Glenn Carroll, Marc Light, Rosemary Vaughan and the anonymous reviewers for helpful comments on earlier versions of this paper. This work was funded by the German Federal Ministry of Education, Science, Research and Technology (BMBF) in the framework of the Verb*mobil* project under grant 01 IV 701 N3.

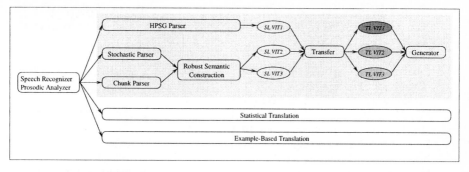

Fig. 1. Combination of Deep and Shallow Analysis in Verb*mobil*

ways. The common interface representation has the advantage that following modules can process input from different analysis modules.

The transfer module should provide a translation for all input representations regardless of their producer and their quality. Hence, transfer should be very robust (see Sect. 3). This is achieved by dynamically relaxing rules which expect a correct input in terms of a given linguistic specification (see Sect. 4). The weakening process is illustrated by an example in Sect. 5.

In transfer, rules with different complexity can be applied. These include fully specified rules, relaxations of these, and default rules. Thus, multiple translations can be produced which have to be ranked with respect to their appropriateness. This is achieved by a filter which optimizes the relation between the input and the number and specificity of the rules which have been applied (see Sect. 6).

2 Supporting Various Inputs

Analysis results to be transferred are encoded in a common format called Verb*mobil* Interface Term (henceforth VIT).[1] A VIT is also used as input to the generator [2]. Fig. 2 shows a VIT for the German utterance in (1).

$$
\begin{array}{llll}
\textit{Ginge} & \textit{dieser} & \textit{Termin} \ \textit{vielleicht?} \\
\text{would be possible} \ \text{this} & \text{time} & \text{maybe} \\
\textit{Would this time be possible?}
\end{array}
\tag{1}
$$

A VIT is a record-like data structure whose fields contain semantic, scopal, sortal, morpho-syntactic, prosodic, discourse and other types of information. These slots can be seen as analysis layers gathering information of different nature which is produced by several modules. Information within and between the slots is linked using constant symbols, called "labels", "instances" and "holes".

Besides pure linguistic information, a VIT contains a unique identifier which encodes the time span of the analyzed speech input, the analyzed path of the original word lattice, the producer of the VIT, the considered language, etc. This ID is used, for example, to synchronize the processing of different analyses.

---

[1] For a more detailed description of VITs, we refer to [5], [14], or [11].

```
vit(vitID(sid(102,a,de,0,4,1,de,y,synsem),     % IDENTIFIER
    [word(ginge,1,[11]), word(dieser,2,[12]),   % WORD LATTICE STRING
     word(Termin,3,[13]), word(vielleicht,4,[14])]),
    index(15,16,i1),                            % INDEX
    [quest(15,h1), vielleicht(14,h2),           % SEMANTICS
     gehen(11,i1), arg3(11,i1,i2),
     dies(12,i2,17,h3), termin(13,i2)],
    [in_g(11,16), in_g(13,17), in_g(14,18),     % SCOPAL CONSTRAINTS
     leq(18,h1), leq(16,h2), leq(16,h3)],
    [s_sort(i1,mental_sit), s_sort(i2,temporal)], % SORTS
    [dialog_act(15,request)],                   % DISCOURSE
    [num(i2,sg)],                               % MORPHO-SYNTAX
    [ta_tense(i1,pres), ta_mood(i1,conj),       % TENSE & ASPECT
     ta_perf(i1,nonperf)],
    [pros_accent(12), pros_mood(15,quest)])     % PROSODY
```

Fig. 2. VIT for Example (1)

The most important information for transfer are semantic predicates in the semantics slot. Each predicate has a unique label, li, as its first argument. Referential predicates introduce an instance, ii, which binds arguments and modifiers. Additional semantic information is provided in the constraints slot. There are "groupings", $in\_g(li,lj)$, and subordination statements, $leq(li,hj)$, which represent underspecified scope, coordination and propositional embedding [6]. Groupings provides a label lj which addresses possible scope domains as a single unit.[2] Scope bearing predicates provide, besides a label, a hole, hi, for their underspecified scope which is constrained by leq relations. They describe indirect (less than) or direct (equal to) subordinations between holes and group labels.

The VIT layers are used to localize the differences in the output of various analysis components. This information is used to guide the relaxation of transfer rules (see Sect. 4). For example, if a parser ignores agreement, we cannot expect the morpho-syntactic slot to be filled correctly. Or if the input consists of single word chunks, no connections between them can be expected.

3 Transfer

This section describes the semantic-based transfer processing with focus on the rule specification.[3] The format of a transfer rule is shown in (2).

$$SL\_Sem \ \# \ SL\_Cond \ TauOp \ TL\_Sem \ \# \ TL\_Cond. \tag{2}$$

---

[2] Groupings can be seen as some sort of UDRS boxes [17].

[3] In fact, transfer rules are encoded by the use of templates [8] which considerably simplify the rule writing, capture generalizations of translation patterns, and ensure the adaptation and reusability of transfer rules independently of the concrete front and back end of the transfer module. For expository reasons, only expanded rules are presented here.

A rule maps sets of source language (SL) predicates (SL_Sem) to sets of target language (TL) predicates (TL_Sem). The operator TauOp indicates the direction of a rule application, i.e., bi-directional (↔) or uni-directional (→ or ←).

In order to restrict the mapping of ambiguous predicates to the appropriate context, the rules are optionally provided with a condition part (SL_Cond and TL_Cond). The # sign separates the condition part from the predicates to be translated. First of all, conditions test information which is encoded in the various VIT layers, such as structural connections, sortal information, co-occurrence restrictions, discourse information, prosodic information, and surface order. But there are also conditions that trigger calls to other modules for providing information which is not part of the actual VIT [9].

For a given SL set of semantic predicates, a rule application reduces the input by the set of semantic entities in SL_Sem if it matches a subset of the input, and if the conditions in SL_Cond are satisfied. Then, the semantic entities TL_Sem are inserted in the TL output. Transfer is complete if the SL input set is empty.

The application of rules is guided by a *specificity criterion* which takes into account the number of predicates in SL_Sem, the number of restrictions in SL_Cond and their specificity. The most complex rule has priority over competing rules (see Sect. 6). Additionally, a transfer rule compiler partially orders the sets SL_Sem and SL_Cond. This makes matching on a given sorted SL input set more efficient. Based on both the specificity of rules and ordered SL sets, the compiler builds a kind of non-deterministic transducer which is used at runtime, see [12].

Currently, the transfer data base contains 8539 rules for a lexicon of about 2500 German and 2000 English words. Concrete numbers of different kinds of rules are shown in Table 1. We consider those rules with only one lexical item to be transferred as simple rules. Complex rules map more than one word at a time. They can be seen as phrasal translation rules. Their number is explained by the high frequency of idiomatic and phrasal expressions in spoken language.

| | Transfer | | |
	German→English	English→German	Total
Transfer Rules	5275	3264	8539
Simple Rules	3671	2200	5871
Complex Rules	1604	1064	2668
Rules with Conditions	3035	950	3985
Rules without Conditions	2240	2314	4554

Table 1. Number of Different Kinds of Rules

The large amount of transfer rules for the considerably small SL and TL lexicons reflects the high context sensitivity of these rules. Nearly half of them involve contextual constraints, see Table 1. Spoken language is highly ambiguous and often redundant. For disambiguation and the deletion of redundant information, a variety of context checks increases the number of rules.

In order to transfer one utterance, the transfer processor needs about 30 msec. in the current prototype. This includes the printing of the output representation, and also its consistency and format checking. The transfer of 11500 utterances takes about 6 minutes on a Sun Sparc Ultra 2.

4 Adapting Transfer Rules to Low-Quality Input

As described in Sect. 2, transfer has to deal with input representations of different quality. However, transfer rules are inherently highly sensitive to changes and differences in the linguistic analyses. If the rule's left hand side (LHS) does not match the input, or rule conditions cannot be satisfied, the rule is not applicable. Therefore, the only way to achieve the desired flexibility is to provide different rules with various degrees of specificity. Certainly, this should not be done by manually multiplying the number of rules according to different input quality. Our solution to this problem relies on two key issues:

- To gain flexibility, fully specified *transfer rules are dynamically relaxed* by reducing their complexity up to a reasonable point.
- To gain robustness, for all predicates an *unconstrained default rule* is provided which covers the most frequent translation correspondence.

Consider the general rule schema in (2). To adjust rules to low quality input, on the one hand, **the SL_Sem of the rule can be weakened**, e.g., (**i**) by ignoring the processing of scopal constraints, or (**ii**) by relaxing the connection between predicates, i.e., ignoring co-references.

On the other hand, SL_Cond **can be relaxed by removing** (**i**) restrictions on scope and subordination between semantic predicates, (**ii**) constraints tested in VIT layers which are not provided by particular analysis modules, (**iii**) tests verified in VIT layers in which the information is not very reliable, e.g., statistically determined dialog act or prosodic information, or (**iv**) conditions verified by expensive calls to external modules, e.g., world or discourse knowledge.

Let us turn to the question on how a dynamic reduction can be controlled. Concerning the information to be removed from a rule, we use, among others, knowledge about its reliability, its frequency of use, the provider of the input, its importance for the generator, and its processing time.

During transfer, a rule r_1 is a relaxation candidate if all semantic predicates in its SL_Sem are elements of the SL input. None of those predicates are removed from r_1. The weakening of r_1 works by removing information on the LHS stepwise until a manually specified rule r_2 with the same information is found. This blocks the relaxation of r_1, and r_2 is given preference. Then, r_2 can be further weakened. This means that if the last condition of a rule was eliminated, the default rule (and not the reduced rule) is applied.

5 Example

We demonstrate the relaxation of a complex transfer rule with the modal particle *vielleicht*. In general, the particle is used to express possibility or likelihood. Then, it corresponds to *maybe* or *perhaps*. However, in spoken German, it is also uttered to signal politeness. In certain suggestions and requests, such as in (1), it is better not to translate it, because in English, politeness is expressed more compactly. The rule in (3) fixes one of the contexts in which *vielleicht* is deleted in the translation.[4] It matches the input VIT in Fig. 2.[5]

$$
\begin{aligned}
&\texttt{vielleicht(L,H),in\_g(L,G),leq(G1,H),leq(G,H1) \#} \\
&\texttt{attitude\_verb(L1,I),L1=<H,dialog\_act(L,request;suggest)} \\
&\texttt{-> leq(G1,H1).}
\end{aligned} \quad (3)
$$

The predicate `vielleicht` is removed if it occurs in an utterance which is assigned the dialog act `request` or `suggest`, and if it contains a verb which expresses an attitude, such as *gehen, passen* and *klappen* ('to be possible' or 'to suit'). These verbs are covered by the predicate `attitude_verb(L1,I)`. Since with *vielleicht* a scopal adverb is deleted, its constraints have also to be removed, i.e., its grouping `in_g(L,G)`, and the constraint for its scope `leq(G1,H)`. We also have to pay attention to the scope constraint `leq(G,H1)`. With the deletion of `in_g(L,G)`, the scope `H1` of another scope bearing predicate which embeds *vielleicht* is no longer bound, i.e., the label chain gets interrupted. To avoid this, `leq(G1,H1)` is inserted on the TL side.[6]

Let us consider how the relaxation of the fully specified deletion rule in (3) influences the translation of *vielleicht* in particular contexts. Since the correct encoding of scopal constraints in the input VIT is often not reliable, we remove these constraints from `SL_Sem` in (4).

$$
\begin{aligned}
&\texttt{vielleicht(L,H) \#} \\
&\texttt{attitude\_verb(L1,I),L1=<H,dialog\_act(L,request;suggest) -> true.}
\end{aligned} \quad (4)
$$

With (4), the deletion of *vielleicht* is still restricted to the appropriate context. But the quality of the output VIT is worsened, since the label chain is interrupted. However, the likelihood of (4) to be applied to real input is much higher than for (3).

Furthermore, the condition part could be weakened. There are a number of possibilities which affect the rule application in different ways. These are discussed below. In (5), the dialog act constraint is removed.

$$
\texttt{vielleicht(L,H) \# attitude\_verb(L1,I),L1=<H -> true.} \quad (5)
$$

Without the constraint on the dialog act, the rule in (5) becomes applicable to utterances which express feedback (6a). The deletion of *vielleicht* would not be appropriate then, since the speaker's doubt is not transmitted into the TL

---

[4] There are further rules that restrict deletions to other contexts, such as predicative constructions with attitude adverbs, suggestions, etc.

[5] The capitalized symbols `L,I,G` and `H` stand for logical variables which are bound to concrete values when applying a rule to a given input.

[6] See [14] for a detailed discussion of a VIT's scope representation.

(6b). Fortunately, the frequency of co-occurrences of *vielleicht* and attitude verbs in dialog acts other than suggestions and requests is not very high.

> (a) *Der Montag würde mir <u>vielleicht</u> passen.*
> Monday   would me maybe   suit   (6)
> (b) *Monday would suit me.*

By leaving out the subordination restriction, L1=<H, as in (7), the information that the attitude verb is in the scope of *vielleicht* is lost.

$$\text{vielleicht(L,H)} \ \#$$
$$\text{attitude\_verb(L1,I),dialog\_act(L,request;suggest)} \ \text{->} \ \text{true.} \qquad (7)$$

Then, rule (7) could also be applied to utterances where the attitude verb is not in the scope of *vielleicht* (8a). Although the deletion of the particle is not desirable here, it does not distort the meaning of the utterance (8b).

> (a) *Wissen sie <u>vielleicht</u>, ob   ihm der Termin passen würde?*
> know you maybe   whether him the time   suit   would   (8)
> (b) *Do you know, whether the time would suit him?*

Finally, the restriction on the type of the verb, `attitude_verb(L1,I)`, could be removed, as in (9).

$$\text{vielleicht(L,H)} \ \# \ \text{L1=<H,dialog\_act(L,request;suggest)} \ \text{->} \ \text{true.} \qquad (9)$$

Then, the subordination constraint also loses its validity. Rule (9) allows the deletion of *vielleicht* in utterances with the indicated dialog acts, as in (10a). In our domain, (9) would apply rather frequently. Although the translation (10b) appears a bit abrupt, in most cases the propositional content is preserved.

> (a) *<u>Vielleicht</u> sollten wir uns mal   treffen?*
> maybe   should we us   some time meet   (10)
> (b) *Should we meet?*

As we have seen with the example above, the relaxation of transfer rules has different effects. In some cases, it leads to overgeneration, in others it does not really harm the translation quality.

$$\text{vielleicht(L,H)} \ \text{<->} \ \text{maybe(L,H).} \qquad (11)$$

To control the process of weakening transfer rules, we follow the principles described in Sect. 4. Relaxation is blocked if the LHS of a relaxed rule is identical to the LHS of another manually specified rule. For example, if the condition part of (4) is removed completely, its LHS is identical to that of the default rule for *vielleicht* (11). Then the default rule is given priority. Hence, the application of a relaxed transfer rule whose conditions were completely deleted cannot occur, because there is always a competing default rule.

6   Ranking of Translations

The application of a set of transfer rules that includes fully specified rules as well as relaxed ones, requires a ranking of the produced translations according to their quality. Our formalization of the ranking is guided by the *specificity criterion* mentioned in Sect. 3, i.e., a translation derived by *as few as possible but most appropriate rules* is likely to have the best quality. In contrast to the scoring device used in the METAL system [3] which selects only the highest scored parsing result for transfer, we exploit the information about the applied transfer rules in order to rate the quality.

Ignoring relaxed transfer rules in the first step, we define a numerical order over competing transfer rules, i.e., rules which share the same semantic predicates in SL_Sem. (12) defines a simple value S_r for a rule r by adding the number of entities used in SL_Sem and in SL_Cond of this rule.

$$S_r = ||\text{SL\_Sem}_r|| + ||\text{SL\_Cond}_r|| \tag{12}$$

Equation (12) can be refined by using knowledge about the different types t of information (see Sect. 4) and by defining individual values for them. These values can be approximated by constants v_t for each information type t. Hence, the value R of a rule r is the sum of the numbers $n_{r,t}$ where information of type t used in r is counted (13).

$$R_r = \sum_t v_t n_{r,t} \tag{13}$$

The information types t and their values v_t can be determined in two completely different dimensions. Concerning linguistic information, these values are tuned with respect to the expected analysis quality and with respect to the structural complexity of a transfer rule, e.g., measured by the number of co-references specified in a rule. On the other hand, we can score information by counting the computational costs. For example, a condition which calls external modules costs more than checking a condition in the current VIT input.[7]

Let us illustrate the computation of S and R using the rules in (5) and (7). In both cases, $||\text{SL\_Sem}_r|| = 1$ and $||\text{SL\_Cond}_r|| = 2$, hence $S = 3$. Let the values for specific information types be as follows: semantic predicate in the mapping part: $v_{sm} = 6$; semantic predicate in the condition part: $v_{sc} = 3$; dialog act

---

[7] To accelerate processing, transfer can be forced to ignore conditions that trigger time consuming external inferences (see Sect. 4).

inference: $v_{da} = 2.5$; scopal subordination: $v_{ss} = 1$. Using these values we get $R_{(5)} = 1v_{sm} + 1v_{sc} + 1v_{ss} = 10$, whereas $R_{(7)} = 1v_{sm} + 1v_{sc} + 1v_{da} = 11.5$. Hence, in this case, (7) would be preferred over (5).

Independent of the method for determining R_r, we can compute the value T of a translation in which l rules r_i were applied (14).

$$T = \frac{\sum_{1 \leq i \leq l} R_{r_i}}{l} \tag{14}$$

Equation (14) adds the values for every rule R_{r_i} used in a derivation and divides the result by the number l of applied rules, i.e., the length of the derivation. From the transfer perspective, T is maximal for translations which are derived by a minimal number of high valued rules.

Let us consider relaxed rules. Obviously, their application reduces the output quality of transfer (see Sect. 5) and should be reflected in the ranking of a rule and the whole translation. (15) defines the relaxation costs C_r for subtracting $s_{r,t}$ pieces of information t in a rule r.

$$C_r = \left(\sum_t v_t s_{r,t} \right) + 1 \tag{15}$$

For the application of fully specified rules, C_r is not taken into account. But once relaxation was necessary, a rule's value R_r^{relax} is determined by $R_r^{relax} = R_r - C_r$ instead of R.

The transfer component ranks the quality by maximizing T for translation alternatives. According to (14), the reduction of a rule value abates the whole translation value. Hence, using original rules higher values are yielded, and, as desired, a better translation quality is achieved. The different transfer outputs are ordered with respect to their scores, and then reported to the generator.

7 Outlook

In this paper we have shown how, in a multi-engine MT system, quality can be balanced against robustness. By relaxing transfer rules which deal with information that is not very reliable, we achieve maximal coverage of the rule base. By subsequently ranking all produced translation alternatives, we have filtered out those translations that correspond best to the particular input quality. The proposed relaxation and ranking method is currently being implemented and will be evaluated at a later stage.

Concerning future research, it would be promising to automatically learn about the reliability of the particular input information required by transfer. The yielded scores could be directly used to improve the control of the rule relaxation. Another question is how the quality measures provided by the transfer module can be used in the final selection among the string outputs delivered by the three different translation engines (see Fig. 1).

References

[1] S. Abney. Partial Parsing via Finite-State Cascades. In *Proceedings of the ESSLLI '96 Robust Parsing Workshop*, 1996.

[2] T. Becker, W. Finkler, and A. Kilger. Generation in Dialog Translation: Requirements, Techniques, and their Realization in Verbmobil. Submitted to "Computational Linguistics", 1997.

[3] W. B. Bennett and J. Slocum. The LRC Machine Translation System. In J. Slocum, editor, *Machine Translation Systems*. Cambridge University Press, 1987.

[4] H. U. Block and T. Ruland. The Verbmobil Stochastic LR-Parser. Siemens AG, Munich, Germany. Undocumented software, 1998.

[5] J. Bos, C. J. Rupp, B. Buschbeck-Wolf, and M. Dorna. Managing Information at Linguistic Interfaces. In *Proceedings of COLING-ACL'98*, Montréal, Canada, 1998.

[6] J. Bos. Predicate Logic Unplugged. In *Proceedings of the 10th Amsterdam Colloquium*, University of Amsterdam, 1996. ILLC/Department of Philosophy.

[7] T. Bub, W. Wahlster, and A. Waibel. Verbmobil: The Combination of Deep and Shallow Processing for Spontaneous Speech Translation. In *Proceedings of ICASSP'97*, Munich, Germany, 1997.

[8] B. Buschbeck-Wolf. Using Templates to Encode Transfer Rules. Verbmobil Report 229, IMS, Universität Stuttgart, Germany, 1998.

[9] B. Buschbeck-Wolf. Resolution on Demand. Verbmobil Report 196, IMS, Universität Stuttgart, Germany, 1997.

[10] A. Copestake, D. Flickinger, R. Malouf, S. Riehemann, and I. Sag. Translation using Minimal Recursion Semantics. In *Proceedings of TMI'95*, Leuven, Belgium, 1995.

[11] M. Dorna. The ADT-Package for the Verbmobil Interface Term. Verbmobil Report 104, IMS, Universität Stuttgart, Germany, 1996.

[12] M. Dorna and M. C. Emele. Efficient Implementation of a Semantic-based Transfer Approach. In *Proceedings of ECAI'96*, Budapest, Hungary, 1996.

[13] R. Frederking and S. Nirenburg. Three Heads are Better than One. In *Proceedings of ANLP'94*, Stuttgart, Germany, 1994.

[14] W. Kasper, J. Bos, M. Schiehlen, and C. Thielen. Definition of Abstract Semantic Classes. Verbmobil Technical Report 61, DFKI GmbH, Saarbrücken, Germany and Universität des Saarlandes, Saarbrücken, Germany and IMS, Universität Stuttgart, Germany, 1997.

[15] H.-J. Kroner and J. Schwinn. Fallbasierte Übersetzung. DFKI GmbH, Kaiserslautern, Germany. Undocumented software, 1997.

[16] M. Light. CHUMP: Partial Parsing and Underspecified Representations. In *Proceedings of ECAI-96 Workshop: Corpus-Oriented Semantic Analysis*, Budapest, Hungary, 1996.

[17] U. Reyle. Dealing with Ambiguities by Underspecification: Construction, Representation and Deduction. *Journal of Semantics*, 10(2), 1993.

[18] M. Schiehlen. Robust Semantic Construction on Partial Syntactic Analyses. IMS, Universität Stuttgart, Germany. Undocumented software, 1998.

[19] C. Tillman, S. Vogel, H. Ney, H. Sawaf, and A. Zubiaga. Accelerated DP-based Search for Statistical Translation. In *Proceedings of EuroSpeech'97*, Rhodes, Greece, 1997.

Parallel Strands: A Preliminary Investigation into Mining the Web for Bilingual Text

Philip Resnik

Department of Linguistics and Institute for Advanced Computer Studies
University of Maryland, College Park, MD 20742, USA
resnik@umiacs.umd.edu.edu
WWW home page: http://umiacs.umd.edu/~resnik/

Abstract. Parallel corpora are a valuable resource for machine translation, but at present their availability and utility is limited by genre- and domain-specificity, licensing restrictions, and the basic difficulty of locating parallel texts in all but the most dominant of the world's languages. A parallel corpus resource not yet explored is the World Wide Web, which hosts an abundance of pages in parallel translation, offering a potential solution to some of these problems and unique opportunities of its own. This paper presents the necessary first step in that exploration: a method for automatically finding parallel translated documents on the Web. The technique is conceptually simple, fully language independent, and scalable, and preliminary evaluation results indicate that the method may be accurate enough to apply without human intervention.

1 Introduction

In recent years large parallel corpora have taken on an important role as resources in machine translation and multilingual natural language processing, for such purposes as lexical acquisition (e.g. Gale and Church, 1991a; Melamed, 1997), statistical translation models (e.g. Brown et al., 1990; Melamed 1998), and cross-language information retrieval (e.g. Davis and Dunning, 1995; Landauer and Littman, 1990; also see Oard, 1997). However, for all but relatively few language pairs, parallel corpora are available only in relatively specialized forms such as United Nations proceedings (LDC, 1996), religious texts (Resnik, Olsen, and Diab, 1998), and localized versions of software manuals (Resnik and Melamed, 1997). Even for the top dozen or so majority languages, the available parallel corpora tend to be unbalanced, representing primarily governmental and newswire-style texts. In addition, like other language resources, parallel corpora are often encumbered by fees or licensing restrictions. For all these reasons, following the "more data are better data" advice of Church and Mercer (1993), abandoning balance in favor of volume, is difficult.

A parallel corpus resource not yet explored is the World Wide Web, which hosts an abundance of pages in parallel translation, offering a potential solution to some of these problems and some unique opportunities of its own. The Web contains parallel pages in many languages, by innumerable authors, in multiple

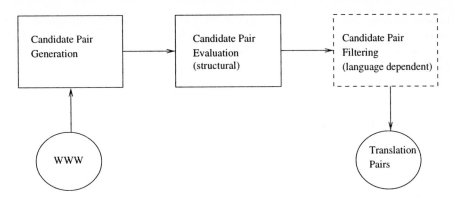

Fig. 1. The STRAND architecture

genres and domains, and its content is continually enriched by language change and modified by cultural context. In this paper I will not attempt to explore whether such a free-wheeling source of linguistic content is better or worse than the more controlled parallel corpora in use today.

Rather, this paper presents the necessary first step in that exploration: a method for automatically finding parallel translated documents on the Web that I call STRAND (**S**tructural **T**ranslation **R**ecognition for **A**cquiring **N**atural **D**ata). The technique is conceptually simple, fully language independent, and scalable, and preliminary evaluation results indicate that the method may be accurate enough to apply without human intervention.

In Section 2 I lay out the STRAND architecture and describe in detail the core of the method, a language-independent structurally based algorithm for assessing whether or not two Web pages were intended to be parallel translations. Section 3 presents preliminary evaluation, and Section 4 discusses future work.

2 The STRAND Architecture

As Figure 1 illustrates, the STRAND architecture is a simple pipeline. Given a particular pair of languages of interest, a *candidate generation* module first generates pairs ⟨url1,url2⟩ identifying World Wide Web pages that may be parallel translations.[1] Next, a language independent *candidate evaluation* module behaves as a filter, keeping only those candidate pairs that are likely to actually be translations. Optionally, a third module for *language-dependent filtering* applies additional filtering criteria that might depend upon language-specific resources. The end result is a set of candidate pairs that can reliably be added to the Web-based parallel corpus for these two languages.

The approach to candidate evaluation taken in this paper has a useful side effect: in assessing the likelihood that two HTML documents are parallel trans-

---

[1] A URL, or *uniform resource locator*, is the address of a document or other resource on the World Wide Web.

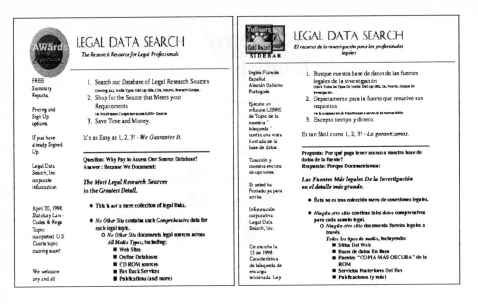

Fig. 3. Example of a candidate pair

For example, Figure 3 shows fragments from a pair of pages identified by STRAND's candidate generation module in the experiment to be described in Section 3. An English page is at left, Spanish at right.[4] Notice the extent to which the page layout is parallel, and the way in which corresponding units of text — list items, for example — have correspondingly greater or smaller lengths.

In more detail, the steps in candidate evaluation are as follows:

1. Linearize. Both documents in the candidate pair are run through a markup analyzer that acts as a transducer, producing a linear sequence containing three kinds of token:

    ```
    [START:element_label]   e.g. [START:A], [START:LI]
    [END:element_label]     e.g. [END:A]
    [Chunk:length]          e.g. [Chunk:174]
    ```

2. Align the linearized sequences. There are many approaches one can take to aligning sequences of elements. In the current prototype, the Unix *sdiff* utility does a fine job of alignment, matching up identical START and END tokens in the sequence and Chunk tokens of identical length in such a way as to minimize the differences between the two sequences. For example, consider two documents that begin as follows:

---

[4] Source: http://www.legaldatasearch.com/.

```
<HTML>                               | <HTML>
<TITLE>Emergency Exit</TITLE>        | <TITLE>Sortie de Secours</TITLE>
<BODY>                               | <BODY>
<H1>Emergency Exit</H1>              | Si vous êtes assis à
If seated at an exit and             | côté d'une...
  .                                  |   .
  .                                  |   .
  .                                  |   .
```

The aligned linearized sequence would be as follows:[5]

```
[START:HTML]              [START:HTML]
[START:TITLE]             [START:TITLE]
[Chunk:12]                [Chunk:15]
[END:TITLE]               [END:TITLE]
[START:BODY]              [START:BODY]
[START:H1]
[Chunk:12]
[END:H1]
[Chunk:112]               [Chunk:122]
```

3. Threshold the aligned, linearized sequences based on mismatches. When two pages are not parallel, there is a high proportion of mismatches in the alignment — sequence tokens on one side that have no corresponding token on the other side, such as the tokens associated with the H1 element in the above example. This can happen, for example, when two documents are translations up to a point, e.g. an introduction, but one document goes on to include a great deal more content than another. Even more frequently, the proportion is high when two documents are *prima facie* bad candidates for a translation pair. For these reasons, candidate pairs whose mismatch proportion exceeds a constant, K, are eliminated at this stage. My current value for K was set manually at 20% based on experience with a development set, and that value was frozen and used in the experiment described in the next section. In that experiment evaluation of STRAND was done using a different set of previously unseen documents, for a different language pair than the one used during development.

4. Compute a confidence value. Let $\langle X, Y \rangle = \{(x_1, y_1), \ldots, (x_n, y_n)\}$ be the lengths for the aligned Chunk tokens in Step 2, such that x_j is not equal to y_j. (When they are exactly equal, this virtually always means the aligned segments are not natural language text. If included these inflate the correlation coefficient.) For the above alignment this would be $\{(12, 15), (112, 122), \ldots\}$. Compute the Pearson correlation coefficient r(X,Y), and compute the significance of that correlation in textbook fashion. Note that the significance calculation takes the number n of aligned text segments into account. The

---

[5] Note that whitespace is ignored in counting chunk lengths.

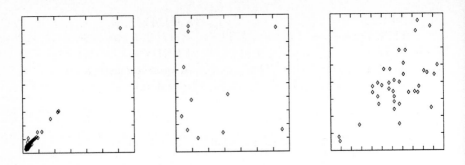

Fig. 4. Scatterplots illustrating reliable correlation in lengths of aligned segments for good translation pairs (left and right), and lack of correlation for a bad pair (center).

resulting p value is used to threshold significance: using the standard threshold of $p < .05$ (i.e. 95% confidence that the correlation would not have been obtained by chance) worked well during development, and I retained that threshold in the evaluation described in the section that follows.

Figure 4 shows plots of $\langle X, Y \rangle$ for three real candidate pairs. At left is the pair illustrated in Figure 3, correctly accepted by the candidate evaluation module with $r = .99, p < .001$. At center is a pair correctly rejected by candidate evaluation; in this case $r = .24, p > .4$, and the mismatch proportion exceeds 75%. And at right is another pair correctly accepted; in this more unusual case, the correlation is lower ($r = .57$) but statistically very reliable because of the large number of data points ($p < .0005$).

Notice that a by-product of this structurally-driven candidate evaluation scheme is a set of aligned Chunk tokens. These correspond to aligned non-markup segments in the document pair. Evaluating the accuracy of this segment-level alignment is left for future work.

2.3 Language-Dependent Filtering

I have not experimented with further filtering of candidate pairs since, as shown in the next section, precision is already quite high. However, experience with the small number of false positives I have seen suggests that automatic language identification on the remaining candidate pairs might weed out the few that remain. Very high accuracy language identification using character n-gram models requires only a modest amount of training text known to be in the languages of interest (Dunning, 1994; Grefenstette, 1995).

3 Evaluation

I developed the STRAND prototype using English and French as the relevant pair of languages. For evaluation I froze the code and all parameters and ran the prototype for English and Spanish, not having previously looked at English/Spanish pairings on the Web.

For the candidate generation phase, I followed the approach of Section 2.1 and generated candidate document pairs from the first 200 hits returned by the Altavista search engine, leading to a set of 198 candidate pairs of URLs that met the distance criterion.

Of those 198 candidate pairs, 12 were pairs where url1 and url2 pointed to identical pages, and so these are eliminated from consideration. In 96 cases one or both pages in the pair could not be retrieved (page not found, moved, empty, server unreachable, etc.). The remaining 90 cases are considered the set of candidate pairs for evaluation.

I evaluated the 90 candidate pairs by hand, determining that 24 represented true translation pairs.[6] The criterion for this determination was the question: Was this pair of pages intended to provide the same content in the two different languages? Although admittedly subjective, the judgments are generally quite clear; I include URLs in an on-line Appendix so that the reader may judge for himself or herself. The STRAND prototype's performance against this test set was as follows:

– The candidate evaluation module identified 17 of the 90 candidate pairs as true translations, and was correct for 15 of those 17, a precision of 88.2%. (A language-dependent filtering module with 100% correct language identification would have eliminated one of the two false positives, giving a precision of 93.8%. However, language-dependent filtering was not used in this evaluation.)

– The algorithm identified 15 of 24 true translation pairs, a recall of 62.5%.

Manual assessment of the translation pairs retrieved by the algorithm suggests that they are representative of what one would expect to find on the Web: the pages vary widely in length, content, and the proportion of usable parallel natural language text in comparison to markup, graphics, and the like. However, I found the yield of genuine parallel text — content in one language and its corresponding translation in the other — to be encouraging. The reader may form his or her own judgment by looking at the pages identified in the on-line Appendix.

4 Future Work

At present it is difficult to estimate how many pairs of translated pages may exist on the World Wide Web. However, it seems fair to say that there are a great many, and that the number will increase as the Web continues to expand internationally. The method for candidate generation proposed in this paper makes

---

[6] A few of the 90 candidate pairs were encoded in non-HTML format, e.g. PDF (*portable document format*). I excluded these from consideration *a priori* because STRAND's capabilities are currently limited to HTML.

it possible to quickly locate candidate pairs without building a Web crawler, but in principle one could in fact think of the entire set of pages on the Web as a source for candidate generation. The preliminary figures for recall and especially for precision suggest that large parallel corpora can be acquired from the Web with only a relatively small degree of noise, even without human filtering. Accurate language-dependent filtering (e.g. based on language identification, as in Section 2.3) would likely increase the precision, reducing noise, without substantially reducing the recall of useful, true document pairs. In addition to language-dependent filtering, the following are some areas of investigation for future work.

- **Additional evaluation.** As advertised in the title of this paper, the results thus far are preliminary. The STRAND approach needs to be evaluated with other language pairs, on larger candidate sets, with independent evaluators being used in order to accurately estimate an upper bound on the reliability of judgments as to whether a candidate pair represents a true translation. One could also evaluate how precision varies with recall, but I believe for this task there are sufficiently many genuine translation pairs on the Web and a sufficiently high recall that the focus should be on maximizing precision. Alternative approaches to candidate generation from the Web, as discussed in Section 2.1, are a topic for further investigation.

- **Scalability.** The prototype, implemented in decidedly non-optimized fashion using a combination of perl, C, and shell scripts, currently evaluates candidate pairs at approximately 1.8 seconds per candidate on a Sun Ultra 1 workstation with 128 megabytes of real memory, when the pages are already resident on a disk on the local network (though not local to the workstation itself). Thus, excluding retrieval time of pages from the Web, evaluating 1 million retrievable candidate pairs using the existing prototype would take just over 3 weeks of real time. However, STRAND can easily be run in parallel on an arbitrary number of machines, and the prototype reimplemented in order to obtain significant speed-ups. The main bottleneck to the approach, the time spent retrieving pages from the Web, is still trivial if compared to manual construction of corpora. In real use, STRAND would probably be run as a continuous process, constantly extending the corpus, so that the cost of retrieval would be amortized over a long period.

- **Segment alignment.** As discussed in Section 2.2, a by-product of the candidate evaluation module in STRAND is a set of aligned text segments. The quality of the segment-level alignment needs to be evaluated, and should be compared against alternative alignment algorithms based on the document-aligned collection.

- **Additional filtering.** Although a primary goal of this work is to obtain a large, heterogeneous corpus, for some purposes it may be useful to further filter document pairs. For example, in some applications it might be important to restrict attention to document pairs that conform to a particular genre or belong to a particular topic. The STRAND architecture of Figure 1 is clearly amenable to additional filtering modules such as document classification incorporated into, or pipelined with, the language-dependent filtering stage.

– **Dissemination.** Although text out on the Web is generally intended for public access, it is nonetheless protected by copyright. Therefore a corpus collected using STRAND could not legally be distributed in any straightforward way. However, legal constraints do not prevent multiple sites from running their own versions of STRAND, nor any such site from distributing a list of URLs for others to retrieve themselves. Anyone implementing this or a related approach should be careful to observe protocols governing automatic programs and agents on the Web.[7]

The final and most interesting question for future work is: What can one *do* with a parallel corpus drawn from the World Wide Web? I find two possibilities particularly promising. First, from a linguistic perspective, such a corpus offers opportunities for comparative work in lexical semantics, potentially providing a rich database for the cross-linguistic realization of underlying semantic content. From the perspective of applications, the corpus is an obvious resource for acquisition of translation lexicons and distributionally derived representations of word meaning. Most interesting of all, each possibility is linked to many others, seemingly without end — much like the Web itself.

Acknowledgments

This work was supported in part by DARPA/ITO contract N66001-97-C-8540, Department of Defense contract MDA90496C1250, and a research grant from Sun Microsystems Laboratories. I am grateful to Dan Melamed, Doug Oard, and David Traum for useful discussions.

Appendix: Experimental Data

At URL http://umiacs.umd.edu/~resnik/amta98/amta98_appendix.html the interested reader can find an on-line Appendix containing the complete test set described in Section 3, with STRAND's classifications and the author's judgments.

References

Brown, P., Cocke, J., Della Pietra, S., Della Pietra, V., Jelinek, F., Mercer, R., & Roossin, P. (1990). A statistical approach to machine translation. *Computational Linguistics, 16*(2), 79–85.

---

[7] See http://info.webcrawler.com/mak/projects/robots/robots.html.

Church, K. W., & Mercer, R. (1993). Introduction to the special issue on computational linguistics using large corpora. *Computational Linguistics, 19*(1), 1–24.

Davis, M., & Dunning, T. (1995). A TREC evaluation of query translation methods for multi-lingual text retrieval. In *Fourth Text Retrieval Conference (TREC-4)*. NIST.

Dunning, T. (1994). Statistical identification of language. Computing Research Laboratory technical memo MCCS 94-273, New Mexico State University, Las Cruces, New Mexico.

Gale, W. A., & Church, K. W. (1991a). Identifying word correspondences in parallel texts. In *Fourth DARPA Workshop on Speech and Natural Language*, Asilomar, California.

Gale, W. A., & Church, K. W. (1991b). A program for aligning sentences in bilingual corpora. In *Proceedings of the 29th Annual Meeting of the Association for Computational Linguistics*, Berkeley, California.

Grefenstette, G. (1995). Comparing two language identification schemes. In *Proceedings of the 3rd International Conference on the the Statistical Analysis of Textual Data (JADT'95)*, Rome, Italy. http://www.rxrc.xerox.com/research/mltt/Tools/guesser.html.

Landauer, T. K., & Littman, M. L. (1990). Fully automatic cross-language document retrieval using latent semantic indexing. In *Proceedings of the Sixth Annual Conference of the UW Centre for the New Oxford English Dictionary and Text Research*, pp. pages 31–38, UW Centre for the New OED and Text Research, Waterloo, Ontario.

LDC (1996). Linguistic Data Consortium (LDC) home page. World Wide Web page. http://www.cis.upenn.edu/~ldc/.

Melamed, I. D. (1996). A geometric approach to mapping bitext correspondence. In *Conference on Empirical Methods in Natural Language Processing*, Philadelphia, Pennsylvania.

Melamed, I. D. (1997). Automatic discovery of non-compositional compounds in parallel data. In *Proceedings of the 2nd Conference on Empirical Methods in Natural Language Processing (EMNLP-97)*, Brown University.

Melamed, I. D. (1998). Word-to-word models of translational equivalence. IRCS technical report #98-08, University of Pennsylvania.

Oard, D. W. (1997). Cross-language text retrieval research in the USA. In *Third DELOS Workshop*. European Research Consortium for Informatics and Mathematics.

Resnik, P., & Melamed, I. D. (1997). Semi-automatic acquisition of domain-specific translation lexicons. In *Fifth Conference on Applied Natural Language Processing*, Washington, D.C.

Resnik, P., Olsen, M. B., & Diab, M. (1998). The Bible as a parallel corpus: Annotating the 'Book of 2000 Tongues'. Submitted.

An English-to-Turkish Interlingual MT System

Dilek Zeynep Hakkani[1], Gökhan Tür[1], Kemal Oflazer[1], Teruko Mitamura[2], and Eric H. Nyberg, 3rd[2]

[1] Department of Computer Engineering and Information Science, Bilkent University, Ankara 06533, Turkey
[2] Center for Machine Translation, Carnegie Mellon University, Pittsburgh PA 15213, USA

Abstract. This paper describes the integration of a Turkish generation system with the KANT knowledge-based machine translation system to produce a prototype English–Turkish interlingua-based machine translation system. These two independently constructed systems were successfully integrated within a period of two months, through development of a module which maps KANT interlingua expressions to Turkish syntactic structures. The combined system is able to translate completely and correctly 44 of 52 benchmark sentences in the domain of broadcast news captions. This study is the first known application of knowledge-based machine translation from English to Turkish, and our initial results show promise for future development.

1 Introduction

This paper describes the integration of a Turkish generation system [2], developed in the framework of an ongoing large-scale research project on Turkish natural language processing, with the KANT knowledge-based machine translation system, developed under the KANT project at Carnegie Mellon University's Center for Machine Translation [7]. The result is a prototype English–Turkish, interlingua-based machine translation system. In order to integrate these independently developed systems, we have designed and implemented a mapping module, using the KANT mapper software developed [4], which transforms the interlingua representation of each sentence to a feature structure (hereafter, f-structure) for Turkish; the resulting Turkish f-structure is then input to the existing Turkish sentence generator, producing Turkish surface forms.

The paper is structured as follows: In Section 2 we give a brief introduction to relevant features of Turkish. In Section 3, we briefly present the architecture and details of the Turkish subsystem comprising the mapper and the Turkish generator. We then present some experimental results, and discuss a set of important issues that we encountered during the design and implementation of the system.

2 Turkish

Morphologically, Turkish is an agglutinative language, with very productive inflectional and derivational suffixation processes by which it is possible to generate thousands of forms from a given root word. A slightly exaggerated example of a Turkish word formation is illustrated by the following nominal:

(1) Ankaralılaştıramayabileceklerimiz
     Ankara-lı-laş-tır-ama-yabil-ecek-ler-imiz
     those whom we can not convert to a citizen of Ankara

Turkish morphotactics are finite-state, and the surface realization of words is constrained by morphographemic processes such as vowel harmony. For details regarding Turkish grammar and word formation rules, one may refer to Lewis [5]; see also Oflazer [10] for a finite-state description of Turkish morphology.

With respect to word order, Turkish can be considered a *subject-object-verb* (SOV) language, in which constituents can change order rather freely in almost all sentential constructions, depending on the constraints of text flow or discourse. The grammatical roles of constituents are identified by explicit morphological case markings rather than their constituent order. For example, the word 'masa' (table), case marked accusative, is a definite direct object. The same word, when case marked dative, expresses a goal (unless it is accompanied by an idiosyncratic verb which subcategorizes for a dative complement)[3,4]:

(2)a. Masa-yı   sil-di-m
       table-ACC wipe-PAST-1SG
       'I wiped the table.'
   b. Kitab-ı   masa-ya   koy-du-m
       book-ACC table-DAT put-PAST-1SG
       'I put the book on the table.'

Word order variation in Turkish is, for the most part, dictated by information structure constraints which capture and encode, to a certain extent, discourse-related factors [15].

3   The Architecture of the System

The system which generates Turkish sentences from interlingua representations consists of 4 subsystems: the mapping system, the sentence generation system, the interface, and the morphological generation system (see Figure 1).

To demonstrate the function of each component, we will use the example sentence:

"Tosco will become the nation's largest independent refinery."

---

[3] From this point on we will give Turkish forms with -'s indicating morpheme boundaries, where necessary.

[4] In the glosses, 3SG and 1SG denote third person singular and first person singular verbal agreement, P3SG denotes third person singular possessive agreement, LOC, ABL, DAT, GEN, ACC denote locative, ablative, dative, genitive, and accusative case markers, PAST denotes past tense, and INF denotes a marker that derives an infinitive form from a verb.

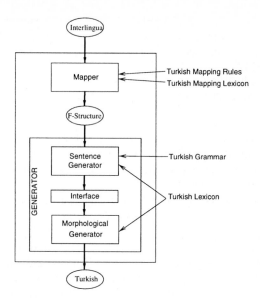

Fig. 1. The Turkish generation system.

The interlingua generated by the KANT analyzer is as follows:[5]

```
(*A-BECOME
 (PUNCTUATION PERIOD)
 (FORM FINITE)
 (TENSE FUTURE)
 (MOOD DECLARATIVE)
 (ARGUMENT-CLASS BENEFICIARY+GOAL)
 (BENEFICIARY (*PROP-TOSCO
               (NUMBER MASS)
               (IMPLIED-REFERENCE +)
               (PERSON THIRD)))
 (GOAL (*O-REFINERY
        (NUMBER SINGULAR)
        (REFERENCE NO-REFERENCE)
        (PERSON THIRD)
        (UNIT -)
        (POSSESSOR (*O-NATION
                   (NUMBER SINGULAR)
```

---

[5] Most of the linguistic features used in the KANT interlingua (e.g., punctuation, form, tense, mood, argument class, number, person) should be self-evident. Some other features are artifacts of KANT's evolution as a technical text system. The IMPLIED-REFERENCE feature is used for nouns (such as the proper noun in the example) which have implicit reference, although they are not marked with a determiner. To promote representational consistency, the same structure (*G-COORDINATION) is used whether or not an explicit conjunction (such as "and") appears; hence in the example the (CONJUNCTION) is NULL.

```
                   (REFERENCE DEFINITE)
                   (UNIT -)
                   (PERSON THIRD)))
         (ATTRIBUTE
          (*G-COORDINATION
           (CONJUNCTION NULL)
            (CONJUNCTS
             (:MULTIPLE
              (*P-LARGE
               (COMPARISON MOST)
               (DEGREE SUPERLATIVE))
              (*P-INDEPENDENT
               (DEGREE POSITIVE)))))))))
```

3.1 The Mapping System

The mapping system produces f-structures for Turkish from the interlingua representations, using a set of mapping rules and a mapping lexicon. For the example interlingua given above, the mapping system produces the following Turkish f-structure:

```
((REL IS-A)
 (ARGUMENTS
  ((SUBJECT
    ((SPECIFIER
      ((DETERMINER ((DEFINITE +)))))
     (REFERENT
      ((AGR ((NUMBER SINGULAR)
             (PERSON 3)))
       (RPROPER +)
       (ARG ((CONCEPT "tosco")))))))
   (PRED-OBJ
    ((SPECIFIER
      ((DETERMINER ((DEFINITE +)))))
     (MODIFIER
      ((QUALITATIVE
        ((ELEMENT
          (*MULTIPLE*
           ((P-NAME "bUyUk")
            (INTENSIFIER ((DEGREE EN))))
           ((P-NAME "baGImsIz"))))
         (CONJ " ")))))
     (REFERENT
      ((SEM ((COUNTABLE +)))
       (ARG ((CONCEPT "rafineri")))
       (AGR ((NUMBER SINGULAR)
             (PERSON 3)))))
     (POSSESSOR
      ((REFERENT
        ((SEM ((COUNTABLE +)))
```

```
       (ARG ((CONCEPT "Ulke")))
       (AGR ((NUMBER SINGULAR)
             (PERSON 3)))))
     (SPECIFIER
      ((DETERMINER ((DEFINITE +)))))))))))
 (VERB ((ROOT TO-BE)
        (SENSE POSITIVE)
        (TENSE FUTURE)))
 (SPEECH-ACT DECLARATIVE)
 (VOICE ((ACTIVE +)))
 (PUNCTUATION PERIOD)
 (S-FORM FINITE)
 (CLAUSE-TYPE ATTRIBUTIVE))
```

A fully detailed discussion of the mapping system is beyond the scope of this paper; in the remainder of this section, we describe how basic sentential components are mapped.

Verb Form Mappings. In order to realize the surface form of a verb in Turkish, it is necessary to determine certain morphological features of the verb in addition to its root, such as voice, polarity, tense, aspect, mood, and agreement features. The voice and polarity information can be directly obtained from the interlingua. The agreement depends on the subject of the sentence. Aspect, mood and tense features depend on the tense, perfective, progressive, and conditional information in the interlingua.

Argument Mappings. In the interlingua representation there is a semantic argument class feature, which states the possible arguments each verb may take. While mapping the arguments of a sentence, this information is used to determine the counterpart of each argument in the f-structure for Turkish. But sometimes, this information may not be enough, in which case, the verb's subcategorization information, and the type of the sentence (e.g., predicative, existential, etc.) and the voice of the main verb in Turkish are also required.

Noun Phrase Mappings. Most of the features for a noun phrase in the interlingua, like definiteness, agreement, quantifier, quantity, and possessor, are directly mapped to their counterparts in the Turkish f-structure.

Prepositional Phrase Mappings. The prepositional phrases which are attached to a noun phrase in the interlingua are mapped to one of the modifiers or specifiers depending on the preposition. The ones which are attached to the verb are mapped to either an argument of the sentence, or a postpositional phrase in Turkish. This selection depends on the preposition in question, and also on certain semantic conditions.

3.2 Sentence Generation System

The sentence generation system was originally designed and implemented by Hakkani and Oflazer [2] for use in a prototype transfer-based human-assisted machine translation system from English to Turkish [14]. This component is implemented using the CMU-CMT Genkit system [13], and is based on a recursively-structured finite state machine (much like a recursive transition network) which handles the constituent order variations of Turkish, implemented as a right-linear grammar backbone.

The sentence generation system receives as input an f-structure representing the content of the sentence, where all lexical selections have been made, and produces as output an f-structure for each word of the sentence, encoding relevant abstract morphological features such as: *agreement, possessive,* and *case* markers for nominals and *voice, polarity, tense, aspect, mood,* and *agreement* markers for verbal forms, as well as markers for *all productive derivations.*

3.3 Morphological Generation System

Morphological realization has been designed and implemented by Oflazer [10] using an external morphological analysis/generation component. This component performs (i) concrete morpheme selection, dictated by the morphotactic constraints and morphophonological context, (ii) handles morphographemic phenomena such as vowel harmony, and vowel and consonant ellipsis, and (iii) produces an agglutinative surface form.

3.4 Interface

The main task of the interface is to collect and send the output of the sentence generation system (which are morphological feature structures), to the morphological generation system in the required format, and then print out the surface form of the translated sentence. For the example sentence at the beginning of this section, the interface produces the following from the output of the sentence generation system:

```
[[CAT=NOUN][ROOT=Tosco][TYPE=RPROPER][AGR=3SG][POSS=NONE][CASE=NOM]]
[[CAT=NOUN][ROOT=ülke][AGR=3SG][POSS=NONE][CASE=GEN]]
[[CAT=ADVERB][ROOT=en]]
[[CAT=ADJ][ROOT=büyük]]
[[CAT=ADJ][ROOT=bağımsız]]
[[CAT=NOUN][ROOT=rafineri][AGR=3SG][POSS=3SG][CASE=NOM]]
[[CAT=VERB][ROOT=ol][SENSE=POS][TAM1=FUTURE][AGR=3SG]]
[PUNC=PERIOD]
```

After sending each word to the morphological generation system, the surface form of the sentence appears as follows:

Tosco ülkenin en büyük bağımsız rafinerisi olacak.

4 Results and Example Translations

For evaluating our prototype system, we have used 52 sentences (646 words) from a corpus of broadcast news captions [9]. Of these 52 sentences, the system was able to translate 44 sentences (85%) correctly and completely. 2 sentences (4%) had missing phrases because of problems with the mapping and sentence generation systems. 6 sentences (11%) could not be translated because of problems with the interlingua and the mapper. The reasons for the missing translations can be summarized as: (i) structural problems in the interlingua, such as incorrect prepositional phrase attachments; (ii) feature mismatches (values stored under wrong features); and (iii) mapper limitations (inability to implement certain mapping operations).

The following examples demonstrate the output of the system.

1. (translate "The company says they have sealed the deal.")
   Şirket onların anlaşmayı imzaladıklarını söylüyor.

2. (translate "Tosco had sealed the deal in World War II.")
   Tosco II. dünya savaşında anlaşmayı imzalamıştı.
   Tosco II. dünya savaşındaki anlaşmayı imzalamıştı.

Note that in the second example there are two valid translations in Turkish corresponding to the attachment ambiguities of the prepositional phrase in the English input. In the first Turkish sentence the prepositional phrase *in World War II* maps to a temporal adjunct, while in the second sentence, it maps to a relativizer noun phrase modifier.

5 Issues and Problems

In this section, we will discuss some issues related to the generation of Turkish text from an interlingua representation, and present how we have handled them. These issues can be categorized into three groups, according to their origin.

While there are challenges to be worked out where the source and target languages differ greatly in their means of realization for the same unit of meaning, our experience has been that the interlingua approach is an advantage when integrating software modules for languages that differ in their grammatical structure. For this reason we feel that our results should encourage others working on dissimilar language pairs to consider the interlingua approach. Many of the general issues listed below (e.g., tense differences, argument mappings, verb mapping, lexical selection) are not specific to English and Turkish, and the approaches described herein can be adapted for use with other language pairs.

5.1 Issues Related to the Differences between English and Turkish

Tense differences. There are some differences between tenses in Turkish and English. Some English tenses do not have exact Turkish counterparts, and vice-versa. An example is the *narrative past tense* of Turkish, which is used when the speaker is talking about a past event, which she has not witnessed herself. Similarly, the past perfect and present perfect tenses of English do not have one-to-one correspondences in Turkish, hence they are mapped to the closest possible Turkish tenses.

Argument mappings. The KANT interlingua categorizes verbs according to their argument classes [6], which facilitates the mapping process. For example, in the case of a verb of argument class AGENT+THEME, agent maps to subject and the theme usually maps to accusative object. But, there are certain verbs that belong to the AGENT+THEME argument class, whose theme maps to a dative object in Turkish. For example despite the fact that the verbs 'break' and 'cause' belong to the AGENT+THEME arguments class, but 'break' in Turkish subcategorizes for an accusative object, whereas 'cause' subcategorizes for a dative object.

(3)a. Kedi vazo-yu   kır-dı.
      Cat   vase-ACC break-PAST-3SG
      'The cat broke the vase.'
   b. Kedi kaza-ya   sebep oldu.
      Cat   accident-DAT cause-PAST-3SG
      'The cat caused an accident.'

Since such subcategorization information cannot be deduced from the interlingua, we introduced a SUBCAT feature. This feature stores the subcategorization information of the verb in the interlingua and is used during mapping. We map the arguments according to this feature, in addition to the argument class of the verb and the voice of the sentence.

Prepositional phrase attachments. Because of the prepositional phrase attachments, some sentences are inherently ambiguous in English. For example, for the English sentence "I saw the girl at home." it is possible to have two different interlingua representations. But, these two interlingua representations will map to different translations in Turkish.

(4)a. Ev-de   kız-ı   gör-dü-m.
      ev-LOC girl-ACC see-PAST-1SG
      '[I] [saw] [the girl] [at home].'
   b. Ev-de-ki   kız-ı   gör-dü-m.
      home-LOC-REL girl-ACC see-PAST-1SG
      '[I] [saw] [the girl [at home]].'

Since the parser produces both interlingua representations, our system produces two surface forms for such sentences.

Additionally, certain prepositional phrases map to different structures in Turkish. A typical example is the preposition 'for'. If it is used for stating a price or a beneficiary, it maps to a dative object in Turkish, otherwise it maps to a Turkish postpositional phrase, whose postposition is 'için'.

(5)a. Kitabı   7 dolara   satın aldı.
   book-ACC 7 dollar-DAT buy-PAST-3SG
   '(He) bought the book for 7 dollars.'

   b. Kitabı   Ali'ye   satın aldı.
   book-ACC Ali-DAT buy-PAST-3SG
   '(He) bought the book for Ali.'

   c. O şirket   için önemliydi.
   He company for important-PAST-3SG
   'He was important for the company.'

We generate the correct sentence by certain semantic checks. It is important to note that it is not always possible to preserve source text ambiguity when mapping to Turkish, because both source meanings cannot be indicated by a single output structure. For this reason disambiguation via semantic restrictions becomes crucial when mapping from English to Turkish.

Verb mappings. There are some verbs whose argument classes depend on their sentential context. For example, the verb 'finish' belongs to argument class THEME/AGENT+THEME in English. In the following sentence, it belongs to the THEME argument class which maps to *bit* in Turkish:

(6)   The film   finished.
      Film bit-ti.
      Film finish-PAST-3SG

On the other hand 'finish' belongs to the AGENT+THEME argument class in the sentence:

(7)   He finished the school.
      O   okul-u   bit-ir-di.
      He school-ACC finish-CAUS-PAST-3SG

As can be seen from the glosses, these verbs have different surface realizations in Turkish. For example, in sentence (7), the verb has a CAUSATIVE marker, which is absent in the sentence (6), although the verbs have the same form in English. This is the case for all of the verbs in this argument class. In order to handle such cases, we make a test in the lexicon and add the causative marker if a verb has an AGENT+THEME argument class.

Lexical selection. Lexical selection is also an important issue for an MT system. As exemplified by (8a), the verb "say" is mapped to Turkish verb "de", while in (8b) it is mapped to the verb "söyle". The rationale for this selection is as follows: if there is a THEME feature in interlingua representation of the sentence, "say" maps to the verb "de", otherwise if there is a complement, it maps to the verb "söyle".

(8)a. John Mary'e   olmaz dedi.
    John Mary-DAT no   say-PAST-3SG
    'John said no to Mary.'

  b. John geldiğini   söyledi.
    John come-INF-ACC say-PAST-3SG
    'John said he came.'

Demonstrative pronoun mappings. Two demonstrative pronouns are used in English to denote singular concepts: 'this' and 'that', used for showing near and far objects, respectively. However Turkish employs three demonstrative pronouns for this purpose: 'bu', 'şu', and 'o', used for showing near, far, and very far objects, respectively. 'This' always maps to 'bu', but 'that' sometimes maps to 'şu', and sometimes to 'o', depending on the context. Since the distance information cannot be deduced as either "far" or "very far" from English, 'that' is always mapped to 'o' in this system.

5.2   Issues Related to the Interlingua

Anaphora resolution. The current KANT parser does not resolve anaphora. This resolution can be critical for Turkish. For instance for the sentence *'Ed read his book.'*, if the writer or owner of the book is Ed himself, the Turkish sentence that must be generated is:

(9)   Ed kitab-ı-nı   oku-du.
    Ed book-P3SG-ACC read-PAST-3SG

Otherwise (i.e. the book belongs to or is written by another person), there must be an explicit pronoun with a genitive marker:

(10)   Ed o-nun   kitab-ı-nı   oku-du.
    Ed he-GEN book-P3SG-ACC read-PAST-3SG

5.3   Issues Related to the Generation and Mapping Systems

Word order variations. The mapping system does not currently produce an information structure (e.g., marking constituents as *topic, focus* or *background*). Such information when available is used by the generator to handle word order variations. So, currently all sentences are produced in the ical order (SOV) in Turkish. The information structure of a sentence can be obtained using syntactic clues in the source language in machine translation [1, 11], or using algorithms that determine the topic and focus of the target language sentences using Centering Theory [12], and given versus new information [3].

Domain differences. The sentence generation system was originally developed for a machine translation system in another domain [14]. Missing parts, like detailed treatment of numbers, were added during the development of the mapping system.

Mapper limitations. Features belonging to the same category are stored in the same slot in the interlingua, using a `:multiple` flag. The problem is that features belonging to the same category in the interlingua may map to different categories in Turkish. Currently, the mapper does not support the operation of extracting individual features under the `:multiple` flag.

6   Future Work

We have presented a system which generates Turkish sentences from interlingua representations. This work is important because it demonstrates the feasibility of rapidly combining independent systems developed at different locations, using interlingua as an intermediary representation. With the implementation of a Turkish mapping component, we were able to construct a prototype English–Turkish machine translation system in about two months.

The coverage, accuracy, and fluency of this machine translation system can further be extended, by adding new and more detailed mapping rules. For the example set of 52 sentences, the output quality of this system is comparable to the output quality of the KANT machine translation system [8] in large-scale domains. To achieve the same output results on a large-scale English–Turkish corpus, significant work must be undertaken to extend the lexicon and mapping rules.

7   Acknowledgments

This research has been supported in part by a NATO Science for Stability Grant TU–LANGUAGE. The authors would like to thank Robert Igo and Krzysztof Czuba for their help with the Turkish lexicon and mapper. We also thank Zelal Güngördü for extensive comments on earlier versions of this manuscript which significantly improved its presentation.

semi-automated methods for transfer lexicon construction. In a six-month effort (with less than 12 person-months, about half of which were academic and half commercial), we were able to quickly develop a system that produces acceptable English to French translations in two limited domains, a battlefield message domain and a weather domain. We also demonstrated limited capability for Arabic (in the weather domain only). The staff included a French (native-speaker) computational linguist who worked on English-to-French transfer and French generation, as well as an Arabic (native speaker) computational linguist for the small Arabic system.

The structure of this overview paper is as follows. In Section 2, we detail the requirements that motivated our experiment. The system is presented in Section 3. We present the parsers, the transfer component, and the generation component in Sections 4, 5, and 6, respectively. We conclude with some observation for the next phase of the project in Section 7.

2 Special MT Requirements

The military has special machine translation (MT) needs which are not being met by currently available commercial MT systems. These needs center around the domain-specific nature of the data the military would like to be able to translate, e.g., battlefield messages traffic, medical diagnosis routines, military training manuals, intelligence reports and briefing slides. In all of these applications, an accurate, efficient MT system would rely heavily on domain-specific vocabulary. In addition, the military often requires translation to or from "exotic" languages which are of little interest to commercial MT providers. For any specific language, for any specific military application, off-the-shelf products could potentially provide a portion of the necessary grammar and vocabulary, but they would have to be augmented extensively with additional domain-specific vocabulary and grammar rules.[1]

In addition to domain-specific requirements and language-specific requirements, the military has another special need which is not shared by the commercial world — the necessity of timely reaction to sudden crises, which can be in any spot in the world and can arise with no warning. A commercial enterprise can spend months gearing up for a new product launch in a new country, and this preliminary planning time can be spent developing support tools such as machine translation components. In a world crisis this is not possible, so tools for quickly adapting an existing system to another language are essential to the military as domain-specific translation.

These special military requirements can be met, we believe, by an MT system which addresses the design goals outlined in Section 1. Specifically, the design goal of lexico-structural transfer will allow us to handle the domain-specific aspect of military translations, and to exploit machine learning tools for the

---

[1] An example of domain-specific grammar is the use of certain types of telegraphic styles in military messages (omission of subjects and of function words). Furthermore, these telegraphic styles are also difficult to handle in target language generation.

acquisition of transfer lexicons. The design goal of using off-the-shelf trainable components will allow us to meet the requirement of rapid configuration of new MT systems for new language pairs and domains.

3   Overview of the System

Skies were clear across the three maritime provinces early this morning.
$\longrightarrow$ Le temps était clair dans les trois provinces maritime ce matin tôt.
Behind this area a moderate flow will cause an inflow of milder air in southwestern Quebec producing mild temperatures on Sunday.
$\longrightarrow$ Une circulation modérée provoquera un afflux du air doux dans le sud-ouest du Québec à l'arrière de cette zone produisant des températures douces dimanche.
Loyalty of local civilian officials is questionable.
$\longrightarrow$ La loyauté des dirigeants locaux civils est douteuse.
The 175tr/9gtd is moving west on e4a48 Autobahn toward Berlin.
$\longrightarrow$ Le 175tr/9gtd se déplace vers l'ouest sur e4a48 autobahn vers Berlin.

Fig. 1. Some sample translations performed by TransLex

TransLex is an English-to-French translation system, with a small English-to-Arabic capability. Some sample French outputs can be seen in Figure 1; a sample Arabic output in Figure 2.[2] The main level of representation in TransLex is a syntactic dependency representation which we will call DSyntS, for *Deep Syntactic Structure* (roughly as defined in (Mel'čuk, 1988)). This level of representation contains all the meaning-bearing words of a sentence (nouns, verbs, adjectives, adverbs, and some prepositions), but no function words (determiners, auxiliary verbs, strongly governed prepositions, and so on). The grammatical contribution of function words (determination, tense, aspect, and so on) is represented through features. The meaning-bearing words are related syntactically using a small set of possible relation labels (essentially, different arguments and generic adjuncts). This level of representation is well suited for MT since it abstracts away from superficial grammatical differences between languages.

TransLex consists of the following components:

- Two parsers (the Collins parser and the SuperTagger from the University of Pennsylvania), each with a converter which converts the output from the parser to the DSyntS. (Two parsers are used only experimentally; in an operational context only one parser is needed, of course.)
- The core transfer component.
- The generator (RealPro) from CoGenTex.

---

[2] No Arabic morphological component was implemented for the generator.

```
==========================================
```
RESULT OF REALIZATION:
```
==========================================
```

كـان جو صافي عبر ال   مقطع ال   بحري ثـلاث هذا صبـاح بـاكـرا .

Fig. 2. Arab translation (without morphology) generated from *Skies were clear across the three maritime provinces early this morning.*

To help us develop the transfer lexicons, we used Sable, a component developed at the University of Pennsylvania. The architecture is shown in Figure 3.

4 Two Parsers

We investigated the use of two parsers, both developed previously at Penn, namely the Collins parser (Collins, 1996) and the SuperTagger with Lightweight Dependency Analysis (Joshi and Srinivas, 1994; Srinivas, 1997). These parsers are rather different: the Collins parser is trained on a corpus annotated with phrase-structure parse trees, and uses the probability of specific word-word dependencies to determine the most likely parse. The SuperTagger is trained on a corpus where each lexical item has been annotated with the tree that is associated with it in a correct Tree-Adjoining Grammar parse - "supertags". It uses only these supertags to heuristically determine the most likely parse. We retrained both parsers on 450 messages from our original 500 message data set. The 50 test messages were selected by randomly removing a few messages from each topic of the training set, with the number of messages being proportional to the percentage of messages in that topic. This is very small training set by typical standards for empirical methods, and the performance of both parsers would improve dramatically given more training data. We also paid special attention to military terminology, and had a canonical expansion for military acronyms, many of which have multiple forms.

Neither parser produces an output in the format needed for our transfer module, which uses dependency structures, DSyntS, (see (Nasr et al., 1997) for details). Therefore, "converters" had to be implemented for both parsers. The Collins parser, which outputs a phrase-structure parse tree annotated with head information, uses the Generic Parse Analyzer (GPA) developed at Penn, which has been specialized for outputting a DSyntS during this project. The SuperTagger/LDA outputs a dependency tree which is based on the derivation structure of Tree Adjoining Grammar; while this representation is very close to the DSyntS, it is not identical (see (Rambow and Joshi, 1996)), so a small converter was needed to bridge the gap.

We hand corrected the parses for the 50 test messages to create a Gold Standard, and then evaluated our two parsers. The Collins parser achieved com-

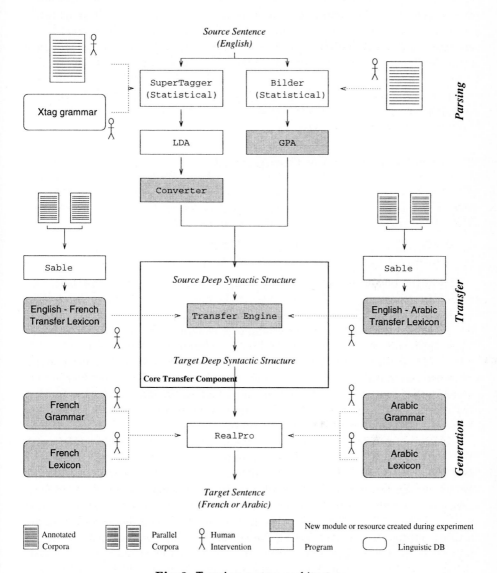

Fig. 3. TransLex system architecture

pletely accurate parses for 72.4% of the sentences, with 85.7% having no more than two crossed brackets. We also evaluated the combination of the Collins parser and the GPA against the same messages annotated for deep-syntactic dependency relations (i.e., a DSyntS) and found that 69% of the correct head-argument and head-modifier relations had been found.[3] The best performance from the SuperTagger, 89% correct SuperTag assignments, came from training it on a combined corpus of 200,000 WSJ words and the 5,000 word (450 messages) training set. At 65%, the performance of the SuperTagger-LDA-converter combination against on the weather corpus was slightly lower than that of the Collins parser with the GPA.

5 The Core Transfer Component

TransLex can draw on several separate transfer lexicons contained in separate files. These transfer lexicons are represented in an easily readable format, the Multi Lexical Base (MLB) format. Here is an example:

```
@ENGLISH: X [class:verb] (ATTR ALMOST)
@FRENCH: FAILLIR (II X [mood:inf])
```

First, the output of the automatic bilingual lexicon extractor (SABLE – see below) is converted into MLB format. At the current state-of-the-art, an automatically induced bilingual lexicon will not contain the detailed structural correspondences necessary for natural language generation in the target language. Thus, the resulting file is then hand-edited by a linguist or domain specialist. Additional MLB files containing translation lexicons can be entirely hand-crafted, or re-used from other related or even unrelated domains. The MLB files are ordered so that in case of multiple occurrence of a key, the different entries for that key are ranked. Finally, the MLB files are automatically processed to generate a fast loadable version of the transfer rules.

SABLE is a tool for analyzing bilingual corpora (or "bitexts") (Melamed, July 1997). SABLE can induce domain-specific bilingual transfer lexicons (Resnik and Melamed, 1997) using a fast algorithm for estimating a partial translation model. A translation model is a set of transfer pairs, consisting of one word from each language which are (in some context in the bitext) a translation of one another. The model's accuracy/coverage trade-off can be directly controlled via a threshold parameter. (By setting the threshold lower, more transfer pairs are proposed, but fewer of these are likely to be correct.) For example, on our battlefield message corpus of about 5,500 words (backed up by the Hansard corpus) we obtained a recall of 73% at a precision of 83%, or a recall of only 32% but at a precision of 91%. This feature makes the model suitable for applications that are not fully statistical such as TransLex.

---

[3] Recall that our transfer representation does not include function words such as determiners, auxiliaries, and strongly governed prepositions, and is thus closer to a representation of propositional content than most syntactic representations. Therefore, the figures reported here for DSyntS accuracy should not be copared to figures for crossing brackets.

6   Generation

For generation, we have used RealPro, CoGenTex's sentence realizer (Lavoie and Rambow, 1997). The input representation for RealPro is precisely the DSyntS formalism which we use for transfer. We have constructed a small French grammar. We based this grammar on the English grammar, which we adapted through successive modifications. We used an off-the shelf morphological component for French. (We did not integrate a morphological component for Arabic – which explains the lack of morphology in Figure 2.)

7   Outlook

Over the next two years, we will be building a more robust MT system based on the approach outlined in this paper, for the language pairs English/Korean and Korean/English. We will be choosing one or two domains, at least one of which will be military.

The work will be carried out in collaboration with Systran, Inc., which will enable us to reuse as much as possible existing resources. We will also be co-ordinating with other government funded English/Korean MT projects at New Mexico State University and Lincoln Labs to avoid duplication of effort. The crucial issues that we will be investigating include to what extent SABLE can be used to build or augment a large bilingual transfer dictionary, and to what extent we can rapidly develop a parser for Korean which can be retrained on different corpora.

Acknowledgments

The work reported in this paper was partially supported by contract DAAL01-97-C-0016 awarded by the Army Research Lab to CoGenTex, Inc., with the University of Pennsylvania as a subcontractor. The work was carried out while Nasr was with CoGenTex. We would like to thank Rich Kaste, project engineer, for his support and feedback. We would also like to thank Benoit Lavoie for his contributions to the implementation of the system, Richard Kittredge for assistance during the project, Aravind Joshi for technical guidance and support, and the Institute for Research in Cognitive Studies at the University of Pennsylvania for facilities.

Bibliography

Collins, M. (1996). A new statistical parser based on bigram lexical dependencies. In *Proceedings of the 34th Annual Meeting of the Association for Computational Linguistics*, Santa Cruz, CA.

Joshi, A. K. and Srinivas, B. (1994). Disambiguation of Super Parts of Speech (or Supertags): Almost Parsing. In *Proceedings of the 17th International Conference on Computational Linguistics (COLING '94)*, Kyoto, Japan.

Lavoie, B. and Rambow, O. (1997). RealPro – a fast, portable sentence realizer. In *Proceedings of the Conference on Applied Natural Language Processing (ANLP'97)*, Washington, DC.

Melamed, I. D. (July, 1997). Automatic Discovery of Non-Compositional Compounds in Parallel Data. In *Proceedings of the ACL-97*, Madrid, Spain.

Mel'čuk, I. A. (1988). *Dependency Syntax: Theory and Practice.* State University of New York Press, New York.

Nasr, A., Rambow, O., Palmer, M., and Rosenzweig, J. (1997). Enriching lexical transfer with cross-linguistic semantic features. In *Proceedings of the Interlingua Workshop at the MT Summit*, San Diego, California.

Rambow, O. and Joshi, A. (1996). A formal look at dependency grammars and phrase-structure grammars, with special consideration of word-order phenomena. In Wanner, L., editor, *Current Issues in Meaning-Text Theory.* Pinter, London.

Rambow, O., Nasr, A., Palmer, M., Bleam, T., Collins, M., Kipper, K., Melamed, D., Park, J., Rosenzweig, J., Schuler, W., and Srinivas, B. (1997). Machine translation of battlefield messages using lexico-structural transfer. Technical report, CoGenTex, Inc.

Resnik, P. and Melamed, I. D. (1997). Semi-Automatic Acquisition of Domain-Specific Translation Lexicons. In *Proceedings of the ANLP-97*, Washington, D.C.

Srinivas, B. (1997). *Complexity of Lexical Descriptions and its Relevance to Partial Parsing.* PhD thesis, Computer Science Department, University of Pennsylvania.

Time-Constrained Machine Translation

Janine Toole, Davide Turcato, Fred Popowich, Dan Fass, and Paul McFetridge

Natural Language Lab, School of Computing Science, Simon Fraser University,
Burnaby, BC, Canada V5A 1S6
toole, turk, popowich, fass, mcfet@cs.sfu.ca,
WWW home page: http://www.cs.sfu.ca/research/groups/NLL/toc.html
&
TCC Communications, 100-6722 Oldfield Road, Victoria, BC, Canada V8M 2A3

Abstract. This paper defines the class of *time-constrained* applications: applications in which the user has limited time to process the system output. This class is differentiated from *real-time* systems, where it is production time rather than comprehension time that is constrained. Examples of time-constrained MT applications include the translation of multi-party dialogue and the translation of closed-captions. The constraints on comprehension time in such systems have significant implications for the system's objectives, its design, and its evaluation. In this paper we outline these challenges and discuss how they have been met in an English-Spanish MT system designed to translate the closed-captions used on television.

1 What is a Time-Constrained Application?

We define an application as *time-constrained* when the user has limited time to process or comprehend the system output. Translated closed captions are a good example of this. Closed captions are presented to the user in parallel with a televised image. In general, the user has no control over the speed of the image or caption flow so he must comprehend the caption in the limited time that the caption appears on the screen. In other words, the translation processing time is not an independent variable, but is specified by the application domain.

Like real-time systems, the class of time-constrained systems includes many types of computer applications. For example, voice-activated telephony systems also impose time constraints on the user - if the user does not respond within a certain period of time, the system disconnects. While we acknowledge that the class of time-constrained systems is large, in this paper we focus on a subset of these applications: time constrained machine translation (MT) systems.

Time-constrained applications, as defined above, should be distinguished from real-time applications. Although the two classes of application share a time-related constraint, there are important differences between them. In real-time MT the constraint is on translation production: translations need to be produced within a given time frame. In time-constrained MT, the stress is on the user's side. The translation must be processed by the user before the next translation appears.

It might be argued that a need for real-time translation is usually related to a need for real-time use of the translations. In this case, real-time applications would also be time-constrained applications. Although this is true in many cases, it is also conceivable to think of real-time MT domains in which there is no constraint on the user's side. The domain of e-mail or web-page translation would probably be one such domain: although the translation needs to be produced as quickly as possible, there is no constraint on the translation processing time. In any case, regardless of whether time-constrained and real-time applications intersect or the former class is a subset of the latter, it is apparent that time-constrained MT doesn't necessarily involve real-time requirements. The translation of closed captions is a clear-cut example. Closed captions can either be translated in real-time or off-line: the former option would be mandatory, for instance, in translating programs captioned in real-time (e.g. news), but in many other situations the translation could be performed off-line. However, in both cases, the use of the translations would happen in the same conditions and the time constraints on the user's side would be the same.

The characteristics of time-constrained MT systems have implications on many levels. Firstly, the objectives of such an MT system differ from a non-time-constrained system. These objectives in turn have consequences for system design and evaluation. These three issues are the focus of this paper. In addition to reviewing these issues, the means by which they are addressed in an English-Spanish MT system is described.

2 Consequences for Translation Objectives

The characteristics of a time-constrained MT system have significant implications for the translation objectives of the system. Typically, when evaluating the acceptability of a translation system, some metric m is chosen and it is assumed that the acceptability of the system is a direct function $F(m)$, where an increase in the value of m indicates an increase in the acceptability of the system. However, a definition of this sort is inadequate when it comes to time-constrained applications. In this domain, it is not just necessary to provide a good translation, whatever definition of 'good translation' one chooses, but it is also necessary that the translation can be processed in the given time frame. In other words, in time-constrained applications acceptability is a function $F(m, t)$ of the chosen metric m and the user's processing time t, where the value of the function increases with an increase in m and decreases with an increase in t - the longer the time that the user needs to comprehend a translation, the less acceptable it is.

As a consequence, the most acceptable system output is not always the most accurate translation, but the translation that provides the best balance between accuracy and comprehensibility within the given time constraints. Since the two requirements might not pull in the same direction, the general task is to maximize the product of both parameters. In other words, a less accurate translation might be preferable to a more accurate one if the cost of a slight accuracy increase is a significant increase in the sentence complexity. The extreme consequence of this requirement is that it is preferable to provide no translation than a complex but scarcely informative translation.

In the domain of closed caption translation, for which we developed an MT system that translates from English to Spanish (see Popowich et al. [10]), there are further factors that interact with those described above in determining what the system output should be like. Most notably, since translations co-occur with a televised image, the user need not rely only on the translated text in order to understand its meaning: users can also employ the visual context to make sense of the translations. As a consequence, an incomplete or vague translation could still be useful to a user. In contrast, the translation of a radio broadcast would not provide such contextual clues to the listener.

The possibility of excluding information in closed captions is endorsed in the captioning guidelines of a major captioning company (see [3]). When editing to maintain a specified reading speed, this guide discourages paraphrasing, replacing a long word with a shorter one, or even cutting a few select words. Instead, the guide suggests that whole phrases should be cut. The guide states that this approach is more effective in reducing the required reading speed (and hence the burden on the user) than the aforementioned techniques. In sum, providing incomplete information in captions is an accepted technique for reducing the burden on the user.

Further information on a user's processing of translated captions was obtained in a market study that was designed to ascertain user acceptability requirements. In this study, focus groups were presented with three different simulations and asked to comment on the translations. One group was presented with a video that simulated 20 percent accuracy. The second group was shown a video that simulated 85 percent accuracy, and the third group was shown a video that had human-translated closed captions (one hundred percent accuracy).

There were three key findings from the study. First, from the user's perspective 85 percent accuracy was indistinguishable from 100 percent accurate translation. Second, unilingual Spanish speakers were more tolerant of errors than bilinguals. Third, and most relevant to our discussion, all speakers were tolerant of text that was grammatically correct although semantically anomalous (although not vice versa). Hence, grammatical output that is not semantically faithful to the original is easier to comprehend than ungrammatical output that is faithful to the original meaning of the utterance.

Therefore, in the domain of caption translation, the goal of achieving a *complete* and *accurate* translation should be weakened to the more modest one of (i) obtaining an output consistent with the input, in the sense that its content may be less specific or informative than the input meaning, and (ii), where a trade off is required the system should find a balance between grammatically accurate and semantically accurate output.

To sum up, the translation objectives in a time-constrained MT sytem differ from those in a non-time-constrained system. In particular, the overall goal of translating in a time-constrained environment is the product of both a positive and a negative requirement: (i) maximizing the amount of accurate information; (ii) minimizing the processing burden on the user. Depending on the particular application, these goals may dictate translation objectives that are quite different from those more generally assumed. In the case of translating closed captions, for example, we identified grammaticality as a particularly important objective and noted that information omission is an accepted technique. The characteristics of other time-constrained MT systems may dictate similar or different translation objectives depending on the particular characteristics of the system and its users. Careful individual analysis of the domain and of the factors affecting users' processing time is required in order to identify the best translation objectives for a particular time-constrained system.

3 Consequences for System Design

In the previous section we identified particular translation objectives that resulted from the unique characteristics of time-constrained systems. In this section we explore the consequences of these objectives for system design and discuss how these challenges have been met in our English-Spanish constraint-based lexicalist transfer MT system. Two variants of the system are mentioned in the following discussion. The first variant is a server-based system which was developed in Prolog and uses a chart parser. The second variant is a real-time system which was developed in C and incorporates the use of pre-computed results (described below).

3.1 Fidelity, Grammaticality, Robustness

The foregoing considerations about an application's goal in a time-constrained environment point towards a special consideration for *grammaticality*. Of course, grammaticality is important in any system. However, what seems peculiar in this domain, is the autonomous relevance borne by this parameter. Given the importance of reducing the user's processing time, grammaticality seems to be the most important requirement for achieving this goal. A grammatical sentence, regardless of its fidelity to the source, is generally easy to make sense of. Therefore, it is of great importance that the translated output is grammatical. In some cases, as already pointed out, this requirement might even override that of fidelity, should the latter require unacceptable processing time on the part of the user.

The constraints posed by the time-constrained environment are not the only ones impacting the design of a system to translate closed captions. Popowich et al. in [10] point out that the fragmented, incomplete, and perhaps ungrammatical nature of the captions themselves dictate that *robustness* is also a very important design objective. Moreover, they argue that the traditional MT dilemma between robustness and *accuracy* should be solved in favor of the former in this domain: a vague translation might still be useful since it is projected with a possibly disambiguating visual image.

In the case of our English-Spanish system, these design objectives have (i) influenced the system architecture, (ii) motivated a multi-engine approach, and (iii) motivated the consideration of input simplification techniques.

System Architecture. The system we developed is a constraint-based, lexicalist transfer system. In the following, the three main system phases: parsing, transfer, and generation are described, along with the choices made in order to meet the different requirements outlined above.

- **Parsing**. In order to meet the robustness requirement, the parser attempts to assign an analysis to all input, grammatical or not. Since parsing is meant to have the broadest possible coverage, it is the task of the subsequent components to make use of the provided parse to produce useful output.
- **Transfer**. The lexicalist approach adopted in transfer is particularly suited to the repair of ill-formed input. Since no structural transfer is performed, the structural flaws of the input sentence can be discarded instead of being transferred across, as long as the transferred lexical information is sufficient to provide the gist of the sentence's meaning. In addition, we take a cautious approach to word sense disambiguation, due to the conservative requirement that an incomplete translation is preferable to a more accurate, but more error-prone, one. Therefore, we tend to preserve ambiguity whenever possible. When this is not possible, multiword lexical entries are used to make translations context-sensitive.
- **Generation**. Generation is the component that enforces restrictions on the output. As explained earlier, output grammaticality is of paramount importance in time-constrained applications. Hence, the system has a restrictive target grammar that ensures that translation candidates fail if they cannot be assigned a grammatical structure.

In addition to these primary modules, we also incorporate a segmenter. The purpose of this module is to split complex input into one or more independent input strings that can be translated separately. These simpler segments have a greater chance of translating accurately. Furthermore, segments that fail to translate can be omitted without the loss of the whole input string.

Multi-engine Approach. As is consistent with recent practice, we make use of a multi-engine approach. In general, a multi-engine approach uses engines in parallel (cf. Nyberg and Mitamura [9]). However, our system consists of two engines in sequence. The first engine comprises a chart parser, transfer component, and chart generator. These components each attempt to find an analysis that encompasses the entire input sequence. If this is not possible, then the second engine comes into play. This engine attempts to find the best analysis using the edges created by the chart parser. This process degrades gracefully to a word-for word translation. The resulting set of edges are transferred to the subsequent transfer and generation components.

The use of two processes is aimed at making the system adjustable to different domains and more flexible in terms of user requirement satisfaction. When high quality output is more crucial, the second process might be switched off so that only utterances for which a full analysis can be found are translated. This approach is particularly effective with the segmenter in place as only those segments of a sentence which fail to translate using the first engine are omitted. This minimizes the amount of information that is not displayed. If robustness is emphasized or the time constraints are less tight, the second process could be activated to translate the problematic segments.

We are also exploring heuristics for a graded use of the second process. The aim of such heuristics is to estimate whether the output of the second process is likely to be useful or not. When it is deemed useful, the output is displayed. If not, this information is omitted.

Input Simplification. Another aspect under investigation is the possibility of simplifying the input, in such cases where a simplification would result in an increase in output understandability, with a minimal loss in informativeness. Unfortunately, in most cases the task is of a complexity comparable to that of fully parsing the input. However, we have implemented some simple heuristics for removing parts of the input when these are likely to increase the processing time without bringing any additional information. This is done mainly with adverbs, particularly when they are unknown to the transfer component, i.e. no translation is provided for them.

3.2 Real-time Translation

A real-time, time constrained system, i.e. one that has time constraints on both production and comprehension, has additional consequences for system design. In such a system, any unusual delay in translation production means a reduction in the time that is available to the user to comprehend the translation. Hence, the system should be designed so as to minimize the time required to produce a translation. In the real-time version of our English-Spanish system, these speed requirements influenced component design.

In order to reduce the time required by the parser and generator, our design incorporates decision trees. The decision tree represents sequences of part of speech tags and the leaves of the tree contain one or more possible parses for this tag sequence. This tree is constructed off-line. At run-time, the tree supplies a number of possible parses for the input tag sequence supplied by the POS tagger. If the lexical entries from the input utterance unify with one of the assigned parses, this parse is used. Since the parses associated with the tag sequences are developed off-line, this method is extremely fast. Initial results indicate that the accuracy of these parse results is comparable to the accuracy of our regular chart parser.

In sum, it is evident from this discussion that our particular translation objectives have affected the system design in several ways. The focus on grammaticality led to a restrictive target grammar to ensure grammatical output. This contrasts with our source language grammar which is designed to parse both grammatical and ungrammatical input. In order to maximize the time available to the user, our real-time system incorporates fast parsing techniques. The possibility of omitting information motivated the multi-engine approach, the incorporation of a segmenter to minimize the amount of information omitted and the focus on system adjustability so that the system can be sensitive to differing user requirements. Letting the translation objectives lead the system design results in a system that is most likely to meet user's needs.

4   Consequences for System Evaluation

The characteristics of a time-constrained system also has consequences for the evaluation of the system. One of the main distinctions in evaluating MT systems, is between *operational* and *declarative* evaluation (Arnold et al. [2]). Under different names and within different classifications, the foregoing distinction seems to be common to most evaluation taxonomies (Hutchins and Somers [5]). As Arnold et al. in [2] put it (p. 4), operational evaluation focusses on the benefits "to be gained by a particular user from using a particular system in a particular situation", whereas declarative evaluation "attempts to move away from the situation of an individual user to give an evaluation based on more general, and widely applicable criteria".

Declarative evaluation and operational evaluation are usually conducted independently with one having little influence over the other. This evaluation pattern is probably influenced by the application domain to which MT is most often aimed, i.e. the translation of documents. For this domain, this model seems to be appropriate: given a source text, the translation accuracy can be appropriately assessed independently of the translation's use. The assessment of the translation's adequacy to the user's requirements and the system's effectiveness in a working environment are separate issues that can be considered independently.

However, in time-constrained systems the two types of evaluation cannot be separated to the same extent. In particular, the characteristics of the operational context influence the type of declarative evaluation that is appropriate. These problems are outlined below.

The most frequently used declarative evaluation metrics are sentence-based metrics where the translation output is evaluated against predetermined scale(s) identifying levels of grammaticality, fidelity, style, etc. However, many of the scales used in non time-constrained systems are inappropriate for time-constrained systems since they identify categories that are not meaningful to a time-constrained user (e.g. Nagao et al. [7]) or apply the scales in ways that are not meaningful in a time-constrained system (e.g. Minnis [6]).

A further problem with the use of text-based metrics in evaluating time-constrained systems, one that is particularly acute in the translation of closed captions, is the choice of test data. With text-based metrics it is preferable to evaluate a randomly selected set of sentences. In this way any idiosyncrasies that are found in one text do not distort the results. However, in the case of the translation of closed-captions this poses a problem since the meaning of a caption is often not clear from the caption alone. Closed captions tend to be short and in many cases they are not complete sentences but phrasal fragments of some kind. Hence, it can be very difficult to evaluate the translation of utterances that are selected randomly since it is only by consulting the surrounding context that the proper interpretation of an utterance can be determined.

A second problem in evaluating time-constrained systems is that, as outlined in section 2, acceptability is not a direct function $F(m)$ of the evaluation metric m, but a function $F(m, t)$ where t identifies comprehension time. The effect of t can only be calculated in an operational context. Hence, while declarative evaluation methods can be used to gauge the degree to which the system measures up against the evaluation scales, they cannot be used to gauge the *acceptability* of a translated sentence.

Further, in the domain of closed captions, there is an additional problem with the use of declarative evaluation techniques to gauge the acceptability of a particular translation. As previously pointed out, in our system the operational context provides the user with additional sources of information: the images and the sound effects. Text, images, and sound effects combine to convey information to the user, who perceives them as a whole. A translation that seems incomplete in isolation may be perfectly acceptable in the context in which it is displayed. Hence, the acceptability of a given translation cannot be accurately judged in isolation from these factors.

In sum, the requirements of a time-constrained system pose two types of problems for evaluation. Firstly, the type of metric used to evaluate the quality of the translation may be inappropriate: many of the scales that are appropriate for other systems are inappropriate for evaluating a time-constrained system. Similarly, the method of application of these scales may not be suitable. Further, the means by which data is selected for evaluation may require modification. Secondly, these declarative metrics provide only a partial picture of translation acceptability since factors from the operational context are not taken into account. Consequently, considerable caution is required in developing an evaluation methodology for time-constrained systems.

The first problem can be resolved by developing an evaluation methodology that is suited to the particular domain. In consideration of our specific domain, in which the end users are exposed to translated closed captions for a very short time, we adopted a very simple metric in evaluating translations, namely, we refrained from adopting multi-point scales, which imply a detailed analysis and are more suitable for written text translation evaluation. Instead, we adopted a three-point scale: the translations are evaluated as either correct (**yes**), acceptable though not ideal (**ok**), or unacceptable (**no**).

Tests are conducted by translating multi-line sections of scripts from randomly selected closed captioned TV programs. This maintains the benefits of randomness while retaining the advantages of sequential text. A native Spanish speaker evaluates the translations on two scales: *grammaticality* and *accuracy*, as is customary in many of the evaluation methodologies proposed in the literature (see Nagao [8], Arnold et al. [1]. Details of our results can be found in [10].

The second problem identified above was that, in the domain of closed caption translation, declarative metrics only give a partial account of the acceptability of a particular translation since the evaluations are done in isolation from the visual context. Performing an operational evaluation provides a partial solution to this problem. However, while operational evaluation provides a direct assessment of quality in terms of user satisfaction, it cannot provide analytical feedback for improving the system. In addition, such tests are expensive and so cannot be done on a frequent basis. As a consequence we rely primarily on the declarative evaluation methodology outlined above. We are in the process of conducting an operational evaluation to establish the relation between our declarative evaluation methods and user acceptability.

In this review we are also experimenting with user reaction to the selective display of translations. Since users are sensitive to the grammaticality of output and have additional sources of information (the visual and aural context), we will test whether user acceptance is increased if we do not display translations which fall below a certain level of confidence.

5 Conclusion

Time-constrained MT systems – those where the user has limited time to comprehend the system output – can be differentiated from other MT systems in terms of the consequences that these systems have for translation objectives, system design, and system evaluation. These consequences, which are the result of the limited time available to the user, may result in objectives, design criteria, and evaluation methodologies that are quite different from those more generally assumed.

A review of these issues suggests, in the spirit of Church and Hovy in [4], that thoughtful consideration should be given to analyzing an application's domain. The tasks of an application vary considerably depending on the domain involved. The success of a time-constrained application relies more in matching the requirements imposed by the domain itself than in fulfilling any abstract, domain-independent metrics.

References

1. Arnold, D., Balkan, L., Lee Humphreys, R., Meijer, S., Sadler, L.: Machine Translation. An Introductory Guide. NCC Blackwell, Manchester-Oxford (1996)
2. Arnold, D., Sadler, L., Humphreys, R.: Evaluation: An Assessment. Machine Translation **8**, (1993) 1–24
3. Captionmax: Suggested Styles and Conventions for Closed Captioning. WGBH Educational Foundation, Boston, (1993)
4. Church, K., Hovy, E.: Good Applications for Crummy Machine Translation. Machine Translation **8**, (1993) 239–258

5. Hutchins, W., Somers, H.: An Introduction to Machine Translation. Academic Press, London (1992)
6. Minnis, S.: Constructive Machine Translation Evaluation. Machine Translation **8** (1993) 67–76
7. Nagao, M., Tsujii, J-I., Nakamura, J-I.: Machine Translation from Japanese to English. Proceedings of the IEEE **74** (1986) 993–1012
8. Nagao, M.: Machine Translation. How Far Can It Go?. Oxford University Press, Oxford (1989)
9. Nyberg, E., Mitamura, T.: A Real-time MT System for Translating Broadcast Captions. In: Proceedings of the 6th MT Summit, San Diego (1997) 51–57
10. Popowich, F., Turcato, D., Laurens, O., McFetridge, P., Nicholson, J.D., McGivern, P., Corzo-Pena, M., Pidruchney, L., MacDonald, S. A Lexicalist Approach to the Translation of Colloquial Text. In: Proceedings of the 7th International Conference on Theoretical and Methodological Issues in Machine Translation, Santa Fe (1997) 76–86

An Evaluation of the Multi-engine MT Architecture

Christopher Hogan and Robert E. Frederking

Language Technologies Institute
Carnegie Mellon University
4910 Forbes Avenue
Pittsburgh, PA 15213 USA
Phone: (412) 268-6593 or (412) 268-6656
FAX: (412) 268-6298
Email: chogan@cs.cmu.edu, ref+@cs.cmu.edu

Abstract. The Multi-Engine MT (MEMT) architecture combines the outputs of multiple MT engines using a statistical language model of the target language. It has been used successfully in a number of MT research systems, for both text and speech translation. Despite its perceived benefits, there has never been a rigorous, published, double-blind evaluation of the claim that the combined output of a MEMT system is in fact better than that of any one of the component MT engines. We report here the results of such an evaluation. The combined MEMT output is shown to indeed be better overall than the output of the component engines in a Croatian ↔ English MT system. This result is consistent in both translation directions, and between different raters.

The Multi-Engine Machine Translation (MEMT) architecture [9] has been used successfully in a number of MT research systems, for both text [11,24] and speech translation [12,26]. As described in the next section, these researchers believe that the MEMT architecture allows one to combine the strengths of different MT technologies while ameliorating their weaknesses.

Up to now, this belief has been justified by argumentation, but not empirical evidence. While at least one of these MEMT-architecture systems was the subject of independent evaluation,[1] this was an overall system evaluation, and thus did not distinguish between the quality of the component engines and any benefit (or detriment) caused by the MEMT architecture. The lack of any rigorous, double-blind evaluation of the MEMT architecture itself was the motivation for our current effort.

We first describe the MEMT architecture and its presumed benefits in general. We then describe the specific translation sources used in this experiment, and discuss the design of our evaluation. We present a detailed statistical analysis of the results. Finally we conclude with the observation that the MEMT system has indeed been shown to produce better output than its component engines.

---

[1] Pangloss participated in the DARPA MT evaluations [11, 28]

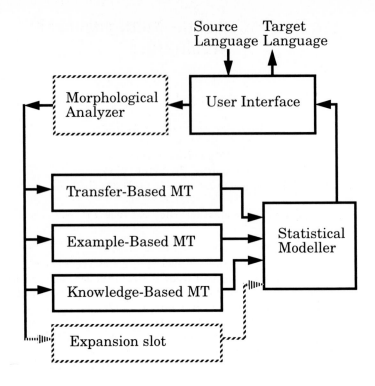

Fig. 1. Structure of MEMT architecture

1 The Multi-Engine MT Architecture

Different MT technologies exhibit different strengths and weaknesses. Technologies such as Knowledge-Based MT (KBMT) can provide high-quality, fully-automated translations in narrow, well-defined domains [21, 7]. Other technologies such as lexical-transfer MT [23, 8, 19], and Example-Based MT (EBMT) [4, 22, 27] provide lower-quality general-purpose translations, unless they are incorporated into human-assisted MT systems [10, 20], but can be used in non-domain-restricted translation applications. Moreover, these technologies differ not just in the quality of their translations, and level of domain-dependence, but also along other dimensions, such as types of errors they make, real-time translation time [26], required development time [12], cost of development, and ability to easily make use of any available on-line corpora, such as electronic dictionaries or online bilingual parallel texts.

The Multi-Engine Machine Translation (MEMT) architecture [9] makes it possible to exploit the differences between MT technologies. As shown in Fig. 1, MEMT feeds an input text to several MT engines in parallel, with each engine employing a different MT technology[2]. Each engine attempts to translate the entire input text, segmenting each sentence in whatever manner is most appropriate for its technology, and putting the resulting translated output segments into a shared chart data structure [16, 29] after giving each segment a score indicating the engine's internal assessment of the quality of the output segment. These output (*target language*) segments are indexed in the chart based on the positions of the corresponding input (*source language*) segments. Thus the chart contains multiple, possibly overlapping, alternative translations. Since the scores produced by the engines are estimates of variable accuracy, statistical language modelling techniques adapted from speech recognition research are used to select the best overall set of outputs [3, 13]. These selection techniques attempt to produce the best overall result, taking the probability of transitions between segments into account as well as modifying the quality scores of individual segments.

Among the differences that one frequently wishes to exploit using the MEMT architecture is the differing trade-off between coverage and quality that exists between different technologies: one would like to cover as much of the input as possible, but still get the highest possible quality for any given segment of the input. While there has been a strong perception that MEMT does provide this benefit, up to now there has never been a rigorous, double-blind evaluation that empirically verified this claim.

2   Experiment Design: Translations

In this experiment, we seek to evaluate the MEMT architecture separately from its implementation with specific translation engines. However, because MEMT performs no translations of its own, only combining and choosing from among the translations provided by other translation engines, it is necessary to include several translation engines in order to perform the evaluation. For this reason, we will simultaneously evaluate the MEMT system as a whole as well as each component translation engine. By comparing the results, we hope to shed light on the contribution of the MEMT architecture to the overall translation process.

The translations to be evaluated will therefore come from three sources. For every source language sentence to be translated, we will first translate it using the entire MEMT system as it is currently designed. Then, we will translate the sentence again using each of the separate translation engines that are part of the MEMT system. The system used for this experiment (the translation component of the DIPLOMAT Croatian ↔ English system [12]) employs two kinds of **translation engines**:

Lexical-Transfer Simple dictionary (word-for-word translation) and glossary (phrase-for-phrase) translation.

---

[2] Morphological analysis, part-of-speech tagging, and possibly other text enhancements can be shared by the engines.

Example-Based MT Translation via partial matching of the input against a parallel corpus (example-base).

These translation engines are described in more detail elsewhere [8,4].

In the MEMT architecture, each translation engine is permitted to hypothesize multiple translations for any sequence of words in the source sentence. The multiple, overlapping translations are sorted out by the language model, which performs a search over the set of available translations to find the subset that exactly covers the input and yields the best combination. When testing the translation engines separately from the MEMT architecture, other means must be employed for sorting out the conflicting translations. For each of the three **translation sources**, the following describes the technique used to obtain a workable translation from among the conflicting possibilities output by the engine.

LEX Using only translations from the Lexical-Transfer engine, perform a random search in the chart of candidate translations. Avoid translations that do not result in a completely translated sentence. There will be more than one possible translation per sentence.

EBMT Using the Example-Based engine, randomly select as many non-overlapping translations as possible. Because Example-Based MT is not able to translate all parts of all sentences[3], there may be parts of the source sentence that are untranslated. Fill gaps in the translation with appropriate selections from the Lexical-Transfer engine. There may be more than one possible translation per sentence.

MEMT The optimal translation as selected by the MEMT architecture. There will be only one translation possible per sentence.

3 Experiment Design: Evaluation

The actual evaluation took the form of a questionnaire, evaluated by native speakers of the target language. Two questionnaires were designed, one for each translation direction: English → Croatian and Croatian → English. The questionnaires had the following format: A series of source-language sentences were presented to the evaluators, each accompanied by four target-language translations. Evaluators were asked to qualitatively evaluate each of the translations based on their knowledge of the target language and the meaning of the source language sentence.[4]

---

[3] The reason for this is that the EBMT engine operates by performing partial matches against its parallel corpus. If no match is found between the input and corpus, or between the source and target sides of the corpus, no translation is produced. On the other hand, the algorithm increases the likelihood that any sentences that do match will be accorded a fairly high quality translation.

[4] Because the native English-speaking evaluators were not bilingual in Croatian, a high-quality human translation of the Croatian sentence into English was provided for them in addition to the original sentence.

3.1 Selection of Translations

In order to reinforce the goal of double-blind evaluation as well as to deal with certain difficulties posed by the translation engines, we used the following algorithm to generate the four translations of each sentence:

1. Randomly place the MEMT translation in
   one of the four slots.

2. If at least one EBMT translation is
   available, randomly select one and
   randomly place it in one of the
   available three slots.

3. For each of the two or three slots still
   empty, randomly generate a LEX
   translation and place it there.

The identity of the source of each of the translations is recorded but hidden from both the evaluator and the researcher.

3.2 Method of Evaluation

Evaluators were asked to evaluate the quality of each of the four translations using a scale from 1 to 5. Due to the often inconsistent intra-sentence quality of MEMT translations, additional scale points are used to distinguish translations that are partly correct from those that are uniformly bad. The scale is given below exactly as it was presented to the evaluators.

5. perfect
4. one or two errors, but otherwise perfect
3. several errors but understandable
2. some parts correct, but cannot understand
1. totally incomprehensible

Because some MT researchers, e.g. [14], have attempted to establish a simplified scale of GOOD, ACCEPTABLE, UNACCEPTABLE (or BAD) in order to encourage comparisons between evaluations of different systems, we would like to suggest that our scale be mapped into the three point scale in the following way: GOOD = 5, ACCEPTABLE = { 4, 3 }, UNACCEPTABLE = { 2, 1 }.

3.3 Evaluators

The evaluators were native speakers of the target languages they were asked to evaluate, and included two speakers of Croatian and two speakers of English. We will denote the evaluators with the labels *cro1, cro2, eng1* and *eng2*. Although one of the evaluators was knowledgeable about the workings of the translator, none had information about the sources of the translations they were asked to evaluate.

The questionnaires were presented to the evaluators as printed versions of HTML pages. The Croatian evaluators were given 500 sentences each, the English evaluators 161 sentences each.[5] Evaluators received only clarification of the meaning of the source language from the researcher.

3.4 Domain

The source language sentences for translation were drawn from the domain of travellers' phrasebooks, a domain closely related to that of the actual system. Phrases to be translated were drawn from available English and Croatian phrasebooks, neither of which had been used in the development of the system.

4 Results

In this section, we present the results of the evaluation. First, we present simple statistics comparing the evaluators and translation engines. We will argue that the simple statistics are not sufficient. We then present a somewhat different approach to measuring the data, and make clear why we believe that it is a superior measure, more accurately reflecting the quantities that we wish to assess.

4.1 Initial Statistics

First let's look at the simple descriptive statistics. We compute averages and standard deviations of the scores $[1\ldots 5]$ assigned by each evaluator {*cro1, cro2, eng1, eng2*} to each translation source {EBMT, LEX, MEMT}.

		cro1	*cro2*	*eng1*	*eng2*	Total
EBMT	mean	2.08	1.98	2.59	2.99	2.20
	stddev	1.13	1.19	1.29	1.20	1.23
LEX	mean	1.66	1.53	2.30	2.68	1.82
	stddev	0.93	0.91	1.32	1.29	1.10
MEMT	mean	1.92	1.86	2.58	2.96	2.10
	stddev	1.12	1.20	1.42	1.29	1.27
Total	mean	1.80	1.70	2.42	2.80	1.96
	stddev	1.03	1.06	1.34	1.28	1.18

Looking at this data, there are two kinds of comparison which are simple to make: comparisons between translation sources and comparisons between evaluators. We would like to raise several issues regarding both of these comparisons.

---

[5] The smaller size of the English evaluation was due to the necessity of providing the English evaluators English translations of the source-language sentences as well as the original Croatian ones.

4.2 Inter-source Comparison

A superficial overview of the data suggests that insofar as quality is concerned, EBMT > MEMT > LEX. Taken at face value, this would seem to suggest that MEMT is contributing negatively to the translation process, that EBMT alone would be superior to the entire system. However, we can statistically test the hypothesis that the means are the same with Student's t test [25, 2]. Doing so reveals that while both EBMT and MEMT are significantly different from LEX[6], they are not distinguishable from one another. Thus, we are prevented from establishing the relative ranking of MEMT against its component engines.

Note that this difficulty is not due simply to the large standard deviations:

> Our first thought is to ask "how many standard deviations" one sample mean is from the other. That number may in fact be a useful thing to know. It does relate to the strength or "importance" of a difference of means *if that difference is genuine*. However, by itself, it says nothing about whether the difference *is* genuine, that is, statistically significant. A difference of means can be very small compared to the standard deviation, and yet very significant, if the number of data points is large. Conversely, a difference may be moderately large but not significant, if the data are sparse. [...] (emphasis original)

[25, pp. 464–5]

Further investigation reveals that the higher quality of EBMT is a result of the way the averages were computed. As stated earlier, this EBMT system cannot provide a translation of every sentence. The averages listed above for EBMT were computed only over those sentences for which an EBMT translation was available. This necessarily results in skewed statistics, since the other translation sources (MEMT, LEX) are forced to provide a translation for every sentence, with no option to "give-up".[7]

One obvious way of dealing with the problem of EBMT is to artificially skew the results back toward what is expected. Assuming that empty translations are evaluated as "totally incomprehensible", we can insert a translation with a score of 1 every time a sentence fails to include an EBMT translation. Doing this produces the following scores for EBMT:

		cro1	cro2	eng1	eng2	Total
EBMT	mean	1.79	1.72	2.07	2.35	1.87
	stddev	1.08	1.11	1.30	1.36	1.17

The data now show that EBMT is performing about as expected as compared to the other translation engines: the average scores are 2.10 for MEMT, 1.87

---

[6] With significance better than $p < 0.001$, which is highly significant.

[7] Not that this would be easy to implement for the other translation sources. The problem of self-evaluation for machine translation is rather difficult, and even EBMT (which does better than most) can only reliably return "yes" or "no".

for EBMT and 1.82 for LEX. The statistical tests now show that MEMT is significantly better than EBMT and LEX, which are not distinguishable from one another. While this establishes that MEMT is useful, we are in the unfortunate situation of being unable to provide a simple, statistically sound ranking of the engines relative to the overall architecture. In addition, this method of "artificial" evaluation seems to us to be an inelegant hack for a problem which may have a better solution.

4.3 Inter-evaluator Comparison

The second interesting aspect of the data presented earlier is that of inter-evaluator agreement. Agreement between human subjects is a well-investigated area in Psychology [18], Sociology [17], Medicine [1,6] as well as Translation [15]. Without delving into the area of agreement measures, it seems to us that it is desirable to have a performance metric for which different evaluations of the same material produce similar scores. A comparison of our evaluators using the mean as a performance metric suggests that, at least quantitatively, the mean does not have the desired property (compare *cro1* 1.80 to *cro2* 1.70 or *eng1* 2.80 to *eng2* 1.96). This highlights a common problem in evaluating translations (*cf., e.g.* [5]), namely that there is no way to ensure that evaluators will agree on what constitutes a certain score. On the other hand, the mean does contain some information about the relative ranking of the sources insofar as all evaluators agree that the ranking of the sources is EBMT $\approx$ MEMT > LEX (or MEMT > EBMT $\approx$ LEX, depending on which set of EBMT scores one believes). The matter at hand is how to reconcile these qualitative agreements into a statistic that also agrees quantitatively.

4.4 A More Informative Statistic

In this section we will present a different kind of statistic, one based on comparisons between translation sources, and comment on the degree to which it solves the problems raised in the previous sections.

Consider carefully the way in which MEMT translates a sentence. The sentence is first translated by all of the translation engines. The candidate translations are scored and placed into a chart structure. The language model then selects the set of translations from the chart that best form a sentence in the target language. Clearly, given this scheme, the MEMT translation can be no better than the best of its engines on a given sentence, for MEMT does no actual translation itself, only using those provided by its engines. We must therefore include in any statistic that measures the effectiveness of MEMT some measure of the translation engines' performance on the same sentence. The metric we suggest is the following: how often does MEMT achieve the best that it is capable of, namely: the best that is available from the translation engines?

We will therefore calculate for each translation source the following statistic: for what percentage of the sentences does this translation source receive a score that is equal to or greater than that of all the other translation sources.

More formally, let $s_1, \ldots, s_N$ be the sentences in the source language to be translated, and $\tau_1, \ldots, \tau_M$ be the available translation sources. Now let $T_i = (t_{i1}, \ldots, t_{iM})$ be the translations into the target language of s_i by each of the translation sources. Finally, let $\Sigma_i = (\sigma_{i1}, \ldots, \sigma_{iM})$ be the scores assigned by the evaluators to each of the translations of sentence s_i. For each translation source $\tau_m \in \{\tau_1, \ldots, \tau_M\}$, we define the following metric:

$$d(\tau_m) = \frac{\sum_{i=1}^{N} \delta(\sigma_{im}, \max\{\sigma_{i1}, \ldots, \sigma_{iM}\})}{N}$$

Where $\delta(i, j)$, the Kronecker delta function, is given by:

$$\delta(i, j) = \begin{cases} 1 & for \quad i = j \\ 0 & for \quad i \neq j \end{cases}$$

This defines a measure in the range $[0,1]$. In the following table, we present the values as percentages.

	cro1	cro2	eng1	eng2	Total[8]
EBMT	55.80%	55.60%	49.69%	46.58%	53.86%
LEX	72.80	69.00	69.57	66.46	70.20
MEMT	73.20	73.00	70.19	70.81	72.47

This statistic appears to be superior to the mean of the score in several ways. Fundamentally, this statistic provides a measure of the degree to which MEMT is doing the job it was designed for: picking the best possible translation, and provides a clear goal (100%) to aim for. This measure is also independent of the actual translation engines used. If more translation engines were used in an evaluation, or different ones, we would expect to be able to compare the results with the current evaluation. In this sense, the statistic is a measure of the MEMT architecture rather than of a particular MEMT system with specific translation engines.

Secondly, this statistic implicitly deals with the problems that arise when translation sources cannot always produce translations, such as is the case for EBMT in our evaluation. Such translation sources are penalized rather severely as the final measures for EBMT (46% – 56%) indicate.

Thirdly, this statistic shows significantly better inter-evaluator agreement than the mean. For those pairs of evaluators that worked on the same material, the maximum difference appears to be about 3%. For the MEMT scores, which are of greatest interest to us, there is remarkable agreement, with less than 1% difference.

These statistics clearly indicate that MEMT is doing its job: it is selecting the best translation available 72.47% of the time.

---

[8] We only report totals across all evaluators. Since our measure is a comparison between translation sources, totals across all translation sources do not make sense.

An Ontology-Based Approach to Parsing Turkish Sentences*

Murat Temizsoy and Ilyas Cicekli

Dept. of Comp. Eng. and Info. Sc., Bilkent University,
06533 Bilkent, Ankara, TURKEY,
{temizsoy,ilyas}@cs.bilkent.edu.tr

Abstract. The main problem with natural language analysis is the ambiguity found in various levels of linguistic information. Syntactic analysis with word senses is frequently not enough to resolve all ambiguities found in a sentence. Although natural languages are highly connected to the real world knowledge, most of the parsing architectures do not make use of it effectively. In this paper, a new methodology is proposed for analyzing Turkish sentences which is heavily based on the constraints in the ontology. The methodology also makes use of morphological marks of Turkish which generally denote semantic properties. Analysis aims to find the propositional structure of the input utterance without constructing a deep syntactic tree, instead it utilizes a weak interaction between syntax and semantics. The architecture constructs a specific meaning representation on top of the analyzed propositional structure.

1 Introduction

One of the main goals of natural language analysis (*NLA*) is to represent the meaning resides in forms of linguistic usage (spoken or written). The general architecture that is utilized in the current art of computational linguistics is based on a layered approach in which structural (morphological and syntactic) analysis is performed without any interaction with information about word senses and semantics. After parsing the structurally-correct analyses of the input sentence, the information attached with semantics is applied to select one among many. Generally knowledge about the real world or the context is not used, and this causes a real problem in disambiguation [8].

Turkish is a free word-order language, and this makes the analysis task even more complicated. Its flexibility in the sentence structure is a result of morphological inflections (suffixation), and their usage generally provide information about semantics (thematic structure of the sentence, tense and aspect of an event, modality, etc.). This information can be utilized in analyzing the propositional structure of a sentence without dealing with the syntactic constituents like subject, direct object, etc. in general. Motivated with this observation, a

---

* This research has been supported in part by NATO Science for Stability Program Grant TU-LANGUAGE.

new approach for parsing Turkish sentences is presented in this paper. It is heavily based on an rich ontology [1, 5], a knowledge resource to represent entities, events, and the relationships between them in a hierarchical structure. The proposed method tries to find the argument structures of predicates, using morphological information and word-order constraints, and successful analyses are reprocessed to construct the possible meaning representations [2, 6]. Syntax is treated as a formalism to propose analysis for noun phrases (denoting world entities), and ontology-based search decides on the acceptance or rejection of those analyses. So, the method never constructs a complete syntactic tree structure, instead uses ontological constraints.

To present the new methodology proposed in this paper, first we introduce some motivations about why such an approach can be utilized in dealing with difficulties arose from the lack of real world knowledge or the context in Section 2. Then, we briefly describe the structure and the knowledge content of the ontology, and the meaning representation which is the output of the implemented system in Section 3. In that section, we also consider the content of the lexicon and its relationship with the ontology. In Section 4, we describe the proposed methodology which is composed of two components: determination of argument structure and concepts found in the input sentence, and construction of the interlingua which is a rule-based constraint-reasoning module. In the last section, we present the conclusion about the described work together with some possible future extensions.

2 Motivation

When we consider the language as a media to exchange information about the real (or some possible) world, the role of a language's structural properties can be reinterpreted as a tool to ease the burden of comprehension (semantic disambiguation). For example, in the sentence "John bought a present for Mary", both entities 'John' and 'Mary' can be the agent of the event 'buy', and it is the syntax that imposes the only interpretation that 'John' is the agent and 'Mary' is the goal. But, language is a phenomenon that cannot be just explained by its structure; it has a close relationship with the real world. There are cases where syntax, even formal semantics, cannot help us to choose one interpretation among many, and it is our real world knowledge that is utilized in selection (at least in preference). For example, consider the following Turkish sentences;

- "Adam kitap okudu"
- "iki kolsuz adam"

In the first sentence, the word 'adam' has two morphological analyses: "the man" and "my island", and both analyses result in syntactically correct sentences. But, only the interpretation "the man read a book" is valid since the event denoted by 'oku' ('read') can only accept a human as an agent, and this eliminates the other interpretation ("my island"). In the second sentence, there are two ways to bracket the noun phrase: [iki [kolsuz adam]] ("two men without hands") and [[iki kolsuz] adam] (semantically ill-defined interpretation, since it requires both the existence and non-existence of arms). But, when we consider a simpler phrase "üç kollu adam", although we cannot safely avoid the interpretation "three men with arm(s)", we generally prefer the other interpretation, "a man with three arms", since "man with arm" is not informative. Note that, in this sentence, the second bracketing is preferred which is not the case for the first one.

Even with these examples, our power in comprehending language is a result of our knowledge about the real world. In fact, we can reach the same conclusion from another perspective which depends on psycholinguistic observations about human performance on linguistic inputs. Although ungrammatical sentences are common in daily speech contexts (unfinished sentences, improper clause embedding, etc.), information loss in such sentences is minimum, if not zero in most of the circumstances. Even the loss of an utterance segment does not generally affect the comprehension (simultaneous speech in groups, sudden noises, etc.). Also, the effect of context and real world knowledge on the seemingly syntactic phenomenon (*Garden Path* effect) [10] is demonstrated in psycholinguistic experiments. The effect of context can be seen in the use of Turkish adjectives as denoting an individual entity in the real world.

– "Küçük kırmızı top gittikçe hızlandı"

In the sentence above, there are four possible interpretations if we are only concerned with the syntactic correctness, and two of them are "the little red thing accelerated as the ball kept going" and "the little red ball accelerated gradually" (note the radical change in interpretation). The first interpretation is possible only if there is a previously mentioned entity that satisfies various constraints (like to be little, to be red, to be in motion, etc.). In all other cases, the second interpretation is preferred, including the null context. But, if those constraints are satisfied, the first interpretation becomes also plausible which means that we have a representation about previously mentioned entities. So, if we are able to represent encountered entities in a sequence of utterances, we can decide which of the interpretations is valid when sentences like the sentence above are uttered.

Started out with these examples in mind, we reach the conclusion that any architecture that is developed for analyzing *NL* inputs should interact with a representation of the real world, an *ontology*, and a representation of the context (the entities and the events encountered so far). Since Turkish has an inflectional morphology [9] that provides information about semantic properties, we think that we can analyze Turkish sentences without constructing their corresponding syntactic tree structure. Syntax is used to provide possible analyses for noun and verbal phrases and to limit semantic interpretations according to word-order constraints. It is the thematic structure of a sentence that is to be found through utilizing word senses defined in the lexicon and the representations of entities and events taken from the ontology. In other words, we propose a new methodology in which there is a weak interaction between syntax and semantics. In addition, there is also an interaction between syntax and context which represents previously encountered entities and events.

3 Ontology and Meaning Representation

Ontology [1, 5, 11] is the knowledge resource that provides the common sense representation of the real world. It is both utilized in constraining the possible interpretations of a sentence and representing the entities and the events encountered in the context. It is built upon proposed abstractions, **concepts**, about entities and events. Note that there is a major distinction between entities (atemporal individuals) and events (temporal phenomena). Concepts denoting entities are defined through a set of features with their value-domains, and those features represent the common sense properties of a group of objects. For example, the concept $HUMAN$ has features like *name, age, gender, occupation*, etc. Some features are given default values (arm-$number = 2$) to make preferences like the ones mentioned in the previous section. An event-concept describes the argument structure (with thematic classifications and constraints on those arguments), the temporal properties, and additional features like entity-concepts. For example, the concept $READ$ has arguments *agent* (limited to $HUMAN$) and *source* (limited to $READABLE$), and its temporal property is *durative*.

Utilized ontology is not just a set of concepts, it defines a highly-connected network among the concepts. The basic connection among concepts is the relationship between an event-concept and its argument entity-concepts. Note that, each event predicates over a limited set of individuals and it is given as the value-domains of its thematic arguments. Ontology also resembles the hierarchical interpretation of the real world through *is-a* relation which defines an inheritance mechanism among concepts. Children concepts define additional features with limitations on the abstraction provided by a parent concept. For example, $HUMAN$ is a $MAMMAL$, which is an $ANIMAL$, etc. So, the previously given features *age* and *gender* of $HUMAN$ is in fact provided by $ANIMAL$. There are also other relations which provide extra interpretations about the real world. For example, the relation between an $INSTITUTE$ and a $HUMAN$ (*boss-of, member-of, student-of*, etc.), or the relation between a $MONITOR$ and a $COMPUTER$ (*is-part-of*) is also defined in an ontology.

As mentioned, ontology is mainly utilized in finding the relations between entities and events. This is extremely useful in comprehending the correct word sense and eliminating some syntactically correct analyses [3]. For example, consider the following three Turkish sentences:

- "John'dan bir mektup *aldım*" ("I *received* a letter from John")
- "Arkadaşımdan bir kalem *aldım*" ("I *took* a pencil from my friend")
- "Marketten bir kalem *aldım*" ("I *bought* a pencil from the market")

In each sentence, the word *'aldım'* is used in three different senses, namely $RECEIVE$, $TAKE$, and BUY. Note that, each sentence has the same syntax, an NP with ablative case (denoting the *source*), an NP with nominative case (denoting the *theme*), and the *VP*. So, it is impossible to get the correct sense from the syntax. But, if we have constraints on *source* and *theme* (such as the *source* of *BUY* must be *SELLER − COMPANY*, and *theme* of *RECEIVE* cannot be in the same location with *agent*, which is a contextual information), then it is easy to eliminate the other interpretations. Similar to this example, the constraint of *READ* (its *agent* must be a *HUMAN*) eliminates the second interpretation of 'adam' ("my island") in the example given in the previous section.

The main purpose of this paper is to analyze Turkish sentences and to represent their intended meaning in an artificial language. So, we need a meaning representation formalism, and we utilize the interlingua representation developed for Microcosmos project in New Mexico State University, called Text Meaning Representation (*TMR*) [2, 6, 11, 12]. *TMR* language is a formalism to represent the relations between events and entities, the semantic properties (aspect, modality, temporal relations, etc.), and pragmatic properties (speech-act, focus, stylistics, etc.). It is heavily based on the ontology, and its propositional content is represented with the concepts from the ontology. It is a frame-based language, and it instantiates the features of the concepts to denote real individuals or events. It may contain several additional frames, besides concepts, to represent other semantic and pragmatic properties. *TMR* is a suitable language for the purposes of this paper since it provides a mechanism to represent the thematic structure of a sentence.

4 Methodology

The computational architecture is based on finding the relationships between the entities (as *NPs*) and the events (as *VPs*) of an input sentence, and these relationships are known as the argument structure of the sentence. To achieve this goal, constraints on events' thematic structures and their value-domains, which are defined in the ontology, are used. In other words, the ontology is the major knowledge resource that guides the analysis. In addition, information about morphological markings and constituent order (although Turkish is a free word-order language, it has some limitations in embedded predicates) are utilized in the analysis. *NP* analysis is generally achieved by the classical *CFG* formalism. The *TMR* structure of an input sentence is constructed after its propositional structure is determined. The computational architecture can be analyzed in three distinct components:

1. **Morphological Analysis:** This phase produces morphologically correct analyses of Turkish words. It is specially important for the current methodology since thematic role of each constituent is explicitly marked in Turkish, and this information is utilized in finding the propositional structure. Also, most of the semantic properties (like tense, aspect, modality, etc.) are explicitly coded through suffixation, and these marks are used in *TMR* construction.

2. **Semantic Analysis:** This phase is the core of the proposed methodology, and it analyzes the propositional structure of the input sentence. It utilizes two knowledge resources, namely the lexicon and the ontology. Its computation is based on a weak interaction between syntax and semantics: syntax proposes *NP* analyses and puts constituent order constraints, and semantics decides on the acceptance or the rejection of the proposed analysis using knowledge from the ontology.

3. *TMR* **Construction:** This phase reanalyzes the constructed propositional structure, uses unprocessed morphological markings, and produces the corresponding *TMR* representation through using map-rules which are relational constraints between *TMR* and Turkish [11, 12]. The core definitions of word senses (without any modifications) are taken from the lexicon where each word sense is defined as a concept instance.

Since morphological analysis is a well known topic with satisfactory computational models, how morphological analysis of Turkish is achieved is not explained here. Morphological analyses of Turkish words are directly taken from an engine developed by Oflazer [9]. In the rest of this section, semantic analysis which is the core of this paper is explained in detail, and *TMR* construction methodology is presented with some examples.

4.1   Semantic Analysis

In order to simplify the presentation, first the core idea of the methodology is presented through demonstrating the analysis of a simple Turkish sentence. Let us reconsider the sentence "adam kitap okudu" with the following morphological analysis:

adam	–	$[root, adam], [category, noun]$	("man")
		$[root, ada], [category, noun], [possessor, 1SG]$	("my island")
kitap	–	$[root, kitap], [category, noun]$	("book")
okudu	–	$[root, oku], [category, verb], [agreement, 3SG], [tense, past]$	("read")

Together with the information from the ontology and the lexicon:

READ			*adam*	$\overset{is-a}{\longrightarrow}$	*HUMAN*		
	agent	*HUMAN*	*ada*	$\overset{is-a}{\longrightarrow}$	*LOCATION*		
	theme	*READABLE*	*kitap*	$\overset{is-a}{\longrightarrow}$	*BOOK* $\overset{is-a}{\longrightarrow}$	*READABLE*	
			oku	$\overset{is-a}{\longrightarrow}$	*READ*		

Only the proposition *READ(agent(adam), theme(kitap))* is plausible because of the constraints of the arguments of *READ*. Note that, this analysis can be achieved without intervening with Turkish syntax, and 'ada' can be directly eliminated since it cannot be an argument of *READ*. In Turkish, constituents can change their position rather freely. For example, "kitap okudu adam" is also valid in Turkish (pragmatic change in the interpretation). This sentence can be analyzed with the same easiness if we are just looking for arguments of the predicate of the sentence.

As mentioned, noun phrases, denoting entities, are marked morphologically in Turkish to introduce their thematic roles, and this should be utilized in sentences like "adam kadına kitabı verdi" ("the man gave the book to the woman") since ontological constraints are not enough to analyze 'adam' ("man") as *agent* and 'kadın' ("woman") as *goal* (both are $HUMAN$). So, if there is only one event in a Turkish sentence and NPs are just single nouns, there is no need for a syntactic parsing to find the propositional content of the input sentence. The propositional content can be found using only knowledge from the ontology and thematic marks of nouns (like nominative, ablative, etc.). In this example, since 'adam' is in the nominative case and 'kadın' is in the dative case, 'adam' must be *agent* and 'kadın' must be *goal* of the $GIVE$ predicate.

But, when the structures of NPs are complicated such as "masanın örtüsü" ("the cover of the table"), "üç kollu adam" ("the man with three arms"), "okul hakkında" ("about the school"), the naive approach above just simply fails. Since each NP denotes an entity in the sentence, a bracketing mechanism is needed to capture complex NPs. This is achieved through syntactic analysis based on a context-free grammar representing Turkish NPs [4]. Since our aim is to find the propositional structure, context-free rules are applied to propose syntactically correct NPs denoting entities, and search for thematic arguments is done on these proposals. For example, consider the Turkish sentence "kadın kırmızı masa örtüsünü yıkadı" ("the woman washed the red table cover"). Syntactic component proposes the NP "kırmızı masa örtüsünü" ("the red table cover") as one entity, and then this proposed NP is attached as *patient* of $WASH$.

$HUMAN$ $\longleftarrow$ [kadın]
$COVER(is\text{-}for(TABLE), color(red))$ $\longleftarrow$ [kırmızı masa örtüsünü]
$WASH(agent(HUMAN), patient(COVER))$ $\longleftarrow$ [yıkadı]

Note that, this architecture forms a weak interaction between syntax and semantics (syntax proposes NP analyses as entities and search for thematic roles decides on their acceptance). In fact, ontology is not only utilized in finding argument structure of an event, but also used to check plausibility of proposed entities. Knowledge about the entity (head of NP) including its features and relations with other concepts is used to check whether proposed analysis can be correctly transformed to a concept instant (like $COVER(is\text{-}for(TABLE), color(red))$ given above). This usage of ontology provides an additional power in disambiguation. Let us reconsider the phrase "iki kolsuz adam" given in Section 2.

[[iki kolsuz] adam]

$Cardinality(arm) = 0$ $\longleftarrow$ kolsuz
$Cardinality = 2 \ \& \ Cardinality(arm) = 0$ $\longleftarrow$ [iki kolsuz]
REJECTED

Same mechanism also rejects the interpretation "my island with three arms" in "üç kollu adam" since the entity $ISLAND$ has no feature to represent *arm*.

Remember that, more informative analyses are preferred over less informative ones, and "üç kollu adam" is interpreted as "the man with three arms" since we have $HUMAN(has\text{-}part(ARM))$ and the analysis of "kollu adam" restates this fact.

Until here, only sentences with one verbal phrase are considered. When there are more than one verbal phrase, even the current architecture has some problems in finding the correct analysis since information about constituent ordering does not exist. For example, consider the following two sentences:

- "Kadın bardağı kıran çocuğa kızdı"
  "The woman scolded the child who broke the glass"
- "Bardağı kıran kadın çocuğa kızdı"
  "The woman who broke the glass scolded the child"

The position change of the word 'kadın' ('woman') radically changes the interpretations of the sentences above, and this is not the kind of information that can be found in the ontology. It is the syntax that changes the interpretation, and it should be added somehow into the architecture. Like case marks in NPs denote the thematic roles of the entities, verbal suffixes present the semantic roles of the events in a sentence in Turkish [4]. Main predicate is always distinguishable from the others and supplementary VPs are marked so that their roles can be found out. For example, $+En$ suffix in Turkish (kıran $\leftarrow$ kır$+En$) is used to express a definite description of an entity which is the *agent* of the event, and it requires the *agent* just after the verb. So, a verb with $+En$ should be analyzed such that next NP is its *agent* and previous entities are to be checked whether they are arguments of the event. Thus, we get the following constituents for the first sentence, and the grouping for the supplementary event $BREAK$.

$$HUMAN_2 \longleftarrow \text{kadın}$$

$$\left.\begin{array}{l} GLASS \longleftarrow \text{bardağı} \\ BREAK \longleftarrow \text{kıran} \\ HUMAN_1 \longleftarrow \text{çocuğa} \end{array}\right\} BREAK(agent(HUMAN_1), patient(GLASS))$$

$$SCOLD \longleftarrow \text{kızdı}$$

Since $BREAK$ has only the arguments *agent*, *patient*, and *instrument*, and 'kadın' as a $HUMAN$ cannot be instrument, it cannot be treated as an argument of $BREAK$. Since constructed proposition is for defining an entity, it is taken out from constituent list, only 'çocuk' ($HUMAN_1$, a concept instance) is left as an entity. So, we have the following constituents and the grouping for the main event $SCOLD$:

$$\left.\begin{array}{l} HUMAN_2 \longleftarrow \text{kadın} \\ HUMAN_1 \longleftarrow \text{çocuğa} \\ SCOLD \longleftarrow \text{kızdı} \end{array}\right\} SCOLD(agent(HUMAN_2), goal(HUMAN_1))$$

Note that, the two events of the example sentence have a common argument, $HUMAN_1$ ('çocuk'), that establishes the connection between the main and the supplementary event. The mechanism just described can be utilized

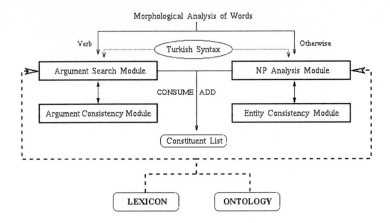

Fig. 1. Architecture of the Semantic Analysis

for other types of relations between events. For example, a verb with the suffix $+H\varsigma$ in Turkish cannot have any other constituent after that verb, so its arguments should be searched in the previously encountered entities and its proposition should be added to the constituent list with erasing all its entities and itself. So, "Annemin Ankaraya *gelişi* beni çok sevindirdi" ("My mother's coming to Ankara made me very happy") is first transformed into analysis "$COME(agent(HUMAN), goal(CITY))$ beni çok sevindirdi", and then the final propositional analysis is achieved. This is the second place where syntax and semantics weakly interact.

As a conclusion, the computational architecture utilizes grammatical rules of Turkish without constructing a complete syntactic tree. Syntax is treated as a tool to help semantic disambiguation, and it proposes *NP* analyses for entities and constraints constituent ordering in cases of more than one event, expressed as *VPs*. But, it is the ontological constraints that decide on the propositional structure. Note that, search for arguments cannot interrupt the application of syntactic rules, it just rejects some proposed analysis. So, the proposed methodology conforms to weak interaction between syntax and semantics. Fig. 1 describes the overall computational architecture.

4.2   TMR Construction

After the TMR construction phase, the overall interpretation of the input sentence is represented in *TMR* formalism [2, 6]. Since arguments of each event with their thematic roles are determined in the previous phase, only the existing semantic (aspect, modality, temporal relations, etc.) and pragmatic (speech-act, stylistics, etc.) properties of the sentence should be introduced into the constructed representation. But, before analyzing these additional information about the utterance, each found entity and event should be represented as a concept instance with a distinct frame. Beside the interpreted structure, each instance should take its definition from the lexicon (feature-value pairs associated with the used word sense) since concepts are proposed abstractions (not word senses). In other words, although 'man', 'woman', etc. are all $HUMAN$, they have different representations in the lexicon to constrain the set of individuals that can be referred with that word sense. Assuming that there is the word 'kadın' in an utterance, the following TMR frame is constructed.

Lexicon Definition				Constructed TMR Frame	
kadın					
$is\text{-}a$	$HUMAN$			$HUMAN_i$	
$definition$	$type$	$common$	$\Longrightarrow$	$type$	$common$
	$gender$	$female$		$gender$	$female$
	age	≥ 17		age	≥ 17

After constructing the TMR frames for entities and events as a first step, semantic and pragmatic properties of the sentence are analyzed through **map-rules** [11] which are content-based (whether a morpheme exists in a specific word, whether analyzed event is punctual or durative, whether constituents are in the default order, etc.) exclusive rules [7]. Each map-rule checks a set of constraints about morphology, syntax, and ontology, and it updates the TMR if those constraints are satisfied. In any TMR representation, temporal and epistemic properties of every event should be provided, and this is achieved by using suffixes of the verb and the event's aspectual properties defined in the ontology. The utilized rules look like the following:

if event is punctual and tense is past
    create frame $aspect((phase, perfect), (duration, momentary), (telicity, false))$
    create frame $temporal\text{-}rel(after, speech, event)$
$else\ if$
    $\vdots$

The information about $speech\text{-}act$ is obtained from the main event (whether sentence is declarative or imperative, which constituent is the scope of the main predicate, etc.). Beside these, constituent order information is utilized to represent the speaker's attitude towards those components. If they are not in the default order, then constituents are attached pragmatic stance, $topic, focus$, and $background$. In addition, the change of speech focus in relative clauses and wh-type questions is represented in $speech\text{-}act$ frame.

5 Conclusion

The role of real world knowledge in comprehending natural language inputs is generally underestimated by the current computational architectures for NL analysis. In this paper, we propose a new methodology for the analysis in which ontology, knowledge resource for representing real world, is the major resource that is utilized, instead of syntactic structure. We choose Turkish as the input language since its inflectional morphology provides enough information about the semantic properties of the components of a sentence. The proposed method is based on finding the argument structures of events using constraints on the thematic structures defined in the ontology.

First, we start with some observations about the language phenomenon which provides enough motivation about the need for an ontology in *NL* analysis. We give examples in which syntactic constraints are not enough to eliminate irrelevant ambiguities. Then, we start with a naive approach which uses just ontological constraints, and new mechanisms are added successively such that our analysis becomes compatible with complex *NP*s and sentences in which there are more than one predicate. The final structure proposes a weak interaction between syntax and semantics, in which syntax just proposes analyses that guide the semantic disambiguation. If semantic analysis is successful, then computational model constructs a specific meaning representation, *TMR*, on top of the analyzed propositional structure.

References

1. J. R. Bateman. Ontology construction and natural language. In *Proceedings of International Workshop on Formal Ontology*, Pauda, Italy, 1993.
2. S. Beale, S. Nirenburg, and K. Mahesh. Semantic analysis in the mikrocosmos machine translation project. In *Proceedings of the 2nd Symposium on Natural Language Processing (SNLP-95)*, Bangkok, Thailand, August 2-4, 1995.
3. B. J. Dorr. The use of lexical semantics in interlingua machine translation. *Machine Translation*, 4:3:135–193, 1993.
4. Z. Gungordu. A lexical-functional grammar for turkish. Master's thesis, Bilkent University, Ankara Turkey, July 1993.
5. K. Mahesh. Ontology development for machine translation: Ideology and methodology. In *Memoranda in Computer and Cognitive Science MCCS-96-292*, Las Crues, New Mexico State University, 1996.
6. K. Mahesh and S. Nirenburg. Meaning representation for knowledge sharing in practical machine translation. In *Proceedings of the FLAIRS-96. Track on Information Interchange, Florida AI Research Symposium*, Key West, Florida, May 19-22, 1996.
7. T. Mitamura and E. Nyberg. Hierarchical lexical structure and interpretive mapping in machine translation. In *Proceedings of COLING-92*, Nantes, France, July, 1992.
8. S. Nirenburg, J. Carbonell, M. Tomita, and K. Goodman. *Machine Translation: A Knowledge-Based Approach*. Morgan Kaufmann, San Mateo, California, 1992.
9. K. Oflazer. Two-level description of turkish morphology. *Literary and Linguistic Computing*, 9:2, 1994.
10. M. Steedman. Computational aspects of the theory of grammar. *An Invitation to Cognative Science, Language*, pages 247–283, 1995.
11. M. Temizsoy. Design and implementation of a system for mapping text meaning representations to f-structures of turkish sentences. Master's thesis, Bilkent University, Ankara Turkey, August 1997.

12. M. Temizsoy and I. Cicekli. A language-independent system for generating feature structures from interlingua representations. In *Proceedings of the 9th International Workshop on Natural Language Generation*, Niagara-on-the-Lake, Canada, August, 1998.

Monolingual Translator Workstation

Guy Bashkansky[1] and Prof. Uzzi Ornan[2],

[1] IBM Haifa Research Lab, MATAM, Haifa, Israel
guy@haifa.vnet.ibm.com
[2] Computer Science Dept, Technion, Haifa, Israel
ornan@cs.technion.ac.il

Abstract. Although the problem of *full machine translation* (MT) is unsolved yet, the *computer aided translation* (CAT) makes progress. In this field we created a work environment for *monolingual* translator[1]. This package of tools generally enables a user who masters a source language to translate texts to a target language which the user *does not master*. The application is for Hebrew-to-Russian case, emphasizing specific problems of these languages, but it can be adapted for other pairs of languages also. After *Source Text Preparation*, *Morphological Analysis* provides all the meanings for every word. The ambiguity problem is very serious in languages with incomplete writing, like Hebrew. But the main problem is the translation itself. Words' meanings mapping between languages is *M:M*, i.e., almost every source word has a number of possible translations, and almost every target word can be a translation of several words. Many methods for resolving of these ambiguities propose using large data bases, like dictionaries with semantic fields based on θ-*theory*. The amount of information needed to deal with general texts is prohibitively large. We propose here to solve ambiguities by a new method: *Accumulation with Inversion* and then *Weighted Selection*, plus *Learning*, using only two *regular* dictionaries: from source to target and from target to source languages. The method is built from a number of phases: (1) during *Accumulation with Inversion*, all the possible translations to the target language of every word are brought, and every one of them is translated back to the source language; (2) *Selection* of suitable suggestions is being made by user in source language, this is the only manual phase; (3) *Weighting* of the selection's results is being made by software and determines the most suitable translation to the target language; (4) *Learning* of word's context will provide preferable translation in the future. *Target Text Generation* is based on morphological records in target language, that are produced by the disambiguation phase. To complete the missing features for word's building, we propose here a method of *Features Expansion*. This method is based on assumptions about *feature flow* through the sentence, and on dependence of grammatical phenomena in the two languages. *Software* of the workstation combines four tools: Source Text Preparation, Morphological Analysis, Disambiguation and Target Text Generation. The application includes an elaborated windows interface, on which the user's work is based. Keywords: machine translation, monolingual user, translator workstation.

---

[1] This paper is a condensed version of the M.Sc. project of Guy Bashkansky, under the supervision of Prof. Uzzi Ornan, which was submitted early in 1995.

1   Introduction

1.1   Translation Methods

Translation methods may be classified according to the role of the computer in the process:

- Non-computerized translation. In this traditional approach the translation is done by a person with command of both languages. The process is costly and time consuming.

- Fully computerized translation. This is translation done completely by a computer, but at present this is the stuff of dreams.

- Partial bilingual computerized translation. A human translator operates a learning interactive system, performs pre-processing and post-processing. Because of the presence of the translator not all the disadvantages of the non-computerized translation method can be avoided, but the work of translation becomes easier.

- Partial bilingual computerized translation (this study). By this method the user does the work in the source language alone, with an interactive learning system, the user need not know the target language. The chief advantage is that no translator need to be employed. There is a risk of stylistic flaws in the translated text even if the text itself is correct morphologically, syntactically, and semantically.

1.2   Preparation and Morphological Analysis of the Source Text

The stage of Hebrew source text preparation is implemented in the software as an ordinary text editor, with load, display and save facilities.

After preparation, the Hebrew text has to undergo morphological analysis, which produces all possible morphological records for every word in the text. This tool also has editor capabilities.

Every word in a non-vocalized Hebrew text has an average of three morphological alternatives. This is because of the lack of lexicographical information in a non-vocalized text and because of the abundance of morphemes and particles that attach to words without a space and thus impede their identification.

In our system the morphological analysis in Hebrew is based on a package developed at the IBM Science & Technology Center in Haifa, which kindly allowed its use. We are indebted to the Center for this. The package is based on a Hebrew dictionary with 20,000 entries, and on knowledge of Hebrew morphology. Meanwhile Prof. Ornan and M. Katz have constructed a different morphological analyzer, based on the use of phonemic writing for Hebrew, see ISO 259-3 and TR #LCL 94-7 (Revised July 1995).

1.2.1   Records of the Morphological Analysis

The grammatical information of each word undergoing morphological analysis is included in a record composed of several fields. Each field represents grammatical information of a different kind, and collectively they represent a distinct alternative of morphological analysis. The table below shows the seven possible morphological analyses for the string "• • • • ". This is a fairly typical case of morphological ambiguity in Hebrew.

Table 1.1: Example of morphological analyses for the string "• • • • "

spell	result	possessive			tense	properties			adja cent	basis	cate-gory	string
		p.	g.	n		per.	gen.	num				
plene	• • • •	2	f	s	*	*	m	s	*	• • •	noun	• • • •
plene	• • • •	2	m	s	*	*	m	s	*	• • •	noun	• • • •
plene	• • • •	*	*	*	past	3	m	s	*	• • • •	verb	• • • •
plene	• • • •	*	*	*	pres.	123	m	s	*	• • • •	verb	• • • •
def.	• • • • •	*	*	*	future	1	mf	p	*	• • •	verb	• • • •
def.	• • • • •	*	*	*	future	1	mf	p	*	• • • •	verb	• • • •
def.	• • • • •	2	mf	s	past	3	m	s	*	• • • •	verb	• • • •

Output of this sort will serve as input for disambiguation; namely, in the translation to the target language both morphological ambiguity in Hebrew as well as semantic ambiguity must be eliminated.

2 Disambiguation

Since almost every word in the source language has multiple mappings in the target language, no reasonable result is obtainable without selection of the appropriate word. In this section we set out the method designed for this purpose, and its use in this study. We call it *Accumulation with Inversion* and *Weighted Selection*, with the addition of *Learning*, and it constitutes the stage of *disambiguation in translation*. Like all the tools in the system, this one also includes editing facilities.

2.1 Stages of Disambiguation

1. *Input.* Input of both a direct (source-target) and an inverse (target-source) dictionaries. Input of records of the morphological analysis of the source text according to user's choice.
2. *Accumulation.* Direct translation of every meaning (source-target dictionary).
3. *Inversion.* Inverse translation of each direct translation (target-source dictionary).
4. *Selection.* Partial disambiguation according to contexts learned previously (see *Learning*). Construction of menus for every ambiguous word. User selection from those menus.
5. *Weighting.* Weighting the results of the selection and final disambiguation.
6. *Learning.* Saving the new contexts learned according to the user's selection.
7. *Output.* Display of the resulting records of disambiguation.

2.2 Dictionaries

The first step in operating the tool for disambiguation is to load the dictionaries. Commonplace dictionaries are sufficient for this purpose, since we only use information found in a very simple regular dictionary. In the experimental dictionaries we constructed, the entries and their translation were taken from the dictionaries Kravitz92 and KS87.

2.2.1 Direct Dictionary

The information contained by the entry in the direct Hebrew-Russian lexicon file is the Hebrew word in regular and phonemic scripts[1], category of the word, its gender and translations. Each word may have several translations, but not less than one. Every suggested translation includes Russian word in Latin transliteration and its gender. This is a fragment of the direct Hebrew-Russian lexicon file:

% Hebrew	Phonemic	Category	Gender
% Russian1			Gender1
% Russian2			Gender2
• • • • •	nittux	n	m
analiz			m
razbor			m
operaci&			f

2.2.2 Inverse Dictionary

Every entry in the inverse Russian-Hebrew lexicon file contains the following information: the Russian word in Latin transliteration, its category, its gender for nouns or the associated lexical case for verbs and prepositions. Each Russian word may have one or more Hebrew translations. Every translation includes a Hebrew word in regular and phonemic scripts, its gender, and list of contexts in which this translation has been verified previously. In the initial dictionary all the lists of contexts are empty, but they fill up as the system is used due to the learning capability. This is a fragment of the inverse Russian-Hebrew lexicon file:

% Russian		Category	Gender			
% Hebrew1	Phonemic1		Gender1	Context11	Context12	...
% Hebrew2	Phonemic2		Gender2	Context21	Context22	...
analiz		n	m			
• • • • •	nittux		m	• • • • •		
• • • • •	bdiqa		f			
razbor		n	m			
• • • • •	pirruq		m	• • •	• • • • •	
• • • • •	birrur		m			
• • • • •	nittux		m	• • • • • • • • •		

---

[1] We use the phonemic script for Hebrew according to the ISO 259-3 standard.

operaci&		n	f	
• • • •	mibca&	m		• • • •
• • • • •	nittux	m		• • • -• • • • •
• • • • •	p&ula	f		• • • •
• • • • •	tif&ul	m		
• • • •	&isqa	f		

2.3 Accumulation with Inversion

We use the term *accumulation* to describe multiplication of meanings of the source word in the course of the morphological analysis and direct translation into the target language. Accumulation requires means for selecting the appropriate word in the target language. The idea of *inversion* that we suggest here is (after direct translation) to continue accumulation *in the reverse direction*, from the target language to the source language. Inverse translations back into the source language are proposed for every suggested translation of every meaning of the source word.

The aim is to get back into the domain of the monolingual user's language so that *the user alone* may select all the words in the source language that are the most appropriate. In this way the ambiguity of the translation to the target language is rendered in the source language.

Accumulation and inversion are carried out according to an algorithm described in the pseudo-code below. Underlined structures are variables, words printed boldface are operations:

input <u>direct lexicon</u>, <u>inverse lexicon</u>, <u>analyzed source text</u>
for each <u>sentence</u> in <u>analyzed source text</u>
    for each <u>word</u> in <u>sentence</u>
        for each <u>meaning</u> of <u>word</u>
            for each <u>source-target entry</u> in <u>direct lexicon</u> **suitable to** <u>meaning</u>
                for each <u>suggestion</u> in <u>source-target entry</u>
                    If in <u>inverse lexicon</u> **found** <u>target-source entry</u> **suitable to** <u>suggestion</u>
                        create <u>connection</u> between <u>target-source entry</u> and <u>suggestion</u>
                        attach <u>connection</u> to <u>meaning</u>

2.4 Selection

2.4.1 Construction of Selection Menus

Every selection menu sets out before the user the suggestions for inverse translation of all the direct translations of all the meanings of a single source word. The menu has no repetitions, and the menu items (more accurately, their links with the translations) are weighted according to the number of appearances and the relative locations in the lexical entries of the corresponding translations. See the pseudo-code below:

for each <u>sentence</u> in <u>analyzed source text</u>
    for each <u>word</u> in <u>sentence</u>
        create empty <u>menu</u>, **zero** <u>ambiguity counter</u>
        for each <u>meaning</u> of <u>word</u>
            for each <u>connection</u> of <u>meaning</u>
                for each <u>inverse translation</u> of <u>target-source entry</u> of <u>connection</u>
                    if <u>item</u> with <u>inverse translation</u> **not found** in <u>menu</u>
                        create <u>item</u> with <u>inverse translation</u>
                    create <u>link</u> between <u>item</u> and <u>target-source entry</u>
                    increment <u>ambiguity counter</u>, **save** it as <u>rank</u> of <u>link</u>
                    if <u>short context</u> of <u>word</u> **found** in <u>contexts list</u> of <u>inverse translation</u>
                        save <u>suggestion</u> of <u>connection</u> as <u>translation</u> of <u>word</u>
      save <u>ambiguity counter</u> as <u>ambiguity rank</u> of <u>word</u>

2.4.2 Example of Selection Menu

Let us look at the underlined word in the fragment: "<u>• • • • • • • •</u>
<u>• • • • • • • • • • • •</u> ". In this case only one morphological record is obtained:
"<u>• • • • •</u>, noun, masculine, plural, possessive suffix: 3rd person, feminine, singular".
Below are the suggested direct translation and inverse translations in the order of
appearance in the lexica:
<u>• • • • •</u> :

    analiz: 1. • • • • •   2. • • • • •
    razbor: 3. • • • • •   4. • • • • •   5. • • • • •
    operaci&:   6. • • • •   7. • • • • •   8. • • • • •   9. • • • • •   10. • • • •

The order of appearance of the suggested translations within lexical entries gives, we
believe, an initial measure of the reasonableness of the suggestions. Therefore, we save the
serial number of the proposed inverse translation as the *rank* of a link between a suggested
direct translation and a suggested inverse translation, for example:

$$\text{rank(link\{analiz,• • • • \})=1 ... rank(link\{razbor,• • • • \})=4 ...}$$
$$\text{rank(link\{operaci\&,• • • • \})=10}$$

The total number of suggested inverse translations constitutes the ambiguity rank of the
source word, so in this case rank(word{• • • • • • • •})=10. These ranks play important role
in the ensuing disambiguation.

The table below presents the menu obtained, including the items, their links, and the
ranks of the links. The algorithm ensures that all the items are different, and that every item
has a link to every suggested direct translation that led to that item.

Table 2.1: Example of menu with items, ties and ranks

• • • •	• • • • •	• • • • •	• • • • •	• • • •	• • • • •	• • • • •	• • • •	items
analiz 1	analiz 2							link rank
razbor 5		razbor 3	razbor 4					link rank
operaci& 7				operaci& 6	operaci& 8	operaci& 9	operaci& 10	link rank

2.4.3 Selection Process by the User

Selection is through windows interface by the user. For every ambiguous word in the source text, the user marks those items on the word menu that he or she prefers as the word's appropriate meanings. The flow of operations in our application's interface is the following.

- The disambiguation tool is activated and occupies the main menu of the application.
- Lexica and analyzed source text are attached; accumulation with inversion and selection menus construction are performed.
- It is possible to page through sentences using the main menu of the application.
- The present sentence of the source text appears in the top window.
- Word in the present sentence may be chosen by mouse or keyboard.
- If the number of suggested direct translations ≥ 2, the word appears in black and can be chosen.
- If the number of suggested direct translations ≤ 1 the word appears in gray and cannot be chosen.
- If the word still was not disambiguated (by context or user's selection), it appears with a mark.
- When user chooses a word, a menu opens with the word's suggested inverse translations (in the source language).
- User selects the appropriate suggestions on the selection menu. The remaining suggestions are rejected.
- When user moves on to the next operation, the selection menu closes and the selection results are saved.

Four cases exist for display and processing of each source word.

1. No suggested direct translations at all are found, then:
   - no solution exists for translating the word;
   - there is no selection menu because no suggested translations exist.

2. Only one suggested direct translation appears, then:
   - a single solution for translating the word exists;
   - there is no selection menu because there is no ambiguity.

3. Several suggested direct translations appear, but the ambiguity can be resolved by the context, then:
   - if the user does not intervene, a solution by the word's context is accepted;
   - the menu exists and may be selected from, if user intervenes.

4. Several suggested direct translations appear, and the ambiguity can't be resolved by the context, then:
   - if user intervenes, disambiguate by his or her selection from the menu;
   - if user does not intervene, disambiguate is according to ranks of links.

A typical picture of the system in the selection stage is presented in the figure below, which is a snapshot of the interface at work.

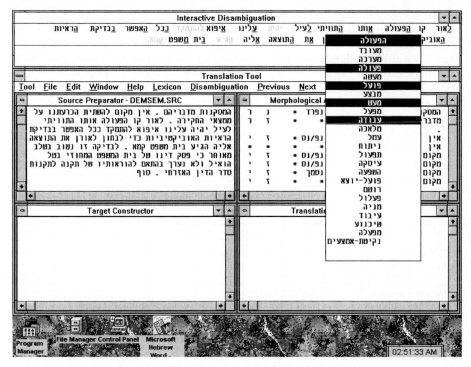

Figure 2.1: Disambiguation interface working example

In the top window (Interactive Disambiguation) which presents the current sentence, the text word • • • • • • was chosen by mouse click, the selection menu has appeared with that word as the title, and from it appropriate suggestions have been selected according to the user's preference. The main MDI (Multiple Documents Interface) window of the application (Translation Tool) embraces the four tools. The active tool at this moment, the disambiguator, presents its main menu, by which one may move to the next or previous sentence, move to the final stage of solution and display, load new lexica and texts, etc.

2.5 Weighting and Resolving of Ambiguities

To conclude the results of selection we weight the links of the items in the menu to the suggested direct translations. In the previous section we presented ranking of links according to order of suggested translations in the lexica. Now we present the technique of weighting and counting the links. A weight of a link is computed as:

$$\text{weight(link)} = \text{choice(item)} * (\text{rank(word)} - \text{rank(link)} + 1) \qquad (2.1)$$

rank(word) - the ambiguity rank of the word, total number of suggested inverse translations;
rank(link) – link's serial number according to the suggested translations order in the lexica;
choice(item) - coefficient of the user's selection for an item: +3 if selected, -1 if rejected.

That is, choice of an item on the menu results in all its links being weighted with positive weights three times larger than their negative weights in the case of rejection. This decision results from the statistical fact that a word in Hebrew has *on average* nearly three alternatives of morphological analysis. Since in a normal text only one meaning is correct, after the accumulation and inversion stages, only about a third of the suggestions deserve attention. Because these suggestions are rejected by the user, an excess of rejections forms against selections. Assuming that positive and negative information are equivalent, we balance the situation with the values chosen for the coefficients.

To conclude the weighting, the weights of the links for all suggested direct translations are summarized, compared, and the maximum is chosen. For our example we obtain the weighting presented in the following table. In this case the translation "razbor" gets the highest score of 63 points, and it is indeed the most appropriate in this context.

Table 2.2: Example of weighting after multiple selection

sum of	• • • • •	• • • • •	• • • • •	• • • • •	• • • •	• • • • •	• • • • •	• • • •	item
weights	✓	✓	✓	✓					choice
analiz 57	analiz 3*(11-1)	analiz 3*(11-2)							link weight
razbor 63	razbor 3*(11-5)		razbor 3*(11-3)	razbor 3*(11-4)					link weight
operaci& 1	operaci& 3*(11-7)				operaci& -(11-6)	operaci& -(11-8)	operaci& -(11-9)	operaci& -(11-10)	link weight

2.6 Learning

In this study, the *short context* of the source word is the basic forms of the neighbouring words. The short context of the word supplies important semantic information (see Levinger92). We use the following hypothesis for disambiguation by short contexts:

> If for one source text word a correct translation T is established, and subsequently among the suggested translations of a second source word that same T is found, then T is a preferred translation for the second word, on condition that in both cases the same short context is present. (2.2)

2.6.1 Learning Short Contexts

The contexts are saved in the inverse lexicon in conjunction with the suggested target-source translations, as shown in Section 2.2.2. The reasons for this are:

- It gives the monolingual user a certain degree of control over the learned knowledge, as every suggested inverse translation and its attached contexts are in the source language.

- The learned context may serve not only for translation of the present source word, but also help when a different source word is found in the same context and the same target language word appears as a possible translation.

Several constraints exist on the learning:

- Learning can occur only after disambiguation. A context is supposed to be a lexical entry, and this can be obtained only after the disambiguation of the neighboring words.

- It should be learned only if the source word appears among the suggested inverse translations of the translation selected in the target language.

- It is worth learning only if it was the user's choice, so essential semantic information has indeed been supplied.

- Even if the software succeeds in disambiguating a word automatically with the help of contexts, the user still must be given the opportunity of intervening through selection.

As we disambiguate morphological and semantic ambiguity "in a single stroke", after disambiguation of the word we do not know which meaning suits the presented translation among the alternatives given by morphological analysis. To learn contexts we have to find their lexical entries, and this provides morphological disambiguation as a by-product.

3   Target Text Generation

To complete the description of the system, we shall briefly describe how a target text in Russian is generated. This part is modular, and can always be replaced by another system.

The input for the target text generation stage is the output of the disambiguation stage, and this input can be inherited from within its internal structures. From that stage we obtain essential semantic information, except for the chosen lexical entry in the target language. To be consistent, we do not use a semantic database at the generation stage either. All that we need for translation is a pair of *regular* and *available* dictionaries.

By giving up databases, we must compromise between the transfer method and the direct method, and depend also on rules specific to the languages involved.

3.1   Completing Syntactical and Semantic Information

In Russian sentence the word-order is allowed to be same as the Hebrew sentence word-order. Russian morphology is extremely rich, therefore generation of a Russian text means first of all the correct choice of the form of each word. This is determined on the basis of the link between semantics and syntax, and in several categories the form of the word is influenced by its semantic and syntactical connection with other words in the sentence. These connections are called *cases*, and they must be determined for proper generation of a Russian sentence.

As noted, we do not obtain a semantic and syntactical analysis from the previous stage. By contrast, morphological generation in Russian clearly requires specific information about every word. To draw this specific information from the records of the morphological analysis of the Hebrew text and from the Russian lexical entries, we propose here the method of *complementary feature flow*.

The idea is based on the intuitive assumption that in a simple Hebrew or Russian text there is a kind of flow of syntactic and semantic features through the sentence. Accordingly, one may *complement* the features of a word with the help of *flowing features*, and at the same time update the flowing features by means of the characteristic features of the word.

3.2 Morphological Generation

The above algorithm enables the conversion of morphological information in a Hebrew text into the morphological information necessary for the generation of its Russian translation, but the generation itself requires an additional effort. The final form of the Russian word is a complex function of category, gender, person, number, tense, case, and basic ending of the word. Usually the significant change is in the word ending. Special treatment is needed for verbs which split into a personal pronoun or an auxiliary word and a verb, and for possessive suffixes that turn into personal pronouns in a particular case.

By this method one can obtain quite good approximation to the Russian morphology, although certain exceptional cases are not covered; however, these are sufficiently close to the obtained theoretical form. Because of the very high redundancy in Russian, these small inaccuracies do not hinder comprehension.

4 Summary

4.1 Conclusion of the Translation Process

Figure 4.1 gives an idea of the look of the system after preparation of the source text, morphological analysis, disambiguation, and generation of the target text. On the Multiple Document Interface (MDI) we constructed, every tool presents its results in its own editing

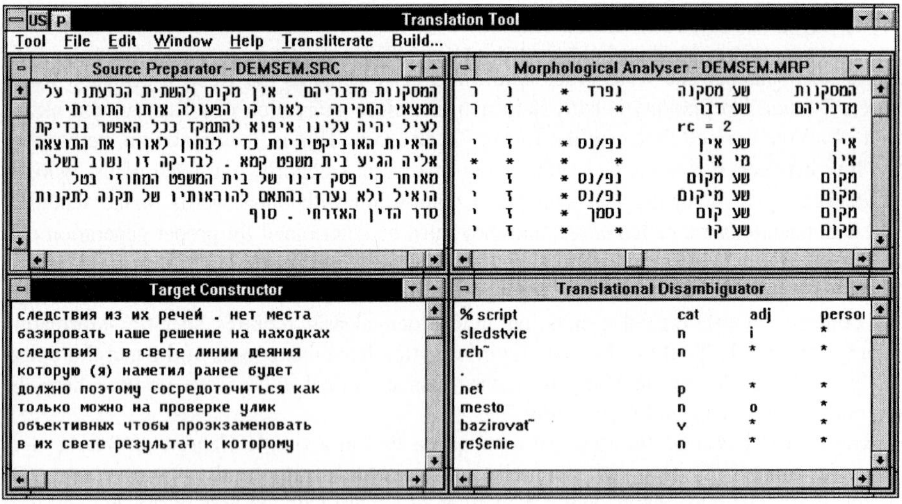

Figure 4.1: A view of the system at text translation completion

window. The main menu allows to access tools, file, edit, window and help services, as well as the facilities of the tool active at the moment. Beginning from the source text, one follows through stage by stage (clockwise in the example) to the target text[1], and thus the goal of the workstation for the present text is completed, and a new text can be started with a "smarter" system.

4.2 Results

These are the principles of the system that allow translations of texts from the user's language to a language in which the user does not master.

1. *Single solution for both morphological and semantic ambiguities* permits omission of a separate stage of morphological disambiguation, and thus reduces the chances of error, diminishes the amount of work to the user, and maximizes use of the interactive work method. This approach is efficient, since "wrong" meanings from the user's viewpoint are eliminated at a glance, and these are usually the meanings that result from semantically inappropriate morphological analyses. The problem of morphological ambiguity in Hebrew is solved as a by-product of the translation.

2. *Accumulation with Inversion* by means of source-target and target-source lexica makes it possible to express semantic meanings of suggested translations in the target language through the source language. As distinct from projects that require creation of huge databases, the dictionaries needed here are regular and available. Unfortunately, we were unable to obtain fully computerized dictionaries for the purpose of academic research, so we had to make do with partial lexica that we compiled manually, and limit the choice of sample translations accordingly. In principle there is nothing to prevent integration of complete dictionaries into the system.

3. *Selection* menus displayed in the source language makes possible intuitive and simple choice of appropriate meanings by the user in the source language. In this way the aim of eliminating the need for the user to know the target language is achieved.

4. *Weighting* of selection of the target word is based on two factors: the weight of the meanings in the order of their appearance in the lexica on the one hand, and user's choice on the other. Thus empirical information provided by the dictionary compilers is exploited. The words selected in this manner prove to be good and to correctly reflect the original semantic meaning.

5. *Learning* mechanism for contexts allows automatic translation not only for the present source word but also for other words for which the same suggested translation is offered as that chosen for the present word. The efficiency of the system increases with use owing to the learning property.

6. *Generation* in the target language is based on several rules for the pair of languages. This approach supplies a readable Russian text that is correct semantically, syntactically and morphologically, but may have stylistic flaws. In any case the test is readable owing to the flexibility and redundancy that is typical in Russian.

---

[1] After the generation stage in Russian, a the Latin transliteration is replaced by Cyrillic script.

4.3 Conclusions

The *chief innovation* in our study is the development of *Accumulation with Inversion and Weighted Selection, plus Learning* method for disambiguation and its application. This technique is based on the use of two *regular* and *available* dictionaries for the pair of languages and operation by a *monolingual* user.

Experiments conducted with the system indicated several of its properties:

1. The user's skill level is not of great importance. He or she must be fluent in the source language and make common sense choices. It's interesting that native speakers of the source language enjoyed a clear advantage over native speakers of the target language who also master the source language. This may be explained in that native speakers are more familiar with the meanings presented in the source language, while knowledge of the target language does not help much in this case.

2. On average, a user spends about 3 min. to translate a text of 100 words.

3. Entirely inappropriate translations were not selected. The weighting method almost always indicates the most appropriate word among those that are left. If several appropriate suggested translations are found, among which the semantic difference is slight or only stylistic, preference is given to the suggested translation that is given before the others in the lexical entry. The quality of the lexicon and ordering of suggested translations in the lexical entries by frequency of appearance are important in such cases for choosing most reasonable translations.

4. The reliability of the lexica is very important. Naturally, it is preferable that in both lexica all the words have as many suggested translations as possible, including slang. On the other hand, it's important that entries in the lexica be balanced, namely that two words with the same degree of ambiguity will have approximately the same number of translations in the lexicon. This holds especially true for the inverse lexicon (target-source) as this sets the sensitivity of the system to the choices made by the user.

5. The *ad hoc* model we used to generate a Russian text proved efficient enough for simple texts. Reliance on the direct dependence between grammatical phenomena in the two languages facilitated the implementation.

6. To obtain the greatest benefits from the system, it must be augmented by complete dictionaries. Such dictionaries are to be found in commercial companies, but they are still not accessible for research purposes. As soon as they are, there will be no need to modify the system but merely to load these dictionaries as the software is being run.

References

CL85   Choueka, Lusignan. Disambiguation by short contexts. *Computers and the Humanities*, 19(3), 1985.

DIS91   Ido Dagan, Alon Itai and Ulrike Schwall. Two languages are more informative than one. In *Proc. of the Annual Meeting of the ACL*, 1991.

GLR88   Igal Golan, Shalom Lappin and Mori Rimon. An active bilingual lexicon for machine translation. In *Proc. of COLING*, 1988.

Nirenburg87 Sergei Nirenburg, editor. *Machine Translation: Theoretical and Methodological Issues.* Cambridge: Cambridge University Press, 1987.

NR87 Nirenburg and Raskin. The Analysis Lexicon and the Lexicon Management System. *Computers and Translation* 2:177-188, 1987.

Ornan86 Uzzi Ornan. Phonemic Script: A central Vehicle for Processing Natural Language - The Case of Hebrew, *IBM Tech. Rep. 88.181*, 1986.

Radford88 Andrew Radford. *Transformational Grammar.* Cambridge University Press, 1988.

Winograd84 Terry Winograd. Natural Language Processing. In *Scientific American*, 1984.

In Hebrew:

Cohen91. Ilana Cohen-Zamir. *Semantic Syntactical Analyzer for Sentences out of Context in Hebrew.* M.Sc. thesis, Technion, 1991.

Dagan92 Ido Dagan. *Multilingual Statistical Approaches to Disambiguation in Natural Language.* Ph.D. thesis, Technion, 1992.

Goldstein98 Lior Goldstein. *Analysis and Generation of the Possessive Inflection in Ultimate-Accented Nouns.* M.Sc. project, Technion, 1992.

Kravitz92 Kravitz Technologies Inc., *Hebrew-Russian-Hebrew Dictionary on ROM card*, 1992

KS87 M. Kleinbart and A. Solomonik, eds. *Hebrew-Russian Dictionary.* Lexicon Publishers, 1987.

Levinger92 Moshe Levinger. *Dispersal of Morphological Opacity in Hebrew.* M.Sc. thesis, Technion, 1992.

Ornan80 Uzzi Ornan. *The Simple Sentence*, 1980.

Ornan87 Uzzi Ornan. Computer processing of Hebrew texts in the basis of single-meaning script. *Mishpatim 17(1)*, 1987.

Ornan92 Uzzi Ornan. Theoretical linguistics and artificial intelligence. In *Hebrew Computational Linguistics*, Israel Ministry of Science and Technology. 1992

Ornan93 Uzzi Ornan. Phonemic transliteration of Hebrew in Latin letters. *Organization of Special Libraries*, 1993.

OK86 Uzzi Ornan and Vadim Kazatzki. Processes of analysis and generation in Hebrew morphology. *13th National Conference on Data Processing*. A.Y.L.A., 1986.

Vinter91 Shuli Vinter. *Syntactical Analysis of Sentences in Hebrew.* M.Sc. project, Technion, 1991.

Shani90 Michal Shani-Klein. *Analysis and Generation of Inflection of Segolate Nouns in Hebrew.* M.Sc. project, Technion, 1990.

Fast Document Translation for Cross-Language Information Retrieval

J. Scott McCarley and Salim Roukos

IBM T.J. Watson Research Center
P.O. Box 218
Yorktown Heights, NY 10598
{jsmc,roukos}@watson.ibm.com

Abstract. We describe a statistical algorithm for machine translation intended to provide translations of large document collections at speeds far in excess of traditional machine translation systems, and of sufficiently high quality to perform information retrieval on the translated document collections. The model is trained from a parallel corpus and is capable of disambiguating senses of words. Information retrieval (IR) experiments on a French language dataset from a recent cross-language information retrieval evaluation yields results superior to those obtained by participants in the evaluation, and confirm the importance of word sense disambiugation in cross-language information retrieval.

1   Introduction

In cross-language information retrieval (CLIR), the goal is to use a natural language query in one language in order to retrieve documents relevant to that query that are written in another language. The widespread availability of World Wide Web search engines and the widespread availability of machine translation (for example, on the Altavista web site) have heightened awareness of the many languages present on the web and the importance of being able to search for and retrieve web pages in other languages. Moreover, the Text REtrieval (TREC) conferences sponsored by NIST now include a crosslingual information retrieval task, which allows many CLIR systems to be evaluated and results compared. There are several possible roles for machine translation in CLIR. Either the queries or the documents may be translated. Clearly translating the queries is computationally easier than translating the entire collection of documents. Translating a large ($\approx$ 1 Gb) document collection is not feasible with many state-of-the-art machine translation systems. On the other hand, it seems likely that the impact on retrieval accuracy of translation errors will be much more severe in query translation than in document translation. In this paper, we present a method of machine translation that is sufficiently fast to translate large document collections, and sufficiently accurate to be used in cross-lingual information retrieval with good results, in fact, better average precision than was obtained by any of the participants on this track at the recent TREC-6 conference.

2 The TREC-6 CLIR Task

The CLIR track at the TREC-6 evaluation provided an opportunity for many different information retrieval systems to be compared over a standard set of queries, documents, and relevance judgments. [1] NIST provided sets of documents in English (AP newswire, 1988-90), French (SDA newswire, 1988-90) and German (SDA newswire, 1988-90 and the NZZ newspaper, 1994). A standard set of 25 queries was also provided, with manual translations of the query set in English, German, French. (Dutch and Spanish translations of the queries were also made available by some of the participants.) After participants submitted results, relevance judgments were made on the pool of results. An average of 56 documents were relevant to each query. Participants were free to participate in any pair of languages, and were encourage to submit monolingual results, also, for comparison, and to improve the pool of relevance judgments. A typical TREC query (Fig. 1) consists of three fields; we will present results for both short (just the <Description> field) and long (all three fields) forms of the query.

<Title> Solar Powered Cars
<Description> Information on solar powered cars.
<Narrative> A relevant document will contain information on research and development on solar automobiles. Solar powered automobiles are part of an effort to popularize alternative energy sources to replace the continued exploitation of the world's finite fossil fuels.

Fig. 1. A typical TREC query

An information retrieval system can be evaluated in terms of recall (percentage of relevant documents returned in the top-N) or precision (percentage of top-N documents that are relevant). A standard metric at TREC is average precision (precision averaged over all relevant documents). We present results (denoted AveP) in terms of average precision, and also in terms of precision at $N = 20$ (denoted P20.)

3 Document translation

We begin the description of our document translation system by briefly reviewing the statistical approach to machine translation as described in [2]. These statistical systems are trained on a parallel corpus of sentences which are known to be translations of each other, and which are aligned on a sentence-by-sentence basis. Canadian parliamentary proceedings recorded in French and English ("Hansards") are one such corpus. Our presentation will assume that we are translating from French to English, but any other pair of languages may be used. An important assumption is that there is an underlying alignment of the words in the French and English sentences. This alignment is regarded as a hidden variable, and is not known a priori. That some sentences in the training corpus are translated "loosely" is not a serious concern; the algorithms discussed below are robust to a considerable amount of noise. We introduce the notation E for a English-language sentence consisting of the words $e_1, ...e_{|E|} = e_1^{|E|}$, and and F for a French-language sentence consisting of the words $f_1, ...f_{|F|} = f_1^{|F|}$. We will generically refer to the alignment of a sentence pair as A. A typical (though incomplete) representation of the alignment is to assign to each word e_i in E an integer $a_i \in \{1...|F|\}$ indicating with which word in the French sentence it is associated. In this representation, it will sometimes be convenient to refer to the number of values of i for which $a_i = j$ as the *fertility* n_j of the j'th word in F. The French sentence is typically augmented with a null word that is aligned to English words that are not aligned with any other words.

In statistical models of machine translation, the goal is to model the conditional probability

$$p(E|F) = \sum_A p(E, A|F) \tag{1}$$

that a human translator would have produced an English sentence E as the translation of a French sentence F. There are many ways to decompose $P(E, A|F)$ into probabilities that are functions of individual words. One such decomposition is

$$p(E, A|F) = \left[\prod_{i=1}^{|F|} p_n(n_i|n_1^{i-1}, F) \right] p(A|N, F) \left[\prod_{j=1}^{|E|} p_s(e_j|e_1^{j-1}, A, F) \right] \tag{2}$$

where the fertilities $n_1, ...n_{|F|}$ are collectively denoted N. This model's prescription for translating a sentence is that first, one picks the fertilities for the French words, then one picks a set of alignments compatible with the fertilities, and lastly one picks the corresponding English words with knowledge of what French words they are aligned to. Different choices for the English words reflect different "senses" or meanings of the French word (i.e. *pomme* may be rendered as *potato* or as *apple* depending upon whether or not it is followed by *de terre*.) We will refer to p_n as the fertility model and to p_s as the sense model. This model is quite similar to Model 3 of Ref. [2] but is trained and decoded in a somewhat different manner, in line with the particular needs of our application. We further assume that an approximate alignment can be easily computed from some other model. An example of such a model is Model 1 of Ref. [2], for which the Viterbi alignment of a pair of sentences can be exactly computed in time proportional to the product of their lengths.

The conditional probabilities in the decomposition Eq. 2 depend upon too many parameters to be modeled. In order to make the computation feasible, we make the following simplifications: since word order plays only a minor role in information retrieval, we will not try to model it. Instead we will simply take $p(A|N, F)$ to be an unspecified constant. (The normalization is never needed.) We expect that the both the fertility associated with a given French word, and also the English words that it translates into, to be primarily dependent on the French word itself, with some variance due to local context. Here we will take local context of a word f_i to be the previous and next non-stop words, denoted f_{i-} and f_{i+}, respectively. (In information retrieval, a stop word is a frequently occurring word such as "a", "and", or "some" which is unlikely to have any value in determining the relevance of a document to a query. Standard lists of stop words are widely available.) Sentence boundaries are marked by an artificial "BOUNDARY_WORD" (which is not a stop word) so that local context is well-defined at the start and end of the sentence. We can now summarize our fertility and sense models in a form suitable for modeling:

$$p_n(n_i|n_1^{i-1}F) \approx p_n(n_i|f_i, f_{i-}, f_{i+}) \tag{3}$$

$$p_s(e_j|e_1^{j-1}, A, F) \approx p_s(e_j|f_{a_j}, f_{a_j-}, f_{a_j+}). \tag{4}$$

The translation model is completely specified by these functions. Note that the two functions that must be modeled are simply conditional probabilities of the occurrence of a word in one language given an ordered triplet of words in another language. The "language" of fertility here is simply a set of small nonnegative integers. This form is practically identical to that of language models, which have extensive use in speech recognition. [3] One minor difference, namely that the the history and future words are in different languages is of no significance, as the words are typically indexed by integers in any event. The other difference, in the order of the words in the history for purposes of smoothing the distribution, is overcome by symmetrizing the distributions with respect to interchange of f_{i-} and f_{i+}.

The procedure for training the translation model is as follows: using an alignment model, find a word-by-word alignment for the training data. For each English word e_i in each of the English sentence, store the following language model events $(n_i, f_{a_i}, f_{a_i-}, f_{a_i+})$ and $(e_i, f_{a_i}, f_{a_i-}, f_{a_i+})$.

With the events that have been stored, build the language models

$$p_n(n_i|f_i, f_{i-}, f_{i+}) \tag{5}$$

$$p_s(e_j|f_{a_j}, f_{a_j-}, f_{a_j+}). \tag{6}$$

Decoding with this translation model proceeds as follows: for each French word f_i, use the fertility model to predict the probabilities of the fertilities n_i from f_i and its local context. Using the same history and the second language model, predict the probabilities for a small number (typically 5) of possible English words. (It is not neccesary to calculate the probability for all words in English. A short list of likely choices is easily obtained by thresholding the alignment model.) It is worth noting that it is not necessary to segment the sentence into short phrases, as is required in some other statistical translation systems. [4]

For comparison purposes, we also consider a simplification of the above model obtained by forcing $n = 1$ for all French words and removing the contextual dependence of the translated word:

$$p_s(e_j|e_1^{j-1}, A, F) \approx p_s(e_j|f_{a_j}). \tag{7}$$

Since there is no contextual dependence, the most likely translation of each word in the French vocabulary may be tabulated in advance. In fact, this simplification is just a statistically constructed dictionary.

For predicting the word-by-word alignments we used Model 1 of Ref. [2]; it was trained on sentences pairs in which the length of both sentences was less than 30 morphs in the Hansard corpus. The corpus had been morphologically analyzed, so that the "words" for the translation model were actually root words ("morphs"). Although the morphological analysis procedure is invertible, the inverse operation was not used because the information retrieval system also used morphologically analyzed text. The sense and fertilities model were also trained on the Hansard. The fertility model was a deleted interpolation 4-gram model [3], and the sense model was constructed from two maximum-entropy [4, 5] trigram models, one for left context and one for right context. The incorporation of the document translation system described above into our information retrieval system is trivial. We simply translated the three years of SDA newswire French and used our information retrieval system on the resulting English text.

4 IR System Description

Our monolingual system is a two-pass system that has been used previously on the ad-hoc tasks of TREC-5 [6] and TREC-6, and in the Very Large Corpus task of TREC-6.[7] The typical preprocessing of documents (in either English or French) consists of tokenizing, sentence-detection, part-of-speech tagging, and morphological analysis to find the root word. Since the translation system translates from morphs to morphs, the document translation step is inserted at this point. The words are then indexed. For each query, the documents are scored according to the widely-used Okapi formula [8] which weighs matching words (and bigrams) according to their frequency of occurence (term frequency) within the document and their rarity with respect to other documents (inverse document frequency.) English bigrams are required to be adjacent; French bigrams are allowed to be separated only by *en*, *de*, or *des*. We also compute a second pass score based on a probabilistic query expansion method. [9] In the crosslingual task, the query is expanded by including words from the original documents, not the translated documents.

5 Results and Conclusions

All of the experiments reported here with our CLIR system have been performed on the TREC-6 task, with English queries and French documents, as this is the most extensive collection of queries, documents and relevance judgments available. Although our principal interest is in crosslingual IR, we present experiments with monolingual IR (French queries, French documents) as baseline. We perform experiments with both long (all three fields) and short (<Description>-field only) forms of the query to test the system with different query lengths.

system	AveP	P20	%base	AveP	P20	%base
crosslingual	0.3054	0.3250	91	0.3400	0.3489	84
monolingual	0.3360	0.4205	100	0.4032	0.4909	100

AveP: average precision
P20:   precision of top-20

Table 1. Crosslingual vs. monolingual (pass 2 IR results): short queries (left), long queries (right)

system	AveP	P20	%base	AveP	P20	%base
dictionary	0.2210	0.2750	73	0.2546	0.3409	68
sensed	0.2637	0.3159	87	0.3003	0.3682	80
monolingual	0.3036	0.4250	100	0.3758	0.4682	100

dictionary: Eq. 7
sensed: Eq. 4

Table 2. Importance of sensing (pass 1 IR results): short queries (left), long queries (right)

Caution must be used when comparing our results with that of the TREC participants. The results reported by the various participants varied widely. Some of the variation in performance is attributable to differences between short and long queries. Results presented here are on the 22 queries for which relevance judgments are available, comparable to other published results. Although our results are after-the-fact, the details of our information retrieval system (mixing coefficients, etc.) were not tuned to the task. Rather they were used as they had previously been calibrated for the English-only ad-hoc task, even though a different calibration might yield superior performance for the French monolingual and English-French crosslingual tasks (a topic for future investigation.)

The translation model achieves both of our goals : speed and retrieval accuracy. Translating the 3 years of SDA newswire (about 250 Mb) required an average of 28 hours for each year of newswire text on an RS-6000 Model 590, or about 7500 words/min. in contrast, the baseline document translation of the German TREC documents was prepared at the University of Maryland and made available to TREC-6 participants. This translation was performed using LOGOS and took approximately 2 months on 5 workstations. [10] Although the tasks are not exactly comparable, a conservative estimate is that the rate of translation achieved by our system is at least 20 times faster. This speedup is obviously of considerable importance if there is a need to perform several translation experiments, or to translate even larger document collections (the English-only ad hoc task involves $\approx 2Gb$ of data.) The system also achieved very good results in terms of average precision of retrieval. Our results exceeded the best results of TREC-6 participants (average precisions of 0.1982 and 0.1946 [1]) by a considerable margin. These results are summarized in Table 1. This level of accuracy was achieved with both long and short forms of the queries.

We also note that the sense and fertility models provided a very significant benefit. (19% for short queries and 18% for long queries.) These gains are considerably larger than the gains made by incorporating bigram information into the Okapi formula. The comparisons here are strictly first-pass (Okapi) scores;

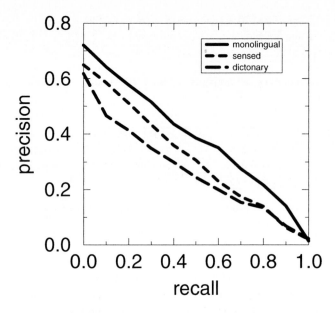

Fig. 2. Precision vs. recall, long queries

in Table 2 we summarize these results and compare them to a first-pass monolingual baseline. The recall-precision graph in Fig. 2 shows that much of the gain is in the precision of highly ranked documents. The gain obviously varied considerably from query to query: Query CL24 (teddy bears / *ours en peluche*) improved from 9% to 55%. We note that even the dictionary translation model returned 13 of 16 relevant documents because it correctly translated *ours*. The big gain in precision comes from finding the correct sense of *peluche* in the context of *ours*.

We have also performed *double*-translation experiments, in which the supplied French form of the query is translated into English with our system, and then this translation is used to retrieve translated documents. Although this is not part of the TREC task, it is of possible relevance to work in multilingual information retrieval systems with more than two languages, in which both query and documents are translated into a third language. Furthermore, it provides another baseline to help assess the loss in retrieval accuracy due to machine translation. In fact, translating both the query and the document improved the retrieval accuracy, to ≈ 95% of the first-pass monolingual results. The output of our machine translator (indeed, any machine translator) has peculiarities of word choice that differ from typical English. A translated query with the same peculiarities as a translated document is a therefore a better match to the set of translated documents than a human-composed query, and is therefore able to retrieve the documents better. An important observation here is that a considerable amount of information survives the translation that is not picked up by the information retrieval system.

In conclusion, we have achieved both of our goals: Our system is capable of translating large collection of documents very rapidly. The translations are sufficiently accurate for our performance on the cross-language information retrieval task to exceed that of any participant at TREC-6. We believe that there are no barriers to incorporating document translation into CLIR, even if corpus sizes are scaled into gigabytes. We look forward to further evaluation of this system in TREC-7.

6   Acknowlegements

This work is supported by NIST grant no. 70NANB5H1174. We thank Martin Franz and Todd Ward for valuable discussions.

References

1. D.Harman and E.Voorhees, "Overview of the Sixth Text REtrieval Conference (TREC6)",in *The 6th Text REtrieval Conference (TREC-6)*.
2. P. F. Brown et al. "The mathematics of statistical machine translation: Parameter estimation", *Computational Lingustics*, 19 (2), 263-311, June 1993.
3. L.R. Bahl, F.Jelinek, and R.L. Mercer, "A Maximum Likelihood Approach to Continuous Speech Recognition", in *IEEE Transactions on Pattern Analysis and Machine Intelligence* 5 (2), 1983.
4. A. Berger, S.Della Pietra, V. Della Pietra, "A Maximum Entropy Approach to Natural Language Processing", in *Computational Linguistics*, vol. 22 (1), p.39 (1996).
5. S.Della Pietra, V.Della Pietra, and J.Lafferty, "Inducing Features of Random Fields", IEEE Transactions on Pattern Analysis and Machine Intelligence, 19 (4), p.380, (1997).
6. E.Chan, S.Garcia, S.Roukos, "TREC-5 Ad Hoc Retrieval Using K Nearest-Neighbors Re-Scoring" in *The 5th Text REtrieval Conference (TREC-5)* ed. by E.M. Voorhees and D.K.Harman.
7. M. Franz and S. Roukos, "TREC-6 Ad-hoc Retrieval", in *The 6th Text REtrieval Conference (TREC-6)*.
8. S.E. Robertson, S. Walker, S. Jones, M.M. Hancock-Beaulieu, M. Gatford, "Okapi at TREC-3" in *Proceedings of the Third Text REtrieval Conference (TREC-3)* ed. by D.K. Harman. NIST Special Publication 500-225, 1995.
9. E.P Chan, S. Garcia, and S. Roukos, "Probabilistic Model for Information Retrieval with Unsupervised Training Data", to appear in *Proceedings, Fourth International Conference on Knowledge Discovery and Data Mining* (1998)
10. D.W. Oard, P.Hackett, "Document Translation for Cross-Language Text Retrieval at the University of Maryland", in *The 6th Text REtrieval Conference (TREC-6)* ed. by E.M. Voorhees and D.K.Harman.
11. B.Merialdo 1990 "Tagging text with a probabilistic model," in *Proceedings of the IBM Natural Language ITL*, Paris, France, pp.161-172.

Machine Translation in Context

Kurt Godden

General Motors
Service Technology Group
MC 480-205-196
30007 Van Dyke
Warren, MI 48090 USA
office: 810-492-7735
fax: 810-492-4252
godden@home.com

Abstract. The Controlled Automotive Service Language project at General Motors is combining machine translation (MT) with a variety of other language technologies into an existing translation environment. In keeping with the theme of this conference, this report elaborates on the elements of this mixture, and how they are being blended together to form a coordinated whole. The primary concept is that machine translation cannot be viewed independently of the context in which it will be used. That entire context must be prepared and managed in order to accommodate MT without undue business risk. Further, until high-quality MT is available in a much wider variety of languages, any MT production application is likely to co-exist with traditional human translation, which requires additional considerations.

1   Introduction

The Controlled Automotive Service Language (CASL) project [1] at General Motors is bringing together a variety of language technologies for the creation, management, and delivery of service information for North American vehicles exported worldwide. These technologies include controlled English authoring, SGML data management, language data management, translation memory (TM), machine translation, as well as traditional human translation and post-editing of machine translation output. Some of these technologies and processes are currently in production at GM's Service Technology Group (STG), but many are not. They are being developed as part of the CASL project and will be integrated into the existing production environment.

In a previous paper [2] I reported on how GM is managing its organizational changes to reduce the business risk of the CASL project, and in this paper I extend that discussion to describe how all of the pieces of the project will come together into a unified whole.

2   Language Management Process Model

Our targeted language management process model is shown at a high level in Figure 1. Single-outlined boxes represent processes or technologies currently in production, while the double-outlined boxes indicate technologies or processes being developed within the context of the CASL project.

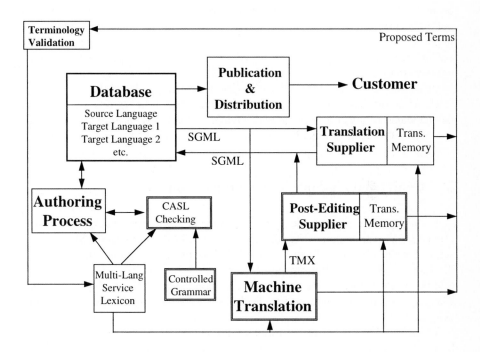

Fig. 1. Consolidated Language Technologies and Processes

In Figure 1, the service information production database is currently based on Ingres and is populated with SGML-tagged data created by authors using ArborText. There are authoring memory tools to allow authors to re-use previously authored source language text when that text also meets their current needs. Document management and versioning is part of this existing data production and management activity. The CASL project is adding all of the subprocesses indicated by the double outlines.

The CASL project is being driven by the potential cost reductions to be gained from the *effective* use of MT for English-to-French translations. However, we recognize that MT cannot be considered independently of its context of use. Minimally, that context must include authoring of the source text, data storage and management, publication, and terminology management as well as the MT process itself. However in the CASL project the context also extends to include controlled authoring, statistical quality control, and the coexistence of MT with human translation, which in turn implies the consideration of translation supplier relations.

If we trace the intended data flow through Figure 1 we can see how MT is situated in a broader context that functions as a *system* [3]. As we currently conceive the process, authors will continue to create source language data as they are today, writing new data when necessary and reusing existing data whenever possible through the use of so-called authoring memory tools to identify relevant information. To the extent that reused data has also been translated in the past, then to that same extent it will not be sent out for translation during the next translation cycle. Thus, authoring memory not only saves authoring resources it also saves on translation resources. One important activity not shown in Figure 1 is author training. Current GM service authors do receive training on how to write for translatability, and are trained on how to conform to the several most important CASL controlled language rules. Anecdotal evidence suggests that authors greatly appreciate being told of the impact of their work upon the ease or difficulty of translation and how writing in a controlled language can result in translation cost savings. One CASL project task is to update and extend this author training.

3   Controlled Authoring and Translation

A major CASL deliverable is the software conformance checker for specially-trained CASL editors to rewrite author text for conformance to the CASL English rule set, followed by author validation of the CASL English for content and check-in to the database. Any database information object that has been so processed will include an SGML tag that indicates its conformance or non-conformance to the CASL rule set. This tag is set by the conformance checker software but used by the MT system (see below).

When data is ready for translation into non-MT target languages, the source language text will be transmitted electronically to a translation supplier. For non-MT target languages, the supplier will employ traditional human-based translation, augmented by TM technology.

When a translation is desired for an MT target language pair (currently only English-French is under development), data will be exported from the database, less those information elements that were previously translated and which were not changed during the previous authoring cycle. The CASL systems administrator will then submit this source data to the MT preprocessor in order to create a list of any remaining unknown words which can then be defined and input to the system. Next all source language translation units will be sent to the Lant®mark MT system for translation. Lant®mark is a METAL-based system from LANT n.v. in Leuven, Belgium. Output from the Lant®mark system will then pass to an outside supplier for post-editing.

This data will consist of both the source and the raw target text from the MT system combined and packaged into TMX standard format. TMX is a new TM data standard developed by the OSCAR consortium of the Localization Industry Standards

Association (LISA). Using TMX format will allow the post-editing suppliers to easily import the data into their existing translator workstations, which in this case will be used as post-editing workstations.

The post-editing supplier, which may also function as a traditional supplier of translation for non-MT language pairs, will use translators to perform the non-traditional role of post-editing output from the MT system. Specially-trained post-editors may be presented with data in one of two different situations. In situation one they will see the English source and the MT-created target language text, when no match was found in the TM system. And in situation two they will see the English source, the TM-matched target language text, and also the MT-created target text. Whichever view they are presented with their task is the same: create a final translation that is acceptable to the client, viz. General Motors.

What is acceptable is defined by three factors which combine to imply a principle of minimal post-editing. A CASL translation will be deemed acceptable if (a) it consists of correct target language terminology, (b) it is grammatical, and (c) it correctly conveys the intent of the source language author. The *style* of the final translation is of secondary importance as long as the technician, who is the final customer of the translation, is able to service the vehicle. We do not expect the CASL post-editors to produce translations in a style typical of those produced by more traditional translators. In fact, to do so would probably entail additional cost and time with no advantage to the technician using that information and would thus be "overengineered".

We are working with Alpnet, a translation supplier, out of their Montreal office to work with us through the end of the CASL pilot in late-1999 to develop the appropriate training for post-editors, recognizing that we are asking them to perform a task for which they have not previously been trained. We also wish to work with Alpnet to develop a pricing model that is appropriate for post-editing of MT output.

It was previously noted that an SGML tag would be set on source language information elements to indicate whether or not they conform to the CASL controlled language rule set. This CASL tag will be used by the MT system in order to make certain assumptions when the tag is set. For example, by convention we are limiting the English word 'since' to its temporal rather than its causal meaning in CASL English. When the CASL tag is set, 'since' will not be treated as an ambiguous term by the MT system, which will translate it only into its temporal sense in French. Such conventional limitations on the source text will form part of the training both for the original authors as well as the CASL editors using the conformance checker.

The core of any MT application from a user's perspective is the lexicon. STG employs a full-time lexicographer to manage the vocabulary development process. English and French speaking automotive technicians are validating terminology from a number of existing sources. Corpus analysis of existing database text also supplies some of the terminology in English. As we enter production with the CASL technology, the lexicographer will also assume responsibility for a feedback process with the post-editing suppliers to continue the terminology validation process.

Successful operation will require more sophisticated pricing models with our suppliers of translation and post-editing work than currently exist. While CASL is still in its pre-production project phase we intend to develop a pricing model with our supplier that encompasses human translation and post-editing of TM and MT output on the principle of minimal post-editing as described above, also factoring in turnaround time and quality.

Working with the post-editors, the translation quality of the raw MT output will be measured in order to provide feedback to LANT for system refinements. In addition, we will measure the quality of the finished translation. Ideally we would use the same metric in both of these quality evaluations. In anticipation of these needs, GM chairs a committee of the Society of Automotive Engineers (SAE) that is charged with developing a quality metric for automotive service information. This committee works under the SAE designation 'J2450' and includes membership from several automotive manufacturers as well as translation providers. Quality control is more than an evaluation metric, however. The quality control processes we intend to use in production have been described elsewhere [4], borrowing statistical process control practices long-established in manufacturing.

4   Deployment

While all of the technologies described here are important, we feel that the key to success of the project lies in how GM prepares its business processes to accept those technologies. This is especially true with respect to deployment of the controlled language checker into the authoring environment. As a result, we have initiated a 'CASL Column' this year in the monthly newsletter that is distributed to all of the 400 service authors in GM. This CASL column will keep authors informed of the activities of the project, its timeline, the expected benefits to the organization, and how it will affect the authors.

We have also had meetings with authoring management and authors to discuss alternative deployment scenarios in order to reach a consensus on how best to increase the probability of success. This involves identification of technical and business barriers and development of barrier removal plans. Key authors are getting hands-on demonstrations of the CASL conformance checker software in order to get their informed feedback and involvement in the process.

These activities are just as important as the development of the technologies themselves. The deployment of technology — MT or any other — necessarily involves its integration into the business environment of the organization. This, in turn, necessarily entails the modification of business practices and daily activities of a wide variety of people. The more change there is, the more potential risk. In recognition of this, STG created a business process reengineering (BPR) [5] team in late 1997 to develop the business processes appropriate for the various language technologies described in this paper. This BPR team is comprised of the key managers for all major business processes involved, and is charged with developing the new business processes in time for the deployment of the technologies in production.

The CASL project's current schedule calls for completion of the technology development during early 1999. The middle half of 1999 is reserved for a 6-month pilot application where, on a small scale, we will operate all of the technologies from authoring through translation while employing the new business processes developed by the BPR team. Production is scheduled for rollout in late-1999.

I have described not only the technologies of the CASL project, but also — and crucially — how the technologies are to operate in a business environment that includes more traditional translation processes. These traditional processes will continue to exist in parallel with the MT and other advanced language technologies of the CASL project. It is imperative that the production workflow not be interrupted as the CASL project is deployed. In order to assure smooth integration, numerous groups must share common goals and cooperate so that the technologies are *purposed* as much as they are *purchased*.

References

1. Means, Linda and Kurt Godden. "The Controlled Automotive Service Language (CASL) Project." Proceedings of the First International Workshop on Controlled Language Applications (CLAW 96). Katholieke Universiteit, Leuven, Belgium. 1996. pp. 106 –114.
2. Godden, Kurt. "Controlling the Business Environment for Controlled Language." Proceedings of the 2nd International Workshop on Controlled Language (CLAW98). Pittsburgh, Pennsylvania. USA. 1998. pp. 185—191.
3. Chambers, George J. "What is a Systems Engineer?" IEEE Transactions on Systems, Man, and Cybernetics. vol. SMC-15, no. 4. July-August 1985. pp. 517–521.
4. Godden, Kurt. "Statistical Control Charts in Natural Language Processing." Proceedings of the First International Conference on Natural Language Processing and Industrial Applications. vol. I. University of Moncton, N.B. Canada. pp. 111–117.
5. Hammer, Michael and James Champy. Reengineering the Corporation: a Manifesto for Business Revolution. HarperBusiness. 1993.

EasyEnglish: Addressing Structural Ambiguity

Arendse Bernth

IBM T.J. Watson Research Center, P.O. Box 704, Yorktown Heights, NY 10598, USA
arendse@watson.ibm.com

Abstract. EasyEnglish is an authoring tool which is part of IBM's internal SGML editing environment, Information Development Workbench. EasyEnglish is used as a preprocessing step for machine-translating IBM manuals. Although EasyEnglish does some traditional grammar checking, its focus is on problems of structural ambiguity. Such problems include ambiguous attachment of participles, ambiguous scope in coordination, and ambiguous attachment of the agent phrase for double passives. Since we deal with truly ambiguous constructions, the system has no way of deciding on the desired interpretation; the system provides the user with a choice of rewriting suggestions, each forcing an unambiguous attachment. This paper describes the techniques for identifying structural ambiguities and generating unambiguous rewriting suggestions.

1 Introduction

EasyEnglish is part of IBM's internal SGML editing environment, Information Development Workbench. EasyEnglish is used as a preprocessing step for translating IBM manuals with the LMT machine translation system [12, 13, 9]. When you want to translate the same text into several different target languages, it is clearly important to improve the translatability before attempting translation. As has often been pointed out (see e.g. [7, 6, 10]), translatability depends on such issues as complexity and ambiguity.

EasyEnglish helps writers improve translatability by checking for both infelicitous grammatical constructions and for structural ambiguity. In addition, EasyEnglish offers extensive vocabulary support. An overview of EasyEnglish can be found in [3]. In [4] it is argued that the EasyEnglish approach is superior to traditional controlled-language approaches and standard grammar checking, and this is substantiated by examples of how preprocessing with EasyEnglish improves the translation quality for our LMT English-German system. In this paper, we will go into more technical detail and describe the way EasyEnglish identifies structural ambiguity from the parses provided by English Slot Grammar (ESG) [11, 14, 15]. We will also describe how EasyEnglish generates its rewriting suggestions. This treatment of structural ambiguity is one of the major advantages of EasyEnglish over other authoring tools (as described in [4]).

EasyEnglish uses a full parse by ESG. The parse that ESG provides is highly detailed and provides accurate information about the structure of the sentence. In cases of structural ambiguity, ESG uses parse scoring heuristics [15] to rank

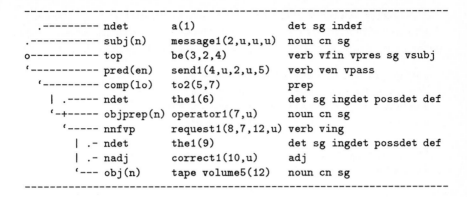

Fig. 1. ESG parse of "A message is sent to the operator requesting the correct tape volume."

the parses according to a specific numeric ranking. ESG parsing heuristics usually arrive at correct attachments in the best-ranked parse; but even when the attachment is incorrect, EasyEnglish can often point out other attachment possibilities to the writer, just by looking at the best-ranked parse. This is unlike some other systems, e.g. the Boeing Simplified English Checker [17], which look at a whole forest of trees.

EasyEnglish has a number of rules identifying structural ambiguity. In most cases, these rules also offer rewriting suggestions. The rewriting suggestions are offered as choices, and the EasyEnglish interface allows the user to select a suggestion and substitute it in the text by mouse-clicking. There are systems, e.g. the *Attempto System* [5], that present the user with a single rephrasing that reflects the interpretation the system arrived at. The user will have to construct a rephrasing that results in the desired interpretation, if the system did not produce the desired interpretation the first time. In other words, the system makes the decision for the user. We think it is more user-friendly to show the user exactly how the construction may be ambiguous and let her make her own choice.

Also, it is safer not to make an absolute decision. Since we deal with truly ambiguous constructions, the system has no way of making that decision. For example, if a present participial clause is attached to the direct object of a verb or a prepositional complement, there will also be the possibility that the participial clause should modify the subject instead. A simplified version of this rule would be:

"If a present participial clause modifies the object or prepositional complement, suggest two rephrasings, one that forces the attachment to the subject, and one that forces the attachment to the object or prepositional complement".

The following sentence, which we will use to illustrate some of the techniques and features of EasyEnglish, illustrates this:

"A message is sent to the operator requesting the correct tape volume."

The problem here is the attachment of the present participle phrase *"requesting the correct tape volume"*. This is pointed out by EasyEnglish as follows:

```
Ambiguous attachment of verb phrase:
"requesting the correct tape volume".
Who/what is "requesting the correct tape
volume", "A message" or "the operator" ?

If "A message" a possible rephrasing
would be:
"A message that requests the correct tape
volume is sent to the operator"

If "the operator" a possible rephrasing
would be:
"A message is sent to the operator that
requests the correct tape volume"
```

It is clearly a problem if such an ambiguity occurs in a technical document! But it is equally clear that it would be very hard for a system to decide automatically on the correct interpretation, [1] and it is for this reason that the rewriting suggestions are offered as choices, and not automatically substituted in the text.

2 Exploring the Parse

Fig. 1 shows the parse for the sentence *"A message is sent to the operator requesting the correct tape volume."* [2] As you can see, ESG decided in favor of close attachment, which is usually a good choice, other things being equal. (There are many attachment heuristics in ESG.) So *"requesting the correct tape volume"* is attached to *"the operator"*. It fills the *nnfvp* slot (nonfinite verb phrase).

ESG parse trees have a network representation that is very convenient for exploration. Table 1 shows the part of the network that reflects the overall structure of the tree and the features for each node (the network has other parts showing other information, e.g. the phrases for each node).

Functions for exploring this network are supplied by the ESG shell. These functions all work off a given node. Among other things, it is possible to test on the slot filled by the node (*netslot[n]*), its mother (*netmother[n]*), and its features (*netf(n)*). It is also possible to get the string corresponding to a given phrase.

---

[1] Our system is based mainly on syntax, without much semantics, since we do not feel that current technologies for semantics offer tolerable efficiency. For a semantics-based approach to natural language understanding in the framework of ESG, see [1, 2].

[2] The structure of the tree should be clear; however, an explanation of the ESG parse trees is given in e.g. [16].

Table 1. Network Representation

n	netmother[n]	netslot[n]	netf(n)
1		2 ndet	det sg indef
2		3 subj	noun cn sg
3		0 top	verb vfin pres sg vsubj
4		3 pred	verb ven vpass
5		4 comp	prep
6		7 ndet	det sg ingdet possdet def
7		5 objprep	noun cn sg
8		7 nnfvp	verb ving
9		12 ndet	det sg ingdet possdet def
10		12 nadj	adj
12		8 obj	noun cn sg

2.1 Nonfinite Clauses

In order to identify the ambiguous construction for the sentence *"A message is sent to the operator requesting the correct tape volume."* it is necessary to go through the following steps:

1. Traverse the network and find a node n that fills slot *nnfvp*. We find that *netslot[8] = nnfvp*.
2. Test the features of n for present participle (*ving*). We find that *netf(8)* includes *ving*.
3. Test that the mother of n is either a direct object or a prepositional complement. We find that *netmother[8] = 7* and that *netslot[7] = objprep* (prepositional object).

This identifies the ambiguity. Then we have to create rewriting suggestions. There are two: One that forces attachment to the subject, and one that forces attachment to the prepositional complement. For the first suggestion, we do the following:

1. Identify the subject by traversing the network and finding the node that fills the *subj* slot. We find that *netslot[2] = subj*.
2. Get the agreement features of the subject. We find that *netf(2)* includes third person (not shown) and *sg*.
3. Call the English generation morphology on the citation form of the participial verb, using the agreement features found in step 2.
4. Put together the rephrasing from the various ingredients: The phrase string for the subject node, the relative pronoun, the finite form of the participial verb, the modifiers of this verb, and the remaining modifiers of the main verb.

These steps give us the desired result:
"A message that requests the correct tape volume is sent to the operator"

It is simpler to create the second rewriting suggestion, since we already identified the object or prepositional complement:

1. Get the agreement features of the prepositional complement and call the English generation morphology on the citation form of the participial verb.
2. Put together the rephrasing from the various ingredients: The sentence up to, but not including, the participial verb, the relative pronoun, the finite form of the participial verb, and the modifiers of this verb.

In this way we get the second rewriting suggestion:

"A message is sent to the operator that requests the correct tape volume."

Introducing restrictive relative clauses in this manner effectively forces the correct attachment. (One might claim that the second suggestion is still somewhat ambiguous, but the preference of close attachment is so strong that we feel this suggestion has a fairly unambiguous structure).

In addition to identifying the ambiguity in terms of *structure*, it is also useful to identify the *location* in the file where the ambiguity occurs. ESG keeps track of the file coordinates for each token in the file, and these are used by EasyEnglish and the interface to highlight the problematic phrase, as well as for substitution of the chosen rewriting suggestion.

2.2 Coordination

Two other types of structural ambiguity that EasyEnglish addresses occur with coordination. Coordination is a major source of ambiguity in parsing and of bad translations by MT systems; disambiguating coordinated phrases is of major importance not only for MT, but for any NLP application. The two types of ambiguity in coordination that EasyEnglish addresses appear in coordinated noun phrases.

The first type is the type of ambiguity that occurs when a conjoined noun group premodifies a noun, and the second type is the type of ambiguity that

```
-----------------------------------------------------------------
o----- top        send1(1,u,6,u,7)    verb vimpr
| .--- ndet       the1(2)             det sg ingdet possdet def
| | .- lconj      data1(3,u)          noun cn sg pl
| .-+- nnoun      or1(4)              noun cn sg
| | '- rconj      information1(5,u)   noun cn sg
'----- obj(n)     sheet1(6)           noun cn sg
'----- comp(lo)   to2(7,10)           prep
  | .- ndet       the1(8)             det sg ingdet possdet def
  | .- nadj       right1(9,u,u)       adj
  '--- objprep(n) person1(10)         noun cn sg
-----------------------------------------------------------------
```

Fig. 2. ESG parse of " Send the data or information sheet to the right person."

occurs when the NP contains a combination of coordinating conjunctions. Both these ambiguities are a matter of scope — in the first case the scope of the premodification, in the second case the scope of the coordinating conjunctions. In both cases the ambiguity is identified by identifying a coordinating conjunction and looking at its potential modifiers. In the parse trees, the modifiers fill the *lconj* and *rconj* slots (left and right conjunct, respectively).

The first case is exemplified by the following sentence:

"Send the data or information sheet to the right person."

The problem here is the scope of *data*; does it modify *sheet* or not? (As can be seen from the parse in Fig. 2, ESG thinks that *data* does modify *sheet*.) The ambiguity is pointed out by EasyEnglish in the following way:

```
Ambiguity in coordinated phrase; possible
rephrasings:
"the information sheet or the data" or
"the data sheet or the information sheet"
```

The first suggestion assumes that *data* does not modify *sheet*, and the scope is effectively disambiguated by reversing the order of the two conjuncts.

The second suggestion assumes that the intention is that *data* actually does modify *sheet*, and this is made clear by distributing the head noun (*sheet*).

The second case of ambiguity in coordination involves the scope of coordinating conjunctions. As an example consider the following sentence:

Open the view and the file or the folder.

(See the parse in Fig. 3.) Here the problem is the scope of the two conjunctions *and* and *or*. Is the intention

Open [the view and the file] or [the folder].

or is it

Open [the view] and [the file or the folder]. ?

In order to disambiguate this type of construction, it is helpful to make the left bracket of the left conjunct of *or* explicit. This can be done by adding a left bracketing conjunction that pairs off *or*, viz. *either*:

```
-------------------------------------------------------------------
o------- top     open2(1,u,4,u) verb vimpr
|   .--- ndet    the1(2)        det sg ingdet possdet def
| .----- lconj   view1(3,u)     noun cn sg
'-+----- obj(n)  and1(4)        noun cn pl
  |   .- ndet    the1(5)        det sg ingdet possdet def
  | .--- lconj   file1(6,u)     noun cn sg
  '-+--- rconj   or1(7)         noun cn sg
    | .- ndet    the1(8)        det sg ingdet possdet def
    '--- rconj   folder1(9)     noun cn sg
-------------------------------------------------------------------
```

Fig. 3. ESG parse of " Open the view and the file or the folder."

```
Ambiguous coordination; possible
rephrasings:
"either the view and the file or the folder"
or
"the view and either the file or the folder"
```

Here, the first suggestion reflects the bracketing first given, whereas the second suggestion reflects the second bracketing.

Similarly, *both* and *and* can be used to bracket a construction where the *or* precedes the *and*:

Open the document or the file and the folder.

Here there are two possibilities for bracketing:

Open [the document or the file] and [the folder].

and

Open [the document] or [the file and the folder].

This is reflected in the following recommendations by EasyEnglish:

```
Ambiguous coordination; possible
rephrasings:
"both the document or the file and the folder"
or
"the document or both the file and the folder"
```

As above, the first suggestion reflects the first bracketing, and the second suggestion the second bracketing. Making the left bracketing explicit when there are more coordinating conjunctions in a sentence effectively disambiguates the scope of the conjunctions.

2.3 Double Passives

Passives are often frowned on by grammar checkers. Whereas EasyEnglish does have the ability to flag passive constructions (and the ability to supply active rewritings, if the agent is available), passive constructions supply a different focus, which can be quite useful in certain circumstances. However, *double* passives introduce an unwanted ambiguity, as exemplified by the following sentence from [8]:

Two cars were reported stolen by the Groveton police yesterday.

The double passive is indicated by the two past participles *reported* and *stolen*, together with the finite verb *were*. This double passive is followed by a *by*-phrase that indicates an agent: *by the Groveton police*. However, the attachment of this phrase is ambiguous. The syntactic preference is for close attachment, meaning that the police did the stealing. But this conflicts with real-world knowledge, and of course this is what makes the sentence funny. Unfortunately, we cannot allow technical documents to be funny at the expense of a potential misunderstanding, so EasyEnglish has to be able to point this out:

```
Ambiguous passive construction.
Is the subject of "stolen":
"the Groveton police"?
```

The parse tree for this sentence is given in Fig. 4, and the rule for identifying the double passive is as follows:

1. Find a node n that is a past participle (*ven*) in predicate position (*netslot[n] = pred*).
2. Test that n has a daughter that fills a complement slot (*comp(en)*) and is a past participle.

It might be noted that we do not try to supply a rewriting suggestion for this type of problem. In this particular case, the best bet would probably be to rewrite the sentence in the active voice, but this is by no means always the case, and we don't think we can reliably supply a good rewriting suggestion.

```
---------------------------------------------------------------
 .------- nadj        two1(1,u,u)          noun num sg pl
 .--------- subj(n)   car1(2)              noun cn pl
o--------- top        be(3,2,4)            verb vfin vpast pl vsubj
'--------- pred(en)   report2(4,u,2,5)     verb ven vpass
 '------- comp(en)    steal1(5,6,2,u)      verb ven vpass
  '----- subj(agent)  by1(6,9)             prep
  | | .- ndet         the1(7)              det sg pl ingdet possdet def
  | | .- nadj         Groveton(8)          noun propn sg
  | '--- objprep(n)   police1(9)           noun cn sg pl
  '----- vadv         yesterday1(10)       noun propn sg tma
---------------------------------------------------------------
```

Fig. 4. ESG parse of "Two cars were reported stolen by the Groveton police yesterday."

3   Conclusion

EasyEnglish is an authoring tool based on a full parse by ESG. Basing EasyEnglish on a full parse by a high-quality, robust, broad-coverage grammar gives a high degree of accuracy in detecting problems [3]. It also allows for good rewriting suggestions, since we have available all the phrasal constituents of the complete syntactic structure. This includes, but is not limited to, all information needed for subject-verb agreement and other inflectional issues.

Identification and disambiguation of ambiguous constructions is important for improving clarity of technical documents in their original English versions; it is also of value as a preprocessing step before translation. Catching problematic constructions in the source language before translation makes it easier for a human translator to arrive at the correct translation. In the context of MT to several languages, as is the case with the use of EasyEnglish for technical documents, it also makes more sense to address as many problems as possible in the source text, thus reducing the need for post-editing translations in several target languages.

Thus structural disambiguation is an important part of EasyEnglish, and one that distinguishes it from the majority of other authoring tools. We have described how EasyEnglish identifies various ambiguous constructions by traversing the ESG parse expressed as a network. The examples given illustrate how the rewriting suggestions supplied by EasyEnglish force an unambiguous interpretation.

References

1. Bernth, A.: Discourse Understanding In Logic. In: Lusk, E. L., Overbeek, R. A. (eds): Procedings of the North American Conference on Logic Programming. MIT Press (1989) 755–771
2. Bernth, A.: Anaphora in Referentially Opaque Contexts. In: R. Studer, R. (ed): Natural Language and Logic: International Scientific Symposium. Lecture Notes in Computer Science, Springer-Verlag, Berlin (1990) 1–25
3. Bernth, A.: EasyEnglish: A Tool for Improving Document Quality. Proceedings of the Fifth Conference on Applied Natural Language Processing. Association for Computational Linguistics (1997) 159–165
4. Bernth, A.: EasyEnglish: Preprocessing for MT. Proceedings of the Second International Workshop On Controlled Language Applications. Carnegie-Mellon University, Pittsburgh (1998) 30-41
5. Fuchs, N. E., Schwitter, R.: Attempto Controlled English (ACE). Proceedings of the First International Workshop On Controlled Language Applications. Katholieke Universiteit Leuven, Belgium (1996) 124–136
6. Huijsen, W.: Controlled Language — An Introduction. Proceedings of the Second International Workshop On Controlled Language Applications, Carnegie-Mellon University, Pittsburgh (1998) 1–15
7. Kumhyr, D., Merrill, C., Spalink, K.: Internationalization and Translatability. Proceedings of the First Conference of the Association for Machine Translation in the Americas. Association for Machine Translation in the Americas, Washington, D.C., USA (1994) 142–148
8. Lederer, R.: Anguished English. Laurel Books, Dell Publishing (1989)
9. Lehmann, H.: Machine Translation for Home and Business Users. Proceedings of MT Summit V. Luxembourg, July 10-13 (1995)
10. Lehtola, A., Tenni, J., Bounsaythip, C.: Controlled Language - An Introduction. Proceedings of the Second International Workshop On Controlled Language Applications, Carnegie-Mellon University, Pittsburgh (1998) 16–29
11. McCord, M. C.: Slot Grammars. Computational Linguistics, Vol. 6. Association for Computational Linguistics (1980) 31–43
12. McCord, M. C.: Design of LMT: A Prolog-based Machine Translation System. Computational Linguistics, Vol. 15. Association for Computational Linguistics (1989) 33–52
13. McCord, M. C.: LMT. Proceedings of MT Summit II. Deutsche Gesellschaft für Dokumentation, Frankfurt (1989) 94–99

14. McCord, M. C.: Slot Grammar: A System for Simpler Construction of Practical Natural Language Grammars. In: R. Studer, R. (ed): Natural Language and Logic: International Scientific Symposium. Lecture Notes in Computer Science, Springer-Verlag, Berlin (1990) 118–145
15. McCord, M. C.: Heuristics for Broad-Coverage Natural Language Parsing. Proceedings of the ARPA Human Language Technology Workshop (1993)
16. McCord, M. C., Bernth, A.: The LMT Transformational System. These proceedings.
17. Wojcik, R. H., Holmback, H.: Getting a Controlled Language Off the Ground at Boeing. Proceedings of the First International Workshop On Controlled Language Applications. Katholieke Universiteit Leuven, Belgium (1996) 22–31

Multiple-Subject Constructions in the Multilingual MT-System CAT2

Munpyo Hong

Institut für angewandte Informationsforschung(IAI) an der Universität des Saarlandes,
Martin-Luther-Straße 14, D-66111 Saarbrücken, Germany
munpyo@iai.uni-sb.de

Abstract. This paper addresses the problems of the so-called 'Multiple-Subject Constructions' in Korean-to-English and Korean-to-German MT. They are often encountered in a dialogue, so that they must be especially taken into account in designing a spoken-language translation system. They do not only raise questions about their syntactic and semantic nature but also cause such problems as structural changes in the MT. The proper treatment of these constructions is also of importance in constructing a multilingual MT-System, because they are one of the major characteristics which distinguish the so-called 'topic-oriented' languages such as Korean and Japanese from the 'subject-oriented' languages such as English and German. In this paper we employ linguistic knowledge such as subcategorization, linear precedence and lexical functions for the analysis and the transfer of the constructions of this sort. Using the proposed methods, the specific transfer-rules for each language pair can be avoided.

1. Introduction

In Korean and Japanese, there are constructions with more than one nominative-NP in a clause. They are referred to as 'Multiple-Subject Constructions(=MSC)' or 'Double-Subject Constructions' in literature. In these languages such grammatical functions as subject and object are marked by case markers assigning nominative and accusative case to the nouns.

Table 1. Some example MSCs in Korean

ku	yeca-ka	ku	namca-ka	cohta.
Det	woman-NOM	Det	man-NOM	like
'The woman likes the man'				

ku	namca-ka	ton-i	manhta
Det	man-NOM	money-NOM	much
'The man has much money'			

ku	aki-ka	son-i	yeypputa
Det	baby-NOM	hand-NOM	beautiful

'The baby has beautiful hands'

ku	ai-ka	mok-i	maluta
Det	child-NOM	throat-NOM	?

'The child is thirsty'

The proper treatment of the constructions is of importance in designing a multilingual MT-System, because they are one of the major characteristics which distinguish the so-called 'topic-oriented' languages such as Korean and Japanese from the so-called 'subject-oriented' languages such as English and German.

In this paper we present the methods for the analysis and the transfer of the constructions of this sort. For the analysis, we divided the constructions into two subcategories. Some of these constructions are lexically-driven, i.e., certain predicates subcategorize for two nominative-NPs. The other sorts are semantically-motivated, namely, some semantic properties of nominative-NPs trigger the constructions.

The MSCs do not only raise the questions of their syntactic and semantic nature, but also cause such problems as structural changes in machine translation(MT). The transfer of the constructions is performed only in the lexical level, so that the complicated structure-changing operations, which make the multilingual machine translation difficult, can be avoided. Because the generation of the target language is triggered only by certain lexical features, the specific structural transfer-rules for each language pair are unnecessary. The proposed algorithm was implemented and tested in the CAT2 multilingual MT-System.[1] Using the proposed methods, we could successfully translate the Korean sentences containing MSCs into English and German. They can also be applied to the Japanese-to-English or Japanese-to-German MT without any serious modification. Before going into the details of the MSCs in Korean, the brief introduction of the CAT2 system will be given in the next section.

2. A Brief Overview of the CAT2 System

The CAT2-System is a transfer-based multilingual MT-System. The only operation in the formalism is unification by which structure-building and structure-transforming rules are applied. It is also stratificational, which means that a constituent structure of the source sentence built by a parser is transformed into the interface structure which is the predicate-argument structure of the source sentence.

To achieve the goal of multilingual translation, the system follows the concept of modularity. It consists of a universal grammar, which is called 'common grammar', language-specific grammars, and lexicons. The universal grammar is a set of princi-

---

[1] CAT2 is both a grammar formalism and an MT-System. More about the CAT2 formalism, cf.[9].

ples and constraints, which, we think, are language-independent, such as head feature principle, subcategorization principle, modifier principle etc. Since every language module has an access to this common grammar, the consistency between language modules can be achieved, and it is simple to add a new language component. Each language module has its specific grammar to which language-specific constraints such as linear precedence belong and the lexicon. Within the CAT2-System English, German, French, Russian, Dutch, Spanish, Arabic, Chinese, and Korean components are available at the moment.

3. Lexically Motivated MSCs

In this chapter three kinds of lexically motivated MSCs are introduced. They are idiomatic expressions, 'psyche'-adjective constructions, and 'exist'-verb constructions.

3.1. Idiomatic Expressions

MSCs are found in some idiomatic expressions. Some examples are shown in table 2.

Table 2. MSCs in the idiomatic expressions

ku	namca-ka	pay-ka	kophuta
Det	man-NOM	stomach-NOM	?
'The man is hungry'			
ku	ai-ka	mok-i	maluta
Det	child-NOM	throat-NOM	?
'The child is thirsty'			

In these examples 'pay-ka kophuta' and 'mok-i maluta' are sentences as themselves and also predicates of the whole sentences taking as their subject the nominative-NP 'ku namca-ka' and 'ku ai-ka'. The idiomatic expressions which allow for MSCs have only two nominative-NPs, i.e., if one more NP with nominative case is attached to the sentence, the sentence will be ungrammatical.

The reason we have to handle these sentences as idiomatic expressions is that they do not show compositionality in building their meanings. At the first example the verb 'kophuta' has no meaning of its own and is only used when combined with the NP 'pay-ka'. The translation pairs in the table 2 also show the lexical gaps between Korean and English. For the analysis of such idiomatic expressions, I suggest an 'Extended Support Verb Construction'. Support Verb Construction(=SVC) is actually composed of a predicative noun which has its own argument structure and a verb which almost lost its original meanings except temporal and aspectual information. The nouns 'pay(=stomach)' and 'mok(=throat)' are not predicative nouns in the traditional sense. However these sentences are similar to SVCs, in that the verbs 'kophuta' and 'maluta' do not have their own meanings and the corresponding translations. Thus I will suggest that the SVC be applied to these expressions, too. The idea of the SVC analysis in CAT2 is that the predicative noun has an argument structure of its own, and the verb shares the argument structure of the predicative noun by the so-called 'argument transfer'.

The noun 'mok(=throat)' takes one argument which bears the 'theme' role and has the nominative case. It also takes a support verb(=*vsup*) 'maluta' as a complement. The verb 'maluta' has no semantic information except temporal and aspectual information {speech=simul, aspect=dur} and inherits the semantic information of the noun by variable binding(SEM). The argument structure of the verb will be unified with that of the predicative noun by the argument transfer(ARG1). The lexical entries for the predicative noun 'mok' and the verb 'maluta' are illustrated in fig.1

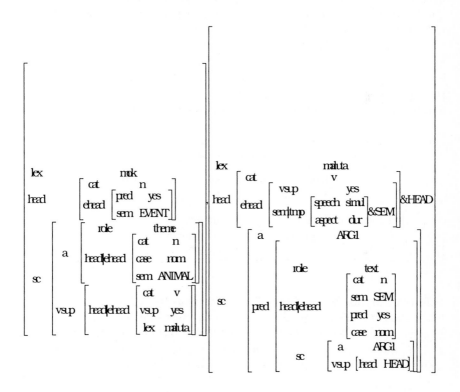

Fig.1. The lexical entries for the predicative noun 'mok' and the verb 'maluta'

For the transfer of SVCs, we only need the predicative noun, discarding the support verb. The semantic information of the verb will not go lost but is stored, as its 'sem' value will be unified with that of the predicative noun by the 'extended head principle' in the CAT2 formalism.[2] The lexical transfer rule for the word 'mok' is illustrated in (1).

$$t\_mok\_thirst=\{lex=mok, head=\{ehead=\{pred=yes\}\}\}.[] \Leftrightarrow \{lex=thirst\}.[] . \quad (1)$$

The English word 'thirst' takes a verb 'be', and it is generated in the intervening stages between the interface structure and the surface structure for the English sentence. The system then generates the correct English translation 'The child is thirsty' for the Korean sentence 'ku aika moki maluta'.

2.2. 'Psyche'-Adjectives and 'Exist'-Verbs

The so-called 'psyche'-adjectives and the 'exist'-verbs also allow for MSCs in Korean. The 'psyche'-adjectives express the emotional state of the subject referent. The 'exist'-verbs are such verbs which can be paraphrased in English and German with 'there are (many) sth.' and 'es gibt (viel) etw.'.

As in the case of the idiomatic expressions, these sentences only allow for two nominative-NPs. These predicates have only two arguments in their argument slot. Therefore if one more argument is attached, it cannot be subcategorized for. However, the problem is how to relate the thematic roles with the appropriate NPs. Because the case information is the only method for it, it is problematic in this case.

Table 3. The possible linkings of the thematic roles into the NPs

silhta(=hate)	<goal,	theme>
	haksayng(student)	swuhak(mathematics)
	*swuhak	haksayng
issta(=have)	<goal,	theme>
	namca(man)	ton(money)
	*ton	namca

In order to link the thematic role to the correct NP we need more than the case information. For this purpose, let us observe the word order in Korean. Korean displays relatively free word order. Except for the fixed word order in a phrase, there are no strict restrictions among the NPs in a sentence. The NPs can be freely scrambled in a sentence without changing the propositional meaning of the sentence.

Table 4. Three possible realization of 'the woman gave the book to the boy' in Korean

ku	yeca-ka	ku	chayk-ul	ku	ai-eykey	cwuessta.
ku	chayk-ul	ku	yeca-ka	ku	ai-eykey	cwuessta
ku	ai-eykey	ku	chayk-ul	ku	yeca-ka	cwuessta.

'The woman gave the book to the boy'

---

[2] About the 'extended head principle' in CAT2, cf.[11]pp.57.

In the table 4 the 3 NPs(ku yeca-ka, ku chayk-ul, ku ai-eykey) can be scrambled without changing the propositional meaning of the sentence('The woman gave the book to the boy')[3], as long as the main verb(=cwuessta) is at the end of the sentence. However, we can observe in the table 5 that MSCs with the 'psyche'-adjectives and the 'exist'-verbs do not allow for this.

Table 5. The relatively strict word order of 'exist'-verbs and the 'psyche'-adjectives

*swuhak-i	ku	haksayng-i	silhta
mathematics-	Det	student-NOM	hate

*ku	chayk-i	ku	namca-ka	issta.
Det	book-NOM	Det	man-	have

The scrambling of the NPs in these sentences is not allowed in contrast to other Korean sentences. This word order constraint can be formulated by f-rules.[4] We introduced a feature 'psy' and 'exist' in order to distinguish the 'psyche'-adjectives and the 'exist'-verbs from the other predicative adjectives and the verbs. The 'psyche'-adjectives have the AV-pair {head={ehead={psy=yes}}} and the 'exist'-verbs {head={ehead={exist=yes}}} in their lexical entries. The other verbs are assigned {head={ehead={psy=no}}} and {head={ehead= {exist=no}}} as a default value by the f-rules (2) and (3).

$$\text{f\_head\_ehead\_psy\_no}==\{head=\{cat=v,ehead=\{psy=no\}\}\}.[] . \tag{2}$$

$$\text{f\_head\_ehead\_exist\_no}==\{head=\{cat=v,ehead=\{exist=no\}\}\}.[] . \tag{3}$$

These f-rules are applied to the lexical items, whilst the default values are assigned to them. The lexical entry for the word 'silhta(=hate)' is illustrated in Fig.2[5].

---

[3] The propositional meaning of a sentence is the meaning only built by its subparts, i.e., without the discourse information such as topics and comments.

[4] The f-rules in CAT2 formalism perform two functions; they can assign default values to the lexical entries, and they can also constrain the object built by the b-rules.

[5] For the ease of implementation, I classified the 'psyche'-adjectives as stative verbs.

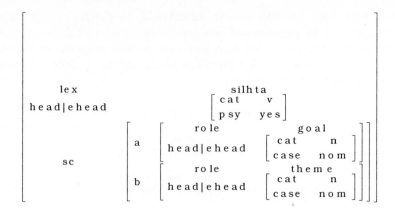

Fig. 2.: The lexical entry of 'silhta(=hate)'

The lexical entries of the 'exist'-verbs look similar to those of the 'psyche'-adjectives, except that they have 'exist=yes' instead of 'psy=yes'. To restrict the mapping between the second nominative-NP and the 'goal' role, a word order constraint was designed with an f-rule in the CAT2 formalism.

$$f\_psy\_exist\_goal\_theme=\{\}.[[\{role=goal,head=\{ehead=\{cat=n,case=nom\}\}\}>> \{head=nil\},\{head=\{ehead=\{cat=v,(\{psy=yes\};\{exist=yes\})\}\}\}]]. \quad (4)$$

This 'f_psy_exist_goal_theme' rule says that if a nominative-NP with the role 'goal' is followed by a 'psyche'-adjective or an 'exist'-verb, it will inevitably fail. It filters out such ungrammatical sentences as in the table 5.

The 'psyche'-adjectives do not pose serious problems in translation. However, some problems arise in translating 'exist'-verbs.

Table 6. The structural changes between Korean and English in the case of an 'exist'-verb 'manhta'

ku	haksayng-i	chinkwu-ka	manhta.
Det	Student-NOM	friend-NOM	have many
'The student has many friends'			
ku	kyoswu-ka	chayk-i	manhta.
Det	Professor-NOM	book-NOM	have many
'The professor has many books'			

As we can see in the table 6, the Korean verb 'manhta' is expressed by a verb(=have) and a modifier of the argument of the verb(=many) in English. Such translational divergencies in MT are treated in most transfer-based approaches by the complex transfer rules. But the drawback of such an approach is well-known[6], i.e., if some complex structural changes are interwoven, the rules often fail to be applied to. To avoid these problems, we try to solve it on the lexical level, maintaining the interface structure of the source language. We assume that the second NP-complement of the verb 'manhta(=have many)' is plural, i.e., if it is a countable noun, its number value will be plural. Thus we encoded the information that the second complement-NP has the AV pair {head={ehead= {sem={bound=many}}}} in the lexical entry of the predicate.

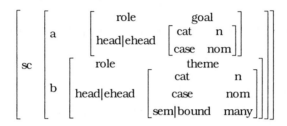

Fig. 3. The subcategorization frame of 'manhta'

The interface structure of the second Korean sentence in the table 6 will then be transferred to the English interface structure without any structural changes as illustrated in the Fig. 4.

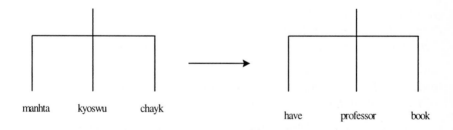

Fig. 4. The Korean and English Interface-Structures for 'The professor has many books'

The AV pair {head={ehead={sem={bound=many}}}} of the second argument, 'book', will trigger the generation of the adjective 'many' before the noun in the generation phase as in the Fig. 5.

---

[6] cf. [4] pp.25.

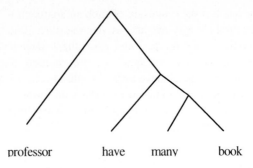

Fig. 5. The constituent structure of 'The professor has many books'

4. Semantically Motivated MSCs

Until now we have observed MSCs triggered by the subcategorization of the predicates. These predicates were either idiomatic predicates or the predicates with the special features, [+psy] or [+exist]. They allow for only two nominative-NPs and no more. But there are other MSCs which do not belong to either group.

Table 7. Some examples of the semantically motivated MSCs

peter-ka	emeni-ka	celmta.			
Peter-NOM	mother-NOM	young.			
'Peter's mother is young'					
hankwuk-i	namca-ka	swumyeng-i	ccalpta		
Korea-NOM	men-NOM	life-span-NOM	short.		
'It is in the case of Korea that men are short-life-span'					
ku	tayhakkyo-ka	tokmwunkwa-ka	2 haknyen-i	yehaksayng-i	yeypputa.
DET	university-NOM	department of German-NOM	sophomore-NOM	female students-NOM	beautiful.
'It is in the German department of the university that the female sophomore students are beautiful'					

These constructions deviate from the lexically driven constructions, in that they do allow for more than two nominative-NPs. Furthermore there do not seem to be common semantic features among the predicates, except that they are all adjectives.

There has been some research about this construction, especially by the GB grammarians. Fukui argued using Japanese examples that in such constructions the NP is adjuncted to the so-called X-bar node and thus a theoretically unlimited number of NPs can be attached to the sentence.[7] However, this argument did not take into account of the semantic aspect of the construction. Because in the case of the first and the second sentence of the table 7, for example, if one more nominative-NP is attached to, it will be ungrammatical as shown in the table 8.

Table 8. Examples of semantically over-saturated sentences

* hans-ka	peter-ka	emeni-ka	celmta.	
Hans-NOM	peter-NOM	mother-NOM	young	
* ilpon-i	hankwuk-i	namca-ka	swumyeng-i	ccalpta
Japan-NOM	Korea-NOM	men-NOM	life-span-	short

Shin pointed out an interesting aspect of this construction in the framework of Montague semantics.[8] According to him, the reason these predicates allow for MSCs is that the type of subject is $<e,t>$, i.e., that of a common noun in the type-theoretical terminology. So it cannot be combined with a predicative adjective, the type of which is also $<e,t>$, so that such sentences cannot have a truth value. To avoid this, the language needs some other devices to restrict the denotation of the NP, the subject of the predicate. Thus if the first sentence table 7 did not have the NP 'peter-ka', the sentence would be ungrammatical, because the subject NP 'emeni' denotes the set of entities which are mothers of someone in a given model.

Table 9. A semantically incomplete sentence

*emeni-ka	celmta.[9]
Mother-NOM	young

The first nominative-NP in the sentence picks up a certain entity in the set of 'emeny(mother)', i.e., 'Peter's mother' to assign the property of 'being young'. It is then a semantically saturated sentence. Thus no NP can be attached to it.

At this point two questions must be answered. Firstly, when can nominative-NPs be attached? Secondly, what is the limit to the number of nominative-NPs which can be attached? My answer to the first question is that the nominative-NP can be attached when the referentiality of the subject NP is not definite or deictically not fixed. As is well known, in Korean and Japanese the existence of a determiner in an NP is not obligatory. In most cases the NPs in these languages are just bare nouns with case markers. The number and the referentiality of these NPs are often deduced from a context. The answer to the second question follows automatically, i.e., if the

---

[7] cf. [5].

[8] cf. [10].

[9] In this paper I do not treat the generic reading of the sentences. Therefore the possible generic reading of the example in table 9, 'every mother in this world is young without exception', is excluded.

referentiality of the subject is definite or deictically fixed, no more nominative-NPs can be attached. In this construction the right most nominative-NP, i.e., the NP which is at the very left of the predicate will be the subject of the sentence, and the others will be only the specifiers of this subject, semantically restricting the denotation of the subject NP. The algorithm we adopt for the analysis of the semantically driven MSC is given in the following.

The algorithm for the analysis of the semantically driven MSCs

In $S_n = NP_{Nom1}$, NP_{Nom2}, $\ldots$, NP_{Nomi-1}, NP_{Nomi}, AP

(NP_{Nomi} abbreviates a nominative-NP in 'i'th position in a sentence)

step 1: if NP_{Nomi} is definite or deictically fixed, then go to step 3

otherwise go to step 2

step 2: set i=i-1, and if i >=1, then go to step 1

otherwise fail[10]

step 3: if i=1, then succeed

otherwise fail

To determine the referentiality and the number of an NP in Korean and Japanese automatically is also a very difficult problem, which can not be handled here.[11] In this paper we simply assume that the referentiality of an NP in Korean is definite in case i) the NP is composed of a noun and a definite article or ii) the NP is a proper name like 'John' or 'ilpon(=Japan)'.

In order to express the underlying semantic relations between the nominative-NPs and to trigger the generation of the tartget expressions, we adopt lexical functions such as 'POSSESS', 'LOCATION' and so on. The semantic relation between these two NPs in the first example of table 7, 'Peter' and 'emeni(=mother)', is that of 'possession' in a broad sense. Therefore the underlying semantic structure of the sentence could be expressed like fig.6.

---

[10] If the rule fails to be applied to, the rescue rules in the CAT2-System are activated for the robustic processing.

[11] About determining the countability and referentiality of an NP in Japanese, cf. [1].

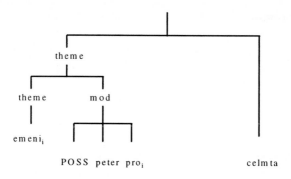

Fig. 6. The interface structure of 'Peter's mother is young'

'POSS' is a lexical function which expresses the 'possessor-possessed' relationship. The idea behind this strategy is that in every language there are some words or morphemes expressing the 'possession' relationship. Therefore it is unnecessary to say explicitly that a word 'A' expressing 'possession' relationship in one language is translated to the word 'B' in another language. What must be said is only that the 'possession'-relationship is transferred to other languages without changes. The Korean interface structure in the fig. 6 will be transferred to the English interface structure without any structural changes. Then the generation module of the target language can generate the corresponding word for the concept. In our system, the English morpheme '-s' is generated for the lexical function 'POSS'.

5. Conclusion

In this paper we showed how MSCs can be handled for the multilingual machine translations. It was proposed that the linguistic knowledge such as subcategorization, the 'extended support verb construction', word orders, lexical functions and the referentiality of nominal phrases can be usefully employed in analyzing and translating the MSC.

Determining the countability and referentiality of an NP in Korean and Japanese automatically is a difficult problem, which is very important for the correct analysis of MSCs. To determine the semantic relations between nominative-NPs is also a very complicated task, for the purpose of which, not only the linguistic approaches but also the statistic methods or example-based approaches can be pursued. They should be done along with the researches about MSCs in future works.

Acknowledgement

I am very grateful to Prof. Dr. Johann Haller, Dr. Oliver Streiter and Catherine Pease at IAI for their valuable comments on the first version of this paper.

References

1. Francis Bond, Kentaro Ogura and Satoru Ikehara(1994): Countability and Number in Japanese to English Machine Translation, Proceedings Vol.1, *COLING 94,* pp.32-38
2. Chang, Seok-Jin(1993): *Information-based Korean Grammar(in Korean)*, Language & Information Research Assn. Seoul
3. Choi, Sung-Kwon(1995): Unifikationsbasierte Maschinelle Übersetzung mit Koreanisch als Quellsprache, *IAI Working Papers Nr.34*, Saarbrücken, Germany
4. Dorr, Bonnie Jean(1993): *Machine Translation: A View from the Lexicon*, The MIT Press
5. Fukui, N(1988): Deriving the differences between English and Japanese: A case study in parametric Syntax, *English Linguistics 5*.
6. Kiss, Katalin E.(1981): On the Japanese 'double subject' construction, *The linguistic review vol.1. NO.2*
7. Brigitte Krenn, Gregor Erbach(1994): Idioms and Support Verb Construction: *German in Head-Driven Phrase Structure Grammar*, pp.365-395, CSLI
8. Mesli, Nadia(1991): Funktionsverbgefüge in der maschinellen Analyse und Übersetzung: Linguistische Beschreibung und Implementierung in CAT2 Formalismus. *Eurotra-D Working Papers 19*. IAI, Saarbrücken, Germany
9. Sharp, Randall(1994): CAT2 Reference Manual Version 3.6, *IAI Working Papers Nr.27*, Saarbrücken, Germany
10. Shin, Soo-Song(1991): *Introduction to unification-based grammar formalism - Lexical Functional Grammar(in Korean)*, Hanshin, Seoul
11. Streiter, Oliver(1996): *Linguistic Modelling for Multilingual Machine Translation*, Shaker Verlag, Germany
12. Oliver Streiter, Randall Sharp, Johann Haller, Catherine Pease, and Antje-Schmidt Wigger(1994): Aspects of a unification based multilingual system for computer-aided translation. In *Proceedings of Avignon 1994, 14th International Conference*.

A Multilingual Procedure for Dictionary-Based Sentence Alignment

Adam Meyers[1], Michiko Kosaka[2] and Ralph Grishman[1]

[1] New York University, NY, NY 10003, USA,
meyers@cs.nyu.edu, grishman@cs.nyu.edu,
[2] Monmouth University, West Long Branch, N.J. 07764, USA
kosaka@monmouth.edu

Abstract. This paper describes a sentence alignment technique based on a machine readable dictionary. Alignment takes place in a single pass through the text, based on the scores of matches between pairs of source and target sentences. Pairings consisting of sets of matches are evaluated using a version of the Gale-Shapely solution to the stable marriage problem. An algorithm is described which can handle N-to-1 (or 1-to-N) matches, for $n \geq 0$, i.e., deletions, 1-to-1 (including scrambling), and 1-to-many matches. A simple frequency based method for acquiring supplemental dictionary entries is also discussed. We achieve high quality alignments using available bilingual dictionaries, both for closely related language pairs (Spanish/English) and more distantly related pairs (Japanese/English).

1 Introduction

Obtaining aligned pairs of source and target language sentences is an important precursor to further work in many natural language processing applications, including corpus-trained (e.g. [9], [12], [17], [1], [8], [3], [20], [21]) and example-based (e.g. [22], [23], [6]) approaches to machine translation. Human translators may also use aligned bitexts to aid them in translating new similar texts. Even if an identical sentence has not been previously translated, translations of similar sentences may be used as models.

Manual alignment unduly constrains the quantity of aligned bitext which can be obtained given limited time and resources. As a result several automatic techniques have been presented in the literature. One of the drawbacks of automated approaches is that they are error prone. Although the errors are low compared to many other computational tasks, there is room for improvement. A high level of performance is desirable since errors in sentence alignment will cause further errors in systems that use the aligned text.

Alignment procedures vary in their ability to handle different types of correspondences between sentences in the source text and sentences in the target text including 1-to-N correspondences, deletions, scramblings and N-to-N correspondences. Virtually all approaches can handle cases where more than one sentence in one text corresponds to a single sentence in the other (1-to-N or N-to-1 correspondences) or in which a sentence in one text corresponds to no sentences in the other text (deletions). Scramblings are cases in which corresponding sentences appear in different orders in the 2 texts, e.g. source sentence 1 corresponds to target sentence 2 and source sentence 2 corresponds to target sentence 1. There were many scramblings in the data used for this paper (as well as the data used for [5]). In principle, the [13], [11] strategies cannot handle scramblings, whereas other strategies can (including ours). It is also logically possible for sets of more than one source sentence to correspond to sets of more than one target sentence (N-to-N correspondences). We are not aware of any papers reporting how they handle these cases, and have not encountered any of these cases in our data. Our approach does not handle these, but others can (e.g. [11]).

Previously reported alignment procedures score how well sets of source and target sentences "match" based on sentence length ([2], [7]), automatically acquired lexical information ([13], [4]), and other sources. [24] and [11] combine automatically acquired lexical information with information from an on-line dictionary. Still other work aligns texts at the word level ([18] [19], [14]). In this paper, we propose an efficient and accurate alignment procedure based primarily on on-line dictionary information.[1] Our procedure handles N-to-1/1-to-N pairings of sentences, scramblings and deletions with very high accuracy. We achieve over 97% precision and 93% recall for alignment of Spanish/English Microsoft help text and are currently extending our system to Japanese/English, where so far we have achieved 90% precision and 75% recall. The disparity between these two results seems to be a function of (1) the complexity of the bitexts; (2) the degree of equivalence of the texts; (3) the syntactic similarities between the source and target languages; and (4) the availability of good translation dictionaries.

We propose a sentence alignment algorithm which can take into account all N-to-1 and 1-to-N matches, where n ranges from 0 (the unaligned case) to some constant (in the texts we looked at, n is never greater than 3). In the next two sections, we will describe two versions of an algorithm for traversing the text and choosing alignments based on a score. The first algorithm only considers 1-to-1 matches and non-matched sentences (1-to-0/0-to-1), whereas the second includes N-to-1 and 1-to-N matches as well (N-to-N matches are not considered). These procedures are independent of the scoring system used. Our scoring procedure is described in Section 4. These procedures assume paragraph aligned texts, with clearly-marked sentence boundaries and without large (ten sentence long) deletions in either text of the bitext.

As pointed out in [11], methods which do not use machine readable dictionaries do not work well with bitexts of unrelated languages, e.g., English/Japanese. This paper shows one way in which available commercial and public domain bilingual dictionaries can be used for text alignment.

---

[1] We do not currently use any n-gram statistics, part of speech tags, or any information other than on-line dictionaries, hand-coded morphological rules and in some cases acquired dictionary entries.

2   The 1-to-1 algorithm

There are one million possible 1-to-1 correspondences in a bitext of one thousand source/target sentence pairs. In practice, however, we do not consider all of these correspondences; it is most unlikely that the first sentence of the source text matches the last sentence of the target text. We have found that considering correspondences within a moving window of ten source and ten target sentences is quite reasonable for the texts we have studied (Spanish/English Microsoft help texts and Japanese/English FOCUS programming manuals). Corresponding sentences are not always in the same sequence in both texts, but we have yet to find cases where they are more than nine sentences apart. In other words, we have not found cases where the $X th$ source language sentence corresponds to the $Y th$ target language sentence and the $X + 1st$ source language sentence corresponds to the Y+Nth target language sentence where $N > 9$. For cases where blocks of aligned text are separated by intervening blocks of 10 or more unaligned sentences, other techniques (such as paragraph alignment) may be used to bring these blocks into alignment, and then the techniques described here can be used to align sentences within corresponding blocks of text.

Our window contains ten source sentences and ten target sentences (initially, the first ten sentences from each file). Call these sentences $S1, \ldots, S10$ and $T1, \ldots, T10$. We fill a 10×10 array with similarity scores (Section 4) that model how well each source sentence matches each target sentence in the window. Using these scores, we determine (in a manner to be described shortly) the best pairing of sentences within this window. In this pairing, either $S1$ and $T1$ match each other, $S1$ and $T1$ match other sentences, or one or both are unaligned. These alignments or nonalignments for $S1$ and $T1$ are recorded. We then delete from the window $S1$, $T1$, and any other sentences with which they aligned, extend the window so that it again contains ten sentences from each file, and repeat the process until the bitext is exhausted.

At each step, our goal is to find the best matches for $S1$ and $T1$. Due to the interdependence of matches, it is not sufficient to select the highest scoring matches among $\{ (S1, T1), (S1, T2) \ldots, (S1, T10) \}$ and among $\{ (S1, T1), (S2, T1), \ldots, (S10, T1) \}$. We must choose the matches for $S1$ and $T1$ that are part of the BEST legal pairing among all sentences in the window, where a pairing is legal only if none of its members are in conflict, e.g., source sentence 1 cannot match target sentence 1 if source sentence 5 matches target sentence 1. The quality of a pairing is determined by the degree to which each source and target sentence is matched with its most preferred partner (based on the similarity scores). We attempt to optimize our choice of pairing based on a version of the Gale-Shapley (cf. [10]) algorithm for solving the stable marriage problem.[2]

Viewed as a version of the stable marriage problem, finding the best pairing of source and target sentences is the same problem as matching a set of potential

---

[2] We also experimented with a definition of best pairing in which the pairing with the highest combined score was assume to be the best pairing. Although the Gale-Shapley based solution produced the best result in some cases, the results between these two approaches were very close.

project bilingual dictionary. Since the bilingual dictionaries only contain the base forms, we must generate all possible base forms for each word in the text before using the bilingual dictionary. For the English, we use the (inflectional) morphological information in COMLEX Syntax ([16]) plus a rule to remove "s" or "es" suffixes from unknown words. For the Spanish, we use some hand-coded rules to remove inflectional endings, add on stem endings and account for the related phonological changes.[8] Since our text contained symbols and mathematical formulas, we also extracted words from these formulas for purposes of matching and allowed a pair of words to match if they were identical. In order to minimize lexical and morphological look up, we generate and update a set of ten hash tables corresponding to the ten source sentences we are considering. Each hash table contains the full set of possible target translations and the number of possible instances of each (so that 1 instance of *el* will match at most 1 instance of *the*, and not 2.).

5 The Distance Parameter

Allowing a window of ten sentences has two effects: (1) it limits the relative difference between a source and target sentence: if the Xth source language sentence corresponds to the Yth target language sentence, the $Xth + 1$ source language sentence may only correspond to the $Yth + K$ target language where $K < N$; and (2) it determines which sentence matches may be part of the maximal pairing. Since a pairing may include matches between sentences within the window of 10, an error may result if source sentence $S1$ seems to match well against target sentence $T10$, even though source sentence $S11$ is a better match for $T10$. For this reason we have parameterized the maximum distance between the source and target in a match (effect 1). Experimentally, the values 6 and 7 produced the best results for our Spanish/English bitext. In the Spanish/English results, we report the results with the distance parameter set to 6. This means that for a given 1-to-1 match (S, T) to be valid the value of $|S - T|$ must not exceed 6. However, the window of 10 allows the 10th source sentence to compete with the 1st source sentence for a match with the 7th target sentence.

6 Lexical Acquisition

We conducted a series of experiments in which we automatically supplemented our bilingual dictionaries. For each pair of sentences which the program aligns, we extract the sets of unaligned source and target words excluding closed class words and compute the product of these sets: a set of source/target word pairs and potential entries in our supplemental bilingual dictionary.[9] Counts of members

---

[8] We purposely overgenerate possible stems, usually producing correct results and nonsense, but no false hits. Therefore nothing is lost by just going for coverage.

[9] It is assumed that exhaustive translations of closed class words already exist in our dictionary and further acquisition would constitute noise.

of each of these 3 sets are kept for the entire alignment. After the bitext is completely aligned, the bilingual dictionary entries are chosen from the set of source/target word pairs (S, W) according to the following criteria: (1) The frequencies of S and W must exceed a threshold (currently 1); (2) The ratio $R_{S,W} = Freq_{(S,W)}/(Min(Freq_S, Freq_W) + 1)$ exceeds a threshold (currently .5), where $Freq_X$ is the frequency of X. If S appears twice, T appears 3 times, and they co-occur twice, then $R_{S,W} = 2/3$.[10] This procedure was used multiple times on the same bitext. Each iteration which enriched the dictionary usually improved the quality of subsequent alignments.

Our acquisition procedure is similar to that of [11], which uses the [13] algorithm to enhance their bilingual dictionary. However, there are two main differences: (1) We acquire dictionary entries from pairs of aligned sentences, whereas they consider pairs of words in sets of candidate sentences, i.e., if the [13] algorithm determines that source sentence $S1$ aligns with some target sentence in the set $\{T1, T2, T3\}$, then each word in these three target sentences is a potential translation for some word in $S1$; and (2) They consider the both $Freq_S$ and $Freq_W$ in determining whether a word pair is added to the bilingual dictionary, whereas we only consider $Min(Freq_S, Freq_W)$.

7 Results

7.1 Spanish/English Microsoft Help Text

We hand-aligned a subset of the Microsoft Excel bitext which included 1341 lines of Spanish text and 1350 lines of English.[11] This was our training data (we debugged and revised the system while examining these data very carefully). Later, we hand-aligned an additional 181 lines of Spanish text with 184 lines of English for test purposes.

On a Quantex PC running Linux, with a 200 MHz Pentium with MMX and 80 megabytes of RAM, the system takes 2 minutes and 49 seconds (real time) to run these the training data using the 1-to-1 algorithm (.125 seconds/sentence) and 6 minutes 18 seconds to run using the 2-to-1 algorithm (.28 seconds/sentence).

The system's performance on the test and training data is given in Tables 1 and 2. MRD refers to our machine readable dictionaries (Collins and Activa). Supp refers to a supplemental dictionary created by looking at pairs of sentences which the system considered unaligned in the earlier runs to determine if additional dictionary entries would help alignment (notice that most of the gains are in recall). Table 1 gives the results of applying our 1-to-1 algorithm and Table 2 gives the results of our N-to-1 algorithm with $N_{MAX} = 2$. Precision and Recall scores are calculated separately for 1-to-1 and 2-to-1/1-to-2 matches.[12]

---

[10] The (+ 1) in the ratio has the effect of preferring pairs with higher frequency.

[11] We have a system of hand tags to indicate scramblings, deletions and N-to-1/1-to-N matches for any value of N. All near translations were assumed to align.

[12] We decided that precision/recall statistics for unaligned sentences were irrelevant. The training corpus contained 7 unaligned source and 13 unaligned target sentences. The test corpus contained 5 unaligned source and 12 unaligned target sentences.

No partial credit is given if the program produces a 1-to-1 match that overlaps a correct 2-to-1 match or if the program produces a 2-to-1 match that overlaps a correct 1-to-1 match (a match $\{X1, Y1\}$ overlaps a match $\{(X1, X2), Y1\}$ and vice versa). For some applications (cf. [15]) such matches would not be considered completely wrong. However, for MT systems which acquire transfer rules on the basis of aligned text, these partial matches are noise.

	1-to-1 Precision	1-to-1 Recall
The Training Corpus		
MRD Only	99.4%	93.3%
MRD Plus Supp	99.5%	99.4%
The Test Corpus		
MRD Only	94.6%	94.6%
MRD Plus Supp	95.7%	96.8%

Table 1. Performance of the 1-to-1 Algorithm for English

	1-to-1 Precision	1-to-1 Recall	2-to-1 Precision	2-to-1 Recall
The Training Corpus				
MRD Only	99.8%	92.8%	0.0%	0.0%
				0 spurious
MRD Plus Supp	99.8%	99.4%	100%	100%
The Test Corpus				
MRD Only	97.7%	91.4%	0%	0%
				0 spurious
MRD Plus Supp	96.6%	91.4%	0.0%	0.0%
				4 spurious

Table 2. Performance of the 2-to-1 Algorithm for English

One of the crucial features of the success of this approach is the availability of an adequate bilingual dictionary. We conducted a further experiment in which we eliminated The Collins dictionary from our system.[13] Then we used our acquisition algorithm (Section 6) to improve these results. As shown in Table 3, the initial results were unexpectedly good,[14] but the performance after acquisition is about as good as the performance using the Collins dictionary. As a further experiment, we edited the acquired dictionary by hand. The results

---

[13] The licensing restrictions of the Collins dictionary limit its use for, e.g., commercial and public domain applications.

[14] The 2-to-1 algorithm was used with the supplemental dictionary.

changed marginally. This suggests that the noise produced from improper lexical acquisition had a minimal effect on the quality of alignment.

	1-to-1 Precision	1-to-1 Recall	2-to-1 Precision	2-to-1 Recall
The Training Corpus				
Initial	99.5%	97.4%	33.3%	80.0%
Post-Acquisition	99.7%	99.1%	57.1%	80.0%
Edited Acquired Dictionary	99.8%	99.4%	100%	100%
The Test Corpus				
Initial	97.7%	91.4%	25.0%	100.0%
Post-Acquisition	97.8%	93.5%	20.0%	100.0%
Edited Acquired Dictionary	96.6%	91.4%	0.0%	0.0% 4 spurious

Table 3. English Results without the Collins Dictionary

7.2 The Japanese/English System

We first segmented the Japanese FOCUS Manual using Kyoto University's Juman version 3.3. We used the segmentation only and ignored the part-of-speech tags. Thus, we did not exclude any word classes (such as the closed class) from alignment. The alignment was based on all the words of the sentences. We hand-aligned Chapters 1, 3 and 4 for use in evaluation. We ran our alignment experiments over the same text. Table 4 shows the size of each chapter in terms of the number of sentences. The dictionary was constructed out of EDR bilingual dictionary and Kyoto University's MU dictionary. The MU dictionary did not help in adding more entries, but provided additional translations to a few existing entries. Similar to the Spanish experiment we added 30 source word/target word pairs that were particular to these texts. The coverage of the words of the text was approximately 50%. Since the translations came from these dictionaries, it could not be guaranteed that the equivalencies were realized in bitexts.

The Number of Sentences		
	Japanese	English
Chapter 1	38	44
Chapter 3	82	88
Chapter 4	128	125

Table 4. Size of FOCUS Text by Chapter

	1-to-1 Precision	1-to-1 Recall	2-to-1 Precision	2-to-1 Recall
Initial	88.9%	65.5%	14.3%	28.6%
Post-Acquisition	90.9%	72.3%	13.6%	42.9%
Edited Acquired Dictionary	89.5%	66.0%	15.8%	42.9%
Post-Acquisition	91.1%	74.3%	13.0%	42.9%

Table 5. Performance of the Japanese Alignment System

Table 5 summarizes the performance of the alignment over the whole corpus. The experiment was run first with only the bilingual dictionary (initial); second, with the automatic lexical acquisition (Post-Acquisition), third, after editing this acquired dictionary (Edited Acquired Dictionary); and fourth, after another automatic lexical acquisition over this correction. The automatic lexical acquisition excluded the closed class from both languages.

While it is not very meaningful to compare results of one project with those of the others because of the different texts, different dictionaries, different amounts of acquired dictionary information, etc., for a lack of better criteria, we present the performance differences with [11]. Comparing the results of Table 5 with [11] on the dictionary experiment alone, we find our precision of 89.0% vs. their precision of 80.2%, and our recall of 66.5% vs. their recall of 74.3%.[15] Recall numbers typically represent the degree of the lexical coverage of the dictionary relative to the texts in question . Given the precision and recall numbers, our initial dictionary probably did not have as good a coverage as [11].

The automatic lexical acquisition did improve the results as shown in Table 5; 11.2% points in precision and over 9.2% points in recall. These improvements are not as dramatic as those reported in [11]. Their precision and recall with the edited acquired dictionary are 93.8% and 95.0%, respectively. They improved in precision by 13.8% and in recall by 20.7%.

We saw no improvements (and no degradation) when nominalizations and adjective/adverb alternations were included in the alignment.

Our alignment procedure seems to do very well for both Japanese and Spanish, even with the bilingual dictionaries that are not very robust. In the case of Spanish, supplementing the Activa dictionary with an automatically acquired dictionary is sufficient to produce a very high-performance alignment system. In the case of Japanese, an existing automatic lexical acquisition system does not seem to produce the results that match those for Spanish.

8 Concluding Remarks

We obtained over 97% precision and 93% recall for aligning Spanish/English Microsoft Excel help text and over 90% precision/75% recall for aligning Japanese/English FOCUS manual text. The differences between our

---

[15] We computed their weighted averages for 349 sentences over 3 types of texts.

Spanish/English and Japanese/English systems are: (1) the particular Japanese/English texts (programming manuals) were more complex than the particular Spanish/English texts (help text); (2) the Spanish/English dictionary was more comprehensive than the Japanese/English dictionary. This point is bolstered by our comparison of our most comprehensive Spanish/English dictionary (which includes Collins) with our less comprehensive Spanish/English dictionary; and (3) Spanish and English are more closely related than Japanese and English.

References

1. Peter Brown, Stephen A. Della Pietra, Vincent J. Della Pietra, and Robert L. Mercer. The Mathematics of Statistical Machine Translation: Parameter Estimation. *Computational Linguistics*, 19:263–312, 1993.
2. Peter F. Brown, Jennifer C. Lai, and Robert L. Mercer. Aligning Sentences in Parallel Corpora. In *ACL91*, 1991.
3. Ralf D. Brown. Example-Based Machine Translation in the Pangloss System. In *COLING96*, pages 169–174, 1996.
4. S. Chen. Aligning Sentences in Bilingual Corpora using lexical information. In *ACL93*, pages 9–16, 1993.
5. Nigel Collier, Hideki Hirakawa, and Akira Kumano. An Experiment in Hybrid Dictionary and Statistical Sentece Alignment. In *COLING-ACL98*, 1998.
6. Osamu Furuse and Hitoshi Iida. Constituent Boundary Parsing for Example-Based Machine Translation. In *COLING94*, 1994.
7. William A. Gale and Kenneth W. Church. A Program for Aligning Sentences in Bilingual Corpora. *Computational Linguistics*, 19:75–102, 1993.
8. Ralph Grishman. Iterative Alignment of Syntactic Structures for a Bilingual Corpus. In *WVLC94*, Tokyo, 1994.
9. Ralph Grishman and Michiko Kosaka. Combining Rationalist and Empiricist Approaches to Machine Translation. In *TMI92*, Tokyo, 1992.
10. Dan Gusfield and Robert W. Irving. *The Stable Marriage Problem: Structure and Algorithms*. The MIT Press, Cambridge, 1989.
11. Masahiko Haruno and Takefumi Yamazaki. High-performance Bilingual Text Alignment Using Statistical and Dictionary Information. *Natural Language Engineering*, 3:1–14, 1997.
12. Hiroyuki Kaji, Yuuko Kida, and Yasututsugo Morimoto. Learning Translation Templates from Bilingual Text. In *COLING92*, 1992.
13. Martin Kay and Martin Röscheisen. Text-Translation Alignment. *Computational Linguistics*, 19:121–142, 1993.
14. Sue J. Ker and Jason S. Chang. A Class-based Approach to Word Alignment. *Computational Linguistics*, 23:313–343, 1997.
15. Philippe Langlais, Michel Simard, and Jean Véronis. Methods and Practical Issues in Evaluating Alignment Techniques. In *COLING-ACL98*, 1998.
16. Catherine Macleod, Ralph Grishman, and Adam Meyers. COMLEX Syntax: A Large Syntactic Dictionary for Natural Language Processing. *Computers and the Humanities*, forthcoming.
17. Y. Matsumoto, H. Ishimoto, T. Utsuro, and M. Nagao. Structural Matching of Parallel Texts. In *ACL93*, 1993.

18. I. Dan Melamed. A Geometric Approach to Mapping Bitext Correspondence. In *Proceedings of the First Conference on Empirical Methods in Natural Language Processing*, 1996.
19. I. Dan Melamed. A Portable Algorithm for Mapping Bitext Correspondence. In *ACL97*, 1997.
20. Adam Meyers, Roman Yangarber, and Ralph Grishman. Alignment of Shared Forests for Bilingual Corpora. In *COLING 1996*, pages 460–465, 1996.
21. Adam Meyers, Roman Yangarber, Ralph Grishman, Catherine Macleod, and Antonio Moreno-Sandoval. Deriving Transfer Rules from Dominance-Preserving Alignments. In *COLING-ACL98*, 1998.
22. Makao Nagao. A Framework of a Mechanical Translation between Japanese and English by Analogy Principle. In Alick Elithorn and Ranan Banerji, editors, *Artificial and Human Intelligence*. Elsevier Science Publishers B.V., Amsterdam, 1984.
23. Satoshi Sato and Makoto Nagao. Toward Memory-based Translation. In *COLING90*, volume 3, pages 247–252, 1990.
24. Takehito Utsuro, Hiroshi Ikeda, Masaya Yumane, Yuji Matsumoto, and Makoto Nagao. Bilingual Text Matching using Bilingual Dictionary and Statistics. In *COLING94*, pages 1076–1082, 1994.

Taxonomy and Lexical Semantics –
From the Perspective of Machine Readable Dictionary

Jason S. Chang[1], Sue J. Ker[2], and Mathis H. Chen[3]

[1] Department of Computer Science, National Tsing Hua University
Hsinchu 30043, Taiwan
jschang@cs.nthu.edu.tw
[2] Department of Computer Science, Soochow University
Taipei 100,Taiwan
ksj@volans.cis.scu.edu.tw
[3] Institute of Information Science, Academia Sinica
Nankang, Taipei 11529, Taiwan
mathis@iis.sinica.edu.tw

Abstract. Machine-readable dictionaries have been regarded as a rich knowledge source from which various relations in lexical semantics can be effectively extracted. These semantic relations have been found useful for supporting a wide range of natural language processing tasks, from information retrieval to interpretation of noun sequences, and to resolution of prepositional phrase attachment. In this paper, we address issues related to problems in building a semantic hierarchy from machine-readable dictionaries: genus disambiguation, discovery of covert categories, and bilingual taxonomy. In addressing these issues, we will discuss the limiting factors in dictionary definitions and ways of eradicating these problems. We will also compare the taxonomy extracted in this way from a typical MRD and that of the WordNet. We argue that although the MRD-derived taxonomy is considerably flatter than the WordNet, it nevertheless provides a functional core for a variety of semantic relations and inferences which is vital in natural language processing.

1 Introduction

Machine-readable dictionaries (MRD) have been regarded as a rich knowledge source from which various relations in lexical semantics can be effectively extracted. Semantic relations derived from MRD have been found useful for supporting a wide range of natural language processing (NLP) tasks. Dictionary is a text whose subject matter is language. The purpose of a dictionary is to provide definitions of word senses and supply knowledge not just about language, but the world [23]. For instance, dictionary entries commonly contain a genus and differentiae, which reveals the classification of things and their relations in the universe. The genus terms in the dictionary entries can be assembled into semantic nets [1, 2, 6] or topical clusters [4] useful for various applications ranging from text understanding [21] to statistical machine translation [12].

Amsler's seminal work on computational analysis of definitions in the Merriam-Webster Pocket Dictionary [2] initiated the interest in using MRD for the theory of lexical semantics [6] as well as for practical NLP tasks. Amsler proposed a simple ATN grammar for processing definitions in the Merriam-

Webster Pocket Dictionary. He demonstrated that structure could be imposed on a dictionary definition by taking advantage of certain regular patterns in definitions. Foremost among these patterns is the pattern of genus-and-species. By extracting and disambiguating genus terms for a pocket dictionary, Amsler demonstrated the feasibility of generating semantic hierarchy from a MRD. Chodorow, Byrd, and Heidorn showed that automatic and semi-automatic procedures could be devised to extract and disambiguate genus so that semantic hierarchies can be generated from full-sized dictionaries [6]. These procedures rely on a parser for definition text in an MRD. However, the state-of-the-art parser has a limited rate of success. Ahlswede and Evens argued that text processing techniques were much simpler and just as effective as parsing in the analysis of dictionary definitions [1].

The genus in the taxonomic relation of genus-and-species can be expressed in terms of word or disambiguated word sense. Vanderwende described a heuristic algorithm [21] for interpreting noun sequences based on semantic relations extracted from the Longman Dictionary of Contemporary English (LDOCE, [18]). Impressive result were reported, despite the fact that these relations are expressed via words rather than disambiguated word senses and only 70% of them are correct. Dolan remarked that it is possible to disambiguate the genus based on a similarity measure between definitions of specific words and those of the genus [7]. Such semantic relations hardly can be viewed as constituting adequate semantics hierarchies. Obviously, there is room for improvement when it comes to the quality of MRD-based semantic relations and MRD-based natural language understanding. The goal of generating highly precise semantic relations for building an adequate taxonomy is still elusive after many years of research.

The three points addressed herein are automatic disambiguation of genus term, discovery of covert categories, and bilingual taxonomy. We argue that we must address these three issues before we can meet the challenge of creating an adequate taxonomy from MRD. We propose a series of simple methods, which rival elaborated parser-based methods in extracting and using rich semantic information in the MRD.

2 Problems in deriving taxonomy from the MRD

In this section, the three issues in extracting and utilizing the semantic knowledge in the MRD are discussed. For each of these problems, the constraints which defy simple solution are addressed.

2.1 Genus term and word sense disambiguation

Genus terms, being general, tend to be very ambiguous and are not always easy to disambiguate. An incorrectly disambiguated genus in a semantic hierarchy leads to a specific word sense being attached to the right word but wrong sense. For instance, one of word senses of *bass* is defined in the LDOCE as *the lowest part in written music*. (All subsequent examples are drawn from the LDOCE unless otherwise specified.) The genus *part* in this case is very ambiguous and not necessarily easy to disambiguate.

Example 1. Ambiguous genus term in a definition.
Definition *bass*   the lowest part in written music.
Definition *part*   (in music) one of the tunes esp. for a particular voice of instrument when put together make up a piece of music.

2.2 Covert categories from overly general definitions

The dictionary often defines a word sense in terms of simple, general words without relying on reader's familiarity with the more specific words. In the case of LDOCE, the defining words are drawn from a controlled vocabulary of some 2,000 words, which obviously does not cover the immediate generalization of any headword. For instance, the LDOCE definition of *historian* reads *a person who studies history* rather than *a scholar on the subject of history*.

Example 2. Members of covert category "person-study-SUBJECT"
Definition *scholar*   a person with great knowledge of, and skill in studying a subject, esp. other than a science.
Definition *historian*   a person who studies history.
Definition *folklorist*   a person who studies folklore.

In this example, the lexicographer uses the overly general concept *person* in the controlled vocabulary to define *historian* instead of its immediate conceptual generalization *scholar*. However, the concept of *scholar* is implicitly reflected in the pattern of *person-study-SUBJECT* in the definitions of *historian*, *folklorist*, etc.

White called such implicit immediate generalization the *covert* category [22]. The author observed that many words are defined by very general words in the Merriam-Webster Modern Pocket Dictionary. For instance, the *plant* words are often defined generally as a kind of *plant*. The definition pattern, *a plant related to the X's*, tips us off to the covert category *X*. This seems to be a general strategy employed by lexicographers in writing dictionary definitions and therefore can be observed in other dictionaries as well. For instance, in the LDOCE, *oregano* and *wolfsbane* are defined as *plant* with an explicit reference to their covert categories, *MARJORAM* and *ACONITE*.

Example 3. Explicitly marked covert category in the definition of the *plant* species

Definition   *oregano*   a type of plant related to MARJORAM and used in cooking.

Definition   *wolfsbane*   a type of flowering plant related to the ACONITE.

However, covert categories are not always marked in the way described by White. For instance, of all words in the overly general class of *person* words, many are defined as *a person who studies* without mentioning the covert category *scholar*. Taxonomy based directly on genus terms without considering the implicit covert category is not satisfactory, since such taxonomy will undoubtedly be too bushy. One can easily come up with cases where inference driven by such a bushy taxonomy might be specific enough for effective natural language understanding.

2.3 Bilingual taxonomy

Despite the potential of a semantic taxonomy for overcoming the language barrier, most studies on taxonomy and related MRD research are monolingual. There has been very little research done on building and using bilingual taxonomies. White pointed out from the anthropological position that one should resist the temptation to regard a semantic taxonomy extracted from dictionary as transcendent of the language of the dictionary [22]. However, he somewhat weakened his position on the ground of practical purposes when it comes to taxonomy of a specific domain. Okumura and Hovy described a heuristic algorithm for linking two taxonomies to build a bilingual taxonomy via a bilingual word list. In this paper, we describe a new approach to building a bilingual taxonomy using a bilingual MRD [17].

3 Deriving taxonomy from MRD

We have alluded to the fact that taxonomy derived directly from headword-genus relations can be problematic due to ambiguous and overly general genus terms. In this section, we describe ways of eradicating these problems. We will also touch on the advantages of using a bilingual MRD in deriving a bilingual taxonomy.

3.1 Genus disambiguation - from tangling web to bush

The focus of deriving taxonomy from MRD is on the semantic information in the definition conveyed by the syntactic head, the genus. Typically, an IS-A relation holds between the headword (i.e. definition entry) and its genus term. For extraction of genus terms, readers are referred to Ahlswede and Evens for detailed discussion [1]. The extracted headword and genus without word sense disambiguation constitutes a tangling web rather than the tree typically required for taxonomy. Dolan proposed a heuristic algorithm for merging closely related senses of a headword based on semantic relation extracted from the definition of such senses. The author noted that a similar idea could be applied to disambiguate genus terms [7]. Chen and Chang described a simple algorithm called *TopSense* for identifying topics relevant to a definition [4]. *TopSense* relies on the fact that, in most cases, the headword, genus and differentiae are related via certain semantic relations which exist implicitly among topical word lists in a typical thesaurus such as the Roget's or Longman Lexicon of Contemporary English (LLOCE, [15]). Therefore, based on this observation, we have come up with a genus disambiguation algorithm along the same line. In a nutshell, the defining words are compared to those of each sense of the genus. The sense of genus is determined in favor of the definition with the most lexical or conceptual overlaps. For instance, in Example 1, the genus *part* of the headword *bass* is found to be intended as the ninth sense of *part* in the LDOCE, since its definition has substantial lexical overlap (*music*) and conceptual overlap (music related terms such as *tune*, *voice*, *instrument*) with the definition of *bass*. Chen and Chang have shown that conceptual overlap can be assessed quite reliably using thesauri such as the LLOCE or Roget's thesaurus [4].

3.2 Discovery of covert categories - from bush to tree

We have noted that genera in dictionary definitions are often too general to be adequate for constructing taxonomy. One should try to find at least one covert category that fits between the headword and genus in taxonomy. Central to identification of covert category is automatic discovery of definition patterns shared by headwords in the same covert category. Furthermore, one word inside or outside of such a category of words should be identified to play the role of immediate generalization in the place of the original genus.

For instance, distribution analysis would reveal that there is a recurrent pattern *person-study-SUBJECT* in a substantial portion of *person* words. Those words constitute a covert category rooted at the word *person*. We should also be able to identify *scholar*, which is implied by all words under the covert category. This is analogous to the situation of finding the most specific generalization (MSG) in unification-based operation.

We observe that there are several cases where the MSG in a covert category can be discovered: (1) MSG is clearly marked in every definition in the category. (2) The definition of MSG is shortest among all definitions in the category. (3) The defining words of the MSG are more general than those in other definitions. (4) The taxonomy rooted at the MSG is the deepest. (5) The covert category is defined by a pattern "*such as …*" following the genus term.

Case 1. MSG is clearly marked in every definition in the category. For the first case, one can easily identify the covert category and insert it as the intermediate layer between the headword and the genus term in the semantic hierarchy. For instance, in both definitions for *cowslip* and *cyclamen*, the covert category PRIMROSE is marked explicitly via the pattern "(a member) of the *X* family." Use of such recurring patterns is a general strategy adapted by lexicographers rather than idiosyncratic property of a specific dictionary. Finding instances and formulating such patterns is not difficult. The intuition is to come up with some pairs of known words and their respective immediate generalizations. This can be used to retrieve definitions of a word containing its immediate generalization. Finally, look for recurring patterns in those definitions. This *folklore wisdom* of discovering patterns yielding taxonomic and other semantic relation is formalized in Hearst [9].

Example 4 (a) Members of the covert category "PRIMROSE"

Definition   *cowslip*   any of several types of small wild plant, esp. a member of the PRIMROSE family which is common in Britain and has sweet-smelling yellow flowers.

Definition   *cyclamen* any of various types of plant of the PRIMROSE family, with thick fleshy roots and white, purple, pink, or very red flowers.

(b) Members of the covert category "cat"

Definition   *lynx*   a type of large strong wild animal of the cat family with long legs and a short tail.

Definition   *serval*   a type of long-legged African animal of the cat family, smaller than a lion, having large ears and brown fur with black markings.

If we have not made use of the covert category, we would have gotten an unduly bushy taxonomy with thousands of nodes rooted at the plain genus terms, *plant* and *animal*.

plant	**animal**
⇨cowslip	⇨lynx
⇨cyclamen	⇨serval

With the covert category, we can approach the kind of depth that is generally expected from taxonomy.

plant	**animal**
⇨ primrose	⇨cat
⇨cowslip	⇨lynx
⇨cyclamen	⇨serval

Case 2. The definition of MSG is shortest among all definitions in the category. The words in a dictionary definition generally work in an intersective way to make the sense more and more specific. The same goes for words in a multi-word lexical noun phrase entry in MRD. Therefore, a shorter head entry or definition usually implies that the word in question refers to a large set of entities and is more general. For instance, the longer definition of *packer* defines it as a

worker in a specific place and performing a specific task. On the other hand, the shorter definition makes *worker* a much larger set of working persons in general. A shorter lexical noun phrase is often more general than a longer one. For instance, the two-word entries, *cocktail dress* and *evening dress* obviously imply the shorter entry *dress*. As far as definition lengths are concerned, *dress* still implies *cocktail dress*, since it has a shorter definition when one disregards the disjunctive differentiae, *or [worn] by special types of people*, which only proves *dress* is a larger set.

Example 5. (a) Members of the covert category "a person who works"

Definition	*packer*	a person who works where the food is prepared and put into tins.
Definition	*worker*	a person or animal who works.

(b) Members of the covert category "dress on occasion "

Definition	*dress*	clothing worn on special occasion or by special types of people
Definition	*cocktail dress*	a short (woman's) dress worn on formal occasions
Definition	*evening dress*	a dress (esp. long) worn by a woman for formal occasions in the evening
Definition	*gown*	a long dress, esp. one worn on formal occasions

Case 3. The defining words of the MSG are more general than in other definitions. Both Cases 3 and 4 demand that taxonomy extraction be a recursive process. If one already has some knowledge of the differentiae in a set of definitions sharing the same recurrent pattern, then it is easy to find the covert category. For instance, it is not difficult to see that the following taxonomy can be extracted from definitions in Example 6.

subject
⇨ **study**
⇨**history**
⇨**folklore**

Example 6.

Definition	*history*	(a study of) events in the past, such as those of nations, arranged in order from the earlier to the later, esp. events concerning the rulers and government of a country, social and trade conditions, etc.
Definition	*folklore*	(the scientific study of) all the knowledge, beliefs, habits, etc., of a racial or national group, still preserved by memory, or in use from earlier and simple times.
Definition	*study*	a subject studied.

With that information, one then can find a definition in the MRD, which is implied by definitions in a given covert category. For instance, *scholar* is implied by all definitions in the covert category of *person who studies*, since its definition contains the word *subject* which is transitively the genus of defining words, *history* and *folklore* in the LDOCE entries of *historian* and *folklorist* respectively.

Case 4. The taxonomy rooted at the MSG is the deepest. Similar to Case 3, sometimes finding the MSG relies on the taxonomic information already known about the head entry. For instance, the MSG of the covert category of working persons is *worker*, which has a similar definition pattern and therefore can be found in the same category. One additional heuristic for identifying the MSG is based on the length of maximum hyponym chain beginning at each word rather than definition lengths as in Case 2. The one with the longest chain tends to be most general. For instance, *worker* is more general than *packer* since many hyponym chains such as (*worker*, *cutter*) and (*worker*, *smith*) begin at *worker* while none begins at *packer*.

Example 7. Entry *worker* is more general than *packer* judging from their hyponyms.

Definition	*worker*	a person or animal who works.
Definition	*packer*	a person who works where the food is prepares and put into tins.
Definition	*cutter*	a worker whose job is cutting cloth, glass, stone.
Definition	*billposter*	a worker who sticks printed notices onto walls.
Definition	*smith*	a worker in metal.
Definition	*laborer*	a worker whose job needs strength rather than skill.

Case 5. The covert category is defined by a pattern "*such as ...* " following the genus term. The MSG of a covert category tends to be technical and not often in use. Lexicographers tend to make the definitions more accessible to the reader via a text generation schema of mentioning one or more specific examples. For instance, in the LDOCE definition of *aphid*, the specific and more commonly known example, *greenfly* seems to bring a much more vivid picture to the mind of the reader. For our purpose, such definitions obviously help to provide an easy way of inserting an additional *aphid* layer for the covert category of insects feeding on plant juice, or *beast of burden* (or *prey*) layer, or *interrogative* layer, for that matter.

Example 8.

Definition	*aphid*	any of various small *insects* (such as the GREENFLY) that live on the juices of plants.
Definition	*greenfly*	a very small *insect* which feeds on the juices from young plants.

Definition	*anthropoid ape*	any of several types of very large *monkey* (such as the CHIMPANZEE and GORILLA) that have no tails and look very much like hairy men.
Definition	*beast of burden*	an *animal* (such as a horse or donkey) which carries things.
Definition	*beast of prey*	an *animal* (such as a lion or tiger) which eats other animals.
Definition	*interrogative*	a *word* (such as who, what, which) used in asking a question stream.

An automatic procedure can be devised to discover these covert categories and insert them into the original taxonomy.

3.3 Bilingual taxonomy from bilingual MRD

Deriving a bilingual taxonomy from a bilingual MRD presents no real technical challenge. In the English-Chinese version of LDOCE (LDOCE E-C, [19]), each definition and example is given a Chinese translation. One simply clears up the translations a bit and posts them to the taxonomy along with the English head entries. Again, one should exercise caution in applying such a bilingual taxonomy, which in White's view [22] is not entirely transcendent of the language of the dictionary, in this case, English. While the taxonomy may do just fine for English-Chinese machine translation, it is obviously problematic when used in the opposite direction, Chinese-English machine translation, or as monolingual taxonomy in Chinese natural language processing.

We have found that the bilingual taxonomy is useful in the corpus-based learning for machine translation. Text and translation alignment (TTA) [11] has been identified as an alternative or supplemental approach to hand-built machine translation system. The crux of TTA lies on taking hold of diverse in-context translations (ICT) of typical source words and phrases. The genus terms and covert categories seem to provide a level of abstraction and classification of word senses and translations to bind ICTs for effective TTA.

4 Challenges to the MRD derived taxonomy

In Section 3, we argued that by identifying covert categories and their MSGs, we can derive a better *folklore* taxonomy from the MRD.

plant	**animal**	
⇨ **primrose**	⇨cat	
⇨cowslip		⇨lynx
⇨cyclamen		⇨serval

However, these are still two layers flatter than the very detailed and technical taxonomy given in the WordNet for *cowslip* and *cyclamen*:

plant ⇨ **herb** ⇨ **vascular plant**
⇨ **primrose**
⇨**cowslip**
⇨**cyclamen**

The WordNet's hyponym chain from *lynx* to *animal*, (**lynx, wildcat, cat, feline, carnivore, placental mammal, mammal, vertebrate, chordate, animal**), is even longer. Does the shorter chain mean that we are extracting from MRD taxonomy inferior to the WordNet? Not really. We argue that all speakers of English are not botany or zoology buffs, therefore language understanding merely requires the kind of folklore taxonomy we would get from an MRD. Sanfilippo and Poznanski pointed out the deficiency of any single MRD and suggested combining multiple MRD sources to derive a better taxonomy [20]. Nevertheless, Vanderwende's impressive success of interpreting noun sequences using directly extracted taxonomic relations is a testament to the effectiveness of folklore taxonomy extracted from a single MRD [21]. In this section, we will show that the covert categories we have proposed to add to the taxonomy can be justified in at least two natural language processing tasks, text and translation alignment and class-based semantic approach to machine translation.

4.1 Natural language understanding and machine translation

Levin advocated that one should extract lexical knowledge base (LKB) rather than just lexical data base (LDB) to support the crucial generalization and inference process which are the hallmarks of productive and novel uses so effortlessly performed by the native speaker of English [14]. The covert categories in LDOCE-derived folklore taxonomy seem to provide an adequate vocabulary for expressing such systematic productive extensions, both syntactical and semantic. That is evident from LDOCE definitions of *shrug, wink, expression* and *signal* shown below.

> **Example 9.** Covert category of *move-BODYPART-as-ACT* corresponds to Levin's GESTURES class
>
> (9.a) Rebecca shrugged.
> (9.b) Rebecca shrugged her indifference.

Definition	*shrug*	to raise (one's shoulder), esp. as an expression of doubt or lack of interest.
Definition	*wink*	to open and close (one eye), usu. as a signal between people.
Definition	*expression*	an act of expressing.
Definition	*signal*	a sound or action intended to warn, command or give a message.

Example 9 shows the covert category of *move-BODYPART-as-ACT* derived from the LDOCE corresponds to Levin's GESTURES class, one of many English verb classes whose members pattern together with respect to diathesis alternation and shared meaning. For instance, intransitive verbs of GESTURE, such as *shrug* and *wink*, frequently show extended use as transitive verb of expression as shown in Examples (9.a) and (9.b).

4.2 Machine translation

Definition, translations and bilingual examples in MRD are found to be very effective knowledge sources for word sense disambiguation and machine translation [3, 5]. The taxonomic information embodied in and extracted from an MRD is not unlike the semantic information employed in long-standing MT systems such as SYSTRAN [8]. Therefore, it is safe to say that machine translation in general requires just the kind of folklore taxonomy one would easily extract from an MRD as described in this paper. For instance, the definitions of *eat*, *acid*, *salad*, and *copper* in the LDOCE E-C are information enough to decide that the word *ate* in sentence, *She ate a lot of salad at lunch* should be translated as • while that in *The acid rain has eaten the copper dome* as • • .

Example 10. Lexical choice for *eat* in machine translation
(10.a) The acid rain has eaten the copper dome. • • • • • • • • • •
(10.b) She ate a lot of salad at lunch. • • • • • • • • •

Definition	*eat*	to take in through the mouth and swallow (solid *food* or *soup*) •
Definition	*eat*	to use up, damage, or destroy (something), esp. by chemical action • • ; • •
Definition	*acid*	a chemical substance containing a particular gas (HYDROGEN) … •
Definition	*salad*	a mixture of foods, usu. mainly of vegetables. • •
Definition	*copper*	a soft reddish metal that is a simple substance easily shaped. •

4.3 Bilingual taxonomy for text and translation alignment

The crux of the problem of text and translation alignment lies on taking hold of the diversity of in-context translations (ICT). The way to cope with a plethora of diverse ICTs must obviously come from a richer and more abstract representation, which provides classification of word senses and translations to bind ICTs. What is needed is a classification binding diverse translations, which is independent of language, part-of-speech, argument structure, etc. The derivation of an ideal classification immediately faces the problem of knowledge acquisition bottleneck. With the genera and covert terms in the bilingual taxonomy, we are able to form genus-based clusters (GBC) of headwords and translations. Table 1 shows some examples of GBC built for LDOCE E-C entries. Clusters based on headword-genus relation seem to lead to far too many possibilities. On the other hand, clusters based on MSG tend to be more focused, leading to lower complexity in TTA. For instance, the possible Chinese translations for *person*-words are too diverse for all of them to be related to *scholar*-words. For instance, none of the *scholar*-words should be, in general, translated as• , • or • . Therefore, it is advisable to discover such covert categories as *SCHOLAR* and associate them with a much more constrained translation cluster for high precision TTA. Table 1 shows that the *SCHOLAR* cluster containing such source word members as *historian* and *folklorist*, indeed has more limited translation members than the *PERSON* cluster.

Table 1. Some examples of the clustering results

GBC	Source word member	Translation member in order of descending frequency
PERSON	novice, prophet, rival, •	• , • , • , • , • , • , • , • , • , • , • , •
SCHOLAR	historian, folklorist, •	• , • , •
WORKER	packer, cutter, •	• , •

However, the procedure described in Section 3 still leaves many words without an immediate generalization and thus lacking direct link to their genus terms. For instance the word *performer* is linked directly to *person* unlike in WordNet. This is justifiable for two reasons. First, these words often do not have well-accepted, consistent means of classification if an immediate generalization is forced upon them. Many different kinds of cross classification are acceptable. So, it might be just as well to leave those words without such a classification and link them to the genus directly. Second, those words tend to have more diversified translations captured by a more general category. For instance, the translation cluster related to *person* words seems to work just fine for aligning *performer* with • .

Example 11. He is a good performer on the cricket field. • • • • • • • •

5 Conclusion

This paper has address issues relating to the problems in building a semantic hierarchy from MRD: genus disambiguation, discovery of covert categories, and bilingual taxonomy. We have demonstrated that distribution regularity in the defining and translation words in GBC of defining terms and translation can be exploited to address these issues. Simple statistics derived from GBC are surprisingly effective for discovering covert categories, building semantic hierarchies, and binding diverse translations in TTA. The automatically derived taxonomy has implication for a wide variety of NLP tasks ranging from understanding to machine translation. The entry words in the taxonomy provide a vocabulary for expressing not only the norm but also productive extensions of semantic word classes in English. They also have great potential for expressing critical lexical transfer portions in the lexicon for machine translation.

The performance of the taxonomy extraction procedures discussed here can certainly be improved by applying stronger analytical methods for dictionary definitions. What we have presented in this paper already constitute a functional core for producing taxonomy useful for a variety of semantic processing tasks and can provide a reasonable basis for lexical semantic theory.

Acknowledgments

This research is partially supported by the ROC NSC grants 85-2213-E-007-042. We are grateful to Betty Teng and Nora Liu from Longman Asia Limited for the permission to use their lexicographical resources for research purpose. Finally, we would like to thank the anonymous referees for their valuable comments. Any errors that remain are solely the responsibility of the authors.

References

1. Ahlswede, T., Evens, M.: Parsing vs. Text Processing in the Analysis of Dictionary Definitions. In Proceedings of the 26th Annual Meeting of the Association for Computational Linguistics (1988) 217-224
2. Amsler, R.A.: A Taxonomy for English Nouns and Verbs. In Proceedings of the 19th Annual Meeting of the Association for Computational Linguistics (1981) 133-138
3. Chen, J.N., Chang, J.S.: Concept-based Adaptive Approach to Word Sense Disambiguate. In Proceedings of 36th Annual Meeting of the Association for Computational Linguistics and 17th International Conference on Computational Linguistics, Montreal Canada (1998) 237-243
4. Chen, J.N., Chang, J.S.: Topical Clustering of MRD Senses Based on Information Retrieval Techniques, Computational Linguistics, 24 (1) (1998) 61-95
5. Chen, J.N., Chang, J.S., Sheng, H.H., Ker S.J.: Combining machine readable lexical resources and bilingual corpora for broad word sense disambiguation. In Proceedings of the Second Conference of the Association for Machine Translation, Montreal, Quebec, Canada (1996) 115-124
6. Chodorow, M.S., Byrd, R.J., Heidom, G.E.: Extracting Semantic Hierarchies from a Large On-line Dictionary. In Proceedings of the 23rd Annual Meeting of the Association for Computational Linguistics (1985) 299-304.
7. Dolan, W. B.: Word Sense Disambiguation: Clustering Related Senses. In Proceedings of the 15th International Conference on Computational Linguistics (1994) 712-716.
8 Gerber, L., Yang, J.: SYSTRAN MT Dictionary Development, In Proceedings of Machine Translation Summit VI, pp. 80-87, San Diego, California, USA (1997)
9. Hearst, M.: Automatic Acquisition of Hyponyms from Large Text Corpora, In Proceeding of the Fourteenth International Conference on Computational Linguistics (1992)
10. Jensen, Karen, Binot, J-L: Disambiguating Prepositional Phrase Attachments by Using On-line Dictionary Definitions. Computational Linguistics, 13(3-4) (1987) 251-260
11. Kay, M., Röscheisen M.: Text-Translation Alignment, Computational Linguistics, 19(1) (1993) 121-142
12. Ker, S.J., Chang, J.S.: A Class-based Approach to Word Alignment, Computational Linguistics, 23(2) (1997) 313-343
13. Klavans, J.L., Chodorow, M.S., Wacholder, N.: From Dictionary to Knowledge via Taxonomy. In Proceedings of the Sixth Conference of the University of Waterloo Centre for the New Oxford English Dictionary and Text Research: Electronic Text Research, University of Waterloo, Canada (1990)

14. Levin, B.: English Verb Classes and Alternations - A Preliminary Investigation. University of Chicago Press, Chicago and London (1993)
15. McArthur, T.: Longman Lexicon of Contemporary English (English-Chinese Edition). Published by Longman Group (Far East) Ltd., Hong Kong (1992)
16. Miller, G.A., Beckwith, R., Fellbaum, C., Gross D., Miller, K.: Introduction to Word-Net: An On-line Lexical Database. CSL 43, Cognitive Science Laboratory, Princeton University, Princeton, NJ (1993)
17. Okumura, A., Hovy, E.: Lexicon-to-ontology Concept Association Using a Bilingual Dictionary. In Proceedings of the First Conference of the Association for Machine Translation in the American, Columbia, Maryland, USA (1994) 177-184
18. Proctor, P., (ed.): Longman Dictionary of Contemporary English. Longman Group Ltd., England (1978)
19. Proctor, P., (ed.): Longman English-Chinese Dictionary of Contemporary English. Longman Group (Far East) Ltd., Hong Kong (1988)
20. Sanfilippo, A., Poznanski, V.: The Acquisition of Lexical Knowledge from Combined Machine-readable Dictionary Sources. In Proceedings of the 3rd Conference on Applied Natural Language Processing, Trento, Italy (1992) 80-87
21. Vanderwende, L.: Interpretation of Noun Sequence. In Proceedings of the 15th International Conference on Computational Linguistics, (1994) 454-460
22. White, J.S.: Lexicon and World Knowledge - Theoretical and Applied Viewpoints, ACL/SIGLEX Workshop on Lexical Semantics and Knowledge Representation, (1991) 139-151
23. Wilks, Y.A., Fass, D.C., Guo, C.M., McDonald, J.E., Plate T., Slator, B.M.: Providing Tractable Dictionary Tools. Machine Translation, 5 (1990) 99-154

Can Simultaneous Interpretation Help Machine Translation?

Dan Loehr

Georgetown University
The MITRE Corporation
1820 Dolley Madison Blvd., McLean VA 22102 USA
loehr@mitre.org

Abstract. It is well known that Machine Translation (MT) has not approached the quality of human translations. It has also been noted that MT research has largely ignored the work of professionals and researchers in the field of translation, and that MT might benefit from collaboration with this field. In this paper, I look at a specialized type of translation, Simultaneous Interpretation (SI), in the light of possible applications to MT. I survey the research and practice of SI, and note that explanatory analyses of SI do not yet exist. However, descriptive analyses do, arrived at through anecdotal, empirical, and model-based methods. These descriptive analyses include "techniques" humans use for interpreting, and I suggest possible ways MT might use these techniques. I conclude by noting further questions which must be answered before we can fully understand SI, and how it might help MT.

1 Introduction

Machine Translation (MT) has not fulfilled the expectations of the past four decades. Although useful, limited systems are in common use today, Fully-Automated High Quality Translation (FAHQT) does not appear on the horizon. In light of this, perhaps a rethinking of the basic approaches to MT is in order.

To this end, a group of researchers[1] at Georgetown University posed themselves the following question: "Should MT translate like people do?". The answer to this question requires further sub-questions, such as "How *do* people translate?", "Should MT be evaluated the same way as humans are?", and "Should MT translate in the same *manner* or with the same *results* as people do?". Each of these sub-questions requires, in turn, still more questions to be answered. Figure 1 below depicts a tree structure of these questions.

---

[1] Those taking part in these conversations were John White, Kathi Taylor, Allan Alderman, Jen Doyon, Greg Roberts, and Dan Loehr. The thoughts expressed in Fig. 1 and in the paragraphs immediately preceding and following it are the collected ideas of this group.

Should MT Translate Like People Do?

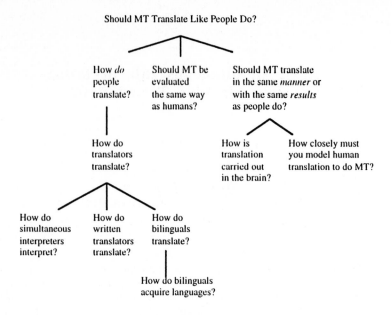

Fig. 1. A Tree Structure of Questions Regarding MT

The bottom-most questions, or *leaves*, are starting points for a re-thinking of the basic approaches to MT. From these leaves, answers might be found which could be bubbled back up the tree, with the ultimate goal of advancing MT by answering the top-most question. Or, further questions (other leaves) might be uncovered which must be answered before we can satisfactorily answer the leaves we started from.

This paper will explore the view from the left-most leaf on the tree: "How do simultaneous interpreters interpret?" It is intended to be a survey paper, capturing the highlights of research and practice in Simultaneous Interpretation (SI), and speculating how these findings might be applied to MT.

This leaf has gone largely unexplored in MT research. As Kay et al [21] remark in a recommendation to the recent MT project Verbmobil:

> One of the things that stands out as remarkable, even against the remarkable history of machine translation, is the fact that almost no professional translators have played a noticeable part in it. Perhaps this is as it should be, but *a priori* it is difficult to see how the case could be made. The linguists and computer scientists that have designed machine translation systems have taken it for granted that they knew what it meant for one text to be a translation of another–either that, or they were defeatist enough to think that the question would not arise in their work. It is not clear what, if anything, they imagined translators did during the years they spent studying their profession.

In sum, Kay et al suggest to Verbmobil: "There is probably some value in asking professional interpreters what they do and how they do it". It is the goal of this paper to do exactly that.

Section 2 below will survey the field, both research and practice, of SI. Skipping ahead, Section 4 will conjecture how the findings of Section 2 might be applied to MT. Sandwiched between these two sections for continuity, Section 3 will note relatively recent work by others along these same lines - that is, applying knowledge about SI to MT. Section 5 will note further unanswered questions below our leaf, and Section 6 will provide concluding remarks.

2   The Leaf: Research and Practice in Simultaneous Interpretation

Although *translation* can refer to both written and spoken media, in practice, *translation* refers to the written medium, and *interpretation* the spoken. (There is a hybrid, *sight translation*, in which the translator reads a written text and speaks the translation aloud). Interpretation itself is broken down into two types: *consecutive* interpretation, in which the interpreter waits for the speaker to pause or to finish before beginning the interpretation, and *simultaneous* interpretation, in which the interpreter speaks the interpretation aloud while the speaker is still speaking, although with a typical delay (or *decalage*) of between three and ten seconds.

Simultaneous Interpretation (SI) is a relatively new phenomenon, existing only since the end of the Second World War. First used at the Nuremberg Trials, it was introduced due to increased international cooperation and the availability of suitable electronic equipment [4]. (SI requires a soundproof booth for the interpreter and earplugs in the audience, so that the sound of the interpretation will not interfere with the sound of the speaker. Prior to this equipment, large conferences relied on consecutive interpretation).

SI is an extremely complex task. At any one time, the interpreter is engaged in at least six activities [30]: listening, understanding, translating, generating output, speaking, and monitoring their own output. This complexity alone is the primary reason I have chosen to study it in light of applications to MT, instead of looking at written translations, which might be considered more similar to Machine Translation. My hunch is that if we can understand such a complex task, then MT might appear simple in comparison. In addition, MT systems are increasingly becoming part of speech-to-speech translation systems (Germany's Verbmobil, Japan's ATR), which more closely resemble SI. Finally, Simultaneous Interpretation carries with it a certain fascination. Lay people, as well as researchers in language, cognitive science, and Machine Translation, all ask the same question: "How do they do it?".

The ultimate answer is to this question is, "We don't know". The cognitive processes underlying interpretation are still a "black box" [36,37]. However, one need not understand the underlying neurological processes to be able to make descriptive observations, arrive at empirical findings, or construct informed models. This section will attempt to describe "How they do it", to the extent it is known, in just these three ways: by anecdotal observation, by empirical research, and through models which attempt to be explanatory.

2.1 Anecdotal Observation

An appropriate place to begin would be to repeat the words of professional interpreters (and translators) when asked, "How do you do what you do?". The forum was the electronic mailing list LANTRA, devoted to such professionals. The answers were varied, but were along the lines of "We don't know", "It's automatic", "It can't be described". This supports findings of cognitive scientists that unconscious, automatic processes cannot be described by the humans carrying them out. The interpreters further volunteered that context was crucial, claiming that this extended to the entire culture of the language being translated, and indeed to all of human experience. When asked what humans do that might be applied to translating machines, the interpreters replied that machines would need such human-like capabilities as handling errorful or incomplete input, failing gracefully, using non-verbal cues, learning, translating incrementally, and, when all else fails, asking for help with an interpretation [24].

An influential book among interpreters learning their trade is Seleskovitch [35], *Interpreting for International Conferences*, in which the author, a professional interpreter and instructor of interpreters, documents her knowledge of her craft. Her instruction can be summed up simply: "Forget the words!". She advocates retaining the meaning of the source language utterance, rather than the lexical items. She argues that concepts (semantic storage) are far easier to remember than words (lexical storage), noting that the average person could relate the plot of a book they had just read, including many details, yet be at a loss to reproduce the text verbatim. Semantic storage also allows the interpreter to tap into concepts already stored in the brain. For this reason, preparation before a conference, by talking to the speaker and by researching the domain of the talk, is vital for interpreters. The concepts gained can be easily reactivated later, rather than having to be constructed during the interpretation. Finally, the use of concepts, rather than words, allows the interpreter to hitch a "free ride" on the brain's natural language-generation ability, by which humans convert concepts to words seemingly automatically. It is for this reason that many interpreters prefer to translate into their native language. Seleskovitch admits that concept-based interpretation may not always be possible. If the interpreter is unable to understand the concept being translated, or is under particular stress, they may resort to word-for-word translations.

Another professional interpreter, who teaches interpretation as well, is Barbara Moser-Mercer. Dr. Moser-Mercer is also active in interpretation research, and has constructed a model of its processes (described in section 2.3). Anecdotally, however, she informs us that simultaneous interpretation must be as automatic as possible ("like stick-shift driving") - there is little time for active thinking processes. She also declares that perfectionists have no place in SI. The question is not avoiding mistakes - it is rather correcting them and moving on when they are made [29].

Lafferty and Bowen (personal correspondence) address a popular question about SI: "How can one begin interpreting a German sentence before hearing the verb at the end?". It is really not such a problem, they explain:

> ... in listening to an English-speaker, do you have to wait for all the words in the sentence before the sentence can make sense? Take the example: "Why did you run the person wearing the hat over?" The verb is "run over", which is quite different from "run" but you have a strong idea of where the verb is going even before it is completed, in part because "run" + person as object of the sentence alerts us to the probable meaning...

They further state,

> Another important difference is that nouns carry much of the weight in a German sentence ... In English ... we prefer to distribute the weight of the sentence over the various parts of speech, and verbs do more work. The idea that we have to wait for a verb before the thought can come across may reflect an English-speaker's expectations ...

This idea of predicting future input is elaborated on by Hönig [16], who states that interpreters, who must keep speaking in the face of incomplete sentences, must either "tread water" (stall while waiting for more input) or "take a dive" (predict the direction of the sentence and begin translating it). He suggests that "diving" is not as risky as it sounds, provided the interpreter has talked with the speaker beforehand, and has what he calls a "text map" of where the talk is headed.

2.2 Empirical Findings

An early researcher into Simultaneous Interpretation was Barik [2]. He reported that interpreters tend to have a decalage (delay) of 2-3 seconds. Noting that this is the average duration of a "speech burst" by the speaker, he proposed that interpreters waited for the conclusions of successive speech bursts before interpreting. This process he called "chunking". Others, including Goldman-Eisler [13], have found that this chunk contains an NP + VP, that is, a clause. Barik notes that if the decalage becomes too long, the interpreter will omit content, while if it becomes too short, the interpreter will commit errors by following the speaker too closely to react to changes.

Chernov [3], noting that interpreters are both listening and speaking 70% of the time, tries to account for this simultaneity by citing neurophysical research which claims that the nervous system has evolved to make fast predictions about external stimuli. This predictive process, at a neural level, is applied to language during interpretation, Chernov argues, and he regards the "prediction of the verbal and semantic structure of the oral message in progress as the most essential psycholinguistic factor explaining the simultaneity in simultaneous interpretation."

Isham [17] confirms Seleskovitch's claim that the meaning, not the words, are what is interpreted. He does so with experiments (his own and that of Jarvalla [18]) in which interpreters are stopped and asked to repeat verbatim as much of the preceding input as they could. They could only repeat verbatim up to the preceding clause boundary - beyond that, they could only repeat the concept of what was said. It is hypothesized that at this point, the input changes from lexical to semantic processing.

A number of cognitive scientists have investigated exactly where in the brain interpretation appears to take place [7,9,22]. Studies have shown that second language ability may be lateralized. It is interesting that many interpreters prefer to keep their headphone on one ear only, saying simply that they "hear" better that way. Researchers believe, however, that this is to take advantage of the ear which inputs to that side of the brain in which the input language "resides". Studies of aphasia have indicated that interpretation ability is not necessarily co-located with language ability. Bilingual aphasics may be able to use either of their two languages but be unable to translate between the two, or be able to translate into a language in which they no longer can spontaneously produce sentences.

Finally, several researchers [26,5] have attempted to uncover the processes of interpretation by using Think-Aloud Protocols (TAP), a cognitive technique in which experts are asked to "think aloud" while they go about their tasks. Obviously, interpreters cannot do this (they are busy speaking their interpretation aloud), so the technique is used with translators. There are obvious problems with this: one is that some processes may be unconscious and thus unavailable to the expert. In addition, there can be a fine line between expert reportage and anecdotal evidence. Nonetheless, if enough subjects are studied in empirical settings, trends can emerge. To this extent, these researchers have found, among other things, that contextual information does indeed play a critical role in interpretation.

2.3 Explanatory Models

In a further attempt to explain what happens in the minds of interpreters, a number of researchers have constructed what they hope to be explanatory models of the underlying processes. None of these has been implemented - Lonsdale's (see below) is perhaps the closest to this goal. Some of these models are based purely on information processing, others on neurophysiology, and still others are rather a hybrid – computer implementations which hope to model the workings of the brain, without necessarily modeling the neurons.

The information processing models include those of Moser-Mercer [30], Gerver [11], Daro and Fabbro [8], and Gile [12]. All of these include constructs found in typical information processing flow diagrams: input buffers, short-term and long-term memory, processing modules, loops, tasks competing for resources, and output generators.

The neurocognitive models include those of Paradis [33] and Gernsbacher [10]. Paradis hypothesizes that bilinguals can not only activate/suppress words (lexical activation) in the neural substrate, but also entire areas of the brain in which different languages are stored. In this way, they can converse in one language or the other by simply activating one area and suppressing the other. In simultaneous interpretation, both areas become activated, although the source language (SL) slightly more so than the target language (TL). Finally, he notes that SI requires not only "automatic" language abilities, but "non-automatic" world-knowledge, which is also activated in his model.

Gernsbacher models comprehension as building mental representations or *structures*. When information arrives, it is either mapped to existing structures, or, if completely unknown or insufficient to make sense of, is used to create a new structure. The building blocks of these structures are smaller *memory nodes*, which are activated by incoming stimuli. Once activated, they are available for cognitive processes. They can also send signals to either enhance or suppress the activation of other memory nodes (and thus, the building of other structures). Gernsbacher claims that suppression is vital to interpretation by reducing the effect of interfering stimuli.

None of the above models has been tested empirically. The hybrid models - computational implementations hoping to model the brain - may soon have this luxury. These include Massaro [28] and Lonsdale [25]. Massaro's is a paper model of what would be necessary to implement a working system, while Lonsdale's is under construction. It is based on the Artificial Intelligence software SOAR, which has been used to model cognitive learning. It has been extended to NL-SOAR, which has language-processing capabilities. Lonsdale's NL-SOAR implementation consists of four modules, three of which will be familiar to MT researchers: a French analyzer, an English generator, and an interlanguage mapping system. The fourth module Lonsdale calls the "SI task control subsystem". This models many of the hypothesized interactions of SI: the decalage, the timing of information flow through the other modules, resource allocation between the modules, and the decision as to when enough of an input "chunk" has been received to begin interpreting. Lonsdale hopes, when the system is finished, to be able to test researcher's hypotheses about these processes.

It may be appropriate to end this section's survey of research in SI with a message echoed in the foreword to nearly every work cited above. Each researcher laments that "we know only a little" - the field is so young and the stuff of inquiry, the mind, so difficult to get at. Nonetheless, I believe we have already encountered a number of techniques which can be applied to machine translation. I will address these in Section 4. But first, let us take a very brief look at the few researchers who have already attempted this task.

3   Previous Work in Applying SI to MT

Although there have been several workshops in which researchers from both interpreting and machine translation have participated (Odense, Denmark 1979 [14], Kent State, Ohio 1995 [6], and Ascona, Switzerland 1997 [31]), the purpose of these was either to foster interdisciplinary research in interpreting (Kent State, Ascona), or simply to have a joint session bringing the fields together (Odense). None of these had a specific focus on applying research and practice from SI to MT. In 1992, however, the EAMT (European Association for Machine Translation) sponsored the first International Workshop on Machine Translation and Translation Theory in Nantes, France, specifically along these lines. A second workshop, by the same name, was held in 1994 in Hildesheim, Germany, and was co-sponsored by the Verbmobil project. Revised papers from these workshops have recently been published, edited by Hauenschild and Heizmann [15].

Noting that MT is migrating towards speech-to-speech translation, Hauenschild and Heizmann stress that it is all the more important for MT to adapt techniques from SI as central, not marginal, to the workings of MT. These include techniques such as incremental processing, ambiguity-preservation, and use of pragmatic factors such as world knowledge or speech acts in a dialogue. Several papers in the collection address these factors: some from the Verbmobil project (which has a formal goal to learn from translators), and some from other researchers.

The first of the Verbmobil papers, Prahl and Petzolt [34], conducted experiments in which translators (using Think-Aloud Protocol) were asked to translate passages in the appointment-scheduling domain of Verbmobil. It was noticed that they made liberal use of world-knowledge - for instance, they translated English "two o'clock" into German "14:00" (2 PM), rather than "2:00" (2 AM). This underscores that any good MT system needs what they call "standard assumptions" (world knowledge). They also noted that if the translators encountered ambiguity, unless it were critical (such as "two o'clock"), they often translated the ambiguity directly. The authors conclude that "relevance" is important, which can be based on the "translation task". Thus, in appointment-scheduling, times are very relevant to the task, and ambiguity should be resolved. Yet irrelevant ambiguity should be preserved.

Another Verbmobil paper is by Hönig [16], whose "text map" (outline of the speaker's talk) I discussed earlier. Hönig makes a specific recommendation for a machine such as

Verbmobil. Prior to its use, have a human pre-load it with a text map of the upcoming translation - Verbmobil can then use this for extralinguistic context.

Of the non-Verbmobil contributions, the first is Amtrup [1], who attempts to implement incremental translation by simply passing incremental stages of a chart parser along to the transfer module of a machine translation system. This of course results in partial meanings and ambiguity which must be resolved later. Fitting nicely with this incomplete meaning is LuperFoy's [27] discourse pegs, which are specifically designed to accommodate partial or incomplete information. Semantic attributes, as they arrive, are hung on "pegs" (place-holders for discourse referents), which can then be later updated as new information arrives. Although at any moment the information state is incomplete, it may be enough to continue translation.

4 The Thread Back to MT: Looking Upward from the Leaf

The question we've been trying to answer on our leaf is "How do simultaneous interpreters interpret?" This question remains unanswered in an *explanatory* sense - that is, we do not know the underlying cognitive processes which guide interpretation. So in this sense, we cannot bubble answers back up the tree to answer our top-most question: "Should MT translate like people do?"

However, we *can* answer this question in a *descriptive* sense. That is, we know the techniques that simultaneous interpreters use. It may not be necessary to know exactly how they implement these techniques. As Kay et al [20] explain:

> Planes do not flap their wings. I am sure you knew that. But I am sure that you also know that statements are not always made for the sake of the new information they convey. This particular one fills a traditional, almost ritualistic, role in a recurring argument about artificial intelligence. He thinks that, if you want a computer to do something that only humans can do, you need to study how humans do it and have the computer follow their example. She replies that what is good for the human may not be good for the computer. Birds provide the existence proof that flight is possible; they may not provide the only way to do it.

Therefore, let us not flap our wings. Rather, let us simply collect the techniques of SI into a "lessons learned", or, if you like, a "bag of tricks", and then pass the whole bag back up the tree. To the top-most question, we can then provide an answer as follows: "If MT *did* translate like people do, here is what it would look like on the surface".

This section, then, will be a convenient re-compilation of sections 2 and 3: the anecdotal, empirical, and model-based "lessons learned" from SI. I will further add guesses at how they might apply to MT - but let me stress - these are guesses at implementation. Actual successful implementation of these techniques awaits the labors of further MT research.

For simplicity, I will present these lessons learned, and guesses at their mapping to MT, in Table 1 below[2].

---

[2] I thank an anonymous reviewer for enhancing the ideas in rows 1, 4, 6, and 7, and suggesting the idea in row 5.

Table 1. Lessons Learned from SI and Possible Applications to MT

Lesson Learned (Technique)	Possible Application to MT (Implementation)
Context is essential, including non-verbal context	Re-double efforts on integration of MT systems with Knowledge-Bases and on multi-modal interpretation
Use dialogue structure	Pre-load system with a "map" of the text to be translated
Translate meaning not words	Go as high up the MT Pyramid as is feasible (at least focus on transfer, not direct, systems)
Handle errorful or incomplete input	Use error recovery techniques, along with partial meaning representations and partial dialogue structures, to at least translate something
Preserve ambiguity if acceptable	Pass ambiguous tokens to target language unresolved
Translate into native language	More emphasis on generation, including corpus-based generation to enhance naturalness
Interpretation must be automatic	Use previously translated phrases as much as possible
Predict input	Use dialogue structure and AI learning techniques, as well as expectation-driven parsing, to predict input
"Chunk" input into clauses before translating	Translate incrementally, but wait for clause boundaries before beginning
Translate incrementally	Use parallel processing, and pass partial results between analysis, transfer, generation modules
Don't be a perfectionist	Allow "good enough" MT (competent and grammatical output)
Fail gracefully	Design system to fail gracefully
When all else fails, ask for help	Design system to ask for help from humans

5   Unanswered Questions: Looking Downward from the Leaf

As discussed, although we have identified techniques of SI which can be applied to MT, we still do not know exactly how simultaneous interpreters do what they do. This, then, constitutes our view downwards from the leaf: further questions to answer.

An obvious leaf might be labeled, "How is translation carried out in the brain?". Although on a separate branch, this question is related to our SI leaf. As mentioned, we have not yet explained how millions of single neuron cells can cooperate to process language. One of the translators on the LANTRA list, when asked "How do you translate?", replied "I read (or hear) stuff, grok it, and type out (or speak) what I grokked, with the awareness that the output is in a different language" [23]. What's going on in this "grok" process?

Another leaf below us has also been mentioned above: "Should MT be evaluated the same way as humans are?". Professional interpreters agree that there is no such thing as an exact translation. Thus, a "translation equivalence" [19] must be defined before we can know what level of translation we're aiming for. If humans do not expect exact translations, should machines?

A whole spray of leaves awaits us regarding certain methods used by professional interpreters. These include techniques such as "use non-verbal input", "learn as you go", "handle incomplete input". How exactly do humans do these things? The view grows leafier.

Yet of all the leaves below us, possibly the largest one contains the question, "How do humans store and process *world knowledge*?". For it is world knowledge which underlies context, and it is context which is critical to any type of translation. In Machine Translation's parent field of Artificial Intelligence, this lack of world knowledge is termed the "common sense knowledge problem". This problem has been the show-stopper in developing anything beyond a limited-domain system which is capable of conversing with humans. The Knowledge Base project Cyc set out to solve this problem by encoding every maxim known to humans in an encyclopedic fashion. Yet after nearly fifteen years of work, Cyc's reasoning powers are still toy-like compared to humans.

It is perhaps fitting to close this section by hearing again from Kay et al [20], this time commenting on that most important leaf: world knowledge. Recall that we launched our investigation of interpretation and machine translation with Kay's words decrying the separation of these two fields, and encouraging their cooperation. Later, we heard Kay wonder whether we would indeed have to "flap our wings", or process world knowledge as humans do. In the end, though, Kay provides a dose of realism:

> What we need to know in order to build a translating machine will not turn out to be an emergent property of any body of existing translations and the only way to make translations of any value is, and always will be, to make them in the way that humans do. The reason is well known if desperately resisted, namely that translation is the quintessential example of what is sometimes called an "AI-complete" problem. What this means is simply that it depends for its solution on solutions to all the other problems in artificial intelligence. In more everyday terms, it means that there is nothing a translator could know, believe, infer, doubt, desire, or fear that might not be crucial at some point in his work as a translator.

In sum, then, we will not have high-quality machine translation until we can learn how humans process world knowledge, and do likewise. As Kay et al [20] summarize:

> .... the translating machine will indeed have to flap its wings.

6   Conclusion

I have looked at simultaneous interpretation in the light of possible applications to machine translation. While explanatory analyses do not yet exist for the processes of human interpretation, descriptive analyses do, arrived at through anecdotal, empirical, and model-based methods. Taking these descriptive "techniques", I have suggested possible ways MT might make use of them.

I have ended by noting that there are many more questions to be answered before we can fully understand how humans interpret, and thus how machines might benefit from this knowledge. Given the limited quality of machine translation, trying to answer these questions is well worth the effort. As Moser-Mercer [32] urges us,

Machine-assisted interpreting projects have so far relied heavily on machine translation research and hardly at all on interpreting research ... limited results in fully
automatic high-quality translation tend to indicate a need to take human strategies
seriously, or at least to give them a second, and closer, look.

References

1. Amtrup, J. (1997). *Perspectives for incremental MT with charts*, in Hauenschild, C.,
   Heizmann, S. (eds.), *Machine Translation and Translation Theory*, Mouton de Gruyter.
2. Barik, H. (1969). *A study of simultaneous interpretation*, Ph.D. Thesis, University of North
   Carolina at Chapel Hill.
3. Chernov, G. (1994). *Message Redundancy and Message Anticipation in Simultaneous Interpretation*, in Lambert, S., Moser-Mercer, B. (eds.) (1994), *Bridging the Gap: Empirical
   research in simultaneous interpretation*, John Benjamins.
4. Crystal, D. (1987). *The Cambridge Encyclopedia of Language*, Cambridge University Press.
5. Dancette, J. (1997). *Mapping Meaning and Comprehension in Translation: Theoretical and
   Experimental Issues*, in Danks, J., Shreve, G., Fountain, S., McBeath, M. (eds.), *Cognitive
   Processes in Translation and Interpreting*, Sage Publications.
6. Danks, J., Shreve, G., Fountain, S., McBeath, M. (eds.) (1997). *Cognitive Processes in
   Translation and Interpreting*, Sage Publications.
7. Daro, V. (1994). *Non-linguistic factors influencing simultaneous interpretation*, in Lambert, S., Moser-Mercer, B. (eds.) (1994), *Bridging the Gap: Empirical research in simultaneous interpretation*, John Benjamins.
8. Daro, V., Fabbro, F. (1994). *Verbal memory during simultaneous interpretation: Effects of
   phonological interference*, in Applied Linguistics, 15 (4). Cited in Lonsdale, D. (1996),
   Modeling SI: A cognitive approach, in Interpreting, Vol. I No. 2.
9. Fabbro, F., Gran, L. (1994). *Neurological and neuropsychological aspects of polyglossia
   and simultaneous interpretation*, in Lambert, S., Moser-Mercer, B. (eds.) (1994), *Bridging
   the Gap: Empirical research in simultaneous interpretation*, John Benjamins.
10 Gernsbacher, M. (1997). *Attenuating Interference During Comprehension: The Role of
   Suppression*, in Moser-Mercer (ed.), *Methodological Issues in Interpreting Research*
   (unpublished).
11. Gerver, D. (1976). *Empirical studies of simultaneous interpretation: A review and a model*,
   in R. Brislin (ed.), *Translation. Applications and research*, Gardner Press. Cited in Moser-
   Mercer, B. (1997), *Process models in simultaneous interpretation*, in Hauenschild, C.,
   Heizmann, S. (eds.), *Machine Translation and Translation Theory*, Mouton de Gruyter.
12. Gile, D. (1997). *Conference Interpreting as a Cognitive Management Problem*, in Danks,
   J., Shreve, G., Fountain, S., McBeath, M. (eds.), *Cognitive Processes in Translation and Interpreting*, Sage Publications.
13. Goldman-Eisler, F. (1968). *Psycholinguistics: experiments in spontaneous speech*, London Academic Press. Cited in Kopczynski, A. (1980), *Conference Interpreting: Some linguistic and communicative problems*, Uniwersytet Im. Adama Mickiewicza W Poznaniu.
14. Hanon, S., Pedersen, V. (eds.) (1979). *Human Translation, Machine Translation: Papers
   from the 10th Annual Conference on Computational Linguistics in Odense, Denmark*,
   Odense Universitet.
15. Hauenschild, C., Heizmann, S. (eds.) (1997). *Machine Translation and Translation Theory*,
   Mouton de Gruyter.
16. Hönig, H. (1997). *Using text mappings in teaching consecutive interpreting*, in Hauenschild, C., Heizmann, S. (eds.), *Machine Translation and Translation Theory*, Mouton de
   Gruyter.

17. Isham, W. (1994). *Memory for sentence form after simultaneous interpretation: Evidence both for and against deverbalization*, in Lambert, S., Moser-Mercer, B. (eds.) (1994), *Bridging the Gap: Empirical research in simultaneous interpretation*, John Benjamins.
18. Jarvella (1971). *Syntactic Processing of Connected Speech*, in Journal of Verbal Learning and Verbal Behavior, 10. Cited in Isham, W. (1994), *Memory for sentence form after simultaneous interpretation: Evidence both for and against deverbalization*, in Lambert, S., Moser-Mercer, B. (eds.) (1994), *Bridging the Gap: Empirical research in simultaneous interpretation*, John Benjamins.
19. Jekat, S. (1997). *Automatic interpreting of dialogue act*, in Hauenschild, C., Heizmann, S. (eds.), *Machine Translation and Translation Theory*, Mouton de Gruyter.
20. Kay, M. (1997). *Interpretation: The Translator and the Fire Hose*, in Moser-Mercer (ed.), *Methodological Issues in Interpreting Research* (unpublished).
21. Kay, M., Gawron, J., Norvig, P. (1991). *VERBMOBIL: A translation system for face-to-face dialog*, Bundesministerium für Wissenschaft, Forschung, und Technik.
22. Lambert, S. (1994). *Simultaneous interpretation: One ear may be better than two*, in Lambert, S., Moser-Mercer, B. (eds.) (1994), *Bridging the Gap: Empirical research in simultaneous interpretation*, John Benjamins.
23. Lane, A. (1997). LANTA List Posting, available at LANTRA List Archives, available at http://www.geocities.com/Athens/7110/lantra.htm
24. LANTRA (1997) List Archives, available at http://www.geocities.com/Athens/7110/lantra.htm
25. Lonsdale, D. (1996). *Modeling SI: A cognitive approach*, in *Interpreting*, Vol. 1 No. 2.
26. Lörscher, W. (1991). *Translation Performance, Translation Process, and Translation Strategies: A Psycholinguistic Investigation*, Gunter Narr Verlag.
27. LuperFoy, S. (1997). *Discourse processing for voice-to-voice machine translation*, in Hauenschild, C., Heizmann, S. (eds.), *Machine Translation and Translation Theory*, Mouton de Gruyter.
28. Massaro, D. (1997). *Information Processing and a Computational Approach to the Study of Simultaneous Interpretation*, in Moser-Mercer (ed.), *Methodological Issues in Interpreting Research* (unpublished).
29. Moser-Mercer, B. (1996). Lecture, Georgetown University.
30. Moser-Mercer, B. (1997). *Process models in simultaneous interpretation*, in Hauenschild, C., Heizmann, S. (eds.), *Machine Translation and Translation Theory*, Mouton de Gruyter.
31. Moser-Mercer (ed.) (1997). *Methodological Issues in Interpreting Research* (unpublished).
32. Moser-Mercer, B. (1997). *Beyond Curiosity: Can Interpreting Research Meet the Challenge?*, in Danks, J., Shreve, G., Fountain, S., McBeath, M. (eds.), *Cognitive Processes in Translation and Interpreting*, Sage Publications.
33. Paradis, M. (1994). *Toward a neurolinguistic theory of simultaneous translation: The framework*, in International Journal of Psycholinguistics, 10. Cited in Moser-Mercer, B. (1997), *Beyond Curiosity: Can Interpreting Research Meet the Challenge?*, in Danks, J., Shreve, G., Fountain, S., McBeath, M. (eds.), *Cognitive Processes in Translation and Interpreting*, Sage Publications.
34. Prahl, B., Petzolt, S. (1997). *Translation problems and translation strategies involved in human and machine translation: Empirical studies*, in Hauenschild, C., Heizmann, S. (eds.), *Machine Translation and Translation Theory*, Mouton de Gruyter.
35. Seleskovitch, D. (1978). *Interpreting for International Conferences: Problems of Language and Communication*, Pen and Booth.
36. Shreve, G., Koby, G., (1997) *Introduction*, in Danks, J., Shreve, G., Fountain, S., McBeath, M. (eds.), *Cognitive Processes in Translation and Interpreting*, Sage Publications.
37. Toury, G. (1982). *A rationale for descriptive translation studies*, in *Dispositio*, 7. Cited in Shreve, G., Koby, G., (1997), *Introduction*, in Danks, J., Shreve, G., Fountain, S., McBeath, M. (eds.), *Cognitive Processes in Translation and Interpreting*, Sage Publications.

Sentence Analysis Using a Concept Lattice

Lebelo Serutla and Derrick Kourie

Department of Computer Science, University of Pretoria, Hillcrest 0083.
[sserutla,dkourie]@cs.up.ac.za

Abstract. Grammatically incorrect sentences result either from an unknown (possibly misspelled) word, an incorrect word order or even an omitted / redundant word. Sentences with these errors are a bottle-neck to NLP systems because they cannot be parsed correctly. Human beings are able to overcome this problem (either occurring in spoken or written language) since they are capable of doing a semantic similarity search to find out if a similar utterance has been heard before or a syntactic similarity search for a stored utterance that shares structural similarities with the input. If the syntactic and semantic analysis of the rest of the input can be done correctly, then a 'gap' that exists in the utterance, can be uniquely identified. In this paper, a system named SAUCOLA which is based on a concept lattice, that mimics human skills in resolving knowledge gaps that exist in written language is presented. The preliminary results show that correct stored sentences can be retrieved based on the words contained in the incorrect input sentence.

Keywords: Concept lattice; machine learning; natural language processing; machine translation; example-based machine translation.

1 Introduction

Grammatically incorrect sentences result from either an unknown (possibly misspelled) word, an incorrect word order or even an omitted/redundant word. Humans are, nevertheless, able to infer the correct meaning of a sentence and other related information and hence facilitate continued flow of communication. How this happens is based on what and how much is known about that language at that particular instance. Having a substantial vocabulary allows for a semantic similarity search to be conducted in order to find out if a similar utterance has been heard before. Knowledge of the syntax of the language facilitates similarity search for a stored utterance that shares structural similarities with the input.

Relying on a syntactic and semantic analysis to match the input against stored knowledge, a 'gap' that may exist may often be uniquely identified. Adequate vocabulary is essential to enable a missing word to be correctly guessed. If, on the other hand, it is difficult to obtain the missing word, then at least the type of the word that is supposed to go into the gap can be determined. Determining a word type, that can be substituted into the place of a knowledge gap, goes a long way in aiding the correct interpretation of a sentence.

In order to guess a missing word or determine its type, substantial knowledge, of a language must be acquired. The knowledge of a language implies knowledge of the semantics, (i.e. vocabulary of words and their meanings) and the syntax, (i.e. how to form valid sentences from the words and their types). This knowledge facilitates sentence interpretation, and therefore communication, even in the presence of grammatical mistakes.

Such interpretation is possible since the search for a matching sentence can easily be directed if much knowledge and lots of example sentences are available. As Ellis (1993) puts it: 'the more comparable objects which are known, the more a query object can be related to database objects, and hence direct the search towards the location in the database where the object fits'.

The human mind may be conceived as a complex network that processes natural language. This language network connects abstractions of words, their meanings, syntax of the language and even dynamic interconnections of words to phrases and sentences that have been conceived before. For instance, humans remember idioms, quotations and what others have said in a conversation. They are able to link words to situations or events that have happened in the past. A name, for instance, might trigger a memory of someone familiar.

We are able to distinguish a new word or a phrase, because it is not in the network. When an incorrect sentence is heard/read, something 'deep inside' tells one that either a verb or a noun, for instance, is missing in the heard sentence. We are able to do this because we can always remember a sentence that shares syntactic similarities with an incorrect one that we are hearing/reading. When processing natural language, humans refer to this network (perhaps subconsciously) for utterance processing.

This paper presents a **Sentence Analysis Using a Concept Lattice (SAUCOLA)** system, based on a concept lattice (CL), for processing grammatically incorrect natural language sentences. It can be a useful augmentation to machine translation (MT) systems since part of the translation involves a re-arrangement of words so that they form comprehensible sentences in the target language. In conventional rule-based MT systems, word re-arrangement often occurs as a result of successively applying a series of re-writing or refining rules. Constructing and maintaining such a rule base significantly increases the complexity of such systems. The SAUCOLA system aims to reduce this complexity by assuming responsibility for word re-arrangement, based on the good sentences retrieved from the stored knowledge.

Handling of grammatically incorrect input is also a concern to MT researchers (cf. (Knight et al. 1995), (Daelemans 1993), (Yamada et al. 1995)) since sentences cannot be parsed correctly. Even grammatically correct sentences that are not recognised by an inadequate MT parser may cause problems. The ability to auto correct input sentences by putting words that may be incorrectly arranged into an arrangement that will be recognised by an MT system's parser for correct parsing and subsequent translation is, therefore, of prime importance.

Rule based MT systems have to be equipped with rules that enable them to deal with all aspects of transforming an input into an acceptable output. Experience with Lexica[1] has shown that rules often work well with sentence constructs with which they were trained. However, when confronted with a slight variation of those sentences, then the result is either a word for word translation, which often contains incorrect word order; an over generation, whereby redundant words are introduced and these have to be pruned off; or an under generation whereby some words have been omitted and thus have to be introduced in order that an acceptable translation can result.

This paper investigates the applicability of a CL as a model of the human network for processing natural language so that grammatically incorrect sentences can be appropriately handled. This will be achieved by finding a sentence in the knowledge base that is as close to the input as possible. This similar sentence will be taken as the best approximation of the input.

A concept lattice, through its embedded indexing mechanism, is able to give nearest neighbours of the input sentence. Once a nearest neighbour has been selected, the input can then be transformed accordingly into a valid and sensible sentence.

The rest of the paper is structured as follows: section 2 brings the current work into perspective by reporting some related research work. Section 3 deals mainly with sentence analysis issues of finding and selecting candidate sentences and how they can be applied in handling the under and over generations in MT. These will be demonstrated for the Sesotho[2]language. In section 4, a brief summary of the current research work is presented. Finally, section 5 concludes by giving future directions into which this research work will move.

2   Related Work

Much research effort in machine learning (ML) has gone into classification. Though the aims were not specifically to support applications in NLP, the resulting algorithms are useful. These algorithms have been widely tested and applied with varying levels of performance. In some cases, satisfactory results have been reported (e.g. (Demiroz and Guvenir 1997), (Wettschereck 1994), (Carpineto and Romano 1993)).

In a broad sense, the classification algorithms can also be seen as partial matching, since they can only predict the class an entity is believed to fall in. Selecting a sentence that is as close as possible to the input is also a classification task, and thus, NLP research can potentially draw benefit from the developed algorithms. This perception is based on the premise that a parse tree can be regarded as a series of classification problems.

In Demiroz and Guvenir (1997), prediction of classes into which input sentences belonged was based on probability. For each class, a probability was calculated and the class that scored the highest probability was taken as the best

---

[1] Lexica is a transfer rule-based MT system developed at the University of Pretoria. It has been used to translate example Sesotho sentences used later in the paper

[2] Sesotho is an African language spoken in Lesotho and many parts of the Republic of South Africa

approximation of the input sentence. The calculation of the probabilities ignored the missing values which could possibly change the probabilities. The algorithm however performed faster and better than the Naive Bayesian Classifier (NBC) and *k- nearest neighbour* classification on feature projections (k-NNFP).

Cardie (1996) and Daelemans et al. (1997) treat ambiguity resolution as a classification problem. In Cardie (1996), this approach resulted in a range of sub-problems in sentence analysis which were previously handled independently to be addressed simultaneously. Also, resources such as tense and voice information, in addition to part of speech information for each word, were made available to, for example, part of speech tagger. In the Kenmore system, it thus became possible for all ambiguities to be treated within a single framework (Cardie 1996).

Classification techniques using a CL have mainly been applied in information retrieval and extraction. They have been found to enhance the browsing capability such that query satisfaction is significantly improved (cf. (Carpineto and Romano 1996a), (Carpineto and Romano 1996b), (Ellis 1993), (Godin et al. 1993)). The results of using a CL to classify and to predict are reported by (Carpineto and Romano 1993). In some instances, results were satisfactory even though some of the data to be classified or predicted contained missing values.

CL's are attractive for classification tasks because they are able to represent all inter-dependencies between features to be recorded and hence a complete inventory among features is obtainable (Oosthuizen 1988). Given a set of features, a set of objects is directly accessed. The CL makes this easy because it is able to contain an exhaustive set of all clusters generated from objects with the named features.

In order to classify an object, as many characteristics as possible that are common between the object and its candidate class must be found since 'close generalisations of objects are better approximations than very general generalisations of objects' (Ellis 1993). A sentence that has to be matched must therefore, have as many words/word types as possible in common with its candidate class (i.e. the class with the largest number of words in common with the input).

Also, the notion of generalisation, which forms the basis for approximate matching, is naturally embedded in a CL. A meet of a given number of features results in a 'unique maximal cluster of objects best matching the volunteered features' or no objects at all, if no meet exists. The spanning concepts of the largest cluster(s) among the given features are then used to obtain the best matching objects' (Oosthuizen 1988).

The notion of approximate matching is important since firstly, a component matching the user's requirements may not exist; secondly, the user cannot know the exact characteristics of the desirable component or entity; and thirdly, the desired component may not be indexed as the user might have thought (Maarek et al. 1991). It is in this spirit that knowledge representation tools should provide for partial matching. The lack of knowledge of Boolean algebra (on the part of the user) can also compound the problem.

It is important for NLP systems to be capable of tackling the problem of missing 'definitive knowledge or knowledge gaps'. To fill a knowledge gap, knowledge based machine translation (KBMT) systems make a random decision (Knight et al. 1995). These random decisions can be guided by mechanisms based upon prediction and partial matching.

3   Sentence Analysis

Conventional MT systems are often guided by statistics in order to choose appropriate word senses [3] during parsing or when carrying out a word mapping from source to target language.

In some instances this may be inaccurate, i.e. the sense associated with the highest statistic might not be the correct one. Other MT systems select the first sense given for a word in a dictionary. Again, this will not necessarily be correct. Incorrect word type choices derived from these approaches usually result in failure of the MT system as it attempts to further parse the associated input sentence.

3.1   General Approach

An MT system is needed that offers an alternative way of handling such ambiguity. During parsing, word sense should not be determined according to the order of look-up in a dictionary (first word first) nor according to some statistically based rule (e.g. most commonly used term), but according to a more general examination of the context in which the word occurs. To be able to do this, account should be taken of known words, word types and legitimate word type ordering in the sentence, just as humans interpret ambiguous parts of a sentence by referring to what is already known about the sentence.

On its own, the lattice structure to be discussed below does not carry information about the order in which words should occur in a sentence. Neither does the lattice contain any explicit information on word types in a sentence. Such information is available in so-called word type vectors (WTV). A WTV [4] is a sequence of word types serving as a template for a set of sentences. For example, ⟨ art, adj, noun, verb, art, noun ⟩ is a WTV for sentences such as:

'A rich man drives a car.'
'A poor student eats a hamburger.'

Using WTV's in combination with a CL appears as a promising approach to the problem of resolving ambiguities, including those arising from errors in

---

[3] The word sense of a word refers to the word type (and possibly also the target language translation) with which the word is associated

[4] WTV's together with their associated set of sentences are reminiscent of concepts (in the ML sense). Each concept is represented by a tuple $\{S_i, W_i\}$, where S_i (an extent) is a set of sentences in a language corresponding to the WTV W_i. In this case, however, the 'intent', W_i, is represented by a sequence of word types, rather than by the more conventionally used set.

the input. A particular kind of CL can be derived from a database of sentences. Words in such a lattice will not be linked to any particular part of speech. As a consequence, the lattice alone cannot be used to disambiguate an input sentence. Instead, word sense determination takes place with reference to a set of WTV's set up from the initial sentence database. Statistical information can also be deployed as an additional measure.

For instance, in disambiguating a sentence containing the word 'love' [5] the lattice will be used as a first line of attack to determine a set of known candidate sentences whose words overlap as far as possible with those in the input sentence. Stored WTV's for these candidate sentences are then brought to bear on the input sentence, providing further information on possibly ambiguous words (such as 'love' as noun or 'love' as verb). Next, the maximum of the probabilities of love being used either as a noun or as a verb is considered.

3.2 Finding Candidate Sentences

Graphically, a concept lattice can be viewed as an acyclic graph linking attributes to their entities via a network of concept nodes. The so-called GRAND algorithm, developed by Oosthuizen (1988), provides a way of setting up such a lattice. In the research described here, the GRAND algorithm is used to construct a special CL, which we shall term a 'sentence lattices'. In such a sentence lattice, each entity is derived from a sentence, being the set of words used in the sentence, rather than the ordered list of words. The set of attributes in the sentence lattice comprises all the words appearing in the various entities.

A sentence lattice is constructed from an original sentence database, S, so that a mapping between each entity and its corresponding sentence can be set up. The WTV associated with each sentence and other relevant information should also be in place. Of course, these mappings are not part of the formal lattice structure. However, unless required by the context, the discussion below will not distinguish between an entity in a sentence lattice and its associated sentence.

The resulting sentence lattice can be viewed as a way of abstracting and organising S so that natural groupings of words emerge as internal concept nodes in the lattice. Because of the lattice properties, any pair of nodes has a unique meet and a unique join. In particular, entities that have words in common will have a unique meet. Such a meet is also, in turn, the join of all attributes corresponding to the words that the entities have in common.

Symbolically the matter may be represented as follows. Consider the set of possible input sentences, G. A mapping from each input sentence onto a set of so-called candidate sentences, C, can be defined, based on the sentence lattice for the sentence database S.

---

[5] The word 'love' can be used either as a verb or as a noun. Whenever a sentence that uses 'love' as a verb is encountered, the statistic associated with 'love' as a verb is incremented. Thus, the stored statistic is the observed frequency of the usage of a word in a particular sense.

Let χ^S be this mapping:

$$\chi^S : G \longrightarrow \mathcal{P}[S]$$

where:

$\mathcal{P}[S]$ is the power set of S

G is a set of input sentences

χ^S is a function that returns a result based on downward closures.

When applied to an argument $g \in G$, the function returns a set, C, of so-called candidate sentences in the sentence lattice derived from S. C is found by determining the meet of all attributes (i.e. words) in g, and then determining the set of sentences in the downward closure of this meet. If this set is empty, (i.e. no sentence in the sentence database is made up of the words in g) then further heuristics should be deployed to identify C.

For example, the set of words constituting g may be reduced by 1, the meet of these words is then found, and the downward closure of the resulting meet is computed. Repeat this for all words in g, and use the union of the downward closures computed in each case as C. Should C still be empty, the entire process could be repeated but with various combinations of 2 words removed from g, then 3, etc. Clearly a context is assumed where there is considerable overlap between words occurring in the input and words in the sentence database.

If too many words have to be removed from g before a non-empty C can be found (say, more than 25% of the words in g) then the sentence database is not appropriate for the domain under consideration.

These candidate sentences constitute 'closest neighbours' in S to the input sentence g. If the input is ill-formed, then a best approximation of the input sentence should be sought from amongst the candidate sentences. This best neighbour is then used as a basis for auto-correcting the input.

3.3 Selecting the Best Neighbour

Serutla and Oosthuizen (1997) suggest that input that cannot be parsed correctly by an MT system normally has one of the following errors: unknown words(s), redundant word(s), omitted word(s), or even incorrect word order. These errors make it impossible for an otherwise applicable rule to match and hence ensure that the input cannot be parsed. Similar errors also occur in the generated or translated sentences of a rule-based MT system. Next, the notion of rank is used to illustrate how the SAUCOLA system could be helpful in resolving under-generation (omitted words), over-generations (redundant words) and incorrect word order in sentences generated by an MT system.

Let

$g \in G$ be some generated sentence.

$\chi^S(g) = C$ is the set of candidate sentences available in S.

$c \in C$ is an arbitrary sentence in C.

$r(s)$ is the rank of an arbitrary sentence s. This is defined as the total number of words in s.

Then the following cases may arise:

1. $r(g) < r(c)$ for all $c \in C$, i.e. the input/generated sentence is shorter than all of its closest neighbours. g is more general than c and is said to subsume c. This case arises when an input/generated sentence has missing word(s). In the context of rule-based MT, the translation mechanism might have failed to generate all the appropriate words required to make the translation sound. For instance, the Lexica English-to-Sesotho translation of the input phrase:

"while the daughter should be trying to read in the garden" (1)

resulted in

"morali lokela be leka ho balile ka teng the ts'imo" (2)

whereas the correct translation is

"ha morali a lokela hore e be o ntse a leka ho bala ka serapeng" (3)

Using (2) as an input to the SAUCOLA system, then (3) would be retrieved, provided it was part of the sentence database initially used.

2. $r(g) > r(c)$ for all $c \in C$, i.e. the input/generated sentence is longer than all of its closest neighbours. This case arises when a generated sentence has at least one redundant word, with the consequence that correctness of the translation is clouded. The problem may also occur in the form of unnecessarily repeated words or phrases in the input or generated sentences under consideration.

The retrieved best approximation of a sentence will help in deciding which word types are not necessary in order that the input can be transformed into an acceptable form. Note that the sentence database contains only those sentences that are 'syntactically and semantically correct'.

An example:

input: but the horse may try to always be fed by the boy first.

output: empa pere e ka 'ka' nna ea leka ho 'be ho' feptjoa ke moshanyana pele kamehla.

required: empa pere e ka nna ea leka ho feptjoa ke moshanyana pele kamehla.

The quoted words in the output are the over-generated ones. By removing them, the required translation is obtained.

3. $r(g) = r(c)$ for some $c \in C$. Here the input sentence has the same length as one of its closest neighbours. g and c are likely to share the same, or nearly the same, syntactic structure. However, one or more of the words in the translated sentence might have been incorrectly selected - either from a dictionary on a first come first serve basis, or from a list of alternatives on the basis of statistical evidence.

But this is not a correct interpretation of how language behaves. It is true that some words are used more frequently than others, and tagging them like that has sometimes worked for MT. The reality, however, is that selection of words is not done in isolation, but is based on what other words are already used in such a sentence. The illustration of this is a choice of a concord when translating Sesotho into English, as can be seen in the following example:

input: I am singing and chewing.
output: Nna kea bina le kea hlafuna.
required: Nna kea bina hape kea hlafuna.

In the above example, the concord 'le' (a translation of 'and') is the first in the dictionary and hence gets picked up and used as a translation of 'and' without paying any attention to the meaning, or what other words in a sentence dictate.

3.4 Additional Considerations

The way in which sentences in S should be selected has not been discussed in great depth. In some applications (e.g. booking systems) a relatively small set of sentences might be available a priori.

In other cases, one might start with a set of WTV's and a small dictionary of words and their possible word types. S could then be generated from this information (even though some sentences might be semantically meaningless, but syntactically correct). For example, the WTV ⟨art, noun, verb, art, noun⟩ and the set of words {boy, girl, sees, the} gives rise to sentences such as 'The boy sees the girl', 'The boy sees the boy', etc.

Furthermore, while the previous discussion referred to 'sentences' throughout, the underlying approach can clearly be applied to phrases well.

Finally, for the sake of simplicity, we have chosen to discuss the sentence lattice in terms of attributes that are made up of words only. There are situations, however, where one might wish to use a word type instead of a word as an attribute. This would be in situations where one could unambiguously link word types to some of the words in the input sentence. An obvious example is having an 'article' attribute, instead of an attribute for 'a' and another for 'the'.

4 Conclusion

This paper is based on the notion that sentence interpretation is a search problem, the search space being the set of all possible sentence interpretations. It is noted that an input sentence can be ill formed with the result that intended meaning is distorted. A mechanism has been proposed to search for the nearest sentence to the input. If found it can be used as a basis to auto-correct the input sentence.

Humans are able to auto-correct such sentences because they have accumulated a valuable sentence database over time. This is coupled with their knowledge of the language syntax and semantics. All these tools are used in interpreting an ill-formed input sentence, so that its correct meaning can be perceived or deduced.

These preliminary results show that even before considering the semantic roles that the words play in various sentences, the retrieved closest neighbours are really similar in many respects to the input sentences. We are taking the structure of the (possibly ill-formed) input sentence and looking for a corresponding structure in our language network. If this structure has been perceived before, it is retrieved; otherwise we perform a network or lattice search for a similar structure in order to interpret the currently unknown input. Eventually, we will bring both the syntax (in the form of WTV's) and the semantics (words and their types) to help us uniquely determine the unknowns in the input and hence interpret a sentence.

5 Future Directions

Since its introduction by Nagao (1984), example-based machine translation (EBMT) has been an active research area in NLP and some research efforts have been published (e.g. Pangloss (Nirenburg 1995), ReVerb (Collins and Cunningham 1996), ALT-J/E (Kaneda et al. 1996). The current approach appears suited in an EBMT context. A source sentence database would have to be aligned with corresponding sentence translations in the target language.

The advantage of this is two fold: firstly, if a source sentence has been perceived before, the aligned translation becomes the required target. It need not be generated. Secondly, if the input sentence shares syntactic similarity (similar WTV) with a stored sentence, then the knowledge used to transform the original source into the aligned target can be used to transform the current input into the required target.

References

Cardie, C.: Embedded machine learning systems for natural language processing: A general framework. LNAI 1040. Springer (1996) 315 – 328

Carpineto, C., Romano, G.: GALOIS: An order-theoretic approach to conceptual clustering. Procs. of ICML'93. Morgan Kaufmann (1993) 33 – 40

Carpineto, C,. Romano, G.: A lattice conceptual clustering systems and its application to browsing retrieval. Machine Learning 24 (1996a) 95 – 122

Carpineto, C., Romano, G.: Information retrieval through hybrid navigation of lattice representations. Journal of Human-Computer Studies 45 (1996b) 553 – 578

Collins, B., Cunningham, P.: Adaptation-guided retrieval in EBMT: A case based approach to machine translation. Procs. of EWCBR'96. LNAI 1168. Springer (1996) 91 – 104

Daelemans, W.: Memory - based lexical acquisition and processing. Procs. of EAMT Workshop. LNAI 898. Springer (1995) 85 – 98

Daelemans, W., van den Bosch, A., and Weijters, T.: Empirical learning of natural language processing tasks. Procs. of ECML'97. LNAI 1224. Springer (1997) 337 – 344

Demiroz, G., Guvenir, H. A.: Classification by voting feature intervals. Procs. of ECML'97. LNAI 1224. Springer (1997) 85 – 92

Ellis, G.: Efficient retrieval from hierarchies of objects using lattice operations. Procs. of ICCS'93. LNAI 699. Springer (1993) 274 – 293

Godin, R., Missiaoui, R., April, A.: Experimental comparison of navigation in a Galois lattice with conventional information retrieval methods. Journal of Man-Machine Studies 38 (1993) 747 – 767

Kaneda, S., Almuallim, H., Akiba, Y., Ishii, M., Kawaoka, T.: A revision learner to acquire selection rules from human made rules and examples. LNAI 1040. Springer (1996) 439 – 452

Knight, K., Chander, I., Haines, M., Hatzivassiloglou, V., Hovy E., Iida M., Luk, S. K., Wjiteney, R., Yamada, K.: Filling knowledge gaps in a broad based coverage machine translation system. Procs. of IJCAI'95 (1995) 1390 – 1396

Maarek, Y. S., Berry, D. M., Kaiser, G. E.: An information retrieval approach for automatically constructing software libraries. IEEE Transactions on Software Engineering 17(8) (1991) 800 – 813

Nagao, M.: A Framework for a mechanical translation between Japanese and English by analogy principle. In Elithorn, A. and Manerji, R. (eds): Artificial and Human Intelligence. Elsevier Publishers (1984) B.V. NATO

Nirenburg, S. (ed.): The PANGLOSS Mark III machine translation system. CMU-CMT-95-145 (1995) Joint Technical Report

Oosthuizen, G. D.: The use of a lattice in knowledge processing. Ph.D. Thesis (1988) University of Strathclyde, Glasgow

Serutla, L., Oosthuizen, G. D.: Using a lattice to enhance adaptation-guided retrieval in example based machine translation. Procs. of SAICSIT'97 (1997) 177 – 191

Wettschereck, D.: A hybrid nearest - neighbour and nearest - hyperrectangle algorithm. Procs. of ECML'94. LNAI 784. Springer (1994) 323 – 335

Yamada, S., Nakaiwa, H., Ogura, K., Ikehara, S.: A method of automatically adapting MT system to different domains. Procs. of TMI'95 (1995) 303 – 310

Evaluating Language Technologies: The MULTIDOC Approach to Taming the Knowledge Soup

Jörg Schütz and Rita Nübel

IAI
Martin-Luther-Straße 14
D-66111 Saarbrücken
GERMANY
email: {joerg,rita}@iai.uni-sb.de

Abstract. In this paper we report on ongoing verification and validation work within the MULTIDOC project. This project is situated in the field of multilingual automotive product documentation. One central task is the evaluation of existing off-the-shelf and research based language technology (LT) products and components for the purpose of supporting or even reorganising the documentation production chain along three diagnostic dimensions: the process proper, the documentation quality and the translatability of the process output. In this application scenario, LT components shall control and ensure that predefined quality criteria are applicable and measurable to the documentation end-product as well as to the information objects that form the basic building blocks of the end-product. In this scenario, multilinguality is of crucial importance. It shall be introduced or prepared, and maintained as early as possible in the documentation workflow to ensure a better and faster translation process. A prerequisite for the evaluation process is the thorough definition of these dimensions in terms of user quality requirements and LT developer quality requirements. In our approach, we define the output quality of the whole documentation process as the pivot where user requirements and developer requirements shall meet. For this, it turned out that a so-called "braided" diagnostic evaluation is very well suited to cover both views. Since no generally approved standards or even valid specifications for standards exist for the evaluation of LT products, we have adjusted existing standards for the evaluation of software products, in particular ISO 9001, ISO 9000-3, ISO/IEC 12119, ISO 9004 and ISO 9126. This is feasible because an LT product consists of a software part and a lingware part. The adaptation had to be accomplished for the latter part.

1   Introduction

MULTIDOC is a European project of the Fourth Framework Programme of the European Commission within the Language Engineering Sector. It is founded on the specific needs and requirements of product documentation expressed by several representatives of the European automotive industry, among them are Bertone, BMW, Jaguar, Renault, Rolls-Royce Motor Cars, Rover, Volvo and others. The focus of the project is particularly on the multilingual aspects of product documentation. Therefore, the general goal is to define and specify methods, tools and workflows supporting stronger demands on quality, consistency and clarity in the technical information, and shorter lead times and reduced costs in the whole production value cycle of documentation including the translation into multiple languages. The results of the project, however, are applicable to any other component or system manufacturing business; thus, they are not restricted to the automotive industry.

The project is divided into two phases: an inception and elaboration phase, the so-called MULTIDOC Concerted Action, and a construction or development phase, the so-called MULTIDOC Project. The first phase has been finished by the end of 1997, and the second phase has started in January 1998.

Evaluation is a task or rather a continuous process that is maintained throughout all project phases, so that a strict user-orientedness is ensured. In the inception and elaboration phase, we assessed several language technology (LT) products and components for their deployment in supporting and enhancing the quality of technical documentation, and to control and streamline the translation process which in most cases is contracted out to translation agencies or translation companies. For this assessment, we defined three so-called diagnostic quality dimensions which form the basis of all verification and validation activities:

1. Process (workflow) quality requirements.
2. Product (documentation) quality requirements.
3. Multilinguality (translatability) quality requirements.

These diagnostic dimensions are iteratively further elaborated and refined during the construction phase. On the one hand, this ensures that we will have quantitatively and qualitatively measurable improvements of the documentation value chain based on the initially stated needs and their associated quality features and characteristics. And on the other hand, this will guide the further development and the adaptation of LT products and components for the task-specific application.

In the remainder of this paper we will describe the prerequisites and the different steps of our evaluation approach. After a brief overview of the main user quality requirements in MULTIDOC which we have identified within the specific domain of technical documentation of Service and Repair Methods (SRM), we elaborate our evaluation methodology and the adopted method and principles. The user requirements have primarily guided the choice of the functionalities of the LT components which will be described subsequently. In the MULTIDOC project, the purpose of evaluating LT components is not to ultimately decide which specific component should win over another. Rather, the evaluation shall result in quantitatively and qualitatively measurable improvements of the whole documentation value chain, and shall also guide the introduction of possible extensions, amendments and improvements to the LT products and components according to user needs and demands. The subsequent sections are dedicated to the discussion of the MULTIDOC evaluation principles (metrics and metric value scales) and the design of the evaluation process. In the last section, we will summarise our findings and draw some further conclusions.

2   Quality Requirements Analysis

Within the MULTIDOC application scenario, we distinguish two types of users:

1. Technical writers as the producers of technical information for automotive service and repair.
2. Technicians and mechanics in automotive workshops as the consumers of technical information in their day-to-day operations.

Both groups have different quality requirements on the technical documentation, and in particular on the different information objects which form the basic building blocks of technical documentation and which are associated to the appropriate car function groups and car components (see below). Technical writers have to produce high-quality documents which have to adhere to the general principles of

- Consistency,
- Comprehensibility,
- Non-ambiguity, and
- Process-oriented preciseness

which all feed into translatability. Technicians and mechanics, on the other hand, are the consumers of this information. Their work is demand-driven; therefore they need:

- Fast and easy access to the right information at the right time (electronic delivery, retrieval software and update mechanism).
- Simple but precise descriptions of, for example, repair procedures.
- Technical information which bridges the chasm between technically correct descriptions and their own perhaps more economic but sloppy workshop jargon.

In the following, we will introduce in more detail the three different quality requirement domains, which we have identified as diagnostic quality dimensions.

2.1   Workflow Quality Requirements

Today, technical documentation is a sequential process performed over several stages with very restricted communication channels between the different stages. The main stage in this process is authoring which is concerned with the actual composing and writing of service information and repair instructions (here, we will only deal with these types of technical documentation because this is the main application area of MULTIDOC). Authoring is preceded by an information gathering and documentation design stage. In this stage, the information from the design and construction departments (product data and service data) is converted into a form suitable for the consumers of technical documentation. In our case, these are workshop technicians and mechanics; in other cases it could be the people of the marketing department, the high level management, or even the car owners. This conversion procedure mainly affects the wording used to describe a certain technical fact, and therefore it is massively terminology related. The terminology concerns not only the naming of car components and car function groups, denoted by nominal terms such as nouns and multiword units, but also the naming of service and repair activities, denoted by verbal terms.

Globally operating car manufacturers are obliged to deliver their technical documentation in SGML (ISO 8879) format in accordance with the Clean Air Act Amendment (CAAA) 1992 as specified in the SAE J2008 norm. The employment of SGML in the documentation process not only has opened the way to view documents in a content-oriented way (see below) as opposed to the predominant layout orientation in Desktop Publishing (DTP) systems but also to deploy the power of SGML to better guide and control the authoring process and the whole documentation value cycle, including maintenance, update and versioning.

With the completion of the authoring stage technical documentation is stored in a document management system (DMS) for the further processing in the so-called acceptance stage, where technical checks and legal checks are performed, and in the editing/formatting stage, where the documentation is prepared for different types of delivery (paper, CD, Web, and so forth). The very last stage in the documentation process is translation which in most cases is done by external translation agencies or translation companies. The translated documents are also stored in the central DMS but there are no sufficient control mechanisms to control the translation process and follow-up translation activities during the documentation maintenance phase.

The most obvious quality requirements for the documentation process are thus derived from the following business problem areas:

- Combination of product data and documentation data.
- Reuse of information.
- Linkage of source language information and target language information.

All three areas benefit from the definition of so-called information objects. Thus, information objects are also one part of the product. They are represented either as a geometric representation (product data diagrams) or as an SGML representation in form of an SGML tagged text unit, and combined through an abstract representation. This view permits the effective, timely and accurate description of the product components and associated service and repair processes, and the ability to manage product documentation as a product.

2.2 Documentation Quality Requirements

During the quality requirements analysis for technical writers, a number of application areas for the employment of LT functionality have been identified; among them the most important are:

- Terminology and abbreviation consistency.
- Spell checking and grammar checking.
- Style consistency, including corporate writing guidelines, i.e. controlled language.
- Intelligent information object search and retrieval.

- Foreign language support in different forms such as bilingual and multilingual glossaries, summarisation, information retrieval and indicative translation.

These areas also contribute to the reusability of the information objects in terms of information structuring (form, not layout, see above), and information content, which aims at conceptually precise descriptions of service and repair operations. For example, if in a repair operation the mechanic has to put away a specific part component of a car before executing a certain repair step, this has to be reflected in the repair information with the right wording and the right sequencing as exemplified in Listing 1.

```
<op_stepgrp id="v114" size="s1">
        <op_step><note> ensure extreme cleanliness</note>
                <op_substep type="disconnect"> ... </op_substep>
                <op_substep type="release"> ... </op_substep>
                <op_substep type="remove"> ... </op_substep>
                    ...
        </op_step>
</op_stepgrp>
```

Listing 1. Step Group Information Object

This SGML excerpt of a repair information object shows how this is achieved. The parameters of the step group pattern (op_stepgrp tag) determine the characteristics of a certain repair operation, which the technical writer has to describe, and which the workshop mechanic has to follow when executing the repair operation. Additional conceptual information specified in the type parameter associated to the op_substep SGML tag triggers the selection of the right wording (terminology and corporate style guidelines) of the repair operation. This then will also control the appropriate and correct translation of this repair operation in a foreign language even if there are cultural differences in service and repair behaviours.

Besides the above introduced principles, the employment of LT in these areas has also an impact on the time and costs. As an example, we will demonstrate that the effective control of terminology helps to reduce costs at a very early stage of the documentation workflow. This is motivated by the costs that are needed to detect and repair a terminology error. Let us assume that a unit cost of one is assigned to the effort required to detect and repair an error during the authoring stage, then the cost to detect and repair an error during the data gathering, harmonisation (synchronisation between product data and product documentation) and documentation design stages (which are similar to the requirements stages in software engineering) is between five to ten times less. On the other hand, the cost to detect and repair an error during the maintenance stage of documentation is twenty times more. The reasons for this large difference is that many of these errors are not detected until well after they have been made. This delay in error discovery means that the cost to repair includes the cost to correct the offending error and to correct subsequent investments in the error. These investments include rework (perhaps redesign) of documentation, rewrite of related documentation, and the cost to rework or replace documentation in the field.

This shows that errors made at early stages in the documentation workflow are extremely expensive to repair. If such error occurred infrequently, then the contribution to the overall documentation cost would not be significant. However, terminology errors are indeed a large class of errors typically found in complex technical documentation. These errors could be between 30 % and 70 % of the errors discovered in technical documentation. It seems reasonable to assume that a 20 % or more reduction in terminology errors can be accomplished at various levels of organisational maturity, in particular with the employment of LT functionality. Because of the multiplying effect, any such reduction can have a dramatic overall effect to our project's bottom line (time and costs, future revenues and increased competitiveness), and thus contributes to the overall documentation quality and the user's satisfaction.

Similar calculations were obtained for abbreviation errors, spell and grammar errors, and style errors, although their correction can only be accomplished during the authoring process, i.e. the writing and composing of the information objects. These examples profile that we are able to define the central and measurable metrics cost and time for the employment of LT components which can be further classified by their contribution to the overall increase of the so-called "hit rate". The "hit rate" is concerned with the measuring of the effectiveness and efficiency of information object search and information object reusability, including the reuse of already translated information objects. This is important because today inefficient search and retrieval facilities contribute to the redundancy of information object storage, which then has an impact on unnecessary follow-up translations causing additional costs.

The information consumers in the automotive workshops need precise information in terms of structure and content at the right time to assure efficient and effective service and repair measures. Here, the LT employment will contribute to certain search and retrieval operations in hotline information applications (see, for example, [8]), including a "translation-on-demand" option in cases where a specific hotline information is not available in a certain language. In the latter application, the maintenance of a terminology repository that also supports domain-specific action and event readings for verbal terms contributes to a successful and terminologically correct "shallow translation" (indicative or informative translation) of the hotline information.

2.3   Multilinguality Quality Requirements

Multilinguality plays a very important role in automotive technical documentation. Today, the automotive industry is faced with the following serious bottlenecks in addition to the above discussed translation related aspects:
- More and more languages in which product documentation has to be published; there is a tremendous increase in Asian and East-European markets.
- Increasing costs of translation.
- Inappropriate lead time of the translation process.

- Poor or no possibility to measure and control the translation process, also in terms of reusing already translated information objects.

The long-term goal within the MULTIDOC project is the definition of a Translation Engineering (TE) methodology and a TE process (method and procedures) which gives up the present way of viewing the documentation process as strictly chronological or linear, not linked with product data environments, and of translation being a separate step at the end of the processing chain. The most important investigation areas to reach this goal are:

- Graphics and other multimedia incarnations, such as video, animation and virtual reality applications, may enrich or even replace text in certain information objects and facilitate new approaches to information production such as symbolic authoring.
- Translation-on-demand policy to allow for an efficient and effective control of the actual translation needs because not all information objects need to be stored in every language that is supported by the business.
- Compilation of documentation from multilingual information objects, either already stored in a foreign language, translated on demand, or generated from an abstract representation; this allows for the simultaneous delivery of multilingual documentation.

Listing 2 below exemplifies that multilinguality can be achieved with the already introduced SGML authoring approach.

```
<op_stepgrp id="v114" size="s1">
        <op_step><note> &note_clean </note>
                <op_substep type="disconnect"> ... </op_substep>
                <op_substep type="release"> ... </op_substep>
                <op_substep type="remove">       <en> ... remove ... </en>
                                                 <de> ... abbauen ... </de>
                                                 <se> ... ta bort ... </se>

                ...
                </op_substep>

        ...
        </op_step>
</op_stepgrp>
```

Listing 2. Multilingual Step Group Information Object

3   MULTIDOC LT Components and LT Quality

3.1   Language Technology Components

An LT component normally consists of a software part and a lingware part to which different evaluation patterns can be assigned. Whereas for the software part developers and users mostly apply the software standards within the ISO 9001 and

SEI/CMM framework, especially the evaluation process is most often carried out in accordance with the ISO 9126 "Software Quality" standard with commercially available source code control products, such as the Logiscope system of Verilog, there is no consensus on "Lingware Quality" evaluation patterns today. The EAGLES initiative has proposed to apply ISO 9126 to Natural Language Processing (NLP) systems ([1]); however, they did not explicitly distinguish between the two parts, and therefore we still do not have measurable metrics for lingware.

Before going into the details of our lingware evaluation patterns, we will list the LT components that we considered in our MULTIDOC evaluation work, and how the evaluation work triggered the further development of these components.

On the one hand, our goal is to support the authoring process along the above mentioned principles, and on the other hand, to foster the process of defining the form and content of information objects and to maintain them through their whole life cycle. For both goals the employment of the following LT products and components is our focus:

- Basic LT components such as morphological, syntactic and semantic analysers and generators for a number of languages including German, English, French, Spanish, Italian, Swedish and some Asian languages, with corresponding dictionaries, including bilingual dictionaries.
- Checking utilities for orthography, grammar, style and consistency derived from (or based on) the basic LT components.
- Translation utilities either derived from the basic LT components or complete MT systems and translation memory (TM) systems.

This selection imposes a distinctive quality degree on the LT products (see below) which cannot be achieved by a monolithic and proprietary system design. Within MULTIDOC we are aiming at distributed system solutions that fit with the targeted distributed documentation environments.

3.2   Language Technology Quality

In our evaluation approach, lingware is defined as the intellectual creation comprising formal natural language descriptions, rules and any data, information and knowledge pertaining to the operation of a natural language processing system. This definition is in accordance with ISO 9000-3 which provides the guidelines for the application of the ISO 9001 standards that are concerned with the development, delivery and maintenance of software. A lingware product then is a language enabled system, i.e. a language technology product or component. It is the complete set of computer programs, procedures and associated documentation and data including the lingware designated for delivery to a user. Now, we are also in the position to define "Lingware Quality" in accordance with ISO 9126, which is the totality of features and characteristics of a lingware product (LT product) that bear on its ability to satisfy stated or implied needs. As with the definition of "Software Quality" this is a very broad and flexible definition which needs further refinement for its actual applicability to an LT product, i.e. a quality model. Instead of evaluating the above listed LT components as they are, i.e. with their built-in general language coverage (vocabulary and grammar), the language resources are continuously enriched with terminology, syntactic, semantic, and translation memory data according to our particular application scenario.

This approach of a cyclic evaluation gave us the possibility to even apply ISO 9126 derived metrics to the lingware part of the components (besides the source code control of the software part), in particular for the ISO quality factors functionality, reliability, usability, efficiency, maintainability and portability, as well as the EAGLES extensions to ISO 9126 customisability and scalability. The results of the cyclic evaluations constantly feed into further refinement and improvement steps. This work also gave us new insights for the future developments of the components, especially for their deployment in networked applications as proposed in [9].

Systems that can be evaluated in this way must be open, extensible and integratable on the software level through the specification of appropriate APIs, and on the lingware level through the specification of suitable "LT APIs" that permit the communication with the existing lingware resources, or through already existing system utilities that allow users to customise the lingware resources or to define their own lingware resources (lingware development environment). An LT API is also provided if the system permits the use of resources according to existing and emerging exchange format standards such as MARTIF (ISO/FDIS 12620) and OLIF ([11], [12]) for terminology and general lexicon resources, the TMX format of the OSCAR working group of LISA for the exchange between TM systems ([13]), and the OpenTag format for text data ([6]). Today, these standards only allow for an ASCII (ISO 8859) based encoding of the data, except TMX which already permits Unicode data encoding (ISO/IEC 10646).

To allow for a strict user-centred evaluation process, we have also included a so-called verification step. In this step the users contribute to the finalisation of the adapted evaluation method and to the definition of the evaluation metrics. The verification process is performed on a theoretical level taking, however, into account the user's genuine working environment as described above.

4   MULTIDOC Evaluation Methodology

4.1   Conceptual Framework

In our evaluation scenario we distinguish three categories for the evaluation:
1. Task which determines the specific requirements in terms of application (domain), system (operating aspects such as resource allocation) and process (workflow integration).
2. Domain which identifies the applicable norms and standards.
3. Safety which defines possible risks and safety levels of a specific workflow.

The basic ingredients that have to be defined and acknowledged by all project partners are:
- Approved terminology for all verification and validation tasks.

- Identified product with its sub-components including an appropriate documentation.
- Process according to the task (verification or validation).
- Testing environment (simulated working environment test, restricted field test, production test).

An additional contribution to our evaluation framework is derived from the ISO 9004 standard for "After Sales Servicing" for the particular areas risks, cost and benefits which play an important role in our industrial task-specific application scenario.

4.2   Diagnostic Evaluation

The evaluation methodology we have adopted within the MULTIDOC project is a diagnostic evaluation. Our definition of this type of evaluation differs from the EAGLES definition ([1]) in so far as we include the user requirements of a task-specific application in our evaluation methodology. This view does not only extend the EAGLES definition, it also permits the application of the ISO 9126 quality model for software systems to lingware systems including lingware developments in a balanced way. We call this a "braided" diagnostic evaluation. It means the systematic and regular application of predefined evaluation principles during the customising phases and scaling phases of a multi-purpose LT product or component. These principles are the central features of continuous quality control, progress monitoring and quality assurance during the evaluation process, and during the further development of the LT component. In this context, the meaning of the term development is twofold. On the one hand, it concerns the software solutions of the system, and on the other hand, the lingware resources such as grammars, lexicons, thesauri, corpora, style rules, test suites, translation modules, and so forth, and the language enabling technologies such as analysers, translators, and generators that implement the language enabled applications. The "braided" diagnostic evaluation methodology is defined in terms of:

- User and developer requirements which define the aimed at or needed functionality and the existing functionality of an LT product or component.
- Evaluation factors with their associated characteristics, metrics and value scales for multi-purpose and task-specific applications in terms of usability (deployment potential), reliability (stability in different application scenarios, see above), efficiency (throughput capabilities according to time and space considerations), maintainability with respect to future customisability and scalability of the LT component. This is accomplished by a quality model that associates to each of the before mentioned quality factors a quality criterion such as readability, testability, integratability, and so forth. If a particular quality criterion is satisfied then the associated quality factor is also satisfied.
- Process steps according to the task-specific evaluation principles consistency, comprehensibility, non-ambiguity, and operation oriented preciseness, which all contribute to the more general principle of translatability.

classes gives hints for further indepth code inspections. In particular, it also helps the developers in streamlining their code (software and lingware).

5.3 Evaluation Procedure

The last step of the evaluation process is the actual measurement of the selected metrics, which is then followed by a rating step. In this assessment step the quality of the LT product is summarised and the specifications for the adaptation process of the existing LT component are defined, i.e. the system "as is" including its language resources, resulting from the evaluation steps performed on a general level, especially metrics such as maintainability, customisability and scalability (see the discussion of APIs above). Based on the results of the evaluation of the current component, specifications can be developed which yield at the optimisation of the system's performance with respect to the predefined evaluation metrics. These specifications relate to concrete requirements resulting from the specific application domain (see above), for example, the treatment of a certain information type, typical linguistic phenomena (controlled language), use of domain-specific terminology, and so forth.

Aspects related to the given information technology infrastructure, for example, a network-based deployment including specific evaluation strategies that could be fulfilled by "intelligent" software agents (see [9]) are also taken into account, as well as time and cost aspects of the product's actual deployment in a corporate environment.

As already outlined above, these evaluation steps are performed in iterative cycles. The continuous communication between the users and the developers ensures that the different evaluation patterns are applied in an optimal way, and that feedback is given on a regular basis. In addition, this processing strategy permits the adaptation or even the redefinition of the evaluation patterns, thus introducing a certain dynamic, i.e. the "braid", into the otherwise static (and perhaps inflexible) evaluation procedure.

6 Conclusion and Perspectives

In this paper we have introduced the MULTIDOC evaluation methodology based on diagnostic dimensions and performed through a cyclic processing technique (method). The utilised methodology is entirely user-centred with additional support through developer oriented requirements to sanction a "braided" evaluation. This approach allows for a clear distinction between the software level and the lingware level in the evaluation process, and the applicability of the ISO 9126 quality model to both levels on a thorough foundation.

The users of the MULTIDOC project agree on the fact that this approach should also be the standard approach to be adopted by LT vendors to support the integration of an LT component into an existing industrial workflow. Today, neither LT vendors nor LT OEM/VAR service providers operate in this way. In this context, the definition of an independent certification procedure seems to be most interesting for LT users.

One of the future next steps is the investigation into automatisable processes to permit the development of source code control facilities for LT components, which are similar to the existing software source code control tools.

Acknowledgements

The MULTIDOC project is partly funded by the European Commission under contracts LE3-4230 and LE4-8323. The content of this paper does not reflect any official statement of the European Commission or the MULTIDOC project partners. The responsibility for the content is solely with the authors of the paper.

References

1. EAGLES: Evaluation of Natural Language Processing System. Final Report, EAGLES Document EAG-EWG-PR.2, Geneva, Switzerland (1995)
2. Haller, J.: MULTILINT - Multilingual Documentation with Linguistic Intelligence. In: Proceedings of 'Translating and the Computer', ASLIB, London, Great Britain (1996)
3. Haller, J. and Schütz, J.: Integration linguistischer Intelligenz in die multilinguale technische Dokumentation. In Proceedings of EUROMAP Forum 'Sprache ohne Grenzen', München, Germany (1997)
4. Maas, H.D.: Multilinguale Textverarbeitung mit MPRO. In: Lobin, G., Lohse, H. Piotrowski, S and Poláková, E. (Eds.): Europäische Kommunikationskybernetik heute und morgen, KoPäd, München, Germany (1998) 167-173
5. Nübel, R.: End-to-End Evaluation in Verbmobil I. In: Proceedings of Machine Translation Summit VI, San Diego, California, USA (1997) 232-239
6. OpenTag - Formal Specifications. Version 1.1b April-22-1998, Last edit: May-01-1998. Available on the Web at http://www.opentag.org/otspecs.htm (1998)
7. Schütz, J.: Language Engineering – Fixing Positions. IAI Memo 0695, Saarbrücken, Germany. Available on the Web at http://www.iai.uni-sb.de/memos.html (1995)
8. Schütz, J.: Combining Language Technology and Web Technology to Streamline an Automotive Hotline Support Service. In: Proceedings of AMTA 96, Montreal, Canada (1996) 180-189
9. Schütz, J.: Utilizing Evaluation in Networked Machine Translation. In: Proceedings of the 7th International Conference on Theoretical and Methodological Issues in Machine Translation (TMI) 1997, Santa Fe, New Mexico, USA (1997) 208-215
10. Schütz, J. and Nübel, R.: Multi-purpose vs. Specific Application: Diagnostic Evaluation of Multilingual Language Technologies. In Proceedings of the 1st International Conference on Language Resources and Evaluation, Granada, Spain (1998) 1251-1254
11. Thurmair, G.: Exchange Interfaces for Translation Tools. In Proceedings of MT Summit VI, San Diego, California, USA (1997) 74-92
12. Thurmair, G., Ritzke, J. and McCormik, S.: The Open Lexicon Interchange Format - OLIF. OTELO Report available on the Web at http://www.otelo.lu (1998)
13. TMX Format Specifications. Version 1.0 November-25-1997. Available on the Web at http://www.lisa.org/tmx/tmx.htm (1997)

Integrating Query Translation and Document Translation in a Cross-Language Information Retrieval System

Guo-Wei Bian and Hsin-Hsi Chen

Department of Computer Science and Information Engineering
National Taiwan University
Taipei, Taiwan, R.O.C.
Email: gwbian@nlg.csie.ntu.edu.tw, hh_chen@csie.ntu.edu.tw
http://nlg3.csie.ntu.edu.tw

Abstract. Due to the explosive growth of the WWW, very large multilingual textual resources have motivated the researches in Cross-Language Information Retrieval and online Web Machine Translation. In this paper, the integration of language translation and text processing system is proposed to build a multilingual information system. A distributed English-Chinese system on WWW is introduced to illustrate how to integrate query translation, search engines, and web translation system. Since July 1997, more than 46,000 users have accessed our system and about 250,000 English web pages have been translated to pages in Chinese or bilingual English-Chinese versions. And the average satisfaction degree of users at document level is 67.47%.

1   Introduction

In the past few years, the World Wide Web (WWW) grows explosively and has become the most useful and powerful information retrieval and accessing system on the Internet. The WWW breaks the boundaries of countries and provides very large online documents (more than 10 million documents) in multiple languages. These multilingual textual resources have motivated the researches in Cross-Language Information Retrieval (CLIR) and online Machine Translation (MT) to build the multilingual information accessing system. Although a number of searching engines and information discovery systems have been introduced on the Internet for users to locate interesting and relevant information, the language barrier becomes the major problem for people to search, retrieve, and understand WWW documents in different languages. That decreases the dissemination power of the WWW to some extent.

To alleviate this barrier, some information providers and WWW servers keep multiple copies of their information in different languages for multilingual service. Due to the dynamic nature of the WWW environment, the provided information is updated frequently. This approach is involved with the data inconsistency problem and the management problem of multilingual documents. How to incorporate the capability of language translation into WWW becomes indispensable for multilingual service. Recently, several online machine translation systems [1-4] have been presented. Traditional MT systems cannot be employed to the WWW directly because they are usually used to translate the written documents in the off-line batch mode. Translation quality is the most important criterion. In on-line and real-time applications, speed performance is also an important factor.

In this paper, we will focus on the following problems to alleviate the language barrier on WWW:

1. Language translation techniques
2. The integration of language translation system and text processing system

The language translation system is proposed to incorporate with the different kinds of text processing systems (e.g., searching engines, text summarization systems, *etc.*). A system integrated MT and IR technologies for WWW (abbreviated as MTIR) is introduced to illustrate our solutions for the mentioned problems. Section 2 describes a general model of the multilingual information system and introduces the architecture of our bilingual English-Chinese system for WWW. We discuss the Chinese-English query translation in section 3. Section 4 specifies how to integrate the query translation of CLIR with several searching engines on WWW. Section 5 describes the online and real-time web translation. Section 6 makes evaluations for such a multilingual information system from different users' viewpoints. Section 7 concludes the remarks.

2 Multilingual Information System

Some of multilingual requirements for computer systems are shown as follows:

1. Data Representation: character sets and coding systems
2. Data Input: input methods and transliterated input
3. Data Display and Output: font mapping
4. Data Manipulation: the application must be able to handle the different coding characters
5. Query Translation: to translate the information need of users
6. Document Translation using Machine Translation (MT): to translate documents

The first three requirements have been resolved by system applications in several computer operating systems. Some of applications and packages can also handle both single-byte and multiple-byte coding systems for Indo-European and Eastern-Asian languages. However, the language barrier becomes the major problem for people to access the multilingual documents. How to incorporate the capability of language translation to meet the requirements 5 and 6 becomes indispensable for multilingual systems.

2.1 Four-Layer Multilingual Information System (MLIS)

Fig. 1 shows a four-layer multilingual information system. We put the different types of processing systems on the four layers:

Layer 1: Language Identification (LI)
Layer 2: Text Processing Systems
Level 3: Language Translation Systems
Level 4: User Interface (UI)

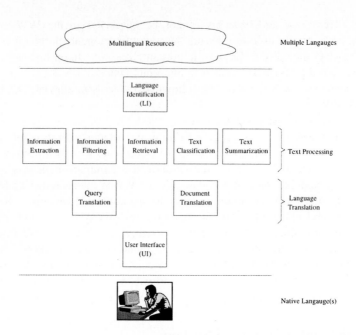

Fig. 1.   A Four-Layer Model of Multilingual Information System (MLIS)

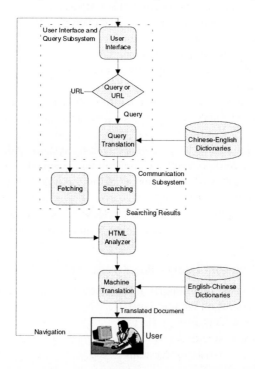

Fig. 2.   The Overall Architecture of MTIR System

Because most of natural language processing techniques (e.g., lexical analysis, parsing, *etc.*) are dependent on the language of processed document, the layer 1 resolves language identification problem before text processing. The language identification system employs cues from the different character sets and coding systems of languages. At layer 2, the systems may perform information extraction, information filtering, information retrieval, text classification, text summarization, or other text processing tasks. Some of the text processing systems may have interaction with another one. For example, the relevant documents retrieved by IR system can be summarized to users. Additionally, a multilingual text processing system should be able to handle the different coding characters to match the requirement 4 (data manipulation). Several searching engines (e.g., AltaVista, Infoseek, *etc.*) have the ability to index the documents of multiple languages. The language translation systems at layer 3 are used to translate the information need of users for text processing systems and translate the resultant documents from text processing systems to users in their native languages. The user interface is the closest layer to users. It gets the user's information need (included parameters, query and user profile) and displays the resultant document to user.

2.2 Bilingual English-Chinese Information System for WWW

On the WWW, the distinct systems can be easily integrated as a larger distributed system using the HTTP protocol. Each system can be involved using an URL of CGI program. First, the CGI program gets input data from the caller. Then the caller gets the resultant document from the server system. Fig. 2 shows the basic architecture of MTIR system. Users express their intention by inputting URLs of web pages or queries in Chinese/English. A Chinese query is translated into the English counterpart using query translation mechanism. The translations of query terms are disambiguated using word co-occurrence relationship. Then the system sends the translated query to the searching engine that selected by user in the user interface. The query subsystem takes care of the user interface part.

The subsequent navigation on the WWW is under the control of the communication subsystem. To minimize the traffic of Internet, a caching module is presented in this subsystem and some proxy systems are used to process the request. The objects in the cache are checked when a request is received. If the requested object is not found, the communication system fetches the HTML file (.htm or .html file) or text file (.txt or .text file) from the neighboring proxy systems or the original server.

The HTML analyzer examines the retrieved file. It divides the whole file into several translation segments for the machine translation subsystem. The HTML tags such as title, headings, unordered lists, ordered lists, definition lists, forms and tables play the similar roles of punctuation marks like full stop, question mark and exclamation mark. In contrast to the above tags, the font style elements, e.g., bold, italic, superscripts, subscripts, and font styles, may produce many unknown words because the whole word is split into several parts. Thus these font style elements should be hidden from the attributed words during translation processing.

After receiving the first translated document, users may access other information through the hyperlinks. We attach our system's URL to those URLs that link to HTML files or text files. Such a way guarantees the successive browses are linked with our system. The other URLs, including inline images and external MIME objects, are changed into their absolute URLs. In other words, the non-textual information is received from the original servers. Our experimental system is accessible with the following URL:

> http://mtir.csie.ntu.edu.tw

3   Query Translation

Several approaches have been proposed for CLIR recently. There are four main approaches for query translation:

1. Dictionary-based approach [5-8]
2. Corpus-based approach [9-10]
3. Hybrid approach (combined dictionary-based and corpus-based) [6]
4. Machine Translation based approach (MT-based) [11]

Because the large parallel Chinese-English corpora are not available, the dictionary-based approach is adopted in our system. The query translation for Chinese-English CLIR consists of three major steps:

1. Word segmentation: To identify the word boundary of the input stream of Chinese characters.
2. Query translation: To construct the translated English query using the bilingual dictionary. The translation disambiguation is done using the monolingual corpus.
3. Monolingual IR: To search the relevant documents using the translated queries.

The segmentation and the query translation use the same bilingual dictionary in this design. That speeds up the dictionary lookup and avoids the inconsistencies resulting from two dictionaries (i.e., segmentation dictionary and transfer dictionary). This bilingual dictionary has approximately 90,000 terms. The longest-matching method is adopted in Chinese segmentation. The segmentation processing searches for a dictionary entry corresponding to the longest sequence of Chinese characters from left to right. After identification of Chinese terms, the system selects some of the translation equivalents for each query term from the bilingual dictionary. The terms of query can be translated in two different levels of dictionary translations: word-level (word-by-word) and phrase-level translations. Those terms, missing from the transfer dictionary, are passed unchanged to the final query.

3.1 Selection Strategies

When there is more than one translation equivalent in a dictionary entry, the following selection strategies are explored.

(1)   Select-All (SA): The system looks up each term in the bilingual dictionary and constructs a translated query by concatenating of all the senses of the terms.

(2)   Select-Highest-Frequency (SHF): The system selects the sense with the highest frequency in target language corpus for each term. Because the translation probabilities of senses for each term are unavailable without a large-scale word-

aligned bilingual corpus, the translation probabilities are reduced to the probabilities of sense in the target language corpus. So, the frequently-used transferring sense of a term is used instead of the frequently-translated sense.

(3) Select-N-POS-Highest-Frequency (SNHF): This strategy selects the highest-frequent sense of each POS candidate of the term. If the term has N POS candidates, the system will select N translation senses. Compared to this strategy, the strategy (2) always selects only one sense for each term.

(4) Word co-occurrence (WCO): This method classifies words on the basis of their co-occurrence with other words. The translation of a query term can be disambiguated with the co-occurrence of its translation equivalents and other words' equivalents. The mutual information (MI) of word pairs reflects the word association norms in one language. If two words x and y have probabilities $P(x)$ and $P(y)$, their mutual information [12] is defined to be

$$I(x, y) = \log_2 \frac{P(x, y)}{P(x)P(y)}$$

This method considers the content around the translation equivalents within the text collection to decide the best target equivalent. The mutual information of word pairs is trained using a window size 3 in the CACM text collection [13]. Totally, there are 247,864 word pairs.

Table 1 illustrates an example for different translation. The Chinese concept '奇異值分解' (jiyi zhi fenjie) and its phrase-level translation 'singular value decomposition' are employed. Four translated representations using different selection strategies on the word-level translation is shown in Table 1 (a). Column 3 shows the translation equivalents in transfer dictionary for the query terms at word-level. Table 1 (b) lists the mutual information of some word pairs of translation equivalents. Most of word pairs have no co-occurrence relations. Considering the example, the equivalent 'singular' of the term '奇異' (jiyi) has the largest MI score with all translation equivalents of other two words.

3.2 Experiments and Evaluations

In the following experiments, the word-level and the phrase-level translations are touched to demonstrate the problems from missing terminology and multi-term concepts. In addition, we will evaluate these selection strategies with the long and the short versions of queries. The short queries are used to simulate the behavior of our methods for WWW. The SMART information retrieval system [14] is utilized to measure the similarity of the query and each document using the vector space model. The query weights are multiplied by the traditional IDF factor. The test collection CACM is used to evaluate the performance of different selection strategies. This collection contains 3204 texts and 64 queries in English. Each query has relevance judgements. The average number of words in the query is approximately 20.

In order to test the effectiveness of query translation, we create the Chinese queries by manually translating the original English queries to Chinese ones. The Chinese queries are regarded as the input queries later. Each Chinese query is translated to four target queries using different selection strategies. The following experiments compare the retrieval performances of the four translated versions of

Chinese queries to the results of the original English queries. One example of the original English query, human translated Chinese version, and translated queries are shown in Table 2. It gives the segmented Chinese string and four automatically translated representations for the CACM Q1. Parentheses surround the English multi-term concepts and the brackets surround the translation equivalents of each term.

To compare the performances of the word-level translation and phrase-level translation, the CACM English queries are manually checked to find the multi-term concepts that are not contained in our bilingual dictionary. These concepts and their translations are added into the bilingual dictionary for the phrase-level experiments. Totally, 102 multi-word concepts (e.g., remote procedure call (遠端程序呼叫), singular value decomposition (奇異值分解), *etc.*) are identified in the CACM queries.

Table 1. Different translations of Chinese concept '奇異值分解' (singular value decomposition)

Table 1(a). Translated representations based on different strategies

Term	POS	SA	SHF	SNHF	WCO
奇異 (jiyi)	N	oddity singularity		singularity	
	ADJ	singular	singular	singular	singular
值 (zhi)	N	value worth	value	value	value
分解 (fenjie)	N	Decomposition analysis dissociation cracking disintegration		decomposition	decomposition
	V	analyze anatomize decompose decompound disassemble dismount resolve	analyze	analyze	
	XV	(split up) (break up)		(split up)	

Table 1(b). The mutual information for some word pairs

word	Equivalents		奇異 (jiyi) w11	w12	w13	值 (zhi) w21	w22	分解 (fenjie) w31	w32	w33	w34	w35	w36
奇異 (jiyi)	oddity	w11											
	singular	w12				6.099		4.115	6.669				
	singularity	w13											
值 (zhi)	value	w21		6.099				1.823	4.377				
	worth	w22											
分解 (fenjie)	analysis	w31		4.115		1.823							
	decomposition	w32		6.669		4.377							
	analyze	w33											
	decompose	w34											
	decompound	w35											
	resolve	w36											

Table 2.   The Chinese query and four translated representations for CACM Q1

Original Query	What articles exist which deal with TSS 'Time Sharing System', an operating system for IBM computers?
Chinese Query	那些文章是有關 TTS '分時系統',一種 IBM 電腦的作業系統
1 Segmentation	那些 文章 是 有關 TTS '分 時 系統', 一 種 IBM 電腦 的 作業系統
2.1 SA	those article [be yes yah yep] about TTS '[minute cent apportion deal dissever sharing] time [formation lineage succession system]', [a ace mono] [class seed] IBM [computer computing] of [(operating system) (operation system) OS]
2.2 SHF	those article be about TTS 'deal time system', a class IBM computer of (operating system)
2.3 SNHF	those article [be yes] about TTS '[minute deal] time system', [a mono] class IBM computer of [(operating system) OS]
2.4 WCO	those article be about TTS 'sharing time system', a class IBM computer of (operating system)

Over a wide range of operational environments, the average terms of user-supplied queries are 1.5 ~ 2 words and rarely more than 4 words.   Hull and Grefenstette [7] work with the short versions of queries (average length of seven words) from French to English in TREC experiments.   But no comparison of the short and long queries is available.   To evaluate the behavior of user's short queries, we make additional experiments to compare with the results of the original long queries.   Three researchers help us to create the English and Chinese versions of short queries from the original English queries of CACM.   For example, the short version of CACM Q1 is "TSS Timing Sharing System".   On the average, the short query has near 4 words, including single-word terms and multi-term concepts.   The short version of English queries is regarded as the baseline to compare the results of translated queries of the short Chinese queries.

The overall results are shown in Fig. 3.   The 11-point average precision [15] of the monolingual short English queries is 29.85%.   It achieves the 83.42% performance of the original English queries.   In word-level experiments, the best WCO (word co-occurrence) strategy gets the 72.96% performance of the monolingual English short version and 65.18% of the monolingual original English version.   In phrase-level, the WCO achieves 87.14% and 74.71% respectively.   The SHF, SNHF, and WCO selection strategies perform better in the long queries than that in short ones. However, the simple SA strategy has opposite result.   Because users give more specific terms in short queries, the SA strategy introduces less extraneous terms to the query.   Alternatively, the phrase-level translation improves the performance up to 14~31% over the word-level translation for Chinese-English CLIR.   Combining the phrase dictionary and co-occurrence disambiguation can bring the performance of CLIR up to 87% of monolingual retrieval in short queries.   Recall that the multi-word concepts and their translations are added to the dictionary in our experiments after the domain experts have examined the queries.   Hence the coverage of bilingual phrasal dictionary will affect the performance of CLIR.   Even though the bilingual dictionary does not contain these multi-word concepts, the WCO method still achieves near 70% monolingual effectiveness for different length of query at word-level translation.

11-point average precision (%)

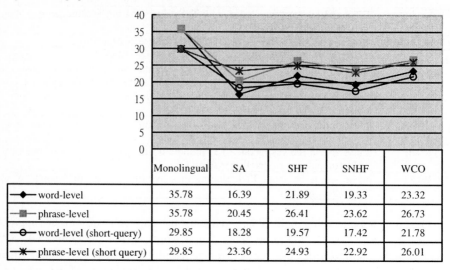

	Monolingual	SA	SHF	SNHF	WCO
◆ word-level	35.78	16.39	21.89	19.33	23.32
■ phrase-level	35.78	20.45	26.41	23.62	26.73
⊙ word-level (short-query)	29.85	18.28	19.57	17.42	21.78
✳ phrase-level (short query)	29.85	23.36	24.93	22.92	26.01

Fig. 3. The comparison of retrieval performances of query translations for the long queries and short queries in different levels of translations

4 Search Engines

Six popular search engines are integrated with language translation in our MTIR system. User inputs query and selects one of the search engines in the user interface. The Chinese query terms will be translated to English ones. After the processing of query translation, our system will send an HTTP request composed of the translated query to the chosen search engine. The retrieved results from the search engine will be translated to the user's native language (Chinese). In general, the CGI program of searching engine processes the HTTP request of query. For instance, assuming "machine translation" is the translated query of the Chinese query "機器翻譯" (jiqi fanyi). The HTTP requests for the CGI programs of several search engines are listed in Table 3. The query words should be separated with the symbol '+' for the standard URL encoding.

Hull and Grefenstette [7] give five different definitions for multilingual information retrieval. The type 4 is "IR on a multilingual document collection, where queries can retrieve documents in multiple languages". How to merge and rank the retrieved documents in different languages is a problem in CLIR. Among these systems, the AltaVista and Infoseek have indexed both the English and Chinese web pages. If a bilingual query ("機器翻譯+machine+translation") is invoked, the two systems will list the relevant documents of both languages. However, the ranking for documents in different languages seems not good. It's still a problem for multilingual IR.

Table 3. HTTP Requests for the CGI Programs of Searching Engines

Search Engine	HTTP Requests for the CGI Programs of Searching Engines	Chinese Indexing
AltaVista	http://www.altavista.digital.com/cgi-bin/query?pg=q&what=web &kl=XX&q=machine+translation&search.x=35&search.y=9	Yes
Excite	http://search.excite.com/search.gw?search=machine+translation	No
Infoseek	http://www.infoseek.com/Titles?qt=machine+translation&col=WW &sv=IS&lk=noframes&nh=10	Yes
Lycos	http://www.lycos.com/cgi-in/pursuit?matchmode=and&cat=lycos& query=machine+translation&x=30&y=4	No
MetaCrawler	http://www.metacrawler.com/crawler?general=machine+translation &method=0&target=&region=0&rpp=20&timeout=5&hpe=10	No
Yahoo	http://search.yahoo.com/bin/search?p=machine+translation	No

5 Document Translation

The requirement for an online machine translation system for users to navigate on WWW is different from traditional off-line batch MT systems.   An assisted MT system should help users quickly understand the Web pages and find the interested documents during navigation on a very huge information resources.   That is, different users' behaviors affect the requirements of machine translation systems.

From users' viewpoint, a high-quality and high-speed online machine translation is required.   However, several steps should be performed after a query is issued.   It takes time for the transfer of the query, the query translation, the retrieval of the document satisfying the query, the transfer of the retrieved document and the document translation.   How to find the tradeoff between the speed performance and the translation performance on the WWW is an important issue.   Besides this issue, our previous work [1] addressed four other issues, including which material is translated, what roles the HTML tags play in translation, what form the translated result is presented in, and where the translation capability is implemented, to design online machine translation systems for the WWW.

Many different approaches to machine translation design have been proposed [16-21].   These include rule-based, example-based, statistics-based, knowledge-based, and glossary-based approaches.   A hybrid approach [22] integrates the advantages of these approaches and tries to get rid of their disadvantages.   A rule-based partial parsing method is adopted and the translation process is performed chunk by chunk. We follow this design strategy and consider the characters of web translation.   The following sections depict the details of analysis, transfer and synthesis modules.

5.1 Analysis Module

At first, we identify the sentence types of source sentences using sentence delimiters. Some structural transfer rules can only be applied to some types of sentences.   Then, we take a morphological analysis.   The words in morphological forms (e.g. +ed, +ing, +ly, +s, *etc.*) are tagged with the morphological tags, which are useful for part-of-speech tagging, word sense disambiguation, and the generation of the target sense using the sense of the root word.

After morpheme processing, the words in root forms are searched from various dictionaries using the longest-matching strategy. There are about 67,000 word entries in an English-Chinese general dictionary and 5,500 idioms in a phrasal dictionary. In addition, some domain specific dictionaries are required for better translation performance. After dictionary lookup, the idioms and the compound words are treated as complete units for POS tagging and sense translation.

For consideration of the speed and robustness issues, a three-stage hybrid method is adopted to deal with part-of-speech tagging. It treats the certain cases using heuristic rules, and disambiguates the uncertain cases using a statistical model. At stage 1, the words with specific morphological tags can be tagged without ambiguities. For example, the word of the pattern ADJ+ly is tagged with RB. The tagging of some morphological words depends on the morphological tag and the POS of its root form. For example, if the dictionary tag of the root of a word (root+er) is JJ, then this word is an adjective. Otherwise, it is a noun. Besides, if a word does not have any morphological tags and has only one POS candidate in the dictionary, then the unique POS is assigned to this word. At stage 2, a pattern matching method that considers the morphological tags of the current and the next words, as well as the POS of the next word, is employed to do the POS tagging. Stage 3 deals with the remaining words, which have not been tagged up to now. A statistical bigram HMM model is followed to solve the uncertain cases.

To reduce the cost of fully parsing in a real-time service, we adopt a partial parser to get the skeletons of sentences. A NP/ADJP finite state machine (FSM) is used to segment the source sentence into a sequence of chunks. This FSM analyzes the tag sequence, and recognizes the fundamental noun phrases and adjective phrases in linear time. Then a predicate-argument detector is followed to analyze the skeleton of sentence [23]. The determination of PP attachment is based on the rule templates [24].

5.2 Transfer Module

The structural transfer, the tense transfer, and the lexical selections touch on the differences of source and target languages. The major structural transfers occur in the comparative clauses, the question sentences, and the modifications of noun phrases. The structure of noun phrases is left-recursion in English, but is right-recursion in Chinese. Due to the recursion in the noun phrases, the transferred target structure is treated as a whole chunk for the subsequent processing. For different tenses, the words "*have*" and "*be*" have different senses in Chinese.

Phrases and idioms are treated as complete units during lexical selection. A bilingual phrase dictionary is employed to produce phrase-by-phrase translation. For those remaining words, several word selection algorithms like select-first, select the-highest-frequency word and mutual information method may be adopted to select the target sense. The select-first method always selects the first translation sense from the candidates with the matched POSes. The second method chooses the target sense with the highest occurrence probability, trained from a large-scale corpus of the target language. The mutual information model considers the content around the words to decide the best combination of target words. Different models access various training tables. The larger the table is, the more time it takes. Section 6 will discuss the time complexity, the table space and the translation accuracy.

5.3 Synthesis Module

The synthesis module deals with word insertion, deletion and word order refinement. For example, if the source word with morpheme tag YJB, is tagged as adverb (RB) and derived from the adjective (JJ) word form, the target sense will be generated in the way of deleting the character "的" (de) and appending "地" (di). The character "的" (de) always appears at the end of Chinese adjectives, and the character "地" (di) at the end of adverbs. In addition, if the present participle and the past participle are tagged as adjective. The character "的" (de) is inserted into the target sense.

Our previous work [1] introduced the generation of bilingual aligned document for web translation system. A bilingual document can be generated and aligned using the HTML block-level tags. Users can read both the English and the Chinese blocks simultaneously. Bilingual aligned document is a better representation scheme when both the translation performance and the speed performance are considered.

6 Evaluation for Multilingual Information System

The implemented system has been opened to Internet users. We analyze each subsystem of MTIR and measure the quantitative evaluation results in 100,000 translated web pages during the last four months of 1997. In such a large experimental resource, a web page has 308.30 words and 101.80 punctuation marks on the average. Total 14.08% of words are in morphological forms, and their root words can be derived from the morphological analyzer. Most of morphological processing (82.21%) is done by the morphological rules and the else is done using the morphological dictionary. Excepting numbers and punctuation marks, the words make up 78.66% of a web page's content. Table 4(a) illustrates the statistical information for the average size of the web pages, the interactions between HTML and MT modules, the HTML tags and the content. Importantly, 11.87% of a web page are unknown words. For example, GeoCities, ICQ, NT, CERN, ASEAN, WinZip, DNS, Pentium, RealAudio, Newswire, QuickTime, NSSDC, AltaVista, Cybertown, MicroSim, HomeBanking, W3C, Hotmail, Website, CNET, ZDNet, RealVideo, Perl, BIOS, AOL, GeoPlus, Win95, and CGI are the terms extracted from the web pages. Most of these unknown words are production names, proper names, technological terms, and web sites.

The overall speed performance depends on the communication, HTML analyzer, and MT subsystem. For the consideration of online and real-time issue, the highest-frequency-word method is adopted for the word selection module. Table 4(b) shows the average processing time for the each subtask of the MT system, and the other two modules on the SUN SPARC station 5. In our system, the average communication time to fetch the requested URL (document) is 44.19 seconds. And 7.81% of requested web pages is time out (exceeding 300 seconds). Recently, a faster proxy system is used to fetch the web pages and the average communication time is reduced to near 20 seconds. After the web pages are fetched, the HTML analyzer parses the HTML structures and calls the MT system to translate the content. On average, these two subsystems take 5.67 seconds to translate an HTML file. In the following, we will discuss the time complexity and the translation quality for the major tasks in MT subsystem.

Table 4. Quantitative Study of Web Translation

(a). Statistical Information for Web Pages and HTML Tags

Size (Bytes)	Call MT (numbers of quasi-sentences)	Numbers of HTML Tags		Content								
		Block-level Tags	Font-level Tags	Anchors	Words	Punctuation Marks	Special Codes (&code)	E-mails	URLs	Hosts	IPs
7037.80	36.53	127.19	96.72	29.41	308.30	101.80	0.12	0.21	0.37	1.43	0.20

(b). Speed Performance of Communication, HTML Analyzer, and MT Subsystem (in seconds).

MT Module									HTML + MT modules	Communication
Dictionary Accessing	Tagging by			Partial Parsing	Transferring			Synthesis	5.67	44.19
	morpheme	rules	HMM		Structural Transfer	Tense Refine	Word Selection			
2.03	0.01	0.01	1.31	0.01	0.00	0.00	0.02	0.01		
3.40										

Table 5. Time Complexity and Translation Quality using Different Word Selection Methods

Evaluation / Word Selection	Table Size (Space)			Speed (Time) in seconds	Translation Quality (Accuracy)
	Entries	Total Frequency	(MB)		
Model 1	none	none	0.00	0.01	62.12%
Model 2	94,531	2,433,670	8.33	0.01	85.37%
Model 3	884,324	2,147,571	80.05	48.72	81.53%

To be an online and real-time service of web translation on Internet, how much time users can endure is an important issue. However, most tasks of natural language processing have the problem of large time complexity. Some tradeoff between speed and quality must be done for the real-time NLP applications. The following shows some discussions. Because the translation quality depends on tagging and word selection in MT system, we evaluate these two major components for the top 30 WWW sites accessed by users of our system. And two additional word selection methods are explored to compare the performances of speed and quality. We assign four graduate and five undergraduate students to evaluate the translation results of these web sites.

With our 3-stage hybrid tagging method, the words of the web page are tagged within 2 seconds. Further, the accuracy of the 3-stage hybrid tagging method is 97.36%. Before the HMM stage, 86.21% of words can be assigned unique POS tags according to the morphological information and tagging rules. For a pure statistical HMM tagger, it spent 12.76 seconds and has 95.02% of accuracy on the average.

Besides, our partial parsing takes about 1 second to get the skeleton of the sentences of the web page. Comparatively, a full parser takes 25 seconds to analyze the sentences.

The cost for the lexical selection is discussed from the factors of time complexity, space requirement, and translation accuracy. Three statistical models, i.e., select-first, the highest-frequency word (word unigram in target language) and word bigram in target language, are evaluated. However, different methods need different training tables to estimate the probabilities. Table 5 lists the table size, the time complexity and the translation quality for different word selection methods. To speed up the processing of the model 2, the target senses of words are sorted by their frequencies. Then, the method 2 has the same efficiency as the method 1. The translation accuracy of model 2 is higher than the model 1 by using the frequently-used words. Model 3 (the more complex selection method) employs the sense association to decide the word meanings for the whole sentence using dynamic programming. It needs to access a bigram table of Chinese words, which is huge with 2,147,571 records. This method takes about 49 seconds to get the translation sequence with the maximum likelihood, but most of time is spent on I/O and only 15% of processing time is used by CPU. Nevertheless, the accuracy of the word selection is lower than the model 2. For one web page, we have to lookup the table 1235.52 times on the average using the bigram model. With MI (mutual information) model, the average number of table accessing increases to 9026.04 for each web page. In other words, the MI model spends about 7 times more than the model 3. The MI model is not suitable for the real-time document translation on web.

Besides the evaluation on the word-level, we provide a questionnaire for Internet users to evaluate the effect of this web translation system on document level. The users can fill in a form containing a sequence of questions to describe their interests, suggestions, and satisfaction degrees about MTIR system. The degrees are varied from 0% to 100% with step 10%. Total 372 users answer the questions. The average satisfaction degree is 67.47%. The satisfaction has shown the importance of language translation in the multilingual information system.

7 Conclusion

The explosive growth of the WWW has brought very large multilingual textual resources to users. How to incorporate the technologies of natural language processing and text processing has shown very important in the information age. In this paper, we have proposed a general model of multilingual information system to integrate the text processing systems and language translation systems. A system integrated MT and IR technologies for WWW (MTIR system) has illustrated our solutions for multilingual services. This system can help users to access and retrieve documents on WWW in their native language(s). Additionally, the online and real-time web translation system can assist the users to understand the web pages during their navigation in the huge information resources. This multilingual system has been developed and evaluated. Several experiments for the query translations of CLIR have simulated and shown the applicability for short queries on WWW. A quantitative study of 100,000 web pages and the 30 top requested WWW sites have reflected the importance of the tradeoff between speed and translation quality for document translation. Additionally, many contemporary terms and proper names can be extracted for dictionary refinement and other NLP researches [25] during users' navigation on WWW using this system.

References

1. Bian, G.W. and Chen, H.H.: "An MT Meta-Server for Information Retrieval on WWW." In *Working Notes of the AAAI Spring Symposium on Natural Language Processing for the World Wide Web*, Palo Alto, California, USA, March, 1997, pp.10-16.
2. David, M.W. and Ogden, W.C.: "QUILT: Implementing a Large-Scale Cross-Language Text Retrieval System." In *Proceedings of ACM SIGIR'97*, 1997, pp.92-98.
3. Gachot, D.A.; Lange, E. and Yang, J.: "The SYSTRAN NLP Browser: An Application of Machine Translation Technology in Multilingual Information Retrieval." In *Proceedings of Workshop on Cross-Linguistic Information Retrieval*, 1996, pp. 44-54.
4. Hayashi, Y.; Kikui, G. and Susaki, S.: "TITAN: A Cross-linguistic Search Engine for the WWW." In *Working Notes of the AAAI-97 Spring Symposium on Cross-Language Text and Speech Retrieval*, 1997, pp. 58-65.
5. Ballesteros, L. and Croft, W.C.: "Phrasal Translation and Query Expansion Techniques for Cross-Language Information retrieval." In *Proceedings of ACM SIGIR'97*, pp.84-91, 1997.
6. David, M.W.: "New Experiments in Cross-Language Text Retrieval at New Mexico State University's Computing Research Laboratory." In *Proceedings of the Fifth Text Retrieval Evaluation Conference (TREC-5)*, Gaithersburg, MD, National Institute of Standards and Technology, 1996.
7. Hull, D.A. and Grefenstette, G.: "Querying Across Languages: A Dictionary-Based Approach to Multilingual Information Retrieval." In *Proceedings of ACM SIGIR'96*, pp.49-57, 1996.
8. Kwok, K.L.: "Evaluation of an English-Chinese Cross-Lingual Retrieval Experiment." In *Working Notes of the AAAI-97 Spring Symposium on Cross-Language Text and Speech Retrieval*, 1997, pp. 110-114.
9. David, M.W. and Dunning, T.: "A TREC Evaluation of Query Translation Methods for Multi-Lingual Text Retrieval." In *Proceedings of the Fourth Text Retrieval Evaluation Conference (TREC-4)*, Gaithersburg, MD, National Institute of Standards and Technology, 1995.
10. Landauer, T.K. and Littman, M.L.: "Fully Automatic Cross-Language Document Retrieval." In *Proceedings of the Sixth Conference on Electronic Text Research*, pp. 31-38, 1990.
11. Radwan, K.: *Vers l'Acces Multilingue en Langage Naturel aux Baess de Donnees Textuelles.* PhD Thesis, Universite de Paris-Sud, Centre d'Orsay. 1994.
12. Church, K. and Hanks, P.: "Word Association Norms, Mutual Information and Lexicography." *Computational Linguistics*, 16(1), 1990, pp. 22-29.
13. Fox, E., ed.: Virginia Disk One, Blacksburg: Virginia Polytechnic Institute and State University, 1990.

14. Salton, G. and Buckley, C.: "Term Weighting Approaches in Automatic Text Retrieval." *Information Processing and Management*, 5(24), 1988, pp. 513-523.

15. Rijsbergen, C.J. van: Information Retrieval, 2nd Edition, London, Butterworths, 1979.

16. Baker, K., et al.: "Coping with Ambiguity in a Large-scale Machine Translation System." In Proceedings of COLING-94, 1994, pp. 90-94.

17. Bennett, W. and Slocum, J.: "The LRC Machine Translation System." *Computational Linguistics*, 11(2-3), 1985, pp. 111-119.

18. Brown, P.; et al.: "A Statistical Approach to Machine Translation." *Computational Linguistics*, 16(2), 1990, pp. 79-85.

19. Mitamura, T.; Nyberg, E. and Carbonell, J.: "An Efficient Interlingua Translation System for Multilingual Document Production." In *Proceedings of Machine Translation Summit III*, 1991.

20. Nagao, M.: "A Framework of Mechanical Translation between Japanese and English by Analogy Principle." *Artificial and Human Intelligence*, 1984, pp. 173-180.

21. Nirenburg, S., et al.: "Multi-purpose Development and Operations Environments for Natural Language Applications." In *Proceedings of Applied Language Processing*, Trento, Italy, 1993.

22. Chen, K.H. and Chen, H.H.: "Machine Translation: An Integrated Approach." In *Proceedings of the 6th International Conference on Theoretical and Methodological Issues in Machine Translation*, 1995, pp. 287-294.

23. Chen, K.H. and Chen, H.H.: "Acquisition of Verb Subcategorization Frames from Large Scale Texts." In *Proceedings of KONVENS94*, 1994, pp. 407-410.

24. Chen, K.H. and Chen, H.H.: "A Rule-Based and MT-Oriented Approach to Prepositional Phrases Attachment." In *Proceedings of the 16th COLING*, 1996, pp. 216-221.

25. Chen, H.H. and Bian, G.W.: "Proper Name Extraction from Web Pages for Finding People in Internet." In *Proceedings of the 10th Research on Computational Linguistics (ROCLING X) International Conference*, 1997, pp. 143-158.

name of a building can either denote the actual building, and is therefore an object name, or if the building refers to a place it belongs to this category.

Group names refer to group or corporate names (*'Quakers'*). This category tends also to intersect with other categories. Returning to the example of the building mentioned above, these can in fact also be used to denote the group of people working inside the building.

Art names cover titles of work-of-arts such as statues, paintings, books, movies, etc. (*'Saint George and the Dragon'*).

Trademark names cover brands and trademarks. This category often intersects with object names (*'Volvo'*).

Historical events names cover battles, specific events of war or peace (*'the Second World War'*).

In our empirical investigation, we found a sliding scale, where the members of several categories seemed to be consistently translated, while others were often subject to translation, and some corresponded with the idea of names as untranslatable language symbols.

1.3 Translate or Transcribe?

From the translator's point of view, the choice between translating or transcribing, that is simply transferring the name as is to the translated text, is often governed by a simple fact: Is there an established translation? If so, use it, if not transcribe the name and where necessary put the translation or a clarification within brackets [1].

As to the terminology in this paper, we distinguish between five different ways of treating a name in the source text, namely transcribing, translating, clarifying, simplifying and omitting. *Transcribing* denotes the exact letter-by-letter transferring of the name into the target text, which means that also Scandinavian letters such as "å", "ä", "ö" will be kept intact. *Translating* will be used when one or more elements of the name is the subject of translation into the target language. *Clarification* is used by the translator in order to make explicit for the reader of the target text something that is implicit in the source name. This often co-occurs with transcribing or translating. *Simplification* is here taken to denote small changes made into a more friendly notation for the target language, for example *"Klason"* becomes *'Clason'*. *Omitting* refers to the cases when the translator for example uses an anaphor instead of a proper name.

In this paper we will use italics with double quotation marks (") to denote a Swedish name example, and italics with single quotation mark (') for English or Italian names. Since the study is based on Swedish original texts, all the target examples are from translated texts.

2 The Retrieval of Names in a Parallel Corpus

2.1 The Method for Automatic Extraction

The simplest method to retrieve names in texts are to look for capital letters appearing in a non-initial sentence position, then eliminate certain exceptions such as *'Mrs.'* and

'*I*'. Unfortunately, this exception list grows very rapidly, especially when dealing with several languages, and the results are not completely reliable. Therefore, according to Bikel et al 1998 [3], we developed another, more complex method, based on statistically significant data in the texts. The basic idea is, that by the assignment of a specific class-tag to each graphematic unit in the text, it becomes possible to identify units that tend to appear together and elements that appear in isolation. This strategy is best known as the n-gram model (see further [4, 39-43]). This is a reimplementation of "Nymble" though adapted to the needs of the texts and the Scandinavian languages. When an element with the class-tag indicating initial capitalization is found, we calculate the probability of it appearing in connection with the preceding word and its associated class-tag. If there is a high probability, the original text unit is annotated as a name.

By comparing names found in the source sentence of an aligned pair with the target sentence, we could get the answer to the question 'is this name transcribed?' If so, we need no further investigation. If not transcribed we need to find out if there is a translation, clarification or simplification present in the target text. If there is a name in the source sentence, not already present in the database, and one name, though different, found in the target sentence, they are taken to be a translation pair. If there is more than one name, then their mutual position will decide which elements to be linked. Though the method is simple, it worked surprisingly well. The difficulties arose when the name was omitted in the target text, and situated somewhere inbetween the positions of the source text names. For such cases, the first name found in the source or target text was said to be the corresponding one.

If a translation was found, the name translation pair was written into a lexical database. For matter of usefulness and simplicity we used the MultiTerm database. The example given below, depict entries in the output files:

<Created By>NameDropper
<Entry Class>10
<Subject>NAMES
<Taxonomy class>Place name
<Svenska>Svartvattnet
<Context> Han for till Svartvattnet och vidare uppåt mot fjället.
<English>Blackwater
<Context> He went to Blackwater and then on up towards the mountain.
Example 1: Lexical entry for a name translation in MultiTerm format.

The information in the lexical entry should be read as follows; The "Created By"-tag is used to indicate that this is automatically extracted information, thereby NameDropper. The "Entry-Class"-tag can be used to filter out information. The number 10 here is used to point out that the information should be handled with caution. The "Subject"-tag is used only to signal names. The "Taxonomy Class"-tag is maybe the most interesting. It follows the taxonomy presented in 1.2 and together with our result from the study shown in 4, we have tried to automatically link each new name to a taxonomy class. The first method for this linking was based on a t-score list from our marked-up corpus, indicating significant words surrounding certain classes. Also certain lexical patterns such as "*the battle of*" or "*X Street*" were used as indicators. All others are given the default class "*Personal names*". The *Svenska*-tag, meaning *Swedish*-tag, gives the Swedish version of the name, followed by a contextual example, namely the first sentence where the new name was found. The *English*-tag shows the English translation of the name followed by the context-tag which gives the English sentence where the name was first found.

3 The Linking of Names in a Parallel Corpus

3.1 The method for translation study

As said before, we use the parallel texts as base material for a descriptive analysis of degrees of translations for our names. All the texts were preprocessed, which means that they were tokenized and aligned at the sentence level.

We structured the names into various classes, at the end summing to 40 classes. Later these classes were generalized and grouped into seven main categories, as described in 1.2. This work had to be done manually since it implied access to information not supplied by the name itself. Often we had to re-examine the texts in order to pick the appropriate category for a specific name. For example, the name "*Ulla Winbladh*", a famous literary person from the work of the Swedish poet Carl Michael Bellman, was found in the name-lists but when checking in the text it referred to a café instead of the person. Even though it was obvious where the name came from, it was not obvious that it had been given a new categorial belonging since it was not supplied with the information given by the attribute 'café'.

Each name that did not have a corresponding, transcribed equivalent in the aligned target sentence, became the object of manual investigation, in order to determine whether it was a case of translation, simplification, clarification or omission. Lastly, the results were counted and investigated as shown below.

4 Specification of Name Translations

On the basis of the seven categories defined above we will describe when the names were either transcribed, translated, clarified, simplified or omitted. As in many earlier studies, we believe this often to be translator dependent, for example the Swedish city "*Göteborg*" which in one novel translates into '*Gothenburg*' and in another is transcribed as '*Göteborg*'. But we also found tendencies that seemed to hold throughout the various novels in the corpus. These tendencies are described below, by examples and quantitative data from the types of names and not tokens (a name is only counted once even though re-occurring in the text). The number of names found was 691, divided into categories and degrees of translation as follows.

Two of our seven categories are subject to constant translation. These are art names as well as historical event names. It can be explained by the fact that these names in all occurrences carry semantic information in addition to their literal realization. To exemplify the category works of art, we have found several names of movies, books and statues, such as "*Kvinnan i sjön*" translated into '*The lady in the lake*', a book title. "*Sankt Göran och Draken*" is translated into '*Saint George and the dragon*', i.e. a statue. The historical events, though very few, are often names of famous battles or war, such as *"slaget vid Jutas"* which is translated into *'the battle of Jutas in Finland'*. Note that this name is translated as well as clarified with the extra information that Jutas is situated in Finland. All the historical events were also translated.

Another category that is often undergoing translation is group names. Again we found that these names tended to have semantic connotations, describing the people in the group. An example of translations in this group is *"Den store Detektiven Allmänheten"*, which is translated into *'The Great General Public'* (the literal translation should be *'the great Detective the Public'*).

The group of object names contains examples in the text referring to object such as ferries which have names even though they are not personified. Most of the examples here were transcribed though a few translations could be found, such as *"Flyvefisken"* becoming *'the Flying Fish'*. A surprising result was found in the intersecting group of trademark names, contrary to the idea of trademark being universal. We found cases where names were neither transcribed, nor really translated either, but rather clarified; for example, the Swedes know very well that a *"PV"* is a famous car from the fifties, though clarified for the target reader as a *'Volvo'*.

Place names can often be found in several bilingual dictionaries, indicating there exists a universal dictionary of place names, covering nations, oceans etc. But in the corpus, we found many local names of small villages, hills, etc, lacking in the universal dictionary. These names can be divided into two groups, those actually meaningful in the source language, for instance denoting topographical features, and those without any connotation. Many place names in Scandinavia indicate the geographical situation, such as *"Kullen"* (*'the small hill'*), *"Sundet"* (*'the channel'*). They become the overlap between names and appellatives since they, if written with small letters only explain where it is situated though with a capital letter they become names. While the first group varied, the second group of place names with no semantic connotation were simply transcribed. This latter group is undergoing further investigations, but the most characteristic clues are presented below.

In our first typicalization of the place names we had 20 different subclasses, including such as cities, nations, working places, lakes, rivers, etc. Many of these subclasses occurred only once or twice in the material, showing the division to be somewhat over-ambitious. Still, by viewing these subclasses we find certain clues which seem to trigger translations. The first group would be international names. They are already part of the bilingual lexicon and as such not a translation problem, like the rest of the names. In the material we found 25% of these marked as being transcribed, but the truth behind that figure is that the Swedish and international name are equivalent. Place names including one element being a colour, have a higher tendency than other place names to be translated (actually 100% in our material). There are several examples in the novels, for example *"Svartvattnet"* becomes *'Blackwater'*. Place names including element of watercourse is also often translated, at least partly, such as *"Lobberåa"* (the -a suffix is northern Swedish dialect) which becomes *'the river Lobber'* and *"Fjällån"* which becomes *'Mountain river'*. In the most extreme case, the name *"Tyresö"* has become *'Tyre Lake'*; however, this is a misunderstanding of the translator since *"Tyresö"* is a suburb, and the last element is *"ö"*, which means *'island'*, though combined with a compound link *"-s"*. Even though the difference between *"Tyresö"* and *"Tyresjö"* is not that great, this is nothing more than an erroneous translation. One more subclass is the one containing elements of animals, which tend to be more often translated than other place names, "*Hundtjärn*" becoming '*Dogmere*'.

The last category to be treated is the most common one, personal names. This group is also the one where the cases of translations are very few. This corresponds to the fact that the group also has the least semantic intensions. Christian names, as well as family names, are static, though not completely without information. For example, they can often give the reader a hint of the person's age and social status. The protagonist of one text carries the name "*Torsten*" which for the Swedish reader indicates that this is a man in his fifties, although this cannot be conveyed in the translated version. Another character is "*Carl*", which is a Swedish royal name. Even though it is common in all social strata, it still gives a view of status and wellbeing, yet again not conveyed in the translation. Family names in Sweden belong to various groups, where the most common are names of the form "*X-son*", simply indicating that in ancient time they were worn by the son of X. Another group are the soldier names, that were given by the king to soldiers of a certain dignity. One example of such a name is "*Stålhandske*", which carries information to the Swedish reader that the person is of Finnish-Swedish origin and a soldier family. However, the name is also built upon the two words "*Stål*", meaning '*Steel*' and "*handske*" meaning '*glove*'. In the translated version of the text we surprisingly found it translated literally into '*Steelglove*'. Of course the name "*Stålhandske*" gives a strong impression, which the translator might have tried to recreate for the target text reader, even though it might have a comic effect on the Swedish reader looking at the target text.

The number of personal names in the study amounts to 246, out of which only 31 are translated and 5 are simplified. On closer look, simplified names are subject to just minor changes, such as "*Klason*" becoming '*Clason*', which might look less odd for an English reader. Even foreign names, non-source and non-target language, fell into this group, for example, the Russian name "*Jurij Tjivarsjev*" became '*Yuri Chivartshev*'. As for the place names, normally there was a trace left in the text by the use of anaphors when a name was omitted.

Among the translated personal names, we found mostly nicknames, such as "*Stickan*" became '*Stiggsy*'. Nicknames that actually have a meaning related to the person in question are rare in the material. One example though is "*D.G.*", an abbreviation for "*Den Gamle*", which was translated into '*O.M.*' as in '*Old Man*'.

We will end by mentioning some problematic cases. In the following examples, the Swedish use of low-case initials differs from that of the other languages studied, i.e., when a noun is derived from a name, as "*darwinist*". Nouns and adjectives originally derived from place names drop their initial capital letter, as for instance "*fagerstahållet*" ('*the direction of Fagersta*'). The same holds for a noun or adjective signifying a religious or political persuasion, names of weekdays, months or festivals in the calendar, i.e., "*katolsk*" ('*Catholic*') or "*påsk*" ('*Easter*').

5 Conclusions

The material of parallel texts is always a well of wonders. In this paper we chose to look more closely upon the topic of names from the parallel point of view. We gave an example of how to automatically retrieve names, which proved to be not without difficulties. We found the following problems to be the most cumbersome ones:
- names in sentence initial position,
- homonyms,
- name phrases,
- names used in compounding words.

Names in the initial position of a sentence are difficult since the capital letters otherwise signaling names is put out of order. The problem is even greater when names and words are homonyms, such as the Swedish name "*Hans*", which also means '*His*'.

Names consisting of several units such as "*Kvinnan i sjön*" ('*The woman in the lake*') are hard to retrieve automatically. Sometimes these name phrases are flagged by using italics or citation marks, though very often no such explicit marks can be found.

The use of compounds in Germanic languages (such as Swedish) can often mislead an algorithm, especially in words where the initial name is compounded with a common word, such as "*Luthagensystemet*" ('*the off-license at Luthagen*'). This is completely nontransparent and without the addition of semantic information it can not be subdivided from the other findings of names in texts.

Translation degree /Name category	Transcribed	Translated	Clarified	Simplified	Omitted
Art name	0	9	0	0	0
Historic event name	0	5	1	0	0
Group name	8	27	4	0	0
Object name	12	5	0	0	0
Trademark name	17	0	4	0	0
Place name	206	140	4	1	2
Personal name	204	31	1	5	5

Table 1. Translation degrees by name categories

All findings in the present study were classified according to the typology described previously, consisting of seven categories with a rather clear cut division. These categories developed during the work and include all names appearing in our material. The results can be viewed above in table 1. Subsequently, we analyzed the data which included 691 unique names. Of these, 447 were transcribed, 217 translated, 14 clarified (4 of the clarified overlapped with the above), 6 simplified and 7 omitted. The categories of historical events, art and group names were most often subject to the traditional concept of translation. Other groups, such as place names were often translated when belonging to one of the following subgroups;

- international names,
- element of color,
- element of animals,
- element of watercourse.

The number of translated names was surprisingly high. However, looking at the texts diachronically, there seems to be a tendency towards a general stylistic and formal simplification of texts, often leaving names transcribed in translated texts.

At present, the most frequently transcribed names were those belonging to the categories of objects and trademarks, as well as personal names, nicknames excluded. This is in accordance with our prejudice, though it is worth noticing that one fifth of the trademarks had been clarified in the texts.

To sum up, we found some of the problems concerning automatic retrieval of names insurmountable. Hence, for a perfect result this phase can only be carried out semi-automatically. A thorough categorization is necessary in order to map translation degrees. Even though we found a tendency towards less cases of actual translations in recent texts, it is still important for the task of human as well as machine translation to formalize rules for name handling.

References

1. Sirkku Aaltonen. Translation of proper names — with special reference to brendan behan's borstal boy and its swedish translation borstalpojken by thomas warburton. In J. Hedberg, G. Korlén, and M. Forsgren, editors, *Moderna Språk*, volume 79, pages 11–19,117–127. 1985.
2. Andrei Bantas. Names, nicknames, and titles in translation. In *Perspectives: Studies in Translatology, 2(1)*, pages 79–87. 1994.
3. Daniel M. Bikel, Scott Miller, Rickard Schwartz, and Ralph Weischedel. Nymble: a high-performance learning name-finder. In *Proceedings of the Fifth Conference on Applied Natural Language Processing*, pages 194–201, 1997.
4. Eugene Charniak. *Statistical Language Learning*. The MIT Press, Cambridge, 1993.
5. Pernilla Danielsson and Daniel Ridings. Pedant: Parallel texts in Göteborg. Research reports from the Department of Swedish, Göteborg University GU-ISS-96-2, Språkdata, 1996.
6. Kerstin Ekman. *Blackwater*. Chatto & Windus, London, 1993. Translator: Joan Tate.
7. Kerstin Ekman. *Händelser vid vatten*. Albert Bonniers Förlag, Stockholm, 1993.
8. Jan Guillou. *Enemy's Enemy*. Höganäs, 1989. Translator: Thomas Keeland.
9. Jan Guillou. *Fiendens fiende*. Bokklubben Bra Böcker, Höganäs, 1989.
10. Lars Gustafsson. *En biodlares dö d*. Natur & Kultur, Stockholm, 1978.
11. Lars Gustafsson. *Morte di un apicultore*. Iperborea, Milano, 1978. Translator: Carmen Giorgetti Cima.
12. Lars Gustafsson. *En kakelsättares eftermiddag*. Natur & Kultur, Stockholm, 1991.
13. Lars Gustafsson. *Il pomeriggio di un piastrellista*. Iperborea, Milano, 1991. Translator: Carmen Giorgetti Cima.
14. Lars Gustafsson. *A Tiler's afternoon*. Harvill, 1991. Translator: Tom Geddes.
15. Luca Manini. Meaningful literary names. In D. Delabastita, editor, *The Translator*, volume 2, pages 161–178. 1996.
16. Velta Rüke-Dravina. Översättning av ortnamn och personnamn i litterära texter. In G. Engwall, & R. af Geijerstam, editors, *Från språk till språk*, pages 230–246. 1983.
17. Maj Sjöwall and Per Wahlöö. *Brandbilen som försvann*. Norstedts Förlag, Stockholm, 1972.
18. Maj Sjöwall and Per Wahlöö. *The fire engine that disappeared*. Victor Goliancz, Ltd, London, 1972. Translator: Joan Tate.

SYSTRAN on AltaVista
A User Study
on Real-Time Machine Translation on the Internet

Jin Yang and Elke D. Lange

SYSTRAN Software, Inc.
7855 Fay Avenue, Suite 300, La Jolla, CA 92037, USA
{jyang,elange}@systransoft.com

Abstract. On December 9 1997, SYSTRAN and the AltaVista Search Network launched the first widely available, real-time, high-speed and free translation service on the Internet. This initial deployment, treated as a global experiment, has become a tremendous success. Through this service, machine translation (MT) technology has been pushed to the forefront of worldwide awareness. Besides growing media coverage, user response during the first five months has been overwhelming. This paper is a study of the user feedback from the MT developer's perspective, addressing such questions as: Who are the users? What are their needs? What is their acceptance of MT? What types of texts are being translated? What suggestions do users offer? Finally, this paper outlines our view on opportunities and challenges, and on how to use this feedback to guide future development priorities.

1   Introduction: Going Live on the Internet

With the goal of "eliminating the language barrier on the Web" [1], AltaVista teamed up with SYSTRAN Software Inc. to offer the first free-of-charge online translation service--*AltaVista Translation with SYSTRAN* http://babelfish.altavista.digital.com. Global accessibility, intuitive ease of use, and near-instantaneous real-time translation speed were teamed up with SYSTRAN's proven MT technology.   Ten major European language pairs are offered in the initial phase, translating English to and from French, German, Spanish, Italian and Portuguese.   The service is available directly from AltaVista's Search Service.   It allows the user to search documents written in any language and translate the resulting hits via a "Translate" link or by importing or typing in any text or providing the URL of any Web page.

The translation site's domain name, *babelfish,* is a concept taken from the book *The Hitchhiker's Guide to the Galaxy* by science fiction author Douglas Adam.   In the book, galactic hitchhikers had an easy way to understand any language they came across: simply popping a "small, yellow, and leechlike fish" (a babelfish) into their ears.   Similarly, the translation service aims to point the way toward the future of a global Internet, giving increased access and understanding to millions of multilingual documents. Today, English is still the dominant language on the Internet (approximately 70%), closely followed by the other major western European languages, but more and more documents are becoming available in a greater variety of languages. Also, the user base is rapidly changing away from that consisting mostly of English speakers.

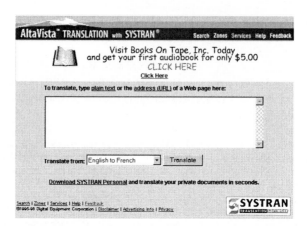

Fig. 1. AltaVista Translation with SYSTRAN as of June 1998.

SYSTRAN had pursued online translation before this service. The first implementation was in France, where SYSTRAN translation systems have been used since 1988 on Minitel, an online service offered by the French Postal Service and widely available to the public on dedicated terminals. Whereas initial usage was by curiosity seekers, translating email and simply experimenting with translation, later usage shifted to more serious translation of mostly business correspondence. The drawback of this service is that it is expensive, relatively slow, and not easily integrated with the PC environment. Since early 1996, SYSTRAN has been offering online translation on the Internet via a service geared mostly toward Web page translation. SYSTRAN is also used on two major intranets: the first within U.S. Government agencies, and the second in Europe, where SYSTRAN has been the official MT system of the European Commission (EC) since 1976. Currently 1,800 professional translators access the EC systems on their internal network, via e-mail.

The AltaVista translation with SYSTRAN has pushed online translation a big step forward, with a good implementation realizing the primary requirements of online translation: speed, robustness and coverage [2]. Also, accessibility pushes it to the forefront of worldwide awareness. Being one of the most trafficked web sites, AltaVista's site makes the service accessible to all, and it is very easy to use. Powerful DEC Alpha servers and the fast AltaVista Search Network complement SYSTRAN's high-speed translation turnover. SYSTRAN's time-tested MT technology provides good quality of translation with a wide coverage using broad and specialized dictionaries and linguistic rules [3]. This truly remarkable combination made the real-time online translation a tremendous success story.

The translation page has been acknowledged as a cool website by various sites (e.g., *What's Cool: Netscape Guide by Yahoo!).* About 14,000 websites already have been found to contain a direct link to the translation page, which helps to generate translation traffic. The media's reaction is explosive, with comments and introduction to the service in particular and MT technology in general (published in assorted newspapers [4] - [13]). The public's reaction is also overwhelming.

2   User Feedback

The translation service has now (at the writing of this paper, i.e. May 1998) been available to the general public for approximately five months. During this time, usage has increased steadily and surpassed more than 500,000 translations per day in May 1998.   User   feedback   is   encouraged   via   two   email   addresses: av_linguistics@pa.dec.com   and   av_trans.support@pa.dec.com,   listed   in http://babelfish.altavista.digital.com/content/feedback.htm.   Concurrent   with   the increase in usage, user feedback also has increased every month. Between January and May, 5005 emails were received concerning linguistic and/or translation comments alone (via av_linguistics@pa.dec.com). This is the set of user feedback discussed in this paper. The following discussion is based on preliminary evaluation of the data.

2.1   First Reaction to the Translation Service

Most users are enthusiastic about the service. People say they never imagined something like this exists. Many who have never used translation software and never considered purchasing one are now trying it out.

> *This is Very Cool!!!! Fantastic! Fantastique! Fantastisch! Fantastico! What else can I say?*

> *And all I can think of is "wow." I know some foreign students this will help tremendously! And I will certainly find it useful in future correspondence with contacts around the globe.*

> *I actually do not know how long you have been offering this service but it is an absolute success! Congratulations on an excellent service which is not only very accurate (I speak several languages myself) but nice and fast as well!! This is the best initiative that I have found on the Internet so far. Keep up the excellent service!*

> *Keep up your efforts, you are needed. Many thanks, even for the funny parts of the translation.*

Another group, especially professional translators, sent angry email to protest against the initiative.

Your "translation program" on the Net is a worthless embarrassment. It is good for nothing, except perhaps for a cheap laugh... I am a better judge of translations than you are. You should hang your heads in shame.

Sorry, no gushing praise. The translation was incomprehensible; half the Portuguese words were not even recognized. Back to the drawing board.

Some are confused, wondering about whether the translation was done by a human or computer.

I would be very interested to know if the entire translation is via software or if natives or language trained staff review the work.

You should fire your translators and hire me.

Also similar to CompuServe's experience [2], many professional translators seize the opportunity to offer their services by sending resumes.

May I suggest, in order to improve the output quality and accuracy of your MAT-based translations, that you maintain the software but add a freelance team of experienced translators, such as myself, as post-output editors?

In summary, user feedback consists of approximately 95% praise, sprinkled with friendly bug reports and suggestions. Less than 5% of users flame the service.

2.2   Acceptance of Machine Translation

CompuServe's two-year on-line experience reported that users were first amazed, then disappointed, and finally pragmatic about the quality of translation [2]. In our experiment, we found that the majority of users are amazingly understanding of MT capabilities and limitations. They are impressed by the capability and even the translation quality.

Some works better that (sic) others. But all told, this stuff is amazing. In the blink of an eye I got most of the gist of something from Italian. Technology can sometimes be breathtaking. This was one of those times for me.

All in all, though, I was impressed at generally good accuracy, keeping the phrases to be translated simple, of course, and the speed: less than 30 sec. at approx. 50kbps.

Many users show that they know what to expect from MT: less than perfect results. They are willing to help.

Generally, I'm impressed. Congratulations! Of course not perfect. But - who knows what you can do in 2 years (or you have already done and not yet disclosed☺). I would like to support you by sending you these little bugs. ...

I could provide you with some software-related phrases and terminology extracted from Italian software source code comments, if it would help you folks to do a better job of translating it to English.

Users also realize the challenges of MT: name handling, idiomatic expressions and context sensitive translations. Some of them even "point out" ways to future success.

Pretty good translations there--I'm impressed. You need some help with the idioms!

I think the context problem would be very difficult to solve but what about a certain idiom library of often used terms?

SUGGESTION: To design a translation mechanism that is grammatically accurate, and accurate in context. Many expressions cannot be translated literally from one language to the next, so I suggest that more careful consideration is given to idiosyncracies and nuances in translations. This will allow you to provide more accurate translations and better service

The positive feedback shows that MT has been accepted as a useful tool in the online environment. It is gaining worldwide popularity, with the "not perfect" quality.

2.3   User Profile

The users of the online translation service are general Web surfers. They belong to the casual users group, who need or want translation on an occasional basis [15] and for broad purposes.

2.3.1 Country of Origin

The majority of feedback comes (in the following order) from the United States, Canada, Germany, Sweden, England, Australia, Netherlands, Italy, France, Brazil, Switzerland, Spain, Norway, Belgium, and Portugal.

2.3.2   Languages Translated and Requested

The user of the service is mostly from English-speaking countries and is concentrating on English and the Western European languages. This is expected since only those languages are offered at this time.

Requests for additional languages show some interesting trends: heavy concentration on Scandinavian languages and even Finnish. This may be due to the fact that a) there are many documents in those languages available on the Internet and few other people can read them, and b) people in Scandinavia and Finland are very actively using the Internet. Other languages requested include Chinese, Japanese,

Korean, Russian, Hebrew and Latin--almost every language that exists. One user suggested a British English to and from American English translator.

2.3.3 Type of Text Translated

Statistics show that 40% of translations are web pages and 60% are text input/copy by users. The analysis of the types of documents translated will be valuable for preparing the MT systems. Such a study is in the preparatory stages and will be the subject of a separate report. For this paper, we summarize the following observations from the user feedback.

The service is often used for translation of personal documents and email judging from requests for colloquial style. One of the most frequent sentences/phrases being translated is *I love you* (the "I" is often in lower case, *i love you*). Other examples include:

> *What's up? Who cares? Where do you live?*
> *Please make yourself comfortable, and allow me to introduce myself.*
> *German: Ich wuensche Dir viel Glueck!*

Idioms and popular expressions are often translated to test the "intelligence" of the systems, including the famous phrase *"The spirit is willing but the flesh is weak"*.

> Brazilian expression: *Em rio que tem piranha, jacare nada de costas.*
> That should translate to: *In River with piranhas, alligator swims on it's (sic) backs*

Vernacular expressions are also being tried and commented upon.

> *We have not been able to express ourselves in the vernacular...i.e. fuck, pussy, fornication. Please note that these words appear in dictionaries and are commonly used in many languages. Thank you for your attention.*

Careful preparation of format filters for preserving HTML formats have made Web page translation popular. Users often send the URL of the page translated with the request to review.

> *I'm *so* impressed with the translation service and thought I'd add a few bits of suggestions to further improve it. (the document I tried translating was http://www..... if you want to double check).*
> *I tried the translation from English to German on my homepage and it turned out [name mistranslated], which is very funny!!! I like your translation very much* ☺

2.4   User Utilization

The usual expectation is that MT, in the online environment, acts mostly as an assimilation tool [2]. Our experience shows that the use of MT is going beyond that. User practice demonstrates five functions for the online translation service.

2.4.1   Assimilation Tool

Information assimilation is the primary purpose of translating web pages. Users find it useful to get the information they want. They don't worry too much about the fine points of the translation, especially if the translation gives a good sense of a foreign language newspaper article [13] or other piece of information.

It does not matter one whit that language translation is not 100%, nor even 90% accurate--getting the "gist" of a foreign-language webpage (and fast!) matches the impedance of web attention spans.

2.4.2   Dissemination Tool

People translating their own web pages hope for greater dissemination of their message. Some users put a link to the translation service page. With a simple click, a personal or business web page can be translated into other language on the fly. This is a sensitive area, since the imperfections of MT may distort the message. Suggestions were made to mark such translations with a warning that it was machine generated.

2.4.3   Communication Tool

Most users are happy to be able to communicate in a language they don't know, and they accept MT as long as the message conveys the idea of what they want to say.

Your software has enabled us to give a much needed job to a woman in our neighborhood (now our housekeeper) who speaks only Spanish. We are able to leave her instructions regularly and she may now ask us any questions she might have. No it isn't perfect, but darn close.

This is the best. I can finally write my grandmother. She doesn't speak English, and I don't speak Portuguese. This is enough to make me cry. Thank you very much.

The translation facility with AltaVista is terrific. It would be great is somebody could build a chat room with built in translation. I would love to converse with somebody who does not speak English. This could be a fun way to learn another language.

2.4.4 Entertainment Tool

One of the most popular usage is back-and-forth translation, where text is translated into and then back from a language. As stated in one of the articles, "The inexactitude of machine translation becomes especially noticeable when a fragment of text is converted from one language to another and then back again, or through several languages, the 'drift' increasing with each pass of the software" [10]. As MT developers, we would like to discourage this practice, especially when users attempt to judge translation quality by evaluations of the "back" translation. However, it has become a very popular entertainment. Even the famous Italian author and poet Umberto Eco could not resist the temptation to play word games with MT [5].

One person has set up a "para-site" called *The AltaVista Language Transmorgradier(sic)* http://www.archive.org/~art/babelphone.html to take advantage of this, allowing surfers to run passages of text through up to five languages with a click. Another person put an "extreme test" *Stress-testing the AltaVista/SYSTRAN language Translator,* http://tbtf.com/aresource/trans.html, to defeat the translator. Various round trips (e.g. multiple round trip through a single language, serial round trip through five languages, etc.) are tried to translate the English idiom "get with child" (i.e. impregnate) back-and-forth. This kind of process is also shared in the user feedback. Poems, jokes, idioms are often tried in this process. One web site contains a Greeting card with the note "Translation courtesy of Alta Vista and Systran": It consists of multiple back-and-forth translations of "Happy New Year".

2.4.5 Learning Tool

Machine translation was never meant to teach language; however, there seem to be users who hope to use it as a learning tool. Students are using it to do their foreign language homework.

> *LOVE your site -- had a lot of fun testing my French! I imagine this will be a great success with the international business community -- not too mention students "helping" themselves with their homework! Wish I'd had it in high school!!!*

> *The only thing that would make it better is if you have an audio where someone could speak the translation so that I would know the proper pronunciation.*

> *I find your service invaluable in untangling Italian verb forms, moods, tenses, etc.*

2.5 Legal Implications

Questions have been brought up regarding the legal implications of MT online, though no answers are provided [14]. We are not going to answer the question of existing and coming legal implications either, but can share some experiences.

Some users point out the need for a clear disclaimer in the online environment. Creation of a detailed and standard disclaimer is a worthwhile task for the MT industry as a whole.

I suggest you attach a detailed disclaimer to this service and seek ways through which the results could be made more flexible and accurate.

Actually, the "about" link does point out the limitations of the product. Relabelling it as a disclaimers would probably make things a little clearer.

Copyright questions have not yet come to our attention. But we had one user who was ready to sue us when he saw the translation of his web page and found the name of his company translated and mangled. Fortunately a quick correction of the problem could be made.

Among the broad usage of the translation service, translation of vernacular expressions is quite active. With current sensitivity to X-rated material on the Internet, we reacted to a mother's complaint when her child translated harmless text and got translations with sexual connotations. The specific example was not given. In fact, some of our dictionaries contain a number of risqué terms, entered during the early days of Minitel usage in France. When we set a switch to hide these terms for the sake of concerned mothers, a number of other users complained that the system couldn't handle the vernacular (see above). Although MT systems don't intend to censor this kind of material, translating them is certainly not the systems' greatest expertise.

3   Possibilities and Challenges

Online translation is a big challenge; it translates uncontrolled language worldwide in real-time, in a public space, and for broad purposes. The early spectacular success is encouraging for various future possibilities. The user feedback provides valuable facts for guiding future development priorities.

- **On-going Improvement of Translation Quality**

The experiment gave us an opportunity to look at translation quality in a new light. On-going improvement of translation quality, has always been, and is of utmost importance. In particular, updating terminology to keep up with the fast-changing Internet is a pressing challenge in the online environment. Also, proper name handling (i.e. human names, company names, street addresses) is a frequent point of concern for the user. Improving the existing complex name handling algorithms is therefore of great importance. Continuous translation quality control is also required along with broadening coverage and enhancing depth.

- **Enhancement of Robustness**

Automatic identification of language, domain, and style level are needed for a translation service catering to such a wide audience. While such parameters can be specified in the regular versions of SYSTRAN, the AltaVista service does not offer choices in the name of ease-of-use. Automatic identification of these parameters would be one more step toward enhanced user friendliness.

Further increasing speed and efficiency, and lifting translation time and size limitations are other items important for the fast turnover of large volume translation.

> *Your translator translated Esperanto as if it were Spanish*

> *Translation of normal English words like "window" is interpreted (in French) as a computer term*

> *Is there a way to request informal translation? Example: I love you Spanish: le amo Informal: te amo*

- **User Involvement**

Users are a valuable resource for the MT developer. Their specific bug reports and general suggestions can be catalogued and acted upon as an important step toward the goal of enhanced quality and coverage. Channeling user input, therefore, is added to the list of tasks for the MT developer.

> *Please, can you write on some FAQ page what kinds of mistakes are most interesting to you? One cannot send you EVERY mistake.*

The AltaVista translation service with SYSTRAN is a good showcase of MT technology. The explosive and positive user feedback shows that MT has proven its worth in practice. Improving translation quality and expanding language coverage are definitely pressing challenges. MT needs to earn its keep, and the best way is through more good implementations [16].

Acknowledgements

We would like to thank Dimitris Sabatakakis of SYSTRAN for his comments and suggestions. We would also like to thank Louis Monier and Henry Story of AltaVista for valuable discussions.

References

1. AltaVista Search Service. 1997. *Eliminating the Language Barrier on the Web. A New Language Translation Service for Web Content Now Available on Digital's AltaVista Search Service.* AltaVista Search Service, Digital Equipment Corporation. White Paper.
2. Flanagan, Mary. 1996. Two Years Online: Experiences, Challenges and Trends. *Expanding MT Horizons: Proceedings of the Second Conference of the Association for Machine Translation in the Americas.* pp. 206-211. October 2-5, 1996. Montreal, Quebec, Canada
3. Gerber, Laurie & Yang, Jin. SYSTRAN MT Dictionary Development. *Machine Translation: Past, Present and Future: Proceedings of Machine Translation Summit VI.* pp. 211-218. October 29 - November 1997. San Diego, CA.
4. Atlantic Unbound. 1997. AltaVista Translation Service. In Web Citations. December 18, 1997
    http://www.theatlantic.com/atlantic/unbound/citaiton/wc971218.htm
5. Maney, Kevin. 1998. Translating via Web is a Hoot as well as a Help. *USA Today.* January 22, 1998.
6. Giussani, Bruno. 1998. Free Translation of Language Proves More Divertimento than a Keg of Monkeys. *The New York Times.* March 10, 1998.
7. Belsie, Laurent. 1998. Translation Software Rides Roughshod over Idiomatic Speech. *The Christian Science Monitor.* March 19, 1998
8. Ament, Kurt. 1998. Real-time Machine Translation on the Internet. 1998. *Intercom.* May, 1998. http://www.infotektur.com/demos/babelfish/en.html
9. Kelly, Tina. 1998. Even Helpful Translation Software Sometimes Weaves a Tangled Web. *The New York Times.* April 30, 1998.
10. Moad, Jeff. 1998. Machine Translation -- the Next Generation.
    http://www.zdnet.com/zdnn/content/pcwk/1504/272427.html.
11. Silberman, Steve. 1998. Speaking in Tongues. *WiredNews*
    http://www.wired.com/news/news/wiredview/story/9369.html.
12. Sullivan, Bob. 1998. Lost in the Translation Software. MSNBC.
    http://www.msnbc.com/news/143457.asp#BODY
13. Kokmen, Leyla. 1998. Speaking the Lingo. The Denver Post Online. August 3, 1998. http://www.denverpost.com/endser/leyla0803.htm
14. Westfall, Edith. Legal Implications of MT On-line. *Expanding MT Horizons: Proceedings of the Second Conference of the Association for Machine Translation in the Americas. pp. 231-232.* October 2-5, 1996. Montreal, Quebec, Canada.
15. Bennett, Winfield Scott. 1997. Learning from Users. *Proceedings of the Second Conference of the Association for Machine Translation in the Americas.* pp. 229-231. October 2-5, 1996. Montreal, Quebec, Canada
16. Gerber, Laurie. 1997. R&D for Commercial MT. *Machine Translation: Past, Present and Future: Proceedings of Machine Translation Summit VI.* pp. 94-97. October 29 - November 1997. San Diego, CA.

Making Semantic Interpretation Parser-Independent

Ulrich Germann

USC Information Sciences Institute,
Marina del Rey, CA
germann@isi.edu

Abstract. We present an approach to semantic interpretation of syntactically parsed Japanese sentences that works largely parser-independent. The approach relies on a standardized parse tree format that restricts the number of syntactic configurations that the semantic interpretation rules have to anticipate. All parse trees are converted to this format prior to semantic interpretation. This setup allows us not only to apply the same set of semantic interpretation rules to output from different parsers, but also to independently develop parsers and semantic interpretation rules.

1 Introduction

Most machine translation systems currently available employ more or less sophisticated glossing techniques: The words and phrases of a source text are replaced by their translations into the target language and rearranged according to syntactic correspondences between the source and the target language. In many cases, this approach leads to acceptable results. For a number of European languages, there are now systems which provide sufficient coverage and quality of translation for applications such as indicative translations and gisting. However, when dealing with languages that show significant differences in their structure, such as Japanese and English, a deeper analysis of the source texts is necessary.

Consider, for example, the following two noun phrases:

(1)

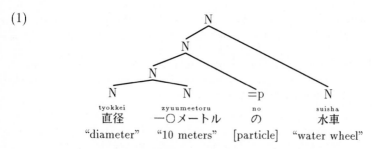

"a water wheel with a diameter of 10 meters"

(2)

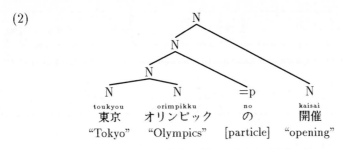

"the opening of the Olympics in Tokyo"

While the syntactic structures of the two noun phrases in Japanese are almost identical, their English translations are quite different in structure. Clearly, the information provided by a syntactic and morphological analysis of the Japanese phrases is not sufficient for accurate translations. However, if we consider the *meaning* of the constituents, we can, with the help of an ontology such as the SENSUS ontology (Hovy and Knight 1993, Knight and Luk 1994), achieve accurate translations into English. For example, SENSUS tells us that *Tokyo* is a location, and *the Olympics* are an event. With this knowledge, we can design a special rule that handles all combinations of locations and events. Similarly, knowing that 'diameter' is an attribute, and '10 meters' is a measurement, we can map a structure of the type [attribute A] + [measurement M] の X into a structure that expresses that X has the attribute A and A measures M (e.g., that the *water wheel* has a *diameter*, and that the *diameter* measures *10 meters*).

At the USC Information Sciences Institute, we are currently developing a system that tries to exploit such knowledge. The GAZELLE machine translation system aims at providing English translations with reasonable quality for unrestricted Japanese newspaper texts via semantic interpretation and subsequent text generation (Knight *et al.* 1995). At this stage, the system translates texts on a sentence-by-sentence basis. Figure 1 sketches the system. After some pre-processing, which ensures the correct character encoding of the input, etc., the input sentence is first segmented and tagged with morphological information, using the JUMAN segmenter/tagger developed at Kyoto University (Kyoto University 1997a). The JUMAN output is then parsed[1] and subsequently interpreted semantically (Knight and Hatzivassiloglou 1995b). The resulting intermediate representation is fed into a text generator, which produces a vast number of potential English renderings of the semantic content of the input sentence (Langkilde and Knight 1998a, 1998b). A statistical extractor picks the most likely rendering based on bigram and trigram models of English (Knight and Hatzivassiloglou 1995a).

---

[1] For parsing, we have used both a bottom-up chart parser with hand-crafted rules and a trainable shift-reduce parser (Hermjakob and Mooney 1997). Originally developed for English, the trainable parser was adapted to Japanese by Ulf Hermjakob, and trained on the Kyoto University Corpus (Kyoto University 1997c), a corpus of 10,000 parsed and annotated sentences from the *Mainichi* newspaper.

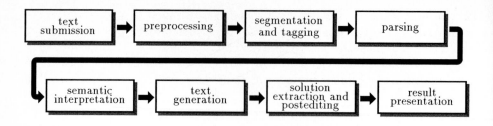

Fig. 1. The machine translation process.

A modular system architecture such as the one above allows us to use and evaluate different engines and strategies for solving particular aspects of the translation task while preserving and reusing as many of the remaining resources of the system as possible. Particularly in the areas of parsing and semantic interpretation, a modular approach is well justified: With more and more raw and annotated data such as corpora, annotated corpora, and treebanks becoming available (Marcus *et al.* 1993, Kyoto University 1997c), trainable parsers (e.g., Collins 1997, Hermjakob and Mooney 1997) have become a feasible and powerful alternative to hand-crafted systems. In contrast, semantically annotated data is still very rare and by no means sufficient as a basis for statistical approaches to semantic interpretation of texts, so that there is currently no serious alternative to a hand-crafted system for semantic interpretation. Even though one could argue — and we do support this argument — that accurate parses often cannot be achieved without the consideration of semantic criteria[2], we nevertheless claim that it is reasonable to perform parsing and semantic interpretation in separate steps. First of all, the amount of knowledge, rules, and processing needed for full-fledged semantic interpretation goes far beyond the requirements for accurate parsing. Therefore, adding semantic interpretation capabilities to an existing parsing system is labor-intensive and expensive, especially when statistical techniques used for parsing have to be coordinated with hand-crafted rules. And secondly, given the number of parsers that are becoming available for Japanese[3], it is highly desirable to be able to interpret output of different parsers with the same set of semantic interpretation rules.

The purpose of this paper is to describe how a system can be designed so that the semantic interpretation of parse trees does not depend on parser-specific

---

[2] A classical example is the sentence pair [*He ate spaghetti with Alfredo sauce*] and [*He ate spaghetti with a fork*], where the decision that the PP [*with Alfredo sauce*] is attached to N' [*spaghetti*], and the PP [*with a fork*] is attached to V' [*ate spaghetti*] can only be made on the grounds that *spaghetti* and *Alfredo sauce* are both some kind of food, whereas a *fork* is a tool for eating.

[3] We are currently aware of the KNP parser developed at Kyoto University (Kyoto University 1997b), and an HPSG parser developed at Tokyo University (Makino *et al.* 1998, Mitsuishi *et al.* 1998), in addition to the parsers currently used in our system (cf. Fn. 1).

characteristics such as the set of category symbols used, or the particular order of attachments within the parse tree. In the remainder of this paper, we first describe how semantic interpretation works and how it is implemented in our system. We then discuss the problems that arise when trying to interpret parse trees robustly, and how these problems can be overcome.

2   Semantic Interpretation

The idea of semantic interpretation is based on the notion of compositional semantics, i.e., the assumption that the meaning of an utterance can be computed by applying combinatorial rules to the meanings of the immediate constituents of the utterance. While semantic interpretation is usually implemented as a bottom-up algorithm, we will discuss the idea of compositional semantics in a top-down fashion in this section.

In a highly simplified framework, we assume that a sentence consists of one or more *basic propositions*. A basic proposition is the claim that a certain predicate or relation holds of, or holds between certain objects in the world. These objects are either sufficiently characterized by linguistic means (such as descriptive phrases that distinguish these objects from others in the respective domain of discourse), or obvious from the context.

For example, the sentence

(3)   *The video lasts about eleven minutes, and [it] describes the company's activities.*

consists of two basic propositions:

(3a)   *The video lasts about eleven minutes.*
(3b)   *The video describes the company's activities.*

(3a) is the claim that the relation *last* holds between the video being talked about and a time span of eleven minutes: *last(video, eleven minutes)*. (3b) claims that the relation *describe* holds between the video and the company's activities: *describe(video, the company's activities)*.

The arguments of the predicates can be further analyzed as restricted variables: *The video* refers to that object X (in the respective domain of discourse) that has the property of being a video: $X \mid video(X)$[4]. Similarly, *the company's activities* are those Y that have the properties of (a) being activities, and (b) being somehow related[5] to the company: $Y \mid (activities(Y) \land be\_related\_to(Y, the company)$. Finally, *the company* is that Z that has the property of being a company: $Z \mid company(Z)$. If we replace the arguments in (3b) by these restricted variables, we get the expression

---

[4]   We do not consider the issue of quantifiers here.
[5]   The specific character of this relation cannot be determined on syntactic grounds. We therefore leave the relation between the company and its activities unanalyzed here.

(3b') *describe* (X | *video* (X),

              Y | (*activities* (Y) $\land$ *be_related_to* (Y, Z | *company* (Z))))

During semantic interpretation, a representation of the content of a sentence is built up by applying combinatorial rules first to the configurations of the individual words and then to the configurations of the higher-level constituents, whose meanings have been determined by previous interpretation steps. The meanings of the individual words are retrieved from a lexicon. As a rule of thumb, noun phrases (*referential constituents*) are interpreted as restrictions of variables, and verbs (*predicative constituents*) as predicates. It is assumed that the predicate–argument relations between the referential constituents and the predicative constituents of a sentence are reflected in its morphological and syntactic structure, so that the range of interpretations that a sentence may have is restricted by its morphological and syntactic properties. As we have seen above, these properties are not always sufficient for an accurate interpretation. In this case, knowledge about the world is utilized.

In the GAZELLE system, semantic interpretation is implemented in the following manner. The parser returns an annotated tree structure. Each node of the parse tree has a category label and a feature structure associated with it, which stores the various properties of the constituent represented by the node. Traversing the tree from the bottom to the top, and augmenting the feature structures associated with the nodes of the parse tree, the semantic interpretation engine gradually builds up an intermediate representation of the semantic content of the sentence, using information from the annotated tree structure, knowledge provided by a lexico-ontological database, and knowledge encoded in the semantic interpretation rules.

A feature structure is a bundle of attribute-value pairs (*features*), e.g. ⟨NUMBER, *sg*⟩, where NUMBER is the attribute and *sg* is its value. A value can be either an atomic feature structure, i.e. an empty bundle of features (which corresponds to an entity that cannot be described in terms of having particular properties), or it can be a complex feature structure itself. Mathematically speaking, features structures are rooted, directed graphs with labeled arcs. Figure 2 shows a feature structure that partially models the English word *sees* in a graph representation and as a so-called *attribute-value matrix* (AVM). The nodes of the graph represent values, the arcs attributes. Each attribute can be identified by its *path*, the sequence of arcs from the root node to the node representing its value. For example, in Fig. 2 the path SYN leads to a complex value representing the syntactic properties of the word *sees*, whereas the path SYN·PERSON points to the 'person' value of the word. By organizing features as a feature structure, features can be grouped and be passed along to higher nodes in the parse tree by declaring *path identity* between an attribute of the mother node and an attribute of a daughter node. Two paths are considered identical if they lead to the same node in the feature structure, i.e., if their values are token-identical. As a matter of convenience, we refer to a feature consisting of an attribute with the path X–Y–Z and its value as the X·Y·Z feature.

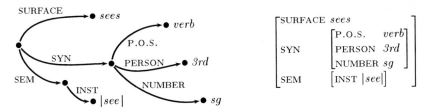

Fig. 2. A feature structure describing the word *sees* in a graph representation (left) and as an attribute-value matrix (AVM; right). Adapted from Germann (1998).

Each semantic interpretation rule consists of two elements: a context-free phrase structure rule which specifies the class of syntactic configurations that the rule should be applied to, and a set of instructions for the manipulation of the feature structures associated with the nodes. Syntactic configurations are identified by the labels of the mother and the daughter nodes in the parse tree. The basic mechanism for the manipulation of feature structures is *unification* (Shieber 1986, Moore 1989). Unification is an operation over two feature structures that returns a feature structure that contains (a) all features that occur in *either one* of the two feature structures, and (b) the unifications of all the features that occur in *both* of them. If the respective values of a feature that occurs in both structures are not unifiable, unification fails. Atomic feature structures are unifiable if they are either type-identical or in a subtype–supertype relationship with respect to a type hierarchy. In the latter case, the result of the unification is the more specific type. For example, the result of the unification of

$$\begin{bmatrix} \text{ATTR1} & A \\ \text{ATTR2} & B \end{bmatrix} \text{ and } \begin{bmatrix} \text{ATTR1} & a \\ \text{ATTR3} & C \end{bmatrix} \text{ is } \begin{bmatrix} \text{ATTR1} & a \\ \text{ATTR2} & B \\ \text{ATTR3} & C \end{bmatrix}$$

if a is a subtype of A. If a and A are not identical or in a subtype–supertype or supertype–subtype relationship, the unification of the two feature structures fails.

The semantic interpretation engine recognizes two kinds of unification instructions. *Conditioned* unification instructions (`<path1> =c <path2|value>`) succeed only if `<path1>` already exists. *Unconditioned* unification instructions (`<path1> = <path2|value>`) will create any path specified if it does not already exist. In order to distinguish the feature structures associated with the different parse nodes, path names are prefixed by the identifiers *x0, x1 ... xn*, where *x0* refers to the root node of the feature structure associated with the mother node in the configuration, and *x1 ... xn* refer to the root nodes of the feature structures associated with the daughter nodes from left to right.

The keyword *xor* in a rule introduces a hierarchical list of sets of instructions for the interpretation engine. The engine applies these sets of rules sequentially until unification succeeds. As soon as a set of instructions succeeds, the engine proceeds to the next configuration in the parse tree.

```
(1)     ((N -> N =p) (*xor* (((x2 bform) =c は)
                            ((x0 bform) =  (x1 bform))
                            ((x0 sem)   = (x1 sem))
                            ((x0 syn focus) = wa)
                            )
                            . . .
                )
        ))


(2)     ((N -> N -n) (*xor* (((x1 lemma)      =c  |*Number*|)
                            ((x2 bform)       =c  "分")
                            ((x0 sem inst)    =   |time unit|)
                            ((x0 sem minute) = (x1 sem))
                            )
                            . . .
                )
        ))


(3)     ((N -> q N) (*xor* (((x1 bform)       =c  "約")
                            ((x0 sem)         = (x2 sem))
                            ((x0 sem mod inst) = |or so|)
                            )
                            . . .
                )
        ))


(4)     ((N -> N N) (*xor* (((x2 sem inst)  =c |time unit|)
                            ((x1 syn focus) =c wa)
                            ((x0 sem inst)  =  |last,measure|)
                            ((x0 sem arg1)  =  (x1 sem))
                            ((x0 sem arg2)  =  (x2 sem))
                            )
                            . . .
                )
        ))


(5)     ((N -> N Symbol) (*xor* (((x2 bform) =c "。")
                                ((x0 sem) = (x1 sem))
                                )
                                . . .
                )
        ))
```

Fig. 4. Excerpts from the semantic interpretation rules applied in the semantic interpretation process sketched in Fig. 3.

With regard to the implementation of a set of interpretation rules, this raises the following questions:

- Which category symbols does the parser use?
- In which configurations do these symbols occur?
- What features does the parser introduce, if any?

One way to answer these questions would be to analyze a sufficient amount of parser output in order to determine which symbols are used, in which configurations they occur, and so on. However, this approach has several disadvantages. First of all, it makes semantic interpretation vulnerable to changes in the parser. Every change in the set of category symbols used, or in the order of syntactic attachments will require adaptations of the semantic interpretation rules. Moreover, once the rules are tailored to one particular parser, switching to a different parser becomes expensive, since the set of rules will have to be ported to the new parser. Finally, depending on the parser, the set of additional features provided may vary considerably. While one parser may use a small set of category symbols and a rich vocabulary of additional features, others may make extensive use of different category symbols and not provide any additional features at all. Overall, this approach turns out not to be an attractive option.

Instead, we established a standardized parse tree format to which the parse trees are converted prior to semantic interpretation. Semantic interpretation then operates over trees in the standardized parse tree format. All features that serve as criteria for semantic interpretation are either introduced by the tree converter (the module that (a) replaces the category labels of the original parse tree with labels that conform to the standardized parse tree format, and (b) integrates additional information from the lexical database), or by the semantic interpretation rules themselves.

The standardized parse tree format is characterized by the following restrictions:

- We restrict the number of immediate constituents for each parse node to a maximum of three, that is, we allow unary ($A \rightarrow B$), binary ($A \rightarrow B\ C$), and ternary ($A \rightarrow B\ C\ D$) phrase structure rules. Ternary rules are restricted to cases of bracketing with symbols that have corresponding left- and-right counterparts such as quotes, parentheses, brackets, etc. All other rules must be unary or binary.
- We restrict the set of nonterminal symbols in the parse tree to the set of basic part-of-speech labels. There are no bar-level distinctions reflected in the labels. The unary sequence N – N' – NP in a parse tree will thus be converted to N – N – N. In our actual system, we distinguish 20 parts of speech,[8] as listed in Fig. 5.
- The label of the mother node in each configuration is unambiguously determined by the following principles. In unary configurations, the label of the mother node is the same as that of the daughter node. In ternary ones, the

---

[8] This part of speech inventory is based on Rickmeyer's (1995) analysis of Japanese.

part of speech	derivational			non-derivational
	lexeme	suffix	particle	
Verb	V	-v	=v	
Noun	N	-n	=n	
Adjective	A	-a	=a	
Nominal Adj.	K	-k	=k	
Adverb	M	-m		
Adnominal	D	-d		
Interjection	I			
Particle				=p
Prefix				q
Symbol				Symbol

Fig. 5. Category symbols used in our semantic interpretation rules.

category label of the middle node prevails. In binary configurations, the label of the mother node is determined by two factors. First, if the configuration contains a lexeme, the label of the mother node is a lexeme symbol. Secondly, the part of speech of the resulting label is determined by the part of speech of the last derivational symbol (cf. Fig. 5). For example, the configuration $N =v$ will be reduced to V by the rule $N =v \leftarrow V$, and $V\ N$ will be reduced to N, whereas the configuration $-v\ -a$ will be reduced to $-a$, because it does not contain any lexeme. The label for the remaining nine possible binary configurations of non-derivational symbols ($=p$, q, $Symbol$) is determined by the label of the left-hand daughter node, except in the case $q \rightarrow Symbol\ q$.

• The part-of-speech classification of the lowest nodes is based on the information from the segmenter/tagger, which we expect to be preserved in the feature structures associated with these nodes. Thus, dependence on information from the parse tree is restricted to knowing in which features of the feature structures this tagging information is stored.

With these restrictions, we have limited the number of possible configurations in a parse tree (including configurations that are completely bogus from a linguistic point of view such as a prefix suffixed to the preceding word) to $k^2 + 2k$, where k is the number of part-of-speech symbols. In our case, with 20 part-of-speech symbols, the number of possible configurations is hence limited to 440: 20 unary rules $X \rightarrow X$, 400 binary rules for every combination of two of the 20 category symbols, and 20 ternary rules $X \rightarrow Symbol\ X\ Symbol$ for bracketing phenomena.[9] Figure 6 shows the complete set of phrase structure rules for the subset { V, N, -v, Symbol } of our set of category symbols.

Since we rely on the parser only for the bare tree structure, while lexical information comes from the segmenter/tagger and the lexicon, and since the

---

[9] For comparison, our current parser employs over 85 category labels, which would increase the number of possible configurations to well over 7000. Of course, most of them will never show up in 'real life', but it is difficult to determine in advance which configurations may or may not occur.

unary rules

V → V	N → N	-v → -v	Symbol → Symbol

binary rules

V → V V	V → V Symbol	N → V N	N → Symbol N
V → N V	V → Symbol V	N → N N	-v → -v -v
V → V -v	-v → -v Symbol	N → -v N	-v → -v Symbol
V → -v V	-v → Symbol -v	N → N Symbol	-v → Symbol -v

ternary rules

V → Symbol V Symbol	-v → Symbol -v Symbol
N → Symbol N Symbol	Symbol → Symbol Symbol Symbol

Fig. 6. The complete set of phrase structure rules for the categorial vocabulary { *V, N, -v, Symbol* }. Our actual set of category symbols consists of 20 symbols.

new parse node labels are assigned to the nodes deterministically based on the principles stated above, we gain a high degree of independence from parser-specific information.

4   Coordinating Parsing and Semantic Interpretation

In order to coordinate parsing with semantic interpretation, the following steps have to be taken:

- If the parser's output does not conform to the structural requirements of our system, the parse trees have to be 'binarized'. This could also be considered a separate 'microparsing' step after some 'macroparsing' accomplished by the first parser. It is currently implemented as part of the parsing process but could also be integrated in the tree conversion step and take place after the category symbols of the lowest nodes in the parse tree have been replaced by our category symbols.
- The category symbols in the parse tree have to be replaced by the category symbols used in semantic interpretation, based on information from the segmenter/tagger, which is preserved in the parse tree, and on the label assignment principles for higher nodes.

Figure 7 illustrates the flow of processing: After parsing, the parse tree is first binarized. The tree converter subsequently replaces the original category labels by labels that conform to the standardized parse tree format and adds information from the lexicon. The standardized, enriched parse tree is then fed into the semantic interpretation engine.

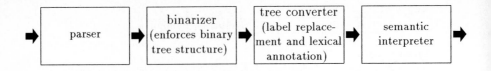

Fig. 7. From parsing to semantic interpretation: Parse trees are first converted to binary format, then category labels are replaced and lexical information is added to the parse nodes. This enriched structure is subsequently fed into the semantic interpretation engine.

5 Summary

We have shown how a semantic interpretation system can be set up to handle output from various parsers by replacing the category symbols provided by the parsers with its own symbols, and by relying only on information provided by the segmenter/tagger and a lexical knowledge base. The advantage of this approach is that the set of semantic interpretation rules can be developed and maintained independently from any specific parser. The costs of the adaptation of a new parser and of the coordination between the parser and the semantic interpretation module are reduced to the creation of mapping tables for symbols on the part-of-speech level and the binarization of the parser's output, if necessary. The modular setup of the system allows us to integrate additional resources as they become available without having to change the actual knowledge base for semantic interpretation.

6 Acknowledgments

The GAZELLE machine translation project is funded by the US Government under contract MDA904-96-C-1077. I am very grateful to Kevin Knight and Daniel Marcu for various comments on earlier versions of this paper.

References

Michael Collins. 1997. Three generative, lexicalized models for statistical parsing. In *Proceedings of the 35th Annual Meeting of the Association for Computational Linguistics (ACL)*.

Christiane Fellbaum (Ed.). 1998. *WordNet*. M.I.T. Press, Cambridge, MA.

Ulrich Germann. 1998. Visualization of protocols of the parsing and semantic interpretation steps in a machine translation system. In *COLING-ACL '98 Workshop on Content Visualization and Intermedia Representations (CVIR '98)*.

Ulf Hermjakob and Raymond J. Mooney. 1997. Learning parse and translation decisions from examples with rich context. In *Proceedings of the 35th Annual Meeting of the Association for Computational Linguistics (ACL)*.

Eduard Hovy and Kevin Knight. 1993. Motivating shared knowledge resources: An example from the Pangloss collaboration. In *Proceedings of the Workshop on Knowledge Sharing and Information Interchange (IJCAI)*.

Kevin Knight, Ishwar Chander, Matthew Haines, Vasileios Hatzivassiloglou, Eduard Hovy, Masayo Iida, Steve K. Luk, Richard Whitney, and Kenji Yamada. 1995. Filling knowledge gaps in a broad-coverage machine translation system. In *Proceedings of the International Joint Conference on Artificial Intelligence.*

Kevin Knight and Vasileios Hatzivassiloglou. 1995a. Two-level, many-paths generation. In *Proceedings of the 33rd Annual Meeting of the Association for Computational Linguistics (ACL).*

Kevin Knight and Vasileios Hatzivassiloglou. 1995b. Unification-based glossing. In *Proceedings of the International Joint Conference on Artificial Intelligence.*

Kevin Knight and Steve K. Luk. 1994. Building a large-scale knowledge base for machine translation. In *Proceedings of the National Conference on Artificial Intelligence.*

Kyoto University. 1997a. Juman. http://www-lab25.kuee.kyoto-u.ac.jp/nl-resource/juman.html. As of 05/22/1997; URL valid on 06/11/98.

Kyoto University. 1997b. KNP. http://www-lab25.kuee.kyoto-u.ac.jp/nl-resource/knp-e.html. As of 05/28/1997; URL valid on 08/24/98.

Kyoto University. 1997c. 京都大学テキストコーパス Version 1.0 (Kyoto University text corpus, version 1.0). http://www-lab25.kuee.kyoto-u.ac.jp/nl-resource/corpus.html. As of 09/23/1997; URL valid on 06/11/98.

Irene Langkilde and Kevin Knight. 1998a. Generation that exploits corpus-based statistical knowledge. In *Proceedings of the 36th Annual Meeting of the Association for Linguistics and 17th International Conference on Computational Linguistics (COLING-ACL).*

Irene Langkilde and Kevin Knight. 1998b. The practical value of n-grams in generation. In *Proceedings of the Ninth International Workshop on Natural Language Generation.*

Takaki Makino, Minoru Yoshida, Kentaro Torisawa, and Jun'ichi Tsujii. 1998. LiLFeS – towards a practical HPSG parser. In *Proceedings of the 36th Annual Meeting of the Association for Linguistics and 17th International Conference on Computational Linguistics (COLING-ACL).*

Mitchell P. Marcus, Beatrice Santorini, and Mary Ann Marcinskiewicz. 1993. Building a large annotated corpus of English: The Penn Treebank. *Computational Linguistics,* 19.

George A. Miller, Richard Beckwith, Christiane Fellbaum, Derek Gross, and Katherine J. Miller. 1990. Introduction to WordNet: an on-line lexical database. *International Journal of Lexicography,* 3(4). ftp://ftp.cogsci.princeton.edu/pub/wordnet/5papers.ps.

Yutaka Mitsuishi, Kentaro Torisawa, and Jun'ichi Tsujii. 1998. Underspecified Japanese grammar with wide coverage. In *Proceedings of the 36th Annual Meeting of the Association for Linguistics and 17th International Conference on Computational Linguistics (COLING-ACL).*

Robert C. Moore. 1989. Unification-based semantic interpretation. In *Proceedings of the 27th Annual Meeting of the Association for Computational Linguistics (ACL).*

Jens Rickmeyer. 1995. *Japanische Morphosyntax.* Groos, Heidelberg.

Stuart M. Shieber. 1986. *An Introduction to Unification-Based Approaches to Grammar.* CSLI, Stanford, CA.

Implementing MT in the Greek Public Sector: A Users' Survey

Athanassia Fourla[1], Olga Yannoutsou[2]

[1,2] Institute for Language and Speech Processing, EUROMAT Office, Artemidos & Epidavrou, 15125, Marousi, Greece

{soula, olga} @ilsp.gr

Abstract. This paper presents the activities of Euromat (European Machine Translation) office in Greece, which has been functioning as a centre for Machine Translation Services for the Greek Public Sector since 1994. It describes the user profile, his/her attitude towards MT, strategies of promotion and the collected corpus for the first three years. User data were collected by questionnaires, interviews and corpus statistics. The general conclusions which have come out from our surveys are discussed.

1. Introduction

This paper presents Euromat Office (*EURO*pean *M*achine *T*ranslation), which functions as a center for Machine Translation Services for the Greek Public Sector. It describes the user profile, their attitude towards MT, strategies of promotion, domain and document type of submitted texts etc.

Before we start we should like to point out the following:

•   the translation services provided are for free and targeted strictly to the Greek Public Sector because of the legal rights the European Commission has over the software
•   a 'reserved' promotion strategy was followed since the team that manned the translation service centre would not be able to handle a very big number of users.

2. Starting up an MT service center

The innovative pilot programme to found a Translation Technology Service Centre for the Greek Public Sector, which would be connected to EC-SYSTRAN via X25, started in 1994 under a Greek Government initiative. The team that had undertaken this goal consisted of two linguists and one engineer, who were trained in Luxembourg in order to staff the centre, while one of the linguists was also specialised in public relations so as to promote the system. In the years that followed another person joined the team for handling hard copy texts (scanning, OCR etc.).This pilot programme can be seen as something special and experimental as it was the very first attempt of the European Committee to make EC-SYSTRAN available to the Public Sector of one of the

Member States. For Greece, too, this was quite innovative as the technological infrastructure of the Public Sector was quite poor at the time. The idea was that raw machine translation would be offered for free and in exchange users would give us feedback in order to improve translation quality.

The experience acquired in introducing new technologies to people unfamiliar with information technology and not particularly computer skilled is the most important thing gained in the past four years. We have come across a variety of situations ranging from the very first time that we introduced the idea of MT to them, to the happy cases of building steady co-operations which resulted in a great contribution towards the development of the system.

The first year was the most difficult one and we had to deal with all popular misconceptions about MT. The hardest problem encountered was to explain the notion of Machine Translation, its purpose, its limits and capabilities. This proved to be harder than expected since information technology is not widespread in the Greek Public Sector and most of its growth occurred after 1994. Problems were encountered even with the computer 'literate' users who had a lot of inhibitions as machine translation systems are not widely known and are often misunderstood.

The second year things ran more smoothly as a relative steady number of users was reached, in spite of the fact that one major problem, when working with the public sector, is the continuous transfer of the clerks, which meant that the whole informative procedure had to start anew if the head of a department changed.

During the third year, EC-Systran users became mostly regular and generally the activities of the office seem to be settled in a 'routine' procedure.

Currently, what we are trying to do is to make users feel 'comfortable' with the system by giving them every chance to realize that they have a significant contribution to the system development. This is done by gathering regularly feedback and terminology, their requests on new language pairs, and by treating them as important agents for the development of the system.

3. Promotional Efforts

The main action lines of the promotion informative campaign were oriented to the Greek Public Servants aiming at transforming their ignorance on Language Technology, and more specifically MT, into knowledge, and their prejudice for computer technology into acceptance.

First of all, we had to start from basics; that is to explain people what machine translation is about and then to introduce them to EC-SYSTRAN. A lot of work had to be done in the direction of solving any possible hesitations from the part of the public sector to co-operate with us and to dissolve any prejudice they may have towards the acceptance of a free service. A point worth mentioning here is that although some services (raw machine translation) were for free, people had many inhibitions even to try the system as they thought that there might be a catch behind it. It was of highest importance to gain their trust, to build and most of all to maintain a relationship of good will and mutual understanding with the Greek public sector.

Various promotion strategies were followed from the beginning of the project involving direct mailing, presentations, information days, distribution of informative leaflets during conferences and other special events, construction of a web page, videos etc.

The first year the pilot phase of the project ran. This was the most difficult period in terms of dealing with a totally unaware target group. We started by mailing a number of letters accompanied by informative leaflets to potential users. Data came from a small database with the names of the public servants who had attended the information day where a demo of EC-SYSTRAN took place before the project began. After letters and leaflets were sent, phone calls both ways followed and presentations for small groups of employees were arranged at their workplaces Whenever an opportunity was given more papers and presentations followed accompanied by informative material.

In the years that followed a web page describing EC-SYSTRAN and the translation services provided was incorporated into ILSP's web page. Furthermore, within the framework of ILSP's general promotion plans, our office advertises its services through a video which presents all the activities of ILSP.

However, the best promotion of the system was through its users as the ones who benefited from our services recommended them to their colleagues from the same or different Public Service.

After the first year the need for promotion in terms of awareness was not so intense. The second year was not a pilot phase any more and we started to expand the range of users. During the third and fourth year, we tried to stabilize our collaboration with the Public Services that had used MT and to keep close contact by advising them on translation issues. In the last two years our goals included less promotion but more work on the direction of identifying our users' problems and keeping them satisfied. We did not want them to believe that once we had ensured their co-operation, their needs were of no interest to us.

For the fifth year, we are planning on developing a user-friendly interface where the users can have direct access and start promoting more the importance of their feedback for the amelioration of the system.

4. The User Profile

In order to reveal the user EC-SYSTRAN profile, surveys were conducted in the form of questionnaires and personal interviews during the last four years.

Regarding their professional activities they are all Public Servants working as translators and administrative staff, coming from all levels of hierarchy from low to top managerial levels. As to the reason they used MT, it was found that while the first year it was for browsing purposes only, as they started to feel more comfortable with it, the next couple of years they used it as draft translation for post processing .

Regarding their attitude towards EC-SYSTRAN at first they seemed rather hesitant. One possible explanation of this could be that public servants in Greece in most cases are not in the least familiar with technology. Another possible consideration is that public employees are in their majority of a certain age and do not always consent to such kind of explorations and innovations. They are mostly conservative and do not dare to experiment even if it is for their own benefit. However, public servants who are keen on trying new tools in order to facilitate their work do exist and experience has shown that once the users become familiar with EC-SYSTRAN's translations they appreciate the help it offers.

In general, having users that are absolutely unaware of what new technologies offer can cause a serious number of problems since they do not understand the procedure, the importance of an 'error free' input text etc. and can easily slander the quality of the translation as they do not feel the logic behind the program.

However, as technology is being widespread, the number of people who really appreciate the facilities of modern technology and acknowledge it is increasing. This applies mostly to users that can now access information written in a foreign language they do not speak. Furthermore, it should be noted that those users who reject translations because of poor quality are very few.

We can identify some major users of the EC MT in terms of Ministries and number of pages translated. Up to March 1997, the system has been used for translation purposes by 16 different ministries. From the percentages of texts and pages given from every ministry we co-operated with, it resulted that there are no important deviations between the percentages of the number of documents and the number of pages given for translation, which means that the ministry which gave the highest percentage of pages for translation (Ministry of Public Order) gave the highest percentage of documents for translation, too. This is interesting from the point of view of regularity; the highest number of pages is not due to an occasional user of the system, but to a regular one.

However, it is also interesting to point out that sometimes a main user does not contribute to the same level towards the domain orientation of the corpus. For example, the main user is the Ministry of Public Order, while the main domain of the corpus is that of aviation. The explanation to this phenomenon is that the texts given for translation from a big organisation like the Ministry of Public Order came from different departments, which means that not all documents were of the same domain, while the main volume of the Ministry of Transportation comes from a single department of the Service of Civil Aviation.

In general, the profile of the EC-SYSTRAN users is changing as time goes by and as they become more familiar with modern technology. Last but not least, we have come to realize that personal contact is invaluable and cannot be replaced by filled in questionnaires.

5. The User Experience

Two direct surveys have been conducted up till now, one before the project started in order to detect the needs for MT in the Greek Public Sector and one after the first full operational year. In addition, personal interviews with the users have been very helpful in forming an opinion as well as statistics that came from our corpus-user database. The latter has been used as an indirect source of information in terms of domain, document type, terminology etc.

Unfortunately, we did not manage to get answers directly from the employees who had used EC-SYSTRAN and did not belong to the upper managerial staff; instead their superiors answered the questionnaires on their behalf giving us what was considered to be a collective answer regarding use, volume, needs etc. This is due to bureaucracy and strict hierarchical order which do not allow direct contact with all the staff. Consequently, we had doubts about the methods used for answering the questionnaires, but when compared with personal interviews, the results were more or less the same.

However, we cannot have an estimation about the average user beliefs of EC-SYSTRAN quality, since the answers varied a lot at this particular question and indicated misconceptions in spite of our informative policy. This survey has shown that the majority of our users expect too much from a machine and many misconceptions are still prominent.

6. Incorporating User Feedback To Improve System Performance

The development of the system is being continued according to the needs and the particularities of the Greek Public Sector. It was often proved to be the case that the more the users of the system got familiar with the concept of Machine Translation, the more willingly they provided feedback.

In particular, the feedback given is mainly terminology from various domains such as agriculture, terms related to fire brigade, criminology, legislation, aviation etc. It is not feasible nor advisable to make global changes to a system from a distance, since the majority of the development team is in another country. Therefore, our job is strictly limited to coding words or expressions in the lexica (STEM and IDLS) as programming needs closer cooperation. The coding is either for general purposes .i.e. we correct translation mistakes and some syntactical or grammatical ones or for specific purposes. In the latter case the topical glossaries for specific domains are enriched. For example, articles treating issues related to athleticism should have a special feature so that common words like 'match' should be translated as 'sports game' and not as 'match stick' etc. In the case of terminological confusion, i.e. when two users provide different terminology for the same word, there is provision for user code.

However, not all needs can be met. While there is great need for translating manuals, a change that would help homograph resolution based on the rule that manuals are usually written in imperative style, could have a disastrous effect since EC-SYSTRAN is based on administrative texts where imperative mood is infrequent.

It is of significant importance to incorporate this feedback into EC-SYSTRAN for two reasons:

1. Translators working in the Public Sector have invaluable experience in the domains they specialize in and the terminology they use is often the result of hard work for many years -if not the work of a life time. Most of the times this terminology is not well-organized and not in any kind of electronic format. Collection of valid terminology is a very difficult task and public employees are often distrustful and reluctant to give their work. Furthermore, correct terminology or simply the use of it, improves the translation quality of a text even if there are syntactical or grammatical errors.
2. Updating the system with the users' own feedback gives them stimuli to provide us with more, as they see the changes in the system and as their work is facilitated.

7. The Input: Domains And Document Type

7.1 Domains

The texts submitted for MT purposes have been composed up till now by 65 different domains. According to the database the most frequently met domain on the basis of pages is 'Aviation' which corresponds to the 15,98% of the total pages translated. However, this is not indicative of the future orientation of the corpus, since those pages are only due to a casual delivery of many aviation manuals, which happened once and it is not likely to be continued. Unfortunately, some major changes to the administration of the aviation service caused the termination of our collaboration. The less common domain is that of fisheries (0,1%).

Another issue of importance is that the maximum number of texts for each domain does not correspond to the maximum number of pages for each domain. So, according to pages the most popular domain is 'Aviation' (2270 pages and 90 texts), however according to texts translated the most requested one is the domain 'Sports' (1540 pages and 93 texts).

7.2 Document type

The most frequent document type in terms of pages is 'manual' with 3,282 pages. This is not surprising as many users express a great need for the translation of manuals although the EC-SYSTRAN is not appropriate for this type of document. The second most frequent document type is 'report' with 2,437 pages and the third most frequent document type is 'recommendation - guidelines', which are common types of administrative texts. However, in terms of number of texts and pages the data are not respective i.e. the most common document type in terms of texts classified under it and the most common document type in terms of pages are not identical. 159 texts are classified under document type 'report', while only 130 texts were classified as manuals. Furthermore, the phenomenon of single occurrences of various document types such as 'circular', 'petition', 'mandate' etc. is also characteristic of our corpus up till now .

8. Conclusion

The experience of Euromat office has definitely put the first stone for the familiarisation of the Greek public servants with the idea of technology in the sector of language engineering. The experiment could be seen two-ways:

• a free trial effort of spreading the notion of MT and language technology before a commercial system is launched in the market. Actually, many requests for translation came from unauthorized users, i.e. from the private sector, who proved to be more informed about technology and willing to try anything.

• a medium for exploring the needs of the Greek Public Sector in terms of office automation

For us, the most important aspect of this project lies with the fact that it tapped an unknown and of course not expressed up till then need. It was exciting to see all this wide range of reaction, ranking between people who were really grateful to the system and people who were almost cursing this thing that wouldn't understand such a simple phrase, or people who were afraid that they would have to do the coding by themselves. However, in most cases, we can say that we acquired lots of new friends and we hope that Language Technology met lots of new friends too.

Public servants in Greece are given almost always the blame for everything bad or wrong in the public sector. This explains at a certain degree why all these people felt a bit confused when offered a service which could relieve them for free from too much work. Nobody else would ever do such a thing for them. So, having an advantage that the private sector didn't have, made them suspicious. Today, we are glad to say that we gained their trust and that we are putting every effort to keep it that way.

In these four years we have contacted lots of users but we still remember the 'pioneers', the ones who trusted us from the beginning and gave us the first texts for translation.

Last but not least, the interaction between the end users and the development team was a fruitful and really interesting experience. Usually, developers and researchers work in isolation without ever seeing or coming into contact directly with the users of their products. Within the Euromat office the opportunity has been given for both developers and users to get in touch with each other. This way, developers got to know and 'face' the users, while the latter had the chance to give their feedback and to enjoy the feeling of their own contribution to a system that they would actually use. Each time a new improved translation was given to a user, after his/her feedback and remarks were incorporated successfully into the system, both sites users and developers enjoyed the results. Today, a big range of enthusiastic users is already created and their comments are most encouraging for the continuation of this effort.

Statistical Approach for Korean Analysis: A Method Based on Structural Patterns

Nari Kim

Institute for Research in Cognitive Science
University of Pennsylvania
3401 Walnut Street
Philadelphia, PA 19104-6228
email: nari@linc.cis.upenn.edu

Abstract. In conventional approaches to Korean analysis, verb subcategorization has generally been used as lexical knowledge. A problem arises, however, when we are given long sentences in which two or more verbs of the same subcategorization are involved. In those sentences, a noun phrase may be taken as the constituent of more than one verb and cause an ambiguity. This paper presents an approach to solving this problem by using structural patterns acquired by a statistical method from corpora. Structural patterns can be the processing units for syntactic analysis and for translation into other languages as well. We have collected 10,686 unique structural patterns from a Korean corpus of 1.27 million words. We have analyzed 2,672 sentences and shown that structural patterns can improve the accuracy of Korean analysis.

1 Introduction

In conventional approaches to Korean syntax analysis, verb subcategorization has generally been used as lexical knowledge [1, 7]. As for the subcategorization of a Korean verb, it declares its complements by representing grammatical morphemes like case postpositions together with the semantic features of their lexical morphemes which are nouns. A problem arises, however, in the syntax analysis using subcategorization when we are given the sentences in which two or more verbs of the same subcategorization are involved. A noun phrase may be taken as the constituent of more than one verb and cause an ambiguity in those sentences. Because subcategorization gives us only declarative knowledge and does not contain any comparable measures, we cannot select the correct structure among possible structures made up of the noun phrase and the verbs. We may be able to adopt a measure based on the similarity between the semantic feature of the questioned noun in the input sentence and those in the subcategorization frames of the involved verbs for comparison [6]. In this case, we should be provided with the semantic features distinct enough to discriminate between the usages of the verbs, for we have to determine which verb takes the questioned noun to construct a phrase structure. A small amount of difference in semantic features cannot be a reliable criterion for selecting a proper structure among candidate structures. Especially in the domain of science or engineering, most of the words used are rather plain. Thus they seldom show mutually discriminative semantic features even though each of them are different in their meanings in reality.

A structural pattern is made up of a head verb and its constituents which repeatedly co-occur in the corpus. The constituents are represented either by grammatical morphemes or by grammatical morphemes and the lexical morphemes combined with them as well. As we acquire structural patterns from a large corpus, we can define *pattern coherency*, a measure of how strongly the constituents and their head verb are structurally related to one another. We can analyze a correct structure by matching structural patterns to Korean sentences and comparing the pattern coherencies of the matched structural patterns, even when the involved verbs are similar not only syntactically but also semantically and have the same subcategorization.

2 Structural Ambiguities in Korean Sentences

We will explain the problem in Korean analysis by considering two Korean verbs, 사용되다(*sayongtoyta*, be used) and 나타나다(*nathanata*, appear). Both of the verbs 사용되다(*sayongtoyta*) and 나타나다(*nathanata*) are commonly used in Korean sentences.

(a) inspection, assembly, experiment, retrieval,
    inquiry, train, calculator
(b) document, text, display, architecture,
    corner, wall painting, industrial product

The nouns in (a) are the examples which have been used as the constituents of the verb 사용되다(*sayongtoyta*) combined with the case postposition '-에(-*ey*)' in our corpus. [1] Similarly, the nouns in (b) are the examples for the verb 나타나다(*nathanata*). The nouns are shown in English translation of the original Korean nouns for understanding. Suppose that the nouns in (a) are used as the constituents of the second verb 나타나다 (appear), and vice versa. This does not cause any syntactic problem and makes sense also. It is because most Korean verbs can be modified by the noun phrases combined with adverbial postpositions such as '-에(-*ey*, locative case),' '-에서(-*eyse*, locative case),' '-로(-*lo*, directional case),' and so on. The noun phrases combined with adverbial postpositions can be either the complements of the verbs or simply the adjuncts of the verbs.

In the syntactic analysis of Korean sentences, it is often the case that a noun phrase has more than one head verb candidate which follows it. If all the candidate predicates take the constituents with the semantic features disjunctive to one another, we can choose one correct structure without difficulty. Unfortunately, however, some of the verbs may take similar and even the same noun

---

[1] The Korean postposition '-에(-*ey*)' can be translated into *in, at, on*, and sometimes even into *to* according to the given context.

for their constituent as shown in the above examples. When those verbs appear simultaneously in a sentence, this causes structural ambiguities. We will show you an example sentence involving such a structural ambiguity.

(1) 이 중에서 정확한 (*i cwungeyse cenghwakhan*)
   these among-Loca be correct-Adnom
   분석 결과를 선택하기 위한 (*pwunsek kyelkwalul sentaykhaki wihan*)
   analysis result-Obj select to
   지식이 필요하다. (*cisiki philyohata*)
   knowledge-Sbj be necessary [2]
   (Some knowledge is necessary to select a correct analysis result among these.)

Sentence (1) has three predicates, 정확하다(*cenghwakhata*, be correct), 선택하다(*sentaykhata*, select), and 필요하다(*philyohata*, be necessary) in it. The noun phrase '중에서(*cwungeyse*, among)' is composed of the noun '중(*cwung*)' and the locative case postposition '-에서(*-eyse*).' [3] While some verbs require a noun phrase combined with the postposition '-에서(*-eyse*)' as their indispensable complement, most Korean verbs can also take the noun phrase combined with '-에서(*-eyse*)' simply as their adjuncts.

When we analyze sentence (1) according to grammar rules or subcategorization, we have three possible structures related to the noun phrase '중에서 (*cwungeyse*).' It is because all of the three predicates in sentence (1) can take the noun phrase combined with the postposition '-에서(*-eyse*)' as their constituent. Moreover, the Korean noun '중(*cwung*)' does not have a semantic affinity with any of the verbs. Consequently, there should be other selectional information besides the subcategorization and semantic features, in order to select the correct structure among candidate structures.

(p1) and (p2), below, are our structural patterns, each of which consists of an individual verb and its possible constituents. Note that the positions of lexical morphemes are described not by specific words but by variables like N1, N2 and N.

(p1) [N1/에서 N2/를 선택하다] [select N2 among N1] (0.660)
(p2) [N/에서 필요하다] [be necessary in N] (0.138)

The values enclosed in parentheses are pattern coherencies, which represent how strongly the constituents and their head verb are structurally related to one another. The pattern coherencies are used as measures to resolve the structural ambiguities. Because the coherency of (p1) is much higher than that of (p2), (p1) is selected as the correct one. Therefore, the noun phrase '중에서(*cwungeyse*, among)' is to be attached to the verb 선택하다(*sentaykhata*, select). A structural

---

[2] Loca : locative, Adnom : adnominal, Obj : objective, Sbj : subjective

[3] '중(*cwung*)' is a noun, though it can be translated into *among*, an English preposition.

pattern can be naturally a translation unit, provided that the corresponding translation is supplemented by a human, as shown in our examples.

We will explain how we acquire structural patterns from a corpus and how we calculate their pattern coherencies in the next section.

3 Structural Patterns

From an empirical standpoint, a sequence of words that we find repeatedly in sentences should be considered to form a kind of syntactical frame. A syntactical frame is what can be applied afterwards to analyzing the structures of other sentences. Thus, we accept the assumption that the words composing a syntactic structure within a sentence appear closer than other unrelated words do. Smadja[9], Grishman[3], and many other studies based on empirical data also have taken this assumption as their basic principle.

3.1 Definition of Structural Patterns

In order to define our structural pattern, we first have to introduce the representational form of a Korean word phrase. A Korean word phrase consists of a lexical morpheme and one or more grammatical morphemes combined with it. It can be represented as follows.

w/g :
$\quad w \in L$
$\quad g \in G \cup \{\lambda\}$
$\quad L$: set of Korean lexical morphemes
$\quad G$: set of Korean grammatical morphemes

In a word phrase w/g, w means a lexical morpheme such as a noun, a verb or an adverb, and g means a grammatical morpheme such as a postposition or an ending. Accordingly, we can define the structural pattern.

Structural Pattern : Let P be $[w_1/g_1 \ ... \ w_n/g_n \ h]$, when $w_1/g_1 \ ... \ w_n/g_n$ are word phrases that are preceding verb h in a sentence. If $Pr(P) \geq \tau$ is satisfied, we call P a *structural pattern* of verb h, where
$\quad Pr(P) = \frac{f(P)}{f(h)}$
$\quad w_i : L \cup M, \ g_i : G \cup \{\lambda\}$
$\quad M$: set of meta variables, for representing meta constituents
$\quad f(x)$: the frequency of word x in the corpus
$\quad \tau$: threshold value$(0 < t < 1)$

In a pattern, lexical morpheme w of a constituent w/g can be either a designated word or a meta variable like N1, N2, or N. We call the former the *lexical constituent* and the latter the *meta constituent* of a pattern. A meta constituent can match any word phrase regardless of its lexical morpheme, if it is combined with the specified grammatical morpheme. Because grammatical morphemes in the Korean language are only a few compared with lexical morphemes, the structural patterns including meta constituents are so productive that we can have high recall in syntactic analysis.

3.2 Acquisition of Structural Patterns

As the Korean language has a head-final characteristic, we can extract pattern candidates by simply collecting the word sequence preceding each verb in the corpus. $\Pr(P)$ is the *pattern probability* of pattern candidate P, which is the proportion of the frequency of P and the frequency of P's head verb in the corpus. Only when a word sequence appears in a significant proportion to the frequency of its head verb, is pattern candidate P accepted as a proper pattern.

The criterion by which we decide whether a pattern candidate can be accepted as a proper pattern or not is an empirically determined threshold value of pattern probability. We fixed the threshold as 0.02, which had shown the best performance in structural attachment through a series of experiments. If the threshold is too high, naturally we get only a small number of patterns from the corpus. In that case, the patterns are insufficient to cover various input sentences; thus they can solve only a small portion of structural ambiguities during syntax analysis. In contrast with this, we get a large number of patterns when the threshold is rather low. But this time, the correctness of structural attachment is not satisfactory because of the erroneous patterns accidentally caught due to the low threshold.

The first step for acquiring structural patterns is Korean tagging. We use the tagger developed by Lee[5]. The tagger analyzes each word phrase and provides us with its part-of-speech, stem, and the grammatical morphemes combined with the stem. In the second step, we extract pattern candidates by collecting the word sequences on the left side of the verbs within a sentence. We generate additional pattern candidates by alternating the lexical morphemes of the extracted word sequences with meta variables. Therefore, if there are n words in a word sequence with the exception of the head word, we have 2^n pattern candidates. We adjust the frequency of the pattern with meta constituents, after any of its lexicalized versions has been accepted as a proper pattern. We call the original lexical morphemes *reference words* of the meta constituents and keep them in the pattern base. If necessary, the reference words are looked up for structural disambiguation.

In the third step, we calculate the pattern probabilities of pattern candidates and filter out the pattern candidates which have lower probabilities than the threshold. We have obtained 10,686 unique patterns from the corpus of 1.27 million words. [4] The number of unique verbs in our pattern base is 4,614. It means that each Korean verb has 3.63 patterns on the average.

Figure 1 shows pattern candidates of the Korean verb 두다(*tuta*, put) and their pattern probabilities. [5]

---

[4] The corpus is collected from the papers in the domain of science and the textbooks of elementary schools.

[5] 에(-*ey*, locative), 를(-*lul*, objective), 로(-*lo*, directional), 기반(*kipan*, basis)

(a) [N1/에 N2/를 두다] $Pr = 0.166$
(b) [N/를 두다] $Pr = 0.105$
(c) [N/에 두다] $Pr = 0.025$
(d) [N/에 기반/을 두다] $Pr = 0.030$
(e) [N1/로 N2/를 두다] $Pr = 0.008$
(f) [N1/로 두다] $Pr = 0.005$

Fig. 1. Pattern candidates of 두다(*tuta*, put)

Pattern candidates (a) through (d) are accepted as proper patterns since their pattern probabilities are higher than the threshold 0.02. Pattern candidates (e) and (f) get lower pattern probabilities. Therefore, they should not be included in the pattern base. Pattern candidate (d) describes a structure that consists of two constituents and the head verb 두다(*tuta*). One of the constituents is a meta constituent 'N/에 (N/*ey*)', and the other is a lexical constituent '기반/을 (*kipan/ul*).' If a lexical word co-occurs repeatedly with a verb, the lexical word can be included in a proper pattern of the verb. The pattern probability of (d) is 0.03. In our experiment, it means that (d) has been found 35 times out of 1,166 total appearances of the verb 두다(*tuta*). The most dominant pattern of 두다(*tuta*) is (a), where both constituents are meta constituents specifying only postpositions. It is because the nouns which can come with 두다(*tuta*) in the frame of (a) vary a lot. Therefore, none of them could obtain significant proportion.

3.3 Pattern Coherency

Pattern coherency is a measure of how strongly the constituents and their head verb are structurally related to one another. Pattern coherency is calculated in this manner: one must check the probability of the occurrence of a given pattern in the whole pattern base while at the same time examining the probability of the occurrence of its head verb in the corpus, and then divide the former by the latter to obtain the value. If a verb has a strong tendency to take a specific constituent, the coherency of the pattern including the constituent is relatively higher than that of other patterns.

Let p be a pattern of verb h. Then the pattern coherency of p, $CO(p)$ is defined in the following formula.

$$CO(p) = \frac{P_{PB}(p)}{P(h)} = \frac{\frac{f(p)}{N_{PB}}}{\frac{f(h)}{N}}$$

where
N : size of corpus
N_{PB} : size of pattern base, $\sum f(p)$
$f(p)$: frequency of p
$P_{PB}(p)$: the probability of p in pattern base
$P(h)$: word probability of h in corpus

Here, we introduced $P_{PB}(p)$ to acquire the probability of pattern p in the pattern base. When we extract patterns from the corpus, we cannot know how big the pattern base will be. Therefore, we calculated approximately the pattern probabilities by dividing the frequencies of the pattern candidates by the size of the corpus. Once the pattern base is constructed, however, we can calculate the exact probability of each pattern in the population of all patterns. Thus, the denominator of $P_{PB}(p)$ should be N_{PB}, the size of pattern base, not N anymore. In our experiment, N and N_{PB} are 1,276,390 and 143,828 respectively.

Figure 2 enumerates the patterns of the verb 나타나다(*nathanata*, appear) and their pattern coherencies. According to the distribution of pattern coherencies in Figure 2, 나타나다 (*nathanata*) comes most frequently with postposition '-에(-*ey*)' in the corpus.

(a) [N/에 나타나다] [appear at N] (1.888)
(b) [N/로 나타나다] [appear to be N] (0.448)
(c) [N/에서 나타나다] [appear in N] (0.333)
(d) [N1/에 N2/로 나타나다] [appear to be N2 at N1] (0.128)

Fig. 2. Patterns of 나타나다(*nathanata*, appear)

Figure 3 shows the patterns of the verb 사용되다(*sayongtoyta*, be used) and their pattern coherencies.

(a) [N/에서 사용되다] [be used in N] (1.236)
(b) [N/에 사용되다] [be used for N] (0.710)
(c) [N/로 사용되다] [be used as N] (0.631)

Fig. 3. Patterns of 사용되다(*sayongtoyta*, be used)

It is noteworthy that the pattern coherency of (c) in Figure 3 is higher than that of (b) in Figure 2, even though the case postposition '-로(-*lo*)' can be attached to both verbs 나타나다(*nathanata*) and 사용되다(*sayongtoyta*). [6] This fact implies that 사용되다(*sayongtoyta*) has a stronger tendency of taking a noun phrase combined with the postposition '-로(-*lo*)' than 나타나다(*nathanata*) does. It coincides with human intuition about the usage of the verbs 나타나다(*nathanata*) and 사용되다(*sayongtoyta*).

---

[6] The meaning of the postposition '-로(-*lo*)' varies according to its head verb as shown in Figure 2 and Figure 3.

4 Structural Attachment Using Pattern Coherency

In syntactic analysis, we apply patterns to input sentences prior to traditional grammar rules. After we recognize the structures of predicates and their nominal modifiers by patterns, other additional constituents such as adverbs or determiners are analyzed by grammar rules. Once all patterns of all verbs in the sentence have been tried to match, we check every noun phrase in the sentence to find out whether more than one pattern matches it. If more than one pattern matches a noun phrase, we select the pattern with higher pattern coherency so that its head verb takes the noun phrase.

We rely on pattern coherencies only when the difference of pattern coherencies is big enough to discriminate between the competing patterns. When the difference is too small to choose a correct pattern, it is necessary to confer a supplementary information, like word similarity. Word similarity is computed between the noun matching a meta constituent and its reference words kept in the pattern base. [7]

For the structural disambiguation, we adopted a concept of *confidence measure*[8]. Since statistical data is usually extracted automatically from large corpora, some erroneous data may be included in it. Confidence measure is an empirically determined threshold by which we can make a reliable decision when we use statistical data.

We have set three kinds of confidence measures: *maximum difference of coherency*, *minimum difference of coherency*, and *minimum difference of word similarity*. If a pattern has a coherency which is higher than that of its opponent by more than the *maximum difference of coherency*(=2.3), we can select the pattern without conferring word similarity. *Minimum difference of coherency*(=0.15) is a confidence measure which is required for a pattern to be selected as a correct one. If the difference of coherencies is between *maximum difference of coherency* and *minimum difference of coherency*, then we should consult the word similarity. When we determine a correct structure by consulting word similarity of patterns, the gaps should be bigger than *minimum difference of word similarity*(=0.015). If none of the cases is satisfied, we simply choose a default structure, where a nominal is attached to its closest predicate [4].

5 Experimental Results

We randomly selected 2,672 Korean sentences from the corpus for the evaluation of our method. The test sentences were excluded from the extraction of structural patterns. The length of sentences ranges from 6 words to 25 words. We will show the accuracy of pattern matching in Table 1. The accuracy of pattern matching

---

[7] We have adjusted the algorithm of Dagan[2] and Yang[10] to our system; any two nouns can be called similar if they share a large part of the patterns in which they have appeared.

is as follows:

$$\frac{\text{\# of structures correctly analyzed by patterns}}{\text{total \# of structures analyzed by patterns}}$$

sent. length	sent.	strs. analyzed by pattern	correct	accuracy
6-10	744	647	636	98.3%
11-15	750	1,135	1,100	96.9%
16-20	709	1,487	1,435	96.5%
21-25	469	1,138	1,076	94.6%
total	2,672	4,407	4,247	96.4%

Table 1. Accuracy of Pattern Matching

The overall accuracy of pattern matching was 96.4%. The accuracy of pattern matching changes according to the length of input sentences. The accuracy decreases when the sentences become longer, because more structural ambiguities exist in longer sentences.

Table 2 shows the accuracy of structural disambiguation. [8] This experiment was done excluding the trivial structures, namely the cases with no structural ambiguity. The accuracy of structural disambiguation is as follows:

$$\frac{\text{\# of ambiguous structures correctly analyzed by patterns}}{\text{total \# of ambiguous structures analyzed by patterns}}$$

sent. length	ambiguities	strs. analyzed by pattern	solved	accuracy
6-10	298	256	245	95.7%
11-15	545	468	433	92.5%
16-20	747	645	593	91.9%
21-25	610	534	472	88.4%
total	2,200	1,903	1,743	91.6%

Table 2. Accuracy of Structural Disambiguation

The experiment achieved 91.6% accuracy in resolving the ambiguities in the structures between nominal constituents and their head verbs. Among the error rate 8.4% in Table 2, 2.9% was due to the deficiency of necessary patterns, because we were not concerned if the verbs in the test sentences were included in the pattern base or not.

---

[8] The number of ambiguities in the second column is the number of ambiguous structures. A sentence may have more than one ambiguity in it.

6 Conclusion

We present a statistical method based on *structural patterns* to select correct structures in Korean analysis. Structural patterns describe the possible constituents of individual verbs, whether they are lexical constituents or meta constituents. We also incorporate the pattern coherency, a statistical measure of how strongly the constituents of each structural pattern are related to one another. Even when we analyze long sentences where two or more verbs of the same subcategorization are involved, we can select a correct structure by comparing the pattern coherencies of the matched patterns.

We acquired 10,686 unique structural patterns from a corpus of 1.27 million words. Using the structural patterns, we have analyzed 2,672 sentences and shown that our method can obtain 96.4% accuracy in pattern matching and 91.6% accuracy in structural disambiguation. These experimental results assure that structural patterns can improve the performance of Korean analysis. Since the acquisition of structural patterns is automatically performed, we can easily apply this method to various domains provided with appropriate corpora.

References

[1] Chang, S. J., *A Fundamental Study on Natural Language Processing*, Project Report, Korean Science and Engineering Foundation, 1989.

[2] Dagan, I., Marcus, S. and Markovitch, S., "Contextual Word Similarity and Estimation from Sparse Data," *Proceedings of the 31st Annual Meeting of the ACL*, pp.164-171, 1993.

[3] Grishman, R. and Sterling, J., "Acquisition of Selectional Patterns," *Proceedings of the 29th Annual Meeting of the ACL*, pp.229-236, 1992.

[4] Kimball, J., "Seven Principles of Surface Structure Parsing in Natural Language," *Cognition*, vol. 2, pp.15-47, 1973.

[5] Lee, H. G. and Kim, Y. T., "A Resolution of Korean Lexical Ambiguities Based on Statistical Information," *Journal of Korea Telecommunications Society*, vol. 19, no. 2, pp.265-275, 1994.

[6] Moon, Y. J., *Design and Implementation of WordNet for Korean Nouns Based on The Semantic Word Concept*, Ph.D. thesis, Seoul National University, 1996.

[7] Seo, Y. H., *Head-driven Korean Parsing Using Semantic Information*, Ph.D. thesis, Seoul National University, 1991.

[8] Shim, K. S., *Structural Disambiguation of to-infinitives Using Expanded Collocation Information*, Ph.D. thesis, Seoul National University, 1994.

[9] Smadja, F., "From N-Grams to Collocation: An Evaluation of Xtract," *Proceedings of the 29th Annual Meeting of the ACL*, pp.279-284, 1991.

[10] Yang, J. H., *A Resolution of Structural Ambiguities in Korean Noun Phrase Coordinates Using Co-occurrence Similarity*, Ph.D. thesis, Seoul National University, 1995.

Twisted Pair Grammar: Support for Rapid Development of Machine Translation for Low Density Languages

Douglas Jones[1] and Rick Havrilla[2]

[1] NLP Research Branch
Department of Defense, Attn: R525
9800 Savage Road Ft. Meade, MD 20755-6000
jones@afterlife.ncsc.mil
[2] R.A. Baruch & Associates
10500 Little Pautuxent Pkwy., Ste. 790
Columbia, MD 21044
rick@afterlife.ncsc.mil

Abstract. We describe a streamlined knowledge acquisition method for semi-automatically constructing knowledge bases for a Knowledge Based Machine Translation (KBMT) system. This method forms the basis of a very simple Java-based user interface that enables a language expert to build lexical and syntactic transfer knowledge bases without extensive specialized training as an MT system builder. Following [Wu 1997], we assume that the permutation of binary-branching structures is a sufficient reordering mechanism for MT. Our syntactic knowledge is based on a novel, highly constrained grammar construction environment in which the only re-ordering mechanism is the permutation of binary-branching structures (Twisted Pair Grammar). We describe preliminary results for several fully implemented components of a Hindi/Urdu to English MT prototype being built with this interface.[1]

1 Introduction

Two major obstacles to building knowledge bases for an MT system are the amount of time it takes to a build high-quality knowledge base and the amount of data that may be required to get started. For languages for which there is a low density[2] of available language resources, these obstacles are especially acute.

---

[1] Our platform for MT prototypes is the Mtendo system, a Java-based implementation of the Gazelle MT system. The underlying Gazelle MT engine is a descendent of JapanGloss, built at the University of Southern California's Information Science Institute under government sponsorship. Gazelle is a hybrid rule-based, statistical MT system using an LFG format for the knowledge bases. It has multiple throughput options: syntactic transfer, word-for-word, and semantic/ontological analysis (see Knight et al. 1995 or http://www.isi.edu/natural-language/GAZELLE.html).

[2] By "low density" languages, also known as "languages of low diffusion", "world minority languages", etc, we mean languages for which major online resources are typically not available.

In this paper, we will first outline the need to develop new ways to acquire linguistic knowledge from a language expert and will describe the status quo for our MT system. Second, we will describe how we are designing the Mtendo Language Tableau as an easier and more effective interface for acquiring lexical and syntactic transfer knowledge. Third, we will describe a set of theoretical constraints on the syntactic knowledge we encode in the Twisted Pair Grammar format. Last, we will summarize our current state, which is fairly preliminary, and outline what we need to do to scale the system up to handle authentic materials, such as newspaper texts and language training materials.

1.1   The MT Language Paradox

Machine translation system builders face a well-known paradox - technology is under continuous development but the languages themselves are relatively constant. It is common for a research team to build a new system release every four to six months. It is also common to spend several years developing robust coverage for a language pair. The consequence is that the knowledge base is rarely in complete synchronization with the MT system. This problem is especially acute for the low density languages, for which MT requirements may be sporadic and for which language expertise may be difficult to find [Nirenburg and Raskin 1998]. If machine translation weren't already hard enough, it is appreciably more difficult for the low density languages.

1.2   Focus on Knowledge Building (KBMT)

To address the problems posed by the MT Language Paradox, we propose to focus efforts more on the knowledge base for an MT system than on the MT system itself. This work falls into the Knowledge-Based MT paradigm (KBMT) [Nirenburg et al. 1992 and Knight et al. 1995]. The main point of this paper is to discuss how a simple knowledge building interface based on Twisted Pair Grammar can simplify knowledge acquisition for low density languages. By design, the language knowledge we build is general purpose. By focusing on the knowledge base, we can update our methods of caching out of that information much easier than we could retool a system-specific knowledge base. Once our knowledge base is built for broad coverage and remains relatively constant for core coverage, we can automatically convert the knowledge sources as new MT resources as needed.

This strategy allows us to make the best use of a language expert's time and expertise. Consider the standard method of training the language expert to build MT system rules directly. Learning to write MT rules can be a very daunting challenge. It can also make it impossible to build an MT system as a short-term project since it may take months to train a language expert to design MT rules. Let us take the Gazelle MT system as a case in point [Knight et al. 1995, Knight and Luk 1994]. To build a Gazelle MT syntactic transfer grammar, there are two types of rules: (1) a "neutral" grammar rule for the source language, (2) glossing rules, which are the "neutral" rules augmented with transfer features [Hatzivassiloglou and Knight 1995]. To augment the MT system, the language expert gathers representative sentences, drawn from grammar books, corpora, and general language expertise, and then writes rules to translate the representative sentences. Care is taken to choose sentences that are as generic as possible, and to write rules which have the broadest coverage possible. As the language expert discovers new target language expressions which fail to translate properly, he or she then either writes new rules, or modifies old rules to extend their coverage. There are advantages and disadvantages with this method.

Advantages include complete control over how the rules are built and full access to the expressive power of the system. Disadvantages include that after a time, it is very difficult to associate particular rules with any particular texts that they are intended to cover. Furthermore, the system becomes too complex to understand (either individual rules become too complicated, or the interaction of simple rules becomes too complicated). The standard remedy to the complexity problem is to develop a corpus of representative sentences, to record the correct MT output, and to test subsequent modifications of the MT system by running it against the corpus, noting any differences that show up. For the improper translations, the language expert carefully examines which rules were responsible, modifies them, and continues to iterate. There is no guarantee that the language expert can tweak the system to handle the entire corpus at once. Our method is to preserve the strengths of this approach (leveraging from extensive language expertise) while avoiding its weaknesses (forcing the language expert to learn system-specific grammar formats, guarantee system consistency, etc.)

1.3   Semi-automated Knowledge Building

We propose here at least a partial remedy to these problems. Rather than build rules directly, we acquire just enough information about a representative translation to automatically construct the MT rules. The Mtendo Sentence Tableau interface[3], shown in Figure 1, is designed for this purpose. The purpose of the Tableau is to encapsulate just as much knowledge as the language expert is willing to commit to. At present, we do not expect the expert to have firm opinions on the clause structure of the sentence, nor do we require an explicit structural analysis. Rather, we expect only that the expert can gloss the source text, annotate it with relevant features (such as number, gender, case, etc.) and re-order the gloss (by dragging word boxes in a graphical user interface) into a reasonably understandable English expression. This expression is then automatically checked to ensure that MT rules can be built from the Sentence Tableau.

---

[3] Two components of the Mtendo interface are shown in Figure 1: the Sentence Tableau and the Generic Rule Generator and Viewer (for viewing the rules automatically generated from the Tableau). These components were built using Java JDK v1.1.6 and the Java Foundation Classes, v1.0.2, by Rick Havrilla and Chris Murphy of RABA Technologies. Doug Jones designed the basic architecture, theoretical framework, and proofs of concept.

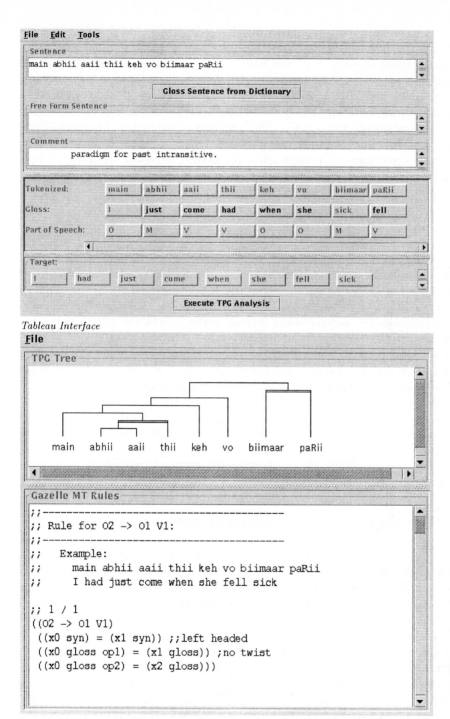

Tableau Interface

Automatic Rule Construction

Fig. 1. Mtendo Language Tableau Interface

The most important step is for the language expert to construct a representative set of sentences that illustrate the essential syntactic structures of the language: these are edited with the Suite Editor. The language expert edits each selected source sentences in the Suite with the Sentence Tableau. For each sample sentence, the system looks up each word in the lexicon. If a word is missing, the tableau prompts the expert to add new words, prompting for headword, gloss, part of speech, and features. The core part of the tableau for building syntactic knowledge is the target translation interface as shown in Figure 1. This translation conforms to the rigid set of constraints discussed below; only target translations that conform to the constraints are accepted by the tableau.

1.4 Avoid Arbitrary Decisions

An essential feature of the system is that the specifics of the MT rules are potentially underdetermined by the tableau. In other words, more than one rule could generate the constituent in the tableau. By focusing on the knowledge over and above the specific requirements of the MT systems, we allow the language expert to cover a lot more ground. We also will allow the expert to avoid arbitrary decisions about the analysis until there is really a need for more information. Consider the case of prepositional phrase attachment: does a PP attach to the verb phrase or does it attach to the sentence? What if the consequences for the choice are not clear? Rather than forcing the expert to make a decision in the absence of good evidence, we can simply ask the expert to provide a compliant translation. As for extracting the MT rule, if there is an ambiguity, we can allow the system to extract rules for both possibilities. Alternatively, we could choose one, either arbitrarily or based on some other principle, and wait for an inconsistency in the MT translation suite.

Let us now step through the theoretical framework that allows us to automatically generate the MT rules.

2 Theoretical Basis for Sentence Tableau

If language is intrinsically organized into binary branching structures, could we use that fact to simplify machine translation? If language is really organized that way [Kayne 1983, Kayne 1994, Chomsky 1995], we can design MT algorithms to exploit that underlying structure to reduce complexity, not only of the core translation algorithms [Wu 1997] but also of the knowledge acquisition process. Following [Wu 1997], we assume that the permutation of binary-branching structures is a sufficient reordering mechanism for MT. Specifically, the core MT process could simply become the permutation of glossed nodes in a binary-branching tree. The proposed "Twisted Pair Grammar" attempts exactly that.

The intended contribution of this paper is to demonstrate broad application beyond the related case of Chinese-English MT [Wu 1997]. Wu proposes a very different sort of solution to the problem of acquiring MT rules: a stochastic inversion transduction grammar is to be automatically acquired from bilingual corpora. Our proposal is neither fully automatic nor stochastic; nonetheless, we share the same assumption about the organization of language: we are both looking for binary branching structures that may be permuted. Contra Wu, however, we expect even languages as different as English and Hindi/Urdu to be composed of similar types of structures. Moreover, we expect to exploit non-superficial regularities to simplify the translation process, even for these very different languages. This paper describes an algorithm for using implicit structure in carefully constructed translations to automatically construct MT transfer rules. The algorithms described in the paper are fully implemented; they generate a complete (albeit simple) knowledge base that enables an MT system to give end-to-end Hindi/Urdu to English throughput.

2.1 Twisted Pair Grammar

Twisted Pair Grammar, a novel contribution in this paper, is a highly constrained environment for building syntactic transfer grammars. It is designed to streamline and expedite MT system building. The essential idea (or hope) is that we can always arrive at a reasonably intelligible translation that conforms to the criteria shown below. We will call these translations "TPG-compliant". The limitations are that all linguistic structures are binary branching and the only word re-ordering mechanism available for the translation process is the permutation nodes in these binary structures. There are no other re-ordering mechanisms.

1. Content words are translated directly.
2. Function words are translated, inserted, or deleted.
3. Words and phrases may be permuted, but only as allowed by permutations of nodes in a binary tree structure assigned to the source text.

Two twisted pair structures are shown below. In the first example, you can see that there are four binary-branching structures that characterize how this sentence is organized. Looking from left to right at the bottom-most level of analysis, the first pair is *'kamre-men' (in the_room)*. The double bar across the top means it is a twisted pair, so to translate that portion, the glosses for those two nodes are permuted. The same goes for *'baiThii hai' (is sitting)*; note the double bar. Those two nodes are themselves permuted, yielding *'is sitting in the room'*. The final remaining pair is a linear pair (not a twisted pair) so it is not inverted, and we get *'Shobha is sitting in the room'* for our translation. A very important point is that what drives the structure-building is not a linguistic analysis of either the source or target texts, but rather, the search for a structure that enables a translation conforming to the TPG constraints listed above. From that point of view, it appears incidental that the structures shown below are plausible on linguistic grounds. However, since the linked correspondences imply a structural relationship for both source and target elements on their own, it stands to reason that the structures are plausible linguistically. The second example illustrates a more complex construction – a sample correlative –, which is still amenable to our analysis. We are currently surveying the core grammatical constructions [Kachru 1980, Barker 1978, Davison 1988, Bains 1989, and

3. Scan the source array from left to right, scanning the target array from left to right, looking for a target cell that matches the gloss for the source cell.
4. When one match has been found, check whether the neighboring cell matches in both the source and target array.
5. If the matching cells are in the same order in both arrays, a linear pair has been found. If the neighboring cells are inverted, a twisted pair has been found.
6. Merge the neighboring cells and repeat until there are no more matching neighboring cells. Cells contain either words or composite cells composed of previous matches.

3.1 A Simple Example

Let us step through the example from Section 2.1, shown below. First, we scan from left to right, looking for two adjacent source words that correspond to two adjacent target words. The two target words may either be in the same order as the corresponding source words (a linear pair), or they may be permuted (a twisted pair). The first pass constructs a prepositional phrase: *kamre* matches *room* and *men* matches *in*. The relevant cells are merged, and in the second pass, the arrays are one cell shorter. Since these cells appear in inverted order in the source array, we construct a twisted pair from the prepositional phrase. For notation, we mark the composite, merged cells in parentheses; twisted pairs are preceded by "*". We continue scanning from left to right at each pass, looking for pairs to merge. On the second pass, we find the verb phrase *(sitting (in the_room))*. The third pass finds the inflected predicate *(is (sitting (in the_room)))*. The fourth pass completes the sentence, discovering the final pair (a linear pair) and the algorithm terminates.

		0	1	2	3	4
First	S:	shobhaa	kamre	men	baiThii	hai
Pass	T:	Shobha	is	sitting	in	the_room
Second	S:	shobhaa	*(kamre men)	baiThii	hai	
Pass	T:	Shobha	is	sitting	(in the_room)	
Third	S:	shobhaa	*(*(kamre men) baiThii)	hai		
Pass						
	T:	Shobha	is	(sitting (in the_room))		
Fourth	S:	shobhaa	*(*(*(kamre men) baiThii) hai)			
Pass						
	T:	Shobha	(is (sitting (in the_room)))			
Final	S:	(shobhaa *(*(*(kamre men) baiThii) hai)				
Pass						
	T:	(Shobha (is (sitting (in the_room)))				

Notice that we managed to create a plausible grammatical structure simply by scanning and matching pairs in these arrays. The essential insight is that the grammatical structure is equivalent to the history of the algorithm that constructed the pairs. Moreover, what drives the meaningful assignment of structure is the discovery of the twisted pairs. Linear pairs, when they occur, contribute only ambiguous structure.

It's worth pointing out that there is more than one possible history that we may be interested in. There are actually two other candidate twisted pairs if we scan exhaustively on the first pass; a spurious one: (men baiThii)*(sitting in) and a plausible one: (baiThii hai)*(is sitting). For the moment, we are ignoring some issues: how to get rid of spurious pairs, alternative treatments of multiple pairs, and what to do if there aren't any pairs. A more sophisticated algorithm will also allow for the deletion and insertion of function words

In fact, the structure we got does not perfectly match the structure shown in Section 2.1. However, what we have is close enough; both are plausible in terms of compositionality. For the moment, let us just proceed with the structure that we found and see what we need to do to automatically generate MT rules from these structures.

3.2   Categorization of Nodes in Structure

So far, we do not have quite enough to go on to create MT rules: the structures are too bare. The Gazelle MT system is based on a constituent grammar (in LFG format). If we add category labels to the nodes in the trees, we will have straightforward constituent trees to work with.

Categorizing the nodes in the tree is simple. For each terminal node, look up the part of speech in the glossary and assign as the category.

For each non-terminal node, assign the category of the higher ranking daughter node. If both categories are identical, assign the shared category. Let us require that we have a glossary that has an entry for each word in the TPG-compliant example pair; each source language entry has to have a target language gloss and a part of speech. That gives us enough information to categorize the terminal nodes.

For the non-terminal nodes, we use the category of the child nodes. To do that, let us further require that categories (parts of speech) are ranked in a total order, for example: *auxiliary < verb < preposition < noun*. We can use this ranking to categorize the rest of the tree: we recursively assign the highest-ranking child-node category to each mother node. We show in Section 3.3), for the category assignment for the prepositional phrase *(in the_room)*, since prepositions outrank nouns, the mother node is categorized as a prepositional phrase (rather than the alternative, a noun phrase). Since verbs outrank prepositions, *(sitting (in the_room))* is a verb phrase, not a prepositional phrase.

What the ranking amounts to is a characterization of headedness: the ranking category is the head. Eventually, we will make fuller use of the idea of a category head.[5] We will use headedness to determine how features are passed through

---

[5] See [Collins 1997] for very productive parsing results making use of headedness in phrases.

the tree to constrain the grammar. For the moment, though, we are just using headedness to determine the category for the mother node.

3.3 Automatic Generation of MT Rules

We still need to construct the MT rules automatically from these trees; the algorithm for that is shown below. We visit each node in the tree and categorize each node as we just discussed. Next, we assign a target gloss for each source node: for the terminal nodes, we simply look up the word in the glossary. For branching nodes, we check whether the node is linear or twisted. For a linear pair, the gloss of the mother node is the gloss of the left node followed by the gloss of the right node. For twisted pairs, the glosses are inverted. Once the glosses have been assigned, creating the actual MT rules is very simple. For terminal nodes, the parent category is simply the lexical category (part of speech). The rule rewrites the category as the string and adds features to encode the gloss, which was assigned directly from the glossary. The branching nodes are only slightly more complicated.

1. Categorize each node in the tree as described above.
2. Visit each node in the tree:
3. For each terminal node, let C and W be the category and word label of the lexical node. Let G be the gloss for W from the glossary. Create a lexical MT rule: `((C -> W)`
   `(X0 gloss) = G))`
4. For each non-terminal node, let M, L, and R be the categories of the mother, left, and right nodes respectively. For a linear pair node, create an MT rule:
   `((M -> L R)`
   `  (X0 gloss op1) = (X1 gloss))`
   `  (X0 gloss op2) = (X2 gloss)))`
   For a twisted pair node, create an MT rule: `((M -> L R)`
   `  (X0 gloss op1) = (X2 gloss))`
   `  (X0 gloss op2) = (X1 gloss)))`

Stepping through the example below, let us see how our algorithm creates the MT rule for the prepositional phrase. The left-hand side of the rule is the parent category, which is PP. The first daughter node is the N and the second is the P. Since this is a twisted pair, the glosses are inverted. The Gazelle MT rules follow the convention of labeling the left-hand side x0 and the daughter nodes X1 to XN [Shieber 1985, Hatzivassigloglou and Knight 1995]. The rule shown below says that the first element of X0's gloss is X2's gloss, and the second element is X1's gloss. That means that the gloss for the postposition comes before the gloss of the noun, so for *kamre men* we get *in the_room*.

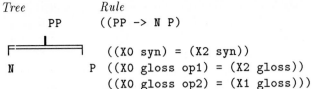

Tree	Rule
PP	((PP -> N P)
	((X0 syn) = (X2 syn))
N ———— P	((X0 gloss op1) = (X2 gloss))
	((X0 gloss op2) = (X1 gloss)))

The rules for the MT grammar that we generated for the sample twisted pair structure are shown below. It is worth pointing out that this simplistic mechanism is creating a rather recursive grammar for our example. We created the rule: `IP->N IP`. Without any further constraints, that allows an arbitrary number of nouns at the beginning of the sentence. For Hindi/Urdu, that is appropriate because the basic clause structure is SOV. The structure here actually predicts scrambling, which is an interesting point but is probably accidental. In any case, the grammar will need additional constraints; the candidate mechanism is feature constraints for the unification mechanisms in the LFG grammar.

```
((PP -> N P)                          ((IP -> N IP)
 ((x0 gloss op1) = (x2 gloss))         ((x0 gloss op1) = (x1 gloss))
 ((x0 gloss op2) = (x1 gloss)))        ((x0 gloss op2) = (x2 gloss)))
((VP -> PP V)                         ((P -> "men")
 ((x0 gloss op1) = (x2 gloss))         ((x0 gloss) = "in")))
 ((x0 gloss op2) = (x1 gloss)))      ((V -> "baiThii")
((IP -> VP I)                          (x0 gloss) = "sitting"))
 ((x0 gloss op1) = (x2 gloss))       ((I -> "hai")
 ((x0 gloss op2) = (x1 gloss)))        ((x0 gloss) = "is"))
```

We are experimenting with variations for the algorithm for constructing rules. On the one hand, we are experimenting with how we create the mother category. The mother needs to be based on which of the left or right daughters is the head. Method 1 is to say that for lexical category L, the mother node is LP (an "L-phrase"). Method 2 is to count the "bar-levels" and create labels "L1", "L2" and so forth. Method 3 is to create a pseudo-categorial grammar category, creating the new label "LR" for lexical categories "L" (left) and "R" (right). Each method is progressively more specific in labeling the mother node for the rules.

On the other hand, we are experimenting with ways to annotate the context-free portion of the grammar with feature notations. Since the MT rules for non-terminal nodes are created automatically, the easiest way to introduce features is to take them from the lexicon and to pass them through the higher level rules. In other words, we will try adding lexical features to constrain the rules. For example, we are generating rules that force the mother category to inherit the syntactic information of the head node ((X0 syn)=(X1 syn)), if the left daughter, X1, is the head, beginning with the lexical entries and working upward. What we need to do next is identify which nodes need to unify this information with something other than a mother-head combination. In other words, we need to encode agreement at some levels in the rule set. Both of these aspects of the rule-generation are still in progress. For the time being, we will comment primarily on the aspects of the system we have presented in relative detail.

To sum up so far: we have an algorithm for discovering implicit structure in example pairs; we have an algorithm for assigning categories and glosses to the nodes in the structures; and finally, we have an algorithm for automatically creating Gazelle MT rules. Ultimately we need to test the resulting MT system for broad-scale coverage and quality. The first step, though, is to determine whether the MT system behaves consistently for the suite of examples we used to create it.

3.4   Testing and Scaling the System

Our preliminary MT knowledge base, which is not yet complete, has over 700 sentence tableaus illustrating both simple and complex features of Hind-Urdu syntax. These tableaus generate a core vocabulary of over 1600 MT lexicon entries and several hundred MT grammar rules (syntactic transfer). Although the system is obviously very small now, we are optimistic that the knowledge base will scale effectively.

As discussed above, we are currently reporting only on the MT grammar rules that are not being marked with feature annotations. In other words, we are describing context-free syntactic transfer rules. The problem, of course, is as soon as these rules are general enough to scale, they overgenerate. Nevertheless, we have tested the rules for internal consistency. In other words, we take an example pair, extract the MT rules, and re-translate the source example. The translation should match the target example. As would be expected, the system consistently translates each tableau sentence perfectly 98% of the time when using only the grammar rules built for that tableau entry. For the two cases in which there is a mismatch in the expected translation, the problem is that a rule overgenerates within the domain of that sentence. This experiment is only a baseline test to be sure that we have not introduced any errors into our tableau. It is not a realistic adequacy test for the system as a whole, though. The issue, of course, is that what we are getting is a grammar for each source language sentence, but what we really want is a grammar for the whole language.

With what amounts to context-free transfer rules, it should not be surprising that quality degrades as the number of MT rules increases when we translate the entire knowledge base suite. Depending upon which of the rule-construction methods we use, from only a small portion to the majority of the test suite sentences are translated perfectly (by string-matching). On the one hand, the test is too rigid: the MT system is designed to yield multiple output, and the top choice is the most fluid [see Knight et al 1994]. On the other hand, the MT system over-generates because the rules really are too general. For example, our tableau has the pair *aap DakTaar and hai* <-> *You are a doctor*, but we get *Is he a doctor* as output. Half of that generalization is actually correct; the pronoun *aap* can mean either *he* or *you*. However, the spurious reordering of the pronoun and verb in the English translation indicates a true overgeneralization. Unfortunately, in many cases, consistency really is degraded. We need to find enough generality inside the specific examples and extract enough implicit structure that applies not only to that example but also to others like it. To achieve better consistency, we are incorporating constraints on the lexicon that propagate appropriately through the unification structure.

We are hoping that a carefully chosen suite of a few thousand sentence tableaus will give us a system with better quality than word-for-word output for newspaper texts. To test this hypothesis, at the same time that we are increasing the quality of translations on the suite itself, we are increasing the lexical coverage of the system. To increase lexical coverage, we are currently building a finite state morphological grammar based on PC-Kimmo, which we have wrapped as a Java module in the Mtendo environment for Gazelle. We are also integrating a large-scale machine-readable dictionary of approximately 50K headwords. With the broad lexical coverage in place, we will compare a direct word-for-word translation with the output we get from Mtendo/Gazelle with the knowledge base built from our Tableaus. To the extent that we are able to produce rough English output that gives a basic understanding of the Hindi/Urdu original, we will consider the system successful.

4   Conclusion

There are also some other important side benefits for focusing on the knowledge building. We can use the knowledge base for multiple MT platforms. By focusing on the knowledge base of TPG-compliant translations, we make the MT system more maintainable. Although the system has been implemented to generate Gazelle MT rules, yielding end-to-end throughput capabilities, we know of no reason why other rule formats could not be generated to drive other MT systems

Moreover, we can share the knowledge bases with other applications, for example, Computer Based Training for foreign language teaching. To the extent that these resources are successful for CBT, we could conceive of building TPG-compliant CBT systems to spin off MT resources instead of the other way around. By stepping back a bit from the specific MT systems, we open up a variety of possibilities.

Acknowledgements

We would especially like to thank Art Becker, Eric Brill, Lynn Carlson, Michael Collins, Jonathan Davis, Laurie Karttunen, Cynthia Kuo, Chris Murphy, Boyan Onyshkevych, Steve Parker, and Annie Zaenen for many helpful comments and discussions. All errors and shortcomings of course are our own.

References

[1989] Bains, Gurprit. 1989. Complex Structures in Hindi-Urdu: Explorations in Government and Binding Theory. Doctoral Dissertation, New York University.

[1993] Barker, Muhamed ABD-AL-Rahman, Hasan Jahangir Hamdani, Khwaja Muhammad Shafi Dihlari, and Shafiqur Rahman. 1993. Spoken Urdu: A Course in Urdu. Volume 1. Spoken Language Service, Inc.

[1995] Brill, Eric. 1995. Transformation-Based Error-Driven Learning and Natural Language Processing: A Case Study in Part of Speech Tagging. (ACL)

[1995] Chomsky, Noam. 1995. The Minimalist Program. Current Studies in Linguistics. MIT Press.

[1997] Michael Collins. 1997. Three Generative, Lexicalised Models for Statistical Parsing. Proceedings of the 35th Annual Meeting of the ACL (jointly with the 8th Conference of the Linguistics. EACL), Madrid.

[1988] Davison, Alice. 1988. "Constituent Structures and the Realization of Agreement Features." Proceedings of the 24th Meeting of the Chicago Linguistic Society, Parasession of Agreement in Grammatical Theory.

[1993] Dorr, Bonnie. 1993. Machine Translation: A View from the Lexicon. MIT Press.

[1994] Fung, Pascal and Dekai Wu. 1994. Statistical Augmentation of a Chinese Machine-Readable Dictionary. Available as cmp-lg/9406015.

[1995] Hatzivassiloglou, Vasileios and Kevin Knight. "Unification-Based Glossing". 1995. Proceedings of the International Joint Conference on Artificial Intelligence (IJCAI).

[1994] Kayne, Richard. 1994. The Antisymmetry of Syntax. Linguistic Inquiry Monograph 25. MIT Press.

[1983] Kayne, Richard. 1983. Connectedness and Binary Branching. Studies in Generative Grammar 16. Foris Publications.

[1994] Knight, Kevin and Steve Luk. "Building a Large-Scale Knowledge Base For Machine Translation. 1994. Proceedings of American Association for Artificial Intelligence.

[1994] Knight, Kevin, Ishwar Chandler, Matthew Haines, Vasileios Hatzivassigloglou, Eduard Hovy, Masayo Ida, Steve Luk, Richard Whitney, and Kenji Yamada. 1994. Integrating Knowledge Bases and Statistics in MT (AMTA-94)

[1995] Knight, Kevin, Ishwar Chandler, Matthew Haines, Vasileios Hatzivassigloglou, Eduard Hovy, Masayo Ida, Steve Luk, Akitoshi Okumura, Richard Whitney, and Kenji Yamada 1995. "Filing Knowledge Gaps in a Broad-Coverage Machine Translation System". (IJCAI-95).

[1998] Nirenburg, Sergei and Victor Raskin. 1998. "Universal Grammar and Lexis for Quick Ramp-Up of MT Systems. (manuscript)

[1992] Nirenburg, Sergei, Jaime Carbonnel, M. Tomita, and K. Goodman. 1992. Machine Translation: A Knowledge-Based Approach. Morgan Kaufmann.

[1985] Shieber, Stuart. 1985. An Introduction to Unification-Based Approaches to Grammar. Center for the Study of Language and Information, University of Chicago Press.

[1995] Wu, Dekai and Xuanyin Xia. 1995. Large-Scale Automatic Extraction of an English-Chinese Translation Lexicon. Machine Translation. 9:3, 1-28.

[1994] Wu, Dekai. 1994. Aligning a Parallel English-Chinese Corpus Statistically with Lexical Criteria. Available as cmp-lg/9406007.

[1997] Wu, Dekai. 1997. Stochastic Inversion Transduction Grammars and Bilingual Parsing of Parallel Corpora. Computational Linguistics. 21(4):377-404.

A Thematic Hierarchy for Efficient Generation from Lexical-Conceptual Structure

Bonnie Dorr and Nizar Habash and David Traum

UMIACS
University of Maryland
College Park, Md 20742
phone: +1 (301) 405-6768
fax: +1 (301) 314-9658
{dorr,habash,traum}@umiacs.umd.edu
WWW home page: http://umiacs.umd.edu/labs/CLIP

Abstract. This paper describes an implemented algorithm for syntactic realization of a target-language sentence from an interlingual representation called Lexical Conceptual Structure (LCS). We provide a mapping between LCS thematic roles and Abstract Meaning Representation (AMR) relations; these relations serve as input to an off-the-shelf generator (Nitrogen). There are two contributions of this work: (1) the development of a thematic hierarchy that provides ordering information for realization of arguments in their surface positions; (2) the provision of a diagnostic tool for detecting inconsistencies in an existing online LCS-based lexicon that allows us to enhance principles for thematic-role assignment.

1 Introduction

This paper describes an implemented algorithm for syntactic realization of a target-language sentence from an interlingual representation called Lexical Conceptual Structure (LCS). We provide a mapping between LCS thematic roles and Abstract Meaning Representation (AMR) relations; these relations serve as input to an off-the-shelf generator (Nitrogen). There are two contributions of this work: (1) the development of a thematic hierarchy that provides ordering information for realization of arguments in their surface positions; (2) the provision of a diagnostic tool for detecting inconsistencies in an existing online LCS-based lexicon that allows us to enhance principles for thematic-role assignment.

Several researchers have proposed different versions of thematic hierarchies (see [9, 4, 3, 13, 18, 7, 22, 21, 1, 2, 8]).[1] Ours differs from these in that it separates arguments (e.g., agent and theme) from obliques (e.g., location and beneficiary) and provides a more complete list of thematic roles (20 roles overall) than those of previous approaches (maximum of 8 roles). We have implemented the approach described here as part of a Chinese-to-English Machine Translation (MT) project

---

[1] For an excellent overview and a comparison of different thematic hierarchies see [20].

at the University of Maryland and we have used the resulting output to guide enhancements to a LCS-based database.

The next section describes our framework for mapping LCS roles to AMR relations. Section 3 introduces the thematic hierarchy used for syntactic realization of arguments. Section 4 describes the implementation, while sections 5 and 6 present the results of testing the implementation, and our conclusions.

2 Mapping LCS Roles to AMR Relations

The input to our MT system is a Chinese sentence that is parsed into a syntactic structure. This is passed to a semantic composition module which creates a corresponding LCS [10, 11, 12].[2] LCS is a compositional abstraction with language-independent properties that transcend structural idiosyncrasies. This representation has been used as the interlingua of several projects such as UNITRAN [6] and MILT [5].

The LCS is passed to a generator which produces an output English sentence by means of two steps: lexical selection and syntactic realization. Lexical selection involves a comparison between LCS components and abstract LCS frames associated with words in an English lexicon. Syntactic realization re-casts LCS-based thematic roles as relations in an Abstract Meaning Representation (AMR), i.e., an unordered tree where the root is a concept and each child is linked by a relation.[3] An intermediate form (LCS-AMR) is produced as a by-product of this mapping between roles and relations. The AMR is as input to the Nitrogen system [15, 16, 17] which provides the mechanism needed for linearization, morphological derivation, word order and agreement.[4] (More details about Nitrogen and AMRs are given in Section 4.1.)

An example of the steps in the conversion from LCS to AMR is shown in (1) below, for the sentence *China arms the coalition*. The LCS can be roughly glossed as "China caused the coalition to go identificationally (or transform) towards being at the state of being armed." From this the agent (China) and theme (coalition) are extracted; these serve as slot-fillers in the LCS-AMR. These are then mapped into their corresponding slots in the AMR.

```
(1) LCS: (CAUSE (Thing China 1)
            (GO Ident (Thing Coalition 2)
              (TOWARD Ident (Thing Coalition 2)
                (AT Ident (Thing Coalition 2)
```

---

[2] The parser and composition module were developed at the University of Maryland.

[3] We also map LCS-based modifiers, quantifiers, and other features into corresponding AMR-based components. For the purposes of this paper, we will focus specifically on realization of LCS arguments.

[4] The Nitrogen generation system was produced at the Information Science Institute at the University of Southern California. We chose to use this system as part of our generation efforts because of its large coverage and accessibility, as well as a balance between knowledge-based and statistical approaches.

```
                    (Property armed 9)))))

LCS-AMR: (A1 / |arm<render|
              :LCS-AG (A2 / |China|  :quant sing)
              :LCS-TH (A3 / |coalition|) :quant sing)

AMR: (A1 / |arm<render|
           :arg1 (A2 / |China| :quant sing)
           :arg2 (A3 / |coalition|) :quant sing)
```

Thematic roles in LCS are represented as integers. In the example above, 1 is used to designate *Agent* and 2 is used to designate *Theme*. Each role has a unique integer.[5] LCS thematic roles are defined to reflect the role taken by the object they refer to in the sentence described by the LCS. There is no built-in information about surface realization of these objects. For example, as shown in 2, a theme can be realized as the subject or the object of a sentence or even as an object of a preposition.

(2) *The girl* walked home.
     We helped *the boy*.
     She nibbled at *a cookie*.

This lack of direct correspondence to syntax is intentional: the LCS is a language-independent structure and positioning of arguments in the LCS is language dependent. The following table displays some of the most commonly used thematic roles, their thematic numbers, their corresponding LCS-AMR relations, and examples of possible realizations.

(3)

Theta Role	#	Abbrev	LCS-AMR Relationn	Possible Realizations
Agent	1	ag	:LCS-AG	Argument: *John* broke the chair.
Theme	2	th	:LCS-TH	Argument: *The boy* went to school.
				Oblique: She nibbled at *a cookie*.
Source	3	src	:LCS-SRC	Argument: She abandoned *the scene*.
				Oblique: We came from *the party*.
Goal	5	goal	:LCS-GOAL	Argument: He entered *the room*.
				Oblique: We are going to *the party*.
Location	11	loc	:LCS-LOC	Argument: *The trees* swarmed with bees.
				Oblique: The bees buzzed in *the trees*.

Realization of thematic roles associated with LCS positions must be provided on a per-language basis. Such information is specified in lexical entries in terms of thematic numbers (see above) coupled with requirements for optionality (:OPTIONAL and :OBLIGATORY), internal/external positioning (:INT and :EXT), and associated prepositions (:COLLOCATIONS). We use a thematic grid as an easy-to-read shorthand to encapsulate all of this information.

---

[5] The exception to this is that *Experiencer* and *Theme* share the integer 2.

The grid includes the thematic roles corresponding to LCS positions in their surface-realization order. A preceding underscore or comma tells whether the thematic role is obligatory or optional, respectively. The thematic grid also includes the particle(s) associated with a particular thematic role. For example, the thematic grid `_ag_th(at),instr(with)` conveys the information that, in English, the agent in the LCS must be realized as the subject and the theme and instrument (when provided) must be realized as obliques (prepositional phrases) in the order given.

In order to create a mapping between LCS-based thematic roles and AMR relations used in the Nitrogen system, we first examined the meaning behind the roles used in these two representations. At first glance, it would appear that they are entirely incompatible: LCS roles are purely thematic with no inherent syntactic ordering information while AMR relations are a mix of syntactic and semantic roles. Moreover, the AMR relations did not allow a specific preposition to be associated with certain oblique relations.[6] If the LCS associates a specific preposition with a certain role, the thematic role must be mapped into the relation `:spatial-location` in the AMR so that a preposition may be specified. This forces all obliques into one relation which, in addition to being inappropriate in many cases (since obliques are not always "spatial" in nature), does not allow for multiple oblique relations. Thus, only one oblique may be produced per sentence.

Our solution is to redefine the mapping between thematic roles and AMR relations to that of mapping between these roles and their surface realizations. We use syntactically-defined AMR relations: `:arg1`, `:arg2`, and `:goal` which refer to argument 1 (or logical subject), argument 2 (or logical object), and goal (the only relation corresponding to the logical indirect object). As for obliques, they will be mapped to two new relations that specify a preposition and its object (`:lcs-prep` and `:lcs-prep-object`). The new relations are then linearized separately, as described in the next sections.

3   Thematic Hierarchy

Once the LCS-AMR relations are identified, the generator must have access to information that establishes the relative ordering of arguments on the surface. A brute force approach to mapping relations to syntactic positions is to associate each verb instance in an AMR with its thematic grid from the associated abstract LCS frame in the lexicon. This method is expensive and inefficient as there are more than 107 distinct grids, each potentially containing several optional items that must be treated separately. Another approach is to induce an ordering among the thematic roles that mirrors their order of realization. Such an ordering may be imposed by means of a thematic hierarchy. As mentioned earlier, several researchers have proposed different versions of thematic hierarchies. An example

---

[6] Nitrogen tends to overgenerate by producing several possible prepositions associated with such relations.

of a simple thematic hierarchy can be the following:[7]

(4) `Agent > Theme > Location`

This means that in the case of an LCS with any two of these three roles, the roles must be realized as argument 1 and argument 2 in the order with which they appear, left to right, in the thematic hierarchy.

We constructed a more comprehensive thematic hierarchy than those proposed previously. To do this, we first extracted all the thematic grids in the verb LCS Lexicon. There were 107 distinct grids, each of which we divided into two partial grids: one for arguments and one for obliques. The relative ordering between obliques and arguments is always the same: arguments are realized closer to the verb and obliques follow. Each partial grid was then ordered topologically.

Initially, the following thematic hierarchy was found for arguments (the roles between the curly braces have equal relative order):

(5) `ag > instr > th > perc > {goal, src, loc, poss, pred, prop}`

Several exceptions were found such as the following:

(6) (i) `The bees buzzed in the trees.`   (ii) `The box contains the ball.`
        `Theme   >       Location`   `Location   >   Theme`

(7) (i) `They deserted the scene.` (ii) `The cop fined John   40 dollars.`
        `Theme >       Source`   `Agent >   Source > Theme`

Cases like (6) above are resolved using the lexical parameter `:EXT`, which is set for Location in (6)(ii). To integrate this solution, we created an intermediate LCS-AMR relation `:lcs-ext` that will replace the original thematic role. This new role is the highest on the thematic hierarchy by definition. Example (7) is the only unresolved ordering. We treat it as an exception that is addressed before everything else. Thus, the final hierarchy for arguments is as follows:

(8)   `special case : ag src th   (in this order)`
      `ext > ag > instr > th > perc >   Everything Else`

As for the ordering of obliques, the following order was established:

(9)   `particle > mod-prop > ag > perc > th > purp > mod-loc >`
      `mod-pred > src > goal > mod-poss > ben`

Note that the order of obliques is not a strict hierarchy but rather a possible topological sort. There are several interdependencies that are hard to resolve using a strict ordering. But for all possible relative orderings, the thematic hierarchy above reflects a correct realization order. Special cases to this hierarchy are found to be alternative possible realizations. For example the following two realizations are correct even though the first one, which appears in the thematic grid is not consistent with the thematic hierarchy used for the obliques:

---

[7] This most closely resembles the hierarchy proposed by [4].

forces Nitrogen to match first with :arg1 then :arg2. If a match is found for :goal, then :arg2 and :goal are swapped as part of the recasting. An additional rule is needed to implement the special case referred to above in (8). An example rule, the one for picking the first argument is shown below in (15). Note that the listing of options reflects the order in the thematic hierarchy.

```
(15) ((x1 :rest)
     (x2 :lcs-ext :lcs-ag :lcs-instr :lcs-th :lcs-perc :lcs-goal
         :lcs-mod-poss :lcs-mod-loc :lcs-src :lcs-mod-pred
         :lcs-loc :lcs-poss :lcs-pred :lcs-prop)
     -> (? (x1 (:add (:arg1 x2)) ?))))
```

The thematic hierarchy for the obliques is implemented differently for two reasons. First, each oblique must be identified by the existence of two relations: the actual thematic role (e.g., lcs-goal or lcs-src) and its corresponding particle relation (e.g., lcs-goal-part or lcs-src-part). Second, the linearization rules for obliques must be associated with each specific preposition. Therefore, there are two sets of rules associated with the realization of obliques. First, there are linearization rules to create the correct sequence of :lcs-prep and :lcs-prep-obj for every possible preposition. And secondly, there are recasting rules to transform the thematic roles and thematic particle roles into :lcs-prep and :lcs-prep-obj. These rules are ordered to reflect the thematic hierarchy of obliques. In (16) we present the two rules that realize a source using the particle "from".

```
(16) ; Linearize with the preposition "from"
     ((x1 (:lcs-prep |from|)) (x2 :lcs-prep-obj) (x3 :rest) ->
      (s (seq (x3 s) (wrd "from") (x2 np))))

     ; Recasting goal and goal particle
     ((x1 :lcs-goal-part) (x2 :lcs-goal) (x3 :rest) ->
      (? (x3 (:add (:lcs-prep x1) (:lcs-prep-obj x2)) ?))))
```

5 Results

The implementation of the thematic hierarchy was tested using a set of 100 randomly selected sentences from a set of 550 examples sentences that are associated with the LCS-based verb lexicon (to exemplify the realization of particular verb classes based on [19]). These sentences were then semi-automatically converted into the LCS-AMR representation. Full realization was performed, i.e., conversion to AMR and Nitrogen's morphological realization. Sample test sentences are given in (17), along with final generation results.

```
(17) (A1 / |place| :LCS-AG (A2 / |he|) :LCS-TH (A3 / |book|)
              :LCS-GOAL-PART |on| :LCS-GOAL (A5 / |table|))

     he placed the book on the table .
```

```
------------------------------------------------------------
(A850 / |hear| :LCS-TH (A851 / |he|)
            :LCS-PERC-PART |about| :LCS-PERC (A853 / |murder|))


he heard about the murder .
------------------------------------------------------------
```

Out of 100 sentences, only one problematic argument assignment was found:

(18) (A1333 / |wink|
          :LCS-TH (A1334 / |she|)
          :LCS-INSTR (A1335 / |eye| :MOD (A1336 / |her|))
          :LCS-PERC-PART |at| :LCS-PERC (A1338 / |him|))

This AMR returned the sentence *her eyes wink she at him* instead of the expected *she winked her eyes at him*. This case revealed an error in the LCS-based lexicon: In all other instances where instrument and theme co-occurred, instrument was higher in the hierarchy. So, the theme (originally the experiencer) must be forced to be external by setting the lexical parameter :EXT (or changing the role assignments, e.g, from theme to agent).

The use of the generator as a diagnostic tool has aided detection of other types of inconsistencies in the LCS-based lexicon. This has allowed us to enhance principles for thematic-role assignment. For example, in an earlier version of the LCS lexicon the following classes of verbs were distinguished by their thematic grids:

(19) (i) _th_loc: bound, bracket, ..., hug, skirt, surround, ring
     (ii) _loc_th: contain, enclose

However, our experimentation with the generator revealed that there would be no principled way to assign reversed roles to objects in sentences such as the following:

(20) (i) The fence (th) surrounded the house (loc)
     (ii) The fence (loc) enclosed the house (th)

Thus, we collapsed the two classes of verbs *contain* and *enclose* into a single class associated with the grid _loc_th.

6 Conclusion

The small test described in the previous section shows that the thematic hierarchy implementation has good coverage over a large sample of the Levin verb classes. Our approach is efficient in that it accesses a single thematic hierarchy rather than individual ordering specifications for linearization of arguments and obliques. Moreover, the approach allows sentences to be produced in a fashion that mirrors that of parsing, with thematic roles corresponding to D-structure positions. Finally, we have used the output resulting from the generator as a diagnostic tool for detecting inconsistencies in an existing LCS-based lexicon and, consequently, enhancing this online resource.

Our future work will involve testing the system on additional data, as well as completely automating the process of generation from Lexical Conceptual structures. Our goal is to produce preliminary results on deployment of an end-to-end Chinese to English machine translation system by the fall of 1998. Further work will focus on other aspects of the generation process, such as improving the performance on grammatical features and modifiers.

Acknowledgments

This work has been supported, in part, by DOD Contract MDA904-96-C-1250. The first author is also supported by Army Research Laboratory contract DAAL01-97-C-0042, NSF PFF IRI-9629108 and Logos Corporation, NSF CNRS INT-9314583, DARPA/ITO Contract N66001-97-C-8540, and Alfred P. Sloan Research Fellowship Award BR3336. We would like to thank members of the CLIP lab for helpful conversations, particularly David Clark, Scott Thomas and Mari Olsen. We would also like to thank Kevin Knight and Irene Langkilde for making the Nitrogen system available and help with understanding the Nitrogen grammar formalism.

References

1. A. Alsina and S.A. Mchombo. Object Asymmetries and the Chichewa Applicative Construction. In S.A. Mchombo, editor, *Aspects of Automated Natural Language Generation*, pages 1–46. CSLI Publications, Center for the Study of Language and Information, Stanford, CA, 1993.
2. C.L. Baker. *English Syntax*. The MIT Press, Cambridge, MA, 1989.
3. J. Bresnan and J. Kanerva. Locative Inversion in Chichewa: A Case Study of Factorization in Grammar. *Linguistic Inquiry*, 20:1–50, 1989.
4. J. Carrier-Duncan. Linking of Thematic Roles in Derivational Word Formation. *Linguistic Inquiry*, 16:1–34, 1985.
5. Bonnie J. Dorr. Large-Scale Acquisition of LCS-Based Lexicons for Foreign Language Tutoring. In *Proceedings of the ACL Fifth Conference on Applied Natural Language Processing (ANLP)*, pages 139–146, Washington, DC, 1997.
6. Bonnie J. Dorr, James Hendler, Scott Blanksteen, and Barrie Migdalof. Use of Lexical Conceptual Structure for Intelligent Tutoring. Technical Report UMIACS TR 93-108, CS TR 3161, University of Maryland, 1993.
7. A. Giorgi. Toward a Theory of Long Distance Anaphors: A GB Approach. *The Linguistic Review*, 3:307–361, 1984.
8. J. Grimshaw and A. Mester. Light Verbs and Theta-Marking. *Linguistic Inquiry*, 19:205–232, 1988.
9. Ray Jackendoff. Grammatical Relations and Functional Structure. In *Semantic Interpretation in Generative Grammar*. The MIT Press, Cambridge, MA, 1972.
10. Ray Jackendoff. *Semantics and Cognition*. The MIT Press, Cambridge, MA, 1983.

11. Ray Jackendoff. *Semantic Structures*. The MIT Press, Cambridge, MA, 1990.

12. Ray Jackendoff. The Proper Treatment of Measuring Out, Telicity, and Perhaps Even Quantification in English. *Natural Language and Linguistic Theory*, 14:305–354, 1996.

13. P. Kiparsky. Morphology and Grammatical Relations. unpublished ms., Stanford University, 1985.

14. Kevin Knight and Vasileios Hatzivassiloglou. Two-Level, Many-Paths Generation. In *Proceedings of ACL-91*, pages 143–151, 1991b.

15. Irene Langkilde and Kevin Knight. Generating Word Lattices from Abstract Meaning Representation. Technical report, Information Science Institute, University of Southern California, 1998.

16. Irene Langkilde and Kevin Knight. Generation that Exploits Corpus-Based Statistical Knowledge. In *Proceedings of COLING-ACL '98*, pages 704–710, 1998.

17. Irene Langkilde and Kevin Knight. The Practical Value of N-Grams in Generation. In *International Natural Language Generation Workshop*, 1998.

18. R.K. Larson. On the Double Object Construction. *Linguistic Inquiry*, 19:335–391, 1989.

19. Beth Levin. *English Verb Classes and Alternations: A Preliminary Investigation*. University of Chicago Press, Chicago, IL, 1993.

20. Beth Levin and Malka Rappaport-Hovav. From Lexical Semantics to Argument Realization. Technical report, Northwestern University, 1996.

21. T. Nishgauchi. Control and the Thematic Domain. *Language*, 60:215–260, 1984.

22. W. Wilkins, editor. *Syntax and Semantics 21: Thematic Relations*. Academic Press, San Diego, CA, 1988.

The LMT Transformational System

Michael McCord and Arendse Bernth

IBM T.J. Watson Research Center, P.O. Box 704, Yorktown Heights, NY 10598, USA
mccord@watson.ibm.com arendse@watson.ibm.com

Abstract. We present a newly designed transformational system for the MT system LMT, consisting of a transformational formalism, LMT-TL, and an algorithm for applying transformations written in this formalism. LMT-TL is both expressive and simple because of the systematic use of a powerful pattern matching mechanism that focuses on dependency trees. LMT-TL is a language in its own right, with no "escapes" to underlying programming languages. We first provide an overview of the complete LMT translation process (all newly redesigned), and then give a self-contained description of LMT-TL, with examples.

1 Introduction

The machine translation system LMT ([10–13, 4, 5, 16]) is the basis of the Personal Translator product [8]. Slot Grammar [9, 14, 15], which is used for source analysis in LMT, is also used as the basis for the EasyEnglish grammar and style checker [1–3]. In the past two years or so we have been reworking Slot Grammar, EasyEnglish, and LMT, mainly because of a re-implementation from Prolog to C. This has given us a good excuse for enhancing some of the design features! For this new version of LMT, we have been concentrating so far on Web page translation as the application (for several language-pair versions).

This paper deals mainly with a particular component of the new LMT, the transformational system, which we believe is of general interest. The system comprises a transformational formalism, called LMT-TL, and an algorithm for applying it. The LMT-TL language is designed to be powerful enough to express all needed source-target transformations, yet simple enough that linguists who know little programming can use it. Pattern matching is a key facility of LMT-TL. LMT-TL does not have "escapes" to an underlying programming language (as is the case e.g. with the transformational system of LMT/Prolog), but is a language in its own right. Primitive operations of LMT-TL can explore, test, and change the transfer tree structure as it is converted from the source language form to the target language form. In order to make the discussion self-contained, we first give a brief description of the overall LMT design in the next section. We wish to thank Sue Medeiros for work on parts of the LMT transfer engine, especially lexical transfer, and to thank Claudia Gdaniec for work on the English→German transformations and lexicons, and for help on the E→G examples in this paper. Gdaniec discusses linguistic issues in English→German translation within this framework [6].

2 Overview of the LMT Translation Process

LMT is a transfer system using four main steps in translation: *Source analysis, lexical transfer, restructuring*, and *target morphological generation*. Let us look at a specific example sentence, following the translation produced by LMT English→German, as we describe these four steps. The English input sentence is: *When asked to read his poems to the audience, John accepted with delight*.

The source analysis produced by ESG (English Slot Grammar) for this sentence is shown in Fig. 1.

```
.------------- vsubconj     when1(1,2)          subconj
| '----------- sccomp(en)   ask1(2,u,3,u)       verb ven vpass
|   '--------- obj(inf)     infto(3,4)          infto
|     '------- tocomp(binf) read1(4,u,6,7,u)    verb vinf
|     | .--- ndet           his1(5)             det pl possdet
|     '----- obj(n)         poem1(6,u)          noun cn pl
|     '----- iobj(p)        to2(7,9)            prep
|     | .- ndet             the1(8)             det sg pl def
|     '--- objprep(n)       audience1(9)        noun cn sg pl
.------------- subj(n)      John1(10)           noun propn sg
o------------- top          accept1(11,10,u)    verb vfin vpast sg
'------------- vprep        with1(12,13)        prep
  '----------- objprep(n)   delight2(13,u,u)    noun cn sg
```

Fig. 1. ESG parse of "When asked to read his poems to the audience, John accepted with delight."

Slot Grammar (SG) analyses show both logical (predicate-argument) structure and surface structure in a single, head-oriented parse tree. In the parse display (illustrated in this example), each line corresponds to a node of the tree. Most nodes (all in this example) correspond to words of the sentence – each the head word of a phrase. The middle column (the *sense* column) of the display shows the word senses chosen for the analysis, together with their *logical* arguments. The first argument is an ID, or "entity argument"; the ID is just the word number in the sentence. The remaining arguments correspond to slots in the complement slot frame of the word sense (as given in the lexical entry for that sense). For a verb, the first of these arguments is the *logical* subject. A u argument signifies that the corresponding slot is unfilled in this sentence. The column to the left of the sense column shows the slots filled by each node, and the accompanying tree lines show the surface structure. The column to the right of the sense column shows the features associated with each node. Logical argument structure in SG analysis includes remote relationships, resulting e.g. from wh-movement and "factoring" of arguments in coordination.

the *mother node*, (4) s: the *slot* that this node fills in the mother node, (5) m: the *modifier list*, and (6) xf: the *lexical transformations* associated with the node.

Let us describe these six fields in more detail. The *head* word of the node is a term representing the target word or multiword (in citation form) associated with that node as head. The *feature structure* is a list (as a term) of feature-value pairs $((feature_1 . value_1) ... (feature_n . value_n))$. Features are names like POS (for "part of speech"), which have associated values (like noun). The *mother node* is another *node* of the tree – the mother of the current node (or nil if the current node is the top node). The *slot* is the Slot Grammar slot (e.g. obj) filled by the current node in the tree. The *modifier list* is a list of *nodes* consisting of the left modifiers of the current node, followed by the current node itself, followed by its right modifiers. The modifiers are given in left-to-right surface order. Many transformations manipulate modifier lists via pattern matching and pattern building. Moving a node in a modifier list means moving the whole tree whose root node is that node. The *lexical transformations* field is a list of "transformation triggers" (explained below) which are associated with the node by the lexical transfer analysis chosen for the node.

Transfer tree nodes actually have other fields besides the above six, but they are largely "hidden" from the transformational formalism.

The transfer tree data structure, being a *list* of nodes, involves of course a certain ordering of the nodes. However, this order should not be confused with the node ordering in modifier list fields of nodes. It is the latter which really determines the surface structure of the transfer trees, which evolves as the transformations operate. The (initial) order on the top level of the transfer tree node list happens to be a "preorder" listing – in which the root node comes first, followed recursively by the list produced for the left modifiers, followed by that for the right modifiers. This ordering determines the order in which each transformation will be tried on tree nodes. However, the transformations should be written so that they do not depend on this ordering. And the design of the transformational algorithm, to which we turn next, seems to make this easy to do.

4 The Transformational Algorithm

In translating a given sentence, the transformational system takes as input the transfer tree that results from lexical transfer, and via the algorithm described in this section, transforms that tree into a final transfer tree that has the desired structure for the target language. Each transformation should be thought of as dealing with a particular *kind* of node – e.g. a verb phrase node. In an (attempted) application of a transformation T, there will always be a *node in focus* for T, which is a parameter in the application procedure called for T. In LMT-TL, the node in focus plays a special role, as we will see. Perhaps most typically, a transformation will change the modifier list of its node in focus. But actually the formalism allows access to any part of the current transfer tree, with the node in focus as a starting point, and a transformation could potentially change any part of the tree.

The transformations themselves (whose form is described in the following sections) are linearly ordered. Normally they are created and stored in a flat file, and the linear order is simply the order in which they appear in that file. The restructuring algorithm is as follows. Indentation is used to indicate statements within a loop.

Initialize the *current transfer tree CT* to the output of lexical transfer.

Run through the transformations T – *only once* – in their given linear order.
A: Run through the list of nodes *N* of *CT*.
Try to apply *T* to *N* with *N* as the node in focus of *T*.
If *T* does apply, set *CT* to the altered transfer tree and go back to A (with the same transformation *T* but at the beginning of *CT*).
Else continue with the next node of *CT* if any.
The final *CT* is the output of restructuring.

5   General Syntax of Transformations

We describe the form of transformations as they appear in a transformation source file. In general, Cambridge Polish (Lisp-like) notation is used, and the transformations are terms.

Each transformation consists of a *transformation name*, followed by whitespace, followed by a *transformation body*. The transformation name must start in column 1, and can consist of any sequence of non-whitespace characters. Non-whitespace parts of the body may not appear in column 1. Comments in the usual form (/* ...*/) are allowed. In the following example, verbfinal is the transformation name, and the body is on the succeeding three lines:

```
verbfinal
    (tf ((POS . verb)(ClLev . dep)))
    (tm (*v1 head *v2))
    (cm (*v1 *v2 head))
```

The *body* of a transformation consists of a sequence of terms called the *transformation elements*. In the preceding example, there are clearly three transformation elements (written there one per line). To apply a transformation, the system tries to execute each of the elements of its body in succession. The transformation *succeeds* if and only if each of the elements succeeds (and we define this recursively below). The attempt at applying a transformation terminates as soon as one of its elements fails.

Transformation elements may be *basic* elements (which is the case in the example just given), or they may be Boolean combinations (with & (*and*), | (*or*), or ¬ (*not*)) of transformation elements.

Each *basic* transformation element is a term of the form (*operation* arg_1 arg_2 ...), consisting of a *(basic) operation* followed by its arguments.

Broadly, operations are of one of two types: *tests* or *changes*. Tests may succeed or fail, but changes always succeed. Changes are final, so all of the discriminating tests for a transformation should be written before any of the changes.

Most basic operations have an initial argument for a node (or list of nodes) that the operation is dealing with. We call this node (or argument) the *subject* node (or argument) of the operation. The notion of *subject node of an operation* should not be confused with the notion of *node in focus of the transformation*. However, these two often coincide in given instances of operations. In this case we usually use the syntactic convention of (a) simply omitting the subject node argument, or else (b) denoting it by the special symbol this. In the verbfinal example above, the subject node is omitted for each of the three operations, and therefore is taken to be the node in focus.

Variables are terms of the form vi where i is 1, 2, 3, ... A variable v may have any of the three prefixes >, <, or *, with the following interpretations, which are relevant to the pattern operations of LMT-TL: 1. $>v$ means assign a value to v (we say v is in *put mode*). 2. $<v$ means get the value of v (we say v is in *get mode*). 3. $*v$ means that v represents a list of nodes (we say $*v$ is a *nodelist variable*). When and whether these prefixes are used will depend on the particular syntactic conventions of each basic operation; we will specify those conventions in the following section. We sometimes call a variable a *simple* variable when there is no prior prefix.

A general convention with basic operations is that if the subject node argument is a nodelist variable $*v$, then the operation will be applied to every node in the list which is the value of v. For example,

```
(cf *v3 ((POS . noun)(Num . sg)(Case . acc)(Gender . nt)))
```

would change the features of every node in the list v3 to those features given in the second argument. If the operation is a test, it must apply successfully to every member of the node list if it is to succeed.

6 Basic Operations

In this section we give an overview of the basic operations of LMT-TL.

There are some simple conventions for naming basic operations. Tests have names starting with t, and changes have names starting with c. When the operation deals with a particular field x of a node (see the field names x given in Section 3), then the name of the operation contains x. For instance, tf tests the features of the subject node, and cf changes the features.

In the formal specification of a basic operation, we will write the subject node argument as *SubjectNode* without further explanation. This argument can (1) be omitted or be the symbol this if the subject node is the node in focus, or (2) be a simple variable, or (3) be a nodelist variable.

We now look in detail at the three of the most useful and interesting basic operations – those related to features, modifier lists, and lexical transformations. Then we give a summary of other available operations.

6.1 Feature Operations

The operation

(tf *SubjectNode Features*)

tests the features of the subject node. The most common form of the *Features* argument is a list of feature-value pairs

$$((fea_1 . v_1) (fea_2 . v_2) \ldots (fea_n . v_n)) \qquad (*)$$

similar to the feature structure of a node, but a "value" v_i can be (1) a constant, or (2) a simple variable, or (3) a put-mode variable $>v$. The operation tf goes through the list and checks that each feature-value pair (*fea . v*) in (*) matches some member of the subject node's feature structure. Note that if v is a put-mode variable, then such matching would bind that variable, so that in this case our "test" can involve an action as well as an ordinary test. The *Features* argument of tf may also be a simple variable, in which case it is evaluated, and a test is made as if its value is of the form (*). Or *Features* may be a variable in put mode, in which case it is assigned the feature structure of the subject node (and the test always succeeds). The operation

(cf *SubjectNode Features*)

changes the features of the subject node to *Features*. The *Features* argument is normally of the form (*) above, where the values are constants or simple variables (which are evaluated before the substitution). *Features* can also be a simple variable, which is first evaluated, and then we proceed as before.

The following example transformation changes the part of speech (of the node in focus) from noun to verb, and changes the features of that verb to be third person and the same number that the noun had, whatever it was. The number is saved in the variable v1 by tf, and then later referred to by cf.

```
nounverb
    (tf ((POS . noun)(Number . >v1)))
    (cf ((POS . verb)(Number . v1)(Person . pers3)))
```

Note that with cf, *Features* will be made the *complete* feature structure of the subject node, so one must take care. Another change operation

(cfx *SubjectNode Features*)

takes a *Features* argument like that of cf, but runs through the pairs in *Features*, and changes (or adds) just those features.

6.2 Modifier List Operations

The test operation

(tm *SubjectNode ModPat*)

tests the modifier list of the subject node. Here *ModPat* is a *modifier list pattern*, which is a list consisting of any of the following five kinds of pattern elements.

(1) A simple variable *v*. This matches the next modifier, and assigns that modifier node to *v*. (2) A nodelist variable *v*. This matches the smallest list of succeeding modifiers that will make the rest of the pattern succeed, and it assigns that nodelist to *v*. (3) The primitive symbol head. This matches the head node of the phrase. (4) A *node test*. This is of the form (*v Test*), where *v* is a variable and *Test* has the form of a transformation body. The *Test* is applied with the current next modifier *m* as *node in focus*, and if this succeeds then the node test succeeds and assigns the node *m* to variable *v*. (5) A nodelist test. This is of the form (*v Test*), where *v* is a nodelist variable and *Test* can have the form of a transformation body. This matches the smallest list of succeeding modifiers *m* satisfying *Test* with *m* as node in focus such that the remainder of the pattern succeeds, and it assigns this nodelist to *v*.

As an example, the modifier test (tm (*v1 head *v2)) matches v1 to the left modifiers and v2 to the right modifiers. In the test

    (tm (*v1 head *v2 (v3 (ts obj)) *v4 (v5 (ts iobj)) *v6))

v3 and v5 should match right modifiers filling the obj and iobj slots, respectively.

The change operation

    (cm *SubjectNode ModPat*)

changes the modifier list of the subject node. Here *ModPat* is a modifier list pattern with any of the ingredients (1), (2), or (3) above, but not (4) or (5) (no node tests or nodelist tests). Such a pattern is used in *building* modifier lists in the obvious way. Nodelist variables are replaced by the lists of nodes that are their values, and such lists are concatenated, etc. The verbfinal example in Section 5 illustrates cm and tm.

6.3 Lexical Transformations

A lexical transfer entry can insert a term called a *(lexical) transformation trigger* as a member of the *lexical transformations* field xf of a node *N*. If a transformation *T* invokes a test

    (txf *N Pat*)

then this test will succeed if and only if *Pat* matches a member of the xf field of *N*; in particular it will succeed if *Pat* matches a lexical transformation trigger that has been placed on *N*. The matching may bind variables in *Pat* which may then be used further in *T*. The most typical case is when *N* is the node in focus for a transformation *T*, and the first element of *T* is a test (txf *Pat*). This is a way of ensuring that *T* will apply only when *T* has been "sanctioned" for the node in focus by the lexicon through insertion of a trigger matching *Pat*. We then call *T* a lexical transformation. We give an example in Section 7.

6.4 Other Basic Operations

There is a large and useful collection of other primitive operations in LMT-TL. These include operations for (1) testing or changing the head word; (2) testing for the mother of a node (or binding a variable to this node, so that one can move upwards in the transfer tree); (3) testing or changing the slot filled by a node; (4) adding, deleting, or copying nodes; (5) navigating the transfer tree; (6) testing various characteristics of the source node that gave rise to a transfer node, such as the source sense and semantic types of the source sense; (7) testing punctuation in the source tree; and (8) performing various debugging operations.

The operations (5) for navigating the transfer tree are named u ("up"), d ("down", any modifier), dl ("down left", any left modifier), and dr ("down right", any right modifier). Each of these operations takes an optional initial subject node argument (which defaults to the node in focus), followed by a *body*, which has the form of the body of a transformation. The operation moves from the subject node to a new node in the tree, in the direction indicated, taking that new node as the node in focus for application of the *body* – which must succeed for the operation to succeed. The downward operations are non-deterministic; they try modifiers in succession until the *body* succeeds.

There are also various abbreviations for combining several operations on the same subject node; for instance (tfm *SubjectNode Features ModPat*) tests both the features and the modifiers of the subject node.

7 Examples

The simple version of a verbfinal transformation given at the beginning of Section 5 moves the verb (matched by head) to the end of any dependent clause (the feature ClLev stands for "clause level"). Of course it is more complicated than that for English→German, since the verb should not move past "heavy" phrases. To show how we can make the transformation more adequate, let us see e.g. how we can prevent movement past relative clauses (filling slot nrel) and clausal adjuncts (filling slot vsubconj):

```
verbfinal
    (tf ((POS . verb)(ClLev . dep)))
    (tm (*v1 head *v2 (v3 (| (ts nrel)(ts vsubconj))) *v4))
    (cm (*v1 *v2 head v3 *v4))
```

Here we have a node test (v3 (| (ts nrel)(ts vsubconj))) which says that the modifier v3 satisfies either of the tests (ts nrel) or (ts vsubconj), where ts tests the slot filled by a node.

The dative transformation for E→G is responsible for moving an indirect object (iobj) before a direct object (obj). Here is a simplified version:

```
dative
    (tf ((POS . verb)))
    (tm (*v1 head *v2 (v3 (ts obj)) *v4 (v5 (ts iobj)) *v6))
    (cm (*v1 head *v2 v5 *v4 v3 *v6))
```

The `sepprefix` transformation is responsible for moving the prefix of a separable-prefix verb to (or towards) the end of a finite independent clause. This movement has constraints similar to those for `verbfinal`. Here is a simplified version:

```
sepprefix
    (tf ((POS . verb)(VInfl . vfin)(ClLev . indep)))
    (th (>v1 : >v2))
    (tm (*v3 head *v4 (v5 (| (ts nrel)(ts vsubconj))) *v6))
    (cadd v7 v1 ((POS . ptcl)) this comp (head))
    (ch v2)
    (cm (*v3 head *v4 v7 v5 *v6))
```

Lexical transfer will produce a head term for a separable-prefix verb in the form (*Prefix* : *Stem*), for instance (ein : willig) for *einwilligen*. So pattern matching in the `th` test assigns the prefix to the variable `v1` and the stem to `v2`. The operation `cadd` creates a new node `v7` for the prefix, filling in the requisite node fields – for instance making `this` (the node in focus) the mother of the prefix. The `ch` operation changes the verb simply to the stem, and finally the `cm` operation places the prefix node appropriately in the verb's modifiers.

Our final example is of a lexical transformation, dealing with the famous problem of translations like *He likes to swim* → *Er schwimmt gerne*. LMT lexical transfer puts a term (verbadv gerne) in the `xf` (*lexical transformations*) field of the transfer node of *like*. Because of this trigger on the *like* node, the `txf` test in the following (simplified) transformation will succeed when this node is in focus, and will bind the variable `v1` to *gerne*. Thus, this transformation is lexically triggered by *like* and any other verb that uses the lexical trigger (verbadv *Adv*). The test `tfm` assigns *schwimmen* to `v5` for our sample sentence. The `cadd` operation creates a new node `v7` for *gerne* as an adverb. Finally, `chm` changes the head word of the focus node to *schwimmen* and adds in the *gerne* adverb as a right modifier in the appropriate position.

```
verbadv
    (txf (verbadv >v1))
    (tfm ((POS . verb))
          (*v2 head (v3
            (tfm ((POS . infto))
                (head (v4 (thsm >v5 tocomp (head *v6)))))))))
    (cdelete v3) (cdelete v4)
    (cadd v7 (ui v1) ((POS . adv)) this vadv (head))
    (chm v5 (*v2 head v7 *v6))
```

8 Conclusion

The LMT transformational component can concentrate largely on structural changes because most disambiguation has been done prior to its operation through Slot Grammar source analysis and slot-based lexical transfer. Nevertheless, re-structuring is a major step in translation which can involve much detail, so a powerful but simple language for writing transformations is called for. LMT-TL fills this bill because of (1) its systematic use of patterns and a powerful pattern matching scheme, (2) its dependency orientation and associated idea of *node in focus*, and (3) an overall economy of design in its syntax and semantics, illustrated by the fact that modifier pattern matching can recursively invoke the full power of transformations.

References

1. Bernth, A.: EasyEnglish: A Tool for Improving Document Quality. Proceedings of the Fifth Conference on Applied Natural Language Processing. Association for Computational Linguistics (1997) 159–165
2. Bernth, A.: EasyEnglish: Preprocessing for MT. Proceedings of the Second International Workshop On Controlled Language Applications. Carnegie-Mellon University, Pittsburgh (1998) 30–41
3. Bernth, A.: EasyEnglish: Addressing Structural Ambiguity. These proceedings.
4. Bernth, A. and McCord, M. C.: LMT for Danish-English Machine Translation. In: Brown, C. G., Koch, G. (eds): Natural Language Understanding and Logic Programming III. North-Holland (1991) 179–194
5. Bernth, A., McCord, M. C.: LMT at Tivoli Gardens. Proceedings of the 11th Nordic Conference on Computational Linguistics. Copenhagen (1998) 4–12
6. Gdaniec, C.: Lexical Choice and Syntactic Generation in a Transfer System: Transformations in the New LMT English-German System. These proceedings.
7. Lappin, S., McCord, M. C.: Anaphora Resolution in Slot Grammar. Computational Linguistics, Vol. 16. Association for Computational Linguistics (1990) 197–212
8. Lehmann, H.: Machine Translation for Home and Business Users. Proceedings of MT Summit V. Luxembourg, July 10–13 (1995) 107–115
9. McCord, M. C.: Slot Grammars. Computational Linguistics, Vol. 6. Association for Computational Linguistics (1980) 31–43
10. McCord, M.C.: A Prolog-Based Machine Translation System. Proceedings of the 1st Conference on Theoretical and Methodological Issues in Machine Translation, Colgate University (1985)
11. McCord, M. C.: Design of LMT: A Prolog-based Machine Translation System. Computational Linguistics, Vol. 15. Association for Computational Linguistics (1989) 33–52
12. McCord, M.C.: A New Version of the Machine Translation System LMT. Literary and Linguistic Computing 4 (1989) 218–229
13. McCord, M. C.: LMT, Proceedings of MT Summit II. Deutsche Gesellschaft für Dokumentation, Frankfurt (1989) 94–99
14. McCord, M. C.: Slot Grammar: A System for Simpler Construction of Practical Natural Language Grammars. In: Studer, R. (ed): Natural Language and Logic: International Scientific Symposium. Lecture Notes in Computer Science, Springer-Verlag, Berlin (1990) 118–145
15. McCord, M. C.: Heuristics for Broad-Coverage Natural Language Parsing. Proceedings of the ARPA Human Language Technology Workshop (1993) 127–132
16. Rimon, M., McCord, M. Schwall, U., Martínez, P.: Advances in Machine Translation Research in IBM. Proceedings of MT Summit III, Washington, D.C (1991) 11–18

Finding the Right Words:
An Analysis of Not-Translated Words
in Machine Translation

Flo Reeder and Dan Loehr

The Mitre Corporation
1820 Dolley Madison Blvd., McLean, VA 22102
{freeder, loehr}@mitre.org

Abstract. A not-translated word (NTW) is a token which a machine translation (MT) system is unable to translate, leaving it untranslated in the output. The number of not-translated words in a document is used as one measure in the evaluation of MT systems. Many MT developers agree that in order to reduce the number of NTWs in their systems, designers must increase the size or coverage of the lexicon to include these untranslated tokens, so that the system can handle them in future processing. While we accept this method for enhancing MT capabilities, in assessing the nature of NTWs in real-world documents, we found surprising results. Our study looked at the NTW output from two commercially available MT systems (Systran and Globalink) and found that lexical coverage played a relatively small role in the words marked as not translated. In fact, 45% of the tokens in the list failed to translate for reasons other than that they were valid source language words not included in the MT lexicon. For instance, e-mail addresses, words already in the target language and acronyms were marked as not-translated words. This paper presents our analysis of NTWs and uses these results to argue that in addition to lexicon enhancement, MT systems could benefit from more sophisticated pre- and post-processing of real-world documents in order to weed out such NTWs.

1   Introduction

The ultimate goal of applying MT systems to real-world data is to have a completely accurate and faithful translation of a given document. One important component [9] of doing so is by having an extensive lexicon. Several options are available when determining which words to add to a lexicon: one might require coverage for a specific domain and utilize existing resources in that domain; one might extract lexical information from a machine readable dictionary (MRD); or one might look at the translations being produced by an MT system and attempt to improve them through manual update. In spite of excellent research in automating the acquisition of lexical information [2,11] a large portion of the work done in MT continues to be accomplished by skilled lexicographers. A lexicographer's time is a precious resource that cannot be wasted weeding through token lists where many tokens are not candidates for update. The problem we face is how to select terms that are appropriate candidates for lexical update in an era of limited resources.

To help lexicographers in this regard, we began an analysis of not-translated words with the view of providing the "best" terms for lexical update. Our assumption is that documents sent for translation reflect items that are important to the user. Therefore, words and phrases that do not translate are the highest priority candidates for lexical update. It could be argued that if users accept a translation with not-translated words, then those words are somehow not important for the gist of the translation. We believe, however, that words found in user documents added to the lexicon will improve translation quality of future documents and, therefore, are a good basis for lexical update. Starting from this premise, we began looking at the not-translated tokens from available systems and undertook work building a prioritized list for lexical update. This paper presents a detailed examination of the words that are marked as not-translated and makes recommendations for both MT system developers and MT evaluators based on this analysis.

2 Previous Work

Work in two areas sheds light on the findings of this study. The first looks towards the evaluation of MT systems from the point of view of lexical coverage. Since this is an area of concern, we looked at existing literature about evaluating lexical coverage. The second area of relevant research was investigated once we started looking at the output of MT systems. Because of the nature of the lists, we examined research in text correction and the types of errors that could interfere with MT.

In the area of lexical coverage evaluation, Volk [10] describes some of the reasons a word might not translate for a group of MT systems. These include: lack of inclusion in the lexicon, incorrect inclusion in the lexicon, as well as wrong forms. Yet Volk's concern with lexical coverage does not address some real-world translation issues. The data in that study was carefully selected and constructed, since his interest was primarily in determining lexical coverage. Additionally, a difference between Volk's study and our is that our study focuses on the inputs that cause words to not be translated.

With her evaluation of MT systems, Flanagan [3,4] describes reasons for errors in translation and in her text on real-world translation expectations, she further elucidates them. The evaluation parameters of MT systems were examined in light of the outputs of translation and the types of errors that can be generated by the translation engine. These include spelling errors, words not translated, incorrect accenting, incorrect capitalization as well as grammatical and semantic errors. This study does not look at the kinds of inputs that can cause failure in a translation process. The second paper examines the quality of inputs into the translation process. In this effort, she argues for pre-editing tools such as spelling checkers and grammar checkers.

In the domain of error correction, Kukich [6,7] presents many sources for error-filled input for many language processing arenas. These range from simple typing errors to cognitive errors. While she addresses only English-language errors, the multi-lingual situation even further complicates error analysis. In addition to traditional insertion, deletion, transposition errors, multi-lingual data can contain transliteration, transcription and code set representation errors. Her work, with along with Flanagan's, directed us in the analysis and evaluation of not-translated words in real-world translations.

These findings are probably not any great shock to most commercial MT system developers. The literature in language processing has shown some of the reasons a word might not be successfully translated or why it might be marked as such. We are looking at the input for the cause of failed translations so that we can weed out those words which are not candidates for inclusion in a lexical update process, since for our purposes, it is important to find which words are the best candidates for lexical update.

3 Approach

We collected a set of documents of the following types: e-mail from discussion lists, World Wide Web (WWW) pages, newspaper articles and general texts. We chose between over 100 documents in each of the following source languages: German, French, Spanish, Italian, Portuguese and Russian. These languages were chosen on the basis of the readily available commercial off-the-shelf (COTS) MT systems. The target language in each case was English. The two systems we used were the UNIX versions of Systran and Globalink.[1] Each system can be tasked to generate a list of not-translated words. We ran the documents through these systems without any pre-processing except encoding conversion and hyphenation removal.

The resulting list of 43,000 not-translated words was then analyzed using a tool we developed for this purpose. The tool first handles the differences in formatting between translation engines, sorting the list by language and removing translation engine markers. Figure 1 shows a sample Systran NTW list in its raw form. Figure 2 shows the same for Globalink. The words in the word list are then converted for code set variations (as some engines return the not-translated words in their own internal encoding), and the word list is sorted again with duplicate entries being removed. Duplication counts are kept, however, to facilitate statistical analysis. Figure 3 shows a cleaned-up list from Systran. Note that any symbols from Figure 1 starting with "$$" are Systran internal tags and are removed from consideration.

$$LN2
From
TRIGANO
<TRIGANO@FRUTC51>
13-DEC-1991
15:36:33.54
$$LN2
presupposees
inferences
$$LN2
Telephone
interessees
$$LN2
$$LN2
TRIGANO
URA
817
Heudiasyc
UTC
649
60206
Compiegne
44
45
02
trigano@frutc51.bitnet
ptrigano@hds.univ-compiegne.fr
$$LN2
$$LN2
$$LN2

LIST OF WORDS NOT FOUND IN SOURCE TEXT	
TIMES	WORDS
3	Ófod
1	Óganisateus
1	Óganizing
2	ÚA
1	ÚDL
1	ÚL
1	Úiveristes
2	Úiversite
4	Úiversity
1	Úiversity's
2	Ófod
1	émail
1	CÓPÚATIÓAL
1	FIRST
1	In
1	Madrid
1	Receipt
1	Third
1	in
1	Andras
1	Bo
1	Fax
2	J'on
1	Noificatio
1	Steven
1	Tel
1	AÚIÓVISÚL
8	ACL
1	ADÍ

Fig. 1. Sample Systran NTW Output   **Fig. 2.** Sample Globalink NTW Output

---

[1] Systran Versions are: French-English, 96-1.8; German-English, 97-1.10; Spanish-English, 97-1.12; Italian-English, 97-1.11; Portuguese>English, 97-1.11; Russian>English, 96-1.7. Globalink Versions are 1993 baseline.

```
<TRIGANO@FRUTC51>
02
13-DÉC-1991
15:36:33.54
44
45
60206
649
817
Compiegne
From
Heudiasyc
inferences
interessees
presupposees
ptrigano@hds.univ-compiegne.fr
Telephone
TRIGANO
trigano@frutc51.bitnet
URA
UTC
```

Fig. 3. Cleaned-Up Systran NTW List

From this list, we then applied various algorithms to categorize the not-translated words. The stages of evaluation include: transliteration or code set problem identification, non-alphabetic sequence identification (to detect non-word tokens), non-source language identification, and acronym detection. Individual statistics are kept for each stage.

4 Results

The first surprise of our effort was the speed with which the list of not-translated words grew. The lists were overwhelming. An original 1 Mb of data resulted in a not-translated word list of 300K. Files of this size imply that we could keep lexicographers busy for years updating new or missed terms. A cursory inspection of the list, however, told us that there were many tokens which were not appropriate for lexical update. Table 1 shows the list of categories for removal, and the approximate proportion of tokens in each from our NTW list. Each of these will be examined more closely.

Table 1. Categories of Not Translated Words

Type of Token	Percentage
Non-word tokens	20%
Transliteration errors	10%
Mixed-language errors	10%
Acronyms	5%
(None of the above)	(55%)

Non-Word Tokens: The non-word tokens can be divided into three general areas: computer-related header information such as e-mail addresses; specialized data representations such as numbers, table labels and corrupted data which caused by OCR errors, and transmission errors (such as spurious control characters and Eudora's automatic conversion to 7-bit formats). The latter group understandably causes particular problems for translation engines. A misplaced control character (as can happen when the 8th bit gets stripped) can cause the translation engine to stop translating. Table 2 illustrates the types of these problems. This type of error accounted for 20% of all our not-found word tokens.

Table 2. Types of Non-Word Errors

Error Type	Example
Scanning error	écrire 6crire
Transmission error	écrire =E9crire
Misplaced control character error	This is ^Z the end.
E-mail address	freeder@123.mit.org
HTTP Markings	</end>
Stripped bits	écrire hcrire

Transliteration Errors: The problem of transliteration or code set representation is an ugly one for MT developers. A code set is an agreed-upon encoding scheme for representing written characters on a computer. Until internationalization tools and methods such as Unicode are widely available, a proliferation of code set representations can cause ambiguity problems [12] as well as failed translations. For instance, despite the fact that approximately 70-80% of our documents were in a standard encoding (ISO-8859-1 or ISO-8859-5), the number of transliteration errors was close to 10%. Table 3 shows the difficulties that can be introduced by code set variations, with errors highlighted in bold.

Table 3. Transliteration Reversal Problem, with errors highlighted in bold

ORIGINAL TEXT
* Als Fazit werden Markierungen für eine **erneuerte** Beruf(ung)spastoral,
* Aufbau eines Freundeskreises: Zu **Altersgenossen** beiderlei Geschlechts werden **neue**, tiefere Beziehungen hergestellt.
* Zum Thema Entwicklungsaufgaben vgl. R. **Oerter**/Eva Dreher, Jugendalter, in: R. **Oerter**/L.Montada (Hrsg.), ...
ISO1   E-Trans
* Als Fazit werden Markierungen fuer eine **erneuerte** Beruf(ung)spastoral,
* Aufbau eines Freundeskreises: Zu **Altersgenossen** beiderlei Geschlechts werden **neue**, tiefere Beziehungen hergestellt.
* Zum Thema Entwicklungsaufgaben vgl. R. **Oerter**/Eva Dreher, Jugendalter, in: R. **Oerter**/L.Montada (Hrsg.), ...
E-Trans   ISO1
* Als Fazit werden Markierungen für eine **erneürte** Beruf(ung)spastoral, ...
* Aufbau eines Freundeskreises: Zu **Altersgenoßen** beiderlei Geschlechts werden **neü**, tiefere Beziehungen hergestellt.
* Zum Thema Entwicklungsaufgaben vgl. R. **Örter**/Eva Dreher, Jugendalter, in: R. **Örter**/L.Montada (Hrsg.), ...

Mixed-Language Errors: Mixed-language documents provide more difficulties for MT, and account for 10% of the NTWs in our analysis. As can be seen in Figures 1 through 3, the proportion of English words in the translation candidates was higher than might be expected. Recall that our source languages were languages other than English. Thus, an English word in the source document would not be in the source language's lexicon, and would therefore be labeled untranslatable. Not-translated words can fall into this category for two reasons. They can either be bona fide loan words, or the source document can contain mixed languages. Web pages are a common example of this. In our analysis, most mixed-language errors were in this latter category. Figure 4 shows this problem.

Ho appena trovato questa frase in un manuale di una macchina utensile che sto traducendo dall'inglese (credo...). Carina, vero? (Ed è solo un esempio...)
- When the spool is operating, confirm the state of operation with a sound of "tak", "tak", "tak".

però poi prosegue (probabilmente riferendosi agli operatori non udenti)

- When confirming is impossible with such sound then visually check the rear of A.T.C.

Fig. 4. Mixed Language Document

Acronyms: Acronyms are another example of tokens which cannot be easily handled. A rudimentary detection of acronyms showed that they accounted for 5% of the words in the NTW list.

In addition to the above categories, there are several other types of words found in NTW lists which we have not yet weeded out, but which we plan to. These include proper nouns and spelling errors.

Proper Nouns: Proper nouns are often marked as untranslatable by translation engines. It can be argued that both acronyms and proper nouns belong in an MT lexicon, but there are practical limitations to this endeavor, as they are a highly productive class.

Spelling Errors: Since spelling errors are difficult to detect, more sophisticated analysis must be performed. According to the literature, spelling errors can be divided into user error (typing), OCR errors, or cognitive errors [7]. Figure 4 demonstrates a sample OCR error for a French text. Certain languages fall victim to specialized errors in this category as well. For instance, German data in upper case present particular problems for translation engines which expect the input to be correctly cased. These cases were counted only if the errors resulted in an obvious non-word, as in Figure 5. Other cases must be handled accordingly.

écrire => 6crire

Fig. 5. Scanning Error of a Word

To sum up, 45% of the words in the NTW list were not translated for reasons other than that they were valid source language words belonging in the MT lexicon. Further analysis may show an even greater proportion of words which are not properly candidates for lexical update.

5 Analysis

The results of NTW analysis suggest several directions for MT developers as well as MT users. The first of these is the need for pre-processing tools. These include not only spelling, grammar and code set correction tools for languages, but also tools which can identify and mark those sections of a document that should not be translated. In addition, MT systems could be equipped with methods of recognizing target language information so that mixed-language documents are not marked as unable to be translated. Such tools would "clean up" the source data before translation, rather than passing problem tokens untranslated into the output.

In terms of MT evaluation, the implication is that we need to carefully prepare a corpus for uniform evaluation. As Flanagan [3] discovered, for practical evaluation, certain error types must be included as separate categories for evaluation, therefore accounting for the nature of real-world data in our evaluations.

6 Future Work

This is by no means a conclusive analysis of not-translated words. Further research will indicate more arenas for pre-processing of translation inputs. One such prospect is automatic detection and correction of spelling errors. Another is proper noun identification and transformation. This work has been shown to be a complex problem [5].

7 Conclusion

While not-translated words can provide a useful measure of translation capability, they are not, as Flanagan [3] described, by any means the sole measure of translation effectiveness. Yet the not-translated word list can measure the ability of the system to pre-process data and to handle error-filled input. The lexical update process continues to be fraught with peril. Finding the right words for lexical update is a challenging process.

References

1. Bech, A. 1997. MT From an Everyday User's Point of View. In *MT Summit*. pp. 98-105.
2. Dorr, B. 1997. Large-Scale Dictionary Construction for Foreign Language Tutoring and Interlingual Machine Translation. *Machine Translation*, vol. 12, no. 1, pp. 1- 55.
3. Flanagan, M. 1994. Error Classification for MT Evaluation. In *Technology Partnerships for Crossing the Language Barrier: Proceedings of the First Conference of the Association for Machine Translation in the Americas*, Columbia, MD.
4. Flanagan, M. 1996. Two Years Online: Experiences, Challenges and Trends. In *Expanding MT Horizons: Proceedings of the Second Conference of the Association for Machine Translation in the Americas*, (pp. 192-197). Washington, DC: AMTA.
5. Knight, K. & J. Graehl. 1997. Machine Transliteration. In *Proceedings of the 35th Annual meeting of the Association of Computational Linguistics*

6. Kukich, K. 1992. Techniques for Automatically Correcting Words in Text. *ACM Computing Surveys*, Vol. 24,, No. 4, Dec. 1992.

7. Kukich, K., 1992. Spelling Correction for the Telecommunications Network for the Deaf. *Communications of the ACM*, Vol. 35, no. 5, May 1992, pp. 80-90.

8. Kumhyr, D., C. Merrill, K. Spalink. 1994. Internationalization and Translatability. In *Technology Partnerships for Crossing the Language Barrier: Proceedings of the First Conference of the Association for Machine Translation in the Americas*, Columbia, MD.

9. Somers, H. L. 1997. The Current State of Machine Translation. In *MT-Summit*. San Diego, Calif. pp. 115-123.

10. Volk, M. 1997. Probing the lexicon in evaluating commercial MT systems. In *Proceedings of the 35th Annual Meeting of the Association of Computational Linguistics*.

11. Wilks, Y., Slator, B., Guthrie, L. 1996. *Electric Words: Dictionaries, Computers, and Meanings*. MIT Press.

12. Yarowsky, D. 1994. Decision Lists for Lexical Ambiguity Resolution: Application to Accent Restoration in Spanish and French. In *Proceedings of the 32nd Annual Meeting of the Association of Computational Linguistics*

Predicting What MT is Good for: User Judgments and Task Performance

Kathryn Taylor and John White

Litton PRC, 1500 PRC Drive, McLean, VA 22102, USA
{taylor_kathi, white_john}@prc.com

Abstract. As part of the Machine Translation (MT) Proficiency Scale project at the US Federal Intelligent Document Understanding Laboratory (FIDUL), Litton PRC is developing a method to measure MT systems in terms of the tasks for which their output may be successfully used. This paper describes the development of a task inventory, i.e., a comprehensive list of the tasks analysts perform with translated material and details the capture of subjective user judgments and insights about MT samples. Also described are the user exercises conducted using machine and human translation samples and the assessment of task performance. By analyzing translation errors, user judgments about errors that interfere with task performance, and user task performance results, we isolate source language patterns which produce output problems. These patterns can then be captured in a single diagnostic test set, to be easily applied to any new Japanese-English system to predict the utility of its output.

The Machine Translation (MT) Functional Proficiency Scale Project

Machine translation (MT) no longer stands alone. The contemporary context for MT is as an integral part of an end-to-end text-handling process, for which the trend is toward less human intervention between the process stages. Documents in any form, including hardcopy, are funneled automatically into a corpus of on-line information made available to monolingual users to work with in their own language. So MT has evolved under the presumption of less human intervention: what is needed now is a more precise judgment of the capabilities of an MT system to produce output suitable for whatever the next step is in a given user's text-handling process.

Monolingual analysts or other information consumers, our target user pool for development of a metric predictive of MT capability, typically perform one or more text-handling tasks using translated material. In this paper we refer to them as users or analysts. Each type of text-handling task (e.g., filtering, detection, extraction, summarization, publication) requires translated text input of a certain quality. For certain of these tasks there is a wide range of acceptable quality, as judged by the accuracy and completeness of MT output, while others require near-human accuracy and fluency.

What is needed is an ordering of the inventory of text-handling tasks, ranging from those with substantial tolerance to poor quality output to those that can only be performed with high-quality output. Also needed is a measure of an MT system's ability to produce suitable output for each of the "downstream" text handling tasks in the inventory, regardless of whether it is a human or automated process. The FIDUL MT Functional Proficiency Scale project (MT Scale, for short), now in the data collection phase, is working toward producing a reusable, efficient and meaningful predictor of the text-handling tasks that an MT system's output will support (White and Taylor, 1998).

Evaluation of MT remains a fundamental issue in the field (Church and Hovy, 1991; Dostert, 1973; Pierce, 1966; Van Slype, 1979). MT evaluation has proven costly and subjective: because there is no one "right" translation, there is great difficulty in creating a reusable, extensible ground truth for evaluation from which a judgment of MT quality can be made. Also, each stakeholder in machine translation evaluation (translators, information consumers, managers, researchers, etc.) needs a different view into MT. Compounding the issues are the radically different theoretical approaches and language pairs, making a single-step, multi-purpose MT evaluation process difficult to envision.

The series of black-box evaluations of the Defense Advanced Research Projects Agency (DARPA) MT initiative within the Human Language Technology (HLT) Program in the mid-1990's (White and O'Connell, 1994; 1996) had as a goal the evaluation of the progress of the core algorithms of the sponsored systems. The diversity of theoretical approaches, language pairs and end-use presumptions were factored out by using a large sample of monolingual end users as raters. The cost was high: in order to counter the inherent subjectivity of judgments about translation, a large number of translations, controls, and decision points had to be maintained. However, the results of this large-scale effort (in terms of the fluency, adequacy and informativeness measures developed) can be reused in this study. For MT Scale, the evaluation question is framed in terms of the user task performance that a particular level of MT output quality allows.

Ideally, an MT evaluation method should be readily reusable, with a minimum of preparation and participation of raters or subjects. To accomplish this, a corpus for which judgments of MT output quality had already been made was reused, namely, the translations of the DARPA MT evaluation series. This corpus was already rated for adequacy, fluency and informativeness. The complete corpus consists of several translations each of approximately 400 newspaper articles, originally in French, Spanish, or Japanese. A great advantage to this corpus is that, for most of these articles, two professionally translated versions were prepared. Two to five machine-translated versions of each article exist, generated either by sponsored research systems or by commercial MT systems.

We will make use of existing resources, such as the DARPA corpus, as accomplish the objectives of the MT Scale project, which are to:

❊ identify the text-handling tasks that users perform with translated material as input
❊ discover the order of text-handling task *tolerance*, i.e., how good a translation must be in order for it to be useful for a particular task;

* analyze the translation problems (both linguistic and non-linguistic) in the corpus used in determining task tolerance; and
* develop a set of source language patterns which correspond to diagnostic target phenomena.

Developing the Task Inventory

Three sources of information for formulating the inventory of tasks that analysts perform using translated material were used: (a) interviews with former analysts (b) unclassified panel discussions during which officials of the intelligence community stated analysis requirements and working analysts described their tasks, and (c) brief interviews with individual analysts, with the cooperation of their senior management.

Interviews with former analysts. Before approaching working analysts about the type of tasks they routinely perform with translated input, project staff interviewed former analysts about their uses of translated material. The interviews with former analysts provided a very preliminary concept of the task inventory and its ordering.

Unclassified panel discussions with officials and working analysts. At government-sponsored program reviews and conferences, analysts often express their "wish lists" for tools and working aids. In defining their needs, they often describe the tasks that they do, and the volume and type of information that cross their desks each day. These discussions provided a general sense of the volume of translated information presented to users and what they needed to do with it.

Brief interviews with individual analysts. A telephone pre-interview survey was formulated to identify analysts by agency and the tasks each performed using translated material. The interview is designed to capture user observations about the role of translation-supported tasks in their day-to-day work, and the quality of translation they perceive as necessary to accomplish those tasks. In the telephone interview, users are asked which text-handling tasks (manual or automated) they typically perform.

The result is a comprehensive list of tasks which are performed using translated material. The tasks identified by individual analysts determine which of the task-based exercises those analysts will perform at the time of the face-to-face interview. At any time during the information-gathering process new tasks may be included in the inventory, and variations of a task category may be ordered within that task category.

Ordering the Task Inventory

To use the task inventory effectively, it is necessary to identify which text handling tasks can be done with relatively poor quality text, and which require high quality text. Certain analytical text-handling tasks require more accurate and fluent material as input than others. It should be possible to rank these tasks on a scale from least tolerant (high end of the scale) to most-tolerant (low end of the scale) of translation errors and omissions. Table 1 shows a hypothetical ranking of tasks from least tolerant (Publishing) to most tolerant (Filtering).

A ranked order of text-handling tasks such as Table 1 implies that an MT system whose output can facilitate tasks on a particular point on the scale should also facilitate tasks lower on the scale, and is unlikely to facilitate tasks higher on the scale. According to Table 1, an MT system that produces a fluent translation (publication quality output) will also support the capture of specified key information from the same translation (extraction). An MT system whose output allows users to recognize that a document is of interest (detection) may not be suitable for capturing all specified key information (extraction), but will perform acceptably for filtering (rapid disposal of irrelevant documents).

Table 1. Preliminary Ranking of Text-Handling Tasks

Task	Description
Publishing	Produce a technically correct document in fluent English
Gisting	Produce a summary of the document
Extraction	For documents of interest, capture specified key information
Triage	For documents determined to be of interest, rank by importance
Detection	Find documents of interest
Filtering	Discard irrelevant documents

As more interview data is gathered and further research performed, there is the possibility that certain tasks may be subdivided. Based on a task description of variations of the extraction task provided at the TIPSTER 18-month meeting, shown in Table 2, Intra-task Ordering - Multiple Levels of Extraction, we became aware that users might draw distinctions between superficial name-spotting tasks and extraction requirements that require a more comprehensive understanding of a text. This raised the possibility that a familiar class of task, upon closer examination, had separate incarnations that could be characterized as less tolerant (deep extraction) and more tolerant (shallow extraction) of MT output errors.

Table 2. Intra-task Ordering - Multiple Levels of Extraction

Type of Extraction	Description
Deep	Event identification (scenarios): the ability to identify an incident type and report all pertinent information
Intermediate	Relationship identification: (member-of, associate-of, phone-number-for)
Shallow	Named entity recognition: (isolation of names of people, places, organizations, dates, locations)

The Face-to-face Interview

At the time of the face-to-face interview, users are asked to perform a variety of activities associated with their specific text-handling tasks, using translations from the DARPA corpus to determine, within the context of their individual ordinary activities, whether they could use a particular translation to do their jobs. There are many issues (e.g., domain knowledge and experience) associated with eliciting this judgment. Many such users have a functional mission (e.g., find information about grain production in Europe) rather than the performance of a text handling task *per se*. The samples presented are general news articles, and are not directly relevant to the domain of their functional task. Human factors effects can also bias the judgment. For example, the user may feel obligated to respond positively when asked "can you do your work with this document" even when he/she actually cannot (M. Vanni, personal communication).

To address these issues, the interview includes three distinct exercise types:

- *The Snap Judgment Exercise - indicating what texts are of sufficient quality that an analyst would be willing to process them further.* Users are asked to make snap judgments about a set of documents, separating out those which might be of good enough quality to enable them to do their jobs.
- *The Task-Specific Exercises - performing a directed task on a set of documents.* Users are given a task that is similar to their ordinary text-handling task, and asked to perform this modified task on a set of translation documents. For example, a user who performs filtering is told to set aside the documents that are definitely not relevant to a given topic. The directed task validates the results of the snap judgment exercise, abstracting away from the domain issue (because the specific task is rather different from their actual tasks) and from several human factors issues.
- *The Rating Reasons Exercise - helping to identify the translation problems which cause a document to be less useful than it otherwise might be for specific tasks.* This exercise is aimed at identifying translation phenomena that should be included in the MT Scale diagnostic test set by capturing the phenomena that disturb users most about the texts they have just tried to make use of in a task-oriented exercise. For example, a user may cite lack of capitalization, transliteration and numerical errors when trying to use a text to perform an extraction task. The significance of these phenomena would be noted for extraction, and source language patterns that produced the errors would become part of the diagnostic test for extraction capability.

Of course, no one group of users will generally require or have expertise in every one of the text-handling tasks that uses translated material as input. Thus the ranked list will be a merged set over a variety of user groups.

The result of these exercises will be a characterization of the relevant text-handling tasks for the subject group of information analysts, ordered by their tolerance to the quality of MT output. It remains to be established whether to expect a single ordering of the text-handling tasks (e.g., that document detection is always more tolerant than extraction), or a non-deterministic order (detection is sometimes less tolerant than extraction in different subject domains, or extraction requirements vary, etc.). It appears, however that even a multi-path ordering, once described, will allow formulation of a scale, as long as there is convergence at either end (a reasonable assumption – topic filtering must always be more tolerant than technical editing).

The next paragraphs describe in depth the exercises that take place at the face-to-face analyst interviews: the snap judgment exercise, the specific task-oriented exercises, and the rating reasons exercise.

The Snap Judgment Exercise

The complaint is often made that MT output little resembles the target language. This lack of resemblance frustrates a native speaker of the language to the point of not being willing to make the effort to try to understand it. The threshold of erroneous output, in the context of a particular downstream task, should indicate the tolerance of that task. In the snap judgment exercise, analysts are asked to separate a set of 15 documents (selected from the DARPA Japanese-English corpus and pre-analyzed for errors) based on a superficial examination and their snap judgment of the overall quality of each document in the set. As a guideline, they are told to spend as much time examining each text as they would skimming an article in a newspaper and deciding whether to read it in depth. They are to divide the texts into three piles: 1) texts that they definitely thought they could process in connection with the task they do, (2) texts they might try to process (3) and texts they would not be willing to process further. The analysts are not pressed for specific reasons for relegating a particular text to a particular pile, but any comments they volunteer are captured.

The main purpose of this exercise is to determine the tolerance level for machine translation output for individual text-handling tasks. Users who perform the same tasks will be expected to have similar sortings of the texts into pile (1), (2) and (3). It is expected that the difference in distribution of piles (1), (2) and (3) among the different tasks will help determine the tolerance of a particular task for a particular quality level of MT output and provide clues to the kinds of MT output errors that affect the use to which an output sample may be put.

The Task-Specific Exercises

In this series of exercises, users perform a task that is similar to one they do daily, using a set of translated documents. The following are examples of some of the task-specific exercises.

The filtering task. For the filtering task, each user is given a set of fifteen texts and given a very broad information category, such as crime, economics, transportation, etc. One by one, the user is asked to categorize each text as being related to the information category, not related to the information category, or say that he/she is unable to tell (cannot be determined). The results of this task will be reported using the measures of recall and precision, i.e., how many of the possible texts related to the information category did the user identify (recall), and how many of the texts the user identified as being related to the information category were actually related (precision). The ground truth for the filtering exercise was determined by a three-member panel who looked at an expertly translated version of the text to determine if the text was related to a broad information category.

The triage task. For the triage task, each user is given an ordered list of 2 to 4 narrowly described categories such as poisonings, foreclosures, airline industry deregulation, etc. The user is asked to organize a group of fifteen texts in the same order as the list, and for texts of the same category, to order the texts by putting the most specific and information-rich texts first. The results of this task will be reported using the measures of recall and precision, i.e., how many of the possible texts related to the more narrowly defined information category did the user identify (recall), and how many of the texts the user identified as being related to the more narrowly defined information category were actually related (precision). The exercise includes elements of the filtering task exercise, but the triage task calls for more in-depth judgments of text content (amount and relevance of usable material) than the filtering exercise.

The extraction tasks. Three levels of exercises are currently envisioned for extraction task, (1) one level will test the reporting of individual entities (names, places, organizations) found in a text, (2) a second level will test the reporting of relationships (person-to-place, person-to-organization. etc.) in a text and (3) the final level will test the recognition of a particular event type and the reporting of standard, pertinent information related to the event (e.g., for a bombing event, the location, date, time, type of device, persons injured or killed, buildings damaged or destroyed, group claiming responsibility). Users will be given guidelines based on the Message Understanding Conference (MUC) Named Entity and Scenario template tasks. The tasks will be scored according to the number of correct fills made from consulting a machine-translated version of a text as compared to the number of fills made by users working from the expert human translations of the same text.

The gisting task. The bracketed version of the DARPA expert translation used to evaluate the adequacy of a translation will be excerpted so that only those brackets that contain information relevant to a summary of the document remain (a three-member panel reached a consensus of which brackets contain information relevant to a summary). The user will be asked to apply the DARPA 1-to-5 adequacy scale ratings to indicate to what extent the information in the selected brackets is present in the aligned paragraphs of a translated version of the document. Low ratings will indicate missing/garbled information, and point to the source language pattern which produced the deficient portions of the translated document.

The publication task. For the publication task, a user will be given excerpts of texts, one at a time, and asked to make any corrections to them that would make them, in the judgment of the user, publication-ready. The user will also be directed to mark excerpts from a text that are publication-ready, or that need only minor corrections to be considered publication-ready in the user's opinion. The user is permitted to "give up on" a text at any point, and move on to another text. This would be a timed exercise, lasting 30 minutes. The number of texts "given up on", would be recorded, as well as the number and type of corrections made by the users to texts.

The Rating Reasons Exercise

This exercise is aimed at identifying the translation phenomena that should be included in the MT Functional Proficiency Scale diagnostic test set.

The rating reasons exercise is a variation of a study conducted to compare the criteria used by American and Japanese English-as-a-Second-Language (ESL) instructors to rate student compositions (Connor-Linton, 1995) The instructors rated compositions and then gave reasons for their ratings. The study demonstrated a correlation between translation concerns and training, related in turn to differences between the Japanese and American instructors.

For the rating reasons exercise, a user is asked to assign overall ratings to texts from the DARPA corpus the analyst has just seen as part of a task-oriented exercise. Then the user is asked to list the three main reasons why the particular rating was assigned. As suggested by the Connor-Linton study, users should react to the material according to their training in the particular text handling task they perform.

As in the Connor-Linton study, reasons are not suggested to the participants, and the reasons may be positively or negatively expressed. All of the ratings reasons are collected and organized into categories by a linguist, and coded with the analyst's task experience and the task exercise for which he/she was a participant. This allows the rating and reason data to be considered on a task-by-task-basis and on an reason-by-reason basis, as a single reason may have been cited by analysts in connection with more than one task.

The purpose of this exercise is to allow the alignment of particular output errors with the success or failure of specific text-handling tasks.

Tasks and MT Output Properties

If it is possible to predict the least tolerant text-handling tasks that a system's output can facilitate, then we will also know that the output is sufficient for all of the more tolerant tasks. The same texts from which the ordering can be inferred also provide evidence of translation problems which indicate the boundary between acceptability for one text-handling task and another.

Developing the diagnostic test that will make that prediction involves identifying the correlation of corpus texts to the task hierarchy, distilling translation problems that appear to be "diagnostic" (i.e., appear to mark the difference between a text being at one level rather than a higher one), and then characterizing those translation phenomena in a compact pattern for the ultimate diagnostic test.

The phenomena encountered are categorized in accordance with established contrastive principles of Japanese and English. Use of the pedagogical models as applied to authentic text has the advantages of exhaustiveness and descriptive adequacy apart from issues in MT theory. Many other phenomena not described in those treatments (since they are unlikely to occur in human translation) are captured; trivial but ubiquitous examples are character conversion errors and punctuation in numerals.

Reusing Translated Terms to Expand a Multilingual Thesaurus

Rocio Guillén

California State University, San Marcos,
rguillen@mailhost1.csusm.edu,
http://www.csusm.edu/A_S/CS/html/rocio.html

Abstract. Multilingual thesauri play a key role in multilingual text retrieval. At present, only a small number of on-line thesauri contain translations of terms in languages other than English. This is the case of the Unified Medical Language System (UMLS) Metathesaurus that includes the same term in different languages (e.g., English and Spanish). However, only a subset of terms in English have a corresponding translation in Spanish. In this work, I present an approach and some experimental results for reusing translated terms to expand the Metathesaurus. The approach includes two main tasks: finding patterns and formulating rules to automate the translation of English terms into Spanish terms. The approach is based on pattern matching, morphological rules, and word order inversion.

1   Introduction

Multilingual text retrieval consists in selecting documents from a collection that may not be written in the same language as the user's query. The term text retrieval has been coined to mean both written text and spoken text retrieval because in linguistics, text can be written or spoken [1]. Two main approaches are considered in cross-language text retrieval: controlled-vocabulary retrieval and free text retrieval [2]. Controlled-vocabulary text retrieval uses a predetermined vocabulary for indexing. The user formulates queries with terms drawn from the same vocabulary. Free text retrieval includes two approaches: corpus-based and knowledge-based. The corpus-based approach focuses on the analysis of corpora and the automatic extraction of information for translation purposes. Corpus-based processing has been used lately to automatically construct thesaurus-like information structures for query expansion (i.e., adding synonyms of terms in the query as found in a thesaurus) [3]. The knowledge-based approach distinguishes between dictionary-based and ontology-based text retrieval. In dictionary-based text retrieval, each term in the query is replaced by a term or set of terms in the chosen language (e.g., see [5]). Ontology-based text retrieval uses mainly multilingual thesauri (for instance, [6]) or multilexical knowledge bases [7]. In this case the use of multilingual thesauri plays a key role [8]. Multilingual thesauri are one type of knowledge structure that have the breadth coverage required in cross-language text retrieval. Unfortunately, this kind of multilingual resources for cross-language text retrieval are scarce. One of the problems is that their construction requires more than the merging of several monolingual thesauri. A true multilingual thesaurus must present a complete conceptual and terminological inventory for each language included. In this way, users will get the same amount of semantic information regardless of the language they use. Partial solutions consist of reusing previously translated terms, and/or expanding and creating multilingual thesauri in various domains. Most of them have been built for retrieving English texts. A small number of on-line thesauri contain terms in other language(s) in specific domains. Among these are the Metathesaurus in the biomedical domain, and EUROVOC in the legal domain. The Metathesaurus of the Unified Medical Language System (UMLS) contains the same term in five different languages (English, Spanish, French, Portuguese, and German). However, only a small subset of the terms in English have a translation in the other languages. Spanish is the language that has the highest number of translated terms. This fact makes the set of English-Spanish terms a good knowledge base to look for patterns from which formulate rules for translating from English to Spanish terms. This allows expanding the thesaurus. The expansion is carried out on a knowledge base created with the existing English and their corresponding Spanish terms. At the end, the generated translations are added to their corresponding English terms. To provide a corresponding Spanish term to those that do not have one, I propose an approach based on morphological rules, word order inversion, and pattern matching using previously translated terms contained in the Metathesaurus.

In the following sections I describe the Metathesaurus, the procedure to discover patterns from the terms that have a translation, and the derivation of a set of rules as a result of such findings. Finally, I present some experimental results, further work, and conclusions.

2 The Metathesaurus

The UMLS has been designed to facilitate the retrieval and integration of information from multiple biomedical resources. The design is based on four knowledge sources. The Metathesaurus is one of them and is the main lexicon component of the UMLS. It is a database of information on concepts that appear in one or more of a number of different controlled lexica and classifications used in the biomedical field. The 1997 version of the Metathesaurus contains 331,756 biomedical concepts named by 739,439 different terms from more than 30 source vocabularies; and it includes translations of its source lexica into Spanish, French, German, and Portuguese. I am using 331,756 different terms in English, and 23,198 different terms in Spanish as input. The Metathesaurus is organized by concept or meaning, and each unique concept name in each language has a unique identifier. Concept names establish the synonymous relationships among all the identifiers and terms that have the same meaning. That is, the concept names link all the different names for the same concept that are included in the thesaurus and specify certain characteristics of each name such as the language of the term.

The work carried out is divided into several stages. First, the input is pre-processed to extract all the English-Spanish pairs from the Metathesaurus (concept names input file). At the same time, all the English entries without a Spanish translation are extracted and stored in a separate knowledge base. In a second stage, a pattern matching algorithm is applied to the English-Spanish pairs to discover candidate patterns. The set of candidate patterns is then examined to formulate translation rules. Order inversion and morphological rules for gender and number are also considered. In a third stage, a number of tests are carried out to evaluate and tune the set of rules. Finally, the set of rules are applied to a set of English terms without a translation to generate new potential entries.

3 Pre-processing the Input

The entries in the concept names input file contain the following data: unique identifier for concept, language of term, term status, unique identifier for term, string type, unique identifier for string, and string [9]. Instances of the entries are shown below. The process of extraction of English-Spanish pairs encompasses the following steps: 1) splitting the input file into two files containing either English terms or Spanish terms considering only the entry with the preferred term (i.e., term status = P); 2) merging the files using the concept unique identifier and discarding all the information except for the string in English and the string in Spanish; 3) storing strings in English without a translation in Spanish in a separate file. Instances of the output are shown below:

Input Entries:

C0000002|ENG|P|L0000002|PF|S0007488|(+)-Cyanidanol|
C0000003|ENG|P|L0000003|PF|S0007489|(+)-Cyanidanol-3|
C0000005|ENG|P|L0270109|PF|S0007491|(131)I-MAA|
C0000005|ENG|S|L0000005|PF|S0007492|(131)I-Macroaggregated Albumin|
C0000039|ENG|P|L0000039|PF|S0007564|1,2-Dipalmitoylphosphatidylcholine|
C0000039|ENG|S|L0000035|PF|S0007560|1,2-Dihexadecyl-sn-Glycerophosphocholine|
C0000039|FRE|P|L0176992|PF|S0241473|1,2-DIPALMITOYLPHOSPHATIDYLCHOLINE|
C0000039|SPA|P|L0336826|PF|S0445131|1,2-DIPALMITOILFOSFATIDILCOLINA|

Output:

English-Spanish pairs

1,2-dipalmitoylphosphatidylcholine|1,2-dipalmitoilfosfatidilcolina
1,4-alpha-glucan branching enzyme|enzima ramificadora de 1,4-alfa glucano
1-carboxyglutamic acid|acido 1-carboxiglutamico
1-methyl-3-isobutylxanthine|1-metil-3-isobutilxantina
1-methyl-4-phenylpyridinium|1-metil-4-fenilpiridinio
1-naphthylamine|1-naftilamina

English terms without a translation

(+)-cyanidanol|
(+)-cyanidanol-3|
(131)i-maa|

4   Pattern Discovery

General methods for pattern discovery have been applied successfully in computational biology [12] and semi-automatic knowledge acquisition [10]. A common goal is to find sets of useful and interesting patterns and rules that occur in data according to some criteria [11]. The pattern discovery method presented in this paper is based on research carried out to discover patterns in sets of biosequences by [13],[14].

An algorithm has been designed and implemented for automatically finding substrings in the English term that map to substrings in the Spanish term. The input is the set of all English-Spanish pairs generated in the pre-processing stage. The algorithm is based on string comparison to find the mismatches between the English and the Spanish terms. Each time a mismatch is found, the pair of strings is realigned to continue the comparison until no more comparisons can be made. A mismatch is then the number of positions in which a pair of strings has different symbols. The mismatches are the candidate patterns from which the translation rules will be formulated.

In order to prevent, to a certain extent, obtaining "bad patterns" (e.g., whole words) or waiting until there are no more characters to compare to realign strings a threshold of four characters is used. If a mismatch is greater than four, the difference is considered to be significant and no good candidate pattern can be obtained. The rationale is that, after running the algorithm a number of times, it was observed that substrings of up to four characters were good candidate patterns. Once a mismatch with fewer than five characters is detected, the strings are realigned to continue the comparison. To carry out the realignment it is necessary to take into account the difference in the length of the strings being compared. The length is also important to determine when the comparison should end. The output of the algorithm is a set of candidate patterns.

There can be more than one mismatch between a pair of strings. For example, taking the following pair as input to the algorithm, it can be observed that there are at least three (in this case different) mismatches:

9,10-dimet*hy*l-1,2-benzant*h*racen*e*
9,10-dimet*i*l-1,2-benzant*r*acen*o*

In the first mismatch the number of positions in which the strings have different symbols is two. That means that from this candidate pattern, a rule can be derived for mapping *hy* to *i*. However, I found that such a pattern is too general. Thus, in order to make a pattern more specific it is necessary to consider the position before and/or the one after the actual mismatch to prevent incorrect mappings. The rule derived is "thyl maps to til".

For the second mismatch the number of positions in which the strings have different symbols is one. That means that another candidate pattern has been found, hence a rule can be derived for mapping h to r. However, since the pattern is even more general, it is necessary to make it more specific. Therefore, "thr maps to tr" becomes the actual rule.

The last case has one position in which symbols differ, the end of both strings. The rule would be "e maps to o". Again, this pattern is too general; hence it is necessary to have a longer substring. The actual rule is "ene maps to eno". This kind of rule can still cause problems in those cases where the gender of the term in Spanish is feminine. One solution would be to add another rule "ene maps to ena". The problem with this solution is that there will be at least two translations for an English term, including the substring "ene". At present, I am considering "ene maps to eno" as the default rule and then applying a morphological rule if necessary, as explained in section 5.

The total number of different patterns found was 2825. The fifteen candidate patterns with the largest number of occurrences are shown in Table 1.

Table 1. Most frequent candidate patterns

English	Spanish	# Occurrences
ine	ina	733
atio	acio	456
in	ina	399
c	co	351
ase	asa	329
nes	nas	281
ins	inas	260
l	les	248
ic	ico	233
ate	ato	219
hydr	hidr	197
one	ona	175
d	de	173
tes	tos	170
ide	uro	160

5 Translating Terms

In the third stage, the set of rules is examined to discard or modify some of them before the actual testing is carried out. The total number of rules at present is 154. The translation process is done in two steps. For each of the English terms, the pattern-based rules are applied first. The translation obtained is then compared to the original Spanish term. If there is a full match, then the process stops. Otherwise, the morphological rules, order inversion rules, and partial matching rules are applied. The translation thus obtained is then compared to the original Spanish term. If there is a full match, then the process stops. Otherwise, the English term replaces the Spanish term. For instance, to illustrate how order inversion rules work take the following terms.

English term	1-carboxyglutamic acid
Original Spanish term	acido 1-carboxiglutamico
Translated term	1-carboxiglutamico acido

The translated term is compared with the original Spanish term to test whether there is a full match. The result is false. Therefore, the order inversion rules are triggered. In the example, the order of the words *1-carboxiglutamico* and *acido* is inverted to obtain *acido 1-carboxiglutamico*. This term is compared with the original Spanish term, and the result is a full match.

The comparison between the original Spanish term and the one generated during the translation process is mainly based on the number of words in the English term. In some cases the comparison is based on the number of words in the Spanish term (the translated one). Further work needs to be done to determine a better criterion to make the comparison. On the other hand, this criterion is used because a distinction is made between correct translations, partial correct translations, and no translation from English to Spanish. The possibilities, depending on the number of words considered thus far, are the following:

- If the number of words is one, the translated term is expected to match the original Spanish term after entering step 1 in the process. The result of the comparison is either true or false. If it is false, there are at least two possibilities to produce a correct translation: a) apply singular/plural rules, and/or b) apply gender rules. The following example illustrates how gender rules work.

English term	dendrites
Original Spanish term	dendritas
Translated term	dendritos

In this example, the result of comparing *dendritos* with *dendritas* is false. The gender rules are triggered, and the "o" in the translated term is replaced by "a". When the translated term an the original Spanish term are compared the result becomes true.

– Whenever the number of words is two, then there are three possibilities to consider: a) a correct translation is produced, b) a partial correct translation is produced, or c) no translation is produced. The result of the comparison for b) and c) is false. So, the Spanish term is moved to step 2 in the process. Order inversion rules are applied first, and a comparison is made. If the result of the comparison is still false, then the rules for gender are applied. Next, a new comparison is made; if the result is false then partial matching rules are applied. To illustrate a case of a partial correct translation take the following example.

English term	acid-base equilibrium
Original Spanish term	equilibrio acido-basico
Translated term	acido-basa equilibrio
Translated term	equilibrio acido-basa
Translated term	equilibrio acido-baso

In the example, order inversion rules and gender rules are applied without generating a correct translation. This triggers the partial matching rules. Word-by-word comparisons are made. For this example, the results of the comparisons yield true for the word *equilibrio*, and false for the word *baso*. Therefore, this is considered a partial correction translation.

– If the number of words in the English term is two, and the number of words in the Spanish term is three, then look for prepositions in the Spanish term. The prepositions considered are *de, del, a, al* and *por*. If one of these prepositions appears in the Spanish term, then the first word translated is concatenated with the preposition. The result is then concatenated with the second word. A comparison is made to test whether a correct translation is produced. If the result of the comparison is false, then the English term replaces the Spanish term. An example illustrating how this case works follows:

English term	action potentials
Original Spanish term	potenciales de accion
Translated term	accion potenciales
Translated term	potenciales accion
Translated term	potenciales de accion

The English term is translated first to *accion potenciales*. The comparison between the translated term and the original Spanish term yields false which triggers rules such as the inversion order rule. The rule is applied and a new comparison is made. The result is still false which triggers other rules. Among them are those that apply whenever there is a difference in the number of words between the English term and the translated term. From analysis of the data it was observed that, in general, whenever the number of words in the English term is two and the number of words in the Spanish term is three, the words in the translated term need to be inverted and a preposition needs to be inserted in between. In the example the preposition that makes the comparison true is *de*.

- If the number of words is greater than two, there are more combinations to test. At this point the work to handle these possibilities is in progress.

6 Experimental Results

Experiments to test the rules were carried out using a file containing 14401 terms from MeSH (Medical Subject Headings) without a translation. The results are shown in Table 2.

The figures presented have been calculated in terms of number of words translated rather than the whole term. The reason is that many of the partial translations may still be useful for retrieval purposes. However, the goal is to generate as many correct translations as possible. To evaluate the results, I am using the translations generated using the Metathesaurus as the baseline (see Table 3). There is not a large difference between the percentages in Table 2 and Table 3. The percentage of the total number of fully and partially translated terms increased by 2% using the test file. If we look at the percentages per number of words, the percentage of one-word full and partial translations increased by 1%, whereas the percentage of two-word full and partial translations decreased by 7%. The rules seem to work well for one word terms which are the largest in number in both files. Thus, it might be better to translate individual words and combine the translations using some heuristics rather than translating compound terms.

Table 2. Results of tests using MeSH

# words English	Total # words	Correct Trans.	%	Part. Correct Trans.	%	No. Trans.	%
1	6095	4136	67	0	0	1959	33
2	4213	1177	28	1718	40	1318	31
3	2249	51	2	not done	0	2198	98
4	1041	4	0	not done	0	1037	99
>4	803	not done	0	not done	0	803	100
Totals	14401	5368	37	1718	12	7315	50

To increase the number of correct translations, all possible valid combinations for English and Spanish should be considered and the following tasks should be carried out: 1) Include dictionaries to translate those terms for which the approach is not applicable. 2) Improve the pattern discovery procedure. 3) Look for

Table 3. Tests using the Metathesaurus

# words English	Total # words	Correct Trans.	%	Part. Correct Trans.	%	No. Trans.	%
1	8744	5802	66	0	0	2942	34
2	6850	2342	34	2838	41	1670	24
3	4023	98	2	not done	0	3925	98
4	1893	3	0	not done	0	1890	99
>4	1688	not done	0	not done	0	1688	100
Totals	21125	8245	35	2838	12	12115	52

better ways to evaluate the results obtained. 4) Automate the process of adding new rules with new versions of the Metathesaurus.

Other experiments are in progress for translating all those English terms without a corresponding Spanish term extracted from the 1997 version of the Metathesaurus (see section 3). In these experiments, the English terms are translated utilizing all the different rules described in section 5. This means that each English term will end up with a set of candidate translations. To determine whether there is a correct translation in the set, a comparison will be made between each of the candidates and the terms in the 1998 version of the Metathesaurus. The process to compare the terms requires several steps: 1) Looking up the English term in the Metathesaurus. 2) If such a term exists, looking up for its corresponding Spanish term. 3) If the Spanish term exists, comparing it with each of the candidates in the set. The process stops when the result of the comparison becomes true or none of the translations are correct.

Further research is planned for the following: a) testing the rules in other domains; b) testing the pattern discovery algorithm in other domains; and c) testing the pattern discovery algorithm in other languages.

7 Conclusion

In this paper I have presented experimental results on an approach for expanding a multilingual thesaurus by reusing translated terms. I have shown that pattern-based rules, morphological rules, order inversion rules and partial matching rules can be applied successfully to translate English terms to Spanish terms. The rules are not applicable in those cases where the two terms are not close, morphologically speaking; hence, the use a dictionary is needed. However, given the fact that many of the biomedical terms are derived from roots common to a number of languages, the approach lends itself to translation and thus extension of multilingual thesauri. Finally, capitalizing on the effort already available will increase the number of resources needed not only in text information retrieval, but also in information extraction and machine translation tasks.

References

1. Soergel, D.: Multilingual thesauri in cross-language text and speech retrieval. AAAI Symposium on Cross-Language Text and Speech Retrieval (1997)
2. Oard, D. W.: Alternative Approaches for Cross-Language Text Retrieval. AAAI Symposium on Cross-Language Text and Speech Retrieval (1997)
3. Sheridan, P., Ballerini, J. P. Experiments in Multilingual Information Retrieval using the SPIDER system. Proceedings of SIGIR-96 (1996)
4. Yang, Y., Brown, R., Frederking, R., Carbonell, J., Geng, Y., Lee, D. Bilingual-corpus Based Approaches to Translingual Information Retrieval. The 2nd Workshop on Multilinguality in Software Industry: The AI Contribution (1997)
5. Ballesteros, L., Croft, W. B. Phrasal translation and query expansion techniques for cross-language information retrieval. AAAI Symposium on Cross-Language Text and Speech Retrieval (1997)
6. Stamatos, E., Michos, S., Pantelodimou, C., Fakotakis, N. TRANSLIB: An Advanced Tool for Supporting Multilingual Access to Library Catalogues. The 2nd Workshop on Multilinguality in Software Industry: The AI Contribution (1997)
7. Gilarranz, J., Gonzalo, J., Verdejo, F. Language-independent Text Retrieval with the EuroWordNet Multilingual Semantic Database. The 2nd Workshop on Multilinguality in Software Industry: The AI Contribution (1997)
8. Nkwenti-Azeh, B. New trends in terminology processing and implications for practical translation. ASLIB (1994) 67–74
9. National Library of Medicine. Unified Medical Language System. 8th Edition 1997. UMLS Knowledge Sources, Documentation (1997)
10. Klemettinen, M., Mannila, H., Toivonen, H. A Data Mining Methodology and Its Application to Semi-Automatic Knowledge Acquisition. DEXA'97 Workshop (1997)
11. Fayyad, U., Piatetsky-Shapiro, G., Smyth, P. From data mining to knowledge discovery: An overview. Advances in Knowledge Discovery and Data Mining (1996) 1–34
12. Brazma, A., Jonassen, I., Eidhammer, I., Gilbert, D. R. Approaches to automatic discovery of patterns in biosequences. Reports in Informatics 113 (1995)
13. Jonassen, I., Collins, J. F., Higgins, D. G. Finding flexible patterns in unaligned protein sequences. Protein Science 4(**8**) (1995) 1587–1595
14. Jonassen, I. Efficient discovery of conserved patterns using a pattern graph CABIOS (1997)

Spicing Up the Information Soup:
Machine Translation and the Internet

Steve McLaughlin and Ulrike Schwall

Lernout & Hauspie (GMS) Munich, Gesellschaft für Multilinguale Systeme mbH,
Balanstr. 57, D-81541 München, Germany
steve.mclaughlin@gmsmuc.de   ulrike.schwall@gmsmuc.de

Abstract. The Internet is rapidly changing the face of business and dramatically transforming people's working and private lives. These developments present both a challenge and an opportunity to many technologies, one of the most important being Machine Translation. The Internet will soon be the most important medium for offering and finding information, and one of the principle means of communication for both companies and private users. There are many players on the Internet scene, each with different needs. Some players require help in presenting their information to an international audience, others require help in finding the information they seek and, because the Internet is increasingly multilingual, help in understanding that which they find. This paper attempts to identify the players and their needs, and outlines the products and services with which Machine Translation can help them to fully participate in the Internet revolution.

1 The Multilingual Internet Marketplace

The Internet was originally a North American invention for an exclusively English-speaking group of users. Communication was the name of the game, and lack of telephone cables or narrow bandwidth were conceived as being the main barriers to growth rather than language. In many parts of the world, of course, reliable access to the Internet still remains a great problem, but these problems of national infrastructure will be overcome, albeit at different speeds. As the Internet becomes increasingly multilingual, the language problem is emerging as the most important hindrance, and this barrier is much harder to surmount. After all, the installation of a fast Internet connection will help non-English speakers receive information more quickly, but it won't help them to understand it.

Once the chauvinistic attitude that "everyone using the Internet should learn English first" has been disregarded as economically and socio-politically outdated, only one conclusion remains: the Internet can only achieve its full global potential through language translation.

But to gain a true picture of what the multilingual marketplace truly consists of, we need to

1. Analyze the language situation and needs on the Internet and
2. Isolate the main groups of Internet players and their requirements.

2 Languages on the Internet

First, let's take a look at rough figures for the most widely spoken world languages:

Rank	Language	Speakers (Millions)
1	Chinese (Mandarin, Wu, Yue)	1.028
2	English	332
3	Spanish	266
4	Bengali	189
5	Hindi	182
6	Portuguese	170
7	Russian	170
8	Japanese	125
9	German	98
10	Javanese	76
11	Korean	75
11	French	72
13	Vietnamese	67

Table 1. Widely spoken languages [1]

This information is interesting as a starting point but cannot be directly mapped onto the situation on the Internet. Bengali and Hindi, for example, play a relatively minor role in terms of Internet content. Obviously a further parameter is required in order to gain a complete picture of an economically, technically and politically driven Internet market: Internet access. The following table shows the population and figures for Internet access for 25 countries. Countries are ranked by the percentage of their population with Internet access.

Rank	Country	Population*	Access**	Access Rank	% Total	Source #
1.	U.S	270,300,000	55,000,000	1a	20.3	(1)
2.	Australia	18,600,000	3,000,000	1c	16.1	(2)
3.	Canada	30,700,000	4,500,000	1d/4a	14.7	(3)
4.	Finland	5,100,000	745,000		14.6	(4)
5.	Sweden	8,900,000	1,300,000	8	14.6	(4)

6.	Norway	4,400,000	601,000		13.7	(4)
7.	Denmark	5,300,000	682,000		12.9	(4)
8.	Switzerland	7,300,000	708,000		9.7	(4)
9.	UK	57,700,000	5,500,000	1b	9.5	(4)
10.	New Zealand	3,600,000	327,000		9.1	(5)
11.	Netherlands	15,700,000	1,390,000	7	8.9	(4)
12.	Germany	82,100,000	6,100,000	3	7.4	(6)
13.	Japan	125,900,000	9,200,000	2	7.3	(7)
14.	France	58,800,000	2,870,000	4b	4.9	(6)
15.	Belgium	10,200,000	478,000		4.7	(4)
16.	Austria	8,100,000	362,000		4.5	(4)
17.	Ireland	3,600,000	145,000		4.0	(4)
18.	Singapore	3,500,000	131,000		3.7	(5)
19.	Italy	56,800,000	1,400,000	6	2.5	(4)
20.	Hong Kong	6,700,000	165,000		2.5	(5)
21.	Taiwan	20,900,000	480,000		2.3	(5)
22.	Korea	67,600,000	1,500,000	5	2.2	(8)
23.	Spain	39,100,000	861,000		2.2	(4)
24.	Portugal	9,900,000	188,000		1.9	(4)
25.	South Africa	42,800,000	600,000		1.4	(9)

Table 2. Internet access

* Source: U.S. Census Bureau
** Defined as persons with *any* type of Internet access
\# Source: (1) Jan-98 MRI
        (2) Sep-97 Roy Morgan Research
        (3) Nov-97 Internet.com
        (4) Dec-97 IDC Research
        (5) Oct-97 IDC Research
        (6) Mar-98 NOP Research Group
        (7) Apr-98 AsiaBizTech
        (8) Nov-97 AsiaBizTech
        (9) Jan-98 Sagonet

These figures show that language demand on the Internet is governed by the availability of the necessary technology on a national level and not by the number of potential users. Of course, countries such as China have an enormous growth potential, assuming that technical, economic and political conditions allow it.

This table is based on countries and not on languages. Nevertheless, we can use this information to build a reliable picture of language ranking on the Internet. The Access Ranking column lists languages in the order of absolute number of users with Internet access. English still has a dominant position and, assuming strong growth in Asia (Chinese) and South America (Spanish) in the next decade, any company providing language support for the Internet will need to cater for the following language combinations (roughly in the order of importance):

English <-> Japanese
English <-> German
English <-> Spanish
English <-> French
English <-> Chinese
English <-> Korean
English <-> Italian
English <-> Portuguese

The figures for the Scandinavian countries would seem to indicate a strong argument for their inclusion in this list. However, English has a strong tradition in the Scandinavian school systems, and the relative importance of these languages will decline as the total number of Internet users worldwide continues to grow.

Another relevant item of information is the Websites distribution per language: Language distribution of Websites is changing rapidly. Up to the present time most of the content was in English and mainly directed to English-speaking (US) users. For non-English-speaking users there was little motivation at all to access the Internet. From 1996 onwards, the situation has started to change dramatically: the growing availability of PCs and deregulation of national telecoms, especially in Europe, has lead to a stronger nationalization of Web content and more localization of Web pages for international audiences.

While between 1980 and the end of 1996 the proportion of English Websites was still above 70%, of the new Websites added in the first two months of 1998 almost 50% were not English [1]. A look at the percentual distribution of Websites in the first two months of 1998 will illustrate the point:

English   53.1 %
Japanese   6.0 %
Swedish   5.5 %
Spanish   3.8 %
German   3.2 %
Italian   1.42 %
Chinese   1.41 %
French   1.25 %
Russian   1.13 %
Korean   0,7 %

These statistics clearly serve to reinforce the need for the language combinations identified above. Russian comes here into play for the first time and will certainly be a growing market force. The situation with regard to Swedish has already been mentioned. It is interesting to note the number of people who can read English is as high as 30% in Northern Europe and as low as 1% in Southern Europe. Of these 30%, many will be educated professionals with Internet access. Although the figures for Arabic are still not significant enough to appear, political and economic forces will certainly make it necessary to offer support for this language in the near future. On the basis of these considerations, the following two language combinations should be added to those listed above:

> English <-> Russian
> English <-> Arabic

3 Translating for the Internet

The type of language translation required within the Internet context is somewhat different from that in more "traditional areas". Even before we deal in detail with the requirements of the individual Internet players, a number of factors can be identified:

- translations must be fast, but may not always need to be perfect.
- a large number of languages must be covered
- translation services must be easily accessible, preferably without leaving the Internet
- pricing and billing must be as automatic as possible and fully transparent.

These factors alone would indicate that human translators can play only a limited role - quite apart from the huge volumes of text involved. This all points to Machine Translation as the only possible solution to many of the enormous language problems the further spread of this medium will bring.

But this enormous opportunity for Machine Translation is also a huge challenge. Unless Machine Translation can be adapted to the Internet situation, it can never achieve its full potential.

- Machine Translation must be a "fully integrated black box". Users will have neither the expertise nor the patience to set switches or choose obscure parameters.
- Lexicons must provide extremely good general coverage with excellent terminology in a few key areas. We cannot expect a user to have linguistic expertise or time to do any linguistic coding.
- Users will normally be satisfied with gist translation but will sometimes require high-quality translations.

In fact, gist translation will often generate the additional need for higher quality translation. A range of translation services (including human translation) must be available when and as needed out of an integrated web-based solution.

4 Internet Players, Language Needs and L&H Technology

When asked to identify the typical Internet user, many people would immediately think of the Surfer. While this is undoubtedly correct, and an enormous market, there are many other players on the Internet scene, each with their own language and translation needs. We will attempt to isolate the different groups of users, analyze their motives for Internet use and define the tools they will need to meet the multilingual challenge.

There are three main groups:
- information gatherers and communicators: this group may be subdivided into private and corporate end-users
- those who use the Internet as a business medium
- those for whom the Internet is a business in itself.

After profiling each of these groups, we will outline the products and services that Lernout &Hauspie have developed to meet their requirements.

4.1 (Semi-)Professional End-Users and Private Consumers

4.1.1 User Profile

This section deals with the typical private or semi-professional Internet user. This group has access to a personal computer with standard PC hardware and software and access to the Internet via a service provider. These people are using the Internet because they want to gain access to information and services. Many will also increasingly use it as a "trendy" communications medium (Email). Access to services and information must be as fast and convenient as possible. For the sake of convenience, this group of users may even be prepared to pay more for Internet-based services.

They have two main language-related requirements:
- the need to find and assimilate information on Web pages in languages they don't understand. This will involve translating search queries and results of searches. Machine Translation will probably be adequate for most purposes.
- a need for occasional translation of non-localized web pages, Emails or smaller to medium-sized documents from their personal computer file system. Depending on the purpose for which these documents are to be used, Machine Translation or human translation will be preferred.

This group of users do not have time or inclination to learn how to use a complex MT product. They will typically also have no easy way of accessing a translator's services. What they require is an application which enables them to translate search queries, results, Web pages, documents and Emails from their own computer. A machine translation will often suffice, but an online link to human translation for occasional use would complement the picture.

4.1.2 L&H Tools
Lernout & Hauspie has the following products and services for this group of users.

iTranslator Client
This subscription service enables the user to access translation services at any hour of the day directly from his or her desktop PC. The user simply chooses the document to be translated, the target language and the "quality" of the translation. Everything else is automatic: the document is transmitted to the Translation Server, processed and then sent back to the Client. Should the user choose a higher quality level than Machine Translation, jobs are routed to a translation agency before they are sent back. If desired, Cost Estimates can be calculated and sent back to the user for approval before a translation is started.

iTranslator Search
This is a client-based subscription service for powerful multilingual Internet searching. The user only needs to input the query in his or her native language. iTranslator Search will do the rest:
- translate the query into all supported languages
- search the Internet (using as many Search Engines as the user wants) for relevant Web pages
- summarize the information found on Web pages and
- (machine) translate the summaries into the user's native language.

As iTranslator Search also includes the Internet Client described above, full translations (machine or human) of complete Web pages or any other documents can also be requested at any time from within the same Client application.

T1 Professional
This disk-based system is aimed at users with more linguistic skills whose main interest lies in translation support rather than multilingual searching. T1 Professional provides a combination of Machine Translation, Translation Memory and Dictionary Lookup facilities for a wide range of applications. With this intuitive and user-friendly system, you can
- translate directly from Microsoft Word and an Internet browser
- add terms to the lexicon
- import and export terminology
- create Translation Memories
- choose from wide range of translation parameters.

The machine translation technology[1] in T1 Professional is used as the core of all other engines in the T1 and iTranslator families.

---

[11] Fur further details of this technology see [Thurmair / Schwall 1997]: *From Metal to T1*, MT Summit VI, San Diego 1997.

4.2 Companies and Corporations

4.2.1 User Profile

Companies and corporations are probably the most intensive information gatherers and communicators on the Internet. They use the Internet as a medium for their own business purposes and will often have their own Intranets. These corporations rely on the Internet for up-to-date information and services so that they can react fast and appropriately to changing business situations. Although other platforms still play some role for corporations, their employees will normally have access to personal computers with standard PC hardware and Windows-based software, sometimes connected to the Internet via high-speed dedicated lines. Most employees will have little or limited linguistic skills, but large companies may have an internal translation group or a long-term relationship with an external translation partner.

Most employees of such corporations will have much the same requirements as those identified for private and semi-professional users in the last section:
- multilingual search facilities with translation of results
- regular need for translations of Web pages, documents and mails.

Access to tools and human resources which support these tasks must be available where and when needed, directly from the user's desk. Machine Translation support should be built into the workflows, and, where needed, access to human translation (whether internal or external) must be fast and convenient.

Those companies with internal human translation services may want to make their services available on an Intranet. And any such department will be interested in automation of the translation process to achieve faster turn-around times. These tools such as Machine Translation, Translation Memory, or terminology bases must be capable of integration into a wide range of workflows. They must also be capable of using the Internet as a transport medium and designed for use with Internet (HTML) documents.

4.2.2 L&H Tools

Many users in this group will have the same type of requirements as private and semi-professional users. They will also wish to utilize the same type of tools described in the previous section:

iTranslator Client: for machine and/or human translation of documents directly from the user's desk. iTranslator Client sends documents for translation to a central translation server, which manages the service requests by dividing them among a number of Machine Translation Engines. Once an engine has completed the execution of a request, the iTranslator Master collects the results and returns them to the iTranslator Client.

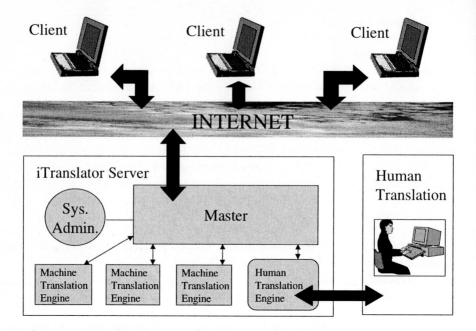

Fig. 1. iTranslator Client

The Human Translation Engine is designed to facilitate the organization and administration of translation jobs which require the services of a human translator. These jobs can consist in either the post-editing of a machine-translated text, or in a full human translation of a text. Both of these job types are performed by a professional human translator.

As we have seen in the previous section, **iTranslator Search** is another tool in the iTranslator family, capable of doing multilingual Internet searching, summarization, and translation of online documents. This tool has the same architecture as iTranslator Client. There are two main components:
- The local client software which provides the interface for query input, document searching, and submission to the server. Summarization is also performed on the client.
- The iTranslator Server (see diagram of iTranslator Client) which distributes the translations over the Engines, manages translation jobs, and maintains customer account information. As query translation has to be performed as rapidly as possible, special Query Engines have been developed for this purpose.

T1 Workgroup

T1 Workgroup has been designed for the corporate user group in which there will normally be access to internal translators or linguistically-skilled employees. T1 Workgroup is a further development of T1 Professional, and offers the complete functionality of the Professional version along with all the advantages of a multi-user system:

- Central lexicons and Translation Memory modules
- User access authorization
- Extended Lexicon Editing and administration options
- An Alignment Editor for help in creating new Translation Memory modules
- Customer and Product settings
- Extendibility to T1 Corporate solutions

In T1 Workgroup, all T1 resources such as lexicons, memories and lookup dictionaries are stored on a central server computer. Except for the lexicon database, Translation Memory and dictionaries used in Lookups, each user will have a full version of T1 on his or her local machine.

Lexicon entries can be kept privately or released for use by all users. One or more users of T1 for Workgroups can be deemed to be Lexicon Administrator. If a Lexicon Administrator is defined, he or she is responsible for reviewing the lexicon work of normal users before it is released for general use.

The basic version of the system will support up to 5 users. This number can be increased by the purchase of additional floating licenses.

T1 Corporate

No two companies are the same, and no two companies have the same translation requirements. Apart from obvious differences such as size, each company or corporation has its own individual profile, the main parameters being line of business and internal organization.

T1 Corporate is not a single off-the-shelf product; it is a customized Intranet solution for companies and corporations assembled together from a range of modules. Modules may be included or omitted from T1 Corporate depending on the translations needs and the company's infrastructure. The T1 Corporate package that is put together for a particular company will depend on the answers to questions such as these:

- Which translation services are required by the company?
- How many users need access to these translation services?
- How many of these users need to be able to add terminology and Translation memory modules to the system?
- Does the company employ in-house translators?
- Which other language tools do users need on a day-to-day basis?

Depending on the company's answers to these and many other questions, the optimum T1 Corporate package will be put together.

Modularity and streamlined architecture are strategic concepts for L&H. This means that packages can include

- the full functionality of **iTranslator Client** and **iTranslator Search** with Servers and any number of desired engines. As T1 Corporate uses IP protocols for data communication, the physical location of the Servers and the Engines is immaterial
- full T1 Workgroup functionality for any number of users
- fully integrated links to in-house or external human translation services.

And as a company grows and it's translation requirements change, further modules may be added to T1 Corporate.

4.3   The Internet as a Business Medium: Content Providers

4.3.1   User Profile

Content Providers utilize the Internet to draw attention to their products or services and to make it easy for consumers to purchase, and the number of Content Providers is increasing dramatically: At the beginning of 1997, IDC Research estimated that there were 70 million Web pages, with that number increasing to 800 million by the year 1999.

Content Providers will often have their own Web servers with fast processors and large storage capacity or they will have their Web pages hosted by a specialized company. In some cases they may even have their own networks (e.g.Bloomberg, ZDNet).

If you want to sell to people, you must make it easy for them to find you and to buy from you. A global audience can be reached most effectively via the Internet, and being able to offer information in a consumer's own language can mean a vital competitive edge. This means translation of Web content into the most important Internet languages - either as a permanent feature of the Website or on-the fly when an Internet user requests such a translation. If the Content Provider wishes to offer translations on the fly, Machine Translation is the only possible course of action. But it must be fast, few Internet users are prepared to wait any length of time online until a translation is ready.

Fast turn-around times are vital, and the large number of Web pages with frequently changing content will mean that human translation will necessarily play a lesser role than in their traditional business areas. Apart from the prohibitive costs that would be involved, it is not easy to find human translators with the necessary Web skills and the normal human translation workflow is too clumsy and time-consuming.

The ideal solution would involve a minimum of effort for Content Providers and allow them to maintain the site in one "master" language. Users would be able to choose the language in which they want to navigate the Website. Hidden from the user's view would be a Machine Translation tool that supports the main Internet languages and

- automatically detect Web pages whose contents have changed and pre-translate them from the master language into all supported languages or
- translates pages on the Website into the user's chosen language on an ongoing basis or as they are accessed (on-the-fly).

Some Content Providers, however, will want to have higher quality (human) translation of key pages on their site. Our ideal tool must therefore allow the Content Provider to control whether a new page is translated by the machine or is automatically routed to a human translator and then transported back onto the site.

4.3.2 L&H Tools

iTranslator Publish

This tool will enable Content Providers to maintain their Web pages in a single language yet offer them to Internet users in any supported languages, with a minimum of effort on the part of the Content Provider and the Internet user.

On the entry page of the Website, the Internet surfer will simply choose the language in which he or she wishes to read the information by simply clicking on the appropriate flag. The first page and any other page on the site which the user moves to will then automatically be presented in the chosen language.

The Content Provider only needs to identify the pages which should be included in the service by using a special marker. These pages can be located on any number of Websites. The desired quality of translation (machine/human) can also be specified for each individual page. Any changes to the content of a page (in the master language) are quickly identified by a special spider mechanism. These pages are then transmitted for translation into the target languages and then written into a special cache or put back to the appropriate location on the Website. This means that the same page is never translated twice and that the translation will be available instantaneously the next time it is accessed.

A machine translation is made of every new page. In the case of pages for which a human translation has been specified, this automatically replaces the machine translation as it becomes available.

This system eliminates the need for on-the-fly translation of Web pages and cuts down the connect time on the part of the user. **iTranslator Publish** uses the same system of servers and Engines as the rest of the iTranslator range, and can be implemented as a service or as a complete inhouse system.

4.4 The Internet as a Business in itself: Service Providers/Search Engines

4.4.1 User Profile

Service Providers are the companies which give people the technical capability of accessing the Internet. Although this is a clearly different group to Content Providers, some companies, such as Compuserve and AOL, fulfil both functions. They will have their own network of powerful web servers. Service Providers are partly financed by regular subscription charges but also want to offer value-added services to increase revenue and attract more subscription customers. More and more Service Providers will be interested in offering translation as a service on their networks - for documents, Emails or discussion groups. After all, the multilingual Internet creates its own translation demand and Service Providers can gain a competitive edge by offering a solution to the problem they exacerbate and at the same time remove an obstacle to further growth. Service Providers may also be interested in offering translation tools for Content Providers which use their networks.

The business of Search Engine providers such as Yahoo and Lycos is to offer searching and indexing facilities to Internet surfers. They are financed by the advertising space they sell on their search engines. As the amount that advertisers have to pay is based on Search Engine accesses, these companies are interested in any services which will increase these figures or generate additional revenue. Support for multilingual searching and translation of results are natural add-ons to Search Engines. They might also want to offer their users natural language front-ends for multilingual searching. This will make the use of the Internet simpler and the results more precise, leading to a greater number of users and larger advertising revenues.

4.4.2 L&H Tools

Many of the products and services in the **iTranslator** range will be of interest to these Internet players.

iTranslator Client for providing translation services to subscribers and surfers as a value-added service or as a competitive advantage.

iTranslator Search to add multilingual search and translation capability. A future version of iTranslator Search will add a natural language front-end to the existing multilingual search tools.

iTranslator Publish as a tool for Content Providers.

5 What's Next?

As we have seen, the solutions currently in place at L&H cover many of the requirements of the players on the Internet scene. And, owing to the **modular** nature of our architecture, it should not prove too difficult to extend our coverage to other related areas such as **Email** or **chat** translation.

Connecting text-based products with **speech** technology would seem a natural development within a company like L&H and should not be such a major challenge. But the heterogeneous user base and diversity of domains mean that bringing **natural language interfaces** to the Internet will represent a major development step.

As to languages, our aim is to cover all the major Internet language pairs identified in this paper. We are also developing other **language combinations** which do not involve English, but these are not primarily intended for the Internet market.

Quality improvement will always remain an important aspect in Machine Translation. Several supplementary strategies are being investigated and may bring considerable advancements in this area.

For Internet purposes, a broad **lexicon and terminology** coverage is vital. In this area, the system has already benefited from the synergy between the Mendez human translation division and our Language Technology division within the L&H group. This co-operation will be intensified.

These close links with human translation also help us in a further way. The growing need for information translation in the Internet context pressurizes users into accepting quality levels that would previously have been rejected. Nevertheless, our strategy is to alleviate any **acceptance** problems by providing, along with Machine Translation, the mechanisms and channels for obtaining higher quality human translations whenever the need arises.

Quite apart from the question of quality, **integration into workflows** is vital to user acceptance of Machine Translation. The easier we make it to use such systems, the more they will became a natural component of everyday applications such as Internet.

References

1. Allied Business 1998, Language Translation, p. 31
2. Allied Business 1998, Language Translation, p. 98

Revision of Morphological Analysis Errors Through the Person Name Construction Model

Hiroyuki Shinnou

Ibaraki University
Dept. of Systems Engineering
Nakanarusawa, 4-12-1
Hitachi, Ibaraki, 316-8511, Japan
shinnou@lily.dse.ibaraki.ac.jp

Abstract. In this paper, we present the method to automatically revise morphological analysis errors caused by unregistered person names. In order to detect and revise their errors, we propose the Person Name Construction Model for kanji characters composing Japanese names. Our method has the advantage of not using context information, like a suffix, to recognize person names, thus making our method a useful one. Through the experiment, we show that our proposed model is effective.

1   Introduction

It is clear that morphological analysis is an important module for an NLP system like the MT system. One problem in the morphological analysis is word segmentation errors caused by unregistered words. Most unregistered words are proper nouns, like place names, organization names, and person names. In this paper, we focus on person names, and propose the Person Name Construction Model to correct morphological analysis errors caused by unregistered person names. This model gives a score to the given word sequence. This score indicates the degree to which the given word sequence appears to be a person's name. By the score, we can extract the name from the morphological analysis result. If the extracted name is not consistent with the morphological analysis result, we revise the result to take the extracted person name into account.

The Person Name Construction Model is based on the heuristic that a person's name is composed of kanji characters which are placed in the first position, the middle position and the last position of the name. For example, in the case of the family name, kanji characters frequently used in the first position are "中", "松" and "長". And in the middle position, they are "谷", "々", "曽". And in the last position, they are "田", "藤", "井". Our proposed model deduces that the character sequences "中谷田", "長藤" and "松曽井", which are a combination of their characters, have the appearance of being names[1]. However, this model tends to judge the given character sequence to be a person's name. So, in order

---

[1] These character sequences are not registered in the dictionary. We don't know whether these character sequences are real person names. However, most Japanese agree that these character sequences seem to be family names.

to remove non-names from the extraction, we also use the heuristic based on the morphological analysis error patterns caused by unregistered person names.

A feature of our proposed model makes no use of contextual clues. Strategies to recognize unregistered words are divided into two types. The one type uses contextual clues, like a suffix (ex. "氏 (Mr.)", "さん (Ms..)"), a prefix (ex. "故 (the late)", "長女 (the first-born daughter)"), the initial phrasing(ex. "社長 (the president)", "大統領 (the President")), a verb (ex. "逮捕される (be arrested)", "殺される (be killed)") and so on in order to recognize unregistered words[3, 8]. Another type uses only clues in the given word sequence, and doesn't use information out of the given word sequence. The former is powerful, and currently the automatic acquisition of such contextual clues is being researched[6, 1, 5]. However we often have the situation without contextual clues. Thus the former strategy needs to have the latter strategy module. For example, in the case of the phrase "～社長 (the president ～)", the "～" part often includes a name. Thus, the phrase "～社長" is a contextual clue to recognize person names. However, the "～" words in this phrase do not always include a person's name. Therefore from only information in the "～" sequences, we must judge whether it includes a person's name or not. Our proposed model is useful in doing this, and can be applied to all sorts of former strategies.

Last we experimented using a small sampling. For morphological analysis errors caused by unregistered person names, our system revised them with 63.8% precision and 72.5% recall. Investigating our system failures, we found most failures acceptable and reasonable. So our proposed model was shown to be useful and effective for the recognition of unregistered person names.

2 Extraction of person names and revision of morphological analysis errors

2.1 Basic procedures

First, we pick out kanji word sequences for doing a morphological analysis of a sentence. Here, we define the term "kanji word" as words composed of kanji characters. For example, for the following sentence (1), we get sentence (2) as the result of a morphological analysis, and we pick out the three kanji word sequences shown in (3).

(1) あの千葉大学の学生が鈴木健四郎社長です
    (That student going to Chiba university is the president Suzuki Kensirou.)
(2) /あの/千葉/大学/の/学生/が/鈴木/健/四郎/社長/です/
(3) /千葉/大学/, /学生/, /鈴木/健/四郎/社長/
    (Chiba university, student, the president Suzuki Kensirou)

A name is extracted from each kanji word sequence if the sequence contains a person's name. If the extracted name is not consistent with the morphological analysis result, we correct the morphological analysis result to account for the extracted name.

Table 1. Person names extracted form kanji word sequences

kanji word sequence	extracted person name
/千葉/大学/	/千葉/ (last name) ...(4)
/学生/	nothing
/鈴木/健/四郎/社長/	/鈴木/健四郎/ (last name/first name)...(5)

For the above example, we have extracted the names shown in Table 1.

From the kanji sequence "/千葉/大学/", we extract the name "/千葉/" as the last name (c.f. (4)). This segmentation is consistent with the morphological analysis result, so we don't revise it. On the other hand, the sequence "/健四郎/", extracted as the first name from the kanji sequence "/鈴木/健/四郎/社長/", is not consistent with the morphological analysis result, in which "健四郎" is segmented into "/健/" and "/四郎/". Therefore, we revise the morphological analysis result to the sequence "/健四郎/".

Next, we describe the procedure to extract the person's name from the kanji sequence. First we extract kanji word subsequences as a part of the given kanji word sequences, and we give each kanji word subsequence a score which indicates the degree to which the given kanji word subsequence appears to be a person's name. Next, we identify the kanji word subsequence as a name if its maximum score goes over a threshold value. The output is the kanji word subsequence recognized as the person's name and classified by type (i.e. last name, first name, or their combination).

Take the case of the kanji word sequence "/鈴木/健/四郎/社長/". We extract kanji word subsequences from its sequence, and get the score for each kanji word subsequence as shown in Table 2. We output the phrase "/鈴木/健四郎/" with the maximum score.

2.2 Person Name Construction Model

Our system computes a score which indicates the degree to which the given word sequence appears to be a person's name. In order to compute the score, we propose the Person Name Construction Model.

Japanese names consist of a last name and first name. Last names can be divided into three character parts: the first position character(LFC), the middle position character(LMC) and the last position character(LLC). For instance, the last name "中曽根" has following the three character parts.

$$LFC = \text{"中"}, \; LMC = \text{"曽"}, \text{ and } LLC = \text{"根"}.$$

In the case of the last name "鈴木", the character parts are:

$$LFC = \text{"鈴"}, LMC = \text{""}, \text{ and } LLC = \text{"木"}.$$

Table 2. Score for the kanji word subsequence

kanji word subsequence	score	extracted name
/鈴木/健/四郎/社長/	0	nothing
/鈴木/健/四郎/	338970480	/鈴木/健四郎/ (last name/first name)
/鈴木/健/	4014368	/鈴木/健/ (last name/first name)
/鈴木/	5296	/鈴木/ (last name)
/健/四郎/社長/	0	nothing
/健/四郎/	43167	/健四郎/ (first name)
/健/	758	/健/ (first name)
/四郎/社長/	0	nothing
/四郎/	5906	/健四郎/ (first name)
/社長/	0	nothing

In the same way, first names can divided into three character parts: the first position character(FFC), the middle position character(FMC) and the last position character(FLC).

Our model assumes that any kanji character "a" has a score which indicates how often the character "a" is used as an LFC. Also the character "a" has scores for LMC and LLC. We define $S_{lfc}(a)$ to be the LFC score for a character "a". We define $S_{lmc}(a)$ and $S_{llc}(a)$ similarly. By the following expression, we define the score $S_l(\alpha)$, which indicates the degree to which a character sequence $\alpha = a_1 a_2 a_3 \cdots a_n$ appears, to be a last name.

$$S_l(\alpha) = \frac{S_{lfc}(a_1) + \sum_{i=2}^{n-1} S_{lmc}(a_i) + S_{llc}(a_n)}{n}$$

In the same way, in the following expression, we define the score $S_f(\beta)$, which indicates the degree to which a character sequence $\beta = b_1 b_2 b_3 \cdots b_n$ appears, to be a first name.

$$S_f(\beta) = \frac{S_{ffc}(b_1) + \sum_{i=2}^{n-1} S_{fmc}(b_i) * S_{fec}(b_n)}{n}$$

Finally, in the following expression, we define a score indicating the degree to which a string α appears to be a last name and a string β a first name.

$$S_l(\alpha) * S_f(\beta)$$

If the length of the character sequence is over 2, we can calculate the score for the character sequence. If the length of the character sequence is 1, i.e. the character sequence is $\alpha = a_1$, we define the scores as follows:

$$S_l(\alpha) = S_{l1}(a_1)$$

$$S_f(\alpha) = S_{f1}(a_1)$$

We will define $S_{l1}(a_1)$ and $S_{l1}(a_1)$ later.

When we are given the kanji word subsequence $P = w_1 w_2 \cdots w_m$, we regard it as the character sequence $P = a_1 a_2 \cdots a_n$. Next we compute each score of $S_l(P), S_f(P)$ and $S_l(a_1 a_2 \cdots a_i) * S_f(a_{i+1} a_{i+2} \cdots a_m)$, and output one with the maximum score.

Finally, we must explain how to construct scores of $S_{lfc}(a_1)$ and so on. In this paper, we used one-year-old newspaper articles as the training corpus. First, we segmented words by morphological analysis for the training corpus. We identified person's names as a result of the morphological analysis, and made a frequency table (T1) for these names. And then we picked out person's names from the dictionary used for morphological analysis and made a frequency table (T2) for these names. T2 always has a frequency of 1. Next we merged T1 and T2, and divided it into a frequency table (TL) for last names and a frequency table (TF) for first names. Further, we divided TL into a frequency table (TL1) for names of the length 1 and a frequency table (TL2) for names of length 2 or over. Similarly, we got TF1 and TF2. Next if the frequency of the name $\alpha = a_1 a_2 a_3 \cdots a_n (n > 1)$ in TL2 is f, we add the value f to the $S_{lfc}(a_1), S_{lmc}(a_2)$, $S_{lmc}(a_3), \cdots, S_{lmc}(a_{n-1})$ and $S_{fec}(a_n)$. We repeated this procedure for all names in TL2. As a result we arrived at scores $S_{lfc}(a), S_{lmc}(a)$ and $S_{llc}(a)$. And we also got scores $S_{ffc}(a), S_{fmc}(a)$ and $S_{fec}(a)$ in this same way.

We defined $S_{l1}(a)$ and $S_{f1}(a)$ to be the frequency of the last name "a" and the first name "a", so these scores can be defined in TL1 and TF1.

Lastly, we explain the case that $S_{*c}(a)$ or $S_{*1}(a)$ is equal to zero. In that case, basically $S_l(\alpha)$ or $S_f(\alpha)$ is defined to be zero. However, if the character sequence α has the following form:

last name + first name,

we used 10 % of $S_l(\alpha)$ as $S_l(\alpha)$, and 10 % of $S_f(\alpha)$ as $S_f(\alpha)$,

2.3 Use of morphological analysis result

The Person Name Construction Model tends to extract too many names from kanji word sequences. This occurs because this model measures the appearance of the person name, although appearance is a weak indication of a person's name. Therefore, it is difficult to judge by only these characteristics whether or not the kanji word sequence is a person's name.

In this paper, we use the result of morphological analysis, together with the Person Name Construction Model. First, we have applied the following heuristics.

H0 Morphological analysis error caused by the unregistered person name includes the kanji word whose length is 1.

For example, the first name "健四郎" is segmented into "/健/" and "/四郎/", but this segmentation is wrong. This morphological analysis error includes the kanji word "/健/" whose length is 1. Most Japanese names have a length of 1,2 or 3. So, if a morphological analysis has incorrectly segmented a part of a person's name, it is clear that a kanji word with length 1 is included.

By using the heuristics H0 and the dictionary, we can judge that a kanji word sequence isn't a person's name. It should be noted that the heuristics H0 does not help us to judge whether a kanji word sequence is a name. If we can judge that the given kanji word sequence isn't a name, the score is zero, and if we cannot judge, the score is obtained by using the Person Name Construction Model.

Next, for the kanji word sequence which includes a kanji word with length 1, we use the following heuristics.

H1 If a morphological analysis error caused by the unregistered person name includes the kanji word whose length is 2, this kanji word is a person's name.

In the above example, the morphological analysis error (segmentation into "/健/" and "/四郎/") for the first name "健四郎" includes the kanji word "/四郎/" with length 2, and this word is a person's name. The heuristics H1 seems tenuous. However we confirmed it to be effective by the following experiment. First we picked person names with length 3 from the dictionary. If the picked word has a character string of $k_1 k_2 k_3$, we made the character strings $k_1 k_2$ and $k_2 k_3$, and checked whether $k_1 k_2$ or $k_2 k_3$ is a person's name. 78.0% of the picked names $k_1 k_2$ or $k_2 k_3$ resulted as person names. This experiment shows that the heuristics H1 is effective.

By using the heuristics H1, we can judge that a kanji word sequence is not a person's name. Again note that the heuristics H1 cannot judge that a kanji word sequence is a person's name. If we can judge that the kanji word sequence isn't a person's name, the score is zero, and if we cannot judge it, the score is obtained by the Person Name Construction Model.

Lastly we use the following heuristics:

H2 "numeral word + suffix word" is not a person's name.

This pattern appears frequently. The kanji word sequence "/千/円/" is an example of this. We assume that these kanji word sequences are not person names.

2.4 Collection of revision error

Even if we use the proposed model and heuristics H0,H1 and H2, some kanji word sequences are judged wrongly as person names. However the frequency of these wrong revision patterns is low, and we gathered frequent revision errors to avoid these errors.

First, we did morphological analysis on a part of the training corpus [2]. Next we revised morphological analysis errors with our system. We collected revised person names, and made a frequency table for the names. Because the frequency of general person names is low, names with high frequency are regarded as wrong

---

[2] 10% of training corpus

Generally, we cannot judge without contextual information whether a proper noun is a person's name or not. Therefore, we cannot avoid the 2nd type error. The recognition of an unregistered word is useful in NLP systems. As for our system, only the 4th error is regarded as a failure.

In conclusion, We should note that our proposed model is useful and effective.

4 Remarks

The aim of our system is the automatic revision of morphological analysis errors caused by unregistered person names. However, our system can be used as the extraction system for person names. In recent years, the information extraction systems have been actively researched[4]. In these systems, it is important to correctly extract person names from texts[7]. Our system is useful in this aspect. The problems of extracting person names are classified into the following 3 types. These type phenomena make it difficult to extract names.

1. Morphological analysis errors cause by unregistered words.
   For example, the right segmentation for the character sequence "鈴木健四郎" is "/鈴木/健四郎/", but a morphological analysis wrongly segments it as "/鈴木/健/四郎/", because the first name "健四郎" is unregistered.

2. Assignment of part of speech fails.
   For example, a morphological analysis correctly segments "細川正" as "/細川/正/", but the part of speech for "細川" is assigned as a general noun. This is wrong. The part of speech for "細川" is the person's name.

3. The word is correctly judged as a person's name upon morphological analysis, but the word is not a person's name in the context.
   For example, a morphological analysis correctly segments "松下塾" as "/松下/塾/", and the part of speech for "松下" is correctly assigned as a person's name. However, in information extraction, the word "松下" should not be extracted as a person's name, because the phrase "/松下/塾/" is the organization name.

Our system can be useful in solving the first problem. The 2nd and 3rd problems cannot be solved without contextual information. Contextual information is also useful for the 1st problem. However, as mentioned in the introduction, even the method using contextual information needs to judge whether the given word sequence is a person's name or not. And our model can be used together with all methods using contextual information. The improvement of the module, which judges whether the given word sequence is a person's name or not, directly improves the extraction system of person names.

A fault of our system is that scores are defined by heuristic method. We should define scores by probability. However, it is unclear how to make the score correspond to the probability, and how to determine probabilities. A definition of the score based on frequency like our system is simple, and works well. Consideration of this aspect will improve our system.

Our model deals with Japanese names and not foreign names. However, foreign names expressed by kanji characters are almost always Chinese names or Korean names. There are a limited number of last names of Chinese and Korean, and there is a heuristic that the length of the last name is 1 and the length of the first name is 2[2]. We believe that it is easy to recognize unregistered Chinese names and Korean names in Japanese texts.

5 Conclusion

In this paper, we presented the method to automatically revise morphological analysis errors caused by unregistered person names. The main part of our method is the module to give the word sequence a score which indicates the degree to which it appears a person's name. To implement this module, we proposed the Person Name Construction Model which applies the heuristic rule on kanji characters composing Japanese names. Through the experiment, we have shown that our proposed model is effective and useful. The problem of our revision system is how to define scores. For this problem, the import of probability may be effective. This is our future task.

Acknowledgments

We used Nikkei Shibun CD-ROM '90 and Mainichi Shibun CD-ROM '95 as the corpus. The Nihon Keizai Shinbun company and the Mainichi Shinbun company gave us permission of use of their collections. We appreciate the assistance granted by both companies.

References

1. Bikel,D., Miller,S., Schwartz,R. and Weischedel,R. : "Nymble: a High-Performance Learning Name-finder", Proc. of ANLP-97, pp. 194–201 (1997).
2. Chen,H-H. and Lee,J-C. : "Identification and Classification of Proper Nouns in Chinese Texts", Proc. of COLING-96, pp. 418–424 (1996).
3. Chen,K-J. and Liu, S-H. : "Word Identification for Mandarin Chinese Sentences", Proc. of COLING-92, pp. 101–107 (1992).
4. Grishman,R. and Sundheim,B. : "Message Understanding Conference-6: A Brief History", Proc. of COLING-96, pp. 446–471 (1996).
5. Sekine,S., Grishman,R. and Shinnou,H. : "A Decision Tree Method for Finding and Classifying Names in Japanese Texts", Proc. of WVLC-6, to appear (1998).
6. Strzalkowski,T. and Wang,J. : "A Self-Learning Universal Concept Spotter", Proc. of COLING-96, pp. 931–936 (1996).
7. Wakao,T., Gaizuska,R. and Wilks,Y. : "Evaluation of an Algorithm for the Recognition and Classification of Proper Names", Proc. of COLING-96, pp. 418–424 (1996).
8. Wang,L-J., Li,W-C. and Chang, C-H. : "Recognizing Unregistered Names for Mandarin Word Identification", Proc. of COLING-92, pp. 1239–1243 (1992).

Lexical Choice and Syntactic Generation in a Transfer System Transformations in the New LMT English-German System

Claudia Gdaniec

IBM T.J. Watson Research Center, P.O. Box 704, Yorktown Heights, NY 10598, USA
cgdaniec@us.ibm.com

Abstract. This paper argues that, contrary to received wisdom in the MT research community, a transfer system such as LMT is well suited to deal with most of the problems that MT faces. It may in fact be superior to other approaches in that it can handle target surface-structure constraints, variation of syntactic patterns, discourse-structure constraints, and stylistic preference. The paper describes the linguistic issues involved in LMT's English⇒German transformational component, its interaction with the lexical transfer component, and types of transformations. It identifies context-dependent and context-independent transformations and among the context-dependent ones, it differentiates between those that are triggered by instructions in the lexicon, by semantic category, by syntactic context, and by setting of stylistic preference. The paper concludes with some examples of divergence between English and German and shows how LMT handles them.

1 Introduction

Development of a full-fledged MT system such as LMT [1] that aims at broad coverage reveals the intricacies of translation generation. I will show the various linguistic levels that play a role in this effort: (potential) lexical transfer, syntactic and surface-structure constraints, morphology, discourse considerations, and finally, stylistic preference. One tenet of this paper is the close interaction of lexical choice and syntactic generation (transformations), with lexical choice offering potential transfers as well as constraining syntactic, discursive, and stylistic realities. I will argue that the transfer-based LMT system has the flexibility and power necessary to generate all possible translations as well as constrain them, because its transfer modules operate on a fully interpreted syntax tree; i.e. they benefit from an analysis that contains and represents both underlying syntactic functions and surface structure. A second focus of this paper is to deepen the understanding of (structural) transformations in the discourse of the MT research community.

---

[1] For a description of the LMT system, see [5, 6].

2   Scope of Transformations

In their Introduction to Machine Translation (1992), Hutchins and Somers describe the necessity of transformations in the following way:

> Structural transfer is necessary when the structure inherited from the source language is inappropriate for the target language. (p. 113)

They use two examples to demonstrate structural transfer rules:

> *Jones likes the film.* ⇒ *Le film plaît à Jones* ⇒ *Der Film gefällt dem* [sic] *Jones.* (p. 113)

Explanation: subject becomes dative object; direct object becomes subject.

> *John likes swimming with his friends in the summer.* ⇒ *John schwimmt im Sommer mit seinen Freunden gern.* (p. 114)

Explanation: main verb demoted to adverb; embedded verb replaces finite verb. Next, they mention the necessity of transformations for divergence in syntactic category:

> As a general rule, for these languages [Indo-European] a verb in the source language corresponds to a verb in the target language, an adjective corresponds to an adjective, a subject-predicate structure remains more or less constant, and so on. Exceptions can be treated by special procedures in 'structural transfer'. (p.140)

Some examples of LMT English-German translations:

> *I am very hungry.* ⇒ *Ich habe großen Hunger.* (adverb ⇒ adjective; adjective ⇒ noun)
> *He said that the decision is tantamount to protecting terrorist organisations.* ⇒ *Er sagte, daß die Entscheidung dem Schutz von Terroristenorganisationen gleichkommt.* (adjective ⇒ verb)
> *You can use the Help key to get additional information, depending on where your cursor is when you press the Help key.* ⇒ *Sie können die Hilfetaste verwenden, um zusätzliche Information zu bekommen, je nachdem, wo Ihr Cursor ist, wenn Sie die Hilfetaste drücken.* (verb ⇒ conjunction)

With regard to style, Hutchins and Somers observe:

> ...more research is needed on computational stylistics, and particularly computational implementations of the findings of comparative stylistics. The need is for methods of ensuring the generation of structures which are idiomatic for the target language, e.g. the 'process orientation' of Japanese, the 'action orientation' of English (...), and the preference in French for more 'dynamic' expressions (...) than in English (...) (p. 143)

In fact, more is at stake than merely a divergence of "orientation." Inside a language, discourse types exhibit particular orientations, such as "nominal" for technical and scientific discourse in German. For instance, the ing-clause in *This command line is especially useful when entering only one or two commands* can be expressed in German as a finite active clause with overt subject,

> *Diese Befehlszeile ist besonders nützlich, wenn Sie nur einen oder zwei Befehle eingeben.* (LMT default)

as a finite passive clause without an overt subject,

> *Diese Befehlszeile ist besonders nützlich, wenn nur ein oder zwei Befehle eingegeben werden.* (LMT if stylistic preference is set = passivevoice)

or as a nominalized infinitive in a more nominal style.

> *Diese Befehlszeile ist beim Eingeben von nur einem oder zwei Befehlen besonders nützlich.* (LMT if stylistic preference is set = nominal). [2]

In Bonnie Dorr's ([3]) categorization of divergences between languages that affect syntactic generation, transformations are necessary for all types of categories: (a) thematic (*Jones likes the film* ⇒ *Jones gefällt der Film*), (b) promotional/demotional (*Jones likes swimming* ⇒ *Jones schwimmt gerne*), (c) structural (*They accessed the files* ⇒ *Sie griffen auf die Dateien zu*), (d) conflational (*They proved his theory wrong* ⇒ *Sie widerlegten seine Theorie*), (e) categorial (*She is thirsty* ⇒ *Sie hat Durst*), and (f) lexical (*They cybercast the news* ⇒ *Sie verbreiteten die Nachrichten übers Internet*). [3] Transformations in the English-German LMT system can generate all six types. [4]

3   Criticisms (and Defense) of Transfer Systems

Hutchins and Somers claim that

> In theory, the deeper the analysis goes, the less likely this problem [the necessity of structural transfer] is to occur, since the deepening analysis aims at neutralising the distinctions between languages. (p. 113)

---

[2] See the exemplary contrastive analysis and discussion of variation and lexical, morphological and surface-structure constraints of English gerund transfer into German in [8].

[3] I use Dorr's divergence types although a comparison of her lexical conceptual structure with McCord's slot grammar (see [5, 6]) is not without problems, as can be seen in the preceding examples. The distinction between conflational and lexical divergence is blurred in a system that does not use an interlingua. Besides, Dorr's English-German example for conflational divergence is not clear: *I like Mary* ⇒ *I habe Marie gern* ([3]:164). *gernhaben* is perceived as one verb in German.

[4] All of these translations are generated by transformations based on transfers and instructions in the bilingual lexicon which are then interpreted and implemented according to the syntactic context.

There are two problems with this claim: First, the deeper the analysis goes and the more removed from any surface structure it becomes, the more surface-structure adjustments are required in generation, whether the output of the analysis is an abstract representation or a syntactic source-language tree. The "problem" of structural transfer may be reduced in a deep analysis, but the necessary text generation would still require transformations to generate surface structures from the deep representation. A transfer system may therefore actually be more economical for languages that have much in common. Second, a deep analysis may lose surface-structure information which may be crucial. Way et al. ([10]:354) argue that a generation module must be able to distinguish between *I permitted John to be examined by the doctor* and *I permitted the doctor to examine John*. Since the representation in LMT retains the surface information – together with the underlying functions – it creates the best of both worlds: *Ich erlaubte, daß John vom Arzt untersucht wird* vs. *Ich erlaubte dem Arzt, John zu untersuchen*.

John Bateman ([2]) claims that the action that transforms the English *John is likely to implement the algorithm* to the German *John implementiert wahrscheinlich den Algorithmus*

> can be seen as problematic in a transfer-based framework that relies on representations less abstract than that of the upper model and SLP (...), because the structures are very different. (p.31)

It turns out that this particular example is, in fact, very simple. It poses no difficulty for a linguistically sound transfer system such as LMT. However, Bateman stops short of discussing the truly complex issues that are involved in the translation of [be likely + infinitive] into German. There are shallow constraints, which an abstract meaning representation might not capture. If *likely* is modified in any way (e.g. *least/less/more/most/very*) or if it occurs in any other tense, German has to make a choice among translations. Three possible ways of expressing the meaning are: (a) *Chancen haben*, (b) *Gefahr laufen*, (c) *es ist wahrscheinlich, daß* + finite clause. The lexical choice depends on the meaning (and connotation) of the embedded clause. If it is seen as negative, (b) is the choice; if it is seen as positive, (a) is the choice; (c) is for neutral meanings.

Bateman ([2]:25) discusses the following example in order to show the superiority of "meaning-based" MT: the categorial divergence in the translation variant *Wegen der elektrischen Entladung brach das System zusammen* (from English: *The discharge of electricity resulted in a breakdown of the system*) as opposed to the structure-preserving, nominal variant *Die elektrische Entladung führte zu einem Zusammenbruch des Systems*. There is no reason why transformations cannot perform this kind of categorial shift, provided the stylistic preference is indicated and all the necessary lexical information is available. These include the verb alternative for the effect (*Zusammenbruch*), the prepositional alternative for the relational verb (*führen*) and all the alternative syntactic categories for what Arnold ([1]) calls the "knock-on" effects. [5] And LMT can actually produce the shift because of the interactive relationship of lexicon and transformations as well as the flexibility of the transformational formalism, which allows both top-down and bottom-up strategies.

This raises another issue: If every cause-effect verb is translated with the preposition *wegen* and a structure-changing verbal construction in order to avoid a nominal style, we lose lexical variety and generate monotony. If the writer of the source document uses different lexicalizations for the same meaning (e.g. *result in*; *lead to*; etc.), we may want to reproduce this variety in our target generation. A more abstract approach would have to have a mechanism in place to avoid monotony. In correspondence with stylistic preference, a transfer system can naturally mirror the writer's lexical variation without having to sacrifice lexical and syntactic choices.

4   Types of Transformations

Instead of using divergence or degree of complexity of transformations, I categorize them in terms of their relationship to context and to how they are triggered. Transformations may be context-dependent or context-independent. In general, context-independent transformations do not allow variation, whereas context-dependent transformations do. Thus the grammar writer has to decide on default translations for those cases where the user does not indicate a stylistic preference.

4.1   Context-independent Transformations

Context-independent transformations are those that are triggered by simple features of nodes in the target tree, regardless of the individual string or the context.

Verb final:

> When Dr. Guillermo Wiese read the advertisement, he knew he had found the solution to his problem. ⇒ Als Dr. Guillermo Wiese die Anzeige las, wußte er, daß er die Lösung für sein Problem gefunden hatte. (LMT translation)

Explanation: every verb in a dependent clause or phrase is moved to the end of the clause or phrase.

Do-support:

> Does that mean that Europe's long-awaited technology market explosion is happening at last? ⇒ Bedeutet das, daß Europas langerwartete Technologiemarktexplosion endlich stattfindet? (LMT)

---

[5] Or domino effect: If the part of speech of the head node is changed, the parts of speech of all its modifiers need to be changed.

Explanation: every bare infinitive that is identified as part of a support-do construction is promoted to replace the governing occurrence of a form of support-do to arrive at a simple tense in German. The original node of the bare infinitive is then deleted from the tree.

Progressive:

> *He was preparing dinner when the children came home.* ⇒ *Er bereitete das Abendessen vor, als die Kinder nach Hause kamen.* (LMT)

Explanation: every ing-verb that is identified as part of a progressive aspect construction is promoted to replace the governing occurrence of a form of *be* to arrive at a simple tense in German. The original node of the ing-verb is then deleted from the tree.

4.2 Context-dependent Transformations

Every transfer-based MT system achieves the preceding context-independent transformations in one way or another. That is not the case with the context-dependent transformations described in this section, however. Some transfer-based systems do not translate the following examples idiomatically. I will show how the English-German LMT succeeds in idiomatic translation in most of the context-dependent cases.

There are four types of context-dependent transformations:

Lexically triggered transformations. e.g. [N1 of N2] becomes [N2N1] compound

> *this type of software* ⇒ *diese Softwareart*
> *these types of software and applications* ⇒ *diese Software- und Anwendungsarten* (all LMT translations)

Non-finite raising construction changes to finite construction with extraposition:

> *He turned out to be the best man for the job.* ⇒ *Es stellte sich heraus, daß er der beste Mann für den Job ist.* (LMT)

Transformations triggered by semantic category. e.g. Present perfective aspect of stative verbs becomes present tense in German:

> *She has known it for many years.* ⇒ *Sie weiß es seit vielen Jahren.*

As opposed to non-stative verbs:

> *She has worked there for many years.* ⇒ *Sie hat viele Jahre dort gearbeitet.* (LMT translations)

Certain possessives modifying nouns of certain semantic types become parts of compounds:

> *Women's soccer was not official until 1996.* ⇒ *Frauenfußball wurde erst 1996 offiziell.*
> *Children's shoes are very expensive.* ⇒ *Kinderschuhe sind sehr teuer.*
> (But note: *My children's shoes* ⇒ *Die Schuhe meiner Kinder*) (LMT translations)

Attributive place name changes to different modifiers:

> *the Berlin mayor* ⇒ *der Bürgermeister von Berlin*
> *the Berlin bear* ⇒ *der Berliner Bär*
> *our Berlin employees* ⇒ *unsere Angestellten in Berlin* (all LMT translations)

Transformations triggered by syntactic context. e.g. Postposed adjectival clause modifier becomes a preposed attributive modifier:

> *Contact the person responsible for maintaining the system.* ⇒ *Wenden Sie sich an die für das Warten des Systems verantwortliche Person.* (LMT)

Or a full relative clause if the adjectival clause is too heavy:

> *Contact the person responsible for maintaining the system that we bought recently.* ⇒ *Wenden Sie sich an die Person, die für das Warten des Systems verantwortlich ist, das wir vor kurzem kauften.* (LMT)

Infinitival noun complement becomes a full relative clause with the subject repeated:

> *The children have only one caregiver to rely on.* ⇒ *Die Kinder haben nur einen Betreuer, auf den sie sich verlassen können.* (LMT)

And:

> *She is the first employee to get a raise.* ⇒ *Sie ist die erste Angestellte, die eine Gehaltserhöhung bekommt.* (LMT)

Transformations triggered by setting of stylistic preference. Based on stylistic preference setting, the English imperative is translated as infinitive or imperative; the register-neutral English address is translated with a formal or informal (singular or plural) form of address; and degree of nominalization is chosen for the translation of English non-finite constructions.

> Imperative ⇒ infinitive vs. imperative;
> *you* ⇒ *du* vs. *Sie* vs. *ihr*;
> ving ⇒ finite active clause with overt subject vs. finite passive clause vs. nominalized infinitive. (See previous example *This command line is especially useful when entering only one or two commands*)

5 Transformations and Interaction with Lexical Transfer

5.1 The Place of Transformations in LMT

In the LMT system, linguistic data and computational methods are separate. The system consists of four major components: source analysis, lexical transfer, structural transfer (transformations), and morphological generation. All stages of analysis are completed before lexical transfer and transformations. The parser's output is a fully interpreted tree representing the source-language sentence, on which both lexical transfer and then syntactic generation operate. Once the transfer words are inserted into the tree, transformations convert it into a target tree. They are written in a special rule-writing formalism and then interpreted by a program written in C. [6] There are at present approximately 160 transformations in the English-German version, each with variants. They are applied in an ordered fashion. The ordering seems relatively intuitive: from substantial syntactic changes (categorial, thematic, and demotional divergence), lexical replacement and additions (structural, conflational, and lexical divergence), to surface-structure changes and finishing touches. [7]

5.2 Interaction of Lexical Transfer and Transformations

The lexical transfer and structural transformation components are computationally and componentially separated but are designed to work closely together. Lexical transfer provides actual and potential transfers as well as instructions for the transformations.

Examples: The transfer for the verb *access* in the bilingual lexicon looks like this: access ⇒ (zu : greifen) (p auf acc) (i.e. greifen + separable prefix zu. Instruction: Insert preposition auf, and set object of preposition to accusative) Output after transformations:

> *They accessed the files.* ⇒ *Sie griffen auf die Akten zu.*
> *The files were accessed.* ⇒ *Auf die Akten wurde zugegriffen.*
> *Which files do you think we expected her to access?* ⇒ *Auf welche Akten glauben Sie, daß wir erwarteten, daß sie zugriff?* (all LMT) [8]

---

[6] See [7].

[7] Hideo Watanabe ([9]:269) finds that "the sequence in which rules are called is a huge and complicated decision network. ... the transfer task is inherently a conglomeration of individual lexical rules. What is worse, these transfer rules must handle not only lexical selection but also structural changes in the target language. From these aspects, the transfer process can be said to fall into a class of problem that can not easily be controlled by the linguistic intuition of grammar writers." Transformations do indeed make up a large and complicated decision network, reflecting the complexity of natural language. But they are not an amorphous conglomeration of individual rules and the process can be controlled, although not easily.

[8] This example demonstrates the superiority of a transfer system that is based on a full syntactic analysis. "files" is recognized as the direct object of "access" in both active and passive sentences as well as in the raised construction and both words get the appropriate transfer accordingly.

Lexical transfer provides the necessary data, in this case: which preposition to insert and which case it governs. The rest is then done by transformations.

The transfers for the verb `fail` in the bilingual lexicon is as follows:

if negated and governing an infinitive ⇒ *(ver + säumen)*
else if governing an infinitive ⇒(instruction: change verb to adverb*nicht*)
else if animate object ⇒ (*ent + täuschen*)
else if object slot is filled ⇒ *fallen* (p *durch* acc) (perfective auxiliary = *sein*)
else if deverbal subject ⇒ (*fehl : schlagen*) (perfective auxiliary = *sein*)
else ⇒ *scheitern* (perfective auxiliary = *sein*)

Output after transformations:

She never failed to pay her bills ⇒ *Sie versäumte nie, ihre Rechungen zu bezahlen.*
She failed to pay her bills. ⇒ *Sie bezahlte ihre Rechnungen nicht.*
I have failed him. ⇒ *Ich habe ihn enttäuscht.*
I failed the exam. ⇒ *Ich fiel durch die Prüfung.*
The planned spacewalk failed. ⇒ *Der geplante Spaziergang im All schlug fehl.*
They have failed. ⇒ *Sie sind gescheitert.* (all LMT)

The lexical transfer component identifies conditions under which particular lexical choices are made and gives instructions for the following component. The transformations read the instructions, and transform the tree accordingly.

6 Examples of Context-Dependent Transformations

In this last section, I will demonstrate a few context-dependent transformations in the English-German LMT system. [9]

6.1 Lexically Triggered Transformations

German compound nouns. Some nouns in the dictionary contain the instruction "change postmodifying prepositional phrase into premodifying noun." To a certain degree, this transformation might be triggered by all nouns with the syntactic category `collective_type_noun` (such as *family, pair, set*; which also require feature raising), but it is also triggered by words such as *list, mode, kind, level, area, source, hierarchy, weapon, confession, trader, imbalance, speed, freedom*, etc. under certain specified conditions. This is what I mean by the "potential" that is sown in the lexicon (see introduction). Whether this potential is realized or not depends on the context in which the noun occurs.

Thus: *We enjoy freedom of speech* will be transformed into *Wir genießen Redefreiheit, We enjoy freedom of speech and movement* into *Wir genießen Rede-*

---

[9] For the specifics of the formalism of the transformation, see [7].

und Bewegungsfreiheit, We enjoy freedom of speech, movement, and emigration into *Wir genießen Rede-, Bewegungs- und Auswanderungsfreiheit,* etc. (all LMT). *We enjoy freedom of stupid speech,* however, will not realize the potential of the compound because specified modification prevents it and it will be translated as *Wir genießen Freiheit dummer Rede.*

The mechanism for this syntactic generation is as follows: Among the rules that transform the prepositional complement daughter(s) of a noun is one that checks for the lexical instruction "compound." It investigates the modifiers of the daughters and if the tests succeed, the preposition is removed, the daughter nodes are moved up in the tree and renamed, moved in front of their mother, and features are changed in order to arrive at the correct combining forms.

English non-finite object clauses. e.g. *We expect the implementation to be completed by the end of the year.* ⇒ *Wir erwarten, daß die Durchführung bis Ende des Jahres beendet ist.* (LMT)

The entry in the bilingual lexicon for *expect* contains an instruction "change infinitive to finite clause." This is an abbreviation for several steps for the transformations: identify the structure (triggered by the instruction from the lexicon), investigate the specifics, transform the tree by adding nodes, attaching the shared object/subject node to the embedded verb as its subject, and changing and unifying features. Since German does not allow raising in these circumstances, the situation becomes more complex in relative clauses and passive constructions:

This is the implementation that we expect to be completed by the end of the year. ⇒ *Dies ist die Durchführung, von der wir erwarten, daß sie bis Ende des Jahres beendet ist.* (LMT) *The implementation is expected to be completed by the end of the year.* ⇒ *Es wird erwartet, daß die Durchführung bis Ende des Jahres beendet ist.* (LMT)

The flexibility of the syntactic generation in the LMT system allows a user not only to customize their lexicon entries but also to customize the "orientation" of their syntax. A user might, for instance, state that they want to avoid passive constructions wherever possible. In this case, the transformation will test for that particular preference setting and transform the passive sentence here into the active-voice variant: *Man erwartet, daß die Durchführung bis Ende des Jahres beendet ist.* (LMT)

English *like* and its complements. The different divergences in translating English *like* into German have been a favorite among MT researchers. (See [3], [4], and others). The bilingual lexicon specifies different transfer words, depending on the type of complementation. If the transfer is *gefallen,* the lexicon specifies the type of thematic divergence and the new roles of the verb's arguments. Transformations map the object of *like* to the subject of *gefallen* and the subject of *like* to the dative object. Then a decision has to be made with respect to word order. The unmarked word order in German is subject before dative object. In the case of *gefallen,* however, object before subject seems the more appropriate discourse structure since it leaves the equivalent of the English subject in the unmarked position for given information. The following examples will show that this default decision to keep the English word order, based on considerations of discourse structure, also solves issues of anaphora and scope of negation. [10]

> *Jones likes the film but not the actors.* ⇒
>> *Jones gefällt der Film aber nicht die Schauspieler.*
>> * *Der Film aber nicht die Schauspieler gefällt/gefallen Jones.*
> *Everybody who has seen the film likes it.* ⇒
>> * *Er gefällt allen, die den Film gesehen haben.*
>> *Der Film gefällt allen, die ihn gesehen haben.*
>> (?) *Allen, die den Film gesehen haben, gefällt er.*
>> *Alle, die den Film gesehen haben, mögen ihn.*
> *I like (it) that she decided to work with us.* ⇒
>> *Es gefällt mir/Mir gefällt (es), daß sie sich entschied,*
>>> *mit uns zu arbeiten.*
>> (?) *Daß sie sich entschied, mit uns zu arbeiten, gefällt mir.*
>> * *Es, daß sie sich entschied, mit uns zu arbeiten, gefällt mir.*
> *I don't like pictures on the walls.* ⇒
>> *Mir gefallen Bilder an den Wänden nicht.*
>> ? *Mir gefallen keine Bilder an den Wänden.*
>> *Bilder an den Wänden gefallen mir nicht.*
>> * *Keine Bilder an den Wänden gefallen mir.*

The English verb *like* has numerous uses, meanings, and contexts. I want to point to one interesting aspect here that it shares with other verbs exhibiting demotional divergence compared with German.

> *They laugh at her because she likes reading novels and listening to classical music.* ⇒ *Sie lachen sie aus, weil sie gerne Romane liest und klassische Musik hört.* (LMT)

as opposed to:

> *She likes reading novels and listening to classical music.* ⇒ *Sie liest gerne Romane und hört gerne klassische Musik.* (LMT)

This non-parallelism can be explained in terms of symmetric coordination and surface structure. In English, both the shared subject and the shared matrix verb are "factored" out of the coordination. The same is true of the German surface verb-last sentence. In the second case, however, the German adverb (*gerne*) that corresponds to the English verb *like* intervenes between the verb and its direct object and can therefore not function as the "factor" anymore. Thus, it has to be repeated inside each list item in the coordination (cf. [11]).

---

[10] I list the following examples in response to Dorr's criticism of the way LMT handles the transfer of *like* to *gefallen* ([3] :255f).

6.2 Transformations Triggered by Semantic Category

[Possessive + Head Noun] construction in English. Normally, a preposed possessive in English becomes a postposed genitive or prepositional phrase in German, e.g. *The world's greatest athlete* ⇒ *Der größte Athlet der Welt*. If, however, the head noun is of the type sports or clothing and the possessive is of the type human_individual or profession, and the modifier is not in itself modified, the possessive becomes the first part of a German compound: *Women's soccer was not official until 1996.* ⇒ *Frauenfußball wurde erst 1996 offiziell.* *Children's shoes are very expensive.* ⇒ *Kinderschuhe sind sehr teuer.* (LMT translations)

The transformation identifies the modifier of a particular head noun (semantic type sports or clothing) and if the test for semantic type human_individual or profession succeeds for the possessive, eliminates the possessive node and changes a feature of the modifier to generate a combining form.

[Noun + Preposition + Noun] construction in English. As I have shown above, there is a list of English nouns that are marked in the bilingual dictionary as inviting compounding in German for this structure. For all other nouns with an [+of+noun] complement, there is the transformation NounOfNoun, which identifies several semantic categories for different processing. I will here list some transformations that make use of semantic types:

If the head is of the semantic type unit of measurement, the transformation deletes the node for the preposition: *three pounds of broccoli* ⇒ *drei Pfund Brokkoli*. (LMT) If the head is of the semantic type title, the transformation changes the preposition into *für*: *She is director of research and development.* ⇒ *Sie ist Direktorin für Forschung und Entwicklung* (LMT)

If the head is of the semantic type place_of_business or occupation/profession and the object of the daughter preposition is of the semantic type field_of_study, the transformation changes the preposition into *für*: *He is the curator of the museum of modern art.* ⇒ *Er ist der Kurator des Museums für moderne Kunst.* (LMT)

7 Conclusion

In this paper, I have described what a transfer system can achieve. LMT can handle difficult translation cases because of: (a) the rich surface and deep structure representation output from the parser, (b) the condition-based transfers in the bilingual lexicon, (c) the wealth of lexical and structural choice used in transformations, (d) the structure of the transformations and their flexibility, (e) the relative ease of rule writing, and (f) the capability of generating variation based on stylistic preference.

References

1. Arnold, D.: Parameterizing Lexical Conceptual Structure for Interlingual Machine Translation. Machine Translation 11 (1996) 217–241
2. Bateman, J.: Towards Meaning-Based Machine Translation: using abstractions from text generation for preserving meaning. Machine Translation 7 (1992) 5–40
3. Dorr, B.: Lexical Conceptual Structure and Machine Translation. Ph.D. Dissertation at MIT (1990)
4. Hutchins, W. J., Somers, H. L.: An Introduction to Machine Translation. Academic Press, London (1992)
5. McCord, M. C.: Design of LMT: A Prolog-Based Machine Translation System. Computational Linguistics 15 (1989) 33–52
6. McCord, M. C.: A New Version of the Machine Translation System LMT. Literary and Linguistic Computing 4 (1989) 218–229
7. McCord, M. C., Bernth, A.: The LMT Transformational System. These proceedings.
8. Mehl, S.: Systematic Alternatives in Lexicalization: The Case of Gerund Translation. Machine Translation 11 (1996) 185–216
9. Watanabe, H.: A Model of a Bi-Directional Transfer Mechanism Using Rule Combinations. Machine Translation 10 (1995) 269–291
10. Way, A., Crookston, I., Shelton, J.: A Typology of Translation Problems for Eurotra Translation Machines. Machine Translation 12 (1997) 323–374
11. Wesche, B.: Symmetric Coordination. Niemeyer, Tübingen (1995)

Translation with Finite-State Devices

Kevin Knight and Yaser Al-Onaizan

Information Sciences Institute
University of Southern California
Marina del Rey, CA 90292
knight@isi.edu, yaser@isi.edu

Abstract. Statistical models have recently been applied to machine translation with interesting results. Algorithms for processing these models have not received wide circulation, however. By contrast, general finite-state transduction algorithms have been applied in a variety of tasks. This paper gives a finite-state reconstruction of statistical translation and demonstrates the use of standard tools to compute statistically likely translations. Ours is the first translation algorithm for "fertility/permutation" statistical models to be described in replicable detail.

1 Introduction

Statistical machine translation (SMT) is a relatively recent approach to the longstanding problem of translating human languages by computer. The designer of an SMT system constructs a general model of how the translation process works, then lets the system acquire specific rules automatically from bilingual and monolingual text corpora (see Figure 1 and 2). These rules are usually coarse and probabilistic—for example, in a certain corpus, *bat* translates as *palo* 71% of the time, and as *murciélago* 29%. The most-established SMT system is based on word-for-word substitution (Brown *et al.*, 1993), although some experimental SMT systems employ syntactic and semantic processing (Wu, 1997; Alshawi *et al.*, 1997; Su *et al.*, 1995). An advantage of the SMT approach is that designers can improve translation accuracy by modestly changing the underlying model rather than overhauling large handcrafted resources.

Unfortunately, SMT has had little impact on machine translation in practice. One reason is that SMT accuracy is not significantly better than that obtained by handcrafting. Another reason is that few people understand SMT techniques like those presented in (Brown *et al.*, 1993), because of their highly mathematical rather than linguistic nature. These mathematical difficulties have slowed duplication and improvement of SMT results.

By contrast, finite-state methods are having a broad effect on various aspects of human language processing (Roche and Schabes, 1997). Techniques for building and composing automata are widely understood, and software toolkits are becoming available to researchers. Finite-state machines offer advantages such as speed, precision, and smooth integration with speech and character recognition.

```
        Garcia and associates .
        Garcia y asociados .

        his associates are not strong .
        sus asociados no son fuertes .

        the company has three groups .
        la empresa tiene tres grupos .

        its groups are in Europe .
        sus grupos estan en Europa .

        its clients are angry .
        sus clientes estan enfadados .

        the associates are also angry .
        los asociados tambien estan enfadados .

        the clients and the associates are enemies .
        los clientes y los asociados son enemigos .

        Carlos Garcia has three associates .
        Carlos Garcia tiene tres asociados .

        the modern groups sell strong pharmaceuticals .
        los grupos modernos venden medicinas fuertes .

        Garcia has a company also .
        Garcia tambien tiene una empresa .

        the groups do not sell zanzanine .
        los grupos no venden zanzanina .

        the small groups are not modern .
        los grupos pequenos no son modernos .
```

Fig. 1. Sample bilingual text corpus used in training SMT systems (adapted from Knight, 1997)

The aim of this paper is to give a finite-state reconstruction of SMT, with three goals in mind. One is to present a new implementation for SMT in which standard algorithms are used to compute probabilities. Another is to present the first translation algorithm for "fertility/permutation" statistical models to be described in replicable detail. Finally, we aim to make SMT techniques more accessible to the wider community.

```
Carlos has strong clients .
its small groups have strong enemies .
Carlos is angry with his enemies in Europe who also sell
        pharmaceuticals .
the pharmaceuticals are with Carlos .
Garcia and associates .
Carlos Garcia has three associates .
his associates are not strong .
Garcia has a company also .
its clients are angry .
the associates are also angry .
the clients and the associates are enemies .
the company has three groups .
its groups are in Europe .
the modern groups sell strong pharmaceuticals .
the groups do not sell zanzanine .
```

Fig. 2. Sample monolingual text corpus used in training SMT systems (adapted from Knight, 1997).

2 Word-for-Word SMT

SMT views any string of words e as a potential translation of any string f.[1] We would like to set up a probability distribution $P(e|f)$ over all pairs of strings, so that given f, we can output the e which maximizes $P(e|f)$. We break this problem down into two simpler problems by using Bayes' Rule:

$$P(e \mid f) \sim P(e) \cdot P(f \mid e)$$

The $P(e)$ factor helps our e output to be natural and grammatical, while the $P(f|e)$ factor ensures that e is normally interpreted as f, and not some other thing.

It is interesting that reasonable translations can come from highly flawed $P(e)$ and $P(f|e)$ estimates. For example, Figure 3 shows several English translations of some French sentence. Translations that pass $P(e)$ are marked with x in the first column; likewise for translations that pass $P(f|e)$.

Both models are flawed. $P(e)$ assigns too much probability to *TV appeared on Jon*, while $P(f|e)$ assigns too much to *Jon appeared in TV*. However, the translation that they both agree on is very reasonable. One goal of SMT is to find probability estimates that are "good enough" to yield acceptable translations.

A common model for $P(e)$ is the word-ngram model, which assigns values to strings based on their sub-sequence frequencies. We turn to models for $P(f|e)$ in the next section.

---

[1] We follow the (Brown *et al.*, 1993) terminology of denoting natural language strings with letters e and f, even if the languages are not English and French. We also refer to e as the source sentence and f as the target sentence, even though the top-level goal will be to translate from f to e.

	P(e)	P(f|e)
Jon appeared in TV.		x
Appeared on Jon TV.		
In Jon appeared TV.		x
Jon is happy today.	x	
Jon appeared on TV.	x	x
TV appeared on Jon.	x	
TV in Jon appeared.		
Jon was not happy.	x	

Fig. 3. English translations of a French sentence scored with models $P(e)$ and $P(f|e)$

Once the general models are in place, we need a training algorithm to fix their parameters, and a "decoding" algorithm for finding the e that maximizes the value of the formula above. We will discuss decoding in our finite-state reconstruction.

3 Translation Models

This section summarizes translation Models 1-3 as presented in (Brown *et al.*, 1993). Each model specifies how to compute a value for any $P(f|e)$ by consulting tables of probabilities. In all three models, a source sentence may produce the same target sentence in several different ways—these ways are covered by different *alignments*. An alignment is a set of connections between source words and target words, normally such that each target word is connected to exactly one source word. We assume that an invisible NULL word exists at the beginning of each source sentence to pick up any "spurious" target words. Here is an alignment between *an old house* and *una casa vieja*:

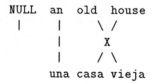

And here is another, less probable alignment:

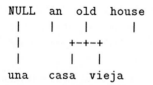

Supposing that e contains l words and f contains m words, there are $(l+1)^m$ conceivable alignments. We refer to an alignment as a, and can write it as a series of values a_j $(j = 1, 2, \ldots m)$, each of which records the source language position that target word j connects to. The job of computing $P(f|e)$ thus becomes:

$$P(f \mid e) = \sum_a P(f, a \mid e)$$

where a ranges over all the conceivable alignments for the pair of sentences. Each model defines the probability of an alignment as a function of the connections it contains, and each does so in a different way.

3.1 Model 1

The first model is based on the following hypothetical translation process: given a source sentence of length l, pick a desired target sentence length m; then, for each target position $j = 1 \ldots m$ choose a connection to source position a_j; and for each target position $j = 1 \ldots m$ choose a target word f_j.

Connections are chosen from the uniform distribution, i.e., a_j may take on any value from 0 to l with equal probability. Word choices are made according to a probabilistic table

$t(f|e)$ = probability that word e gets translated as f

We can write

$$P(f, a \mid e) = c \prod_{j=1}^{m} t(f_j \mid e_{a_j})$$

where alignment a is a series of values a_j $(j = 1 \ldots m)$, and c relates to the positional connections and to choice of m itself.

To get a formula for computing $P(f|e)$, we sum over all possible alignments a, as shown above.

Notice that in this hypothetical process there is no notion of consuming the source sentence word by word and producing the target sentence. Instead, all source words must remain available for consultation. Also notice the process chooses a number m which subsequent steps must remember and adhere to. These properties make Model 1 unattractive for finite-state modeling.

3.2 Model 2

This model is the same as Model 1 except that the value of an a_j is not chosen uniformly. It depends on j, as specified in another probabilistic table:

$a(i \mid j, l, m)$ = alignment probability of position j

This allows the model to express a preference that words at the beginning of a target sentence tend to get connected to words at the beginning (or end) of a source sentence. Here

$$P(f, a \mid e) = c \prod_{j=1}^{m} t(f_j \mid e_{a_j}) \prod_{j=1}^{m} a(a_j \mid j, l, m)$$

3.3   Model 3

Model 3 is based on a very different hypothetical translation process. For each e_i, we choose a *fertility* ϕ_i that dictates how many target words will connect to it. For each $i = 0, 1, \ldots l$ and each $k = 1, 2, \ldots \phi_i$, we then choose a target word τ_{ik}. Finally, we permute all these words.

Fertilities for $e_1 \ldots e_l$ are prescribed by the probabilistic table

$n(\phi \mid e) = $ fertility of word e

The fertility of the NULL word (e_0) depends on the length of the target sentence, because longer sentences have more spurious words. Model 3 introduces a single probability

$p_1 = $ NULL word parameter

and its opposite $p_0 = 1 - p_1$. A fertility of ϕ_0 is selected with probability

$$\binom{m'}{\phi_0} p_0^{m' - \phi_0} p_1^{\phi_0}$$

$m' = \sum_{i=1}^{l} \phi_i$ is used as an approximate target-sentence length, because m itself is unknown until we choose ϕ_0. Actual target words τ_{ik} are chosen from table $t(f|e)$ as in Model 1.

The final permutation assigns a value π_{ik} (from 1 to m) to each target word. Model 3 reverses the position-mapping probabilities from Model 2, so that π_{ik} ($i > 0$) are assigned according to the table

$d(\pi_{ik} \mid i, l, m) = $ distortion of position i

Words generated from NULL ($i = 0$) are free to roam unbound by the d-table. Of the ϕ_0 spots left vacant in $\pi_i k$, there are $\phi_0!$ ways to arrange the NULL-generated words. A particular selection contributes an additional $1/\phi_0!$ factor to the d probabilities.

The target sentence has $f_{\pi_{ik}} = \tau_{ik}$ for each $i = 0, 1, \ldots l$ and each $k = 1, 2, \ldots \phi_i$.

For any source sentence, a choice of fertilities, translations, and permutation pick out both a target sentence and an alignment. For example, if $e = $ *an old house* and we choose $\phi_0 = 0$, $\phi_1 = 1$, $\phi_2 = 1$, $\phi_3 = 1$, $\tau_{11} = $ *una*, $\tau_{21} = $ *vieja*, $\tau_{31} = $ *casa*, $\pi_{11} = 1$, $\pi_{21} = 3$, $\pi_{31} = 2$, then we obtain the first of the two alignments shown in Section 3.

Several sets of choices may correspond to the same alignment. For example, the alignment

seems to require

$$\tau_{11} = cinturon, \tau_{12} = de, \tau_{13} = seguridad$$
$$\pi_{11} = 1, \pi_{12} = 2, \pi_{13} = 3$$

but

$$\tau_{11} = de, \tau_{12} = cinturon, \tau_{13} = seguridad$$
$$\pi_{11} = 2, \pi_{12} = 1, \pi_{13} = 3$$

produces the same thing.

(Brown *et al.*, 1993) note that the permutation process can generate non-strings—if every π_{ik} is chosen to be 5, then all target words will be piled up in position 5. Model 3 is therefore said to be *deficient*.

All this leads to:

$$P(f, a \mid e) = \binom{m - \phi_0}{\phi_0} p_0^{\,m-2\phi_0} p_1^{\,\phi_0} \cdot$$

$$\prod_{i=1}^{l} n(\phi_i \mid e_i) \prod_{i=0}^{l} \phi_i! \cdot$$

$$\prod_{j=1}^{m} t(f_j \mid e_{a_j}) \cdot$$

$$\frac{1}{\phi_0!} \cdot \prod_{j:a_j \neq 0} d(j \mid a_j, l, m)$$

This formula, somewhat daunting at first, is explained by the finite-state reconstruction of Section 6. There we achieve the same values for $P(f, a|e)$ without carrying out any combinations or factorials, and we compute $P(f|e)$ without explicit reference to alignments at all.

4 Alternative Models

We will look at two alternatives to Model 3 not documented in (Brown *et al.*, 1993). One replaces the $d(\pi_{ik}|i, l, m)$ table by a simpler $d(\pi_{ik}|i)$ table. The other disposes of distortion probabilities altogether. Each of the $m!$ possible permutations is deemed equally likely (probability $= 1/m!$), and

$$P(f, a \mid e) = \binom{m - \phi_0}{\phi_0} p_0^{\,m-2\phi_0} p_1^{\,\phi_0} \cdot$$

$$\prod_{i=1}^{l} n(\phi_i \mid e_i) \prod_{i=0}^{l} \phi_i! \cdot$$

$$\prod_{j=1}^{m} t(f_j \mid e_{a_j}) \cdot$$

$$\frac{1}{m!}$$

This last version of Model 3 is not deficient—it does not allow target words to be stacked on top of one another. Of course, it does not capture word-order effects in translation, leaving source language word order up to the language model $P(e)$.

5 Finite-State Devices

A weighted finite-state transducer is one way of implementing a probability distribution over pairs of strings. It is a state-transition diagram whose arcs have labels of the form $x{:}y/w$, where x is an input word, y is an output word, and w is a numerical weight. Either x or y may be the empty token ϵ.

To get $P(f|e)$, we find a path whose input-word sequence matches e and whose output-word sequence matches f, then multiply the weights of the arcs along that path. Actually, we must find *all* such matching paths and sum their contributions—there may be more than one way to produce f from e, just as there is more than one way to throw a seven with two dice. To ensure compliance with the laws of probability, we require that all arcs leaving state s with input word x have w's that sum to one.

Transducers can be composed algorithmically (Pereira and Riley, 1997). If one transducer implements $P(x|y)$ and another implements $P(y|z)$, then we can compute a third transducer implementing $P(x|z)$. This allows a cascade of small transducers to simulate a big one.

If we supply an input string to a transducer, we get a network of all possible outputs, with arc-probabilities. Likewise, if we supply an output string, we get all possible inputs. More generally, we can supply a network of possible outputs and get a network of possible inputs.

Finding a most-likely input or output sequence (also known as "decoding") is a kind of shortest-path graph problem.

6 Finite-State SMT

We will now effect the Model 3 translation process using finite-state devices. Rather than constructing one giant transducer, we will construct a cascade of simple transducers that ultimately leads us from a source sentence to a target sentence.

Figure 4 shows the plan. There are four transducers in the translation model. If we insert *Mary did not slap the green witch* at the top of the cascade, many Spanish sentences could come out the bottom, each with probability $P(f|e)$. One is shown here. Likewise, if we insert *Mary no daba bofetada a la bruja verde* at the bottom, many English sentences could come out the top, each with its own $P(f|e)$.

Model 3 does not generate very good target sentences, even when the permutation process is moderated by the distortion table. So in practice, we will use the cascade only in these ways:

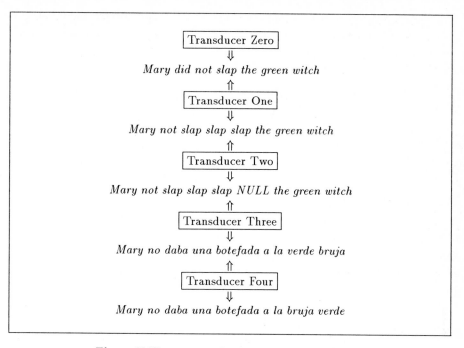

Fig. 4. SMT as a cascade of finite-state transducers.

Fig. 5. One alignment for a pair of sentences.

- For a given pair (e, f), estimate $P(f|e)$.
- For a given target sentence f, find the most likely source sentence $\hat{e}$:

$$\hat{e} = \frac{\text{argmax}}{e} P(e) \cdot P(f \mid e)$$

For the latter task, we add a source language model to the top of the cascade.

6.1 Transducer Zero

This transducer—actually an acceptor—assigns a probability to any source sentence. Although many acceptors are possible, we will assume a word-trigram model with *deleted interpolation* smoothing (Jelinek and Mercer, 1980). Here is a piece of this acceptor:

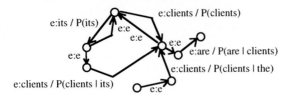

6.2 Transducer One

This transducer determines fertilities for words on its input. If the fertility of an input word is zero, the word is dropped in the output (e.g., *did*). If the fertility is one, it is copied. Otherwise, the word is duplicated, triplicated, etc. Here is a piece of this transducer:

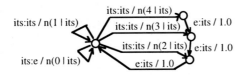

We might say this transducer converts English to *Enggglis*. The connection between English and Enggglis sentences is usually clear, although in an occasional pair like *I had had it* and *I had had had it*, it is not obvious what fertilities were employed.

6.3 Transducer Two

This transducer sprinkles NULL words throughout an Enggglis string. More precisely, before copying each input word to the output, it emits NULL with probability p_1. Here is a piece:

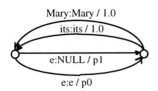

6.4 Transducer Three

Here, we simply substitute target words for source words, one-for-one, according to $t(f|e)$:

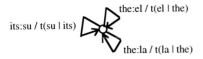

the:el / t(el | the)

its:su / t(su | its)

the:la / t(la | the)

We can call the output *Spanglish*, because it is Spanish written with English word order.

6.5 Transducer Four

The final task is to permute a Spanglish sentence into a Spanish one. Here we will assume that all permutations are equally likely, as in Section 4. Unfortunately, no practical finite-state transducer can do this work. But because we are at the end of the road, we can do this with a non-finite-state algorithm. Given a particular Spanish sentence, we build a finite-state acceptor that includes all permutations of it. Each permutation is a potential Spanglish antecendent. Of particular interest are the ones for which simple word substitution yields good English.

Here is a permutation acceptor for *la casa vieja*:

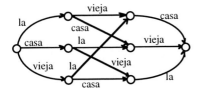

Permutation acceptors have 2^m states.

6.6 Computation of P(f, a | e)

Next, we determine the probability that a particular target sentence will be generated from a particular source sentence. We first confine ourselves to transductions that correspond to a single alignment a. Recall that the same alignment may be produced from different choices of word translations (τ) and permutations (π).

If we take a to be the alignment shown in Figure 5, then there are 48 ways to produce *Mary no daba una bofetada a la bruja verde* from *Mary did not slap the green witch*. To see this, first consider that *slap* could translate to *bofetada daba no* in Spanish, and get permuted back to *no daba bofetada*. There are 6 (3!) such ways this could happen. Also consider that NULL could appear in any of eight positions, produce the Spanish word *a*, then get permuted back into the fifth position in the Spanish output. Each of the 48 sequences has the same probability, so that:

$$P(f, a \mid e) = 48 \cdot$$

$$\prod_{i=1}^{7} n(\phi_i \mid e_i) \cdot$$

$$p_0{}^7 p_1{}^1 \cdot$$

$$\prod_{j=1}^{9} t(f_j \mid e_{a_j}) \cdot$$

$$\frac{1}{9!}$$

This is the same value we get from the $P(f, a|e)$ in Section 4:

$$P(f, a \mid e) = \binom{9-1}{1} p_0{}^7 p_1{}^1 \cdot$$

$$\prod_{i=1}^{7} n(\phi_i \mid e_i) \prod_{i=0}^{7} \phi_i! \cdot$$

$$\prod_{j=1}^{9} t(f_j \mid e_{a_j}) \cdot$$

$$\frac{1}{9!}$$

because $\phi_4 = 3$. Tracing the finite-state composition gives an intuitive picture of the factorials and combinations in the $P(f, a|e)$ formula.

6.7 Computation of P(f | e)

To compute $P(f|e)$ using the finite-state cascade, we create two acceptors, one for e (single-path), and one for f (permutational), add them to the beginning and end of the cascade (omitting Transducer Zero), then compose all six automata. The resulting transducer will contain a path for each way of producing f from e. To get $P(f|e)$, we sum the weights of all these paths. This computation makes no reference to alignments, but computes the same value as summing $P(f, a|e)$ over all possible alignments a.

7 Translation Algorithm

In this section, we show how sample translations are produced by the finite-state cascade. We have trained a translation Model 3 on the bilingual corpus shown in Figure 1, and a trigram language model on the monolingual corpus in Figure 2. We store the training results as finite-state automata.[2]

Computing the most-likely source language translation for f is similar to computing $P(f|e)$. We don't know e, but we can constrain it using a source language model. We again compose all six automata, but instead of summing the path weights, we extract the k highest-probability paths. This gives us a k-best list of possible translations.

One of our aims in giving this Model 3 translation algorithm is to fill a gap in the translation algorithm ("decoding") literature. Unfortunately, (Brown *et al.*, 1993) never published a replicable fertility/distortion translation algorithm, and subsequent papers have focussed on simpler Model 2 variants (Wang and Waibel, 1997), syntactic models (Wu, 1996), and cases without word-order variation (Tillmann *et al.*, 1997).

We now translate some novel sentences not seen in training.

ORIGINAL:
la empresa tiene enemigos fuertes en Europa .

AUTOMATIC TRANSLATIONS:
the company has strong enemies in Europe . 8e-08
the company has strong enemies in Europe . 2e-08
the company has strong enemies in Europe . 1e-08
the company has strong enemies in Europe . 8e-09
the in Europe company has strong enemies . 5e-09
the company has strong enemies in Europe . 5e-09
the company has strong enemies in Europe . 4e-09
the enemies in Europe company has strong . 4e-09

Notice that the k-best list includes repetitions. This is because we search for the best paths rather than the best sequences. Our smoothed language model

---

[2] **Implementation note.** We follow (Brown *et al.*, 1993) in Viterbi-style training, as the EM algorithm is too expensive even for this small corpus. We bootstrap initial parameters using Models 1 and 2. Our initial Model 3 training employs several simplifications: (1) we initialize fertilities for e_i based on the lengths of the sentence pairs in which it occurs, without consulting the t or a tables, (2) we do not use NULL, (3) we only use the immediate alignment neighborhood around the Model 2 Viterbi alignment (no pegging), (4) our parameters are stored in two-level hash tables in LISP.

On the other hand, our finite-state tools are reasonably complete. Our C++ implementation includes composition of weighted transducers and acceptors (Pereira and Riley, 1997) with full handling of ϵ-transitions. It includes forward-backward learning, which we use here to train and smooth our trigram language model. It also includes a k-best path extractor that follows the recently discovered $O(m + n \log n + kn)$ algorithm of (Eppstein, 1994). This toolkit has been used for several MT-related tasks and is available for research purposes.

offers several paths that produce the same e, and we have already seen the multiplicity of paths relating a particular pair e and f. We typically ask for a large k and compress the result by summing identical sequence weights and resorting.

We can study the translation process more closely by inspecting the intermediate structures that get produced as our target sentence makes its way up the cascade. Our 8-word sentence first becomes a 256-state/1024-arc/40320-path permutation acceptor. Just before composition with the source language model, there are over 300 million English sentences (paths), stored in a 1537-state/3586-arc acceptor. The language model assigns low probability to most of these sentences, but does not actually filter any of them out.

Here are two more translations:

```
ORIGINAL:
sus grupos pequenos no venden medicinas .

AUTOMATIC TRANSLATIONS:
its small groups do not sell pharmaceuticals .
its small groups sell pharmaceuticals not .
its small groups sell not pharmaceuticals .
its small groups do not sell pharmaceuticals .
its small groups do not sell pharmaceuticals .
its not small groups sell pharmaceuticals .
its small groups sell pharmaceuticals do not .
its small groups sell pharmaceuticals not .
```

The composition automatically inserts the zero-fertility word *do* in every position of every permutation, and this proves useful to the source language model.

```
ORIGINAL:
los asociados estan enfadados con Carlos .

AUTOMATIC TRANSLATIONS:
the associates are angry with Carlos .
the associates are angry with Carlos .
the associates are with Carlos angry .
the Carlos associates are also angry .
Carlos the associates are also angry .
the Carlos Garcia associates are angry .
the Carlos has associates are angry .
the Carlos is associates are angry .
```

In this translation, the Spanish word *con* is unknown, never seen in training data. This would normally block the finite-state composition, but we have augmented our word-translation transducer to allow *any* English word to produce *con* (at low probability). The source language model uses context to select the translation *with*.

8   Better Finite-State Models

The previous section did not employ distortion probabilities. We can implement a $d(j|i)$ table by adding more transducers to the cascade. Source words are followed by source position indicators (like *spos-6*) that are carried along during the fertility and translation stages. Later, they are probabilistically converted to target position indicators (like *tpos-5*). Permutation acceptors must include target positions after every word, to match the output of the $d(j|i)$ transducer.

We can also address some problems with Model 3. For example, a word's different fertilities are not tied to its different translations. When used as a noun, *slap* has a fertility of only one; and it never translates to *daba*, only to *botefada*. While this information is not available from the probability tables, it is available from the bank of most-probable alignments. We could revise our fertility transducer to replace *slap* with either *slap-1* or *slap-3* (instead of triplicating the word). Then our word translation device would convert *slap-3* into a sequence of three target words, and *slap-1* would simply go to *botefada*.

Model 3 is also loose about phrasal translation. If *una*, *daba*, and *botefada* are spread widely within a sentence, *slap* still becomes a candidate source word. It may be clear from inspecting the alignments, however that these three words are always produced adjacent to one another. In that case, our word translation device could produce a token like *daba_una_bofetada*. This would incidentally account for order within a phrase—Model 3 does not distinguish between orderings like *modern post office* and *post modern office*. We must add information to the permutation acceptor, e.g., by adding arcs for known phrases:

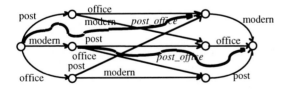

Tokens like *post_office* and *daba_una_bofetada* would then incur single rather than multiple distortion costs. This last consideration motivates Models 4 and 5 of (Brown *et al.*, 1993).

9   Discussion

We have presented a reconstruction of statistical machine translation in terms of cascaded finite-state automata, and we have shown how these automata can be used in translating sentences and calculating conditional probabilities. We use general composition and decoding algorithms that are also useful in a wide range of other applications.

There are several interesting questions. First, will the finite-state composition scale up to large vocabularies and sentence lengths? (Brown *et al.*, 1993) employ an undocumented suboptimal search and report search errors, so scale is clearly a problem. On the other hand, finite-state cascades have been shown to greatly reduce memory requirements for speech recognition, and there now appear to be pruning and lazy composition methods that find approximate best paths in the face of overwhelming possibilities. It is interesting to consider the development of general methods versus MT-specific solutions. Of course, if MT-specific knowledge could reduce the size of the permutation acceptors, that would help greatly.

Another question is: can finite-state methods be used in model training as well as decoding? Forward-backward training is problematic for a couple of reasons. One is the existence of many local minima. A second is the fact that training consists of input sequences paired with output permutation acceptors (not sequences).

However, it may be practical to use finite-state cascades to compute $P(f|e)$ during training iterations. Further, it may be possible to use k-best lists to locate a subset of alignments for which to collect parameter counts at each iteration. This could call into question the idea of summing over alignments—why not sum over paths?

Of course, alignments are useful for other things (such as sense-tagging), but when transducer composition employs a judicious naming scheme for result-states, alignments are recoverable from paths.

Finally, it is interesting to consider the probabilistic integration of speech and character-recognition—or of any other process that presents ambiguity, such as part-of-speech tagging, sense tagging, morphological analysis, accent restoration, and spelling correction.

References

H. Alshawi, A. Buchsbaum, and F. Xia. 1997. A comparison of head transducers and transfer for a limited domain translation applications. In *Proc. ACL*.

P. F. Brown, S. A. Della-Pietra, V. J. Della-Pietra, and R. L. Mercer. 1993. The mathematics of statistical machine translation: Parameter estimation. *Computational Linguistics*, 19(2).

D. Eppstein. 1994. Finding the k shortest paths. In *Proc. 35th FOCS*.

F. Jelinek and R. L. Mercer. 1980. Interpolated estimation of Markov source parameters from sparse data. In *Pattern Recognition in Practice*. North-Holland, Amsterdam.

K. Knight. 1997. Automating knowledge acquisition for machine translation. *AI Magazine*, 18(4).

F. Pereira and M. Riley. 1997. Speech recognition by composition of weighted finite automata. In E. Roche and Y. Schabes, editors, *Finite-State Language Processing*. MIT Press.

E. Roche and Y. Schabes, editors. 1997. *Finite-State Language Processing*. MIT Press.

K.-Y. Su, J.-S. Chang, and Y.-L. U. Hsu. 1995. A corpus-based two-way design for parameterized MT systems: Rationale, architecture and training issues. In *Proc. TMI*.

C. Tillmann, S. Vogel, H. Ney, and A. Zubiaga. 1997. A DP-based search using monotone alignments in statistical translation. In *Proc. ACL*.

Y. Wang and A. Waibel. 1997. Decoding algorithm in statistical machine translation. In *Proc. ACL*.

D. Wu. 1996. A polynomial-time algorithm for statistical machine translation. In *Proc. ACL*.

D. Wu. 1997. Stochastic inversion transduction grammars and bilingual parsing of parallel corpora. *Computational Linguistics*, 23(3).

Lexical Selection for Cross-Language Applications: Combining LCS with WordNet

Bonnie Dorr and Maria Katsova

UMIACS
University of Maryland
College Park, Md 20742
phone: +1 (301) 405-6768
fax: +1 (301) 314-9658
{dorr,katsova}@umiacs.umd.edu
WWW home page: http://umiacs.umd.edu/labs/CLIP

Abstract. This paper describes experiments for testing the power of large-scale resources for lexical selection in machine translation (MT) and cross-language information retrieval (CLIR). We adopt the view that verbs with similar argument structure share certain meaning components, but that those meaning components are more relevant to argument realization than to idiosyncratic verb meaning. We verify this by demonstrating that verbs with similar argument structure as encoded in Lexical Conceptual Structure (LCS) are rarely synonymous in WordNet. We then use the results of this work to guide our implementation of an algorithm for cross-language selection of lexical items, exploiting the strengths of each resource: LCS for semantic structure and WordNet for semantic content. We use the Parka Knowledge-Based System to encode LCS representations and WordNet synonym sets and we implement our lexical-selection algorithm as Parka-based queries into a knowledge base containing both information types.

1 Introduction

This paper describes experiments for testing the power of large-scale resources for lexical selection in machine translation (MT) and cross-language information retrieval (CLIR). We adopt the view that verbs with similar argument structure share certain meaning components [9], but that those meaning components are more relevant to argument realization than to idiosyncratic verb meaning. This distinction mirrors the difference between *semantic structure*, which contributes to structural positioning of arguments, and *semantic content*, which is specific to individual verb meaning.[1]

First, we verify the hypothesis that these two meaning types are distinct by demonstrating that verbs with similar argument structure as encoded in Lexical Conceptual Structure (LCS) [5, 6, 7] are rarely synonymous in WordNet [11, 12, 13]. We then use the results of this work to guide our implementation of

---

[1] See [10] for more details about the structure/content dichotomy.

an algorithm for cross-language selection of lexical items, exploiting the strengths of each resource: LCS for semantic structure and WordNet for semantic content.

We use the Parka Knowledge-Based System [8, 17] to encode LCS representations and WordNet synonym sets (synsets).[2] Our lexical-selection algorithm is based on Parka-based queries into a knowledge base containing both information types. An input source-language sentence is represented as a LCS; target-language words are then retrieved using LCS-based graph-matching coupled with further refinement by WordNet links.

The advantage of this approach is that it provides a framework for implementing large-scale *event-based* selection using both information types. Event-based selection refers to retrieval on queries that are verb-based clauses (such as 'The soldiers *attacked* the city') or deverbal noun phrases (such as 'The soldier's *attack* on the city'). The benefit to using both LCS and WordNet in event-based retrieval is that the syntactic properties of a word (e.g., that *attack* is a verb in the clause and a noun in the deverbal phrase) are suppressed while more relevant properties are brought into focus: (1) argument structure—that 'soldier' and 'city' are the primary components of the *attack* event; and (2) meaning—that *attack* is closer in meaning to *assault* than to *criticize*. We view the combination of WordNet and LCS as a first step toward evaluating the utility of these two resources for Cross-Language Information Retrieval (CLIR), a large-scale information search task in which the query may be posed in a natural language that is different from that used in the documents [3, 4, 14, 15].

The next section describes our initial experimentation to validate that verbs with similar argument structure are rarely synonymous. Section 3 describes the implementation of a lexical-selection algorithm that exploits this result. Section 4 discusses the impact of the LCS-WordNet combination on the lexical-selection task and describes our future directions.

2 Mono-Lingual and Cross-Lingual Validation of Structure/Content Distinction

We have conducted experiments to verify the hypothesis that verbs with similar argument structure as encoded in Lexical Conceptual Structure (LCS) are rarely synonymous in WordNet. Our experiments were run first mono-lingually and then cross-lingually. An important by-product of these experiments is that, by inducing a reduction in ambiguity for the mono-lingual case, we can achieve more precise results in the cross-lingual case. The idea is that disambiguation of a source-language term reduces the potential "fan-out" in the target language, thus achieving precision close to that of the mono-lingual case (as in traditional single-language IR techniques where no linguistic techniques are used).

We ran experiments with three verbs: *sap*, *walk*, and *close*. We constructed sentences and corresponding input LCSs for each case:

---

[2] Parka KB provides a very convenient mechanism for studying structural properties of the verbs and to implement fast searching techniques. It also provides a foundation for handling large-scale cross-language resources.

(1) (i) He sapped my strength
```
[CAUSE
  ([Thing HE],
   [GO Ident
      ([Thing STRENGTH],
       [TOWARD Ident
          ([Thing STRENGTH],
           [AT Ident
              ([Thing STRENGTH], [Property SAPPED])])])])]
```
(ii) Florinda walked across the street
```
[GO Loc
   ([Thing FLORINDA],
    [TOWARD Loc
       ([Thing FLORINDA],
        [ACROSS Loc ([Thing FLORINDA], [Thing STREET])])],
    [Manner WALKINGLY])]
```
(iii) He closed the door
```
[CAUSE
  ([Thing HE],
   [GO Ident
      ([Thing DOOR],
       [TOWARD Ident
          ([Thing DOOR],
           [AT Ident
              ([Thing DOOR], [Property CLOSED])])])])]
```

In each of these cases, the semantic structure is encoded in the argument structure itself, e.g., the primitive GO takes as its two arguments a Thing (DOOR) and a Path (TOWARD). The semantic content is encoded as a LCS constant, respectively: SAPPED, WALKINGLY, and CLOSED.

Our experiments were run first on an English database of 54,000 LCS entries that includes verbs, nouns, adjectives, and prepositions. Using a relaxed version of the graph-matching technique described in [3, 4], we ignored constant positions and extracted only those LCSs that structurally matched the input LCS. Consider the verb *sap*. Out of 54,000 LCSs, only 149 match the LCS in (1i). These include verbs like *clean, clear, drain, empty*, etc. We then checked the synonymy relation in WordNet for these graph-matched verbs. The verb *sap*, as used in the LCS above, corresponds to synset 00657546.[3] The only verbs among the 149 graph-matched verbs in this synset are *sap* itself and *drain*. Thus, for this case, we found that semantic-structure/semantic-content overlap occurred in only 2 out of the 149 cases (including *sap* itself).

The full set of results for *sap*, *walk*, and *close* are given in Table 1. Note

---

[3] The synset numbers are taken from Version 1.5 of WordNet, available at http://www.cogsci.princeton.edu/~wn. Synset numbers were assigned to LCS templates by hand: each template was human-annotated with as many WordNet synsets as were applicable. (See [1] for more details.)

Verb	Synset(s)	Graph-Matched	Same Synset
sap	00657546	149: clean, clear, drain, empty, erase, reduce,...	2: drain, sap
walk	01086212 01089891 01116106 01086031	272: amble, approach, creep, go, leave, saunter,...	1: walk
close	00772512 00773754	918: collapse, fold, shut, smooth, split,...	2: close, shut

Table 1. Mono-Lingual Generation of Matching Terms

that in each case, the number of graph-matched possibilities is radically reduced (918 down to 2 in the case of *close*), thus supporting our hypothesis that the overlap between semantic structure and semantic content is rare. The two cases where there is more than one overlapping verb (*drain* overlaps with *sap* and *shut* overlaps with *close*) are true cases of syntactic and semantic interchangeability with respect to their usage in the examples given in (1).

In our cross-lingual experiment, we ran the same algorithm on the three LCSs above to produce Spanish target-language equivalents. Our Spanish LCS lexicon has approximately 40,000 LCSs and, as in English, each entry human-annotated with as many WordNet synsets as were applicable.[4] The results in Table 2 show that we were able to restrict the fan-out from Spanish to English words at least as well as in the mono-lingual (English-to-English) case.

We undertook additional experimentation with WordNet to determine if it would be reasonable to produce more target-language candidates, e.g., one link away (hypernymy) from each verb's synset. We found that the candidate set did not grow drastically: one additional term for *sap* (*reducir* = reduce) and one additional term for *close* (*tornar* = change). Further investigation would be required to determine the usefulness of terms generated using other types of links (e.g., hyponymy, troponymy) as well as different distances from the matched target-language candidate. Measures of success would presumably vary on the application: MT would, perhaps, require more refined matching than CLIR. In the next section, we will examine cases where the one-link (hypernym) approach is used to select target-language terms in cases where no synsets match those of the source-language term.

---

[4] Unlike the English, the Spanish LCS lexicon includes only verbs and nouns (which is the reason for the size discrepancy), but this difference is inconsequential for the event-based experiments reported here. See [2] for more details regarding the annotation of Spanish verbs with WordNet synsets.

Verb	Synset(s)	Graph-Matched	Same Synset
sap	00657546	358: agotar, desaguar, escurrir, evacuar, reducir, vaciar, zapar,...	1: escurrir
walk	01086212 01089891 01116106 01086031	136: andar, caminar, correr, ir, pasear,...	2: andar,caminar
close	00772512 00773754	1554: alterar, cerrar, clausurar, concluir, convertir, disminuir, separar, tapar, virar,...	4: cerrar, clausurar, concluir, tapar

Table 2. Cross-Lingual Generation of Matching Terms

3 Implementation of Lexical Selection Algorithm

Having tested the utility of accessing semantic content independently from semantic structure, we have implemented an algorithm for cross-language selection of lexical items, exploiting the strengths of each resource: LCS for semantic structure and WordNet for semantic content. We use the Parka Knowledge-Based System to encode LCS representations and WordNet synonym sets and we implement our lexical-selection algorithm as Parka-based queries into a knowledge base containing both information types.

Parka is a frame-based knowledge representation that is intended to provide extremely fast inferences and accommodate very large knowledge bases (KBs), on the order of millions of frames. Frames are used to specify categories, instances, and predicates to Parka. Predicates represent relations among entities. The relations being used in our algorithm are binary predicates. We created two tools, one for converting files with LCSs into Parka-based assertions and one for updating the KB (adding new LCSs). We have built Parka KBs for the entire English and Spanish lexicons. We also have transferred all the definitions from the English and Spanish WordNets into Parka-WNet KB.

The basic procedure on the graph-matching (structural) level is the following: Given a composed LCS for a source-language sentence, extract all possible LCSs whose structure covers that of the composed LCS except for the constant position. We implement this procedure by processing the query on each tree level of an LCS representation. Queries are designed to capture only the structural properties of a LCS.

Consider example (1ii) given earlier. The LCS entry for the word *walk* is shown here:[5]

---

[5] The [AT] node is a generic positional primitive that matches any number of other positional primitives such as ACROSS, OVER, etc.

(2) [GO Loc
        ([Thing X],
        [TOWARD Loc ([Thing X], [[AT] Loc ([Thing X], [Thing Y])])],
        [Manner WALKINGLY])]

At the highest level, the GO Loc node, there are 1059 matching LCSs in the lexicon. For example, the verb *swim* shares this node with *walk*. Moving to the next node level, there are 4399 matches (because all possible matches on two levels are included for each LCS candidate), but the number of possible words has decreased. In general, the algorithm processes the effective query which is optimally constructed for each LCS tree. It extracts all the structural matches of the source LCS on all the tree levels.[6] Finally, the graph-matching procedure extracts the matching target-language words. In the case of *walk*, there are 272 candidates as was indicated in earlier in Table 1.

In order to further reduce this set, we use WordNet as the basis of a more refined lexical selection. For example, suppose we are trying to eliminate *correr* (= *run*) as a target-language candidate. We use WordNet to check for similarity between *runningly* and *walkingly* (or, more precisely, the lexemes themselves: *run* and *walk*). Because *run* is not in any of the synsets containing *walk*, the verb *correr* is ruled out. By contrast, the verbs *andar* and *caminar* are in synsets that include *walk* (both occur in 01086212 and 01086031), so these two verbs are selected as a match.

In addition to cases where target-language terms occur in the appropriate synset(s), we also examined cases where no synsets match those of the source-language term. There are two such cases, one in which there is a LCS that matches exactly (both in structure and in content) and one in which there is no LCS that matches exactly (i.e., the structure matches, but not the content). Thus, including the case where there are matching synsets, there are three cases to consider:

1. If the LCS matches exactly and there are shared synsets, return matching words with shared synsets. For example return *escurrir* for *sap*; *andar, caminar* for *walk*; and *cerrar, clausurar, concluir, tapar* for *close*.
2. If the LCS matches exactly and there are no shared synsets, return words that match exactly. For example, return *fortalecer, fortalecerse*, and *confirmar* for *strengthen*.
3. If the LCS does not match in content, return one-link hypernyms of structurally matching words. For example, return *reír* and *reírse* for *giggle*.

In the last case above, we determine the closeness of semantic content using an information-content metric approach (cf., [16]), i.e. selecting those words with the shortest (weighted) distance in WordNet between the mismatched LCS constant

---

[6] Theoretically, Parka provides utilities to process N-level queries, where N is the depth of the LCS tree. However, due to memory limitations, large-scale application of our algorithm requires that we restrict the number of levels. Thus, at each recursive tree level, we limit our processing to one- or two-level queries.

and the corresponding lexemes. As a first approximation to this, we used the one-link (hypernym) approach to select target-language terms.[7]

Consider the following examples corresponding to the last two cases above:

(3) She strengthened her muscles

```
[CAUSE
  ([Thing SHE],
   [GO Ident
     ([Thing MUSCLE],
      [TOWARD Ident
        ([Thing MUSCLE],
         [AT Ident ([Thing MUSCLE], [Property STRENGTHENED])])])])]
```

(4) Mary giggled at the dog

```
[CAUSE
  ([Thing DOG],
   [GO Perc
     ([Thing MARY],
      [TOWARD Perc
        ([Thing MARY],
         [AT Perc ([Thing MARY], [Thing DOG])])])],
   [Manner GIGGLINGLY])]
```

There are 1554 LCSs in the Spanish lexicon that match the composed LCS structurally in (3). However, none of these correspond to words that share the synsets (00131909 and 00132257) associated with *strengthen* in the composed LCS. Thus, we select only those words whose lexical entry matches the composed LCS exactly, both in structure and in content (i.e., including the constant **STRENGTHENED**). The three words that match exactly are *confirmar* (= confirm), *fortalecer* (= fortify), and *fortalecerse* (= fortify oneself).

In the case of (4), there are 36 LCSs in the Spanish lexicon that match the composed LCS in structure (but not in content). Some examples are: *bufar* (= snort), *cacarear* (= cackle), *gritar* (= howl), *jadear* (= gasp), *reír* (= laugh), *reírse* (= laugh over), and *sonreír* (= smile). However, only *reír* and *reírse* correspond to words that share the synset (00020446) which is a hypernym (one link away) of the set associated with *giggle* in the composed LCS; thus, these two words are selected.

A summary of the last two cases is shown in Table 3

4 Conclusions and Future Work

We have demonstrated that verbs with similar argument structure as encoded in LCS are rarely synonymous in WordNet. We exploit this result in the task

---

[7] Hypernym links tie a word to its more general counterpart, e.g., *laugh* is a hypernym of *cackle*.

Verb	Synset(s)	Graph-Matched	Same Synset
strengthen	00131909 00132257	1554: alterar, confirmar, fortalecer, fortalecerse, modificar, tornar,... **Exact:** confirmar, fortalecer, fortalecerse	0:—
giggle	00019651	36: bufar, cacarear, gritar, jadear, reír, reírse, sonreír,...	0:— **One link away:** reír reírse

Table 3. Generation of Verbs with no Matching WordNet Synsets

of lexical selection, using LCS graph-matching to determine the closeness of semantic structure (argument structure in the LCS for the events) and WordNet links to determine the closeness of the semantic content (the constant in the LCS for verbs).

The combination of LCS and WordNet allows us to cover a variety of different cases that otherwise would not be handled by either knowledge source alone. In particular, we have shown that there are cases where LCS graph-matching alone is sufficient for selecting target-language terms, e.g., for *strengthen*, where WordNet does not provide a synset-based equivalent in Spanish. We have also shown that there are cases where WordNet is critical to the final selection of target-language terms, e.g., for *walk*, where numerous exactly matched LCSs in Spanish can restricted by a handful of shared WordNet synsets, and for *giggle*, where there are no exactly matched LCSs in Spanish but there exists a small set of related WordNet synsets.

Our future work will generalize the one-link synset matching by integrating a probabilistic technique based on insights from [16], which focuses on nouns. We will implement an analogous information-content metric method for verbs using Parka utilities. We will then extend this combined approach to the task of noun selection. This will involve construction of a probabilistic mapping from Spanish nouns (taken from a Kimmo-based lexicon) and WordNet senses. We expect nouns and verbs to be characteristically opposed in their requirements with respect to the resources we use. In particular, WordNet is hierarchically shallow for *verbs*, but this is counter-balanced by the richness in argument structure provided by the LCSs. In contrast, LCSs are shallow for *nouns*, but this is counter-balanced by the deep hierarchical structure of nouns in WordNet.

Acknowledgments

This work has been supported, in part, by DARPA/ITO Contract N66001-97-C-8540. The first author is also supported by DOD Contract MDA904-96-C-1250,

Army Research Laboratory contract DAAL01-97-C-0042, NSF PFF IRI-9629108 and Logos Corporation, NSF CNRS INT-9314583, and Alfred P. Sloan Research Fellowship Award BR3336. We would like to thank members of the CLIP lab for helpful conversations, particularly Jim Hendler, Philip Resnik, Wade Shen, and Scott Thomas.

References

1. Bonnie J. Dorr and Douglas Jones. Acquisition of Semantic Lexicons: Using Word Sense Disambiguation to Improve Precision. In *Proceedings of the Workshop on Breadth and Depth of Semantic Lexicons, 34th Annual Conference of the Association for Computational Linguistics*, pages 42–50, Santa Cruz, CA, 1996.

2. Bonnie J. Dorr, Antonia Marti, and Irene Castellon. Spanish EuroWordNet and LCS-Based Interlingual MT. In *Proceedings of the MT Summit Workshop on Interlinguas in MT*, San Diego, CA, October 1997.

3. Bonnie J. Dorr, Antonia Marti, and Irene Castellon. Evaluation of euro wordnet- and lcs-based lexical resources for machine translation. In *Proceedings of the First International Conference on Language Resources and Evaluation*, Granada, Spain, 1998.

4. Bonnie J. Dorr and Douglas W. Oard. Evaluating resources for query translation in cross-language information retrieval. In *Proceedings of the First International Conference on Language Resources and Evaluation*, Granada, Spain, 1998.

5. Ray Jackendoff. *Semantics and Cognition*. The MIT Press, Cambridge, MA, 1983.

6. Ray Jackendoff. *Semantic Structures*. The MIT Press, Cambridge, MA, 1990.

7. Ray Jackendoff. The Proper Treatment of Measuring Out, Telicity, and Perhaps Even Quantification in English. *Natural Language and Linguistic Theory*, 14:305–354, 1996.

8. Brian Kettler, William Anderson, James Hendler, and Sean Luke. Using the parka parallel knowledge representation system (version 3.2). Technical Report CS TR 3485, UMIACS TR 95-68, ISR TR 95-56, University of Maryland, 1995.

9. Beth Levin. *English Verb Classes and Alternations: A Preliminary Investigation*. University of Chicago Press, Chicago, IL, 1993.

10. Beth Levin and Malka Rappaport Hovav. The Elasticity of Verb Meaning. In *Proceedings of the Tenth Annual Conference of the Israel Association for Theoretical Linguistics and the Workshop on the Syntax-Semantics Interface*, Bar Ilan University, Israel, 1995.

11. George A. Miller. Dictionaries in the Mind. *Language and Cognitive Processes*, 1:171–185, 1986.

12. George A. Miller. WordNet: An On-Line Lexical Database. *International Journal of Lexicography*, 3:235–312, 1990.

13. George A. Miller and Christiane Fellbaum. Semantic Networks of English. In Beth Levin and Steven Pinker, editors, *Lexical and Conceptual Semantics, Cognition Special Issue*, pages 197–229. Elsevier Science Publishers, B.V., Amsterdam, The Netherlands, 1991.

14. Douglas W. Oard. *Multilingual Text Filtering Techniques for High-Volume Broad-Domain Sources*. PhD thesis, University of Maryland, 1996.

15. Douglas W. Oard and Bonnie J. Dorr. Evaluating Cross-Language Text Filtering Effectiveness. In *Proceedings of the Cross-Linguistic Multilingual Information Retrieval Workshop*, pages 8–14, Zurich, Switzerland, 1996.

16. Philip Resnik. Using information content to evaluate semantic similarity in a taxonomy. In *Proceedings of IJCAI-95*, pages 448–453, Montreal, Canada, 1995.

17. Kilian Stoffel, Merwyn Taylor, and James Hendler. Efficient management of very large ontologies. In *Proceedings of AAAI-97*, 1997.

Improving Translation Quality
by Manipulating Sentence Length

Laurie Gerber

SYSTRAN Systems Inc.
7855 Fay Avenue, Suite 300
La Jolla, CA 92037
619-459-6700 ext 119
lgerber@systransoft.com

Eduard Hovy

Information Sciences Institute
4676 Admiralty Way
Marina del Rey, CA 90292-6695
310-822-1511 ext 731
hovy@isi.edu

Abstract. Translation systems tend to have more trouble with long sentences than with short ones for a variety of reasons. When the source and target languages differ rather markedly, as do Japanese and English, this problem is reflected in lower quality output. To improve readability, we experimented with automatically splitting long sentences into shorter ones. This paper outlines the problem, describes the sentence splitting procedure and rules, and provides an evaluation of the results.

1. Introduction: Long Sentences in Translation

The sentence is a somewhat puzzling construct; on the face of it, a sentence is one of the most clearly articulated notions in linguistics, yet grammars that adequately cover real-world texts (such as newspaper articles), in which sentences of 50 words or longer are fairly routine, is still a goal that eludes computational linguists and MT system grammarians -- in fact, no complete grammar of any human language has ever been produced, despite decades of work by many talented people, which prompts [Nunberg 90] to make a distinction between the sentence as a unit of formal linguistic inquiry (what he calls the 'lexical sentence') and as a unit of written text (what he calls the 'text sentence'), and to devote portions of his book on punctuation to illustrate that the notion of what constitutes a sentence is not clear, having varied across the centuries (see chapter 7) -- a fact also stated in [Levinson 86], who suggests that the text sentence as a construct (in English) arose during the 17th century.

While words and paragraphs both seem natural units to many linguists[1], the definition and length of the sentence seem to depend as much on prosody, rhythm, and style, on surrounding context in dialogue, and on the balance between the lengths of surrounding sentences, as they do on actual content, a fact that poses something of a challenge to grammarians:

---

[1] Michael Halliday to Eduard Hovy; personal communication; 1988.

Bloomfield's classic definition of a sentence [Bloofield 33] "...an independent linguistic form, not included by virtue of any grammatical construction in any larger linguistic form" (which fails, as pointed out in [Gunter 74], because it disallows the grammatical connection between a question and its elliptical response, as in A: "who can see the boy?" B: "the man" or B: "he"); or Quirk et al's formulation of a sentence so that it must contain a verb [Quirk et al. 85] (which fails for the same reason);

and to educators teaching good writing:

"The first principle of rhythm in writing, to capture the basic rhythm of speech, is variation of sentence length... the ear must rule -- and the ear must be attuned to the sound of the full paragraph." [Vaughan Payne 65; italics in original] and "Another obvious way to emphasize a sentence, of course, is to make it noticeably longer or shorter than other sentences around it." [Weathers and Winchester 78], both of whom provide excellent writing suggestions without ever saying precisely why or when you make long or short sentences, and how long the sentences should be.

The alert reader will have noticed that the above paragraphs are each a single sentence. Possibly, the reader will also have felt a slight sense of strain, as verbs and phrases kept piling up. This sense of strain is a real phenomenon: psycholinguistic research in the 1970's illustrated convincingly that human sentence processing is sensitive to boundaries of sentences, clauses, and (to a lesser degree) phrases [Fodor et al. 74]. But apart from implications that the things introduced in a new sentence somehow 'get settled' when the period (sentence end) is reached, there seems to be a dearth of clear, explicit, models of what exactly the function of the sentence break is, and why or where one should place sentence breaks for optimal understandability.

All this may seem very academic. But the problem of sentence scoping raises its head in translation of texts with long sentences (such as newspaper articles), or of transcriptions of speech (such as parliamentary speeches, in which the sentence scoping patterns differ across languages). For example, the Canadian Parliamentary records, bilingual in French and English, exhibit a sentence-alignment mismatch of over 10%; that is to say, at least every tenth sentence of English is, in translation, either combined with a neighbor or split into separate sentences.

The question is: why? How does sentence length matter? Should an MT system be aware of sentence length?

Clearly, overlong sentences can be difficult to read; overlong sentences in bad translation almost certainly so. An analysis of real-world MT system output of Japanese newspaper text illustrates the point. Figure 1 contains several passages of text, with system translation. Figure 2 contains the same texts, after human insertion of sentence boundaries and appropriate rearrangement of misplaced words.

研究開発に投じる資金はおよそ２兆円と見込まれ、政府を

中心として、広く内外からの資金調達の検討、地方公共団
体との連携等を図り、国民の理解と協力を得て研究開発を
推進する必要がある。

It is necessary for the fund which is thrown to research and development to be estimated, approximately 2,000,000,000,000 Yen to assure the examination of raising of funds from the inside and outside and the cooperation et cetera with the municipal corporation widely with government as the center, to obtain understanding and cooperating of the people and to promote research and development.

一方、長距離の飛行については、現在の亜音速機は、例え
ば東京～ニューヨーク間の飛行時間が１２時間にも達する
ことから、飛行時間短縮の要求が大きく、超音速機開発を
はじめ２１世紀に向けた新規プロジェクトの開発機運が高
まっている。

On one hand, development opportunity of the new project to which as for the present subsonic plane, from the fact that for example flight time between Tokyo - New York reaches to as many as 12 hours, demand for flight time shortening is large concerning the flight of long distance, directs to 21 century including supersonic aircraft development has increased.

今後、大陸間を中心とした超距離航空輸送の増大が確実視
されており、２１世紀初頭には３００席で５００～
１０００機の超音速輸送機の需要が期待できる。

In the future, increase of the super distance aeronautical transport which centers on between the continents can be considered for certain, can expect to 21 century beginning demand for 500 - 1000 supersonic transport planes with 300 seats.

Fig. 1. Text samples containing long sentences.

The same sentences, after light postediting by a human:

Funds invested in research and development are estimated at approximately 2,000,000,000,000 Yen. With government as the center, investigation of fundraising widely inside and outside, as well as cooperation with municipal corporations is planned. It is necessary to promote research and development by obtaining the understanding and cooperation of the people.

On one hand, for the present subsonic plane for long-distance flights, because the flight time between Tokyo - New York reaches to as many as 12 hours, demand for flight time shortening is large. Development opportunities for new projects which aim toward the 21 century, including supersonic aircraft development, have increased.

In the future, the increase of long-distance aeronautical transport which centers on intercontinental travel can be considered for certain. You can expect demand for 500 - 1000 supersonic transport planes with 300 seats in the beginning of the 21st century.

Fig. 2. Text samples from Figure 1, after human insertion of sentence breaks and appropriate placement of words.

Without resorting to theory (whatever there is on the subject), one can imagine plausibly that people find shorter sentences easier to understand because they do not have to remember as many verbs, each (or many) of which may be the appropriate predicate for the many noun phrases and adverbs, or so many NPs, each of which may be the appropriate anchor for the many relative clauses.

Analogously, one can argue that MT systems will find shorter sentences easier to process because there are simply fewer attachment points for the various constituents, and hence fewer potential ambiguities, or (in cases of incomplete knowledge) fewer options to guess among. In addition, shorter sentences have the advantage over longer ones of grouping together more reliably and closely the sentence fragments that the systems may simply be unable to attach. In other words, a short sentence gives the system more points at which to clear the stack, and gives the reader more resting points at which to figure things out.

To test this argument, we studied the effects of splitting sentences prior to translation, using a commercial MT system to convert arbitrarily selected Japanese newspaper text into English.

2. Some Problems in Translating across Sentence Boundaries

The work described here is part of a collaboration between members of the research staff of SYSTRAN, one of the oldest MT companies in the world, and members of the Machine Translation project at the Information Sciences Institute of the University of Southern California.

SYSTRAN Software, Inc. (SSI): SSI's system development process is highly refined and efficient, making it possible to quickly and efficiently build and upgrade the capabilities of MT systems. Recently, SSI has placed a high priority on focused research that will lead to the introduction of new techniques and tools. A partnership with a research group is an ideal avenue for this. If successful, a collaboration would provide improved output quality for the J-E system, with the further possibility of implementing the new technology also in other language pairs.

Information Sciences Institute of USC (ISI): Over the past two decades, USC/ISI has performed research on text planning and generation, automated text summarization, multilingual information retrieval, and, since 1989, Machine Translation. The Penman sentence generation system [Penman 89] was a benchmark generator up to 5 years ago; the NITROGEN generator [Knight and Hatzivassiloglou 95] is a robust

Our analysis of sentences indicated that it is fairly easy to identify the conditions under which a sentence can be split with a high chance of translation success. Note that this module is invoked after homograph resolution (so that reliable part of speech information is available), and before clause analysis (so that the subsequent analysis of the sentence will result in a normal, complete clause structure); for a description of the steps in SYSTRAN analysis, see [Hutchins & Somers 1992] or [Yang and Gerber 1996]. These conditions, incorporated into rules, are:

- The original sentence is a minimum of 20 words long

- Either: a continuative or infinitive form verb phrase is found followed by a comma, or a clause conjunction is found

- The verb phrase is not functioning as an adverbial/extended particle (e.g., *ni tsuite,* "concerning")

- The resulting new sentence will be at least 7 words long

We provide an example, using a simplified notation. For the following input sentence:

今後、大陸間を中心とした超距離航空輸送の増大が確実視されており、２１世紀初頭には３００席で５００～１０００機の超音速輸送機の需要が期待できる。

the initial analysis phase produces the following sentence structure (clause level information only):

今後、 1) Sentential adverb: "in the future"

大陸間を中心とした 2) Relative clause: "which centers on intercontinental

超距離航空輸送の増大が確実視されており、 3) Independent clause #1, receives potential inflection from clause #2. The verb "consider to be certain" is continuative and followed by a comma.

２１世紀初頭には３００席で５００～ 4) Independent clause #2, with potential form verb "can expect..."

１０００機

の超音速輸送機の

需要が期待できる。

After applying the rules the above structure is replaced by the following two:

Sentence 1:

今後、   1) Sentential adverb: "in the future"

大陸間を中心とした   2) Relative clause: "which centers on
intercontinental"

超距離航空輸送の増大   3) Main clause still receives potential
が確実視されている。   inflection from final clause. The
predicate "consider to be certain" is
now in a sentence-final form.

Sentence 2:
２１世紀初頭には   4) Independent clause #2, with
３００席で５００〜   potential form verb "can expect..."
１０００機   Subject "you" is supplied in synthesis.
の超音速輸送機の
需要が期待できる。

These two structures give rise to the following sentences:

In the future, increase of the super distance aeronautical transport which centers
on between the continents can be considered for certain. You can expect to 21
century beginning demand for 500 - 1000 supersonic transport planes with 300
seats.

Had no splitting been applied, the system would have produced:

In the future, increase of the super distance aeronautical transport which centers
on between the continents can be considered for certain, can expect to 21
century beginning demand for 500 - 1000 supersonic transport planes with 300
seats.

4. Analysis

In our experimentation with sentence breaking, we used a corpus of several hundred
newspaper texts selected from three domains. Financial and Aerospace texts from

various Japanese newspapers and reports manually input at SYSTRAN over the past 6 years; and newspaper texts used in the DARPA MT evaluations during 1990-94.

Starting with the DARPA texts, we first translated the texts using SYSTRAN in the normal way, then marked all the sentences in the corpus for sentence length (in words), and then for each text sorted the sentences by size. We grouped the sentences into length categories (3 - 10 words, 11 - 20 words, and so on). Our goal was to see if there was any discernable length-based threshold for either understandability; presence of breakable sentence structures; or feasibility of using our hypothesized break points.

As part of this analysis, we analyzed 15 to 25 of the sentences in each length category and used the 5-point rating system described in Section 6 (in which 1 is best) to evaluate the sentences before they had been split. The results were:

Sentence length (words)	Average rating	% of sentences with break points
3-10	3.0	0%
11-20	2.8	21%
21-30	3.0	36%
31-40	2.7	46%
41-50	3.5	50%

As expected, we found that longer sentences do indeed have more break points; but unexpectedly, we observed that very short sentences did not have noticeably higher quality, and that sentences in the range of 31 - 40 words were still quite readable.

Analysis indicated that the very short sentences are often titles written in a telegraphic style that is difficult to translate. In addition, short sentences contained an inordinate number of not-found-words (particularly people- and place-names), as well as colloquialisms and informal usage (the sort of phonetic collapsing and ellipsis Japanese speakers use informally was transcribed literally in quoted text).

Our explanation for the readability of mid-length sentences is that as more substance appears in the sentence, minor flaws are less noticeable, since the key words allow one to infer the (major) meaning. However, this does increase the amount of inference required, and may introduce a sense of strain. We did not try to measure the strength of the sense of strain!

5. Evaluation

We wished to measure the increase in readability due to sentence splitting (if any). We performed two evaluations.

5.1 Evaluation 1

We had the system translate 221 randomly selected long Japanese sentences from the DARPA newspaper corpus, first without the Splitter and then with it.

We then counted the number of sentences that were actually split, tabulating the number of times they were split. Of the 221 sentences, 124 were split, multiple times in some cases. The results indicate that the rules given in Section 4 are about 80% successful at locating break points.

To measure the improvement in readability, we created two test sets (A and B) of 24 text fragments, each containing equally many split and unsplit sentences. The sentences were extracted at random from the above-mentioned corpus. The two sets were duals; where set A contained a split fragment, set B contained its unsplit equivalent, and vice versa. The sequence of split/unsplit sentences was determined by a random number generator. We gave these sets (either A or B, but not both) to each of 10 subjects for evaluation. The subjects were graduate students or professional researchers with native or near-native English ability. They were instructed as follows to read and score each fragment on a five-point scale:

> Please read the following paragraphs one at a time. After reading each paragraph, please score it by making a mark on the appropriate line. Please do not make more than one mark; if you can't decide, choose the upper category. Here is an example:

> When 10 years ago, active service is retreated, simultaneously, it called in the team companion of Koshien institute high era. The same club was formed.

> 1. _____ Perfectly clear, and perfectly grammatical
> 2. _____ Somewhat clear, and not perfectly grammatical
> 3. __X__ Hard to understand, though patches make sense
> 4. _____ Mostly unclear, only small patches of sense
> 5. _____ Incomprehensible; total spaghetti

Their ratings, given in Table 1, were rather puzzling:

Sentence type	Test set A		Test set B	
	Ave score	Variance	Ave score	Variance
Split	3.1500	0.0678	3.2833	0.0044
Unsplit	3.2667	0.0983	3.1667	0.0861
Unsplit - Split	0.1167		-0.1170	

Table 1. Scores for evaluation 1.

The subjects in Test Set A performed as expected: split sentences scored somewhat lower (i.e., were somewhat more understandable) than unsplit ones. But the subjects in Test Set B performed contrary to expectation, by about the same amount -- they believed that the unsplit sentences were *easier* to understand than the split ones!

The only certain conclusion to draw from this evaluation is that neither the number of test sentences nor the number of subjects was large enough. It is also not unreasonable to suspect that splitting sentences does not, for the current quality of SYSTRAN J-E output, make much difference in understandability. Since the average sentence scores lie between 3 and 4 in all cells in the above table, the sentences are, at best, hard to understand on average anyway.

5.2 Evaluation 2

In order to explore this mystery, we had the system translate several hundred sentences from all three domains mentioned in Section 5, both with and without the Splitter module. We then randomly extracted 36 sentences - 12 from each domain: 4 short (11 - 20 words) sentences, 4 medium-length (41 - 50 words), and 4 long (more than 70 words). Again, as above, we constructed two dual test sets, randomly varying the order of sentence lengths and domains, so that each subject saw 18 split and 18 unsplit sentences, equally many of each domain, and equally many of each length category. Each subject saw two different examples of any combination of split-domain-length parameters.

Split sentences		Domain				
		DARPA	Aerospace	Financial	totals	ave score
	Short	55	47	64	166	2.767
	Medium	71	48	63	182	3.033
Length	Long	65	59	57	181	3.017
	Totals	191	154	184		
	ave score	3.183	2.567	3.067		

Unsplit sentences		Domain				
		DARPA	Aerospace	Financial	totals	ave score
	Short	67	55	56	178	2.967
	Medium	73	50	67	190	3.167
Length	Long	70	61	51	182	3.033
	Totals	210	166	174		
	ave score	3.500	2.767	2.900		

Tables 2 and 3. Results of evaluation 2.

5 subjects received Test set A and 5 others Test set B. All subjects held at least a Master's degree, and were native or near-native speakers of English. They were not informed of the purpose of the test, but were asked simply to rate each (set of) sentence(s) on the same scale as in the previous experiment.

The results were less disappointing than in the previous evaluation, though not startling. Tables 2 (split) and 3 (unsplit) list the total scores per sentence category, for 4 sentences in each cell, each seen by 5 people. As is clear from the tables, there were some differences between the scores of split and unsplit sentences. For the DARPA and Aeronautical texts, as expected, split sentences scored better than unsplit ones, by 0.317 and 0.2 per sentence respectively. However, for the Financial texts, the unsplit sentences scored higher than the split ones. We are not sure what to conclude from this counterhypothetical result.

Also, paradoxically, the largest score improvement occurred when *short* sentences were split, while the rates were essentially equal with the splitting of long sentences!

6. Conclusion

Though the first evaluation was inconclusive, we take the second, more thorough, evaluation to show that our starting hypothesis, that breaking up long sentences during translation will improve the overall quality, is most probably correct.

We can think of several reasons why our results are not more pronounced. First, it is possible that the one condition we did not compensate for -- the fact that the sentences, split and unsplit, occur in isolation in the evaluation, instead of inside their natural context -- might weaken the effect of increased understandability. Second, it is possible that the sentence-splitting points used in our algorithm are not fully adequate, and that other, more sophisticated methods will perform better at separating sentences and then generating good cross-sentence links, using discourse cue phrases. The discourse structuring methods of [Marcu 97] come to mind, as example. Third, it is possible that short sentences are indeed easier to understand, but only when the translation quality reaches a certain level; in other words, that the somewhat low level of output quality of today's system blocks evaluators from noticing the improvements due to sentence shortening.

Whatever the reason, we feel that this experiment has been a valuable experience for us, and we hope that it may inspire others to perform additional experiments and prove or disprove the sentence-length hypothesis once and for all.

References
1. Bloomfield, L. 1933. *Language.* New York: Henry Holt.
2. Fodor, J.A., T.G. Bever, and M.F. Garrett. 1974. *The Psychology of Language.* New York: McGraw-Hill.
3. Gunter, R. 1974. *Sentences in Dialog.* Columbia, SC: Hornbeam Press.
4. Hovy, E.H. and L. Gerber. 1997. MT at the Paragraph Level: Improving English Synthesis in SYSTRAN. In *Proceedings of the 4th Conference of Theoretical and Methodological Issues in Machine Translation* (TMI). Santa Fe, New Mexico.
5. Hovy, E.H. and C-Y. Lin. 1998. Automated Text Summarization in SUMMARIST. In M. Maybury and I. Mani (eds), *Advances in Automatic Text Summarization.* MIT Press, to appear.
6. Hutchins, J. and H. Somers. 1992. *An Introduction to Machine Translation.* Cambridge: Academic Press Limited.
7. Knight, K. and V. Hatzivassiloglou. 1995. Two-Level, Many-Paths Generation. In *Proceedings of the 33rd Conference of the ACL* (252-260).

8. Knight, K., I. Chander, M. Haines, V. Hatzivassiloglou, E.H. Hovy, M. Iida, S.K. Luk, R.A. Whitney, and K. Yamada. 1995. Filling Knowledge Gaps in a Broad-Coverage MT System. In *Proceedings of the 14th IJCAI Conference.* Montreal, Canada.
9. Levinson, J. 1986. *Punctuation and the Orthographic Sentence: A Linguistic Analysis.* Ph.D. dissertation, City University of New York.
10. Marcu, D. 1997. The Rhetorical Parsing, Summarization, and Generation of Natural Language Texts. Ph.D. dissertation, University of Toronto.
11. Nunberg, G. 1990. *The Linguistics of Punctuation. CSLI Lecture Notes 18*, Center for the Study of Language and Information, Stanford University.
12. Penman 1989. The Penman Documentation. Unpublished documentation for the Penman Language Generation System, USC/Information Sciences Institute.
13. Quirk, R., S. Greenbaum, G. Leech, and J. Svartvik. 1985. *A Comprehensive Grammar of the English Language.* London and New York: Longman.
14. Vaughan Payne, L. 1965. *The Lively Art of Writing.* Chicago: Follett Publishing Company.
15. Weathers, W. and O. Winchester. 1978. *The New Strategy of Style.* McGraw-Hill.
16. Yang, J. and Gerber L. 1996. *SYSTRAN Chinese-English MT System.* In *Proceedings of the International Conference on Chinese Computing 96.* Singapore.

Machine Translation among Languages with Transitivity Divergences Using the Causal Relation in the Interlingual Lexicon

Yukiko Sasaki Alam[1]

Dept. of Foreign Languages and Literatures
San Francisco State University
1600 Holloway Avenue
San Francisco, CA 94132
yukiko@sfsu.edu

Abstract. This paper proposes a design of verb entries in Interlingua to facilitate the machine translation (MT) of two languages with transitivity divergence as derived from their shared and individual linguistic characteristics. It suggests that the transitivity difference is best treated with verb entries containing information of the causal relation of the expressed events. It also demonstrates how the proposed design of verb entries gives a principled treatment of aspect divergence in semantically corresponding verbs of a source language (SL) and a target language (TL). Although the current paper focuses on English and Japanese, the proposed treatment should be applicable to the MT of similarly divergent languages, since the proposed lexicon in language-independent Interlingua contains information on causal relations of events as necessary to bridge the transitivity difference.

1 Introduction

Pursuant to a principled treatment of transitivity and aspect divergences of an SL to a TL, the present paper offers a design of verb entries intended to be language universal in nature and which thus belong in Interlingua. The proposed design is formulated on the following assumptions:

(1)

    a. For economy, language-independent grammatical knowledge should be stored in Interlingua Grammar, not in each individual language grammar.

    b. Causal relations of events are language-independent knowledge, and hence should be stored in Interlingua.

---

[1] I wish to thank two anonymous reviewers of AMTA 98 for their valuable comments on an earlier version of this paper. Usual disclaimers apply.

c. Semantic depth of the Interlingual representation should vary according to the linguistic distance between an SL and a TL.

Although the present article deals with problems related to the semantics of verbs, it does not discuss verb classes[2] or word meaning per se. Language-independent representation of word meaning remains among the most difficult problems of MT.[3] Along the lines of such deep knowledge base models as KBMT [2, 12], PIVOT [10], ATLAS [15] and UNITRAN [3, 4], the current paper takes the view that a deeper knowledge representation is required for high quality multilingual MT translation.

Intransitive verbs discussed here are the so called *unaccusative* verbs, which are nonagentive intransitives implying a change of state. The present paper discusses a treatment of transitivity divergences between transitive verbs and such unaccusative intransitives in English and Japanese. It does not discuss the so called *unergative* verbs which are agentive intransitives implying an undelimited event. Nor does it discuss the position of a verb in the transitivity spectrum depending upon such factors as the reduction of the grammatical object, or the definiteness or indefiniteness of the implicit or overt object.[4]

The current theory is expressed within the framework of Lexical Functional Grammar (LFG) [8] for the formalism that allows an explicit representation of the interaction and autonomy of syntactic, functional/grammatical and semantic components of grammar.

The second section presents data on the transitivity divergence of English and Japanese while the third section presents a proposed design of verb entries and demonstrates the step-by-step translation process. The fourth section shows that the proposed design of verb entries also helps the resolution of the aspectual divergence of English and Japanese. Finally, the fifth section concludes with a discussion of the advantages of the proposed design of lexical entries for verbs in Interlingua.

2   The Data

Ikegami [6] characterizes English and Japanese as a DO language and a BECOME language respectively. It is often the case that the Japanese counterpart of an English sentence with a transitive verb is a sentence with an intransitive verb. For instance, although the English sentence (2) has three hypothetical Japanese translations, (3a), (3b) and (3c), only (3c) is acceptable:

(2)   *The wind opened the door.*   (Transitive)

---

[2] See [9] for a discussion of classes of Japanese verbs in terms of such syntactic regularities as case assignment and case alternations.

[3] See [1: 82-83, 11: 51, 14, 17] for the discussion on this topic. Also refer to [7] for a list of relation concepts and attribute concepts for the Interlingual representation of words.

[4] See [13] for a discussion of this issue.

(3) a. *Kaze-ga   doa-o   ake-ta.   (Transitive)
        wind-SUBJ   door-OBJ   open-PAST
        'Wind opened the door'

     b. *Doa-ga   kaze-de   ake-rare-ta.   (Passive)
        door-SUBJ   wind-BY   open-PASS-PAST
        'The door was opened by wind.'

     c. Kaze-de   doa-ga   ai-ta.   (Intransitive)
        wind-CAUSE   door-SUBJ   open-PAST
        'The door opened due to wind.'

The awkwardness of (3a) and (3b) is due to the fact that the logical subject of the Japanese transitive verb *ake* 'open (tr)' should denote an animate agent. This is similar to the volitive restriction that applies to the English verb *murder*, as illustrated below:

(4) a. *Malaria murdered John.   (Transitive)

     b. *John was murdered by malaria.   (Passive)

     c. John died from malaria.   (Intransitive)

The animate restriction on the agent subject is a general rule in Japanese grammar, giving rise to a relatively frequent use of intransitive verbs in Japanese, a factor contributing to the characterization of Japanese as a BECOME language.

Due to the animate restriction on the agent subject, the English transitive verb does not often have a transitive counterpart in Japanese: for instance, Japanese has a verb equivalent to *murder*, but not one equivalent to *kill*, which allows the subject to be inanimate. Thus, the most plausible counterpart Japanese sentence of (5) would be (6), a sentence with an intransitive verb:

(5) Malaria killed John.

(6) Zyon-ga   mararia-de   shin-da.
     John-SUBJ   malaria-CAUSE die-PAST
     'John died from malaria.'

Hence, a systematic transitivity conversion between verbs belonging to this category in the two languages is in order.

3   The Proposal

3.1   Verb Entries in Interlingua

A pressing question would be which component of grammar is responsible for the transitivity conversion. This paper maintains that the Interlingual lexicon needs to contain information on the causal relation of events and that the transitivity conversion is carried out according to this information. For instance, the following information should be present in the lexical entry for the verb meaning 'kill' in the Interlingual lexicon:

(7)   Lexical Entry for KILL in Interlingua

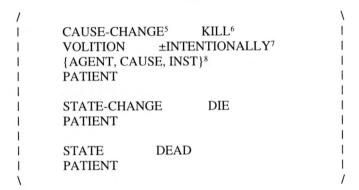

```
/                                                                              \
|        CAUSE-CHANGE⁵        KILL⁶                                             |
|        VOLITION       ±INTENTIONALLY⁷                                         |
|        {AGENT, CAUSE, INST}⁸                                                  |
|        PATIENT                                                               |
|                                                                              |
|        STATE-CHANGE         DIE                                              |
|        PATIENT                                                               |
|                                                                              |
|        STATE           DEAD                                                  |
|        PATIENT                                                               |
\                                                                              /
```

3.2   Translation Process for the Interlingual Representation

What follows is a process of forming an Interlingual representation of (5), *Malaria killed John*. First, by referring to English phrase structure rules and the lexical entry for *kill* in (8) and (9), the sentence is parsed into the c(onstituent)-structure and the f(unctional)-structure illustrated in (10):[9]

(8)   English Phrase Structure rules[10]

```
S       ->      NP              VP
                (SUBJ)
VP      ->      V               NP
                                (OBJ)
```

(9)   Lexical Entry for *kill*

---

[5] CAUSE-CHANGE is ACCOMPLISHMENT in Vendler's terminology of verb aspect [16].

[6] For the sake of convenience, English is used to represent the meaning in Interlingua.

[7] "±" indicates that this event takes place with or without someone's intention.

[8] The curly brackets indicate that any of the three thematic relations can be an argument of the verb KILL. INST stands for INSTRUMENT. The names of the thematic relations follow conventional ones which attempt to capture prototypical semantics of the arguments and adjuncts of verbs.

[9] See [8] for the exposition of the technical terms, *c-structure* and *f-structure*, in Lexical Functional Grammar (LFG).

[10] This is a simplified set of English Phrase Structure rules for the description of the current task.

kill [V; KILL (x, y); CAUSE-CHANGE][11]

(10) Grammatical representations of *Malaria killed John*

a. c-structure

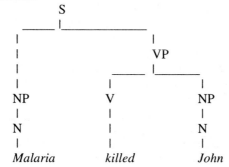

b. f-structure

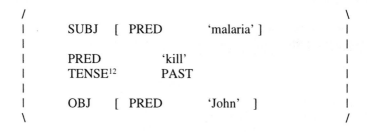

Next, since the meaning of *kill* is KILL, from the lexical entry for KILL in Interlingua in (7), the thematic relations of the two arguments of *kill* are identified as PATIENT and one of AGENT, INST and CAUSE.[13] In order to form the Interlingual representation of the English sentence, the values of the thematic relations must be determined. This determination is carried out by the Linking rule which operates according to Prominence Hierarchies, which are specified in Interlingua because they are largely language-independent, with exceptions such as 11b-ii, which in this case is specific to languages like English:

(11) Prominence Hierarchies for Linking

a. Grammatical Relation Hierarchy

SUBJECT > OBJECT > OBLIQUE

---

[11] This lexical entry contains minimally necessary information for the current discussion.

[12] For the sake of simplicity, I omit the process of the morphological parsing of the tense inflection.

[13] The concept of thematic relation is equivalent to that of Fillmore's Case [5]. The term *thematic relation* is employed here due to its current prevalence in the linguistic literature.

b. Thematic (Relation) Hierarchy

    i.   AGENT > PATIENT > {INST, CAUSE}
   ii. {INST, CAUSE} > PATIENT (Language-specific rule)

Because English allows the logical subject of a sentence to be the INST or CAUSE argument (in addition to the AGENT argument allowed by many languages including Japanese), it has two sets of the Thematic Hierarchies: one which is language-independent (11b-i) and one which is language-specific (11b-ii). As the value of SUBJECT is MALARIA, which is an INANIMATE entity, and the sentence is not passive, the Thematic Hierarchy (11b-i) with AGENT as the most prominent grammatical relation is not used, the one (11b-ii) with INST or CAUSE as the most prominent grammatical relation employed instead. Furthermore, for the thematic relation, CAUSE is selected between INST and CAUSE, because MALARIA does not denote a CONCRETE entity, which is a required feature for INST. The choice of the Thematic Hierarchy having the most prominent CAUSE or INST over the one having the most prominent AGENT leads to the cancellation of the symbol "+" in "± INTENTIONALLY". Now that the values of CAUSE and PATIENT are identified from the Linking rule, the following Interlingual representation is formed:

(12) Interlingual Representation of *Malaria killed John*

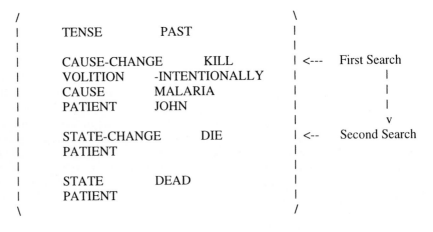

```
/                                              \
|    TENSE          PAST                        |
|                                               |
|    CAUSE-CHANGE        KILL                    | <---   First Search
|    VOLITION      -INTENTIONALLY               |          |
|    CAUSE         MALARIA                       |          |
|    PATIENT       JOHN                          |          |
|                                               |          v
|    STATE-CHANGE        DIE                     | <--    Second Search
|    PATIENT                                     |
|                                               |
|    STATE         DEAD                          |
|    PATIENT                                     |
\                                              /
```

3.3   Translation Process for Generation

Once the Interlingual representation of the English sentence is created, a search begins for the counterpart Japanese verb of KILL. Because there is no verb which means killing unintentionally, the search fails. Next, a second search begins by going to a deeper level of the Interlingual representation: to the Japanese correspondent of DIE, which is listed as an event resulting from killing. Since Japanese has the verb *shin* which means 'die', the search concludes successfully:

(13)   Lexical Entry for the Japanese verb *shin* 'die'

shin   [V; DIE (x); STATE-CHANGE]

Next, the Linking rule which operates on the Prominence Hierarchies repeated in (14) determines the grammatical relations of the CAUSE and PATIENT arguments:

(14)   Prominence Hierarchies for Linking

a. Grammatical Relation Hierarchy

SUBJECT > OBJECT > OBLIQUE

b. Thematic (Relation) Hierarchy[14]

AGENT > PATIENT > {INST, CAUSE}

Since the PATIENT argument is more prominent than the CAUSE argument, the Linking rule assigns it to SUBJECT. In addition, as *shin* 'die' is an intransitive verb, the CAUSE argument is not assigned to OBJECT, but to OBLIQUE.

Given the grammatical relations SUBJECT and OBLIQUE, *Zyon* and *mararia* receive their appropriate syntactic cases, based upon the following case assignment rules:

(15)   Japanese Case Assignment rules[15]

Assign the SUBJECT CASE *ga* to the SUBJECT argument
Assign the OBJECT CASE *o* to the OBJECT argument
Assign the CAUSE CASE *de* to the CAUSE argument

---

[14] Note that there is a difference between English and Japanese Thematic Hierarchies. The unitary Japanese Thematic Hierarchy is assumed to be responsible for the absence of the CAUSE or INST (logical) subject. Compare this to the English binary Thematic Hierarchies.

[15] I use CASE to indicate the syntactic case, which is an incarnation of a semantic thematic relation.

was used when processing SDA/NZZ documents in the original German, and no techniques for splitting German compounds were implemented.[3]

2.1 Same Language Query (SLQ)

To approximate an upper bound for the performance of any CLIR system, we compared the retrieval effectiveness of our four experimental approaches with the retrieval effectiveness achieved by using queries that are given in the same language as the documents. For example, the CL01 "title query" would be presented as [waldheim affair] when retrieving English AP documents and as [die affaire waldheim] when retrieving German SDA/NZZ documents.

2.2 Dictionary-Based Query Translation (DQT)

By far the most commonly used query translation approach is to replace each query term with appropriate translations that are automatically extracted from an online bilingual dictionary (c.f., [6, 1]). The usual approach is to automatically extract a bilingual term list from the dictionary entries, so for translating queries from English into German for retrieval from the SDA/NZZ collection we used an online bilingual term list developed by Stefan Büdenbender.[4] That term list contains 131,274 bilingual pairs in which each pair consists of one word or phrase in English and the corresponding word or phrase in German. The number of unique words in the list is far smaller than 131,274 because many words appear in several bilingual pairs and the number of unique stems is smaller still because the dictionary contains multiple morphological variants for many of the words. The pairs were initially sorted in lexicographic order based on the English terms and we used the same dictionary to translate queries from German into English for retrieval from the AP collection after resorting the pairs by the German terms.

It is common for a single word to have several translations, some with very different meanings. Bilingual dictionaries typically seek to help users select appropriate translations of individual words by embedding the word in a representative phrase, and this practice was present in the bilingual term list that we used. It is not at all clear how one should design an algorithm to extract only the "appropriate" translations using this information, so we have implemented six simple dictionary-based query translation techniques that together explore the effects of winner-take-all, word-match and stem-match approaches. We illustrate the effect of each technique with a German translation of the English CL01 title query given above.

Single Word (SW) Bilingual term lists provide no obvious basis for selecting a single translation when more than one alternative translation for a word

---

[3] We tried a small German stopword list in our TREC-6 experiments and found that it hurt average precision somewhat in most cases [10].

[4] The bilingual term list is available at http://www.bg.bib.de/~a2h6bu/

is encoded in the list. In SW we arbitrarily choose the first exact single whole-word match in the list.[5] The list is sorted in alphabetical order, and we expect this technique to perform about as well as any other arbitrary choice of a single word. Words which are not found in the dictionary are retained unchanged, a simple cognate matching strategy that often works well for proper names.

[waldheim affäre]

Single Word, Stemmed (SWS) The bilingual term list we have used contains several morphological variants for each word rather than a single entry for a root form, but it is possible that some required morphological variants may not be present. Accordingly, for the SWS technique we first seek an exact match for each term, and if that fails we stem every word in the bilingual term list and in the query and then try the matching again.[6] If that fails we retain the word unchanged in the hopes of a cognate match.

[waldheim affäre]

Every Word (EW) SW involves arbitrary choices, but information retrieval algorithms are able to accept multiple possibilities. Thus, the more common technique for using bilingual term lists has been to retain every possible translation when more than one alternative is present in the list. In the EW technique we replace each word with every exact single whole-word match in the bilingual term list.

[waldheim affäre angelegenheit ereigneis geschäft handlung sache]

Every Word, Stemmed (EWS) EWS is the stemmed variant of EW, in which we retain every exact single stem match in the dictionary. This is done in a single pass, rather than the two pass approach used in SWS, since that approach seems to better match the idea of "every" possible translation.

[waldheim affäre angelegenheit angelegenheiten ereigneis geschäft handlung sache]

Every Phrase (EP) Like many dictionaries, our bilingual term list contains phrases in addition to single words. Phrases are ignored, however, on the source language side of the bilingual term list in the preceding techniques since only single word matches are used. Because some query words may appear only as part of a phrase, in the EP technique we include the translation any time the query word exactly matches any word in the bilingual term list, regardless of whether that word appears alone or as part of a phrase. In order to prevent an explosion of nuisance matches, words which appear in our stopword list are not translated.[7]

---

[5] An "exact" match is one in which the two character strings are the same length and each character in the two strings matches. A "whole word" is any whitespace-delimited string of characters that appears in the document.

[6] Stemming is an automatic suffix removal technique. We used the Porter stemmer for English that is available from ftp://ftp.vt.edu/pub/reuse/IR.code/ for this purpose.

[7] Stopwords are common words that are of little benefit to information retrieval. We used the standard English stopword list supplied with the Inquery system for this purpose.

[waldheim affäre angelegenheit ereigneis geschäft handlung
sache ehrensache familienagelegenheit liebesglück es war eine
abgekartete sache es ging heiss her liebesaffäre liebeserlebnis
techtelmechtel staatsangelegenheit das ist meine sache]

Every Phrase, Stemmed (EPS) EPS is the stemmed analogue of EP in which
we retain every exact stem match in the bilingual term list, regardless of
whether the stemmed word appears alone or as part of a phrase. Again, only
one pass is needed.

[waldheim affäre angelegenheit angelegenheiten ereigneis
geschäft handlung sache ehrensache familienagelegenheit
liebesglück es war eine abgekartete sache es ging heiss her
liebesaffäre liebeserlebnis techtelmechtel mein
privatangelegenheiten staatsangelegenheit staatsangelegenheiten
bescherung das ist meine sache seine angelegenheiten in ordnung
bringen geschäfte abwickeln]

In every case we replace each word in the query with the corresponding word or
phrase in every matching bilingual pair to produce a version of the query that
can be compared with the documents in the collection. In addition to simple
word-to-word mappings, word-to-phrase mappings are possible (and, in fact,
common), so translated queries are typically longer than untranslated queries
and the translated queries sometimes contain repeated words. Furthermore, the
translated queries often contain multiple words with the same stems, and in
English (but not in German) these words will be treated by our information
retrieval system as if they are identical.

2.3 MT-Based Query Translation (MQT)

Machine translation systems seek to translate documents from one language
to another, either as an aid for human translators or for direct use as a fairly
rapid and inexpensive rough translation. This provides an obvious approach to
query translation, but we are aware of only one prior experiment to use such a
technique [11]. In that experiment, Radwan and Fluhr compared the retrieval
effectiveness of queries translated from French into English by the SYSTRAN
machine translation system with the effectiveness of their EMIR dictionary-
based query translation system using a version of the small Cranfield collection
for which French queries were available. In that study they found that the EMIR
was more effective than their MT-based query translation technique using SYS-
TRAN. Our experiments offer some insight into the performance of a MT-based
query translation approach on larger test collections.

The Logos machine translation system that we used for our experiments is
a commercial product that is designed to assist human translators by automatically preparing fairly good translations of individual documents.[8] The system is

---

[8] Logos Corporation, 111 Howard Boulevard, Suite 214, Mount Arlington, NJ 07856
USA

typically used by translation bureaus and other organizations as the first stage of a machine-assisted translation process, and we have previously used it for cross-language routing experiments [7]. The Logos system includes extensive facilities for adding domain-specific technical terminology and new linguistic constructs, but for the experiments reported here we used only the machine readable dictionaries and semantic rules that are delivered as standard components of the product.

We used the Logos system to translate English queries into German for use with the SDA/NZZ collection and to translate German queries into English for use with the AP collection. Since the Logos system is designed to generate readable translation, it generates only a single "best guess" translation for any input. Thus MT-based query translation is most similar to the DQT-SW technique in which a single candidate translations is retained.

2.4 MT-Based Document Translation (MDT)

Our MT-based document translation approach parallels the design of our MT-based query translation design. We have selected English as a query language and translated each SDA/NZZ document into English as a preprocessing step. We then indexed the translated document collection and used English queries for the retrieval experiments. Essentially the preprocessing step reduces cross-language retrieval to a (possibly degraded) monolingual case. We used four SPARC 20 workstations and a fifth workstation that was upgraded from a SPARC 5 to a SPARC Ultra 1 after about three quarters of the documents had been translated.[9] Translation of the 48 months of newswire stories contained in the SDA and NZZ collections using these machines required approximately 10 machine-months, and successful translations were obtained for 251,572 documents. The remaining 268 documents were omitted from the translated collection.

2.5 Foreign Language Query (FLQ)

Monolingual information retrieval systems sometimes produce useful results because of fortuitous matches between words in different languages, proper names that are rendered in the same way in different languages, and foreign language terms in the documents that happen to be in the query language. For example, the English version of the CL01 title query shown above contains the proper name "Waldheim" which also often appears in relevant German documents. In order to establish a practical lower bound on retrieval effectiveness we have used both untranslated queries and untranslated documents to reveal the effect of these cognate matches.

3 Results

Table 1 summarizes the non-interpolated average precision results for the SDA/NZZ collection using every technique, averaged over the 21 topics for which relevant

---

[9] The translated documents are available to TREC participants from NIST.

documents are known. For title queries the advantage of same language queries over four of the eight CLIR techniques is statistically significant (with 95% confidence), as is the difference between three of the CLIR techniques and foreign language queries, but the available 21 queries are not sufficient to produce statistically significant differences among the CLIR techniques that we have tested. It does appear, however, that DQT-SW is no worse than the more commonly implemented DQT-EW technique, and that the same pattern is evident in the stemmed variant of each technique and with long query as well. These figures are averaged over 21 queries, however, and that obscures query-by-query variations. DQT-SW obtains this average performance by doing quite well on some queries and quite poorly on others. Since the average precision is much closer to zero (the minimum possible) than to one (the maximum), the potential gain for an individual query is far greater than the potential loss. Thus, a few exceptionally good translations could account for this effect. So in one sense, this result points up a weakness in the average precision measure. Viewed from another perspective, however, our result suggests that seeking an improvement over arbitrary choice may be as useful as the more common approach of seeking to cut down on the number of translations selected (c.f., [1]).

Technique	Query Length	
	Title	Long
SLQ	0.2480	0.2396
DQT-SW	0.1749	0.1342
DQT-SWS	0.1542	0.0969
DQT-EW	0.1778	0.1312
DQT-EWS	0.1363	0.0827
DQT-EP	0.1152	0.0165
DQT-EPS	0.1172	0.0182
MQT	0.1668	0.1561
MDT	0.1761	0.2171
FLQ	0.0307	0.0117

Table 1. Non-interpolated average precision for the SDA/NZZ collection, averaged over 21 topics.

Machine translation also seems to be doing well. On long queries, MT-based query translation outperforms every DQT technique. Title queries, which are all three words or less, lack the same effect. That is not surprising, since the machine translation system that we used is designed to perform best on well formed sentences. The effect of greater context is also apparent in the performance of MT-based document translation, which outperforms MT-based query translation on both title and long queries. This difference may, in fact, be understated somewhat because our experience suggests that English to German translations are noticeably better in many cases than German to English translations with the system that we used. Since MT-based query translation used English to German translations and MT-based document translation used German to English translations, we might have seen an even bigger advantage for MT-based document translation with a more evenly balanced translation performance.

In order to seek confirmation for these results we applied three of our CLIR techniques to the English AP collection. Table 2 summarizes the non-interpolated average precision results for that collection, using DQT-SW, DQT-EW and MT-based query translation. DQT-EP was omitted because we lacked a usable stopword list in German, the stemmed variants were omitted because both German stemming software and a compound splitting technique would have been needed, and replicating MT-based document translation was impractical within the time frame of this study. For those techniques that we were able to easily implement, the same trends were evident on the AP collection as on the SDA/NZZ collection. Again, DQT-SW was no worse than DQT-EW, and that MT-based query translation performs somewhat better than either of those techniques on long queries. Thus although we have not obtained statistically significant results, we now have some reason to believe that two of our most important observations are repeatable.

| Technique | Query Length | |
	Title	Long
SLQ	0.3449	0.3958
DQT-SW	0.1982	0.1154
DQT-EW	0.1805	0.0710
MQT	0.1928	0.2455
FLQ	0.0105	0.0132

Table 2. Non-interpolated average precision for the AP collection, averaged over 21 topics.

4 Conclusions

We have conducted an extensive evaluation of eight cross-language information retrieval techniques and found some interesting results. When using a bilingual term list that contains morphological variants rather than root forms, we have seen that matching exact words is better than matching stems. We have seen the same result with a different bilingual term list in a different language pair (English and Spanish) [5], so there is reason to believe that this result will generalize to other bilingual term lists and evaluation collections. Perhaps our most surprising result is that arbitrarily choosing a single translation for each term produces the same average precision as the more common use of every possibly translation. Although we believe that to be an artifact of the average precision measure, it does offer an interesting perspective from which to think about the design of dictionary-based query translation techniques. Finally, and perhaps most importantly, we have observed that a sophisticated machine translation system can outperform simpler techniques for cross-language information retrieval. Our inability to easily replicate the MT-based document translation experiment on the AP collection (an estimated 10 machine-months of computation would have been required) speaks volumes about the practical limitations of that approach, however. But as machine translation becomes faster, we have demonstrated one way in which those powerful capabilities might be used. It is clearly possible to exploit these same resources that we have used to craft more sophisticated techniques. For example, we could take advantage of redundancy in the bilingual term list to improve our translation choices in the DQT-SW method. And in MT-based query translation and MT-based document translation we could preserve some additional terms in the face of unresolvable ambiguity by coupling the translation and retrieval systems more tightly. Our encouraging results suggest that these would be promising directions for future work.

Acknowledgments

This work has been supported in part by DARPA contract N6600197C8540, the University of Maryland General Research Board, and the Logos Corporation. The author is grateful to Bonnie Dorr for her extensive comments on an early version of this paper, Paul Hackett for implementing dictionary-based query translation, Scott Bennett and Harriet Leventhal for their assistance with the Logos translation system, James Allan for help with Inquery configuration, and Fred Gey for making us aware of the German bilingual term list that we used.

References

1. Ballesteros, L. and Croft, W. B. (1997). Phrasal translation and query expansion techniques for cross-language information retrieval. In *Proceedings of the 20th International ACM SIGIR Conference on Research and Development in Information Retrieval.* http://ciir.cs.umass.edu/.
2. Buckley, C., Mitra, M., Walz, J., and Cardie, C. (1997). Using clustering and SuperConcepts within SMART: TREC 6. In *The Sixth Text REtrieval Conference (TREC-6).* National Institutes of Standards and Technology. To appear. http://trec.nist.gov/.
3. Carbonell, J., Yang, Y., Frederking, R., Brown, R. D., Geng, Y., and Lee, D. (1997). Translingual information retrieval: A comparative evaluation. In *Proceedings of the Fifteenth International Joint Conference on Artificial Intelligence.* http://www.cs.cmu.edu/afs/cs.cmu.edu/user/ralf/pub/WWW/papers.html.
4. Davis, M. and Ogden, W. C. (1997). Quilt: Implementing a large-scale cross-language text retrieval system. In *Proceedings of the 20th International ACM SIGIR Conference on Research and Development in Information Retrieval.*

5. Dorr, B. J. and Oard, D. W. (1998). Evaluating resources for query translation in cross-language information retrieval. In *Proceedings of the First International Conference on Language Resource Evaluation*. http://www.glue.umd.edu/~oard/.

6. Hull, D. A. and Grefenstette, G. (1996). Querying across languages: A dictionary-based approach to multilingual information retrieval. In *Proceedings of the 19th Annual International ACM SIGIR Conference on Research and Development in Information Retrieval*. http://www.xrce.xerox.com/people/hull/papers/sigir96.ps.

7. Oard, D. W. (1997a). Adaptive filtering of multilingual document streams. In *Fifth RIAO Conference on Computer Assisted Information Searching on the Internet*. http://www.glue.umd.edu/~oard/.

8. Oard, D. W. (1997b). Alternative approaches for cross-language text retrieval. In *AAAI Symposium on Cross-Language Text and Speech Retrieval*. American Association for Artificial Intelligence. http://www.glue.umd.edu/~oard/.

9. Oard, D. W. (1997c). Serving users in many languages: Cross-language information retrieval for digital libraries. *D-Lib Magazine*. http://www.dlib.org.

10. Oard, D. W. and Hackett, P. G. (1997). Document translation for cross-language text retrieval at the University of Maryland. In *The Sixth Text REtrieval Conference (TREC-6)*. National Institutes of Standards and Technology. To appear. http://trec.nist.gov/.

11. Radwan, K. and Fluhr, C. (1995). Textual database lexicon used as a filter to resolve semantic ambiguity application on multilingual information retrieval. In *Fourth Annual Symposium on Document Analysis and Information Retrieval*, pages 121–136.

12. Soergel, D. (1997). Multilingual thesauri in cross-language text and speech retrieval. In *AAAI Symposium on Cross-Language Text and Speech Retrieval*. American Association for Artificial Intelligence. http://www.clis.umd.edu/dlrg/filter/sss/papers/.

Lexicons as Gold: Mining, Embellishment, and Reuse

Keith J. Miller and David M. Zajic

The MITRE Corporation, 1820 Dolley Madison Boulevard
McLean, VA 22102-3481
{keith, dmzajic}@mitre.org

Abstract. Given the high labor costs of developing new lexical resources for Machine Translation (MT) and language processing systems, it is desirable to make the most of those resources already in existence. This paper describes the work being carried out on two MT projects that share a common goal: the creation, maintenance and reuse of lexical information. This goal calls into play a range of tasks from dictionary mining of machine-readable dictionaries (MRDs) to the definition of a repository capable of housing this diverse lexical information. This paper outlines the two efforts, focusing on the problems encountered and the intermediate results achieved. While the ultimate goal of the automated processing of on-line resources into multi-purpose lexical repositories is far from being achieved, our experience has shown that there are significant applications that can make use of the partially processed information produced en route. We will describe our experience with two projects, with a focus on one which utilized multiple lexical resources to provide the basis for two natural language processing (NLP) tools: a segmenter and a glosser for Thai. Finally, we make recommendations for future resource development, with a view toward mitigating the difficulties of merging information from diverse sources.

1 Introduction

As one instance of the 'knowledge acquisition bottleneck', the creation of lexicons suitable for use in machine translation systems is a time-consuming, expensive task. Methods employed for lexicon creation include manual entry and enhancement of lexical entries, mining of domain-specific corpora for lexical information, and dictionary mining (of machine-readable dictionaries (MRDs)). Naturally, any tools or methodologies that expedite the lexicon creation process will be welcomed in the MT community. Likewise, lexical resources, once they are created, are valuable commodities and must be amenable to reuse.

Despite earlier optimism, and some significant progress in automatically extracting lexical information from online sources [7, 8], no one has yet been successful in transforming MRDs into MT lexicons fully automatically. As Kilgarriff notes in [4], automatic extraction techniques are not yet suited to tasks in which deep semantic information will be necessary. Nonetheless, it will be shown that while, like the goal of fully automated machine translation, the goal of extraction of machine translation lexicons from online resources is far from being realized, it is possible to benefit from the incremental success that has been obtained.

The two projects discussed in this paper have as common goals the acquisition, maintenance, and reuse of online lexical resources.

2 Common Ground

The two independent projects discussed in this paper are the following
- The LSB Project: creating a resource that will enable the sharing and reuse of lexical information.
- The QuickMT project: pursuing the more controversial goal of extracting information usable in the MT process from machine-readable dictionaries.

The lexicon-related tasks from these two projects will be discussed in turn, with special attention given to the process and the difficulties encountered in the QuickMT project. This discussion will be followed by descriptions of the practical successes that have resulted from these projects, even in their current intermediate stages of development. Finally, with an eye toward the next step of our work, we will discuss the problems of merging information from disparate lexical resources, and close with some considerations in the creation of the resultant unified lexical resource.

2.1 The LSB Project

Many MT systems and other NLP tools provide ways for users to create supplementary lexicons to augment and possibly override entries in the proprietary lexicons that come with the system. Users may create very large and high-quality domain-specific lexicons with their own dictionary creation tools. If a new NLP tool becomes available, the user will certainly want to retain the benefits of having the domain-specific lexicon he or she has developed, but will not want to undergo the expense of recreating it for each different tool. The Lexicon Service Bureau (LSB) project addresses this issue. We are developing an architecture for storing this data in a system-independent form, and examining possible uses for such data. The concept of the LSB can be compared to two features of word processors: first, the ability to save a document in a system independent form (text only); and second, the ability to load a text only document and store it in the system's own format.

[3] addresses the issue of MT lexicon reuse among users of Japanese-English commercial MT systems. They propose an SGML tagged basic format containing information that all MT systems can handle. An environment for creating lexicons in this format is provided, and the developers of the various MT systems are encouraged to provide tools for writing to and reading from this format. In contrast to this work, which is prescriptive in nature, the LSB is concerned primarily with the reuse of existing lexical information from sources such as MRDs and existing user-created lexicons.

Furthermore, MT lexicons are not the only possible reuse targets for the LSB. Any NLP system requiring a lexicon, such as spelling correction or optical character recognition, can potentially benefit from LSB's generation of lexical information specific to the needs of that application.

It is our intention that the LSB will store lexical data acquired from many different sources and for many different languages. The design of the internal representation must be extremely flexible, to accommodate the wide variety of information in existing resources which will feed the LSB, the differing requirements of various NLP systems which will draw on the contents of the LSB, and, of course, the substantial variation in lexical characteristics of human languages. Our solution is to make the representation as generic as possible. Two levels of entities are being modeled: lexical entries and languages. The languages put constraints of the contents of the lexical entry instances. A lexical entry consists of generic information and language-specific information. Information which we believe will apply to almost all lexical entries in any language constitutes the generic section. This includes a unique id, a surface form, a syntactic category, a source, a word/phrase indicator, a domain, and a (possibly null) pointer to another lexical entry from which the entry was derived and the type of derivation. All other information is language-specific, and is stored in the form of feature-value pairs. One lexical entry will typically have many feature-value pairs associated with it. The language model specifies the features that are relevant for each syntactic category in the language, and the valid values for those features. For instance, nouns in Spanish bear the feature GENDER, and the valid values are MASCULINE and FEMININE. Feature-value pairs my be grouped together into clusters, for cases such as German adjectives, where a surface form of an adjective is characterized by a composite of case, gender and number, but not necessarily by any one of these alone. Normalizing our data schema in this manner does have a cost in retrieval time and maintenance of data integrity. We feel that gains in storage space (i.e. reduction in the number of empty fields) and the flexibility to modify the language models to accommodate new input formats and new output requirements outweigh the costs. Language models for English, Russian, German, Spanish, and French have been specified, based on the EAGLES Multext project [2]. Within the LSB, groups of lexical entries form monolingual lexicons. Within the LSB, groups of lexical entries from one language are grouped into monolingual lexicons. Any translation information, as from a bilingual lexicon or a legacy user-created domain-specific MT lexicon, is stored separately in the form of translation links. Each direction-specific language pair is represented by its own set of translation links, which are based on [1]. T-links can be used to express a variety of translation relationships more complex than simple translation equivalence.

The ultimate goal of the LSB project is to develop a unified lexical resource from which application- and domain-specific lexicons for many NLP applications can be generated. At present, each new lexical resource in the LSB is represented by its own monolingual modules. For instance in the case of MT, if a Spanish-English lexicon, a French-English lexicon and a German-English domain-specific lexicon are all added to the LSB, there will be one each Spanish, French and German monolingual lexicons, and three different English monolingual lexicons. The next phase of our research will address the issue of merging monolingual lexicons while maintaining necessary linguistic information and avoiding duplicate entries. Word sense disambiguation will be the major difficulty in this process.

2.2 QuickMT

The QuickMT project has as its goal the development of software tools and methodologies that will facilitate the rapid development of MT systems for low-density languages. Translation of Thai into English has been chosen as a testbed for the first phase of the project. In later phases, the tools and methodologies developed during this phase will be evaluated based on their effectiveness in the rapid development of MT systems for other low-density languages. Given that our focus is low-density languages, large machine tractable lexicons are not likely to be available. Thus, one of our tasks is to develop methods and tools to facilitate the rapid development of such lexicons. We assume in our methodology that the following resources will be available:

- at least one machine-readable bilingual dictionary,
- a native (bilingual) speaker of the low-density language who can verify or refute observations made by
- a computational linguist, who may or may not be the same person as the native informant.

As demonstrated in the literature, unstructured information can be as useful as highly structured MRDs in the lexicon creation task [5, 6]. In our case, we had access to the data sources shown in Table 1. Additionally, we had access to English word lists with part of speech information, which could be loosely classified as a structured data source.

Table 1. Data sources used.

Data Sources	Information Content/Used
A. Structured Data Sources SGML-tagged Thai-English dictionary SGML-tagged English-Thai dictionary	Thai words, POS, glosses more Thai words, and glosses – (by inversion)
B. Unstructured Data Sources Thai newspaper text, unsegmented Thai newspaper text, hand-segmented List of Thai words retrieved from WWW	Thai free text (test, training data partitions) Thai words, POS, glosses Unverified Thai words (no gloss, no POS)

Figure 1 represents the processing flow and merging of information in deriving a large (>55000 entries) Thai word list, augmented with part of speech (POS) information and glosses. The principal methodology involved two steps. The first was the enrichment of the wordlist during each phase of processing with all the information that could possibly be extracted or inferred from combinations of the source data. The second step then focused on the filtering of the final wordlist by distilling out the most reliable information, resulting in the most complete and reliable lexical resource possible. This flow and the associated subtasks are depicted in the diagram as follows:

1. Structure parsing: Begin with the Thai-English Dictionary; extract Thai word list (entries) with English translations (glosses) and part of speech information.
2. Structure Inversion and Augmentation: Extract word list from English - Thai Dictionary, and invert to create Thai word list with English glosses, subject to certain stipulations. If the Thai entry is not segmented, use the word lists and the entries extracted from the Thai - English dictionary to segment and invert as many

entries as possible. Quality control and disambiguation of competing sources are handled during the distillation and filtering phase.

3. Merge and Fuse Structures: Further augment this information with word lists extracted from hand-segmented Thai free text (unstructured). This yields Thai word lists with POS and gloss information. Further leverage off of English word lists with POS and the English - Thai dictionary to induce POS for Thai words.

4. Distill and Filter: Using a priority scheme to distill the most reliable information out of the augmented lexicon, create the final filtered Thai lexical resource. The output of this entire process is a Thai - English lexicon, including POS information and glosses for each Thai word.

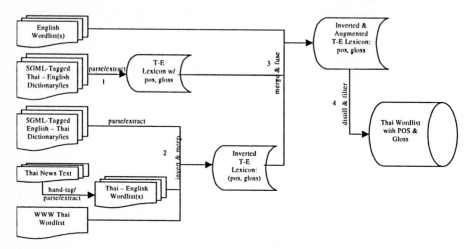

Fig. 1. Processing flow for lexicon creation in the QuickMT project.

We have made considerable progress with 1 and 2 above, and are currently using very simple, stand-in methods for 3 and 4, which are the subject of current research.

Figure 2 contains a portion of the lexical entry for the Thai word ดี from the SGML-tagged version of the dictionary. A typical entry contains the Thai spelling of the word, the Thai part of speech, and one or more senses consisting of (sometimes several) translations for the Thai word. The entry may also contain "phrases" or usage examples for a particular sense of a word, as is demonstrated in ความดี ("goodness"), under the second sense of the first entry for ดี. These phrases may or may not be compositional, and may translate to one word, several words or entire sentences. It is our intent to more fully exploit these usage examples in subsequent processing of the dictionaries; however, at this stage, we are simply extracting the usage examples as separate entries, labeling them as phrases or idioms when appropriate. We take the additional (somewhat risky) step of attempting to infer part of speech information for the Thai segment when the Thai entry is a single word that translates into a single English word.

`<SUPERENTRY>`
 `<ENTRY N="1">`
 `<FORM><ORTH`
 `LANG="tha">`ดี`</ORTH></F`
 `ORM>`
 `<GRAMGRP><POS>V</POS>`
 `</GRAMGRP> <SENSE`
 `N="1"> <TRANS>to`
 `be<DEF>good</DEF>`
 `<DEF>fine</DEF>`
 `<DEF>nice</DEF>`
 `</TRANS>`
 `</SENSE>`
 `<GRAMGRP><POS>sV</POS>`
 `</GRAMGRP>`
 `<SENSE N="2">`
 `<TRANS>`
 `<DEF>well</DEF>`
 `<DEF>nicely</DEF>`
 `<DEF>nice and (e.g.`
 `cool)</DEF>`
 `<DEF>quite</DEF>`
 `</TRANS>`
 `</SENSE>`
	`<RE TYPE="phrase">`
	 `<FORM> <ORTH`
	 `LANG="tha">`ความดี`</ORTH>`
	 `</FORM>`
	 `<TRANS>`
	 `<DEF>goodness</DEF>`
	 `<DEF>virtue</DEF>`
	 `<DEF>good</DEF>`
	 `</TRANS>`
	 `</RE>`
	 `[...] </ENTRY>`
	 `<ENTRY N="2">`
	 `<FORM>`
	 `<ORTH`
	 `LANG="tha">`ดี`</ORTH>`
	 `</FORM>`
	
	 `<GRAMGRP><POS>N</POS></G`
	 `RAMGRP>`
	 `<TRANS>`
	 `<DEF>gall bladder</DEF>`
	 `</TRANS>`
	 `</ENTRY>`
	 `</SUPERENTRY>`

Fig. 2. MRD entry for Thai word ดี.

Note that in this initial pass, only one SGML tagged Thai dictionary was used. The merging of information from more than one Thai dictionary introduces considerably more complexity, as is discussed toward the end of this paper, and is the subject of the next phase of research. Furthermore, the glosses contained in the resulting Thai-English lexicon are unanalyzed phrases of the type normally found in dictionaries intended for human consumption. For example, the lexical entry for ชืด extracted from the SGML-tagged version of the dictionary (see excerpt below) contains the gloss "to be tasteless", without any indication of which portion of the translated phrase is to inflect (if any), or whether the sense of "tasteless" in question refers (for example) to people, to food, or both. This is due to the way in which information was extracted from the SGML-tagged version of the dictionary. Text enclosed between <DEF> ... </DEF> tags was not further analyzed, but was imported unmodified into the Thai - English lexicon. Note that a more thorough processing of all senses in the lexical entry may enable the marking of the portion of translation subject to inflection as well as the inference that this particular Thai word deals with food, and not with people, jokes, etc.

The lack of inflectional information in the entry for ชืด is in contrast to the information extracted for the Thai word ดี ("good/well/gall bladder"). The portion of this lexical entry extracted from the SGML excerpt in figure 2 is included in figure 4 below. In this lexical entry, the infinitive portion of the verbal meaning is separated from the (in English) adjectival complement. Note that this is not due to any special processing on our part, but to the fact that this information was separated out in the SGML original.

```
<ENTRY><FORM>
   <ORTH LANG="tha">ชืด</ORTH> </FORM>
     <GRAMGRP><POS>V</POS></GRAMGRP>
     <TRANS> <DEF>to be tasteless</DEF>
     </TRANS>
   <SENSE> <FORM>
   <ORTH LANG="tha">เย็นชืด</ORTH>
   </FORM>
     <GRAMGRP><POS>V</POS> </GRAMGRP>
     <TRANS>to be<DEF>stone cold</DEF>
             <DEF>cold and tasteless</DEF>
   <NOTE TYPE="hint">of food which should be
       served hot</NOTE>
</TRANS></SENSE></ENTRY>
```

SGML version

```
#S(WORD :HEAD ("ชืด") :W-CLASS (#S(W-
CLASS  :POS  ((TE28-DICT  ("vi")  ("vt")))
:TRANSLATIONS (#S(TRANS :TRANSLATIONS
("to be tasteless"))) :SOURCE TE28-DICT)) :MAIN
T)
```
**Extracted Thai-English Lexicon (LISP
structure)**

Fig. 3.

```
#S(WORD :HEAD ("ดี") :W-CLASS (
   #S(W-CLASS :POS ((TE28-DICT ("vi") ("vt")))
:TRANSLATIONS (#S(TRANS :TRANSLATIONS
("good" "fine" "nice") :TEXT ("to be"))) :SOURCE
TE28-DICT)
      #S(W-CLASS :POS ((TE28-DICT ("secv")))
:TRANSLATIONS (#S(TRANS :TRANSLATIONS
("well" "nicely" "nice and (e.g. cool)" "quite")))
:SOURCE TE28-DICT)
      #S(W-CLASS :PHRASE ("ความดี")
:TRANSLATIONS (#S(TRANS :TRANSLATIONS
("goodness" "virtue" "good"))) :SOURCE TE28-DICT)
[…]
      #S(W-CLASS :POS ((TE28-DICT ("n")))
:TRANSLATIONS (#S(TRANS :TRANSLATIONS
("gall bladder"))) :SOURCE TE28-DICT) […] ) :MAIN
T)
```

Fig. 4.

Another point of note is that, as in the QuickMT project mentioned above, the question of what constitutes a lexical entry was not always clear-cut. As is hinted at above in the discussion of usage examples, the mapping between an entry in the SGML version of the dictionary and the Thai - English lexicon was not always one-to-one. The SGML version of the dictionary, being intended for human use, was organized in the way that people are accustomed to using dictionaries (at least in languages with alphabetic writing systems): by headword, with sub-entries for various senses of the word, including the senses associated with the various parts of speech. Usage examples and other related words were also included under the headword's entry. For the purposes of the MT lexicon, we maintain the relationship between a headword and its various part of speech homonyms. Usage examples, however, are extracted as separate lexical entries. It is also sometimes necessary to split other information out into a separate entry. For example, a word may be listed as having a special meaning only in a given phrase or context. In some cases, it is warranted to split that phrase out into a separate entry. In other cases, it is a question of a compound word, which is then merged with the entry for the appropriate headword.

We have observed that mining MT lexicons from MRDs is not just a matter of parsing the MRD, even when the MRD appears to be in a highly structured form (e.g. SGML-tagged). A principal reason for this, but one that is often overlooked, is that the organization of MRDs is essentially different from that of MT lexicons, the structure of each reflecting the purpose for which it is intended. Furthermore, simply converting the structure of the MRD into a format usable by an MT system is not sufficient. MRDs contain much more information than simple part of speech and word-for-word translation information. Translations are often phrasal and complex, and entries contain explanatory information and cross-references to other entries as well as other meta-information that would not be useful in its raw form, but all of which could be useful in the building of an MT lexicon.

Sifting the Sand from the Gold

Even though the simple processing completed thus far has not resulted in fully automating the production of an MT lexicon from an MRD, we have achieved some intermediate results which have been incorporated into very useful applications. Specifically, we have been able to use the information mined from the MRD to produce a system that segments Thai free text (which is normally written without spaces between words). We can further make use of the value added by the gloss and part of speech information extracted from the MRD, so that in addition to simply providing a segmented Thai sentence, we can provide a POS-tagged gloss as well. This tagged gloss may be enough for the user to get the gist of an otherwise unintelligible text, and enable him/her to decide whether it is worth committing the resources necessary to obtain a full translation.

The LSB project has also seen positive results even at its present state of development. A large lexicon created by a user for a particular syntactic-transfer-based MT system has been used to populate two monolingual lexicons within the LSB and the translation links between them. The contents of the LSB were then used to create a domain-specific lexicon for a different syntactic-transfer-based MT system, and for a government off-the-shelf substitution-based MT system.

Future Directions and Conclusion

The previous sections have demonstrated that although there are complexities involved, it is possible to extract from online bilingual dictionaries information that is useable for various facets of machine translation. Note that, in the case of the QuickMT project, although there were many types of information used in developing the final lexical resource (e.g. wordlists, Thai free text, tagged Thai text), only one complete Thai-English dictionary was used. Obviously, it would be desirable to be able to enrich the final resource with additional Thai-English dictionaries, if they are available. This raises questions related to the problem of merging entries from two or more dictionaries. While there were complications to be addressed in the merging of data from several sources that were "data-poor" (with respect to explicit lexical information) with the "data-rich" Thai-English MRD, these issues were resolved in ways that promoted the complementary use of the information contained in the various sources. The problems associated with combining and reconciling information from two data-rich sources (two MRDs, for example) are of a much higher complexity.

When considering the merging of two data-rich sources, two principal problems are

- deciding when two senses of a word are similar enough that it is unnecessary to include a distinct entry for each, and
- if two entries are warranted, deciding on the relative prominence, priority, or likelihood that should be assigned to each.

Thus, the focus in the next phase of our research will be on combining multiple online lexical resources by distilling out the most reliable and useful information from each.

In conclusion, we would like to suggest several guidelines that may prove useful to developers of unified lexical resources. These guidelines are not innovations, but we present them here as ideals that, based on our experience, are difficult, though still desirable, to achieve.

1. Facilitate the merging of information from various sources in a way that maximizes usability while minimizing information loss. Information sources and consumers have differing specifications and requirements regarding the way in which information is represented. As a simple example, part of speech codes may vary from one system to another, and mappings between codes of two systems are not always one-to-one. It is a nontrivial matter to develop a neutral representation that will both maintain the level of granularity originally present in the disparate information sources and enable the generation of information containing all and only the distinctions that are useful to the information-consuming system. This issue is further discussed in [3].

2. Ensure that the design is general enough to allow for the variation both in the information types that are provided by various sources and in information types that are required by the disparate systems subscribing to the information provided. This issue is related to but distinct from the issue of providing a neutral mapping for codes and other information contained in a resource. Here, we are concerned with developing a structure that is flexible enough to account for the fact that languages encode information differently, information sources provide varying types of information, and information consumers require varying types of information. Thus, one machine translation system may require that verbal entries

contain case frame or other subcategorization information, whereas another does not. Likewise, an MRD may provide high-level ontological information for nouns or information concerning irregular verb forms, or some other information not consistently provided. In the case of mining the information from MRDs, one solution would be to ignore such information in the name of maintaining unity in the lexical resource. We suggest that a better solution is to accommodate such variation in knowledge sources. In some cases, such as in the case of differing information required by the MT systems, ignoring the differences is not an option; the variation must be accounted for.

With these ideals in mind, we are currently devising a methodology to facilitate the acquisition and enable the sharing of lexical information between MT systems as well as other NLP tools.

References

1. Copestake, A. and Sanfilippo, A.: "Multilingual Lexical Representation". Building Lexicons for Machine Translation, Papers from the 1993 AAAI Spring Symposium. AAAI Press, Menlo Park, California. 1993.
2. EAGLES, Expert Advisory Group on Language Engineering Standards: Synopsis and Comparison of Morphosyntactic Phenonmena Encoded in Lexicons and Corpora. A Common Proposal and Applications to European Languages. Technical Report EAG-CLWG-Morphsyn/R, ILC-CNR, Pisa 1996.
3. Kamei, S., Itoh, E., Fujii, M., Hirai, T., Saitoh, Y., Takahashi, M., Hiyama, T., & Muraki, K.: "Sharable Formats and Their Supporting Environments for Exchanging User Dictionaries among Different MT Systems as a Part of AAMT Activities". Proceedings of Machine Translation Summit IV, San Diego, California, 1997.
4. Kilgarriff, A.: "Foreground and Background Lexicons and Word Sense Disambiguation for Information Extraction". Proceedings of the International Workshop on Lexically Driven Information Extraction. Frascati, Italy. July 1997. pp. 51 - 62.
5. Melamed, I.D.: "A Word-to-Word Model of Translational Equivalence". Proceedings of the 35th Conference of the Association for Computational Linguistics (ACL'97). Madrid, Spain. 1997.
6. Melamed, I.D. & Resnik, P.: "Semi-Automatic Acquisition of Domain-Specific Translation Lexicons". Proceedings of the 5th ANLP Conference. 1997.
7. Vanderwende, L.: "Ambiguity in the Acquisition of Lexical Information". Proceedings of the AAAI 1995 Spring Symposium Series, working notes of the Symposium on Representation and Acquisition of Lexical Knowledge. 1995. pp. 174 - 179.
8. Wilks, Y.A., Slator, B.M, & Guthrie, L.M.: Electric Words: dictionaries, computers, and meanings. MIT Press. Cambridge, Massachusetts. 1996.

System Description/Demo of Alis Translation Solutions Overview

Nathalie Côté, Trans., MBA[1]

[1]Product Specialist, Translation Solutions, E-mail: ncote@alis.com
Alis Technologies Inc.
100 Alexis Nihon Blvd.
Suite 600
Montreal, Quebec
Canada H4M 2P2
www.alis.com

Abstract. Part software, part process, Alis Translation Solutions (ATS) address the language barrier by tightly integrating a variety of language tools and services which include machine and human translation, on-line dictionaries, search engines, workflow and management tools. During the AMTA-98 conference, Alis Technologies is demonstrating various applications of ATS: Web and Intranet Publishing, Web Browsing, Company Document Circulation, E-mail Communication and Multilingual Site Search.

1. Introduction

Unlike the printed word, information found on the Internet, intranets and in electronic mail transmissions is dynamic. It changes constantly in order to keep up with today's fast-paced business world. It's now humanly impossible for conventional translation methods to manage such vast amounts of information.

2. Alis Translation Solutions

Part software, part process, Alis Translation Solutions (ATS) address the language barrier by tightly integrating a variety of language tools and services which include machine and human translation, on-line dictionaries, search engines, workflow and management tools. ATS helps organizations to achieve more efficient global communications by allowing users to understand information previously beyond their reach.

ATS allows users to request, through an intuitive interface which they may call upon as needed, the translation of any type of text appearing on their screen. This text can be an HTML document from the Internet or an intranet, E-mail, or an electronic document from a word processor or other applications. Through that interface, users can determine their translation parameters such as the desired target language and the quality level required. Based on those parameters, the ATS system then processes the request, either with automated translation and editing tools, or a human translation service. The users automatically receive the translated text on their screen, *in the same format as the original text.*

The process part is related to the professional services, and the software part uses Alis Technologies core technology and linguistic tools.

The Alis core technology and language expertise is tightly coupled with our partners solutions. Our partners include human translation teams, machine translation vendors, linguistic tool vendors, workflow management developers, among others.

The combination of Alis' rich language expertise along with the wide network of partner solutions equals a unique ability to respond to the complex technical demands of customers entering new cultural markets.

This combination also creates an opportunity for customers to access unparalleled best-of-breed solutions. Our partners include Alphabyte, Interwoven, Lexi-tech&TransLex, Microstar, Mitsui, Moovmento, NeocorTech, Systran, Toshiba, Transparent Language, Triad Data, Verity, Vignette, Weblations, Xerox, and the list is growing.

3. ATS Core Technology

ATS provides a single point of entry for multiple machine translation engines and language-handling technologies. This solution exceeds stand-alone language applications in flexibility, translation quality and cost-effectiveness because ATS core technology is an open architecture. It allows easy additions and upgrades, is scalable to accommodate a large number of users, and offers the choice of multiple tools for best possible translation quality and lower translation costs.

The ATS server integrates multiple machine translation engines, human translation services, translation memory, workflow management, Web site management and multilingual search engines. The server provides the ATS linguistic layer and resides along side the HTTP server (Apache-based) and the SMTP server.

4. ATS Linguistic Tools

As ATS provides linguistic solutions for specific language problems in large organizations, linguistic software services development is demand-driven. The framework provided by the ATS architecture gives Alis the ability to integrate, as required, different linguistic technologies and build *best of breed* solutions.

Completing the Alis Translation Solutions is a wide array of linguistic tools to increase productivity and to help improve the quality of automated translation. Most of them are used to pre-process text before it is run through machine translation. The list of these tools is ever expanding.

4.1 Language Identifier and Code-Set Detection

This is an assistant application that can quickly identify the source language of a document by analyzing a small number of phrases. In a situation like surfing the Internet, where any site and any document can be translated, knowing the source language of the document allows the system to match that information with the language pairs available for translation. It can then automatically show the users the target languages to which they have access. Alternatively, if the users have captured their preferences (e.g. target language - always translate into French) either on their machine or on the server, this will keep them from having to indicate the language pair every time.

4.2 Multilingual Search and Query Expansion

This particular application is designed to allow users to enter a search query in their own language, search content in a different language, and obtain the results in their own language. The query string itself is automatically translated before performing the search, and the resulting summaries are translated back into the language of the query. In the end, users are presented with the resulting documents in the same language as that of their initial query.

4.3 Accent Tools

For languages that use accented characters (e.g. French), this type of application can be used prior to machine translation to ensure all accents are correctly used. If the system has identified the language as French, for example, this utility can be run automatically on the input text. This tool is especially useful in the case of e-mail translation, since accents are sometimes lost in the transmission.

4.4 Word Dictionaries

These dictionaries allow the user to simply look up a word in different languages. This can be useful as an alternative to translation when the user has some understanding of the source language and just wants to look up a few words, or to further understand a document.

4.5 Structured Languages

This application allows a corporation to define a set of restricted vocabularies to be used in documents submitted for translation. It then checks the documents to ensure that they comply with the vocabulary before they are sent to a translation engine. The application can also generate an appropriate set of input parameters for the translation engine to guarantee a high-quality result. This type of application is best in situations where a restricted vocabulary is already in use (e.g. technical publications).

4.6 Part of Speech Identifiers

These utilities are run as a pre-edit filter on the text to be translated. They identify and tag certain parts of speech such as proper nouns (e.g. names) so the translation engines do not translate them.

Other Utilities

In order to create the best quality translation output possible, Alis has also created other utilities which may be included in the ATS solution. Examples of these are special HTML filters (e.g. inclusion of graphic first paragraph characters in translation, or cleanup of HTML tags), Meta-dictionaries that can be used by all engines, and others that can be used for re-tagging and re-punctuating translation output.

In each case, Alis Technologies uses its existing, in-house methodology for a thorough evaluation process of each application or service, in order to integrate the best linguistic tools available into the solution. This evaluation process is based on the characteristics of the linguistic such as domains covered, input format, output quality and on systems of representation of information, quality and size of lexicons, etc. The core technology then provides a uniform client interface to all these integrated linguistic services.

5. Professional Services

Besides the extensive integration of various components, the services offered by Alis' team of experts make ATS unique.

Services range from consultation to customization, quality assurance, implementation, maintenance, support and training, and play a large part in making every ATS a turnkey, worry-free solution.

System Demonstration
SYSTRAN® Enterprise

Christian Raby

SYSTRAN Software, Inc.
7855 Fay Avenue, Suite 300, La Jolla, CA 92037 – USA
craby@systransoft.com

1 Introduction

SYSTRAN® Enterprise responds to the demands of today's fast paced international business environment and is tailored for use on an intranet, extranet or LAN.

2 System Builder and Contacts

SYSTRAN Software, Inc.

Director of Product and Technical Services: Imed Fehri - ifehri@systransoft.com

Director of Sales & Marketing: Reba Rosenbluth - rrosenbl@systransoft.com

3 System Category

SYSTRAN® Enterprise is now in beta-testing at SYSTRAN's La Jolla facilities and is scheduled for commercial release as follows:

Commercial release (Phase I):   September 28, 1998
Commercial release (Phase II):   October 30, 1998

4 System Characteristics

The system includes 21 domain-specific topical glossaries, which follow: Automotive, Aviation / Space, Chemistry, Colloquial, Computers / Data Processing, Earth Sciences, Economics / Business, Electronics, Food Science, Legal, Life Sciences, Mathematics, Mechanical Engineering, Medicine, Metallurgy, Military

Science, Naval / Maritime, Patent / Abstracts, Photography / Optics, Physics / Atomic Energy, and Political Science.

SYSTRAN® Enterprise supports ANSI, ASCII, HTML, RTF, and SGML file formats.

5   Resources

SYSTRAN's methodology is a sentence by sentence approach, concentrating on individual words and their dictionary data, and on the parse of the sentence unit, followed by the translation of the parsed sentence. Three major groups describe the SYSTRAN architecture: Dictionary, Systems Software and Linguistic Software. Each of these consists of a great number of modules which all work together to create a fully automatic MT (Machine Translation) system.

All of SYSTRAN's dictionaries are integrated into the above process. Included are single-word/stem dictionary and an expression dictionary. The latter includes idioms, phrases, grammar rules for lexical disambiguation, as well as rules which can influence the parsing process. It should be noted that SYSTRAN is presently restructuring all of its dictionaries and their user interface. SYSTRAN's new dictionaries are scheduled for release in early 1999 and will allow the full range of expression coding.

SYSTRAN parses with a battery of procedural modules which resolve, step by step, various syntactic and semantic relationships and assign structure within the sentence. The SYSTRAN parser is deterministic in nature, so each module makes firm decisions and passes the results on to the next module. The advantage is that every sentence, even an incomplete or malformed one, will be parsed and therefore translated. The disadvantage of such determinism, is that incorrect decisions may be passed on and compounded from module to module. SYSTRAN is able to soften this by several mechanisms that flag uncertain decisions. SYSTRAN's final step in this checking process is a Filter program which identifies the major parse errors.

After a parse of the input sentence has been constructed, algorithms for the construction of a translation are invoked. Translation information, on both the word and expression levels, is derived during dictionary lookup and the parsing phases of the translation, for use by two distinct Transfer and Synthesis modules. The Transfer component performs situation-specific restructuring, depending on the degree of difference between source and target languages. It is the only module, besides the dictionary, which relates to both source and target language, and it is rather small when the two languages are closely related.

Following this, the Synthesis module generates the target language strings which correspond to the information provided by all previous modules. Synthesis is a source-language independent module. The Synthesis modules contain sophisticated algorithms for creating specialized target language constructs, such as negation, questions, verbs with their complete morphology, placement of adverbs, and articles etc.

6   Minimum System Requirements:

TCP-IP network
486 Intel or compatible
32 MB RAM

Server:

15 MB of hard disk space per language pair
Windows NT 4.0 or higher

Client:

Windows 95, 98 or NT 4.0

7   System Description:

Tailored for use on an intranet, extranet or LAN, SYSTRAN® Enterprise provides users with easy access to the translation server from any worldwide client operating on a company network through an IP address. SYSTRAN® Enterprise features include:
- TCP-IP based
- Multi-threaded
- Provides concurrent user configurations
- JAVA client
- Documented API to write CGI scripts
- Capability of specifying desired translation servers

SYSTRAN Enterprise will be available in the following language pairs:
English<->French
English<->Italian
English<->German
English<->Spanish
English<->Portuguese
English<->Japanese
Chinese->English
Russian->English

A full demonstration of SYSTRAN® Enterprise along with detailed features and benefits will be presented at the AMTA '98 in Philadelphia.

Integrating Tools with the Translation Process

Edith R. Westfall

TRADOS Corporation, 803 Prince Street, Alexandria, VA 22314
703-683-6900 (v), 703-683-9457 (f)
edith@trados.com

System Developers: TRADOS GmbH

Hackländerstrasse 17, D-70187 Stuttgart, Germany
+49 (711) 168 77-0 (v), +49 (711) 168 77-50 (f)
E-mail: info@trados.com
Web: http://www.trados.com

Abstract. Translation tools can be integrated with the translation process with
the goal and result of increasing consistency, reusing previous translations, and
decreasing the amount of time needed to put a product on the market. This
system demonstration will follow a document through the translation cycle
utilizing a combination of TRADOS Translator's Workbench 2.0 (translation
memory), machine translation, and human translation.

Type: System description/demo

Primary software in demonstration: TRADOS Translator's Workbench 2.0

North American Sales and Support

East:
803 Prince Street
Alexandria, VA 22314
703-683-6900 (v)
703-683-9457 (f)

West:
1250 Oakmead Parkway, Suite 210
Sunnyvale, CA 94086
408-524-2975 (v)
408-524-2974 (f)

System information

Recommended system requirements:

	Minimum	Recommended
OS	Windows 95/NT	Windows 95/NT
CPU/Speed	Pentium 133	Pentium 233
RAM	16	32 or more

Hard disk	15 MB for installation	40 MB for a large bilingual TM database with 130,000 translation units.
Monitor		17"
Network	10 Mbit/s Ethernet	100 Mbit/s Ethernet
Additional software	MS Word 6.0 (MS Word 7.0 for Japanese, Chinese, Korean)	MS Word 7.0 MultiTerm '95 Plus!

System characteristics

The following formats can be used with Translator's Workbench either directly or with a filter: Word, RTF, RC, PageMaker, HTML, SGML, FrameMaker, Interleaf.

The size of the databases created by Translator's Workbench and MultiTerm '95 Plus! is unlimited.

Translator's Workbench and MultiTerm '95 Plus! are language independent. If the operating system supports a language then TRADOS products can work with the language (with the exception of bi-di languages)

Demonstration Overview

The TRADOS suite of translation tools can be integrated into the translation process in conjunction with machine translation (MT) to enhance the translation process. This system demonstration will follow a document, in this case a product description, through the translation cycle. It will start with an evaluation of the document and then continue through the steps of the translation cycle – analysis by Translator's Workbench, MT, and interactive use of Translator's Workbench to complete the translation. In this demonstration, the following assumptions are held: the document is in Word 8 (Word 97), some terminology has been collected in MultiTerm, and a translation memory database has been created and some translation units added.

System Overview

Translator's Workbench is a commercial translation memory system. As a translation memory system it is designed to aid the translation process to increase efficiency and consistency of work for human translators. Although it can be used in conjunction with machine translation, it is not an MT system. Translator's Workbench does not create sentences; rather it finds the closest available match from a database of completed work. By using a database of translations created by human translators the editing required is minimized.

Using translation memory in conjunction with machine translation plays to the strengths of both of these tools – good quality translation from human translators and the speed of machine translation. Using MT together with translation memory minimizes the impact of the variable quality of MT.

MultiTerm promotes consistent terminology through its integration with Translator's Workbench. MultiTerm is a concept-oriented database designed specifically for building and managing terminology. Each entry is free form and can contain translations, definitions, attributes, or graphics. Up to 20 languages can be included as well as synonyms, cross-references, examples, and identification of the source for the information.

Process

Table 1. Explanation of codes

Code	Usage	Description
<Author>	The creator of the translated segment.	MT! indicates that the translation was created by an MT program
<USE>	source language	U.S. English
<FRE>	target language	French

The tools-integrated translation process is as follows:
Review the source file.
• What program was used to create the product description?
Which translation memory database should be used?
• Use "analyze" function in Translator's Workbench with a specific translation memory database.
Export the unknown segments.
• Choose export type for MT system.
  • Translator's Workbench generates a file for use by the MT system. See example 1 – the source segment is repeated as a placeholder for the translated segment.
    Example 1:   <Author>MT!
                   <USE>Product Description
                   <FRE>Product Description
Translate the exported text with the appropriate machine translation software.
• During the translation process, the source text, which has been acting as a placeholder, will be replaced with a generated translation. Machine translation software analyzes the source segment, parses it, and translates the segment
    Example 2:   <Author>MT!
                   <USE>Product Description
                   <FRE>Description au produit
Import the translated file into your translation memory.
• These translated segments are merged into the designated translation memory database and are available for use.
• These segments are flagged with <Author>MT!.

Use Translator's Workbench in the interactive mode to translate the product description.

- Resize the Translator's Workbench and word processing program windows.
  - Translator's Workbench should take up one-third of the screen.
  - Word processing program should take up the remainder of the screen.
- Translations are suggested by Translator's Workbench.
- The author tag lets you know who (or what) is responsible for the translation. This information lets you decide on the degree of editing necessary.
  - Use personal knowledge of translator's abilities.
  - Be aware that MT created the segment. Translator's Workbench allows the user to assign a "penalty" for translation segments created by MT. By using this option the user can make sure that MT segments are not 100% matches.
- Formatting is preserved.
- MultiTerm entries for words in active sentence are displayed.
  - Use terminology consistent with client preferences.
  - Check terms chosen by machine translation system.

Print or otherwise display the document for final proofing of both translation and layout.

- You can enter the edits for the translation.
- These corrections are saved in the translation memory database.

Advantages of integration of Translation Memory and Machine Translation

By using a tools-integrated translation process rather than a manual, non-tools process, the following steps are saved:

- Identifying reusable translation text
  - Analyzing what is different about this product description versus previously translated documents.
- Reformatting document
  - Cutting and pasting
  - Reapplying styles
- Checking consistency of translation
  - Need to check the consistency of translation is diminished.
- Checking terminology
  - Quicker verification of appropriate terminology.

Review

The following components of the TRADOS suite of translation tools have been demonstrated:

- Translator's Workbench

- Multilingual translation memory.
- Storage of user-defined administrative information in translation memory.
- Fuzzy matching for quick access to sentences, phrases, and terminology.
- Fuzzy match differences highlighted in various colors.
- Integration with word processors.
- This demonstration covered one European language. However, Translator's Workbench supports all European languages, including non-Latin languages such as Russian and Greek and DBCS languages such as Japanese as both source and target languages.
- Automatic identification and substitution of numbers.
- Configurable sentence segmentation.

- MultiTerm '95 Plus
  - MultiTerm can manage up to 20 languages simultaneously (including non-Latin languages such as Russian and Greek and DBCS languages such as Japanese).
    - Terms are indexed in all languages so the user can instantly switch from one language pair to another. Other data fields can be indexed also.
  - Attributes
  - Search capabilities
  - Network capability

Conclusion

The translation process, when viewed in its entirety, provides many opportunities for the integration of translation tools. A large volume of translation lends itself to using either translation memory or machine translation. However, as this example shows, the TRADOS suite of translation tools together with MT can be integrated into translation process to have a greater impact.

The resulting savings in time and increase in consistency is important as the volume of translation grows. TRADOS Translator's Workbench is a tool that increases in utility over time. As source and target segments are saved, the chance to leverage previous translations expands.

Key to the integration of translation memory and other translation tools is the process. That is, having a series of steps that are followed consistently. A process also means that the timesavings and other positive impacts can be measured – a very important consideration in the budget-conscious business world.

EMIS
A Multilingual Information System

Bärbel Ripplinger

IAI, Martin-Luther-Straße 14, D-66111 Saarbrücken, Germany
babs@iai.uni-sb.de

Abstract. The objective of the EMIS project is the conception and realization of a web-based multilingual information system on European
media law with the following functionalities:
- search by words, a combination of words, phrases or keywords
- guided search by using a so-called *thematic structure*
- cross language retrieval of documents in different languages with one
  monolingual query by using language processing and MT technology
- exploitation of additional information for the retrieved documents,
  which is stored in a database
- structured representation of the document archive, the so-called *dogmatic structure*
- multilingual user interface.

System builder and contact: The development of the information system
EMIS is carried out by the Institute for Applied Information Sciences (IAI).
For further information contact the author.

System category: EMIS is an ongoing joint industrial research project of the
Institute for Applied Information Sciences (IAI) and the Institute for Eu-
ropean Media Law (EMR) funded by the German Ministry of Economics.
(Start: November 1996, End: Mid 1999.)

System characteristics: The project aims at the conception and realization
of a multilingual information system in the *domain of European media law*.
The system will provide multilingual search, cross language retrieval and
navigation functionalities for an archive of documents accessed by a multilingual user interface using a standard browser.

Resources: At present the database consists of 166 media law texts from different European countries and the European Union in the languages German,
English and/or French. The texts from the EU exist in all three languages
and are used to build up bilingual thesauri on the one hand and for relevance
feedback to improve recall and precision on the other. The documents are
stored in a relational database (ORACLE), together with additional information about the law.
For the retrieval, EMIS makes use of the following monolingual and reversible
bilingual lexicons (the domain dependent entries are used as thesauri):

de	38200 morphemes	
en	37500 morphemes	
fr	58000 morphemes	
de-en	433900 lexemes	(2100 media law terms)
de-fr	26700 lexemes	(1900 media law terms)
en-fr	39300 lexemes	(4100 media law terms)

Hard- and software: The prototype presented here and the final system run entirely on a webserver, so the end users need only a standard web browser. The system modules are platform independently implemented in C, Perl and JavaScript: The development is performed on a Unix Workstation and the final system will run on an NT-Server. An intended EMIS intranet application will even run without ORACLE.

Functionality description: The core component of EMIS is the multilingual *cross language retrieval* which is enhanced by linguistic processing i.e. by a morpho-syntactic analysis applied to the documents and to the queries, and the relevant bilingual dictionaries. The languages covered by the project are German, English and French.

System internals: In the EMIS project a cross language retrieval is done by query translation. This query translation is for keywords implemented by using multilingual thesauri (see Resources) and for free text retrieval by a simple MT tool which is part of the **Mpro** program package: a development of the IAI [1].

To improve the query translation from the interface language into the other working languages, the translation is done domain dependently. If there are translations in the given context - in the EMIS system the domains are *media law, telecommunications,* and *general law* - these are preferred. If no such translations are available all others found in the bilingual dictionary are used for retrieval. Multi-word units or phrases will be translated compositionally if there are no translations of the whole expression. The user gets informed about the 'unauthorized' status of these translations.

EMIS provides the user with several possibilities to access the documents. The first three represent a kind of retrieval by concepts and the last one a cross language free text retrieval.

Retrieval using the 'dogmatic structure'

The dogmatic structure gives an overview of all existing media laws in Europe and the European Union. For each country the relevant documents are listed sorted into particular law areas. Clicking on a document the user can view the whole text at once or read paragraph by paragraph.

Retrieval using the 'thematic structure'

The EMR as the domain expert in the project has developed the so-called *thematic structure*; this hierarchical structure represents the domain by different topics. The upper structure consists, for instance, of the following concepts: *Broadcasting, Multimedia, Youth Protection, Media Concentration, Financing and Telecommunications.* These concepts are refined in the lower levels. By clicking on a concept the user will get documents relevant to this topic. Compared to the first retrieval functionality the user will get here, for instance, all the documents from all countries relevant to telecommunications (and not only one).

The base thematic structure (in all working languages) and the classification of the documents along the different themes is carried out manually because expert knowledge is absolutely essential. The thematic structure itself will be automatically generated.

Keyword retrieval

For the text retrieval by keywords traditional multilingual thesauri are used for the document indexing. In the current state of the system the keywords are assigned by the domain experts only in German. The multilingual thesauri are used to translate the particular query and retrieve the relevant documents. For the future, it is foreseen that the linguistic analysis described below will be used together with the thesauri to extract the keywords automatically. First attempts to perform automatic indexing have been completed successfully within another project of IAI.

Free text retrieval

The retrieval approach used in this project takes advantage of linguistic processing technologies. Using the Mpro tool every document is morpho-syntactically analyzed. The tool performs a part-of-speech tagging, a lemmatization, an analysis of homographs (optional) and for German texts also a compound analysis.

In the following examples, a German (1), an English (2) and a French (3) word analysis are given:

```
(1) {ori=Rundfunkanstalt,wnra=1,wnrr=1,snr=1,c=noun,
     lu=rundfunkanstalt,s=loc&ag,t=rundfunk#anstalt,cs=n#n,
     ts=rundfunk#anstalt,ds=rundfunk#anstalt,ls=rundfunk#anstalt,
     ss=medium#loc&ag,w=2,lngs=germ#germ}
```

```
(2) {ori=Broadcasting,wnra=1,wnrr=1,snr=1,c=noun,s=ation,
     lu=broadcasting, ds=broadcast~ing}
```

```
(3)  {ori=Radiodiffusion,wnra=1,wnrr=1,snr=1,c=noun,s=process,
      lu=radiodiffusion,ds=radiodiffuser~ion,nb=sg,g=f}
```

Indexing: The results of the document analyses are used to generate different indexes. For German texts, three indexes are used: the first is an index generated by using the 'lu-feature' (i.e. the lexical unit), the second is generated from the 'ls-feature' which indicates the derivation of the lexical unit and the third is built up using the 't-feature' which marks the possible normalized word parts of a compound (in cases of simple words, the value of the t-feature is the same as the value of the lu-feature).

For English and French two indexes are generated at a time, the first takes the lu-feature and the second the ds-feature (the derivation).

Function words are excluded from the indexing process.

The algorithm: Each query, which can be a simple word, a multi-word unit or a phrase, undergoes the same morpho-syntactic analysis as the documents. From the output of this analysis the values of the lu-, t-, and the ls-features or the lu- and the ds-features are used to search the indexes. The result of the access with the lexical unit (lu) of the lu-index represents the number of exact matches. The access of the ls-index with the value of the ls-feature results in a list of documents which contain words with the same derivation as that of the query. Here, some wrong results can occur if the derivation denotes a homonym. For example, the search for *publicity* contains all occurences of *public*. At present we are investigating whether the integration of semantic information (s, ss-features) into the search process can solve this problem. As the result of the access of the t-index we will get a list of all compounds containing the input as part. If the query consists of a compound (mostly relevant for German), for all parts of the compound extracted from the t-feature and the corresponding derivations (extracted from the ls-feature) an access to the ls/ds-index and the t-index is performed. The first results in a list of documents where the compound occurs with its parts. For instance, for the query *Jugendschutz (youth protection)* the list contains hits like *Schutz der Jugend/protecting of the youth* or *die Jugend schützen/protect the youth*. The search space in these cases is one single sentence (i.e. the unit Mpro marks as sentence). By accessing the t-index for all parts, the result is a list of documents containing semantically similar terms. For the example of *Jugendschutz*, hits are *Kinderschutzbund/children protection organization, Jugendarbeit/youth work*.

The different result lists represent equally the different relevance of the hits which will also be clearly represented in the output.

If the input is a multi-word unit (English/French compound) or a phrase all function words are removed and the remaining meaning-bearing words undergo the procedure described above. Additionally the units must be within a particular environment within one sentence to be an exact hit. This environment is computed using a rule of thumb, i.e. the length of the environment corresponds to three times the number of units. All other hits are collected in a second list which represents the minor relevance of those documents.

References

1. D. Maas, 1996: MPRO – Ein System zur Analyse und Synthese deutscher Wörter, in: **R. Hausser (ed): Linguistische Verifikation**, Max Niemeyer Verlag, Tübingen 1996

An Open Transfer Translation

Jorge Kinoshita

Escola Politécnica da Universidade de São Paulo
Departamento de Computação e Sistemas Digitais (PCS) - Brazil
email: jkinoshi@pcs.usp.br URL: http://jk.pcs.usp.br

Abstract. We are developing an English-Portuguese Transfer Machine. The transfer machine operates in three phases: the analysis phase is done according to a dependency grammar, the transfer phase is done according to a transfer dictionary and the generation phase conjugates the Portuguese words. The user interface is done through the web. Our system is "open" because the user can view intermediate structures generated by the system and change the database system in order to correct the text during the revision process.

1 Introduction

We are developing an English-Portuguese [?] transfer machine based on some presuppositions: (1) we do not need to get perfect texts translations. Our aim is to speed the translation process performed by humans. (2) two related words (a bigram) in an English sentence defines a good context and hence, it is possible to associate a good translation to the bigram. A database of bigrams and their translations (which we call, "a transfer dictionary") can be used in the analysis phase (the more bigrams are found in the analysis, the better) and in the transfer phase (in order to translate bigrams). (3) instead of revising the text that was automatically translated, the user should revise the transfer dictionary. When the user changes one entrance in the dictionary, the system shows how the entire text is modified due to this alteration. For instance: the system can wrongly translate "home page" to "página (page) do(of) lar(home)" The correct translation is "home page" (The Brazilian Portuguese keeps the English term). If the translation "home page" → "home page" is added to the dictionary, all the occurrences of "home page" will be automatically revised; then speeding the translation process.

The translation process that is performed automatically consists of :

(1) link the words of an English sentence in pairs (by some dependency grammar). It is possible to associate a relation-tag (kind of linkage) to a bigram. For instance in "spread-wing", the relation-tag is VB/NN that means "verb-object".
(2) translate the bigrams according to the dictionary.

The translation process that is performed manually consists of: (1) select an wrong translation of an word or bigram and correct it. (2) submit the correction to the system which will correct the necessary portions of the text. (3) repeat the two former steps until no improvement can be made. (4) correct manually all sentences of the text (this will not change the database system). For instance: the anaphora, ellipses and idiomatic expressions are difficult to be handled by bigrams.

2 The Transfer Dictionary

In the transfer dictionary, it is possible to declare the translation of:

(1) a **bigram** (two words). Example: "give up → desistir". In this example two words are translated as a single word. It is possible to add and delete words and even change words position.

(2) a **partial bigram** (one word and its relation-tag to the head). Examples:

(A) "like -VB/NN → gostar-de" : the verb "like" when linked to its object is translated as "gostar" plus the preposition "de" that is inserted before the translated object. If no object exists, the preposition "de" is not inserted.

(B) "it -PRP\R → -" : the pronoun "it" behaving as a subject is deleted in Portuguese translations.

(3) a **single word** according to its tag. Example: "like VB → gostar".

It is also possible to rearrange the sentence according to the Portuguese syntax based only on the relation-tag. For instance, in Portuguese, adjectives generally follow the noun and this is handled looking at the relation-tag JJ\NN (adjective-noun).

The dictionary follows a syntax that is beyond the scope of this article.

3 The Translation

Translation is done automatically in 3 phases:

- **analysis**: link each word to its head (one word, the root of the sentence, does not have a head). For instance, the sentence "the boy sold a new house" is analyzed as in Table 1.

Table 1. Analysis Result

pos	head	tag	word
1	2	DT	the
2	3	NN	boy
3	0	VBD	sell sold
4	6	DT	a
5	6	JJ	new
6	3	NN	house

Table 2. Transfer Result

pos'	pos	head	tag'	word'
1	1	2	DT	o
2	2	3	NN	menino
3	3	0	VBD3s	vender
4	4	6	DTf	um
5	6	3	NNf	casa
6	5	6	JJf	novo

where:

pos = word position in the sentence; *head* = head of the word; *word'* = Portuguese word in infinitive form.

The structure shows how words are linked to each other. For instance, "house" is the object of "sold" because the word 6 has the word 3 as its head. The tags follow the TREEBANK [?] notation.

- **transfer**: The input is the structure generated by the analysis and the output is a sequence of words in Portuguese but in the radical form as it is shown in Table 2.

The translation of bigrams is done in a top-down direction because it is easier to handle the movement of words and phrases around the head-word. The statements used from the transfer dictionary are presented in Table 3.

Table 3. Rules

$JJ\backslash NN$: % + %
a DT : um
boy NN : menino
house NN : casa.f
new JJ : novo
sell VB : vender
the DT : o

- **generation**: After the transfer phase, the words must be conjugated according to their tags and the result is: "o menino vendeu uma casa nova".

Revision. The revision is done interactively with the system: **1-system** displays all the translated text. **1-user** selects the sentence of the text that he intends to fix. **2-system** displays the analysis and transfer structures. **2-user** selects any word of the transfer structure (for instance, the word "house"). A selection of one word implies in the selection of a bigram: the word and its head (ex: house and sell). **3-system** displays all possible entrances of the transfer dictionary related to the selection; in this example, to the word "house", to the bigram "sell-house", to "house" behaving as an object and to "sell" behaving as a transitive verb. The system also displays blanks to be filled by the user if there is lack of some entrance in the dictionary (which normally happens, specially for the bigram translation). For instance, let us suppose that the translation of "house" were not declared. Its translation appears as a blank enabling the user to provide new information. **3-user** corrects the system database. **4-system** looks in the text for all possible cases where it can be applied. This process does not imply in redoing all translation again.

The system keeps all intermediate structures of the parser and transfer phases in a database. This is done because: 1) as the system is designed to be in internet, it must attend many users. A user must not block any process during his interaction to the intermediate structures of his text. 2) any user alteration that affects the intermediate structures can be checked very fast; otherwise the system would have to generate all the structures again. 3) the intermediate structures in a database can be used as a noted corpus providing information for future programs.

4 Conclusion

Our transfer mechanism is based on simple operations on bigrams. The simplicity of the formalism suggests that it could be applied (or easily adapted) to projects that have an analysis similar to that provided by dependency grammars (ex: Link Grammar [?]). The user needs to be prepared to use the system. He needs to know the rule syntax for deleting English words, adding Portuguese words, reordering the words in Portuguese, etc. In a future version, a more user-friendly interface will be created. Today, the system allows many users changing the database and working on the same translation. The problem is that a user can damage the translation of other users. In a future version, we are planning to have some mechanism of controlling versions in order to recover to previous states. Today, the system registers in a file the operations performed by all users. This file will be used to recover to previous states.

System builder and contact: the author.

System category: research vehicle.

System characteristics: translation of technical texts (given in HTML or plain text). The system is treating 50 sentences per minute in its automatic translation (Pentium MMX 200MHz: local test). This result must be seen with care: the output still requires a lot of revision work and there were many small phrases (titles) that were counted as sentences.

Resources: word-net1.6 [?], and GDBM files of around 1.7 Mbytes for dictionaries and a small grammar of 50Kbytes.

Hardware and software: Pentium PC; operating system: Linux RedHat 4.2.

Functionality description: Today our system does not speed the translation process. The revision phase requires a lot of work because: (1) our database is still very poor. Today the purpose is to create mechanisms to control it. (2) the parser needs to be improved.

acknowledgement: FAPESP - Fundação de Amparo à Pesquisa do Estado de São Paulo

References

1. KINOSHITA, J.: Aspectos de Implementação de Uma Ferramenta de Auxílio à Tradução Inglês-Português. Tese de Doutorado, Departmento de Computação e Sistemas Digitais da Escola Politécnica da Univesidade de São Paulo, Brazil (1997)
2. PENN TOOLS. http://www.cis.upenn.edu/ adwait/penntools.html, (1998)
3. SLEATOR, D. D. K.; TEMPERLEY, D. : Parsing English with a Link Grammar. Pittsburgh, Canegie Mellon University, sleator@cs.cmu.edu (1991)
4. MILLER, G.A. ET AL.: Introduction to WordNet: an on-line lexical database. Princeton University, http://www.cogsci.princeton.edu/ wn/, (1993)

TransEasy: A Chinese-English Machine Translation System Based on Hybrid Approach

Qun Liu[1] and Shiwen Yu[2]

[1] Institute of Computing Technology, Chinese Academy of Sciences,
P.O.Box 2704, Beijing 100080, China
liuqun@mtgroup.ict.ac.cn
[2] Institute of Computational Linguistics, Peking University,
Beijing 100871, China
yusw@pku.edu.cn

Abstract. This paper describes the progress of a machine translation system from Chinese to English. The system is based on a reusable platform of MT software components. It's a rule-based system, and some statistical algorithms are used as heuristic functions in parsing as well. There are about 50,000 Chinese words and 400 global parsing rules in the system. The system got a good result in a public test of MT system in China in Mar. 1998. It is a research vehicle up to now.

1 Introduction

The current level of Chinese-English machine translation is much lower than that of English-Chinese machine translation in China [1], because the analysis of Chinese is more difficult than that of English. There are several commercial Chinese-English MT systems in the software market, but most of them are of little practical use value.

TransEasy is a new Machine Translation System from Chinese to English we developed. We try to make it a practical Chinese-English MT system.

The basic information of the system is as follows:
- System Name: TransEasy
- Developer: Institute of Computing Technology, Chinese Academy of Sciences
  Institute of Computational Linguistics, Peking University
- System Builders and contacts:
  Qun Liu, Shiwen Yu, etc. (the authors of this paper)
- System Category: research vehicle
- System Characteristics:
  Translation Speed: about 40,000 Chinese Characters per hour
  Domains Covered: no specific domain
  Input Formats: plain text
  Output Quality: about 70% of the translations are understandable

- Resource: Lexicon: 50,000 entries of Chinese Words
  Rulebases: less than 400 rules in the global parsing rulebase
- Hardware and Software: IBM/PC compatible
  Windows 95 or NT with Chinese environment (GB Code)

2 General MT Development Platform

The development of the Chinese-English MT System is based on a General MT Development Platform [7].

The development of a MT system is tedious work. MT systems for different language pairs, or even MT systems of different kinds, have many common data structures and algorithms. Making these data structures and algorithms reusable, will greatly reduce the work of development. The Platform provides this kind of reusability. The Platform contains a lot of software components. These software components implement the most frequently used data structures and algorithms in MT systems. The relations between these software components are clearly defined. These software components can be used independently. The platform supports the development of MT systems of different language pairs, and provides the API functions for specified natural language. The software components are easily extended to fit different types of MT systems.

3 Algorithms

We use the transfer approach in the system. The process of the translation is: morphological analysis, structural analysis, transform, structural generation and morphological generation

The morphological analysis of Chinese is much more difficult than that of English. There are two kinds of ambiguities in this phase: segmentation ambiguity and tagging ambiguity. The morphological analysis of this system includes four steps:

1. overlapped words processing and dictionary consulting
2. rule-based disambiguation of segmentation
3. rule-based disambiguation of tagging
4. statistical disambiguation of segmentation and tagging

In the last step we use a HMM model. A threshold is used to discard the tags with low probability [8]. Because we use a nondeterministic algorithm, we need not to eliminate all the ambiguity in this phase. The ambiguities that cannot be eliminated are kept to the phase of structural analysis.

The structural analysis relies mainly on syntax features and uses the semantic information for reference. Semantic analysis is done simultaneously with the syntactic analysis.

A modified Chart Parsing algorithm is used in the structural analysis phase. We use a statistical algorithm to improve the efficiency of parsing. A probability is given to each potential node by scoring function, which use PCFG as the model [8]. When the parsing of the source sentence failed, a kind of "soft failure" technique is used to give the most likely result.

In the phases of transform and structural generation we use the algorithm which we call it "local sub-tree transform algorithm".

4 Knowledge Bases

There are 10 knowledge bases of different kinds used in the system.

Language model is very important in machine translation. We defined a special knowledge base called *Language Model* to define all the lexical, syntactic and semantic categories and attributes of source and target languages. All the linguistic symbols used in other knowledge bases must be defined in the Language Model. The language model of this MT system chiefly originates from the "Grammatical Knowledge Base of Contemporary Chinese"[10]. The analysis of this MT system relies mainly on syntax features and uses the semantic information for reference.

There are six *rulebases* used in different phases of the translation. The rules in rulebases are global rules, which are available in all situations. Local rules, which are restricted with certain word, are stored in the dictionary. The format of global rules and local rules are the same. The basic format of all the rules is: *Pattern + Unification Equations,* somewhat like the format of rules in LFG grammar.

A bilingual *dictionary* is used in the MT system. It contains not only the meaning items, but also the local rules restricted with the words.

The *example base* is actually a corpus for the MT system. On one hand, it stores collected bilingual text. On the other hand, it stores the entire sentences that have been translated by the MT system. The source text, target text, source trees and target trees are stored. Users can modify the translations and trees stored in it. The example base is used to evaluate the translation of the system and to generate the statistical data that is used in the scoring functions in lexical analysis and parsing. We are developing another example-based translation engine for this system at the same time.

The statistical database stores the statistical data used in the scoring functions in lexical analysis and parsing. The data is generated from the example base.

5 Current State and Future Works

A training set of 4,000 Chinese sentences has been used to train the system. These sentences are selected on purpose, which cover the most frequently used patterns of sentences in Chinese. About 90% of the translations of the sentence in the training set are understandable, which means people may know the meaning of the source text from the target text. In the open test of Chinese-English Machine Translation Systems held by the Steering Committee of Chinese Hi-Tech R&D Plan in March 1998, this system got a good result, about 71% of the translation is understandable. Usually the result English sentences are not very proper in grammar. The most common mistakes are on articles, number of nouns and tense of verbs, because there are no corresponding linguistic features in Chinese and it is very difficult to generate these features in the translation properly in high correctness.

The future work we plan to do includes: use more Chinese sentences (about 10,000) to train the system, expand the corpus, improve the statistical algorithm, and add an example-based translation engine.

6 Acknowledgements

This project is supported by the Chinese National High-Tech R&D Plan. The development of this system is under the leadership of Prof. Xiang Zhang. We would like to thank all the members of our research group, especially Weidong Zhan, Ying Liu, Baobao Chang, Bin Wang, Hui Wang, Qiang Zhou and Yu Ye for their hard work on the project.

References

1. Duan Huimin and Yu Shiwen, Test Report on MT Systems, on (Chinses) Computer World Newspaper, 1996.3.25, p183. (In Chinese)
2. Feng Zhiwei, New Discussion on Machine Translation of Natural Language, Press of Language and Character, 1995. (In Chinese)
3. Feng Zhiwei, The Computer Processing of Natural Language, Shanghai Press of Foreign Language Education, 1996. (In Chinese)
4. Gazdar G., Mellish C., Natural Language Processing in Lisp, Addison-Welsley Publishing Company, 1989
5. Kay, Martin, Unification in Grammar, In V.Dahi & P.Saint-Dizier(Ed.) Natural Language Understanding and Logic Programming, Elseview Science Pub, 1985.
6. Liu Qun, Zhan Weidong, Chang Baobao, Liu Ying, The Computational Model and Language Model of a Chinese-English Machine Translation System, Advance on Intelligent Computer Interface and Application, Press of Electronic Industry, 1997. (In Chinese)
7. Liu Qun, Zhang Xiang, Research Method Based on Software Component for Machine Translation, Language Engineer, Press of Tsinghua University, 1997. (In Chinese)
8. Liu Ying, Liu Qun, Zhang Xiang, Chang Baobao, A hybrid approach to Chinese-English machine translation, IEEE ICIPS'97 Conference, 1997.
9. Shen Yang, Zhen Ding'o (Ed.), Research on Valence Grammar on Modern Chinese, Press of Peking University, 1995. (In Chinese)
10. Yu Shiwen, Specification on "Syntax Information Dictionary on Modern Chinese", Journal of Chinese Information Processing, Vol 10, No 2, pp1-22, 1996. (In Chinese)
11. Yu Shiwen, Some Aspect on Computational Linguistics, Applied Linguistics, No. 3, 1993. (In Chinese)

Sakhr Arabic-English Computer-Aided Translation System

Achraf Chalabi

Sakhr Sotware,Sakhr building,Nasr City,Free Zone,Cairo,Egypt Tel : 202 2749929
email: ac@sakhr.com

Abstract. Automation of the whole translation process using computers and machine translation systems did not fulfil, so far, the ever-growing needs for translation. On the other hand, Computer-aided translation systems have tackled the translation process by first concentrating on those mechanical tasks performed during the translation, then by gradually automating those intelligent (creative) tasks. This has resulted in useful systems that both increase translator's productivity and guarantee better consistency across translation jobs. This paper describes Sakhr Cat system which has been specifically designed to support document, web page translation and software localization for the Arabic-English language pair

Introduction

Sakhr CAT system is a computer-aided translation program, supporting bidirectional bilingual translation between English and Arabic. It is fully integratable with MS Word. The CAT program also supports translation from English or Arabic to any single-byte target language with less features.

The different components of the system are designed in such a way to support normal document translation , web page translation and software localisation.The system consists of five major components, following is a detailed description of each one.

Workbench

Sakhr system is the first to apply natural language processing (NLP) technologies with both Arabic and English as source languages. Sakhr CAT Workbench has built in many of its proprietary linguistic engines, including the Arabic Morphological Analyzer, English Stemmer, Arabic Automatic Diacritizer, English Homograph Resolver and Idiom Parser.

Translator's productivity and consistency are enhanced throughout translation work by avoiding repetition of identical or similar tasks. The CAT program achieves this by automatic building translation memories that store translations on-line and provide users with potential translations, via the fuzzy/identical matcher, while working on any given text.

Workbench main features

- Translation memories: from Arabic or English to any single-byte language.;
- Powerful linguistic-based fuzzy matching for both Arabic and English;
- MS Word: serves as the default editor & Network environment support;
- Automatic surface translation & Fuzzy search in translation memories;
- Dictionaries & translation memories can be imported, exported and updated;
- Graphical browsing of differences between source, matched and target units;
- User-defined matching and segmentation criteria & Help file localization;
- Simultaneous access to multiple translation memories & dictionaries;
- Merge & Reverse Source-Target Languages of translation memories;
- Individual translation memory labelled with control information (client name, project name, date, translator name,…) ;
- Off-line translation with user-defined color scheme for different actions;

Dictionary

Sakhr CAT dictionary is a bidirectional, bilingual (Arabic/English) general domain dictionary, especially designed to plug into Sakhr CAT Workbench. It fully utilizes all mechanisms of linguistic processing performed in the Workbench, such as morphological analysis, part-of-speech disambiguation, shallow word-sense disambiguation, idiomatic expression detection and others.

Sakhr CAT Dictionary entries are represented as stems, creating a favorable environment for dictionary accessibility to all varieties of word inflections. This is crucial for handling Arabic, a highly inflectional language, and is a great addition for handling English inflections.

Two idiom dictionaries are integrated with the CAT Dictionary. They include nominal, adjectival and adverbial expressions and cover extensively common English phrasal verbs and verbal idioms.

Dictionary main features

- 40,000 Arabic stem entries & 40,000 English stem entries;
- 40,000 Arabic common expressions & 20,000 English common expressions;
- Automatic inflection-to-stem transformation of source language words;

- Automatic transformation for verb tense and noun number ;
- Part of speech tagged entries for both A/E & User-defined word class filters;
- Classification of senses for polysemous entries;
- Unidirectional (E>A) phrasal verbs and verbal idiom detection;
- Bidirectional (A<>E) nominal, adjectival and adverbial idiom detection;
- User-defined display features & Update utility for dictionary translations;
- Drag and drop from dictionary into Workbench;

Aligner

Sakhr CAT Aligner significantly reduces the time required for alignment by performing automatic segmentation of both source and target documents, then mapping units based on a highly intelligent lexical matcher.

This intelligent utility helps producing Translation Memories (TM) out of previously translated documents, Web pages or application resources. Building a translation memory out of previously translated documents is an extremely effective way for storing completed data and re-using it in subsequent translations. Consequently, TM increases productivity in future translation jobs. The Aligner also provides a graphical user-friendly interface to post-edit the results of the automatic mapping.

Aligner Main features

- Automatic segmentation of source and target texts with user-defined criteria;
- Automatic mapping based on multiple dictionary driven lexical matching;
- User-defined matching criteria & Text, HTML and application resources support;
- Automatic alignment for resources directly from EXE, DLL and OCX files;
- Automatic generation of translation memory in original and reverse directions;
- Automatic alignment for both Arabic and English, plus full environment available for manual alignment of other language pairs;
- Easy-to-use graphical user-interface for post-alignment tasks;
    - Edit / Split / Merge / Link / Unlink units
    - Hold/Resume job

Software Localisation

Resource CAT simplifies and speeds up the time-consuming task of localizing into other languages, especially Arabic, all resources of software applications.

Assisted by the highly-productive CAT Workbench environment, the user takes advantage of previously developed translation memories to complete the translation task rapidly and efficiently, while building new translation memories or inserting new translation pairs into existing ones.

Software Localisation features

- Full integration with Sakhr CAT Workbench;
- Automatic extraction of text units from RC, DLL , EXE and OCX files;
- Automatic injection of translated units under Windows 95 or Windows NT;
- Off-line translation & Automatic generation of project-specific glossary;
- On-line validation tests such as:
  - Differences in the number of hot keys, truncated text in dialog boxes;
  - Hot keys inaccessible from the keyboard;
  - Duplicate hot keys & accelerator keys in dialog boxes or menus;
- On-line WYSIWYG preview of translated dialog boxes and menus;
- English to Arabic terminology dictionary for computer domain;
- Localization from A/E to any single-byte language supported with less functions;

Web page translation

Sakhr Web CAT is a web-specific CAT component that plugs into Sakhr CAT Workbench. Localizing a web page involves translating its textual content. Since the textual content represents on the average over 80% of a web page, translation represents, in most of the cases, the bulk of a web page localization job.

During the preparation phase, the Web CAT automatically extracts all translatable texts from the HTML file, segments them into units based on user-defined segmentation criteria, and displays the text along with its segmented units in an easy-to-use, multi-window interface. The user is totally freed from having to laboriously extract and segment translatable units from the HTML file.

Web page translation main features

- Automatic text extraction from web pages & Automatic text segmentation;
- User-defined segmentation criteria & Off-line translation;
- Original and translated pages can be previewed using any Internet browser;
- Automatic replacement of translated text, preserving original formats;
- Web page translation from Arabic or English to any single-byte language is also supported with less functionality

System Description/Demo of Alis Translation Solutions Application : Multilingual Search and Query Expansion

Nathalie Côté, Trans., MBA[1]

[1]Product Specialist, Translation Solutions, E-mail: ncote@alis.com
Alis Technologies Inc.
100 Alexis Nihon Blvd.
Suite 600
Montreal, Quebec
Canada H4M 2P2
www.alis.com

Abstract. Alis Technologies partnered with Verity to develop a new multilingual search and retrieval technology. This tool enables the translation of search queries into multiple languages, and allows the search results to be translated back into the language of the query. This important component of the Alis Translation Solutions, a family of products and services designed to provide the highly tailored and integrated translation solutions that large corporations require, will be demonstrated at AMTA-98.

1. Introduction

Multilingual search is becoming a typical requirement among global corporations, as Web sites and intranets are growing larger, more complex, and contain information in several languages. For potential customers or employees from around the world, finding the information they need within the Web site or intranet of a multinational can represent quite a challenge, as only parts of the total content might be available in certain languages.

Alis Technologies partnered with Verity to directly address the need for international companies to provide access to information across a growing span of languages. The addition of the Search Information Server nicely rounds out Alis Technologies' Web solution by enabling people to gain full multilingual access to Web documents. By extending queries across different languages, one can obtain a much more complete set of qualified search results.

2. Multilingual Search and Query Expansion

Alis' and Verity's new multilingual search and query expansion technology is an important component of the Alis Translation Solutions (ATS), a family of products and services designed to provide the highly tailored and integrated translation solutions that large corporations require. This particular application is designed to allow users to enter a search query in their own language, search content in a different language, and obtain the results in their own language. The query string itself is automatically translated before performing the search, and the resulting summaries are translated back into the language of the query. In the end, users are presented with the resulting documents in the same language as that of their initial query.

If potential customers enter a search string, say, in French, and get a negative search result because the information they want happens to be indexed only in English on the site, chances are they will move on to the Web site of a competitor. To increase, or even maintain, their customer base, corporations need to provide access to all the information on their Web site, regardless of the language of that information.

2.1 ATS Benefits for Multilingual Search and Query Expansion

By allowing customers and employees to search in any language:
- A global corporation can expand its customer base or maintain customer satisfaction by giving Web site visitors access to the information they are looking for, regardless of the language in which the information is stored.
- It can reduce customer support costs by giving access to support information in the language(s) that customers understand.
- It can facilitate worldwide human resources management by allowing employees to access corporate and HR information in their own language.

3. Translation Flow

As shown in Figure 1, the multilingual search application allows users to enter a search query in their own language (say French), search content in another language (say English), and obtain the results in their own language (French). The query string itself is automatically translated (in this case, into English) before the search is performed, and the resulting summaries are translated back into the language of the query (French). In the final steps of the search, users are presented with the complete document in the same language as that of their initial query (French).

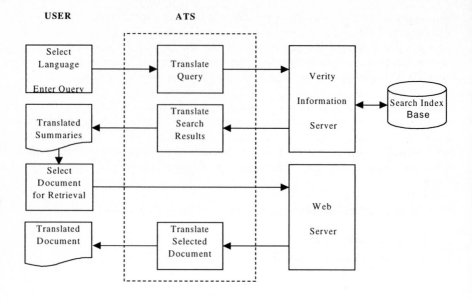

Fig. 1. Multilingual search translation flow

3.1 Functionality Description

Building a tool to expand multilingual queries requires both technical and linguistic analyses. On one hand, the use of bilingual dictionaries can be improved by allowing the multilingual search tool to indicate both the query in the user language and the equivalents in the target language. On the other hand, Alis uses machine translation engines to translate the retrieved texts back into the user's language. Our goal is to maximize the effectiveness of full machine translation and dictionary look-up for the task of multilingual query expansion search and retrieval.

Step 1. The query is made in the user language.
Step 2. The query is expanded into the target language.
Step 3. The search is made for documents in both languages.
Step 4. Documents not in the user language are automatically translated.
Step 5. All documents are returned in the user language, categorized by domains.

Linguistic Challenges
The search performs homograph disambiguation and expansion by domain. Then the query is translated into all alternative synonyms. Errors can occur when the query's particular meaning is not the most commonly used in general language. Also, a number of queries using adverbials and prepositions are multi-word expressions. Therefore, they may or may not be properly translated and return false searches. The demonstration will show how these challenges are addressed in ATS.

4. Environment

Alis Translation Solutions are designed to be modular and scalable. ATS links machine translation engines, language-handling routines and system administration tools, along with optional dictionaries, human translation services and workflow management software. They allows users to display, create and exchange information in a multitude of languages.

ATS server software provides the ATS Linguistic Services Layer and resides along side the HTTP server (Apache-based) and the SMTP server.

Other components of ATS include:
- Machine translation (MT) engines
- Dictionaries
- Pre-editing software tools
- System operation monitoring tools

Lecture Notes in Artificial Intelligence (LNAI)

Vol. 1395: H. Kitano (Ed.), RoboCup-97: Robot Soccer World Cup I. XIV, 520 pages. 1998.

Vol. 1397: H. de Swart (Ed.), Automated Reasoning with Analytic Tableaux and Related Methods. Proceedings, 1998. X, 325 pages. 1998.

Vol. 1398: C. Nédellec, C. Rouveirol (Eds.), Machine Learning: ECML-98. Proceedings, 1998. XII, 420 pages. 1998.

Vol. 1400: M. Lenz, B. Bartsch-Spörl, H.-D. Burkhard, S. Wess (Eds.), Case-Based Reasoning Technology. XVIII, 405 pages. 1998.

Vol. 1404: C. Freksa, C. Habel. K.F. Wender (Eds.), Spatial Cognition. VIII, 491 pages. 1998.

Vol. 1409: T. Schaub, The Automation of Reasoning with Incomplete Information. XI, 159 pages. 1998.

Vol. 1415: J. Mira, A.P. del Pobil, M. Ali (Eds.), Methodology and Tools in Knowledge-Based Systems. Vol. I. Proceedings, 1998. XXIV, 887 pages. 1998.

Vol. 1416: A.P. del Pobil, J. Mira, M. Ali (Eds.), Tasks and Methods in Applied Artificial Intelligence. Vol. II. Proceedings, 1998. XXIII, 943 pages. 1998.

Vol. 1418: R. Mercer, E. Neufeld (Eds.), Advances in Artificial Intelligence. Proceedings, 1998. XII, 467 pages. 1998.

Vol. 1421: C. Kirchner, H. Kirchner (Eds.), Automated Deduction – CADE-15. Proceedings, 1998. XIV, 443 pages. 1998.

Vol. 1424: L. Polkowski, A. Skowron (Eds.), Rough Sets and Current Trends in Computing. Proceedings, 1998. XIII, 626 pages. 1998.

Vol. 1433: V. Honavar, G. Slutzki (Eds.), Grammatical Inference. Proceedings, 1998. X, 271 pages. 1998.

Vol. 1434: J.-C. Heudin (Ed.), Virtual Worlds. Proceedings, 1998. XII, 412 pages. 1998.

Vol. 1435: M. Klusch, G. Weiß (Eds.), Cooperative Information Agents II. Proceedings, 1998. IX, 307 pages. 1998.

Vol. 1437: S. Albayrak, F.J. Garijo (Eds.), Intelligent Agents for Telecommunication Applications. Proceedings, 1998. XII, 251 pages. 1998.

Vol. 1441: W. Wobcke, M. Pagnucco, C. Zhang (Eds.), Agents and Multi-Agent Systems. Proceedings, 1997. XII, 241 pages. 1998.

Vol. 1446: D. Page (Ed.), Inductive Logic Programming. Proceedings, 1998. VIII, 301 pages. 1998.

Vol. 1453: M.-L. Mugnier, M. Chein (Eds.), Conceptual Structures: Theory, Tools and Applications. Proceedings, 1998. XIII, 439 pages. 1998.

Vol. 1454: I. Smith (Ed.), Artificial Intelligence in Structural Engineering. XI, 497 pages. 1998.

Vol. 1456: A. Drogoul, M. Tambe, T. Fukuda (Eds.), Collective Robotics. Proceedings, 1998. VII, 161 pages. 1998.

Vol. 1458: V.O. Mittal, H.A. Yanco, J. Aronis, R. Simpson (Eds.), Assistive Technology in Artificial Intelligence. X, 273 pages. 1998.

Vol. 1471: J. Dix, L. Moniz Pereira, T.C. Przymusinski (Eds.), Logic Programming and Knowledge Representation. Proceedings, 1997. IX, 246 pages. 1998.

Vol. 1476: J. Calmet, J. Plaza (Eds.), Artificial Intelligence and Symbolic Computation. Proceedings, 1998. XI, 309 pages. 1998.

Vol. 1480: F. Giunchiglia (Ed.), Artificial Intelligence: Methodology, Systems, and Applications. Proceedings, 1998. IX, 502 pages. 1998.

Vol. 1484: H. Coelho (Ed.), Progress in Artificial Intelligence – IBERAMIA 98. Proceedings, 1998. XIII, 421 pages. 1998.

Vol. 1488: B. Smyth, P. Cunningham (Eds.), Advances in Case-Based Reasoning. Proceedings, 1998. XI, 482 pages. 1998.

Vol. 1489: J. Dix, L. Fariñas del Cerro, U. Furbach (Eds.), Logics in Artificial Intelligence. Proceedings, 1998. X, 391 pages. 1998.

Vol. 1495: T. Andreasen, H. Christiansen, H.L. Larsen (Eds.), Flexible Query Answering Systems. Proceedings, 1998. IX, 393 pages. 1998.

Vol. 1501: M.M. Richter, C.H. Smith, R. Wiehagen, T. Zeugmann (Eds.), Algorithmic Learning Theory. Proceedings, 1998. XI, 439 pages. 1998.

Vol. 1502: G. Antoniou, J. Slaney (Eds.), Advanced Topics in Artificial Intelligence. Proceedings, 1998. XI, 333 pages. 1998.

Vol. 1504: O. Herzog, A. Günter (Eds.), KI-98: Advances in Artificial Intelligence. Proceedings, 1998. XI, 355 pages. 1998.

Vol. 1510: J.M. Zytkow, M. Quafafou (Eds.), Principles of Data Mining and Knowledge Discovery. Proceedings, 1998. XI, 482 pages. 1998.

Vol. 1515: F. Moreira de Oliveira (Ed.), Advances in Artificial Intelligence. Proceedings, 1998. X, 259 pages. 1998.

Vol. 1529: D. Farwell, L. Gerber, E. Hovy (Eds.), Machine Translation and the Information Soup. Proceedings, 1998. XIX, 532 pages. 1998.

Vol. 1531: H.-Y. Lee, H. Motoda (Eds.), PRICAI'98: Topics in Artificial Intelligence. XIX, 646 pages. 1998.

Lecture Notes in Computer Science